Congregational chapel, Saltaire. (380)

ROYAL COMMISSION ON THE HISTORICAL MONUMENTS
OF ENGLAND

An Inventory of

Nonconformist
CHAPELS

and

MEETING-HOUSES

in the North of England

Christopher Stell

London: HMSO

©Crown copyright 1994

ISBN 0 11 300041 3

British Library Cataloguing in Publication Data
A CIP catalogue record for this book is
available from the British Library

Printed in the United Kingdom for HMSO
Dd 295291 C8 6/94

CONTENTS

LIST OF ILLUSTRATIONS

(illustrations are exterior photographs unless otherwise stated)

CHAIRMAN'S FOREWORD

This third volume of the Nonconformist Chapels and Meeting-houses of England once again illustrates the rich variety in date and style which is to be found in the buildings of the many different branches of nonconformist practice. In the North of England, no less than in those areas of the country already covered, the richness of this architectural inheritance is readily apparent. The buildings listed span a period of over three centuries and stretch from those of traditionally vernacular style to major works by architects of national repute.

The survey on which the volume is based has been carried out and prepared for publication on behalf of the Royal Commission by Mr C. F. Stell. The Commissioners are indebted to him for the care, attention and scholarship which he has brought to this field of study, in which he is acknowledged as a leading authority.

The importance of this series of Inventories, of which a fourth volume to cover Eastern England is now in progress, has been manifest in various ways. As a permanent record, together with the archive on which it is based, it includes many buildings which have disappeared or been altered in recent times. It stimulates public awareness and draws attention to the continuing need for vigilance in the face of changing attitudes to religion and the use of religious buildings.

A concern which has been expressed previously over the survival of some of the better examples of this class of building continues to be felt, but with greater optimism for the future. Some evidence of improvement in the care and maintenance of chapels and meeting-houses has become apparent, both from the availability of repair grants from public and charitable sources and from a wider appreciation of their architectural merits. It is hoped that changes which are being proposed in the legislation regarding the ecclesiastical exemption which has, hitherto, posed a serious threat to the future of important listed interiors, will reduce some of the more tragic losses of this kind. The formation, announced as this volume passes through the press, of the Historic Chapels Trust to parallel the Redundant Churches Fund for nonconformist buildings, is another recent development in this field which gives cause to hope for a more secure future for some of the buildings recorded in this Inventory.

The detailed archive on which this published account is based will be available for inspection by arrangement with the National Monuments Record at the offices of the Royal Commission.

PARK OF MONMOUTH

PRINCIPAL MONUMENTS

List of monuments described in this Inventory that were recommended by the Commissioners as being 'most worthy of preservation'. (For the complete list for England see the Forty-second Interim Report of this Commission, Command No. 9442, 1985.)

Monument numbers, in brackets, are followed by page references.

ACKNOWLEDGEMENTS

Throughout the fieldwork and preparation of the Inventory of which this volume forms a part the author has been greatly assisted by the kindness and consideration of many friends and acquaintances. Some have already been named in preceding volumes, others have helped in many ways not only by the provision of information but also in eliminating errors which might otherwise have remained unnoticed.

Once again Mr David Butler generously placed his particular knowledge of Friends' meeting-houses at the disposal of the Commission and has offered helpful advice based on his own researches. The interest and support of Dr Clyde Binfield has been a great encouragement throughout, not least from his particular acquaintance with the many and varied facets of nonconformist life. Grateful thanks are due to Mr Alan Rose and the Rev. Dr Ian Sellers for advice and assistance relating to entries in Lancashire and Cheshire and to Mr W. John Smith of Middleton for the discussion of further buildings in that region. For much valuable information on the Methodist chapels of north-east England the author has long been especially indebted to Mr Geoffrey Milburn, while for much general encouragement and more particularly for expending time and trouble on reading and commenting on the sections for Berwick-upon-Tweed and other parts of Northumberland especial thanks are due to the Rt. Hon. Alan Beith M.P.

In attempting to do justice to the great wealth of chapels in Yorkshire the writer is much indebted to Mr Colin Dews who made many welcome suggestions for the improvement of the coverage of that county; also to Mr Donald Raine whose knowledge of nonconformity in Bradford has been of great benefit to this work.

Many others whose names are not recorded here have materially assisted in supplying information or commenting on particular points. The officers and members of the various nonconformist historical societies have again made positive and helpful contributions during the progress of the work.

To the ministers, church officers and others who, over many years, have had to suffer unexpected and sometimes untimely requests to inspect their premises, and have responded with almost uniform kindness, most grateful thanks must be expressed; without their co-operation this volume could not have been produced. To the staff of Dr Williams's Library the writer remains permanently indebted for their invaluable and cheerful assistance and interest as the work has progressed.

Of the staff of the Royal Commission particular acknowledgement is made of the documentary research of Dr Bridgett Jones, who retired in 1992, and to the staff of the photographic section whose work has greatly enhanced the value of this volume. Thanks are also extended to the Commission's editorial staff, managed by Miss Kate Owen, for seeing the volume through the press, to Mrs Susan Whimster for editing the text and to Mrs Ann Hudson for compiling the index.

C. F. S.

EDITORIAL NOTES

Denominational names used are generally those in use when the buildings were erected. Methodist chapels appear under the name of the original society where this could be ascertained. Presbyterian and Congregational chapels now used by the United Reformed Church (URC) are so indicated in the text. No general attempt is made to distinguish the present grouping of continuing Congregational or Baptist congregations not involving a change in their principal designation; most of the latter, where not otherwise stated, will be found to be of Particular Baptist origin. Unitarian and Free Christian congregations appear under their proper historical appellations.

The name 'meeting-house' or 'chapel', although not generally given, should be assumed to be included as appropriate in the heading of each entry. The designation 'church', as increasingly applied indiscriminately to ecclesiastical structures, is avoided as incorrect and tending to ambiguity in the present context. 'Former' indicates that the building is now used by another stated denomination or for other purposes. Closure or demolition is noted where this could reliably be determined but, in view of the time which has continued to elapse since many of the records were made, further changes will inevitably be found to have taken place.

The measured drawings are reproduced to uniform scales of 12 and 24 feet to the inch (1:144 and 1:288). Sequence hatching has been adopted throughout: the original or principal work is indicated in solid black, secondary work by cross-hatching and later minor additions by single-line hatching; where necessary this is more fully explained in the accompanying text. Dimensions are quoted in the text for most monuments built prior to 1800; these are internal unless otherwise stated, the length of the principal axis of the original pulpit or rostrum being given first.

Historical information concerning the origins and development of individual congregations necessarily derives in the main from published sources. The accuracy of these varies considerably and although they have been used with caution some errors may remain. Corrections or comments on any statement in this Inventory will be gratefully acknowledged.

Boundary Changes. The arrangement of the Inventory follows that of the previous volumes, being by historical county and civil parish, the names and boundaries being taken as those obtaining immediately prior to local government reorganization in 1974. The changes affecting the volume area, which have been considerable, are indicated on the map (p. xxii). These comprise the conflation of Cumberland, Westmorland, the Lonsdale district of Lancashire N of Morecambe Bay, and the extreme NW corner of the West Riding of Yorkshire to form a new county of Cumbria; the formation of separate counties of Merseyside and Greater Manchester from the industrial or more urbanized areas of south Lancashire and adjoining counties, of Tyne and Wear and Cleveland from parts of Northumberland, Durham and the North Riding of Yorkshire centred respectively on the conurbations around Newcastle upon Tyne and Middlesbrough, and the separation of the manufacturing districts of the West Riding to form South Yorkshire and West Yorkshire; the major part of the East Riding has been joined with parts of North Lincolnshire to create the county of Humberside and the remaining parts of the North Riding together with substantial portions of the other Ridings have become North Yorkshire. Other changes which leave Cheshire, Durham and Northumberland still substantially recognizable in area as well as name, but which give the name of Lancashire to a county whose boundaries accord only slightly with the historic County Palatine, are too numerous to set out in greater detail. Changes of county name within the area of the present Inventory are indicated in italics under the county headings or beside individual parish names.

Conversion Table

1 inch = 25.4 mm

1 foot (12 inches) = 304.8 mm

1 yard (3 feet) = 914.4 mm

1 mile (1760 yards) = 1.6 km

PREFACE

The north of England is characterized in the minds of many as the home of 'dark Satanic Mills' and huge chapels where augmented choirs vie with each other in interminable and painful renderings of 'The Messiah'. Nothing could be further from the truth. The rich variety of building styles and denominations is as great, if not greater, than in any other part of the country. The rise of Puritanism within the Established Church is seen in the early history of many dissenting congregations whose occupancy of several chapels-of-ease, notably in Lancashire, was terminated only with difficulty. The retention by nonconformists of the Ancient Chapel of Toxteth, in Liverpool, Lancashire (118) is particularly remarkable, as is the survival of the two Commonwealth chapels at Bramhope and Great Houghton in the West Riding of Yorkshire (77, 148). The subsequent establishment of numerous Presbyterian congregations, many now Unitarian, which still possess important early chapels, is best seen in Lancashire at Rivington (215) and in the group of chapels in Cheshire of which Knutsford (60) is the best preserved. The chapel of 1692–3 in St Saviourgate, York (1), is of particular interest in illustrating the high expectations of the Presbyterians to be the *alter ego* of the Establishment.

At the other extreme we see in the north Lancashire fells around Swarthmoor evidence of the development of the Society of Friends; their many surviving meeting-houses bear witness to the peculiar attraction of Quakerism amongst the yeomen and small farmers of the Lake District. Further north, in Cumberland and especially in Northumberland, the influence of Scottish Presbyterianism becomes apparent together with the various secessions from which the Established Church in North Britain suffered in the eighteenth century and later.

The 'new dissent', centred around the rise of Methodism, found fertile ground in the growing manufacturing districts of Lancashire and Yorkshire. Here the Moravian Church was also active, building outstanding settlements at Fulneck in the West Riding of Yorkshire (335), and Fairfield, Lancashire (77), as well as other smaller chapels. Allied to them were the congregations formed by Benjamin Ingham, some of which remained independent or passed into the hands of the Sandemanians; a few are mentioned here.

Chapels of the nineteenth century and after are most prominent in the urban areas where all denominations erected buildings whose size now causes embarrassment to many of their possessors. Some of the smaller chapels of the early years of the century continue the styles of the previous century but it is to the work of named architects and notable benefactors that attention is constantly drawn: to such buildings as the Congregational/URC chapel in Saltaire, Yorkshire, West Riding (380), Christ Church, Port Sunlight, Cheshire (11), or the seaside extravaganza at Fairhaven, Lancashire (133).

The criteria adopted here, as for the previous volumes in the series, are set out more fully in the earlier prefaces. Particular attention has been given to buildings dating from before 1800 but none of importance dating from before 1850 has knowingly been omitted. Some earlier buildings demolished prior to the commencement of the survey are also included. Later chapels up to 1914 have been noted so far as space and opportunity have allowed and wherever possible all monuments listed have been personally inspected, if briefly, by the author.

In the Preface to the second volume attention was drawn to the threats of demolition or unsympathetic conversion to which chapels and meeting-houses are especially subject. This is again painfully apparent with the loss by denominational indifference of such notable buildings as Matthew Henry's Chapel, Chester (24), or Risley Chapel, Lancashire (66), by arson of the Catholic Apostolic Church in Liverpool, Lancashire (121), or by conversion as at the Independent Chapel, Heckmondwike, Yorkshire, West Riding (191), to name but a few. The continued threat to this unique architectural heritage is now, if belatedly, being recognized; the unsympathetic excesses of some congregations are about to be restrained; and the formation of the 'Historic Chapels Trust' as a nonconformist equivalent to the Redundant Churches Fund, gives grounds for hope that the attention now being drawn to them will permit the survival, intact and preferably in use, of at least some of our most outstanding nonconformist chapels and meeting-houses.

CHRISTOPHER STELL

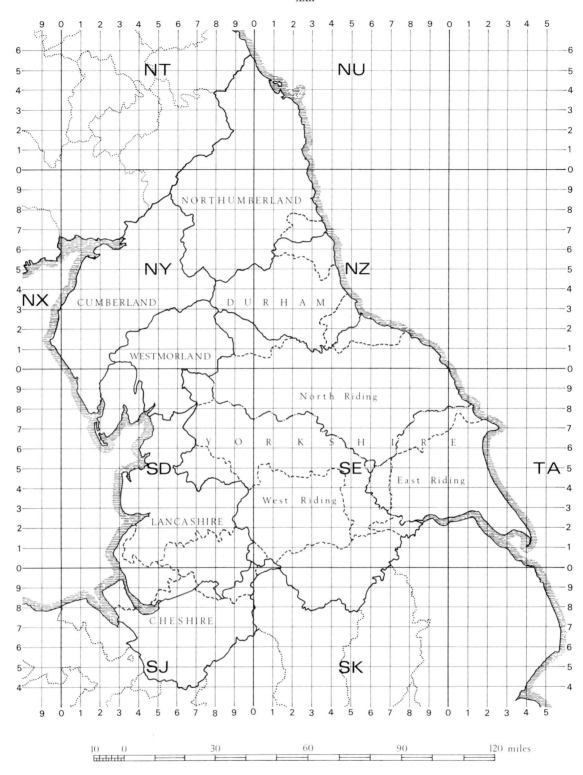

Map showing county boundaries: the subdivisions of Yorkshire are shown by interrupted lines and alterations post-1974 by broken lines. The grid on this map is the National Grid taken from the Ordnance Survey map with the permission of the Controller of Her Majesty's Stationery Office, ©*Crown copyright.*

AN INVENTORY OF

NONCONFORMIST CHAPELS AND MEETING-HOUSES

IN THE NORTH OF ENGLAND

CHESHIRE

A strong nonconformist presence, predominantly Presbyterian, is evident from the late 17th century particularly in the eastern parts of the county within the orbit of Manchester. An early instance of the formation of an Independent congregation is at Dukinfield (39) where the private chapel of the Hall served as a meeting place from 1640–1. At Chadkirk use of a remote chapel-of-ease was secured for a time under the protection of a sympathetic magnate, although the society was eventually forced to move to Hatherlow (15). A similar origin is seen in the congregation at Hale Barns (49) where possession of Ringway Chapel was retained until 1721–2. Of the new chapels built in the late 17th century three are particularly notable for their similarity in date and style, long and narrow on plan and with external gallery staircases at each end. The first of these was built at Macclesfield (71) in 1690, shortly followed by Knutsford (60), which is the best preserved of the group, and within 4 years by Dean Row (145), which suffered a drastic rearrangement in 1844–5. The greatest recent loss has been in Chester where Matthew Henry's Chapel (24) of 1700, a building of considerable size and importance, was demolished c.1965 without adequate record. The Presbyterian chapel in Nantwich (106) of 1725–6, much altered in the mid 19th century, has also been demolished as has the smaller Cross Street Chapel in Sale (122) of 1739. After 1840 much work was done by congregations, many of which had become Unitarian, on repairing or altering the meeting-houses in their charge. At Allostock (3) the little building of c.1700 survived its transformation into a school and latterly to a private house but at Dukinfield (40) and Gee Cross (55) the 18th-century meeting-houses were entirely rebuilt. At Wheelock Heath (50) the Presbyterian meeting-house of 1704–5 survived until 1860 when the Baptist church which had long been in possession found the need to replace it.

Evidence of Baptist activity in the county is apparent from 1663, when the burial-ground at Hill Cliffe (8), south of Warrington, was first acquired, although the meeting-house has been rebuilt. The chapel at Great Warford (47), of 1712, is of exceptional interest as the conversion of a timber-framed barn, though comparable in its proportions

with the group of three Presbyterian chapels mentioned above. The early 18th-century chapel at Brassey Green (136) and the former General Baptist chapel at Nantwich (101) are indicative only of the varied fortunes of successive users. Of greater rarity is the former Johnsonian chapel at Millington (89), of 1759.

Baptist concern for the provision of burial-grounds, at Hill Cliffe, and in 1689 at Mottram St Andrew (100), is comparable with that felt by the Society of Friends. The Quaker burial-ground at Middlewich with its associated meeting-house (88) has disappeared almost without trace, but at Whitley (142) the walled enclosure remains a little over one mile W of the meeting-house at Frandley (7). This last was rebuilt in the late 19th century and little remains of 18th-century or earlier Quaker building in the county. The meeting-house at Morley (148) was converted to cottages in 1830, the small meeting-house in Macclesfield (77) of 1705 has been much altered and that in Nantwich (103) is hardly remarkable. Only the Wilmslow meeting-house (149) of 1830 is of any real architectural merit.

Two small former Methodist chapels of 18th-century date survive at Mottram in Longdendale (63) of 1791, and Knolls Green (94) of 1783, both considerably altered. The chapel of 1784 in Stockport (130) has been demolished, the large Sunderland Street chapel in Macclesfield (78) has been closed, while in Chester (26) the chapel of 1811 by Thomas Harrison, succeeding an octagon of 1765, has been re-fronted, as has the chapel of 1808 in Nantwich (104). The most complete surviving example of Wesleyan architecture is Brunswick Chapel of 1823 in Macclesfield (79), a town pre-eminent for its nonconformist buildings, where the former New Connexion chapel in Park Street (80) of 1836 proclaims the past strength of other branches of this denomination. The origin of the Primitive Methodist Connexion at Mow Cop (112) should not be overlooked nor the historical importance of the chapel at Englesea-brook (141) where one of its founders is buried.

Cheshire Congregationalism found renewed vigour in the early 19th century although some of its churches, such as Tintwistle (134), could trace their origins to the 17th century. Their principal chapels of the early 19th century have, almost without exception, been demolished or transferred to other uses. St George's Chapel, Macclesfield (75), a proprietory chapel of 1822–3, soon passed to the Established Church and its successor in Roe Street (76) suffered eventual closure, though its classically designed front of 1829 remains unaltered. To these must be added Queen Street, Chester (25), of 1838, and Monks Lane, Nantwich (102), of 1842. The first stylistic diversion from the accepted Georgian canon was to be seen at Runcorn (118), where a generous patron preferred a late Gothic style. More ambitious was Rake Lane, Liscard (139), of 1841–2, where the benefactor included a substantial tower. In a smaller Congregational chapel of 1843 at Parkgate (107), which eventually passed to the Church of England, the architect tried hard to make its mediaevalism more than superficial even to the cast-iron tracery of its windows, but in Crewe (97) the first chapel of 1847 still succeeds in being amusing rather than archaeological. The chapel at Bowden Downs (5) of 1848, which is more advanced in style, has also passed out of the denomination.

The Gothic Revival in Cheshire was principally upheld, at least at its commencement, by the Unitarians who, even before the security of the Dissenters' Chapels Act, had rebuilt Dukinfield Old Chapel (40) in the lancet style with internal fittings of exceptional interest. The passing of the act was celebrated by the rebuilding of Hyde Chapel (55) in 1846 in a very correct and scholarly manner, as well as by the repair of some other of the older meeting-houses. Later in the century, at Altrincham (4) and at Hyde (57), the

work of the Unitarian architect Thomas Worthington should be noted. At the same period W. F. Poulton designed two chapels for Congregationalists in Crewe (98) and Stalybridge (127) but the two most outstanding buildings of this denomination are of even later date, the benefactions of the industrialist W. H. Lever. The first of these, built in 1902–4 to serve his model village, is Christ Church, Port Sunlight (11), a Gothic 'parish church' on an Independent trust; the second, built in 1906–7 in his home village of Thornton Hough (133), is a rare but entirely successful essay in the Romanesque.

Little need be said of the smaller chapels in the county, though the three-bay Wesleyan chapels at Poole Green (114) of 1834 and at Key Green, Congleton (32) of 1845 are good of their kind. The usual building material throughout most of Cheshire is a dark brown brick which is in evidence from the earliest period. In the later 19th century polychrome brickwork was used to good effect in the Primitive Methodist chapel in Tiverton (137) of 1864, similarly at Winsford (153) and more stridently by the Congregationalists at Over (152) in 1865–8. Stone was used at King Edward Street, Macclesfield (71) in 1690 and remained available in the hilly regions on the eastern edge of the county. At Parkgate in the Wirral (107) and at Runcorn (118) sandstone of excellent quality was used in the early 19th century. Some stone slate roofs have survived but much replacement by the ubiquitous Welsh slate has left relatively few examples of the use of other roofing materials.

ACTON

(1) WESLEYAN, Acton Bridge (SJ 592758). Opened 1832.

ALDERLEY EDGE

(2) WESLEYAN, Chapel Road (SJ 845782). Gothic, with corner tower and broach spire, by Hayley and Sons, 1863.

ALLOSTOCK

(3) ALLOSTOCK CHAPEL, Chapel Lane (SJ 745713). A small dissenting congregation formed in 1690 came by the early 19th century to be associated with the Presbyterian, latterly Unitarian, society in Knutsford, with which it shared a minister. A barn was registered in 1692 possibly for this congregation and the present chapel erected c.1700. In 1846 a school was established, the chapel altered to serve as a school-room in which occasional services continued to be held, and a master's house built at one end. The building remained in scholastic use until 1983.

The chapel is a small rectangular building with brick walls and roof formerly covered with stone slates but now largely replaced by blue slate. The SE front has a central doorway covered by a large porch built in 1898 and two windows with segmental-

arched heads. The NW wall has two windows with rebuilt heads formerly flanking the pulpit. Windows were inserted in the SW wall in 1898.

The interior (22ft by 39½ft) has been entirely refitted; galleries were removed after 1822. (Converted to private house c.1985, NW wall partly rebuilt and monuments obliterated)

Former Presbyterian chapel, Allostock.   (3)

Monuments: in burial-ground (1) Sarah, daughter of Samuel and Elizabeth Hockenbul, 1788; (2) John Minshull, 1788 (Urwick (1864) also notes monuments internally to the Rev. Samuel Garside, 1716, and Mrs Mary Garside, 1718).

Cong. Mag. III (1820) 399–400. Evans (1897) 4. *Inquirer* 1 October 1983. Payne (1934) 6–7, 64–9. Urwick (1864) 412–17.

ALTRINCHAM   *Greater Manchester*

(4) ALTRINCHAM CHAPEL, Dunham Road (SJ 766880). A 'Presbyterian' chapel built in Shaws Lane in 1814, demolished since 1964, was superseded by the present Unitarian chapel in 1872. The chapel, of brick with steeply pitched roof, polygonal E end and traceried windows, was designed by Thomas Worthington. *Plate*: includes two cups and a plate, 1815.

Evans (1897) 5. Godfrey, P.B., *Unitarianism in Altrincham 1814–1964* (1964). *UHST* IV (1927–30) 62.

(5) Former CONGREGATIONAL, Bowden Downs (SJ 762874). The church originally meeting here was formed about 1839 when a chapel 'at the foot of the Downs' was acquired. The present chapel was built on a new site in 1848 and enlarged in 1868; it was closed *c.*1970 but reopened after 1978 by a recently formed independent society.

The chapel, of stone in the Gothic style, comprises an aisle-less nave of six bays to which two-bay galleried transepts and a short sanctuary were added in 1868. The SE front has a window of five lights with cusped tracery above a porch built 1921; two orignal porches remain in the second bay of the side walls. The interior has a gallery at the SE end, of two bays with provision for staircases at the S and E corners.

Fittings – *Glass*: in SE window, two tiers of figures below canopies, *c.*1900. *Monuments*: in chapel (1) John Spier Herod, 1851, with crest; (2) Rev. Alexander Mackennal, 27 years pastor, 1904, and Fanny his wife, 1903. *Pulpit*: stone, semi-octagonal with ogee-arched traceried panels, and twin staircases. *Sculpture*: on wall behind pulpit, five panels copy of 'Singing Boys' by Della Robbia; in nave, statue 'The sisters of Bethany', by J. Warrington Wood, 1869. *Seating*: plain pews without doors, *c.*1868 (removed *c.*1982).

Nickson, C., *Bygone Altrincham* (1935) 174–91. Powicke (1907) 89–94. Urwick (1864) 380–2.

(6) Former METHODIST, Regent Road (SJ 766877). Built 1788, superseded in 1866 by a chapel in Bank Street. The first chapel later became All Saints' mission church; it was demolished 1964.

Nickson (1935) op. cit. 208–9, 214–15.

ANTROBUS

(7) FRIENDS, Frandley (SJ 636792). The site was acquired in 1676 when an existing building appears to have been converted for meetings. A new meeting-house and separate stable block were built in 1726; a drawing of 1858 shows the meeting-house as a building with two tiers of mullioned windows and a chimney stack above the SW gable. The present building of 1881–2 is of stock brick with three-bay sides divided by stepped buttresses and paired lancet windows. At the E end behind the stand are three graduated lancets; at the other end is a small gallery above a vestibule.

The former stable of 1726 to the SW is of brick with a platband at first-floor level. An external staircase at the N end leads to the upper floor. In the gabled ends are small oval windows. Lower windows have been inserted on the W side.

Fittings, in meeting-house – *Seating*: open-backed benches *c.*1881–2. *Table*: oak with turned legs, 17th-century. For *burial-ground see* WHITLEY (142).

APPLETON

(8) BAPTIST, Hill Cliffe (SJ 611852). A church of which John Wigan, doyen of early Baptist activity in the vicinity of Manchester, may have been a founder, acquired the present site in 1663 as a 'burial-place for Anabaptists and such other of the congregational way in Cheshire and Lancashire as wish to bury there'. A new meeting-house on the site was registered in 1694 and in the 18th century the church was at the centre of the spread of Baptist preaching throughout the region. The former meeting-house, said to have been long and narrow ('48ft by 18ft'), was widened by 12ft in 1801. It was replaced in 1841 by the present chapel of brick and slate. The N front is gabled with two doorways and a central window.

Baptist chapel, Hill Cliffe, Appleton.   (8)

Monuments: in burial-ground (1) Maria Heslopp, 1664/5; (2) Elizabeth Pycroft, 1714 (this last was maliciously recut *c.*1905 to give a false date of 1522; other spurious 16th-century dates have also been reported).

Cong. Mag. III (1820) 569. Kenworthy, J., *History of the Baptist Church at Hill Cliffe* (*c.*1900). Urwick (1864) 403–4, 459–61. Whitley (1913) 51 and *passim*.

AUDLEM

(9) BAPTIST (SJ 663436). The Particular Baptist church formed 1814 joined the General Baptist New Connexion in 1844. The chapel rebuilt in 1840 of brick and slate has round-arched windows alternating with rendered pilasters. Pedimented front of three bays.

Urwick (1864) 140–1. Whitley (1913) *passim*. Wood (1847) 233.

BADDILEY

(10) WESLEYAN, Ravensmoor (SJ 620507). Red-brick front with large wheel-window in gable; 1878.

BEBINGTON   *Merseyside*

(11) CHRIST CHURCH, Port Sunlight (SJ 339845). Built in 1902–4 at the expense of W. H. Lever (Lord Leverhulme) as an

Former Congregational chapel, Bowden Downs. (5)

Christ Church (URC), Port Sunlight.   (11)

undenominational Free Church, with strong Congregational (now URC) connections, for his new industrial model village. The architects were William and Segar Owen. The building, in the late perpendicular style, has walls of local red sandstone and stone-slated roofs; it comprises a long nave of five principal bays with aisles, transepts, vestries, choir, polygonal chancel, and a short tower at the SE corner containing eight bells. An elaborate memorial to Lady Lever was built against the W end in 1914.

Nicholson and Spooner (c.1911) 104–8.

BOLLINGTON

(12) Former CONGREGATIONAL, Wellington Road (SJ 935780). Gothic, with corner turret and spire, by W. Williamson of Manchester, 1868. Now converted to offices.

CYB (1867) 362. Powicke (1907) 173–7. Urwick (1864) 251.

(13) WESLEYAN, Wellington Road (SJ 931779). Gothic, with thin octagonal corner tower and spire, by William Waddington of Manchester, 1886. Two pairs of mid 19th-century gate piers in front survive from previous chapel.

BOWDON   Greater Manchester

(14) PRESBYTERIAN, Delamer Road (SJ 764873). 'Trinity' URC built 1872 for Presbyterian Church in England, Gothic with corner tower and broach spire enriched with gabled openings.

BREDBURY AND ROMILEY   Greater Manchester

(15) HATHERLOW CHAPEL (SJ 935904). A strong local support for Puritanism, encouraged by the Bradshaws of Marple Hall, secured to nonconformist ministers the use of the small timber-framed chapel of Chadkirk (SJ 940902), where they were reported as preaching in 1669. In 1688 the Rev. Gamaliel Jones, although a dissenter, appears to have been appointed minister at Chadkirk and on 16 July 1689, the chapel was registered as a nonconformist meeting-house. About 1704–5 Jones and his Presbyterian or Independent supporters were dispossessed of the old chapel, much of which was rebuilt in 1747, and in 1706 they built a new meeting-house 600 yards NNW at Hatherlow.

The original Hatherlow chapel was a long building of stone '60ft by 29ft' in four bays with an octagonal bell-cote at one end of the roof. After the erection of the present chapel in 1846 the former was converted for use as a school-room; it was demolished in 1911 and replaced by a new Sunday-school on the roof of which the form of the earlier bell-cote has been reproduced. The chapel of 1846 (now URC) S of the former, of stone with lancet windows, has a turret above the principal entrance supported by flying buttresses.

Fittings – Bell: loose in chapel, uninscribed, perhaps from former meeting-house. Monuments: in chapel (1) Ormerod Heyworth, Liverpool merchant, 1851, and Elizabeth his widow, 1860. In burial-ground, N of chapel, stones of late 18th century and after include (2) Rev. John Meldrum, 28 years minister, 1814, and Jane his wife, 1807. Pulpit: loose in chapel, octagonal with two tiers of bolection-moulded fielded panels and moulded capping, early 18th-century from former chapel.

Cocks, J., Memorials of Hatherlow and the Old Chadkirk Chapel (1895). Cong. Mag. III (1820) 457–8. L & CAST XXVII (1909) 71–8. Powicke (1907) 189–94. Richards (1947) 89–90. Urwick (1864) 312–32.

BRERETON

(16) WESLEYAN, Brereton Heath (SJ 802652). Dated 1834, enlarged 1930.

BROXTON

(17) PRIMITIVE METHODIST, Brown Knowl (SJ 495536). 'Ebenezer Chapel', rebuilt 1913, has tablet from former chapel of 1836 reset in back wall.

WHSP XXXVII (1967–70) 57.

BULKELEY

(18) Former PRIMITIVE METHODIST, Mill House (SJ 530550). Low walls of large sandstone blocks, blocked doorway in gabled end to road, now converted to garages. Early 19th-century, superseded 1861.

(19) PRIMITIVE METHODIST, Wrexham Road (SJ 532545). Jubilee Chapel of brown brick with gabled front of three bays dated 1861. Sunday-school gallery with balustraded front behind pulpit.

BURLAND

(20) Former PRIMITIVE METHODIST (SJ 602535). Brown brick with tablet in front pediment dated 1833. Tall round-arched windows in side walls. Drastically altered since 1971 on conversion to house.

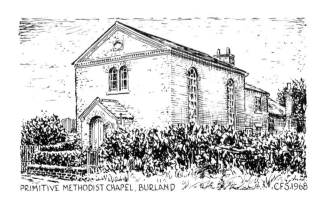

PRIMITIVE METHODIST CHAPEL, BURLAND   CFS.1968

BURWARDSLEY

(21) PRIMITIVE METHODIST (SJ 522566). Rusticated ashlar, wide eaves and shaped barge-boards; dated 1843.

CAPENHURST

(22) CALVINISTIC METHODIST, Two Mills (SJ 353736). 'Bethesda Chapel' of brick with round-arched windows and cast-iron frames was built in 1855 and enlarged to the front in 1913.

CHEADLE AND GATLEY   *Greater Manchester*

(23) CONGREGATIONAL, Gatley (SJ 844886). A small three-bay chapel of brick with round-arched windows was built in 1779, a school-room was added to the N *c*.1820 and rebuilt in 1871. The chapel was entirely refitted and a porch built in 1882. In 1937 it was superseded by a new chapel on a fresh site; the former building remained in use for social purposes until 1967 when it was sold. Demolished before 1969.

Powicke (1907) 187–9. Shercliff, W.H., *Gatley United Reformed Church 1777–1977* (1976). Urwick (1864) 337–8.

CHESTER

(24) MATTHEW HENRY'S CHAPEL, Trinity Street (SJ 403664). Demolished *c*.1965 when the then Unitarian congregation moved to a new chapel in Blacon Point Road (SJ 379676). The chapel built in 1700 for a Presbyterian society then under the pastorate of the Rev. Matthew Henry was a large building '60 feet square' of brick with slated roofs. It was originally approached from Crook Street. The W front of three separately gabled bays originally had a central entrance and two tiers of arched windows. The roof was supported by two parallel arcades each with two tall timber columns supporting the valley beams. The pulpit between arched windows on the longer N wall faced a S gallery which was inserted in 1707 to accommodate the members of a formerly separate dissenting congregation; E and W galleries also existed in the early 19th century. The chapel was much altered at various times: in 1844 it was re-pewed and classrooms built below the S gallery; in 1862 the W front was refenestrated; the roof was reconstructed and coved ceilings introduced in 1899; and in 1908 the S gallery was removed to be replaced by taller rooms and a small E gallery substituted. (The Blacon Point chapel was sold 1988 to an Evangelical congregation)

Fittings – *Books*: Matthew Henry, *Commentary on the Bible* (6 vols., one dated 1721), formerly chained. *Monument*: Matthew Henry, minister 1687–1712, 1714, erected 1862; *Plate*: includes

Matthew Henry's Chapel, Chester (Roberts, 1901).   (24)

two-handled gadrooned cups of 1703 and 1723. *Pulpit*: hexagonal on stem and flared base with panelled back-board and canopy, 1700; contemporary spiral balusters are reused in pulpit staircase and communion rails. *Seating*: chairs, five 18th-century.

Cong. Mag. III (1820) 222–6, 281. Evans (1897) 44–5. *Inquirer* 27 February 1988. Roberts (1901). Tasker, W. W., 'Matthew Henry's Chapel', *Chester & N. Wales Archaeol. & Hist. Soc. Jnl.*, NS XXII (1918) 172–96. *UHST* V (1931–4) 188–91. Urwick (1864) 28–38.

(25) Former CONGREGATIONAL, Queen Street (SJ 408666). A new society, gathered about 1768 and formally constituted in 1772, built the first chapel on this site in 1777. The original chapel '60ft by 46ft' was virtually rebuilt in 1838 by enlargement to front and rear. The E front of ashlar is of five bays with two tiers of sash windows, pedimented end bays and a three-bay Doric portico below the centre. A contemporary lecture hall with attached Doric columns and entablature adjoins to the S (derelict 1971) and there is a small burial-ground to the north.

Cong. Mag. III (1820) 281–3. Powicke (1907) 127–31. Roberts (1901) 140–62. Urwick (1864) 38–47.

Former Congregational chapel, Queen Street, Chester.   (25)

(26) WESLEYAN, St John Street (SJ 40726625). Methodists formerly meeting in a private house and barn built an octagonal chapel in 1765 which stood on or near the site of the Calvinistic Methodist chapel in City Road (SJ 411666). The present building, of 1811 by Thomas Harrison, has brick walls with lunette windows to the gallery. The front wall, originally semicircular with a central entrance and date tablet above, was rebuilt in 1906; the tablet has been reset at the rear.

Bretherton, F. F., *Early Methodism in and around Chester, 1749-1812* (1903). Urwick (1864) 47-9. *WHSP* XXV (1945-6) 83-4.

CHORLEY

(27) METHODIST NEW CONNEXION, Lindow End (SJ 822788). 'Stanley Chapel', brick with tall narrow windows, dated 1830.

CHURCH HULME

(28) Former FREE METHODIST, Holmes Chapel (SJ 764667). Low pedimented front with defaced tablet formerly inscribed 'DEO DEDICATUM A.D. MDCCCL'. Converted to commercial use 1974-6.

CHURTON BY FARNDON

(29) PRIMITIVE METHODIST, Churton (SJ 417565). Three-bay gabled front with later porch; opened 1832.

CONGLETON

(30) Former CONGREGATIONAL, Mill Street (SJ 858632). The chapel built in 1790 for a newly formed congregation was superseded by a new chapel in Antrobus Street in 1877. It was subsequently sold for use as a Masonic Hall and now carries this name with the date 1878. The walls are of brown brick and the roof is covered with slates. The front wall is gabled, of three bays with a central doorway between windows, now blocked, and three upper windows with four-centred arched heads and intersecting glazing bars. Traces of similar windows remain in the rear wall. The side walls have two bays of windows with flat-arched heads. The chapel was described in 1820 as being '42 feet by 36, with three galleries'.

Cong. Mag. III (1820) 401-2. Powicke (1907) 184-7. Urwick (1864) 159-61.

(31) CONGREGATIONAL, Antrobus Street (SJ 856631). Big gabled front of three bays with paired entrances and octagonal corner tower, spire removed. By William Sugden of Leek, 1876-7, superseding chapel in Mill Street.

(32) WESLEYAN, Key Green (SJ 892638). Broad three-bay ashlar front with half-hipped slate roof, round-arched windows and doorway with reeded architrave; dated 1845.

COOLE PILATE

(33) FREE METHODIST (SJ 651472). Broad three-bay front with porch and round-arched windows. Dated 1850.

CREWE (*see also* MONKS COPPENHALL)

(34) WESLEYAN, Slaughter Hill (SJ 736555). Brick with square tower above entrance, ball finials to parapet and short spire. Dated 1909.

CROWTON

(35) PRIMITIVE METHODIST, Ainsworth Lane (SJ 579746). Much altered, perhaps with former three-bay front to lane; tablet 1840 reset.

CUDDINGTON

(36) FREE METHODIST, Mill Lane (SJ 596723). Opened 1849, much altered.

DELAMERE

(37) CALVINISTIC METHODIST, Willington Lane, Boothdale (SJ 529675). Three-bay gabled front with round-arched doorway and pointed-arched windows with intersecting cast-iron glazing bars. Lozenge-shaped tablet inscribed 'Delamere CHAPEL Erected 1817'.

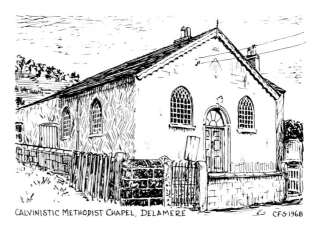

CALVINISTIC METHODIST CHAPEL, DELAMERE   CFS 1968

(38) METHODIST NEW CONNEXION, Willington (SJ 532669). Gabled front with traceried cast-iron window frames, dated 1823.

DUKINFIELD   *Greater Manchester*

(39) DUKINFIELD OLD HALL CHAPEL (SJ 935970). The private chapel of Dukinfield Old Hall, standing N of the now demolished house, was used from 1640-1 by an Independent congregation formed by Samuel Eaton, chaplain to Colonel Robert Dukinfield, and following their removal to Stockport *c.*1653 by a remnant of more questionable orthodoxy until the Restoration. It was registered as a meeting-house in October 1695, probably for the Presbyterian society which built a new chapel in 1707-8 (*see* (40)), but then passed out of regular use until 1872 when it was bought by a newly formed Congregational church. The chapel was then repaired and incorporated as a transept into a much larger chapel, designed by H. J. Paull, which remained in use until *c.*1977 when both

Old Hall Chapel, DUKINFIELD   *Cheshire*

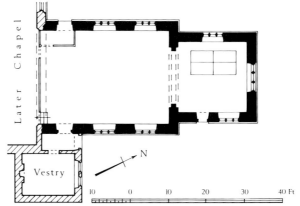

Dukinfield. Old Hall Chapel. From SE. (39)

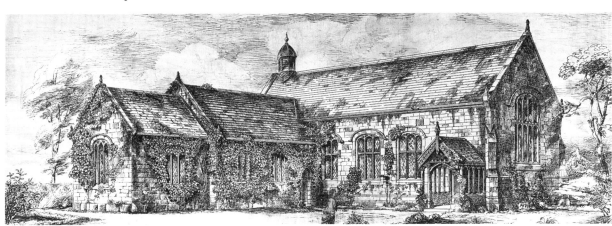

Dukinfield. Old Hall Chapel. From NE. (39)

buildings were gutted by fire. (Later chapel since demolished, earlier building derelict)

The former chapel, built in the mid 16th century, has stone walls; the roof, now tiled, was originally covered with stone slates. The building comprises a small square chancel and aisle-less nave, with windows of three graduated round-arched lights and an E window of slightly greater elaboration. The S doorway of the chancel has a segmental-arched head and N and S doorways at the W end of the nave had round-arched heads, the former destroyed by stone robbing in 1978. The W wall of the nave was removed in 1872–3 and the W window reset in the S wall of the new building; a small vestry to the S also incorporates some reused material. A hexagonal wooden bell-cote formerly stood above the W gable. The roof structure was entirely renewed in 1872–3. The chancel arch is semicircular of two chamfered arches dying into the responds. The remains of a timber screen were removed in 1872.

Floorslabs: in chancel below later boarded floor (1) Susanna, daughter of Sir Robert and Lady Susanna Dukinfield, 1722; (2) Martha, daughter of Sir Robert and Lady Susanna Dukinfield,

Dukinfield Old Chapel. From SW. (40)

1723, fragmentary; (3) Sir Robert Dukinfield, Bart., 1729.

  CYB (1874) 418–19. Gordon (1896) 7–31. Halley (1869) I: 294–5. Nightingale V (1893) 311–13.

(40) DUKINFIELD OLD CHAPEL (SJ 944979). The Presbyterian congregation, latterly Unitarian, originated about 1677

following the death of John Angier, who had succeeded in maintaining a nonconforming ministry at the chapel-of-ease at Denton. His nephew Samuel Angier, failing in an attempt to succeed his uncle, opened a barn at Denton and later his house and a barn at Dukinfield for use as a meeting-house, and may for

Dukinfield Old Chapel.   (40)

a few years from 1695 have used Sir Robert Dukinfield's chapel.

The first chapel on the present site, built in 1707–8, was a long building aligned N–S with a tall pedimented porch centrally to the W with twin doorways and surmounted by a bell-cote; the pulpit was against the E wall. A rebuilding proposed in 1838 was rendered imperative by severe storm damage the following January, and the present chapel designed by Richard Tattersall of Manchester was opened 26 August 1840. The W front was rebuilt and extended in 1892.

The chapel has stone walls and slate roofs. The original building is cruciform with tall lancet windows in the transepts and N and S aisles with clerestory windows above the arcades. The later W front has a traceried window above the entrance flanked by buttresses rising to octagonal turrets. The interior has a rib-vaulted plaster ceiling. Galleries around three sides are continuous across the transepts. At the E end is an organ chamber with vestry below. The pulpit, set high in an elaborate screen wall in front of the organ, is approached directly from the vestry.

Sunday-school, 200 yards S, at corner of Town Lane and Pickford Lane, was built in 1810, enlarged 1820, 1839, and further extended to the rear in 1881. The original building, of three storeys, has a symmetrical frontage of three bays with a round-arched doorway with rusticated stone surround. (School buildings demolished since 1984)

Fittings – *Font*: hexagonal stone pillar, *c*.1840. *Glass*: original plain quarries and red glass borders with bottle-glass roundels; some later glass of 1881 and 1899 by Comère and Capronnier of Brussels. *Monuments*: in chapel (1) Joshua Rylance, 1804; (2) William Hampson, 1834; (3) John Dukinfield Astley, 1813; (4) John Astley, artist, 1787, erected 1802, signed 'Fisher, York'. In burial-ground, E of chapel (5) Francis Dukinfield Astley, 1825, and William Astley, 1843, tall monument in railed enclosure, with four Ionic columns supporting pedimented sides and surmounted by a draped urn, with shield-of-arms; (6) Rev. John Gaskell, 1836, Ann his wife, 1832, and an infant. S of S transept (7) Samuel Angier, 1713, table-tomb with Latin inscription; (8) Rev. William Buckley, 1752, Judith his widow, 1766, and their children Betty, 1787, and Rev. William Buckley, 1797, table-tomb; (9) William Dukinfield Bart., 1735, table-tomb; N of N transept (10) John Leech, 1822, Elizabeth his widow, 1826, *et al*. In Sunday-school (11) John Whitaker, 1856.

Paintings: in vestry, of former chapel, 1839; in manse, portrait of Samuel Angier, aged 74. *Plate*: includes a two-handled cup of 1690 given by Samuel Angier 1713. *Pulpit*: octagonal with arcaded sides and decorated canopy. *Seating*: in gallery, large box-pews *c*.1840; lower seating renewed 1892. *Sculpture*: in W vestibule, grotesque headstops flank inner doorway.

Evans (1897) 78–80. Gordon (1896). Nightingale V (1893) 280–95. Tayler, H. S., *Dukinfield Old Chapel Sunday School, Century Souvenir* (1900). *UHST* VI (1935–8) 246–50.

(41) METHODIST NEW CONNEXION, Wellington Street (SJ 939983). 'Bethesda' chapel, by John Eaton of Ashton-under-Lyne, 1840–1, with tall lancet windows. (Rebuilt 1977–8)

Rose, E. A., *Methodism in Dukinfield* (1978).

(42) MORAVIAN, Old Road (SJ 944981). A religious society formed in 1740 joined the Moravians in 1743. The first meeting-

Moravian chapel, Dukinfield.   (42)

house was built in 1751 and a settlement was established around the chapel which remained until 1785, when it was removed to Droylsden, Lancashire. A second chapel replaced the former in 1826 and that was superseded by a third in 1859. The latter, demolished in 1973, was of brick with stone dressings and 'long and short' quoins at the front.

The burial-ground, W of the chapel, contains numbered grave-slabs including 'No 1 John Line 1756' (date altered to 1754).

England (1888) 3–14, Pls. 1, 2. McQuillan, T., *Two Hundred Years of Christian Witness: A Brief Account of the Story of the Moravian Church in Dukinfield* (1950).

DUNHAM-ON-THE-HILL

(43) WESLEYAN (SJ 473729). Brown brick on sandstone plinth, round-arched windows with later frames. Dated 1843.

ELTON

(44) PRIMITIVE METHODIST (SJ 458754). Small three-bay brick chapel dated 1845 adjoining earlier barn.

FADDILEY

(45) Former WESLEYAN (SJ 591531). Gabled front with bell-cote, pinnacles and rose window; dated 1873. (Entirely re-fronted since 1977 on conversion to house)

FRODSHAM

(46) WESLEYAN, Five Crosses (SJ 525769). Yellow brick, Gothic, opened 1885. Former chapel 100 yards NE with pedimented front and round-arched windows; dated 1858.

GREAT WARFORD

(47) BAPTIST (SJ 816770). The church, which was in existence by the late 17th century, is reported to have met in various places including 'Norbury House' and Pownall Brow Farm. In 1689 land was acquired in Mottram St Andrew (*see* (100)) for use as a burial-ground and in 1712 the present site in Merriman's Lane, then occupied by a barn and cottage, was acquired to provide a permanent meeting-place. The barn was converted to a meeting-

Wesleyan chapel, Faddiley, before and after conversion to house (45)

Baptist chapel, Great Warford, front. (47)

Baptist chapel, Great Warford. (47)

Baptist chapel, Great Warford, rear. (47)

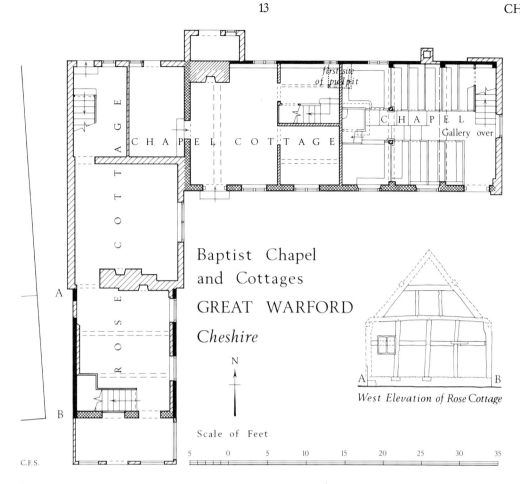

Baptist Chapel
and Cottages
GREAT WARFORD
Cheshire

N

West Elevation of Rose Cottage

Scale of Feet

5   0   5   10   15   20   25   30   35

C.F.S.

house and the cottage remained in use variously altered until 1979. The church was much reduced in support by 1757, when a new minister, John Taylor, briefly attracted greater numbers before a charge of 'unbecoming conduct' divided the congregation; he is credited with 'restoring' the meeting-house with a 'dado of plaited rushes' and his successor, Thomas Holt (*c*.1788–1831), with laying a brick and plank floor in lieu of strewn rushes. A further period of depression was followed in 1838 by a second revival resulting in 'extensive repairs' said to have been carried out in 1845.

The meeting-house retains the basic timber-framed structure of the 16th-century barn from which it was converted, but the S and W walls were rebuilt in brickwork in 1712 or later and the E end wall similarly replaced *c*.1881. The roof is covered with local stone slates in graduated courses. The building was subdivided in the early 19th century and the W half converted to serve as a house for the minister or caretaker.

The S front has a segmental-arched doorway at each end and four intermediate bays of windows, those to the left in two tiers, with one upper window blocked; the two bays remaining to the meeting-house were similar but two tall triangular-headed windows were substituted in the late 19th century. The N wall of exposed timber-framing with brick infilling has at the centre two upper windows which formerly flanked the pulpit.

The interior (originally 15ft by 40ft) had E and W galleries of

which the former remains with an open front of flat shaped balusters. After subdivision the pulpit was re-sited in the NW corner and later removed to its present position; the former sites are outlined in the wall plaster. The roof is ceiled at collar level and one queen-post truss remains with two additional supports below the tie-beam. The W half, now a cottage, is of two storeys with a floor inserted at gallery level. One roof truss with cambered tie-beam remains in a corresponding position to that in the meeting-house.

'Rose Cottage', SW of the meeting-house, is a one-bay timber-framed building of the 16th century of one storey and attic, formerly thatched but with a tiled roof of lower pitch constructed in the late 19th century when a three-storeyed extension was made to the rear. (Cottage demolished 1979)

Fittings – *Baptistery*: an open stone-built baptistery reported to have existed in Foden Lane about a mile NE can no longer be located. *Inscriptions*: on two pierced circular metal plates attached to S doors, perhaps door-pulls with rings missing, 'NOTHE 4 1712', possibly for November the 4; on tablet in blocking of upper window, 'W/BC/1813' for Warford Baptist church; on back of pew, 'TG'. *Monuments*: in burial-ground to S (1) Samuel and Martha Rile, 1771; (2) Joshua Wood, 1790, Hannah his widow, 1798, *et al.*; (3) Joshua Wood, 1729, Elizabeth his widow, 1736, *et al.*; (4) Sarah Bower, 1766, reused stone with earlier date 'HB 1671'. (*See also* (100).) *Pulpit*: square, with

Baptist chapel, Great Warford. Sundial. (47)

fielded-panelled front and wide book-rest renewed on N side, early 18th-century, narrow back-board with early 19th-century moulded border. *Seating*: two ranks of pews with ends tenoned to floor rails, early 18th-century with backs and doors later. *Sundial*: stone pillar with horizontal brass dial inscribed 'This pillar was erected by Thos. Holt minister of this place March 30th, 1813'.

Richards (1947) 383–5. Urwick (1864) 280–3. Whitley (1913).

(48) Former WESLEYAN (SJ 817769). Dated 1843; much altered on conversion to house.

HALE
Greater Manchester

(49) HALE CHAPEL, Hale Barns (SJ 791855). The early 16th-century chapel of Ringey or Ringway, an unendowed donative

originally in the gift of the Earls of Derby, became the home of a Puritan congregation in the 17th century and continued as a seat of nonconformist worship until 1721–2. When the protection of the lords of the manor was eventually withdrawn and the former building transferred to the Church of England, the present site, a field named the Butts or Buttsfield, was acquired and a chapel built on it which was registered 16 July 1723. The congregation, which is described as Presbyterian in the trust deeds, came to accept a Unitarian ministry by the 19th century.

The chapel, of brick with a slate roof, was altered in 1885–98 by the rebuilding of the vestry, the insertion of a doorway at the E end in place of the former entrances and the removal of a W gallery. The broad S front of six bays has four large segmental-arched windows between two orginal doorways, now blocked. An external gallery staircase, perhaps an addition, formerly projected from the W end bay which had an upper doorway and small gallery window to the right. The W end is gabled and was earlier surmounted by a bell-cote now rebuilt in altered form at the opposite end; a Venetian window of *c*.1890 replaces a tall window with wood frame divided by two mullions and three transoms. The E wall has a segmental-arched window, reduced in height, above the inserted entrance. The N wall originally had four windows matching those to the S and two smaller windows flanking the pulpit.

The interior (25½ft by 49½ft), from which a ceiling may have been removed, has three king-post trusses to the roof; the central pulpit and much of the seating remains in its original position.

Fittings – *Bell*: in bell-cote over E gable. *Chairs*: two, early 18th-century. *Collecting Shovels*: three, shallow square trays with handles, 18th-century. *Communion Table*: with turned legs and plain stretchers. *Glass*: in W window, figure of Charity flanked by angels playing musical instruments, by Burne-Jones executed by Morris and Co., 1906. *Paintings*: in vestry (1) portrait of unknown man, oil on canvas, early 18th-century; (2) water-colour drawing of chapel and Sunday-school 1860, by R. H. Wolff. *Plate*: includes four two-handled pewter cups, early 18th-

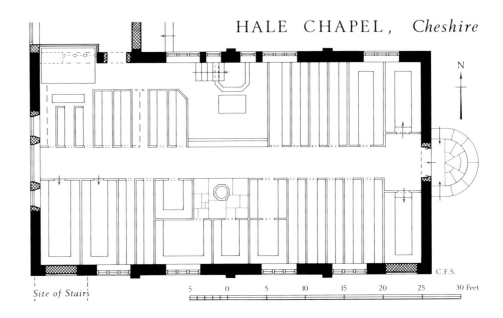

HALE CHAPEL, *Cheshire*

Site of Stairs

century and two tall cups and plate dated 1801, 1804. *Pulpit*: with inlaid bolection-moulded front panel, fluted angles, back-board, and octagonal canopy, early 18th-century, reduced in height; flat balusters reset in staircase. *Sundial*: on S wall, square stone dial, Roman numerals repainted as Arabic, dated 1812.

Evans (1897) 97–9. Gordon, A., *The Story of Hale Chapel and its Ancestry* (1924). Urwick (1864) 382–9.

HASLINGTON

(50) GENERAL BAPTIST, Wheelock Heath (SJ 751574). The plain brick chapel of 1860 replaces a Presbyterian meeting-house of 1704–5, closed 1773 and reopened by Baptists in 1790. *Monuments*: in burial-ground, from 1813.

Urwick (1864) 190–2. Whitley (1913). Wood (1847) 233.

(51) CONGREGATIONAL, The Dingle (SJ 737563). Brick with pointed windows; modern tablet dated 1810 but reported 'opened April 1813'. (URC).

Cong. Mag. III (1820) 456–7.

(52) PRIMITIVE METHODIST, Bradeley Road (SJ 737560). Chapel dated 1868; Sunday-school adjacent 1890 on site of 1860 chapel.

(53) PRIMITIVE METHODIST, Winterley (SJ 747575). Chapel of 1873 replaces 1834 building; Sunday-school adjacent 1903.

HATHERTON

(54) PRIMITIVE METHODIST, Crewe Road (SJ 684473). Three-bay chapel built 1850, enlarged 1898.

HYDE   *Greater Manchester*

(55) HYDE CHAPEL, Gee Cross (SJ 953934). The influence of John Angier, the nonconforming curate of Denton, and the work of his nephew Samuel Angier amongst others, encouraged the formation of a separate Presbyterian society (latterly Unitarian) at Gee Cross. The present site was acquired in 1708 and some intention to supplement rather than supplant the provision of the established church may be detected in the trust deed: this empowered the trustees 'to builde a chappel thereupon for the use . . . of oulde people and children of the inhabitants of the three towns of Hyde, Werneth and Haughton by reasons that those three towns are soe far distant from their parish churches'. The chapel was virtually rebuilt in 1767 in brick of four bays with a bell-cote.

In 1844 a further rebuilding was proposed and the present chapel on an adjacent site was erected in 1846–8. This is of stone and slate in the 14th-century Gothic style by Bowman and Crowther. It comprises a nave with N and S aisles, chancel, S porch, and W tower with broach spire. The E window is of five lights with wheel tracery. The nave has an open timber roof. The N and S arcades have pointed arches below paired clerestory windows.

Fittings – *Communion Table*: stone, on five legs, elaborately painted and gilded. *Font*: stone, octagonal with detached shafts and enriched bowl; crocketed wooden cover. *Glass*: by Warrington of London and Waites of Newcastle upon Tyne.

Hyde Chapel, Gee Cross.   (55)

Inscription: internally above N doorway, recording the date of erection, 1846 'Under the Protection of that Act of Public Justice Stat. vii and viii Vict. c. xlv Which secures to Nonsubscribing Dissenters peaceful Possession Of the Chapels and Endowments of their pious Forefathers.' *Monuments*: in chancel (1) Samuel Ashton, 1812, and Mary his widow, 1825. In extensive burial-ground many monuments mainly of 19th century. *Painting*: water-colour of former chapel, 1846. *Seating*: pews with doors extend across full width of nave.

Evans (1897) 109–10. Middleton, T., *A History of Hyde Chapel* (1908). *UHST* VII (1939–42), 70.

(56) CONGREGATIONAL, Stockport Road (SJ 955942). 'Zion Chapel' built 1847–8 for seceders from the now-demolished Union Street chapel, brick with hipped roof, bays divided by pilasters.

Powicke (1907) 205–6. Urwick (1864) 350.

(57) UNITARIAN, Flowery Field (SJ 945955). Built 1878 by Thomas Worthington for a congregation formed in 1831. Prominent battlemented tower at SE corner. Polygonal chancel, nave with galleried transepts and small rear gallery.

Evans (1897) 110–11.

KINGSLEY

(58) Site of FRIENDS, Meeting-house Lane (SJ 531748). Burial-ground now garden surrounded by low sandstone wall. Inscription on two stones in NE wall: 'Easterly edge of site of Friends Meeting House built 1686 taken down 1856 by order of Cheshire Monthly Meeting'.

(59) FREE METHODIST, Blakelees (SJ 542750). Opened 1843; three-bay front, altered.

KNUTSFORD

(60) BROOK STREET CHAPEL (SJ 754783). Although a Pres-byterian presence in Knutsford is known from 1672, when two of the ejected ministers, Hugh Henshaw and Peter Leigh, took

out licences to preach here, the development of a substantial society was delayed by the existence of an evangelical ministry at the parochial chapel. When the curate, Rev. Kettleby Turner, died in 1687 to be replaced, after a dispute involving the rights of the inhabitants to appoint a successor, by a man less sympathetic to nonconformist susceptibilities, support for the existing society was much increased and a pastor appointed. In January 1690 the house of Isaac Antrobus was registered for meetings, to be followed shortly afterwards by the erection of the present chapel in one of the adjoining fields. The chapel was registered in January 1694 and the trust deed of 7 March 7 William III (1695) refers to an earlier agreement allowing the congregation to build the chapel at their own expense. The development of a heterodox ministry from the mid 18th century and the subsequent arrival of other denominations has left the chapel entirely in Unitarian hands.

The chapel, standing well back on the S side of the street, is of brick, the roof is covered at the front with stone slates but the rear slope was re-covered in blue slates in 1888. The windows throughout are of two lights with rendered mullions and surrounds and with plain brick labels to the lower stage. The broad N front has porches at each end incorporating gallery entrances and rebuilt external staircases; between the two tiers of windows are two smaller windows, perhaps inserted in the early 18th century to light the pulpit. The S wall has six windows in two irregularly spaced tiers. The E and W ends are gabled, the former having an exposed roof truss with three-light timber window above the tie-beam, but the latter was rebuilt in brickwork in the late 19th century.

The interior (22½ft by 54ft) has a flat plaster ceiling probably added in the 18th century. An original gallery around three sides has a front of flat shaped balusters; the gallery columns have all been renewed except one in the SW corner now enclosed within a vestry which, with a W vestibule, was separated from the body of the chapel in the 19th century. The lower seating and the

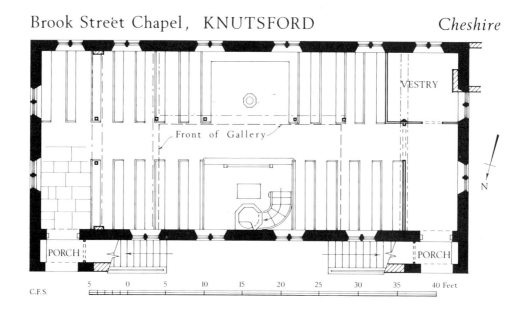

Brook Street Chapel, KNUTSFORD   *Cheshire*

VESTRY

Front of Gallery

PORCH   PORCH

N

5   0   5   10   15   20   25   30   35   40 Feet

C.F.S.

Brook Street Chapel, Knutsford.   (60)

pulpit were renewed in 1859, the former pulpit was transferred to Renshaw Street Mission, Manchester, which was founded in that year. The roof is supported by three intermediate trusses with tie and collar-beams, struts, diagonal ridge and two purlins with wind-braces to each slope.

Fittings – Books: about a hundred volumes of chapel library 'established October 1st 1833'. In 1730 four volumes of Richard Baxter's *Practical Works* were donated of which two were (1934) reported to survive with 'the remains of the fastenings'. *Clock*: in gallery, on S wall, by Luhard Luhardson, 18th-century. *Monuments*: in chapel, said to include two stones to John Long, 1674, and E [ ] his wife, 1651, brought from the parish churchyard 1859, also a brass to Isaac Antrobus, 1734, with Latin inscription. In burial-ground N of chapel many flat slabs of 18th century and later, also monument to Rev. William Gaskell, 1884, Elizabeth his wife (the novelist, Mrs Gaskell), 1865, and their daughters. *Plate*: includes a small two-handled cup of 1694. *Seating*: in gallery, panelled pews of late 17th-century type.

Evans (1897) 124–5. Payne, G. A., *An Ancient Chapel* (1934). Payne, G. A., *250th Anniversary of Brook St Chapel, Knutsford* (1939). Richards (1947) 376–8. UHST VII (1939–42) 179–80. Urwick (1864) 437–48.

(61) WESLEYAN, Princess Street (SJ 751786). Gothic, with corner tower formerly with spire, 1864 by T. R. Clements. Reset against tower, three stone steps from which John Wesley is reputed to have preached, 20 March 1738.

LITTLE LEIGH

(62) BAPTIST, Shutley Lane (SJ 620770). Dated 1829; enlarged and altered.

LONGDENDALE   *Greater Manchester*

(63) Former WESLEYAN, Stalybridge Road, Mottram in Longdendale (SJ 993957). The chapel, built in 1791, was sold to the Methodist New Connexion in 1803. In 1841 the congregation overwhelmingly supported the popular preacher, Joseph Barker, following his expulsion from the Connexion and obtained a lease of the chapel. The 'Barkerites' were dispossessed in December 1845 (*see* (64)), the chapel was briefly reopened by the New Connexion, then let to the Mormons and finally to the Independents, who bought it in 1852 and added a Sunday-school alongside in that year.

The chapel has stone walls covered with later rendering, and a

former WESLEYAN CHAPEL, MOTTRAM   CFS1972

slate roof formerly with a 'cupola' or bell-cote. In 1835 the walls were heightened and a gallery added. The E and W walls each have three round-arched windows; the entrance is at the S end. The interior (33ft by 24ft) has a S gallery supported by two fluted cast-iron columns. The original pulpit has been partly covered by modern boarding. Major alterations to the interior were proposed 1979.

WHS, L & CJ II (1970–4) 185–9.

(64) CHRISTIAN BRETHREN, Hyde Road, Mottram in Longdendale (SJ 992956). The 'Barkerite' congregation from the foregoing, who from 1841 had adopted the title 'Christian' or 'Christian Brethren' as their peculiar designation, removed to a new building 150 yards SW of the former opened November 1846. There they established close links with neighbouring Unitarian congregations from which they were theologically indistinguishable.

The chapel, of stone with a hipped slate roof, is of two storeys with a broad front of six bays to the street. It was particularly intended to provide for the needs of a large Sunday-school and is inscribed 'Mottram Christian Sunday School for Children of all Denominations Built by Subscription A.D. 1846'.

Evans (1897) 178. Petts, G. W., *The Origin and Rise of Hyde Road Christian Church, Mottram-in-Longdendale* (1954).

(65) METHODIST NEW CONNEXION, Spring Street, Hollingworth (SK 004963). Stone with hipped slate roof, opened 1830. Three-bay front with two tiers of Venetian windows in centre bay; continuous gallery.

Monuments: in burial-ground, of early 19th century and later include Hugh Lawton, 1834, *et al.*, table-tomb erected 1860.

LYMM

(66) STRICT BAPTIST, Cherry Lane (SJ 664850). Built 1819. Brick with round-arched windows; porch added and interior refitted 1889.

Paul (1961) 302–6.

(67) BAPTIST, Higher Lane (SJ 686867). The chapel, built in 1850, has walls of sandstone and a decorative slate roof. The side walls of four bays divided by stepped buttresses have two-light traceried windows. The interior has an open timber roof; a stone pulpit in the SE corner and two ranks of box-pews with doors removed are contemporary with the building. The baptistery is in a room at the E end separated from the chapel by a segmental arch closed with shutters.

(68) CONGREGATIONAL, Brookfield Road (SJ 680873). Stone, formerly with a patterned slate roof now tiled, and double bell-cote at S corner now removed; five-bay sides with paired lancets. Built 1862–3, by Edward Walters. (URC)

CYB (1963) 331. Powicke (1907) 107–9. Urwick (1864) 455–6.

(69) PRIMITIVE METHODIST, Eagle Brow (SJ 681872). The chapel dated 1897 stands alongside the former chapel of 1849. The latter, of stone with a gabled brick front formerly with a central entrance, has pointed-arched windows with moulded labels.

Sellers, I., Jackson, M. and Thomas, G., *Methodism in Lymm 1786–1986* (1986).

(70) INDEPENDENT METHODIST, Cherry Lane (SJ 675869). 'Sion Chapel' dated 1849; three-bay front with lancets.

MACCLESFIELD

(71) KING EDWARD STREET CHAPEL (SJ 91657385). John Gartside, a Presbyterian licensed as a preacher in 1672 in Macclesfield, Mottram and Gawsworth, may have laid the foundations for this congregation, which in 1690 had a Congregationalist, Joseph Eaton, as its minister. Unitarian doctrines came to be favoured by the society in the late 18th century resulting in a Trinitarian secession *c*.1777. A second Unitarian chapel was opened in Parsonage Street in 1859 by opponents of the long-established patronage of the Brocklehurst family at the old meeting-house, but the two congregations reunited in 1896.

'Back Street Chapel', as it was called until 1825, stands on the S side of the street concealed behind a line of buildings. The chapel was opened on Bartholomew's day 1690, and registered 15 January 1691. The interior was refitted and the cross gallery removed *c*.1840 and the lower seating was again renewed in 1930. The walls are of sandstone laid in shallow courses and the roof is covered with blue slates. The broad N front has entrances in the end bays covered by two-storeyed porches similar to those at Knutsford (60) with external gallery staircases. Two tiers of windows of two and three lights with stone mullions, some replaced in timber, have altered frames and lowered cills. The S wall is of eight bays with two tiers of windows. The end walls are blank and covered by later building.

Presbyterian chapel, King Edward Street, Macclesfield. (71)

The interior (21¼ft by 60½ft) has galleries at the E and W ends, with cusped panelled fronts of c.1840. The pulpit, set centrally against the N wall, has at the back an elaborately panelled Gothic 'reredos' of c.1840; this was altered in 1929 to obscure four of the front windows. The roof is supported by three trusses, partly exposed where the ceiling was raised to collar level.

Fittings – *Baptismal Basins*: (1) shallow pewter dish, 18th-century; (2) pottery fontlet and cover dated 1842, reproduction at one-eighth full size of font in St Mary Magdalene Church, Oxford. *Chair*: with elaborately carved rails, panelled back, arms terminating in human hands, said to be by William Leicester, 1688. *Clock*: on front of E gallery, dial with arched head, 18th-century. *Paintings*: in vestry, oil portraits of Thomas Culcheth, minister 1717–51, and his wife. *Plate*: includes a pair of cups of 1727. *Pulpit*: octagonal with bolection-moulded panels, domed canopy with inlaid soffit, 1690; clerk's desk in front, 18th-century. *Rainwater-head*: centrally on N wall, lead, dated 1690. *Seating*: in E gallery, open-backed benches with panelled ends, c.1840.

Evans (1897) 160–2. Richards (1947) 378–80. *UHST* (1951–4) 142–7. *Urwick* (1864) 223–35.

(72) BAPTIST, St George's Street (SJ 918731). 1873, Italianate, with continuous oval gallery and circular pulpit.

(73) CONGREGATIONAL, Park Green (SJ 918734). The Trinitarian seceders from King Edward Street built a chapel in Townley Street in 1788, which was enlarged in 1789 and further enlarged or rebuilt in 1810; it was superseded in 1876–7 by Park Green chapel designed by C. O. Ellison.

The former 'Ebenezer chapel', standing behind its successor, is a plain building of brick with a gabled front and central entrance. The interior (57½ft by 36ft) has a gallery around three sides with a late 19th-century cast-iron front. A large Sunday-school building stands adjacent. (URC)

Cong. Mag. III (1820) 625–6; *CYB* (1877) 484–5. Powicke (1907) 206–10. Urwick (1864) 236–47.

(74) SUNDAY-SCHOOL, Roe Street (SJ 916735). A large building of brick in ten bays of four storeys was erected for inter-denominational use in 1813. Sectarian rivalry led to Independent services being held there until 1823, when they were transferred to St George's Chapel.

Cong. Mag. II (1819) 122; III (1820) 626–7.

(75) ST GEORGE'S CHAPEL, High Street (SJ 919730). Built in 1822–3 for the congregation gathered at Roe Street by Rev. R. S. McAll. The cost of erection was largely met by the sale of shares, the shareholders having the right of ministerial appointment. In 1827 the proprietors declined to support a candidate proposed by the majority of the attenders and proceeded to transfer the chapel to the Church of England, to which it now belongs; a new Independent chapel was built in Roe Street (*see* (76)).

The chapel has brick walls and a slate roof. The N front of three bays, with a pediment pierced by an arch over the centre bay, has two round-arched doorways in an open Doric porch with Venetian windows above. The side walls have two tiers of windows in seven bays. A chancel has been added at the S end. The interior has a coved plaster ceiling and a gallery around three sides supported by fluted cast-iron columns.

EM NS VI (October 1828) 445. Powicke (1907) 210. Urwick (1864) 248–9.

(76) Former CONGREGATIONAL, Roe Street (SJ 915735). The chapel was built in 1829 to designs by a Mr Stringer, for the seceders from St George's Chapel. After c.1930 it became 'St Albans parochial hall' and has subsequently been altered for use by the Salvation Army. The walls are of brick with an ashlar front and the roof is hipped and slated. The front of five bays has round-arched upper windows. The interior has been subdivided and no original fittings remain. Contemporary cast-iron railings and gate piers stand adjacent to the street.

EM NS VII (September 1829) 414–15. Powicke (1907) 210–12. Urwick (1864) 248–53.

Former Congregational chapel, Roe Street, Macclesfield.　(76)

(77) FRIENDS, Mill Street (SJ 917735). The meeting-house, standing behind buildings on the E side of the street, was built in 1705 and greatly enlarged to the S c.1916. The E wall is of coursed sandstone rubble, the S wall has been removed, and the other walls are obscured by later buildings; the roof is slated and gabled to east and west. No original windows remain. The interior (originally 36¼ft by 21¼ft) has a W gallery with an early 19th-century balustraded front. The stand, formerly at the E end, has been removed. The roof is supported by two original exposed queen-post trusses. A *burial-ground* surrounding the meeting-house has been mostly built over but two large ledger stones remain (1) Thorp family, 1828–60; (2) Martha Hanson, 1852.

(78) Former WESLEYAN, Sunderland Street (SJ 920734). Methodist preaching commenced about 1743 and shortly afterwards a stable was converted for use as a preaching-house. This was exchanged in 1750 for a cottage similarly converted and by a new chapel in 1764. The first chapel on the present site was built in 1779 and visited by John Wesley in the following year. Serious structural defects became apparent in January 1798 during a crowded service led by Dr Coke and the chapel was rebuilt in its final form.

The chapel, completed in December 1799, was closed in 1969. The walls are of brick and the roof is hipped and slated. The W front to the street is of four bays with two tiers of pointed-arched windows. The N and S walls, which are similarly fenestrated,

Wesleyan Chapel, Sunderland Street, MACCLESFIELD, *Cheshire*

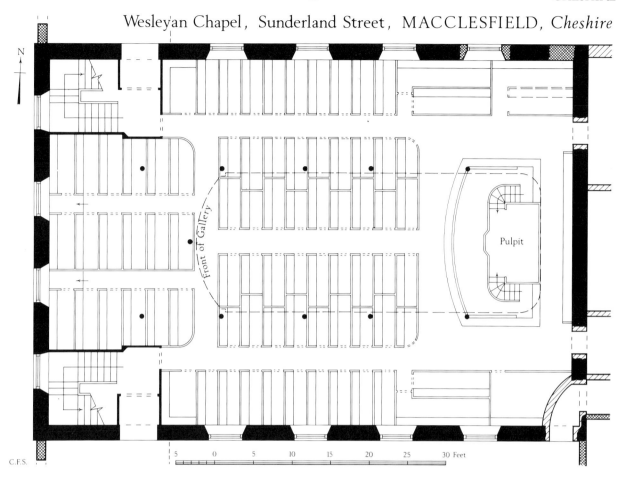

N

Front of Gallery

Pulpit

5 0 5 10 15 20 25 30 Feet

C.F.S.

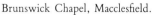

Brunswick Chapel, Macclesfield. (79)

Former Methodist chapel, Park Street, Macclesfield. (80)

have entrances in the foremost bays approached through arched gateways from the street. The interior (67¾ft by 47¼ft) has a continuous gallery supported by cast-iron columns. In 1902 an organ recess was constructed at the E end at gallery level and a rostrum pulpit was probably also inserted at that date. The original box-pews remained to the lower floor but the gallery

pews were renewed in the late 19th century.

Dolbey (1964) 77–8.

(79) WESLEYAN, Chapel Street (SJ 91957300). 'Brunswick Chapel', built in 1823, has walls of brown brick. The front wall of five bays with two tiers of round-arched windows has a three-bay pedimented centre and a formerly open semicircular porch

with Doric columns and entablature. The side walls, originally of six bays, have been extended by two further bays to the rear. The interior has a continuous gallery; the pulpit and seating were replaced in the late 19th century.

(80) Former METHODIST NEW CONNEXION, Park Street (SJ 918731). Built 1836. Brick with five-bay front, two tiers of windows and flanking entrance and staircase wings. Now in commercial use.

(81) PRIMITIVE METHODIST, Beech Lane (SJ 916741). Brick with three-bay gabled front dated 1830. Round-arched windows with altered glazing.

(82) Former FREE METHODIST, Park Green (SJ 91957321). Four-bay front with three tiers of windows between three-storeyed wings. Inscribed band below cornice, now defaced, dated 1858. Now in commercial use.

(83) Former CHAPEL, Parsonage Street (SJ 91827322). Plain brick with two tiers of round-arched windows, three-bay gabled front. Built 1806 for evangelical dissenters.

MARPLE   *Greater Manchester*

(84) CONGREGATIONAL, Marple Bridge (SJ 966893). The church, now URC, which originated in the late 17th century first met in a barn at Mill Brow where a chapel was built in 1716. A new chapel was built on the present site in Hollins Lane in 1787; it was enlarged in the early 19th century and superseded by the existing chapel in 1885. Gothic by Barker and Ellis of Manchester on steeply sloping site; Sunday-school 1905.

Monuments: in burial-ground, many ledger stones of late 18th century and later, broken in pieces and rearranged in long flights of steps.

Urwick (1864) 332–5.

(85) Former PRIMITIVE METHODIST, Moor End Road, Mellor (SJ 987886). Low stone building with arched doorway in gabled end and tablet dated 1827. Now used by Scouts.

(86) UNITED METHODIST, Newhouse Hill, Mellor (SJ 985885). Gabled ashlar front with rusticated quoins and two tiers of short round-arched windows. Opened 1845. *Monument*: in front of chapel, Thomas Knowles Waller, Wesleyan local preacher, 1864, 'in 1817 he settled at Mellor where he established the first Sunday School and Methodist services'.

(87) WESLEYAN SUNDAY-SCHOOL, Marpleridge (SJ 963871). 'Mount Pleasant Sunday School' adjacent to the site of a chapel of 1876, now demolished, was built c.1842.

MIDDLEWICH

(88) Site of FRIENDS, Newton Bank (SJ 699663). A meeting-house registered in 1692 but of uncertain date was closed c.1790 and later used for a British School; it subsequently served (1863–83) as a Free Methodist chapel but has long been demolished. In a 19th-century brick boundary wall incorporating some earlier material is a reset sandstone lintel inscribed 'SOCIETY OF FRIENDS 1690'.

Urwick (1864) 175.

MILLINGTON

(89) Former BAPTIST, Arthill (SJ 725855). A congregation of

Johnsonian Baptists formed in the mid 18th century acquired the present site 'part of a close called The Meadow . . . containing 8 roods 29 yards of Cheshire measure' in 1759. The meeting-house, registered in October 1759, eventually became a preaching-station for Higher Lane Chapel, Lymm, but closed c.1924. It was subsequently used as a workshop. In 1987 the whole property was under conversion to a private house.

The original building (39ft by 19¾ft externally), of brick and slate, incorporated minimal living accommodation at the E end; in the early 19th century this was extended with the addition of a cottage of two storeys with a wing projecting to the N, and an external staircase was provided for separate access to the gallery room.

In the S front are two wide round-arched windows with keystones and separate chapel and cottage doorways. Two large windows on the N side have plain arched heads. In the original E end wall, now internal, are two former gallery windows with segmental-arched heads and keystones.

The interior, of three bays, had a flat plaster ceiling inserted in the mid 19th century. The pulpit stood at the W end between two small upper windows. At the opposite end is a gallery with plain boarded front and false panelling, now closed above; the original access appears to have been by a staircase in the cottage for which the gallery may have served as additional accommodation. All seating has been removed but the stone paving of a central aisle remains to the lower floor with brick floors below side pews.

The roof is supported by two king-post trusses with bent principals.

Monuments: in burial-ground to S, include some table-tombs and ledger stones of exceptional size, (1) Ann, wife of Joseph Blease of Bollington, 1760, 'She being the first corps interr'd in this Yard'; (2) Isaac Cheetham, 34 years minister, 1800, table-tomb; (3) William Hazeldine, 1823, sandstone slab (6ft 4in. by 8ft 8in. by 4in.); (4) Joseph Forrest, 1826, and Ann his widow, 1830 (6ft 5in. by 8ft 8in.).

Dawbarn, R. (ed.), *History of a Forgotten Sect of Baptised Believers Heretofore Known as "Johnsonians"* (nd, ?c.1910). Urwick (1864) 450. Whitley (1913) 66, 124, 151.

(90) CONGREGATIONAL, Bucklow Hill (SJ 731833). Low brick pedimented front of three bays, built 1835. Porch added c.1885; horizontal cornice of pediment removed. (URC)

Powicke (1907) 97–101. Urwick (1864) 437.

(91) Former WESLEYAN, Booth Bank (SJ 725853). Tablet from 1834 chapel recording John Wesley's preaching at Booth Bank Farm, 1747, reset below motorway bridge.

MINSHULL VERNON

(92) CONGREGATIONAL, Cross Lane (SJ 678606). Built 1809–10, greatly altered and refenestrated c.1880. Original round-arched window with wooden Y-tracery in N gable. (URC)

Powicke (1907) 161–6. Urwick (1864) 183–6.

(93) Former WESLEYAN, Bradfield Green (SJ 681593). Broad three-bay front with later porch.

MOBBERLEY

(94) Former METHODIST, Knolls Green (SJ 803795). The chapel,

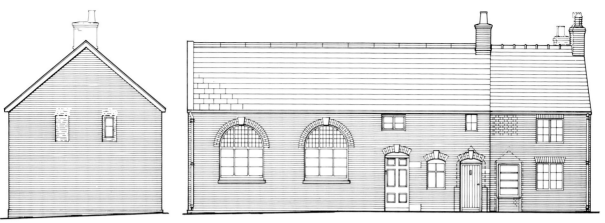

West Elevation   *South Elevation*

Section aa   *North Elevation*

Former Baptist Meeting-house at Arthill
MILLINGTON, *Cheshire*

5   0   5   10   15   20   25   30   35 Feet

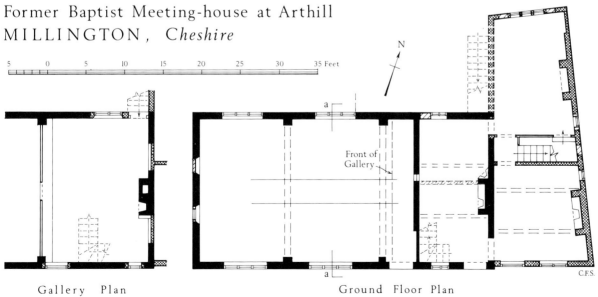

Gallery Plan   Ground Floor Plan

Former Methodist chapel, Knolls Green, Mobberley. (94)

built in 1783 for Methodist preaching and subsequently occupied by the Methodist New Connexion, was reopened by Independents by 1803 and formally transferred to Congregational trustees in 1806. It is a small building of brick, with a slate roof that rises above the line of the adjacent 18th-century cottages to the right and of the Sunday-school of 1902 to the left which replaces a pair of similar cottages. The SW front has been refenestrated in the late 19th-century with two pointed-arched windows and a gallery window above a wooden porch. The rear elevation is generally similar. The interior (26¾ft by 21ft), largely refitted in the late 19th-century, has an original NW gallery with fielded-panelled front and later fretwork embellishment.

Chandelier: in school-room, brass, six-branch with gadrooned body inscribed 'THE GIFT OF MR HENRY RIDGEWAY OF MOBBERLY. 1783'.

Dolbey (1964) 71. Powicke (1907) 104–5. Urwick (1864) 285.

MONKS COPPENHALL (*CREWE*)

(95) GENERAL BAPTIST, Union Street (SJ 706550). 1883–4 by J. Wallis Chapman. Octagonal timber-framed lantern.

(96) BAPTIST, West Street (SJ 699561). 1900 with 1895 Sunday-school behind. Cast-iron arcades with provision for side galleries. *Organ*: domestic chamber-organ by Alex. Young and Sons, Manchester, 1897, with elaborately painted case and monogram. 'J B F', formerly at Berkeley Towers.

(97) Former CONGREGATIONAL, Edleston Road (SJ 704555). The present site on the W side of the road, originally Oak Street later Exchange Street, was bought in 1841 by the Cheshire County Union, although the chapel was not built until 1847. In 1868 services were transferred to the Town Hall and elsewhere prior to the erection of a new chapel 'at the top of Victoria Street' (*see* (98)). The former building was then sold for commercial use. It was reopened by Christadelphians in 1930.

The chapel, of brick with stone dressings and a slate roof, is a late Gothic *jeu d'esprit* with a battlemented E front divided by panelled pilasters, and with ogee labels above doorway and windows. A shield-shaped tablet in the gable carries a defaced inscription. The side walls each have four windows with pointed-

Former Congregational chapel, Edleston Road, Crewe. (97)

arched heads and cast-iron frames. The interior has a moulded and panelled ceiling; no gallery or original fittings survive.

Chaloner, W.H., *Crewe Congregational Church, 1841–1947* (1947). Urwick (1864) 148.

(98) CONGREGATIONAL, Hightown (SJ 701558). Red brick in utilitarian Lombardic style, 1869–70, by W.F. Poulton, replacing the foregoing. (URC)

Chaloner (1947) op. cit. *CYB* (1870) 378.

(99) Former PRIMITIVE METHODIST, Ramsbottom Street (SJ 697561). 'Heath Memorial', dated 1874; arcaded entrance. (Derelict 1977)

MOTTRAM ST ANDREW

(100) BAPTIST BURIAL-GROUND (SJ 876782). Land adjacent to 'Oak Cottage' was bought in 1689 and placed in trust in 1691 for the use of the church now meeting at Great Warford (47). It is described as a close called 'The Sandfield, 32 yards long and 20 yards wide at one end and two and a half yards wide at the other end besides the ditch'. A stone near the entrance erected 1933 is inscribed 'GREAT WARFORD BAPTIST CHAPEL BURIAL GROUND FOUNDED 1689'.

Monuments: (1) Joseph Burges, 1745, headstone; (2) Thomas Falkner, Elizabeth his wife and their sons Samuel and John, all 1757; (3) Thomas Eaton, 1710; (4) Margret (*sic*), wife of Thomas Eaton, 1709; (5) Mary Haywood, 1706; (6) Dorothy Preston, 1701.

NANTWICH

(101) GENERAL BAPTIST, Barker Street (SJ 651522). The meeting-house, demolished in 1957, is said to have been built in

1725 on a site formerly the property of Samuel Acton, a tobacconist and person of means, who also served as minister. The subsequent appointment of a Particular Baptist pastor led to a decline in attendance, and about 1770 the building was let to the Methodists, who used it until 1808. An attempt to re-establish the General Baptist church was made in 1812, when the meeting-house was reopened with help from the New Connexion church at Barton in the Beans, Leicestershire. The acceptance by the pastor, John Cooper, and his successors of Unitarian doctrines led to the expulsion of the church from the Connexion in 1833, and before 1840 to the demise of the society. The third and existing Baptist church was formed here in 1862, removing in 1873 to a new chapel in Market Street (SJ 65185242), after which the building passed to secular use.

The meeting-house was a small building of brick and tile about 32ft long with segmental-arched windows and renewed frames. The roof structure in three bays appears to have had wind-braces to the lower purlins.

Monuments: Hall (1883) records a wall monument, re-sited in the school-room of Market Street chapel, to Lydia wife of John Goodale, 1746. Elizabeth Minshall, widow of John Milton, is said to have been buried here in 1727, but no reliable evidence is available.

Hall (1883) 393–7. *Nantwich Chronicle* 5 October 1957. Shaw, W.S., *A Short History of the Nantwich Baptist Church* (1953). Taylor (1818) II: 262n, 377–82. Urwick (1864) 134–5. Whitley (1913). Wood (1847) 208. Wright, E.H., *Hospital Street Methodist Church and Circuit, 1808–1958* (1958).

(102) Former CONGREGATIONAL, Monks Lane (SJ 653523). The church originated with the itinerant preaching of Captain Jonathan Scott and first met in 1780 in a converted coachmaker's shop in Barker Street. The first chapel, built in 1801 in Church Lane, was superseded by the present building in 1842. The church (now URC) has met since 1974 in the Baptist Chapel, Market Street, and proposals for the conversion of the Monks Lane Chapel into four houses were made in 1980.

The chapel has brick walls and a slate roof. The N front, in red brick laid to Flemish bond, is of three bays with a pediment. The side walls of brown brick have two tiers of round-arched windows in four bays. Minor extensions to the S were made in the late 19th century and in 1903 a large Sunday-school (demolished since 1971) was built to the west. The interior has a gallery around three sides with original box-pews; the lower pews were renewed in the late 19th century. The pulpit at the S end, standing on four Ionic columns, has a contemporary panelled front and stands in front of a later organ recess.

Monuments: in chapel (1) John Ramsay, 1834; (2) Andrew Ramsay, 1835, *et al.*; (3) Gilbert Ramsay, 1857, signed 'Knowles, Manchester'; (4) Robert John Cumming, 1852; (5) Henry Hilditch, 1834, and Mary his widow, 1866; (6) Sarah, daughter of Rev. Peter Henshal, 1823, painted board; (7) Elizabeth Smith, 1814; (8) Rev. Robert Smith, 40 years minister, 1822; (9) Edgar Whitfield Sadler, 1854; (10) Henry Kitchen, 1821, painted board. N of chapel (11) John, Andrew and William Ramsay, early 19th-century, 'removed from Church Lane Chapel and interred here August 21st, 1907'. W of chapel (12) Joseph

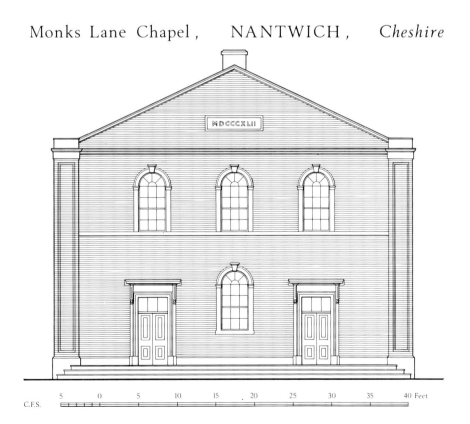

Monks Lane Chapel,   NANTWICH,   *Cheshire*

MDCCCXLII

C.F.S.   5   0   5   10   15   20   25   30   35   40 Feet

Jackson, 1876, Ann his wife, 1855, and Samuel their son, 1849.

Hall (1883) 398–400. Powicke (1907) 158–61. Urwick (1864) 135–8.

(103) Former FRIENDS, Pillory Street (SJ 652521). The meeting-house, built in 1725 on land acquired the previous year, was repaired and altered c.1850. Meetings ceased in 1922; the building was converted to a theatre in 1983. The walls are of brick and the roof is tiled. The original structure is rectangular (38½ft by 20½ft) with a gabled entrance wing of c.1850 on the E side. The N wall has been rebuilt. Windows have flat-arched heads and later sashes. The interior, largely refitted c.1850, is divided into two rooms. The principal room has a stand at the N end with a dado of reused 18th-century fielded panelling behind. The gallery at the S end has a stepped floor; the panelled front was formerly closed with removable shutters.

The roof is supported by two original trusses incorporating some reused material; that over the main room has a tapered king-post and braces, the other above the gallery front has tie and collar-beams.

Monuments: in former burial-ground, now car park, uniform 19th-century headstones reset against N boundary wall.

Hall (1883) 397–8.

Former Friends' Meeting house, NANTWICH   *Cheshire*

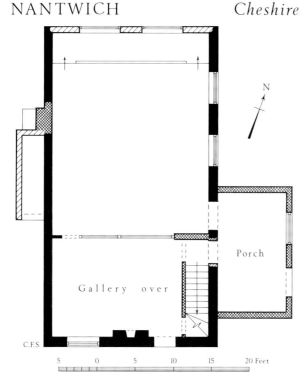

(104) WESLEYAN, Hospital Street (SJ 653522). The chapel, built in 1808 for the society formerly meeting in the General Baptist Chapel, is said to have copied the design of one recently built in Wagg Street, Congleton. The walls are of brick and the roof is hipped and slated. The side walls are in three bays with two tiers of round-arched windows. A further bay was added to the front in 1876, the original front was of five bays with a three-bay pediment. The interior, refitted in 1876, has a gallery around three sides supported by cast-iron columns.

Hall (1883) 400–3. Wright (1958) op. cit.

(105) PRIMITIVE METHODIST, Welsh Row (SJ 646524). The chapel built in 1840, superseding a building in Marsh Lane converted in 1826, has a three-bay pedimented front with double doors under a wide central archway. Galleried interior refitted late 19th century.

Hall (1883) 403.

(106) PRESBYTERIAN, Hospital Street (SJ 654522). In 1672 Robert Fogg, ejected Rector of Bangor Isycoed, Flintshire, was licensed as a Presbyterian preacher and his house and two others in Nantwich registered as meeting-houses. Matthew Henry preached here in 1686 'to a considerable company', probably at the Presbyterian meeting-house in Pepper Street, which was formally registered in 1689: that building, originally a malt-kiln, was afterwards converted to a warehouse and finally replaced by a pair of cottages. The site for a new meeting-house at the corner of Hospital Street and Pratchitts Row was acquired in March 1725, and the building erected between 4 May 1725 and 18 May 1726. It stood concealed behind a timber-framed building, next to the street, demolished c.1850, in which Joseph Priestley, minister 1758–61, kept a school to augment his income. The society supported Priestley's religious opinions, becoming Unitarian in its later days; it suffered greatly from lack of support, and although efforts were made to repair the fabric and the fortunes of the society at several periods from the mid 19th century onwards, the cause was abandoned about 1965 and by 1968 the building had fallen into a derelict condition.

The chapel, registered in April 1726, has brick walls with stone dressings at the front and a slate roof with central valley at collar level. Major repairs carried out in 1847–9, after the building had become structurally unsafe, included the entire renewal of the roof structure, partial rebuilding of the S wall and a reversal of the internal fittings. The pulpit, formerly at the S end, was re-sited against a new partition wall inserted to separate the N end and form a vestibule with large school-room above. In 1896 a two-storeyed school building was added as a front wing, partly obscuring the original frontage, and some minor refurbishing was carried out inside the chapel.

Prior to 1896 the N wall had two shaped gables which concealed the ends of the double roof; these gables had been rebuilt in 1870 and may not therefore represent the original design. Between the two entrances was a pair of round-arched windows with keystones, the frames renewed in 1870, and in 1896 the surviving window was subdivided at the level of the inserted floor. Two small windows above the doorways were inserted c.1849. The side and rear walls have each two round-arched windows with keystones; the N window on the W side has been blocked and an upper window inserted.

The interior (42¾ft by 37¼ft) was formerly divided into three bays by two pairs of oak posts with quadrant-moulded corners which supported the earlier roof structure. One pair remains embedded in the inserted partition wall. The other pair was

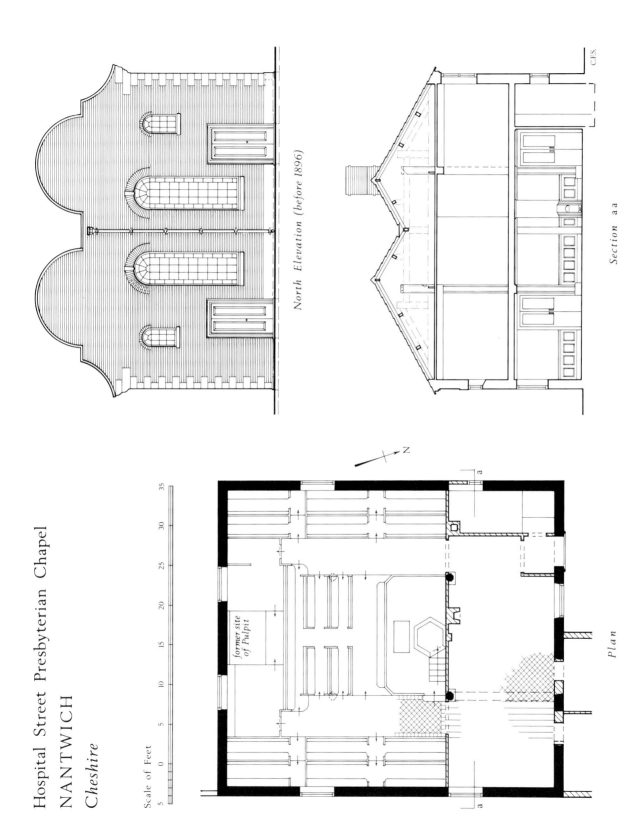

Hospital Street Presbyterian Chapel
NANTWICH
Cheshire

Scale of Feet

North Elevation (before 1896)

Section a a

Plan

former site
of Pulpit

replaced by two queen-post trusses and the reduced area of the chapel covered by a flat plaster ceiling with moulded and enriched cornice. It is possible that the former ceiling may have been vaulted above the central space. (Chapel demolished 1970–1)

Fittings – *Monuments*: in chapel on S wall (1) Rev. James Hawkes, 23 years minister, 1846, and Ann his wife, 1826; (2) Peter Barron, 1831, and Mary Street his wife, 1821; on E wall (3) John, son of Rev. Thomas and Elizabeth Haynes, 1758, small brass plate. In burial-ground, against S wall (4) Elizabeth, wife of John Bolland, surgeon, 1850; (5) Joseph Hassal, 1833, Sarah his widow, 1843, and Emma Vaughan, their daughter, 1829. (Hall (1883) also records (6) Ann, wife of Thomas Cooke, 1834). *Seating*: against E and W walls, two tiers of pews, partly reconstructed, include much early 18th-century fielded panelling, fronts renewed. The centre pews also incorporate original material.

Evans (1897) 178–80. Hall (1883) 383–92. Urwick (1864) 115–34. Minute books from 1847 in Cheshire County Record Office.

NESTON-CUM-PARKGATE

(107) Former CONGREGATIONAL, Parkgate (SJ 279783). A chapel opened in 1809 was superseded by the present building in 1843. About 1863 this was sold to a Presbyterian church, some of the proceeds being used to build a new chapel in Lymm. The chapel is now used by the Church of England as 'St Thomas's Church'.

Sandstone walls and slate roof. Gabled NE front with low battlemented porch and lancet above flanked by plain shields. Side walls of five bays with lancet windows, blind in the end bays.

Former Congregational chapel, Parkgate. (107)

Window frames of cast-iron with floral patterned tracery. Small burial-ground to NE with seven monuments.

Urwick (1864) 66, 456.

NETHER ALDERLEY

(108) Former METHODIST NEW CONNEXION, Soss Moss Hall (SJ 829759). A brass tablet in the kitchen records the use of the room as a Methodist preaching-place from 1835 to 1940.

ODD RODE

(109) WESLEYAN, The Bank (SJ 845573). Rendered walls; three-bay gabled front with lancet windows; dated 1839.

(110) PRIMITIVE METHODIST, Mow Cop (SJ 855572). Large plain brick 'Primitive Methodist Memorial Chapel' built 1860, enlarged 1882, replacing a small chapel of 1841. Date tablet from first chapel reset in side wall.

Kendall (1905) I: 22.

(111) FREE METHODIST, Mount Pleasant (SJ 849567). Dated 1856, porch 1903.

(112) MONUMENT, Mow Cop (SJ 857574). A modern inscription W of The Folly commemorates the Camp Meeting held here 31 May 1807 by the originators of the Primitive Methodist Connexion.

PICKMERE

(113) WESLEYAN (SJ 694772). Small chapel built 1826, perhaps with central entrance; variously altered and rear wing added 1928.

POOLE

(114) WESLEYAN, Poole Green (SJ 636558). Brick with hipped slate roof, broad three-bay front with Gothic traceried panels to central doorway; dated 1834. Pulpit at S end renewed, original tripartite panel with swag ornament on wall behind.

WESLEYAN CHAPEL, POOLE GREEN CFS 1968

PRESTBURY

(115) WESLEYAN, Bollin Grove (SJ 901772). Opened 1816. Cottage attached at end.

RAINOW

(116) WESLEYAN, Walker Barn (SJ 954738). Stone walls and roof, pointed windows. Gabled front dated 1863.

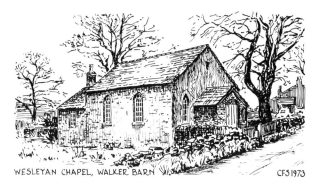

WESLEYAN CHAPEL, WALKER BARN CFS 1973

ROWTON

(117) WESLEYAN, Moor Lane (SJ 451645). Brown brick and slate, three bays with four-centred arched windows and shaped gable towards road, dated 1865. Small school-room wing to left.

RUNCORN

(118) CONGREGATIONAL, High Street (SJ 514830). The congregation originated in 1829 by secession from St John's Countess of Huntingdon's chapel. St Luke's chapel, Mason Street, was built for the seceders in 1830 (rebuilt 1934) but in 1834 a more suitable chapel was provided by a private benefactor. 'Bethesda Chapel' was erected on a new site at the expense of John Tomkinson of Liverpool, a quarry owner who supplied the

Bethesda Chapel, RUNCORN, *Cheshire*

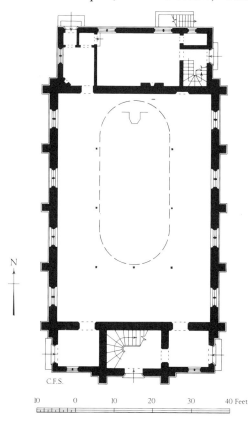

C.F.S.

10   0   10   20   30   40 Feet

Bethesda Chapel, Runcorn. (118)

Bethesda Chapel, Runcorn. Detail of parapet. (118)

stone for the Liverpool Custom House and St George's Hall. The foundation stone was laid 25 August 1834, and the building completed by 29 September 1835, at a cost of £6,000. The chapel remained Tomkinson's property until 1851, when financial difficulties obliged him to sell it to the congregation. The interior was severely damaged by fire in 1891.

The chapel has walls of sandstone ashlar and a slate roof. The body of the chapel is of four bays with two tiers of windows of two lights with rectangular labels, two-stage buttresses, and a battlemented parapet which continues up the front and rear gables. The S front has a central porch of two storeys enclosing the gallery staircase and lower porches to each side. A vestry bay at the N end, also dated 1835, has a plain parapet and two shields to the N carved with grotesque heads. All the windows have cast-iron frames.

The interior has a continuous round-ended gallery supported by cast-iron columns of quatrefoil section. An organ recess with plaster barrel-vaulted ceiling was constructed behind the pulpit *c*.1891 replacing first and second-floor rooms at the N end. The roof is supported by three trusses and is ceiled at collar level. (Demolished *c*.1976)

Monuments: in burial-ground SE of chapel (1) John Tomkinson, 1865, and Elizabeth his widow, 1868, table-tomb; N of chapel (2) Margaret (Pullan), wife of Rev. William Robinson, 1837, and Jane Pullan her sister, 1868; (3) Mary Martyn, widow of Rev. William Robinson, 1886.

Powicke (1907) 137–40. Urwick (1864) 457–9.

(119) Former WESLEYAN, Main Street, Halton (SJ 53958180). Rendered front with pedimented gable dated 1818; converted to cottages after erection of present chapel in 1875.

RUSHTON

(120) Former WESLEYAN (SJ 576638), with two round-arched windows each side of large gabled porch, dated 1840. (Converted to house since 1969)

SALE   *Greater Manchester*

(121) WESLEYAN, Northenden Road (SJ 797916). 'Trinity Chapel', built 1875 by Pennington and Bridgen of Manchester.

Brick with an ashlar front, pedimented entrance front of five bays with two giant Ionic columns *in antis*. Galleried interior with domed centre to ceiling. (Demolition proposed 1978)

(122) Former PRESBYTERIAN, Chapel Road (SJ 787924). The chapel was built in 1739 for a society which previously met in a building nearby in Cross Street, and which continued to use the name 'Cross Street Chapel' for subsequent buildings. In 1876, after the society had adopted Unitarian beliefs, a new chapel was built in Atkinson Road. It was rebuilt after a fire in 1896 and

Former Presbyterian meeting-house, Sale.   (122)

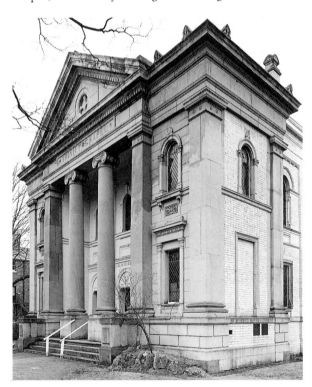

Trinity Chapel, Sale.   (121)

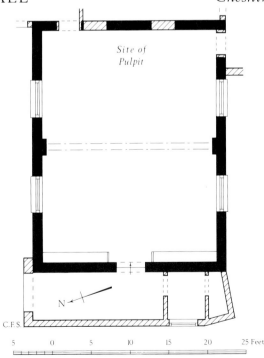

Former Presbyterian Meeting-house
SALE   *Cheshire*

Site of
Pulpit

N

C.F.S.

5   0   5   10   15   20   25 Feet

closed before 1969. The former chapel was used for Sunday-school purposes and later by the St John Ambulance Brigade.

The walls are of brown brick in Flemish bond with some glazed headers and rusticated sandstone quoins; the roof is covered with stone slates to the S but the N slope has been relaid with Welsh slate. The entrance in the gabled W wall, now covered by a lean-to shed, has a semicircular arched head with keystone and impost blocks; above it is a window with similarly arched head and two further windows of a like kind in the N and S walls; these last have hung sashes with original softwood glazing bars. The E wall is covered by a 19th-century extension but the marks of two rectangular windows which flanked the pulpit are visible internally. The interior (29¼ft by 22½ft) has no original fittings. The roof is supported by a central truss and ceiled at the level of the lower purlins. Below the feet of the truss are pilasters with Roman Doric capitals. (Demolished c.1970)

Evans (1897) 216–17. Pipkin, J., *Cross Street Chapel, Cheshire* (1925). Urwick (1864) 366–7.

SANDBACH

(123) CONGREGATIONAL, Hope Street (SJ 757608). 'Hope Chapel', dated 1836 and opened in 1837, was built for a congregation, now URC, formed in 1807. Walls of brown brick with an intermediate platband interrupted by tall round-arched windows, but perhaps originally with two tiers of windows. Gabled front of three bays with round-arched doorway, side to road with three windows and paired doorways under a three-centred arch. Sunday-school behind dated 1893.

Monuments: in chapel yard (1) Rev. William Silvester, 1846, table-tomb; (2) Rev. William Rhodes, 21 years minister, 1870, and Margaret his wife, 1865, table-tomb; also numerous headstones reset around boundary walls.

Cong. Mag. IV (1821) 49. *EM* NS XV (November 1837) 535–6. Powicke (1907) 167–70. Urwick (1864) 192–3.

(124) Former INDEPENDENT, Forge Fields, Wheelock (SJ 750592). Brick with narrow front, swept gable, and two tiers of round-arched windows, upper windows altered. Built 1842, superseded 1892. Now in commercial use.

Urwick (1864) 195.

SOUND

(125) Free METHODIST (SJ 626480). Small chapel with low hipped roof and later porch. Original date tablet reset in boundary wall 'METHODIST CHAPEL ERECTED 1838 BY JOS. CARTLIDGE'.

SPURSTOW

(126) PRIMITIVE METHODIST (SJ 556570). Broad three-bay front; entrance originally in slightly projecting gabled centre. Built 1844, enlarged 1905.

Lucas, G. A., *Spurstow Methodist Church, 1844–1944* (1944).

STALYBRIDGE   *Greater Manchester*

(127) CONGREGATIONAL, Melbourne Street (SJ 963985). Decorated Gothic with big gabled front divided by buttresses and twin-arched outer porch with date 1861. By Poulton and Woodman, superseding a chapel of 1835.

CYB (1862) 293. Urwick (1864) 352.

STOCKPORT   *Greater Manchester*

(128) ST PETERSGATE CHAPEL (SJ 894902). The chapel, built 1842 for a Presbyterian, latterly Unitarian, congregation formerly meeting in a chapel of 1722 in High Street, was demolished in 1971.

Evans (1897) 231–3. *UHST* III (1923–6) 148–52, 272–6, 285. Urwick (1864) 293.

(129) Former FRIENDS, Lower Hillgate (SJ 898902). A meeting-house was built on the E side of the street in 1705–6 and shops erected in front in 1810. Rebuilt 1900 with two gables to street and pointed-arched windows. Burial-ground at rear with nine ledger stones c.1830–50. Sold 1959.

Cheshire Notes and Queries VI (1903) 149–50.

(130) Former METHODIST, Lower Hillgate (SJ 898902). N of (129) facing Garnett Street, the chapel was built in 1784 to replace one of 1759, and was demolished c.1970–5. Brick with three-bay gabled front and simple Venetian windows centrally to gallery and below.

L & CAST LXXVIII (1975), Fig. 2 facing p. 30.

SUTTON

(131) Former SUNDAY-SCHOOL, Sutton Lane Ends (SJ 928709). Front of six bays with two doorways and windows in arched recesses. Defaced tablet 'ERECTED by VOLUNTARY CONTRIBUTIONS AD 1838'.

TARPORLEY

(132) GENERAL BAPTIST (SJ 554623). The first chapel, built 1832 for a church formed in 1817 at Brassey Green (*see* (136)), was superseded by the present building in 1865–6. The chapel, designed by 'Mr Jones of Eaton', has a brick gabled front with flanking buttresses formerly terminated by pinnacles and a pyramidal finial at the apex.

Jupe, M. R., *Tarporley Baptist Church* (1966). Thomas, M. F., *Brassey Green & Tarporley: A Baptist History* (1984). Whitley (1913) 223, 357. Wood (1847) 210.

THORNTON HOUGH   *Merseyside*

(133) CONGREGATIONAL (SJ 304810). 'St George's Church', of 1906–7, is an accomplished essay in the Romanesque manner by J. Lomax Simpson for W. H. Lever (Lord Leverhulme). It comprises an unaisled nave, transepts, apse, and short crossing tower. The elaborately decorated interior retains all its original fittings. (URC)

CYB (1908) 163–4.

TINTWISTLE   *Derbyshire*

(134) CONGREGATIONAL (SK 024973). The formerly Presbyterian church originated in the late 17th century as a result of the preaching of William Bagshawe, 'The Apostle of the Peak'. About 1689 a barn on the present site was acquired for use as a meeting-house and this was superseded by a new building in 1763. The chapel was entirely rebuilt in 1811, the seating capacity increased in 1837 and the structure 'renovated' in 1891.

The chapel, of stone with a hipped slate roof, has a front of three bays with two tiers of Venetian windows in the pedimented centre bay and shallow porches with Tuscan columns and open

Congregational chapel (URC), Thornton Hough. (133)

Congregational chapel, Tintwistle.   (134)

pediments in front of the two entrances. A Venetian window centrally in the rear wall at gallery level has been blocked. An inscribed tablet in the front wall was (1972) obscured by a neon cross. A detached Sunday-school N of the chapel was rebuilt in 1820 and enlarged 1853. (Chapel demolished *c*.1975–80)

Brass: in chapel, to Rev. William Hudson, 30 years pastor, 1811, small grave plate with later tablet below recording his founding of the Sunday-school in 1788, 'the oldest in the district'.

EBENEZER CHAPEL, TINTWISTLE   CFS1972

Cong. Mag. IV (1821) 102–4. Powicke (1907) 235–8. Urwick (1864) 352–61.

(135) WESLEYAN (SK 026974) 'Ebenezer Chapel', built 1830, has a broad three-bay front with pedimental gable and pointed-arched doorway and windows with multiple intersecting glazing bars. (Becoming derelict 1972)

TIVERTON

(136) BAPTIST, Brassey Green (SJ 527607). A strong Baptist element appears to have existed in this district in the late 17th century and the registration of the house of Edward Allen in January 1692 may have been for a Baptist congregation. The first meeting-house on this site is said to have been built about 1700 by Thomas Walley, the building long continuing the private property of his descendants. The present chapel may date from *c*.1742 and be the 'new erected building at Bresne Green in Tirreton' registered January 1743. The Particular Baptist church survived with difficulty in the late 18th century until, under the long ministry of Cornelius Gregory, a General Baptist society was formed in 1817, after which the principal centre of activity passed to Tarporley (*see* (132).)

The meeting-house, standing on a secluded site, has walls of early 18th-century brickwork; the roof was covered in slate in the 19th century. The principal part of the building is of two bays with gabled end walls clasping brick buttresses at the corners and a flat buttress centrally on the N side. The entrance at the W end has a segmental-arched head and in the gable above is a circular opening covered by a modern external shutter. Two segmental-arched windows in the N wall (formerly with leaded lights in 18th-century frames), one in the S wall and two windows at the E end which formerly flanked the pulpit have been partly blocked in brickwork in recent years. A two-storeyed cottage adjoins at the E end of the S side. The interior (20½ft by 16½ft) has been subdivided.

Monuments: in burial-ground (1) Stephen Cawley, 1773, and Ann his widow, 1774, flat slab; (2) John Walley, 1796, Ann his widow 1809, and Ann their daughter, 1773, table-tomb; (3) headstone W of chapel with enigmatic inscription 'Ah! M. S. In 77 & 77./Of what could dy./Death the Bereav'd/Yet, on other terms/more vivid Lives than/Mortals ever Breathd'.

Cong. Mag. III (1820) 400. Jupe (1966) op. cit., 3–7. Thomas (1984) op. cit. Urwick (1864) 144–7.Whitley (1913) 124, 160, 232. Wood (1847) 210.

(137) PRIMITIVE METHODIST (SJ 551604). Polychrome brickwork, gabled front with finial and with inscribed scroll above upper windows dated 1864.

UTKINTON

(138) PRIMITIVE METHODIST, Cotebrook (SJ 571653). Rusticated sandstone walls, three-bay gabled front dated 1843.

WALLASEY   *Merseyside*

(139) CONGREGATIONAL, Rake Lane, Liscard (SJ 308932). The chapel was built in 1841–2 by John Astley Marsden of Liscard Castle, a brush manufacturer and member of the Congregational church which met in Great George Street, Liverpool. Marsden had previously acquired some memorabilia of Dr Isaac Watts

Rake Lane Congregational Chapel, Liscard
WALLASEY
Cheshire

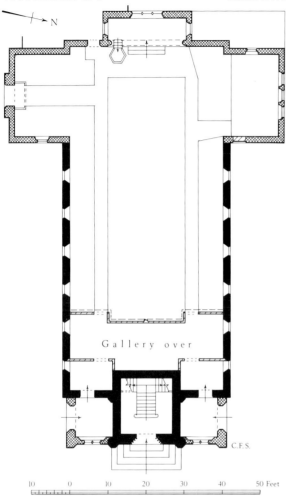

Gallery over

10 0 10 20 30 40 50 Feet

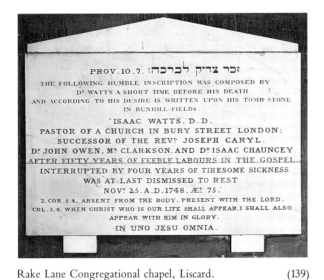

PROV. 10.7.

THE FOLLOWING HUMBLE INSCRIPTION WAS COMPOSED BY
D͂ WATTS A SHORT TIME BEFORE HIS DEATH
AND ACCORDING TO HIS DESIRE IS WRITTEN UPON HIS TOMB STONE
IN BUNHILL-FIELDS.

ISAAC WATTS, D.D.
PASTOR OF A CHURCH IN BURY STREET LONDON:
SUCCESSOR OF THE REV͂ JOSEPH CARYL.
D͂ JOHN OWEN, M͂ CLARKSON. AND D͂ ISAAC CHAUNCEY
AFTER FIFTY YEARS OF FEEBLE LABOURS IN THE GOSPEL
INTERRUPTED BY FOUR YEARS OF TIRESOME SICKNESS
WAS AT LAST DISMISSED TO REST
NOV͂ 25.A.D.1748. ÆT 75.
2.COR.5.8. ABSENT FROM THE BODY, PRESENT WITH THE LORD.
COL.3.4. WHEN CHRIST WHO IS OUR LIFE SHALL APPEAR,I SHALL ALSO
APPEAR WITH HIM IN GLORY.
IN UNO JESU OMNIA.

Rake Lane Congregational chapel, Liscard. (139)

from the latter's chapel in Bury Street, St Mary Axe, London, comprising a memorial tablet, the pulpit, and Sir Thomas Abney's pew; these he incorporated into the new chapel. Although opened in September 1842, the interior furnishings do not appear to have been completed until the following year. Major alterations carried out about 1888 included a considerable westwards extension with the addition of transepts and a shallow chancel, the removal of the original side galleries, and the construction of two outer porches. The chapel was closed *c.*1969.

The walls are of squared sandstone and the roof is slated. The original building is of six bays with lancet windows to the side walls and battlemented parapets. The E front is dominated by a central tower of three stages with octagonal corner buttresses and a two-centred arched doorway which gives access only to the gallery staircase. The interior has an E gallery only. The roof is supported by collar-beam trusses and ceiled on the line of the roof slope.

Fittings – *Monuments*: in chapel (1) Dr Isaac Watts, 1748, plain tablet repeating the inscription on his monument in Bunhill Fields, London; (2) James Marsden, 1840, and Hannah his widow, 1841, buried in Newington Chapel Yard, Liverpool, erected by their son John Astley Marsden. *Pulpit*: hexagonal, wood, 1888, entirely encasing Dr Watt's pulpit. *Sculpture*: on W wall of chancel, bas relief 'copied from one in the Cantorium or Singing Gallery in Florence Guildhall', given by Mrs T. Raffles Bulley, *c.*1888.

[Abbott, G. A.] *Liscard Congregational Church* (1942). Urwick (1864) 93–4.

WEAVERHAM

(140) WESLEYAN, Forest Street (SJ 613741). Brick with terracotta dressings, 1878.

WESTON

(141) PRIMITIVE METHODIST, Englesea-brook (SJ 752515). The chapel has brick walls and a tiled roof. It was built in 1828, extended to the front and much altered in 1832 and a Sunday-school hall erected alongside in 1914. Major repairs and partial conversion to a museum of Primitive Methodism were undertaken in 1983–6.

The original structure had thin walls of 9in. brickwork with low rectangular windows in the side and rear walls visible internally during the latest repairs. In 1832 the front was brought forward by 7ft, an external skin of 4½in. brickwork was added to the side walls for half their former length, and the earlier windows altered.

The front wall of 1832 is gabled with two tiers of hung-sash windows and a reset or renewed tablet dated 1828. Inside is a rear gallery of 1832 supported by two marbled columns and having three ranks of contemporary box-pews. The pulpit and other fittings date from the late 19th century.

Monuments: in burial-ground (1) Hugh Bourne 'chief founder of the Primitive Methodists', 1852, James his brother, 1860, Sarah, wife of the last, 1853, also John Walford, 1869, and Sarah his widow, 1870, short obelisk above tall square base with corner buttresses, signed 'John Walford, *Architectus*'; (2) in chapel, John Dean, 1841, floorslab.

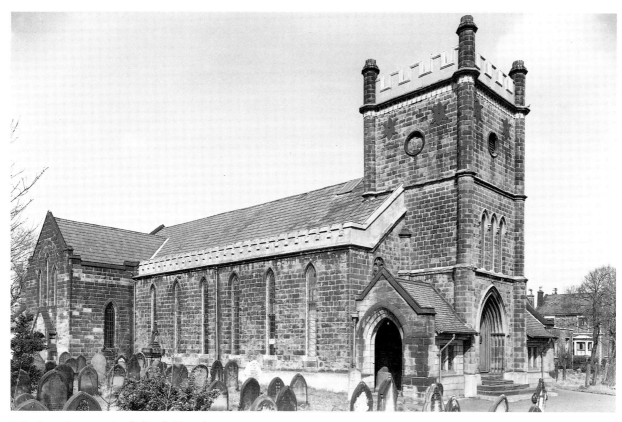

Rake Lane Congregational chapel, Liscard.   (139)

Primitive Methodist chapel, Englesea-brook.   (141)

WHITLEY

(142) FRIENDS' BURIAL-GROUND, Village Lane (SJ 616797). Square enclosure bounded by 19th-century sandstone wall; in use from 1657. *Monuments*: (1) John Starkey Gent., 1686, ledger stone, below the inscription is a small shield charged with a stork. Also small slabs 1849–1951 and unmarked mounds.

(143) WESLEYAN (SJ 613812). Rendered walls and slate roof, broad three-bay front with small porch. Opened 1802, interior refitted late 19th century with stepped seating right of entrance.

WILDBOARCLOUGH

(144) WESLEYAN, Gradbach (SK 001665). Stone with three-bay gabled front, dated 1849.

WILMSLOW

(145) DEAN ROW CHAPEL (SJ 871816). The Presbyterian, latterly Unitarian, congregation originated in the late 17th century probably as a result of the preaching of Robert Bird, ejected curate of Birch Chapel, Manchester, who was licensed as a preacher at Wilmslow in 1672. The formal organization of the society is thought to date from 1688, when Bird's son Eliezer was appointed minister. The meeting-house, built *c*.1694, was registered in January 1695. From the late 18th century the congregation greatly declined and were almost extinct by 1843 when the building had become very dilapidated. A major restoration was then carried out including internal refitting and rearrangement, the formation of two school-rooms at the E end

Dean Row Chapel. (From Nightingale V (1893) 95.)   (145)

and a large gallery to the west. Some further alterations to the fittings were made in 1902.

The chapel has brick walls and the roof is covered with stone slates. The broad S front has external gallery staircases at each end with entrances below to the body of the chapel. Between the staircases are two tiers of windows, four to the lower floor and six above, all of two lights with rendered mullions. Above the lower windows is a continuous brick label. The N wall of six bays was strengthened by the addition of three buttresses in the mid 19th century. The middle bays project slightly and have a pair of cross-framed pulpit windows above a range of lower windows with continuous brick label; the side bays also have two upper windows at the ends of the former galleries. The E and W walls are gabled with ball finials and have each two upper windows but with lower windows at the E end only. A brick bell-cote on the W gable with a single bell was rebuilt in 1910 in memory of the architect Thomas Worthington.

The interior (23ft by 60ft) was greatly altered in 1844–5. It originally had a gallery around three sides with the pulpit centrally on the north. In the alterations the S gallery was removed, the E gallery occupying one and a half bays was closed to form two storeys of school-rooms, and the pulpit re-sited at the E end of the remaining chapel. The W gallery remains supported by two wooden posts with quadrant-moulded angles; an entrance lobby and small room were formed below the gallery.

Fittings – *Communion Table*: in vestry, oak, late 17th-century. *Doors*: four, in S wall, late 17th-century. *Monuments*: in burial-ground (opened 1751) – N of chapel (1) Rev. George Chadwick, minister nearly 17 years, 1803. S of chapel (2) Rev. Hugh Worthington, 1773; (3) Frances, daughter of Rev. William and Sarah Brocklehurst, 1787; (4) Rev. William Brocklehurst, minister nearly 38 years, 1786, Sarah his wife, 1769, and Mary their daughter, 1758; (5) William, son of Rev. William and Sarah Brocklehurst, 1772; (6) Rev. John William Morris, 1843, Elizabeth his widow 1846, *et al*. W of chapel (7) John Clark, 1754; (8) Lydia, daughter of Joseph Barrow, 1781. *Pulpit*: reset in NE corner, wood, octagonal with two tiers of panels, late 17th-

century. *Seating*: remade *c*.1848 incorporating old material. *Sundial*: in burial-ground, pillar with three dials erected *c*.1871.

Arnold (1960) 94–5, 106–7. Burgess, W. H., *The Story of Dean Row Chapel, Wilmslow, Cheshire* (1924). Evans (1897) 65–6. Nightingale V (1893) 95. Richards (1947) 381–3. Urwick (1864) 270–7.

(146) NORCLIFFE CHAPEL, Styal (SJ 834835). The chapel was built in 1823–4 by Samuel Greg, owner of Quarry Bank Mill, who appointed a Baptist minister. In 1833 a Unitarian minister succeeded to the charge who, from 1843, held the pastorate jointly with Dean Row. The chapel, which remained in Unitarian hands, was greatly altered in 1867. In 1979 it became the property of the National Trust, who own the whole of the village.

The walls are of brick and the roof is covered with stone slates. There is a bell-cote above the SW gable. The original chapel was of three bays with an entrance in the NE end. The original side windows have flat-arched brick heads, the frames have been replaced by paired stone lancets. In 1867 the chapel was extended to the SW and a chancel added, buttresses were built against the side walls and a timber-framed porch erected on the SE side.

Evans (1897) 235–6.

(147) CONGREGATIONAL, Chapel Road (SJ 843806). The church, now URC, originated in 1844 and the chapel was erected in 1846–8 on land given by John Jenkins of Fulshaw Hall. The chapel, of stone with lancet windows, was designed by John Rogers; it was much enlarged in 1868 by the addition of a polygonal organ apse and galleried transepts, and in recent times by a large vestibule in front.

Lazonby, W., *Pleasant Pastures: The History of Wilmslow Congregational Church, 1844–1946* (1946). Powicke (1907) 241–4. Urwick (1864) 277–8.

(148) Former FRIENDS, Morley (SJ 832820). The meeting-house, registered in January 1694 as 'a new erected piece of building in Pownall fee, Wilmslow parish', was converted to three cottages about 1830 when the society built a new meeting-house in Wilmslow. It was converted to a single dwelling, 'Penn Cottage', *c*.1960.

Brick walls with slate roof, gabled ends. Segmental-arched windows with renewed frames. Much altered and gable wall rebuilt.

(149) FRIENDS, Altrincham Road (SJ 840811). Built 1830 to replace the foregoing. Brick with sandstone dressings and hipped slate roof. Broad N front of five bays with round-arched windows and central entrance. The interior is divided by a central passage with the main meeting-room of two bays to the E, a smaller room to the W and a separate room at the W end added in 1881 with a lower annexe beyond. In the burial-ground to E are some large 19th-century ledger stones.

(150) WESLEYAN, Hough (SJ 855782). The chapel was built in 1838 for use by a Sunday-school commenced in 1835 and for preaching services. The walls are of brick and the roof slated. The original front faced E and had a central doorway with fanlight between two round-arched windows. In the later 19th century the entrance was re-sited in the gabled S wall between a pair of inserted windows and a large tablet above the original entrance

Congregational chapel, Over.   (152)

inscribed 'WESLEYAN *SUNDAY SCHOOL* 1838' reset in the gable.

   Banks, J., *Hough Chapel 1838–1988* (1988).

(151) WESLEYAN, Styal (SJ 837835). Brown brick with double-gabled slate roof, converted 1837 from an existing outbuilding, extended to rear and variously altered. External staircase to gallery and upper rooms at front.

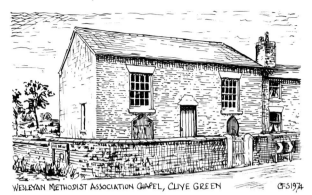

WESLEYAN METHODIST ASSOCIATION CHAPEL, CLIVE GREEN   CFS1974

WINSFORD

(152) CONGREGATIONAL, Over (SJ 640659). 'Providence Chapel', built in 1814–15, was superseded in 1865–8 but survived in Sunday-school use until 1880. The present chapel, by John Douglas of Chester, has walls of red and yellow patterned brickwork in the Lombardic style with an arcaded loggia entrance.

   Parker, T. N., *A Brief History of Over Congregational Church 1814–1964* (1964). Powicke (1907) 161–6. Urwick (1864) 180–2.

(153) PRIMITIVE METHODIST, High Street (SJ 645662). Gabled front of polychrome brickwork with small bell-cote and scrolled inscription dated 1870.

(154) WESLEYAN METHODIST ASSOCIATION, Clive Green (SJ 678651). Broad three-bay front, doorway with shaped lintel and altered inscription. Dated 1849.

WITHINGTON

(155) WESLEYAN, Lower Withington (SJ 814698). Opened 1808, enlarged and porches built late 19th century. *Monuments*: in front of chapel (1) Samuel Gallimore, 1820, *et al.*; (2) Ann, wife of Thomas Wood, 1813, *et al.*

CUMBERLAND

Cumbria

Although adjacent to the Scottish border the county cannot compare with Northumberland in the degree to which orthodox Presbyterianism found continuing favour. The former meeting-houses of that denomination at Brampton (20) and Great Salkeld (55), of the early 18th century, are of local interest, as is the later survival at Maryport (87), and those buildings which were or became Congregational are of wider significance. Of the latter, Redwing Chapel at Garrigill (5) of 1756 and Park Head Chapel near Kirkoswald (79), dating in part from the early 18th century, were worthy examples with a refinement of detail remarkable in such relatively remote situations; both have unfortunately been sold during the course of this survey.

The principal importance of the county, however, lies in the number of surviving Friends' meeting-houses, mostly of 18th-century date, many of which are now closed and converted to other uses. Of the score or so recorded here which incorporate work of the 18th century or earlier, that at Pardshaw of 1729 (47) is perhaps the most interesting. The two earliest are Whelpo (27) and Kirkbride (77) both of 1698, but for architectural merit and as evidence of the prosperity of the Society in the first half of the 18th century, those at Moorhouse of 1733 (25) and Sikeside of 1736 (63) are pre-eminent. Although support seriously fell away later in the century, the meeting-house at Thornyland (104) was rebuilt *c.*1773, and Wigton (114), of 1830, is evidence of a continuing witness.

The late 18th century saw the beginning of much renewed activity by various denominations, the fruits of which can be seen in the many chapels erected in the following century. The former Countess of Huntingdon's chapel at Bootle (15), of 1780, was one early product of this revival; another was the Lady Glenorchy's Chapel in Workington, now rebuilt (118). The earliest remaining Methodist preaching-house in the county, of 1797 in Cockermouth (38), typifies in its location the self-effacement of many early societies and contrasts

markedly with the assurance of its mid 19th-century successor (39). The only two Baptist chapels recorded, at Little Broughton (21) and Oulton (117), were of interest primarily for the early origins of their respective churches, but the many other small early 19th-century chapels, particularly those of Wesleyans and Primitive Methodists, as well as Congregationalists and others, mark the zeal which their respective denominations displayed for the evangelization of the countryside. Some of these chapels have simple three-bay fronts, as at Distington (50), of 1830, while others, such as Warwick (108), display greater architectural pretension. Many have exceptionally large inscription tablets of varied shape – a quatrefoil on the Congregational chapel of 1844 at Allonby (1) and an octagon at Aspatria (9), together with sometimes lengthy scriptural quotations. Some village chapels built by Wesleyans in the later 19th century are notable because they appear to comprise a nave and chancel, although on closer inspection the 'chancel' is found to serve as a school-room: examples are at Kirkoswald (81) and Glassonby (53, 54). Town chapels of the 19th century exhibit a variety of architectural styles, from the rare Jacobean of Lowther Street, Carlisle (30), of 1843 by a Scottish architect, to the Italianate Wesleyan chapel at Penrith (97) of 1872, superseding a Georgian chapel which still stands, and another at Workington (119) of 1890. The Gothic style was used in an imaginative manner at Cockermouth (36) in 1850, in a formerly unspoilt chapel which has suffered a major internal conversion in recent years; later examples are generally of a more pedestrian character with indifferently designed towers and spires.

Most of the buildings listed have stone walls, some of sandstone, others of rubble frequently covered with rendering, and with few exceptions roofs are slate covered. Brickwork appears from the late 17th century (77) but is rare, occurring only in the coastal areas of the north west and as far inland as Brampton (20).

ALLONBY

(1) CONGREGATIONAL (NY 082434). Small chapel near N end of village. Rendered walls and slate roof gabled to N and S, side-entry porch and quatrefoil tablet above with date 1844 and text from Heb. 10:25. Pointed-arched windows with moulded labels and intersecting glazing bars.

(2) FRIENDS (NY 082435). The meeting-house, 200 yards N of the above, has rendered rubble walls and a stone slate roof. The S and W sides facing the road are unfenestrated. The N part of the present building comprises a low-built cottage of two rooms, probably of 17th-century date, converted for use as a meeting-house in 1703. In 1725, or possibly 1732, a larger room was

added to the S, approximately 22½ft square, and in the 19th century a passage and the present entrance were built along the W side of the original cottage. The interior has been refitted and the windows, all of which face E, were altered in the 19th century. A partition of hinged shutters divides the two principal rooms at the S end. The burial-ground, detached to N, has a high rubble wall to the W with a gateway with chamfered jambs and lintel.

Butler (1978) 32–4.

ALSTON WITH GARRIGILL

(3) CONGREGATIONAL, Alston (NY 719466). A tall plain building of rubble with a hipped slate roof, opened 1805 and 'considerably enlarged' in 1821, was built for a section of the church meeting about Alston Moor. Altered three-bay two-storeyed front wall with traces of two entrances replaced by central doorway. Two pointed-arched windows at rear flank the pulpit.

CHST IV (1909–10) 254–9. *Cong. Mag.* V (1822) 162–3.

(4) FRIENDS, Alston (NY 719464). The meeting-house, on the SW side of Front Street, has rubble walls and a stone slate roof. It was built in 1732 and heightened in 1762–4, the outline of the

Friends' Meeting-house, Alston,
ALSTON WITH GARRIGILL, *Cumberland*

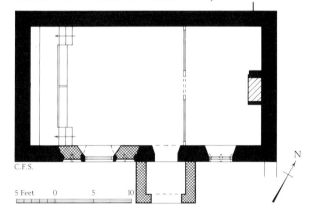

C.F.S.

5 Feet   0   5   10

former gables remaining visible in the end walls. Meetings ceased in 1902 but were resumed *c*.1985.

The front wall, facing SE, originally had three two-light mullioned windows and a doorway between. An upper gallery window to the right of the entrance was added in 1764. In the 19th century a porch was added and the original dated door lintel reset; the lower window to the right of the porch was replaced by a hung sash and a larger sash window was inserted to the left between the other pair of windows, which were then blocked.

The interior (30ft by 15ft) has the principal room at the SW end with a smaller room to the NE, above which was a gallery. The ceiling of the NE room was raised in the 19th century and the gallery reduced to loft space.

Butler (1978) 17–19.

(5) REDWING CHAPEL, Garrigill (NY 739418). The Congregational church meeting about Alston Moor was formed in the late 17th century and a meeting-house erected in 1695 at Loaning Head. In the early 18th century the congregation was described as 'generally labourers in the lead mines'. The present chapel, NW of the village, was built in 1756.

The chapel stands in a stone-walled enclosure close to the river South Tyne. The walls are of rubble and the roof is covered with stone slates. The entrance in the E gabled wall has a stone lintel carved with the date of erection. Four windows, on the S side only, have round-arched heads and hollow-chamfered jambs with pins for external shutters; hung sashes with intersecting glazing bars are of a later date.

The interior (18¾ft by 36¼ft) has a stone-flagged floor, plastered walls with rows of iron hat pegs and a flat plaster ceiling. The original pulpit at the W end has bolection-moulded panels and fluted corner pilasters; the back-board is elaborated with a round keystoned arch supported by fluted Roman Doric pilasters. A later clerk's desk stands in front of the pulpit. Seating comprises two ranks of box-pews with fielded-panelled backs and panelled doors; a large table-pew at the W end spans the full width of the chapel. *Monuments*: in burial-ground, headstones of 18th century and later. (Chapel closed and sold since 1964; substantially intact 1991)

CHST IV (1909–10) 254–9. *Cong. Mag.* V (1822) 162–3.

(6) Former WESLEYAN, Garrigill (NY 743421). 'Rebuilt 1859'.

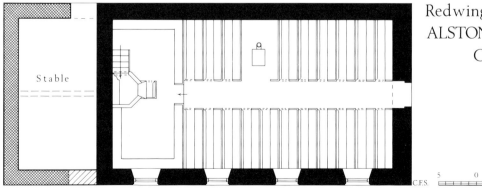

Stable

Redwing Chapel, Garrigill
ALSTON WITH GARRIGILL
Cumberland

N

Scale of Feet

5   0   5   10   15

C.F.S.

Redwing Chapel, Garrigill. (5)

(7) WESLEYAN, Lowbrownside (NY 710442). Three-bay rendered front of 1848 altered 1894. Date tablet with name 'EBEN EZER' [*sic*] over site of original central entrance.

(8) WESLEYAN, Nentsberry (NY 764453). Rubble walls and stone slate roof, two round-arched windows in front and rear walls. Dated 1825.

ASPATRIA

(9) Former CONGREGATIONAL (NY 143419). The chapel, now in commercial use, was built in 1827 at a cost of £300. The walls are rendered and the front has a pedimental gable ornamented with three pyramidal finials. Two pointed-arched windows with intersecting glazing bars flank a late 19th-century Gothic porch. An octagonal date tablet in the gable carries a text from Luke 15:7.

    CYB (1872) 322; (1894) 207–8.

Former Congregational chapel, Aspatria.   (9)

(10) PRIMITIVE METHODIST, Queen Street (NY 152421). Gabled Gothic front with vacant bell-cote and canted corners, dated 1895.

BEWALDETH AND SNITTLEGARTH

(11) FRIENDS' BURIAL-GROUND, Bewaldeth (NY 21103495). Rectangular enclosure bounded by rubble walls and a stream to S, purchased 1659 and a meeting-house for 'Isel meeting' erected at W end 1687. No monuments or recognizable structural remains of meeting-house, which was demolished before 1865.

    Butler (1978) 55–6.

BEWCASTLE

(12) PRESBYTERIAN, Blackpool Gate (NY 533780). Gothic, with rusticated stone walls and small bell-cote with one bell. Built 1891 on a new site superseding a meeting-house of 1790. *Plate*: in URC History Society collection, includes a pair of pewter cups of 1789 and contemporary flagon. (URC)

    Cong. Mag. V (1822) 163–4. Herdman (1901) No. 33.

BLENNERHASSET AND TORPENHOW

(13) Former CONGREGATIONAL, Blennerhasset (NY 180416). Built 1828 for church formed 1718. Rendered walls, originally with three pointed-arched windows at front and entrance in lean-to porch at gable end. Altered on conversion to house.

    Cong. Mag. V (1822) 164.

BOLTONS

(14) Site of FRIENDS, Bolton Low Houses (NY 239442). Irregular enclosure bounded by rubble walls incorporating in NE corner fragments of the N and E walls of a meeting-house of 1701–2, demolished 1904.

    Butler (1978) 31–2.

BOOTLE

(15) BOOTLE CHAPEL (SD 108882). The chapel was built and later endowed by Joseph Whitridge and was opened 30 July 1780 for the use of the Countess of Huntingdon's Connexion (now URC). It has rendered rubble walls and the slate-covered roof is hipped at the front. The front wall facing E has three round-arched upper windows above a central doorway between two rectangular windows. A tablet over the entrance is inscribed: '*THIS* Place of Divine Worship was founded by Mr. Joseph Whitridge of London *Anno Domini* 1780'. The N and S walls have round-arched windows. Adjacent to the W is a double-fronted house dated J W 1780 and beyond it a cottage dated I A 1808.

    The interior ($32\frac{1}{4}$ft by $23\frac{1}{2}$ft) has a flat plaster ceiling and wide coved cornice. It was largely refitted in the late 19th century with pitch-pine pews and a low rostrum pulpit. A gallery at the E end has been removed.

Bootle Chapel (URC).   (15)

Fittings – *Books*: (1) Clement Cotton, enlarged etc. by Samuel Newman, *A Large and Complete Concordance* (1643); (2) Anthony Burgess, *Spiritual Refining or a Treatise of Grace and Assurance ... 120 Sermons* (1652); (3) Isaac Ambrose, *Looking unto Jesus, A View of the Everlasting Gospel ...* (Glasgow, 1758); (4) *Book of Common Prayer* (1788) inscribed 'This book belongs to Bootle Chapel 1834'. *Monuments*: externally against E wall (1) Rev. Daniel Gray, 26 years minister, 1808; (2) James Brockbank of Beckside, 1822; N of chapel (3) Joseph Whitridge of Mill Holme, 1793, Bridget his wife, 1786, and children William, Joseph and Jane.

Cong. Mag. V (1822) 164–5. Seymour (1839) II: 465–6.

BOTHEL AND THREAPLAND

(16) Former PRIMITIVE METHODIST, Bothel (NY 182389). Plain building with gabled front, oval tablet dated 1836 above site of entrance.

(17) WESLEYAN, Bothel (NY 181389). Rubble and slate with ashlar dressings and pointed-arched windows; opened 1882.

BRAMPTON

(18) BETHESDA HALL (NY 528611). Mid 19th-century meeting-house of the Christian Brethren. Four sash windows above central entrance in rendered front; rear entrance at upper level.

BETHESDA HALL, BRAMPTON   CFS·1970

(19) Former CONGREGATIONAL (NY 531611). Zion Chapel, built 1818, has a gabled front with two round-arched windows and two-storeyed porch.

Cong. Mag. V (1822) 165.

(20) PRESBYTERIAN (NY 531611). The congregation (now URC) traces its origins to the ejection in 1662 of the vicar, Nathaniel Burnard, who continued to preach in the locality. The former meeting-house of 1722 (30¾ft by 36¾ft), now almost entirely surrounded by later buildings and completely refurbished for use as a hall, has brick walls and a hipped slate roof. The principal front faced S and had four three-centred arched upper windows, of which three remain visible. Access was originally from the SW corner of the present site where the outer gateway is inscribed 'PRESBYTERIAN CHURCH BUILT 1722 REPAIRED 1851'. The present chapel, which stands adjacent, was built in 1854 in the Gothic style with a considerable donation

from Robert Barbour of Bolesworth Castle, Cheshire, and contains a monument to the benefactor.

Fittings – *Painting*: water-colour, of former meeting-house, shows roof with double gables to E and W, S front with four bays of arched windows at two levels and arched doorway between bays 1 and 2 from W; house adjacent to N. *Royal Arms*: 1801–37, Hanover escutcheon lacks Electoral Bonnet or Crown.

Cong. Mag. V (1822) 165. Penfold, H., 'Brampton Presbyterianism, 1662–1780', *C & WT*, NS III (1903) 94–125.

BROUGHTON

(21) BAPTIST, Little Broughton (NY 080316). The chapel was built in 1806 replacing an earlier meeting-house for a church which originated in the mid 17th century. Rendered walls with four original round-arched windows, one later in rear extension, all with late 19th-century Venetian-tracery frames. *Monuments*: in burial-ground, loose against boundary wall, (1) John Fletcher, 1769, Elizabeth his wife, 1765, and Abraham their son 'mathematician', 1793, headstone; (2) Rev. Samuel Blenkinsop, 1734, capstone from table-tomb; (3) John, son of John Metcalf of Camberton, 1744, headstone; (4) John Wheelwright, 1711/12, capstone from table-tomb.

Cong. Mag. V (1822) 214–15. Whitley (1913) 334.

(22) FRIENDS, Little Broughton (NY 078317). A meeting-house built in 1687 was rebuilt in 1742 and drastically altered in the late 19th century. It has rendered walls and a slate roof; the entrance was on the N side, three altered windows remain in the S wall and a fourth was replaced in the 19th century by two doorways inside a porch. The interior (49ft by 18¼ft) is divided into two rooms by a partition of double-hung shutters. Late 19th-century tablet in W wall with date 1687. (In use 1990 by Broughton Evangelical Fellowship)

Butler (1978) 52, 54–5.

(23) WESLEYAN, Great Broughton (NY 073315). Chapel built 1846, rebuilt 1884.

(24) PRIMITIVE METHODIST, Little Broughton (NY 078318). Built *c*.1884, enlarged 1908; round-arched doorway and windows with bevelled keystones and imposts.

BURGH-BY-SANDS

(25) Former FRIENDS, Moorhouse (NY 336567). The meeting-house is a large building of brick with stone dressings; the roof is covered with stone slates and green lakeland slate. It was built in 1733 to replace a building of 1681 and continued in Quaker use until 1913; it has since been used by Methodists and latterly for farm storage. The front wall, facing N, has five principal windows with rectangular stone frames and original sashes with softwood glazing bars; the doorway, W of centre, has a moulded architrave and round-arched head with keystone dated 1733. The S wall has a small doorway opposite the front entrance. At the W end of the N and S walls are two two-light mullioned windows below the eaves to serve a former gallery. A stable, also of brickwork, was added at the W end in the later 18th century.

The interior (58ft by 23½ft) is divided into two rooms by a partition with fielded-panelled shutters. The larger room to the E has a flat plaster ceiling. The stand or ministers' gallery at the E

Former Friends' meeting-house, Moorhouse. (25)

Former Friends' Meeting-house, Moorhouse, BURGH BY SANDS, *Cumberland*

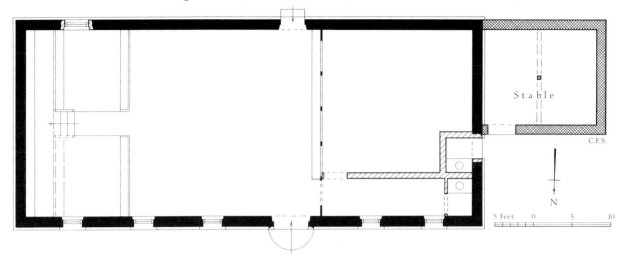

Stable

C.F.S.

N

5 Feet 0 5 10

end remains partly intact and has an open front of flat shaped balusters. Two fixed benches with open backs remain. The W room has been altered and a gallery over it removed. The roof has five king-post trusses, the ends now supported by internal buttresses carried by stone blocks which project from the wall faces.

A small burial-ground on the opposite side of the road, 200 yards N, is dated 1694.

Butler (1978) 9–11.

CALDBECK

(26) Former FRIENDS, Gillfoot (NY 347383). The meeting-house was built in 1729 for the use of monthly business meetings. It was later used for worship but that use ceased in 1913. The building was subsequently converted to cottages and it now retains little of its original character. The walls are rendered and the roof is partly covered with old slates. The original front faced NE and had a doorway, now altered to a window, between two pairs of windows with ashlar surrounds and pins for external shutters.

Butler (1978) 76–7.

(27) Former FRIENDS, Whelpo (NY 310396). The meeting-house, dated 1698 above the present NE entrance, was registered in April 1699. It ceased to be used for regular meetings in 1846 and was then converted to a cottage, Carlisle Friends retaining the right to meet in a room at one day's notice. It is a long low building with rendered stone walls and a roof covered with old slates. Two windows in the front wall were added or altered *c*.1846 but four original windows remain at the back.

Butler (1978) 71–2.

(28) WESLEYAN, Caldbeck (NY 322401). Rendered walls with ashlar corner strip and slate roof. Gabled front with later porch. Three round-arched side windows and large tablet 'Remember now thy Creator, 1832'.

(29) WESLEYAN, Hesket Newmarket (NY 342386). Stone walls with ashlar quoins and slate roof. Three round-arched windows in S wall and small bell-cote on E gable. Opened 1840.

CARLISLE

(30) CONGREGATIONAL, Lowther Street (NY 402558). The church now meeting in Lowther Street originated in a cause founded by Lady Glenorchy in 1781 for 'Protestant Dissenters of the Presbyterian or Independent persuasions'. In that year she bought a small meeting-house (now demolished) in Annetwell Street, which had been built *c*.1778 for a small Presbyterian congregation attached to the Associate (Burgher) Presbytery of Glasgow, and was the property of Rev. Alexander Waugh. The meeting-house remained in the possession of Lady Glenorchy's trustees until 1816, when it was transferred to a Congregational trust.

The chapel in Lowther Street, designed by Mr Nichol of Edinburgh, was opened 19 March 1843, partly refitted in 1864–5, and further altered internally in 1901. It has a stone front of three bays with tall windows and a shaped central gable, all in the Jacobean style with strapwork ornament above the windows. The interior has galleries around three sides supported by tall wooden columns of quatrefoil section which rise to ceiling level. The central space is spanned by a plaster barrel vault.

Plate: includes a pair of Sheffield-plate cups of the late 18th century.

Black (1906) 327–8. *Cong. Mag.* V (1822) 215–19. Thomas, J. and Porteus, C. A., *Memorials of Lowther Street Congregational Church, Carlisle, 1786–1936* (1936). Thompson, D. P., *Lady Glenorchy and her Churches – The Story of Two Hundred Years* (1967) 45–8, Pl. 21.

(31) Former FRIENDS, Fisher Street (NY 400561). A meeting-house in the Abbey Close, bought in 1653, was lost to Friends at the Restoration. In 1681 a burial-ground was acquired at the NW end of Fisher Street and in 1702 a small building close to a second burial-ground further along that street was obtained for use as a meeting-house; this was enlarged in 1711 to accommodate the Yearly Meeting for the Northern Counties. It was subsequently sold to Methodists and rebuilt.

The third meeting-house, on a new site further E, was erected in 1776–7. Additional rooms were built against the street

Congregational chapel, Lowther Street, Carlisle.

(30)

frontage in 1864 to the designs of James Stewart. In 1963 a fourth meeting-house was constructed on the site of the first burial-ground (NY 399562) and its predecessor is now used as a club.

The third meeting-house is almost entirely obscured by later structures. It has brick walls with some ashlar dressings and a hipped slate roof. The front elevation had three tall windows and a doorway to the right; all these openings were designed to have semicircular arched heads with keystones and with external shutters to the windows, but it is thought that cheaper trabeated openings may have been substituted during the course of erection. The surviving doorway at the front has rusticated stone jambs and a lintel incorporating a keystone dated 1776.

The interior (49ft by 30ft) has a corridor on the SE side with a narrow gallery above; the remainder of the space is divided into two square rooms which formerly had a continuous stand along the NE side. The rooms are separated by a partition of vertically sliding shutters with further shutters opening from the corridor. The gallery front was replaced by a thin cast-iron balustrade in 1864.

Butler (1978) 1–7.

(32) WESLEYAN, Fisher Street (NY 400561). The Methodist Central Hall of 1922 replaces a chapel of 1817, itself the successor to a chapel of 1786 which stood on the opposite side of the road. The site was earlier occupied by the Friends' meeting-house of 1702.

(33) PRESBYTERIAN, Fisher Street (NY 399561). The church (now URC), which originated in the late 17th century, allied itself to the Scottish Secession Church in 1809 eventually becoming a part of the Presbyterian Church of England. Until 1736 it occupied a meeting-house near the West Walls, removing thence to a chapel on the present site which was rebuilt in 1856 and again replaced in 1894–5 by the existing galleried structure in the Gothic style, to the designs of T. Taylor Scott.

Cong. Mag. V (1822) 216–17. Mackelvie (1873) 121–2.

(34) PRESBYTERIAN, Chapel Street (NY 402561). The chapel, built in 1834 for a congregation of the established Church of Scotland, has walls of ashlar and a slate roof. The front wall has a simple pediment, central doorway and three round-arched windows. Inside is a round-ended gallery supported by fluted cast-iron columns.

CASTLE SOWERBY

(35) Former FRIENDS, Sowerby Row (NY 398390). A small meeting-house of 1713, closed by 1773 and latterly used as an outbuilding of Row Foot Farm appears to have been demolished since 1977.

Butler (1978) 69–71.

COCKERMOUTH

(36) CONGREGATIONAL (NY 119308). The church (now URC) formed 2 October 1651 with George Larkham, curate of Cockermouth, as pastor, claims to be the oldest Independent Church in Cumberland. A burial-ground was given in 1669. A meeting-house opened in 1687 was superseded in 1719 by another

on a new site which now stands behind the present chapel of 1850, when it was converted for use as a Sunday-school. A secession in 1765 resulted in the erection of a second meeting-house, the 'High Meeting', the older being referred to as the 'Low Meeting'. The two societies reunited in 1782.

The former meeting-house has rendered walls with some exposed stone dressings including rusticated angle pilasters. The S front, now gabled but perhaps altered, has two round-arched windows flanking the probable site of the entrance and two plain windows above; re-erected at one side is the original porch with two substantial stone columns supporting a lintel with the date 1719. Centrally in the N wall is a round-arched doorway. The interior (32ft by 42ft) has been entirely refitted but the original moulded plaster cornice remains.

The present chapel, opened 11 September 1850, is said to have been designed by a Mr Eaglesfield although it bears a very close resemblance to the former Baptist chapel of 1842–4 in Myrtle Street, Liverpool, by W.H. Gee (Whitley (1913) 260). The chapel has a triple-gabled S front of ashlar of three bays with pinnacles and pointed-arched windows with cusped tracery. The side walls have two-stage buttresses and lancet windows. The interior has matching N and S galleries, the former behind the pulpit having vestries below. The seating is almost entirely original with box-pews to the lower floor and S gallery and open-backed benches to the N gallery. (Interior now totally altered and subdivided, new entrance pierced below central front window)

Fittings – *Collecting Shovels*: set of five, wood with circular decorations, *c*.1850. *Monuments*: on N wall (1) Rev. James Muscutt, pastor, 1819; against S wall of former meeting-house (2) John, son of James and Jane Fell, 1843, *et al*.

Clark, J.B., *The Story of the Cockermouth Congregational Church, 1651–1951* (1951). *Cong. Mag.* V (1822) 272–8. Lewis, W., *History of the Congregational Church, Cockermouth...* (1870).

(37) FRIENDS (NY 124305). The meeting-house, largely rebuilt in 1884, replaced buildings of 1782 and 1688, each of which had fallen into disrepair. The present building is a low structure of

Congregational chapel (URC), Cockermouth.   (36)

stone with Renaissance details, divided internally by counter-weighted shutters into two equal rooms with a continuous stand along one wall. The E and S walls incorporate part of the 1782 structure.

Bradbury, J. B., *Cockermouth Quaker Meeting* (1988). Butler (1978) 48–51.

(38) Former WESLEYAN, High Sand Lane (NY 12053078). Although a Methodist society was in existence here by 1768, the first regular preaching-house was provided only in 1797 by the purchase and conversion (or rebuilding) of 'old maltkilns'. This building, superseded by a new chapel in 1841 and subsequently used by Brethren and others for social purposes, is named 'Victoria Hall'. It stands on the W side of the lane concealed behind other property. The walls are of random rubble with squared stone dressings and the roof is slated. The S front, gabled and with modern rendering, has a central doorway and a pair of square gallery windows. In the N wall is a pair of round-arched windows formerly flanking a pulpit. The interior (33¼ft by 24½ft) has a contemporary gallery around three sides supported by four substantial timber columns.

Burgess (1980) 9.

(39) Former WESLEYAN, Market Street (NY 123307). Large chapel built in 1841 to replace the foregoing, superseded 1932 by a new building in Lorton Street and converted 1934 for use as the Town Hall. Rendered walls with two tiers of windows above a basement. Three-bay front with central doorway and round-arched windows. Rear wall to S has a Venetian window at the back of the former communion area and altered windows above. The interior, although subdivided for office use, retains the principal structure of a continuous oval gallery supported by cast-iron columns.

Former Primitive Methodist chapel, Crosby. (40)

1973 and entirely refenestrated. *English Heritage Magazine* (September 1992) 23; (December 1992) 27, 32.)

CULGAITH

(41) WESLEYAN, Blencarn (NY 639311). Red sandstone with three-bay front, pointed-arched openings and gabled porch; date tablet for 1840.

(42) WESLEYAN, Culgaith (NY 609297). Red sandstone and slate roof with stone slate verge; three-bay front with wide doorway and tablet dated 1830.

(43) Former WESLEYAN, Skirwith (NY 618327). Red sandstone with pointed-arched windows with stone Y-tracery. S front of three bays and gabled porch, dated 1868. Small octagonal turret on W gable.

Former Methodist chapel, Cockermouth. (39)

Wesleyan chapel, Skirwith. (43)

CROSSCANONBY

(40) Former PRIMITIVE METHODIST, Crosby (NY 075384). The chapel has rendered walls and a slate roof. The NW front of three bays with round-arched openings has a date tablet of 1863 with a text from Ps. 46: 1, 4. (Converted to two-storeyed cottage since

DALSTON

(44) Former WESLEYAN, (NY 368502). Behind other buildings on W side of the Square. Low sandstone walls, gabled front with blocked doorway and partly defaced tablet 'Methodist Chapel 1825'.

(45) Former WESLEYAN (NY 368497). Built 1851, of stone; transferred to United Methodist Free Church and extended to front in red brick 1903. In Methodist use.

Burgess (1980) 53–4.

DEAN

(46) FRIENDS, Eaglesfield (NY 093280). The meeting-house, built in 1711 solely for meetings for burial, stands within an older burial-ground, in use from c.1670. It was registered in April 1712 although the internal fittings were not completed until c.1728. The walls are of rendered rubble and the roof is covered with local slates. It comprises a single room, described in the building accounts as '12 yards long and 8 yards wide within the walls and 4 yards high the side walls'. The two longer side walls have opposed entrances and three windows each of two lights with chamfered stone mullions. In the NE wall are two similar

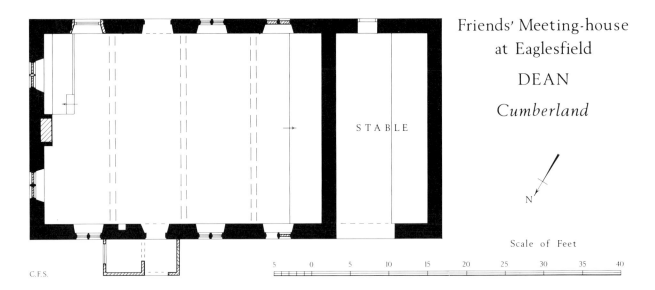

Friends' Meeting-house
at Eaglesfield
DEAN
Cumberland

STABLE

N

Scale of Feet

5   0   5   10   15   20   25   30   35   40

C.F.S.

Former Friends' meeting-house, Eaglesfield. (46)

windows blocked in old brickwork and separated internally by a fireplace which divides the stand. A stable or hearse-house was added to the SW end later in the 18th century. The burial-ground to the SE is bounded by an 18th-century wall and gateway to the road with lintel dated 1693. (Converted to house *c.*1978 with inserted rooflights, unsympathetic external rendering and loss of fittings)

Fittings – *Inscription*: on lintel of SE doorway, 'JOHN BARN/Gave 40 li To Build This House. 1711'. *Monuments*: in burial-ground, 19th-century and later headstones, and flat or cambered ledger stones. *Seating*: benches with open backs and shaped ends, 18th-century.

Butler (1978) 57, 59–60.

(47) FRIENDS, Pardshaw (NY 104254). The meeting at Pardshaw derived from one which commenced in 1653, the earliest to be formed in Cumberland. A meeting-house was built near the

Friends' meeting-house, Pardshaw.   (47)

Friends' Meeting-house at Pardshaw, in the Parish of DEAN,   *Cumberland*

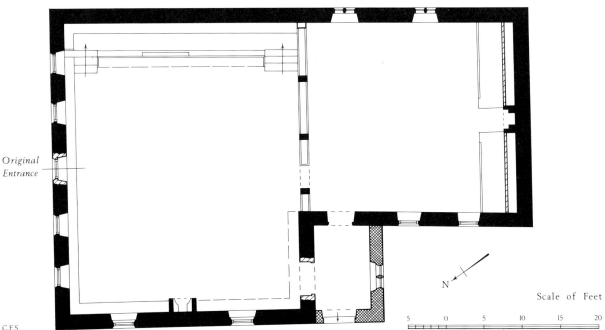

Original Entrance

N

Scale of Feet

5 0 5 10 15 20

C.F.S.

present site in 1672 and enlarged in 1705. In March 1726/7 a parcel of arable ground was bought in a place called 'Guards', about 59 yards long containing 1 rood 15 perches on which the present building stands. The large meeting-house was built first, in 1729, and the small meeting-house added immediately afterwards reusing material from the previous building. A meeting-house certificate was issued in February 1729/30. A porch was added between the two meeting-houses in 1740 and in 1850 the entrance to the large meeting-house was closed and a new doorway pierced from the porch. A free-standing range of stables had been built to the NW in 1731; this was enlarged to the NE in 1745 to provide a school-room and again in 1774.

The building is L-shaped and has rendered rubble walls and a slate roof. The large meeting-house (36½ft by 30ft), facing NE, originally had a central doorway flanked on either side by two windows with moulded stone frames which had a central mullion and transom; there were two similar windows in the NW wall. All these windows were altered in the mid 18th century, when wooden sashes were substituted, and in 1850 a matching window replaced the original doorway. The small meeting-house (27ft by 24ft) has two similarly altered windows in the NW wall and two windows of two lights in the opposite wall. The two rooms are divided by a double partition with fielded-panelled shutters; each room has an original fireplace, that in the small meeting-house separates the two halves of the stand. The roof is supported by braced king-post trusses.

Fittings – *Inscription*: on lintel of stables, date '1672' in raised characters, partly recut, probably from the former meeting-house. *Monument*: in burial-ground, to John Dalton, born at Eaglesfield 1766, buried at Manchester 1844. *Seating*: in large meeting-house, open backed benches, some with overhanging ends, 18th-century.

Butler (1978) 40–6.

(48) WESLEYAN, Eaglesfield (NY 094282). Rendered walls, gable entrance with later porch, round-arched windows. Built 1845.

DEARHAM

(49) PRIMITIVE METHODIST (NY 071361). Built 1856, altered and enlarged 1899 including three traceried Gothic windows facing road. Derelict 1973.

DISTINGTON

(50) WESLEYAN (NY 006235). Rubble with ashlar dressings and slate roof. Three-bay front with pilaster strip at one corner and platband joining heads of two rectangular stone-framed windows. Central doorway with large tablet above bearing two texts and date MDCCCXXX. Two round-arched windows in gable wall to left.

(51) Former PRIMITIVE METHODIST, Common End (NY 005227). Set back in terrace, three-bay front of rubble with round-arched windows, one altered, date tablet 1838. Converted to cottage since 1984.

EMBLETON

(52) WESLEYAN (NY 176306). Gothic, rebuilt 1904, with oval date tablet of 1863 reset in front wall.

Wesleyan chapel, Distington. (50)

GLASSONBY

(53) WESLEYAN, Gamblesby (NY 609394). Gothic chapel of 1864, sandstone, gable end with finial, three-bay side with central porch; school in attached pseudo-chancel.

WESLEYAN CHAPEL, GAMBLESBY C.F.S·1990

(54) WESLEYAN, Glassonby (NY 576390). A smaller version of the foregoing, dated 1869.

GREAT SALKELD

(55) Former PRESBYTERIAN (NY 547369). A Presbyterian congregation meeting in Great Salkeld from the late 17th century may have originated as a section of a church which met 'in and about Kirkoswald'. A meeting-house was built at Plumpton in 1709 (*see* (62)) and another at about this time at Great Salkeld, the two congregations being intimately connected.

The early 18th-century former meeting-house at Great Salkeld, superseded in 1876 when the latterly United Presbyterian congregation built a new chapel in the village, stands in a field ¼ mile W of the latter. It has walls of sandstone rubble; the roof, formerly covered with stone slates, has been removed. The S wall, altered by the insertion of a wide doorway, had an entrance close to the W end with a single-light window to the left and three two-light mullioned windows to the right. Traces of further windows remain in the N and W walls and a narrow window high in the E wall. The interior (36¼ft by 17¾ft) was originally open to the roof and wall plastering remains inside the

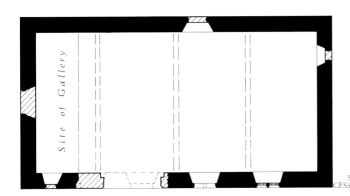

Former Presbyterian Meeting-house
GREAT SALKELD
Cumberland

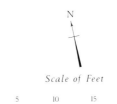

N

Scale of Feet

E and W gables, but mortices in the surviving tie-beams indicate the later insertion of a flat plaster ceiling.

C & WT, NS VIII (1908) 41–54. *Cong. Mag.* V (1822) 557.

(56) WESLEYAN, Salkeld Dykes (NY 545365). Snecked rubble walls and stone slate roof, gable entrance with semicircular Gothic label over doorway enclosing date 1832. Two rectangular windows in plain stone frames to side walls.

GREYSOUTHEN

(57) Site of FRIENDS (NY 073295). A meeting-house built 1742 and closed 1871 was derelict by 1961, when the property was sold. The site is now occupied by a modern bungalow.

Butler (1978) 60–2.

(58) Former WESLEYAN, Chapel Terrace (NY 072294). Dated 1833.

GREYSTOKE

(59) WESLEYAN, Little Blencow (NY 454328). Small two-bay stone chapel with pointed-arched windows, lean-to porch dated 1877 and tall iron finial on rear gable.

HAYTON

(60) WESLEYAN, Corby Hill (NY 480570). Red brick with lancet windows, dated 1894; attached at rear former chapel with round-arched windows, of mid 19th century.

HAYTON AND MEALO

(61) Former CONGREGATIONAL, Hayton (NY 105414). Small red-sandstone chapel with pointed-arched doorway and two windows to right, other openings altered on conversion to cottage. Tablet in front wall dated 1844.

HESKET

(62) WESLEYAN (NY 476389). A Presbyterian meeting-house at Brockley Moor or Plumpton (NY 480384) was built in 1709, probably by a section of the Kirkoswald church. It was a small building with rubble walls and a stone slate roof, a single round-arched window in the front wall and a plain doorway with dated lintel at one end of the same wall. The building was bought by Wesleyans in 1888, who removed to the present chapel on a new site in 1905; it has since been demolished. Incorporated in the front wall of the present chapel is the former lintel dated 1709.

C & WT, NS VIII (1908) 41–54.

HETHERSGILL

(63) Former FRIENDS, Sikeside (NY 446665). The meeting-house, built in 1736 to replace one of 1688, was closed in 1913 and is now used for farm storage. It has walls of sandstone ashlar and a slate roof. The front wall has three windows and a doorway between, all with round-arched heads and keystones; the other walls are unfenestrated. The E and W gables have parapets with moulded corbels. The interior (45½ft by 24ft) was formerly divided by a partition W of the entrance, the smaller W room having a corner fireplace with moulded stone jambs. The roof is supported by three king-post trusses. The burial-ground at Megs Hill (*see* (78)) appears to have been used by this meeting.

Butler (1978) 11–13.

Former Friends' meeting-house, Sikeside.   (63)

(64) Former WESLEYAN, Ullermire (NY 465668). Stone walls and slate roof. Ashlar front with tablet dated 1833 between two round-arched windows with keystones and impost blocks. Entrance through later porch in gable wall to left. (Derelict 1970)

HOLME ABBEY

(65) WESLEYAN, Abbey Town (NY 173508). Red sandstone with pointed-arched windows and gabled porch. Dated 1869 on wall anchors.

HOLME ST CUTHBERT

(66) Former FRIENDS, Beckfoot (NY 093496). The meeting-house was built in 1745 and registered at Quarter Sessions January 1746/7. It was closed in 1940 and converted to a private

house in 1970 including the shortening of the S end by 12 feet. It has rendered walls, principally of brick, and a slate roof. The only windows, in the E wall, have chamfered sandstone jambs and appear to have been altered in the 19th century. Against the W front is a later gabled porch with two inner doorways. The interior is divided into two rooms by a stone wall pierced by three openings with hinged shutters. The roof above the larger room to the S was supported by two braced king-post trusses. A free-standing stable has a cruck-trussed roof. Burial-ground to S with a few uniform headstones.

Butler (1978) 28–9.

(67) WESLEYAN, Old Mawbray (NY 086466). Rubble walls, rendered at front and slate roof. Three-bay N front with later porch, large oval tablet dated 1843 and two pointed-arched windows with intersecting glazing bars. Pulpit against E gable wall.

HUTTON

(68) PRESBYTERIAN, Penruddock (NY 425275). The congregation originated in the late 17th century. A meeting-house at Penruddock was registered in April 1704 and a trust deed of 1712 refers to it as 'lately erected and built by Isaac Noble'. The present building, which stands on the same site, is believed to date from 1789. For a period in the early 19th century the church was Independent; it later joined the United Associate Presbytery of Annan and Carlisle. (Now URC)

The chapel has rendered rubble walls and a slate roof. It is gabled to N and S and the front E wall has three round-arched windows with keystones and impost blocks and a gabled porch. In the W wall are three narrow pointed-arched windows. The interior (37ft by 18ft) was entirely reseated in 1864 and has a rostrum pulpit at the S end.

Fittings – *Collecting Shovels*: pair, rectangular wooden box with long handle, 2½ft overall, 19th-century. *Monuments*: in chapel (1) Rev. John Miller, 32 years minister, 1862; in burial-ground (2) Rev. Robert Roberts, 24 years minister, 1806, and Elizabeth his widow, 1831; (3) Rev. Andrew Rattray, '17 years Independent minister of this chapel', 1829. *Pitchpipe*: early 19th-century.

C & WT, NS V (1905) 150–71. *Cong. Mag.* V (1822) 555–6. Mackelvie (1873) 122–3. *PHSJ* I (1914–19) 128–34.

Presbyterian chapel (URC), Penruddock.　　　　(68)

(69) Former WESLEYAN, Beckces (NY 419278). Rendered walls and slate roof, built in 1840, now a cottage. Two widely spaced windows in front wall, original porch against E gable wall.

IRTON WITH SANTON

(70) WESLEYAN, Santon (NY 102017). The chapel has walls of rendered rubble with a slate roof. Three-bay front to S with plain stone frames to rectangular windows and doorway; large tablet above entrance with text and date 1828. Original pulpit at E end, late 19th-century pews replacing stepped seating at W end. Cottage of slightly later date to E covering one original window in end wall. (Chapel closed and fittings partly dismantled 1970)

Clock: on W wall, in kidney-shaped case, signed 'Plasket Thompson, Whitehaven'.

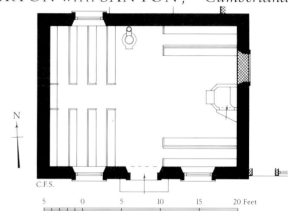

Wesleyan Methodist Chapel, Santon
IRTON WITH SANTON, Cumberland

Wesleyan chapel, Santon.　　　　(70)

KESWICK

(71) BETHESDA FREE CHAPEL, High Street (NY 26752325). Random rubble with gabled front, central doorway with four-centred arched head between windows with moulded labels. Small gallery along one side only. Tablet in front dated 1851.

(72) BRETHREN, St John's Street (NY 26782335). Small upper

room with two windows above carriage entrance, late 19th-century.

(73) Former FRIENDS, High Hill (NY 262239). The meeting-house, built in 1715, was no longer in use by c.1775. It was subsequently used as a school; in the late 19th century it was converted into three cottages and now comprises one dwelling, 'Quaker Cottage'. It has rendered rubble walls and a slate roof. Little evidence remains of its original fenestration.

Butler (1978) 51–3.

(74) WESLEYAN, Southey Street (NY 268234). Stone Gothic, gabled front dated 1863, transeptal rear extension added 1909.

(75) PRIMITIVE METHODIST, Tithebarn Street (NY 264235). Chapel at corner of Heads Road, rubble with ashlar dressings, three-bay gabled front with deep eaves and round-arched windows. Dated 1869. Sunday-school behind, 1894.

KINGWATER

(76) Former WESLEYAN, Nickie's Hill (NY 540670). Altered three-bay front, dated 1838.

KIRKBRIDE

(77) FRIENDS (NY 228561). The meeting-house, which stands on the SE side of an unsurfaced lane on the W side of the village, was built in 1698. Regular use ceased in 1854 but occasional meetings continued for at least a further fifty years. The walls are of brickwork with stone dressings to doorways and windows.

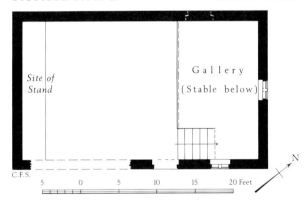

Friends' Meeting-house,
KIRKBRIDE   *Cumberland*

The roof, now largely fallen in, is covered with local slates with a verge of stone slates. The entrance, to the left of which was formerly a pair of two-light mullioned windows, is in the SE wall; a doorway on the NW side gives access to a stable beneath a low NE gallery. The interior (31ft by 17½ft) comprises a single room with a stand at the SW end opposite the gallery. (Derelict 1970)

Butler (1978), 30–1.

KIRKLINTON MIDDLE

(78) Former FRIENDS, at Megs Hill (NY 436665). The burial-ground at Megs Hill, an almost square enclosure with stone boundary walls, has been in use since c.1689, the date of the first deed, in conjunction with the meeting-house at Sikeside (63). A further deed of 17 January 1749/50 refers to the 'new built school house and Meeting house with the New Close or inclosed burial ground adjoining on the East at Megs Hill . . .'. The meeting-house, which adjoins the NW corner of the burial-ground, was in use only for meetings for burial. It was sold in 1964 and is now used for farm storage. The building dates from 1749 and has brick walls of this period but the roof has been re-covered. The only traces of original openings are three narrow segmental-arched windows in the E wall, one of which has been altered to form a doorway giving direct access to the burial-ground. The S wall has been much altered by the insertion of a wide cart entrance. The interior (35ft by 15⅔ft) has two roof trusses with tie-beam and collar-beam. One seat remains which has a tall back probably from the front of a divided stand.

Butler (1978) 15–16.

KIRKOSWALD

(79) PARK HEAD CHAPEL (NY 588421). The Congregational church formerly meeting at Park Head derives from a church 'at Huddlesceugh, Parkhead and Kirkoswald' which met first at Melmerby in or about 1653; a meeting place is said to have been built at Huddlesceugh for George Nicholson under James II's Indulgence (1687), and the oldest portion of the present chapel may be of this date. The chapel was rebuilt in 1711.

The chapel stands 2 miles E of Kirkoswald and ½ mile W of Huddlesceugh Hall; it has rubble walls and a slate roof. Traces of former quoins in the gable-end walls show that it was originally a long narrow building 39½ft by 15ft externally but widened on the S side by a further 10⅓ft in the 18th century. The N wall is pierced by four plain round-arched windows and the S wall by four windows of greater elaboration having hollow-chamfered jambs comparable with Redwing chapel (*see* (5)). The corners of the extension have rusticated quoins, and a round-arched doorway centrally in the E wall is also of the date of the enlargement. The interior has a flat plaster ceiling; the pews and rostrum pulpit date from a late 19th-century refitting. (Converted to house since 1975. End walls rendered, rectangular sashes inserted in windows and arched heads blocked; all

Congregational chapel, Park Head.
Before conversion to house.   (79)

monuments and interments cleared from burial-ground)

Monuments: On W wall behind pulpit (1) William Jameson, yeoman, of Scales, 1840, Thomas Jameson Esq., of Scales, 1843, and Hannah his widow, 1863; in burial-ground, several thick sandstone headstones of 18th century and later including the following with brass inscription tablets (2) Joshua Gibson, 1767, recording a bequest of £12, (3) Rev. James Scott, 9 years minister, 1815, and his children Matthew and Sarah.

Cong. Mag. V (1822) 387–9.

(80) Former CONGREGATIONAL, Kirkoswald (NY 554412). Small red-sandstone chapel built 1864. Broad three-bay front with pointed-arched doorway and two-light windows. Interior, now gutted, had stepped seating to right of entrance and pulpit to left.

CYB (1867) 356.

(81) WESLEYAN, Kirkoswald (NY 554414). Red-sandstone chapel of four bays with tall gable finial, gabled porch and pointed-arched windows with Y-tracery. School in attached pseudo-chancel. Dated 1871.

(82) WESLEYAN, Renwick (NY 597435). A chapel of 1818 was rebuilt in a free Gothic style in 1903–5. A plain school-room of 1863 is attached to the rear.

LAZONBY

(83) WESLEYAN (NY 547396). Small chapel dated 1850, gabled front and porch with cusped arched doorway.

LONGTOWN

(84) UNITED METHODIST, Albert Street (NY 381684). Banded red and yellow brickwork, 1865.

(85) PRESBYTERIAN (NY 379689). A Presbyterian chapel was built in 1798 and a society was still in existence *c.*1822 but the present building appears to have been erected for a new congregation which originated in 1832. The building is inscribed 'United Secession Church 1834' and has been associated successively with the United Associate Presbytery of Annan and Carlisle, the United Presbyterian Church, the United Free Church and, since 1929, the Church of Scotland. The chapel, which stands on a concealed site behind buildings on the E side of the main road, has walls of red sandstone. The W front is gabled with central doorway and window over. The N and S walls have each two pointed-arched windows with intersecting tracery. Between the S windows is a tablet inscribed 'W G 1834' and near the W end of that wall is a blocked doorway.

Black (1906) 329–30, 360. *Cong. Mag.* V (1822) 386. Mackelvie (1873) 123–4.

LORTON

(86) WESLEYAN (NY 161258). Rendered rubble and slate, three-bay front with round-arched windows and later porch; dated 1840.

MARYPORT

(87) Former PRESBYTERIAN, John Street (NY 035366). Maryport was developed in the mid 18th century and the first Presbyterian meetings commenced in 1773 in a house on the North Quay. In 1777 a meeting-house was built which remains behind other buildings on the N side of John Street. This cost £120 and a collection towards the expense is recorded in the chapel register of Market Place Chapel, Kendal. The congregation was associated with the Church of Scotland. About 1821 a division occurred, the seceders who allied themselves to the United Secession Presbytery of Annan and Carlisle eventually built a chapel in Crosby Street (*see* (88)). In 1888 the two congregations reunited at the latter; the John Street meeting-house was subsequently occupied by the Salvation Army and is now in industrial use.

The building has sandstone rubble walls and a later gabled brick wing at the front incorporating the entrance and gallery staircase. The original windows in the W wall have plain stone surrounds, but the fenestration has been much altered. The meeting-house, initially 25ft by 34¾ft, was enlarged by 13⅓ft to the E in the early 19th century and a gallery built; the line of the extension is marked internally by wooden columns. A floor has been inserted at gallery level but a portion of the fielded-panelled gallery front remains and the site of the pulpit at the N end is still discernible. The roof is supported by king-post trusses.

Fittings – *Monuments*: a few 19th-century sandstone headstones remain SE of the chapel. *Plate*: in URC History Society collection, includes a pair of Sheffield-plate cups dated 1776.

Black (1906) 328–9. *Cong. Mag.* V (1822) 664. Jackson, H. and Jackson, M., *A History of Maryport* (*c.*1960) 27–8. Nicholson and Axon (1915) 350.

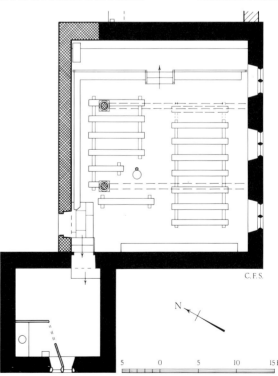

Friends' Meeting-house at Mosedale, MUNGRISDALE   *Cumberland*

C. F. S.

N

5   0   5   10   15 Feet

(88) PRESBYTERIAN, Crosby Street (NY 036367). Built in 1831 for seceders from John Street. Rendered walls, slate roof and lancet windows; enlarged to front in sandstone, tower added *c*.1888. *Monuments*: reset to N, sandstone headstones (1) Thomas Grierson, 1831, signed 'R. Crosthwaite'; (2) Esther Moncrieff, 1849, signed 'Asbridge'. (Demolition proposed 1980)

 Mackelvie (1873) 122.

(89) CHURCH OF CHRIST, Furnace Road (NY 036364). Built 1861, inscribed 'The Disciples were called Christians'.

MATTERDALE

(90) WESLEYAN, Ulcat Row (NY 405225). Random rubble and slate, two arched windows in N and S walls, side-entry porch to E; opened 1848.

MUNCASTER

(91) Former BIBLE CHRISTIAN, Ravenglass (SD 084963). Rendered walls, round-arched windows. Built 1872 and later converted to Workingmen's Institute, porch added 1898 and floor inserted.

MUNGRISDALE

(92) FRIENDS, Mosedale (NY 357322). The meeting-house was registered in July 1702 and slightly enlarged to the NW later in the 18th century. Regular meetings had ceased by 1865 although some religious use continued, latterly as a chapel-of-ease to Mungrisdale, until 1970. Meetings were resumed in 1973. The seating was of particular interest.

 The walls are of rubble, partly rendered, and the roof is

Friends' meeting-house, Mosedale.   (92)

covered with local slates. The principal room (23ft by 26⅔ft) has three two-light windows in the SE wall with chamfered mullions and hinges for external drop-shutters; the floor is paved with sandstone flags. Two Tuscan columns of sandstone support the roof at the line of the extension. The stand, at the NE end, has a divided front of flat shaped balusters and a fielded-panelled back to the seat. The seating in the body of the room is in two ranks, partly altered in the NW section and since 1970 more drastically changed; the seats comprise wooden benches, without backs until 1884, fixed to moulded oak sleepers. *Burial-ground* 100 yards E on opposite side of main road, small walled enclosure with chamfered jambs to entrance; no monuments.

Butler (1978) 73–6.

OUSBY

(93) WESLEYAN, Melmerby (NY 616373). Sandstone walls and slate roof, mid 19th-century, renovated and refitted 1882. *Collecting Shovels*: pair, oval with long handles, 19th-century.

PENRITH

(94) CONGREGATIONAL, Duke Street (NY 513304). Red sandstone Gothic with corner tower and spire, 1865–6 by George Watson of Penrith, replacing a chapel of 1824. (URC)

Cong. Mag. V (1822) 554–5. CYB (1867), 359–60.

(95) FRIENDS, Meeting-house Lane (NY 516304). Friends bought an existing property, Layne House, in 1699 and converted it for use as a meeting-house. The thick stone outer walls of this building (48ft by 19½ft) remain but without datable features. A wing added to the SW in 1803 has a plain stone-framed doorway between two windows.

The interior was largely refitted in 1803; minor rooms at the extremities of the original house have galleries above with balustraded fronts and were formerly approached by upper doorways in the NE wall. The stand with central entrance is set against the NE wall between the galleries and faces the wing which forms an integral part of the principal room.

The roof structure of the original house includes four trusses with paired principals, three with corner braces and one with a collar, and a diagonally set ridge, possibly 16th-century. Traces of the former attic rooms of the original house remain at the NW end.

Butler (1978) 84–8.

(96) Former WESLEYAN, Sandgate Head (NY 517304). Zion chapel, at the bottom of Fell Lane N of Sandgate, was built in 1815 for a society which previously met in the school-room of Mr Varty. In 1872, when the Wesleyans removed to Drovers Lane (*see* (97)), the chapel was sold to the Primitive Methodists; it is now in use by the Assemblies of God. The walls are of rubble, rendered on the principal elevations, with painted stone dressings. The front wall has a simple pediment with date tablet of 1815, rusticated quoins, platbands at gallery and eaves level, three bays of round-arched windows and a central doorway with Tuscan columns and open pediment. The interior has an original gallery around three sides; other fittings date from the late 19th century.

Judge, G. H. B., 'The beginnings of Methodism in the Penrith district', *WHSP* XIX (1933–4) 153–60.

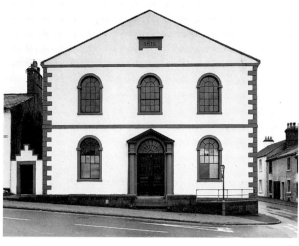

Zion Chapel, Penrith.   (96)

(97) WESLEYAN, Drovers Lane (NY 515306). Large Italianate chapel of red sandstone at the corner of Wordsworth Street, built 1872 to replace the foregoing.

(98) PRESBYTERIAN, Lowther Street (NY 516306). The congregation (now URC) originated in the late 17th century, eventually joining the Associate (Burgher) Presbytery of Selkirk and subsequently the United Presbyterian Church. The church occupied rented property until *c*.1785, when a meeting-house was built in Rowcliffe Lane. The present chapel, built in 1864 on a new site, is of sandstone with lancet windows.

Colligan, J. H., *Penrith Presbyterian Church* (1908). *Cong. Mag.* V (1822) 554. Mackelvie (1873) 120–1.

PLUMBLAND

(99) INDEPENDENT (NY 153392). Small chapel with pointed-arched windows; dated 1847.

SCALEBY

(100) WESLEYAN, Scaleby Hill (NY 440636). Low-built white-washed rubble walls with dressed stone quoins and hipped slate roof. Front wall to N has two pointed-arched windows between later ashlar porch. Date tablet of 1828 on W wall. Interior refitted late 19th century. *Collecting Shovel*: octagonal metal tray with two wooden handles.

SEBERGHAM

(101) WESLEYAN, Welton (NY 352444). Rubble and slate. Opened 1834.

SETMURTHY

(102) Former FRIENDS (NY 197319). Low building of 1799 converted to cottage after 1828 with later two-storeyed extension.

Butler (1978) 57, 58.

SKELTON

(103) PRIMITIVE METHODIST (NY 437357). Rubble with rendered gabled front, round-arched windows. Dated 1865.

Former Friends' meeting-house, Thornyland.   (104)

SOLPORT

(104) Former FRIENDS, Thornyland (NY 458739). The meeting-house, standing on a remote site and now used as a shelter for farm animals, was built in 1773 to replace one of 1698. Regular use ceased c.1870 although occasional meetings by Friends and Wesleyans continued until the end of the century. The walls are of rendered rubble with sandstone dressings and the roof is hipped and slated. The front faces S and has three wide segmental-arched windows and doorway between. The interior (40⅓ft by 24¼ft) is divided by a partition with vertically sliding fielded-panelled shutters; the smaller room to the E has an original fireplace with stone hob grate. A date stone of 1698 is reset externally in the E wall. The roof is supported by five king-post trusses.

Butler (1978) 13–15.

Former Friends' meeting-house, Scotby.   (107)

THRELKELD

(105) Former WESLEYAN (NY 347269). Small chapel of 1843 converted to cottage c.1970.

WALTON

(106) PRIMITIVE METHODIST (NY 521646). Porch between lancet windows. Dated 1858.

WETHERAL

(107) Former FRIENDS, Scotby (NY 442551). The erection of a meeting-house at Scotby was proposed in 1717 and the building completed in the following year. In 1740 a stable was added at the SW end and in 1743 the principal room was ceiled; a ceiling was added to the 'little end of the Meeting-house' in 1765. The meeting ceased in 1913 and the building is now in use as a workshop.

The walls are of brick with stone dressings and there is some stone in the lower courses at the rear; the roof is covered with slates and has a verge of stone slates. The front wall, facing SE, has a chamfered plinth, doorway with chamfered jambs and lintel and two windows to the right and one to the left, perhaps formerly of two lights but now with mullions removed. The interior (35¾ft by 22ft) has no original fittings but traces remain of a partition to the left of the entrance and of the site of the stand at the NE end with window behind. (Conversion to residential accommodation proposed 1987)

Burial-ground to S with short oval-sectioned cylindrical 19th-century gravestones.

Butler (1978) 7–9.

(108) Former WESLEYAN, Warwick (NY 465567). The chapel, now in secular use, was built in 1847. The front, of squared stone, is pedimented and occupied only by a giant doorway

Former Methodist chapel, Wetheral. (108)

(13ft 8in. high) with bracketed cornice. At each side are lower pedimented wings or lodges. The side walls, partly of brickwork, have two tiers of windows.

WHITEHAVEN

(109) CONGREGATIONAL, Scotch Street (NX 975181). Large Gothic chapel by T. Lewis Banks with corner tower and elaborate interior, built 1874. The former meeting-house, built for the Countess of Huntingdon's Connexion in 1793, which stood on the NE side of Duke Street was bought by this congregation in 1819; it was subsequently occupied by the Salvation Army. (Closed c.1970)

Cong. Mag. V (1822) 670–1. CYB (1872), 416.

(110) Former FRIENDS, Sandhills Lane (NX 973182). The erection of a meeting-house in Whitehaven was under consideration from 1713 but the project proceeded slowly; the land was acquired by 1716 and collections were made towards the cost of the work in 1724 and 1726. The principal structure was complete by 1725 and a gallery around three sides was added in 1784. Since 1931 the building has been used by the Brethren.

The meeting-house has rendered rubble walls and a double slate-covered roof with twin gables to SW and NE. The SW elevation is approximately symmetrical with two doorways incorporating windows above, each flanked by a pair of windows. The interior (54ft by 35⅔ft) had a row of four 'great stone pillars' on the main axis to support the roof, but two are now replaced by steel and the others removed. A screen with hinged shutters divides the meeting-house into two unequal parts. There was a continuous stand against the SE wall; the gallery on the other three sides is supported by quatrefoil-sectioned iron columns.

Butler (1978) 62–4.

(111) WESLEYAN, Lowther Street (NX 975180). Gothic, with corner tower; walls faced in polygonal masonry. Built 1877, by T. Lewis Banks, replacing a chapel in Michael Street.

(112) PRESBYTERIAN, James Street (NX 972179). The church (now URC) originated in the late 17th century, at first in connection with the congregation at Cockermouth. The first meeting-house, in Market Place, was built in 1694, enlarged c.1755 and further altered in 1857 by the addition of a Gothic front. A secession occurred in 1775 resulting in a second chapel in High Street, but the congregations reunited in 1895. The present chapel, a Gothic structure with corner tower, stands on the original site.

Plate: (in URC History Society collection) includes a pair of mid 18th-century pewter cups.

CHST III (1907–8) 224–5. Cong. Mag. V (1822) 665–6.

WIGTON

(113) CONGREGATIONAL, Water Street (NY 257484). The early history of orthodox dissent in Wigton is obscure; although the congregation (now URC) claims to have been founded in 1666, the present church seems to have been formed c.1816 and the chapel built in 1834. The chapel is a tall building of sandstone ashlar with two tiers of windows above a basement storey; the front has a plain pediment and central doorway with consoles supporting a cornice; below a window to the right is a memorial to Rev. John Walton, 1849 'one of the founders and first Pastor of the Independent Church in this town ... 1816 to 1826'. Another inscription records that the chapel was opened 8 October 1834. The interior is lofty and has a gallery around three sides.

Cong. Mag. V (1822) 713.

(114) FRIENDS, West Street (NY 253483). The meeting-house built in 1830, possibly designed by William Alderson, superseded one of 1707, which itself replaced an earlier building. The walls are of red sandstone and the roof slate-covered and hipped towards the front. The S front, of ashlar, is terminated by rusticated pilasters and pierced by three windows with tapered

Friends' meeting-house, Wigton. E side. (114)

architraves. A later pent roof along the E side covers the two entrances to the two equal parts into which the building is divided. The rooms are separated by a shuttered partition which can be lowered into a pit beneath the floor. There is a continuous stand along the W side. *Burial-ground* to N with uniform headstones. (Meeting-house much altered internally 1988)

Butler (1978) 23–8.

(115) WESLEYAN, High Street (NY 256482). Sandstone Gothic; built 1882–3 to replace a chapel in George Street.

(116) Former PRIMITIVE METHODIST, New Street (NY 254486). Red sandstone, dated 1864, much altered.

WOODSIDE

(117) Former BAPTIST, Oulton (NY 244508). The only early 18th-century Baptist congregations in Cumberland were at Egremont and jointly at Oulton and Broughton, the Great Broughton church claiming to date from 1648. A house in Oulton was registered for Anabaptists in April 1712, and other certificates are dated 1720 and 1724. An inscription on the present chapel records that it was built in 1722 and rebuilt in 1832. 'Tabor Chapel' is a small building with rendered brick walls and a stone slate roof; gabled front of three bays with large oval tablet above doorway. By 1901 the chapel had passed to the Primitive Methodists and it is now in secular use. (Demolished *c*.1985)

BM (1842) 29–30. *Cong. Mag.* V (1822) 386–7.

WORKINGTON

(118) LADY GLENORCHY'S CHAPEL, South William Street (NY 001288). The Low Meeting-house was built in 1780 for a mixed congregation of Independents and Presbyterians with substantial assistance from Lady Glenorchy. The church later became Congregational (now URC). The chapel was enlarged in 1855 and largely rebuilt in 1884. The front is of yellow sandstone with dressings of red sandstone, in three principal bays with a

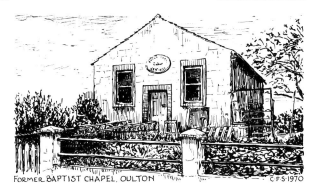

FORMER BAPTIST CHAPEL, OULTON C·F·S·1970

gabled centre and two tiers of windows. The rear wall incorporates two blocked round-arched windows with pins for external shutters which may date from the late 18th century. Free-standing at rear, 'Congregational Sabbath School erected 1878'.

Monuments: in burial-ground, uprooted and loose against boundary walls (1) Thomas Commings, 1807, Deborah his widow, 1816, John their son, Attorney at Law, 1794, and Margaret Ruth their niece, 1798; (2) Daniel Matthewson, shipwright, 1803, Ann his widow, 1819, and James their son, 1802; (3) John Irving, ship-owner 'who died of the Spasmodic Cholera', 3 August 1832, and Margaret his widow, 1860; (4) William Rees, deacon, 'who died of the Spasmodic Cholera' 4 August 1832; (5) Peter Sands, 1782; (6) John Watte, 'late Collector of the Customs in Workington', 1840.

Cong. Mag. V (1822) 714. Thompson, D.P., *Lady Glenorchy and her Churches – the Story of Two Hundred Years* (1967).

(119) WESLEYAN, South William Street (NY 001289). Elaborate Italianate chapel of 1890 in red and yellow sandstone by Charles Bell. Gabled S front with big Venetian-traceried window above altered entrance, tall domed tower at SE corner.

The county of Durham, thinly populated until the development in the 19th century of the mineral resources along its eastern seaboard, does not figure prominently in the early history of dissent. Only nine licences were taken out under the Indulgence of 1672, of which seven were for Presbyterians; a few Quaker meetings were in existence in the late 17th century, and Baptists were represented by the Hexham church which exercised an influence over both sides of the Derwent. The Baptist chapel at Hamsterley (26), one of the principal monuments in the county, was erected by one branch of this church. Evidence of early Presbyterian activity is to be seen at the western extremity of the county in the former meeting-house at Ireshopeburn (43), while at Swalwell (62) the oldest recently surviving chapel in the county, of 1750, was erected by another Presbyterian society which had formerly met in more rural surroundings. The development and vicissitudes of a town congregation are epitomized in the history of the Claypath church in Durham (13), where the mid 18th-century meeting-house still remains behind the present chapel. Evidence of the early spread of Methodism is to be found in the chapels at Newbiggin, in Teesdale (37), and at High House, in Weardale (45), both of 1760 although now much altered, and at Wolsingham (65) of 1776.

The 19th century produced few chapels of note outside the major towns. A group of four buildings in Sunderland (52, 53, 54, 57) together with one in Darlington (11) show a marked similarity in design with a front of five bays and pediment over the middle three. That the Friends' meeting-house in Sunderland (54) should have been so designed presents an unexpected conformity while its internal arrangements, as repeated later at Darlington (10), although suited to Quaker practices, are typical only of the North of England. Few chapels of a strongly stylistic character were noted, although Renaissance elements predominate. The earliest Gothic motifs occur in the two pointed-arched windows at the former Congregational chapel at Staindrop (39) of 1827; the most fully developed building in this style is St John's, Ashbrooke Road, Sunderland (55), built by the Wesleyans in 1887–8.

Throughout the county stone is the most commonly used walling material, but brickwork is found in eastern districts from the mid 18th century (13, 62) and is common to most of the 19th-century buildings in Darlington and Sunderland. Roofs are almost entirely slate-covered, stone flags survive only rarely (26, 43) and pantiles in two minor instances (26, 27), although they may also have been the original covering at Swalwell (62).

BARNARD CASTLE

(1) CONGREGATIONAL, Hall Street (NZ 051165). The church, now URC, was formed in 1815. A nonconformist congregation existed here in the late 17th century, fostered by the preaching of the ejected incumbent John Rogers and subsequently supported by ministers from Cotherstone, Yorks. N.R. A chapel was built

CONGREGATIONAL CHAPEL, BARNARD CASTLE   CFS 1974

in Newgate in 1813 superseding various temporary premises; the present building, dated 1836, built on an extension of a site originally intended only for a Sunday-school, was opened 18 April 1837. The walls are of squared stone with gables to N and S having moulded eaves corbels. The entrance in the N wall has a round-arched head and a fanlight with intersecting glazing bars. The windows in two tiers have plain stone lintels and hung sashes with small panes.

EM (October 1837) 485–6. Smisson, E.A., *The Way We Have Come...Barnard Castle Congregational Church* (1936).

(2) Former METHODIST, Broad Gates (NZ 051162). The former preaching-house, built in 1764, is now subdivided and converted to dwellings. It was built with the assistance of voluntary labour and opened by John Wesley 13 April 1765. In 1823 it was superseded by a new chapel in The Bank. Later occupants included an Infants school and, for a brief period, the Congregational Sunday-school; it also appears to have served as a meeting place for a Unitarian society formed about 1842.

The building (43½ft by 34¼ft externally) has rubble walls and a slate roof. It stands partly above an alley which passes below the S

Former Methodist chapel, Barnard Castle.   (2)

side from which cellars under the remainder of the building are approached. The E and W walls are gabled; the latter has an arched entrance to the alley and formerly had a large round-arched window centrally to the upper room. The S front, facing the garden of the former preacher's house, had four similarly arched windows now lowered or altered and upper windows inserted. The N and E walls may not have had original fenestration but some upper windows on the N could date from an early 19th-century refurbishment.

Inscription: in E wall, stone with date '1764'.

Curnock (1938) V: 110. Evans (1897) 10. Smisson (1936) op. cit. 13. Steele, A., *History of Methodism in Barnard Castle...* (1857) Frontis.

BISHOP AUCKLAND

(3) Former WESLEYAN, West Auckland (NZ 181263). Behind buildings on N side of main street, three-bay front dated 1827.

(4) PRIMITIVE METHODIST, Etherley Dene (NZ 192290). Three-bay front with four-centred arched openings, gabled end walls. Dated 1869.

CHESTER-LE-STREET

(5) CONGREGATIONAL, Low Chare (NZ 276514). Three-bay gabled front with round-arched openings and a circular window over the entrance. The original date tablet is inscribed 'BETHEL 1814', two later tablets above the windows have 'REMODEL-LED 1860'. (URC)

(6) Former WESLEYAN, Low Chare (NZ 276514), immediately SE of the above, was built in 1807 and superseded by a new chapel in Station Road in 1880. It has been occupied by the Salvation Army since 1923. The chapel has stone walls and a gabled front with a central doorway with moulded stone architrave between two plain windows.

CONSETT

(7) WESLEYAN, Iveston (NZ 139503). Stone and slate; L-shaped

plan with later gabled wing. Tablet with winged cherub's head dated 1837.

CROOK AND WILLINGTON

(8) PRIMITIVE METHODIST, Emmerson Street, Crook (NZ 166355). Ashlar front with rusticated lower stage and big pediment, dated 1868.

DARLINGTON

(9) Former BAPTIST, Archer Street (NZ 288148). The chapel, built in 1847 for a congregation originally formed in 1810, was converted to a Masonic Hall *c.* 1871 and has subsequently been much altered by enlargement and refenestration. The walls are of brown brick and traces of round-arched windows remain in the side walls, the front windows have been altered. The chapel was superseded in 1871 by a new building in Grange Road (NZ 287142) designed by William Peachey.

B.Hbk (1871) 256. Bartlett, G. W., *The Baptist Church in Darlington, A Centenary Record of its Rise and Progress* (1910).

(10) FRIENDS, Skinnergate (NZ 287144). A large double-gabled meeting-house built in 1768 and enlarged in 1793 which stood on the present site behind a row of cottages on the W side of the street was almost entirely rebuilt in 1846. The street frontage is now occupied by a forebuilding of brick in five bays having a central entrance flanked by a pair of Doric columns. The meeting-house behind has a broad gabled rear wall facing the large burial-ground; the side wall to the N is of 18th-century brickwork.

Friends' meeting-house, Darlington.   (10)

The interior comprises two formerly identical parallel rooms separated by a partition of vertically sliding shutters capable of being raised into the roof space. At the W end of each room is a continuous stand with partly balustraded front, gated entrances and continuous coved canopy. At the E end was a gallery approached by a double staircase in the lobby. Major alterations in recent years have included the conversion of the gallery to

Friends' meeting-house, Darlington. Interior before alteration.   (10)

separate rooms, the introduction of suspended ceilings and the removal of most of the stand from the N room.

FHSJ XXIV (1927) Frontis. Lidbetter (1961) Fig. 29.

(11) WESLEYAN, Bondgate (NZ 286147). The chapel, dated 1812, was designed by William Jenkins. It has walls of brown brick and a hipped slated roof. The E front, of five bays with two tiers of round-arched windows with altered frames, has a pediment over the three slightly projecting middle bays and a central entrance with fanlight flanked by a pair of tall columns with Greek Doric capitals and Tuscan bases.

The interior, which has a gallery around three sides, was entirely refitted in 1885. (In 1993 further alterations in progress included the stripping out of the fixed seating to the lower floor and the provision of ancillary accommodation next to the entrance)

Communion Chairs: pair, backs carved with representations of communion cups in low relief, *c*.1840 (from the former Free Methodist 'Paradise Chapel' of 1840 in Coniscliffe Road (NZ 286143), demolished since 1972).

(12) WESLEYAN, Haughton Le Skerne (NZ 310160). Brick with pedimented gable dated 1825. Front with two altered round-arched windows. Sunday-school adjacent built 1900.

DURHAM

(13) CONGREGATIONAL, Claypath (NZ 276427). The church (now URC) meeting in Claypath originated as a Presbyterian congregation in the late 17th century. Some Arian influences are traceable in the late 18th century, and to these may be ascribed the commencement of a separate Independent church which in 1783 was meeting in a chapel in Framwellgate. The Presbyterian cause was further weakened about this time by a protracted lawsuit over the removal of a minister, and in 1804 the church appointed the Independent minister to serve concurrently as its pastor. Two meeting-houses remained in use until 1821 when the Claypath building was adopted as the sole meeting place of the then united Congregational church. The Claypath meeting-house, which had been rebuilt in 1751, was repaired and a gallery added to accommodate the enlarged congregation. In 1885–6 a much larger chapel was erected in front of the old building, which was further altered for Sunday-school use in 1903 following the sale of a building in Gilesgate.

The former chapel, of 1751, is a plain building of dark brick with a slate roof. The front wall facing S towards Claypath is concealed behind a line of shops and houses and is now partly covered by the later chapel. Two tiers of round-arched windows with keystones remain at one end but the original entrance does not survive. The E and W walls are gabled and have round-arched windows without keystones; a segmental-arched outer doorway was pierced in the W wall *c*.1885. Two tall semicircular-headed windows in the longer N wall flank the original site of the pulpit and are embellished internally with moulded architraves, imposts and keystones. The interior ($35\frac{3}{4}$ft by $42\frac{1}{4}$ft) has been entirely reconstructed and a floor inserted.

Wesleyan chapel, Bondgate, Darlington.   (11)

Former Congregational chapel, Claypath, Durham.   (13)

The present chapel, opened 1 September 1886, has walls of Hebburn stone with Dennick stone dressings and a slate roof. It was designed by T. H. Gradon in the early Decorated style and has a tower with prominent stone spire at the SE corner.

Plate: includes a pair of cups of 1647, with traces of gilding, engraved with shield-of-arms and later inscription 1775.

CYB (1886) 223–5; (1887) 258. Derbyshire, H., *A History of the Congregational Church, Durham* (*c*.1930).

(14) BETHEL CHAPEL, North Road (NZ 270426). The Methodist New Connexion chapel, dated 1853, is a stone building with a pediment and giant order of Roman Doric pilasters continued around the three exposed sides. The front, of three bays with two tiers of windows, has a tall pedimented porch with Ionic columns.

(15) PRESBYTERIAN, Waddington Street (NZ 267427). Stone, with octagonal corner turret and spire. Built 1872. (URC)

Hawkins (1973) 79–92.

EGGLESTON

(16) BAPTIST, Egglesburn (NY 983246). Small chapel, dated 1872. Secondary doorway to former Reading Room inscribed with the name of the periodical *British Workman*.

Bethel Chapel, North Road, Durham.   (14)

(17) WESLEYAN (NZ 001238). Three-bay front of coursed rubble with rusticated quoins and two tiers of windows; dated 1828. Sunday-school 1881 adjacent.

Former Presbyterian chapel, Ellison Street West,
Gateshead.   (25)

ETHERLEY

(18) WESLEYAN, High Etherley (NZ 165281). Late 19th-century
with reset tablet of 1829 in front wall.

(19) PRIMITIVE METHODIST, Toft Hill (NZ 162281). Tall five-bay
gabled front dated 1879.

FOREST AND FRITH

(20) WESLEYAN, Forest (NY 871295). Low three-bay gabled
front dated 1867.

GAINFORD

(21) Former CONGREGATIONAL (NZ 171169). Built 1849, greatly
altered c.1950–60 on conversion to houses. Former Sunday-school
at rear.

(22) WESLEYAN (NZ 170168). Small chapel facing the green.

Rendered front with three round-arched windows; oval tablet
above doorway dated 1834. Side entrance to Sunday-school dated
1897.

GATESHEAD   *Tyne and Wear*

(23) CONGREGATIONAL, Bensham Road (NZ 252629). The
chapel, on the S side of the road, was built in 1872 for a newly
formed congregation. It was designed by J. P. Pritchett of
Darlington in the Decorated style, and has a gabled front with
five-light traceried window, and a corner tower and spire.
(Demolished 1973)

   CYB (1873) 419–20.

(24) Former METHODIST NEW CONNEXION, Sheriff Hill
(NZ 265606). Zion chapel, Sodhouse Bank; dated 1836.

(25) Former PRESBYTERIAN, Ellison Street West (NZ 254632).
Early 19th-century chapel, latterly in commercial use. An almost
square building of brick with a hipped roof; three bays of round-
arched windows in two tiers above a basement, the front divided
by a platband below the upper windows. (Demolished since
1982)

HAMSTERLEY

(26) BAPTIST (NZ 119311). The church traces its origins to the
Baptist church in Hexham which was founded in 1652 and early
in its existence suffered from the attentions of the pretended
convert 'Joseph Ben Israel'. This church, which drew members
from a very considerable area, divided in 1655 into two sections,
Hexhamshire and Derwent, and these gradually crystallized into
more localized units, of which Hamsterley was one; until 1785 it
was associated with Rowley (31). The first meeting-house at
Hamsterley was built in 1715; it was rebuilt in 1774 and no traces
of the former building survive.

   The meeting-house and the former manse adjacent to the W
form a single structure with rubble walls and a stone-slated roof.
The end walls, now covered by later buildings, are gabled and
have stone copings and moulded kneelers. The front wall, which
faces S, has two tall windows with round arches and keystones;
to their right is a similarly arched doorway with keystone
inscribed with the date 1774 and the name 'BETHEL' in Hebrew
characters. The rear wall has two sash windows close below the

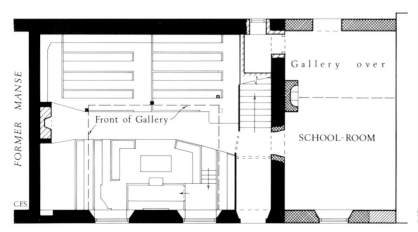

Baptist Meeting-house
HAMSTERLEY
Durham

N

Scale of Feet

5   0   5   10   15   20

Baptist meeting-house, Hamsterley. (26)

eaves. A small two-storeyed wing to the E occupying a gap between this and an adjacent house was added *c*.1800; it has rubble walls and the roof is covered at the front with stone slates but with pantiles at the rear; the first floor has been partly removed internally and the front windows have been replaced by a single tall sash.

The interior of the chapel (22¼ft by 30¼ft) has a wide staircase to the gallery immediately opposite the entrance, with square balusters and plain handrail. The gallery, which extends around three sides, is supported on square wooden posts and has a fielded-panelled front. The pulpit between the windows on the S side was replaced in the 19th century by a wide rostrum but the original pedimented back-board remains. The seating throughout is original with shaped ends and panelled backs, and includes a table-pew in front of the pulpit. At the W end of the lower floor is an original fireplace with stone surround.

Fittings – *Books*: remains of an extensive theological library including works of the 17th and 18th centuries. *Candle Sconce*: on pew W of pulpit, with two scrolled brass branches, 18th-century. *Hat Pegs*: in gallery, notched wooden pegs. *Monuments*: in front burial-ground (1) George Dowson, 1777, and Joseph, son of John Dowson of Maland, 'whose death was occasioned by the breaking of a Grindstone at Bedburn Mill, May 6th 1796'; (2) Thomas, 1775, Edward, 1782, and Jane, 1791, children of Cockrell and Hannah Readshaw; (3) John Hall, 1781, and Ann his widow, 1798; (4) Rev. Isaac Garner, 1758, Ann his widow, 1806, and Dorothy their daughter, 1833; (5) Jane, 1776, and Mary, 1777, daughters of Robert and Jane Morgan; (6) Thomas Morgan, 1786, and Mary his wife, 1785; (7) Lucy Jopling, 1776; (8) Joseph Little, 1776.

Twitchett, F. G., *A Short History of Rowley Baptist Church, 1652-1952* (1952).

HARRATON   *Tyne and Wear*

(27) Former WESLEYAN, Chartershaugh, Fatfield (NZ 307535). Rendered brick walls and pantiled roof, broad three-bay front; early 19th-century. John Wesley is reputed to have used a former engine-house at Chartershaugh pit as a preaching-house.

HARTLEPOOL   *Cleveland*

(28) INDEPENDENT, Durham Street (NZ 528340). Rendered front of three bays with giant pilasters and pediment, two tiers of windows, and central doorway with consoles and cornice. Tablet dated 1843.

(29) Former WESLEYAN, Victoria Road (NZ 508326). Large prominently sited chapel of 1871–3 by Hill and Swann of Leeds. Five-bay front with two tiers of round-arched windows and three-bay pedimented portico with giant Corinthian columns.

HASWELL

(30) WESLEYAN, Church Street (NZ 374431). 'Wesleyan Chapel erected 1849'; rendered walls, gabled three-bay front with round-arched openings.

HEALEYFIELD

(31) BAPTIST, Rowley (NZ 087480). The church originated as a branch of the Hexham church, founded 1652; until 1785 it was linked with Hamsterley (26). The first meeting-house at Rowley, built in 1717, was rebuilt in 1823–4. Alterations in 1864, when the chapel was enlarged, and in 1890, when a school-room block was erected on the site of the vestry and stable, and a general refitting at the latter date, have left little beyond the masonry of the early 19th-century walls. The building is a long low rectangle with a slated roof, and has a gabled side-entry porch at the junction of the two principal parts.

Twitchett (1952) op. cit.

HOUGHTON-LE-SPRING   *Tyne and Wear*

(32) Former METHODIST, Newbottle (NZ 338516). The chapel, now used for storage, has a 20th-century tablet in the front wall inscribed 'Wesley Methodist Church, 1786', the probable year of erection. It has walls of rubble, squared in the front, and grey ashlar dressings. The gabled S front has a central doorway with moulded imposts and round-arched head with prominent long and short voussoirs. Two large windows, similarly arched, are now blocked. The side and rear walls also have round-arched windows but of less elaboration. A low vestry wing extends beyond the E side; further outbuildings at the rear are dated 1872.

HURWORTH

(33) WESLEYAN (NZ 302102). Opened 1827. Late 19th-century brick gabled front with lancets.

MIDDLETON IN TEESDALE

(34) Former BAPTIST, Hude (NY 947257). The chapel, now used as a Masonic Hall, was built in 1827 for a church founded in that year. It has stone walls and a hipped slate roof. The front wall has a shallow round-arched recess enclosing the doorway, over which is a defaced inscription.

(35) WESLEYAN, Chapel Row (NY 948254). Five-bay pedimented front with two tiers of round-arched windows and paired doorways. Dated 1870.

(36) Former PRIMITIVE METHODIST (NY 950254). Gabled front,

Wesleyan chapel, Victoria Road, Hartlepool.   (29)

dated 1872, formerly incorporating 1839 tablet from earlier chapel now reset in front of Wesleyan Chapel. (Converted to offices since 1972) *Weathervane*: on rear gable.

NEWBIGGIN

(37) METHODIST (NY 916277). The chapel, 100 yards NE of the main road, is reputed to have been built in 1760 and is claimed to be the oldest Methodist chapel in existence with an unbroken record of service. The walls are of rubble with an ashlar front to the SW added in 1860; the roof is slate-covered. The original walling is exposed at the rear and at the NW end; one blocked window in each of these walls dates from *c*.1760, but in alterations which marked the centenary the walls were heightened and two round-arched windows were inserted in the back wall. The front wall, rebuilt when the chapel was slightly enlarged on this side, is of three bays with round-arched doorway and windows; an inscription above the doorway reads 'WESLEYAN CHAPEL/ERECTED 1760 ENLARGED 1860'. A later house and school-room adjoin at the SE end.

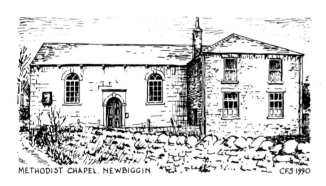

METHODIST CHAPEL, NEWBIGGIN   CFS 1990

The interior (41ft by 25ft), entirely refitted in 1860, has a rostrum pulpit at the NW end facing stepped seating. The former *pulpit* with two stages of fielded panels and moulded cornice stands in one corner. *Love-feast Cups*: (1) white glazed pottery with dark-green floral pattern, two handles, stem and base, bowl inscribed 'LOVEFEAST'; (2) white glazed pottery with bands, two handles, mug-shaped body inscribed on two faces '*Love Feast/God is Love*'. Both early 19th-century.

Dolbey (1964) 73–4, Pls. 5, 6 (sketch plan).

SPENNYMOOR

(38) BAPTIST (NZ 258338). Brick gabled front dated 1875 with three arched recesses enclosing elaborately moulded doorway and windows.

STAINDROP

(39) Former CONGREGATIONAL, Queen's Head Wynd (NZ 127207). The former chapel, latterly used as a workshop, is dated 1827 and has rubble walls with ashlar dressings and a slate roof. The front and rear walls are similarly fenestrated with a centrally placed tall window with two-centred arched head and intersecting glazing bars flanked by two tiers of rectangular windows; in the front wall are two plain doorways, one blocked. The gabled end walls have parapets and moulded stone kneelers.

A chapel of the late 19th century 50 yards S was demolished *c*.1970.

(40) Former FRIENDS, 20 North Green (NZ 127206). The meeting-house, which stands on a concealed site, was built in 1771 superseding earlier meeting places in Raby and Staindrop. Meetings ceased *c*.1889 and, although they resumed for a few years in the early 20th century, the building was sold about 1974 and has since been converted to a house.

The walls are of rubble with a broad front of squared stone and the roof is pantiled. In front is a low gabled porch with a plain sash window in the walling to the left. The end walls are gabled and have shaped kneelers, one dated 1771.

(41) Former WESLEYAN, North Green (NZ 129206). Gabled front with wheel-window above porch. Dated 1869.

(42) PRIMITIVE METHODIST (NZ 130207). Three-bay gabled front with four-centred arched openings. Dated 1861.

STANHOPE

(43) Former PRESBYTERIAN, Ireshopeburn (NY 866386). A cottage and outbuildings at the W end of the village immediately W of the bridge over Ireshope Burn are claimed to have served as a Presbyterian meeting-house from the early 18th century until 1827 and to have been provided during the ministry, here and at Garrigill, Cumberland, of Adam Wilson, 1719–38.

The building, which has rubble walls and a stone-slated roof, was built in 1687 as a single-storey dwelling, the steeply pitched roof of which is visible in the present gable walls. The original entrance on the N side, now blocked, has a stone lintel inscribed with the initials 'I¹B' and date 'OC Y 21 [October Yᵉ 21] 1687' and carved with representations of a hammer, claw, and pincers. The house was heightened in the early 18th century, the W half now used for storage becoming a cottage of two storeys with a fireplace to the only room on each floor; the E half, which has an upper floor inserted in the early 19th century, was probably converted to cottage use *c*.1827 and alterations to the windows in the S wall suggest its possible prior use as a small meeting-house.

Clack and Pattinson (1978) 93. *CHST* IV (1909–10) 255; V (1911–12) 23–6. Dawson, L., 'Early Methodism in Upper Weardale', *WHS, NEB* XXII (September 1974) 23.

(44) Former PRIMITIVE METHODIST, Brotherlee (NY 925377). Two small round-arched windows in gable end, front altered. Built 1850, converted to garage after 1960.

Clack and Pattinson (1978) 79–80.

(45) METHODIST, High House (NY 873385). The chapel on the N side of the road E of Ireshopeburn was built in 1760 but heightened, extended to the E, entirely refenestrated and refitted in 1872. The walls are of squared stone with later ashlar dressings. The entrance is at the E end; traces of two original windows remain in the N wall.

The interior (originally about 29ft by 33ft) has a gallery around three sides. Some late 18th-century fielded panelling is reset as a dado to the ground floor.

Fittings – *Clarinet*: attached to organ case. *Clock*: in vestry, late 18th-century. *Collecting Shovels*: wood, with shaped handles and shallow box.

Clack and Pattinson (1978) 57–9. Dolbey (1964) 69.

(46) Former PRIMITIVE METHODIST, Rookhope (NY 940427). Broad front with rusticated stone dressings and four narrow round-arched windows. Built 1863 to supersede a chapel of 1836.

Clack and Pattinson (1978) 77–8.

(47) Former WESLEYAN, Chapel Street, Stanhope (NY 997394). Built 1800 for a society in existence by 1785; it was superseded in 1871 by the present chapel nearby and has since been converted to a pair of cottages, Nos. 16 and 17. Traces of two tall windows remain in the front wall and of a smaller upper window above the original doorway to the right.

Clack and Pattinson (1978) 45–7.

(48) PRIMITIVE METHODIST, Wearhead (NY 861393). Built 1825–6. Broad SW front of three bays with two tiers of windows, later two-storeyed annexe to right. Interior, refitted in the late 19th century, has a gallery with open cast-iron front around three sides and a wide rostrum pulpit with a later organ recess built behind.

Clack and Pattinson (1978) 82–3.

(49) Former WESLEYAN, Westgate (NY 908385). The chapel, built in 1791, is a substantial structure of stone with a hipped slated roof. The original front wall is of three bays with a wide round-arched central doorway and two tiers of windows. One window above the doorway has been blocked and a small tablet dated 1791 has been partly defaced. At the rear is a later wing for vestry and organ chamber; the main range has also been extended to provide ancillary accommodation. The chapel was closed in 1938 and has more recently been converted to four houses.

Clack and Pattinson (1978) 50–1.

(50) PRIMITIVE METHODIST, Westgate (NY 906380). Large broad-fronted chapel of five bays built 1871, by George Race junior and Atkinson, with smaller building alongside altered to match but reputedly the former chapel of 1824.

Clack and Pattinson (1978) 78–9.

STANLEY

(51) WESLEYAN, Burnopfield (NZ 176568). Gabled front with three graduated lancets and tablet inscribed in lettering of early 19th-century character 'WESLEYAN CHAPEL 1775'. Rebuilt 1880, some older masonry incorporated at side.

Bethesda Free Chapel, Tatham Street, Sunderland. (52)

SUNDERLAND *Tyne and Wear*

(52) BETHESDA FREE CHAPEL, Tatham Street (NZ 401568). The Independent chapel was built in 1844 for Rev. A. A. Rees, a former Anglican, nicknamed 'The Pope of Tatham Street'. The church is now Baptist. The front wall of brick is of five principal bays; the three middle bays are pedimented and have two tiers of windows with renewed frames and a central entrance. Across the head of the recessed centre bay is a large tablet bearing the chapel name in bold raised letters.

(53) BETHEL CHAPEL, Villiers Street (NZ 401571). The chapel was built in 1817 to the designs of a Mr Hogg for Independent seceders from the Presbyterian meeting in Robinson's Lane; the church moved to a new building in the later 19th century and the chapel subsequently passed into commercial use. The walls are of rubble, rendered at the front, and the roof is slate-covered. The wide front wall, of five bays with two tiers of windows, has a pediment over the three middle bays and an entrance in the slightly recessed centre bay with a segmental-arched window above. (Demolished 1979)

Bethel Chapel, Villiers Street, Sunderland. (53)

(54) FRIENDS, Upper Nile Street (NZ 401569). The meeting-house, erected in 1822, superseded a building of 1718 on the N side of High Street of which the burial-ground was still visible *c*.1905. The walls are of brick with rendered dressings and the roofs are covered with slates. The E front, of five bays with a three-bay pediment, has a central doorway with incised line ornament on jambs and lintel, the latter bearing the date of erection. Two segmental-arched windows flank the entrance, three similar windows above and blank panels over. The blank end bays are terminated by rusticated pilasters.

The interior has a lobby at the E end with gallery above, the remainder being divided into two meeting-houses of equal size by a tall wooden partition with movable shutters. There is a continuous two-stage stand along the W wall. Late 19th-century extensions include, S of the meeting-house, a circular committee room, octagonal externally, with a domed roof, and to the N a hall, beyond which is a caretaker's house of two storeys, built *c*.1822. The whole complex is surrounded by a tall brick boundary wall. (Demolished *c*.1976)

Friends' meeting-house, Sunderland.   (54)

Wesleyan chapel, Ashbrooke Road, Sunderland.   (55)

(55) WESLEYAN, Ashbrooke Road (NZ 396559). The Society meeting here originated in a chapel which stood at the corner of High Street West and Sans Street, Bishopwearmouth (NZ 401572), built in 1793. Following the transfer of the congregation, 'Sans Street Chapel' served as a city-centre mission, for which purpose it was altered and refronted in 1903; it was closed in 1963 and has since been demolished.

'St John's, Ashbrooke', of 1887–8 by Robert Curwen, is a large building of stone in a 14th-century Gothic style comprising a nave of five bays with a clerestory, aisles, two transepts each of two bays, and a tower at the N corner; the tower, of four stages, is surmounted by a tall stone spire with corner pinnacles. In each transept is a gallery recessed behind the arcades. *Pulpit*: with handrail in the form of a brazen serpent.

Milburn. G. E. (ed.), *St John's, Ashbrooke: A Church and its Story* (1988).

(56) WESLEYAN, Middle Herrington (NZ 359531). Rubble with lancet windows; 1839 rebuilt *c*.1855 with later additions.

(57) Former PRESBYTERIAN, Villiers Street (NZ 401570). 'St George's Chapel', as this was originally called, was built in 1825 for a congregation which originated in 1739 by secession from the Corn Market Chapel, and which formerly met in Robinson's Lane. In 1890 this congregation removed to a new chapel in Belvedere Road and the Villiers Street building, renamed St James's, passed to another body of Presbyterians which had previously occupied meeting-houses in Borough Road (Smyrna Chapel) and Spring Garden Lane.

Former Presbyterian chapel, Villiers Street, Sunderland.   (57)

The chapel has an ashlar front, squared rubble sides and a slate roof. The front wall is of five bays; the three middle bays, divided by pilasters carrying an entablature and pediment, have two tiers of windows, round-arched at the sides, and segmental-arched of two orders above the central entrance. The date MDCCCXXV appears in raised letters on the pediment. In front are contemporary iron railings, gates and scrolled overthrow.

Plate: (in URC History Society collection), pewter flagon from Robinson's Lane meeting-house dated 1766. (Also in this collection is a pewter cup, 1815, and flagon, 1797, from the former Maling's Rigg chapel in Sunderland.)

Middlemiss, J.T. and Hyslop, R., *A Short History of Presbyterianism in Sunderland* (1897). Milburn, G.E., *Church and Chapel in Sunderland 1780-1914* (1988). *PHSJ* III (1924-7) 242-4. Sunderland Antiquarian Society, *Antiquities of Sunderland* V (1904) 50-69; VI (1905) 9-36.

(58) PRESBYTERIAN, 'St George's', Stockton Road (NZ 396563). Built 1889-90, by John Bennie Wilson, to supersede the former St George's Chapel in Villiers Street. Large building of red sandstone with nave, transepts and square tower with impressively tall open upper stage and pyramidal roof. (URC)

Hawkins (1973) 206-7. Hyslop, R., *Two Hundred Years: 1739-1939, Being the Story of St George's Presbyterian Church, Sunderland* (c.1939).

TOW LAW

(59) WESLEYAN, Dan's Castle (NZ 118395). Opened 1846; stone panel over entrance inscribed 'Wesleyan Chapel'.

URPETH

(60) Former WESLEYAN, Beamish (NZ 218546). The chapel, formerly standing in the village but now rebuilt in the Beamish Open Air Museum, is of rubble with pointed-arched windows and a gabled porch at one side. It was built in 1854 and rebuilt to the present size in 1876. In 1904 a new chapel was erected adjacent to one end, replacing a two-storeyed cottage; this chapel was not re-erected in the museum, its place being taken by a modern vestry designed and fitted in the style of 1876.

WEST RAINTON

(61) Former WESLEYAN (NZ 322467). Stone with four lancets in each side wall. Built c.1860 but incorporating tablet inscribed 'EBENEZER 1822'. (Derelict 1973)

WHICKHAM   *Tyne and Wear*

(62) Former PRESBYTERIAN, Swalwell (NZ 204623). The Presbyterian church meeting at Swalwell (latterly URC, closed c.1986) originated in the late 17th century and gathered first at Ryton Woodside (4 miles W); in 1750 a meeting-house was built in Swalwell on land the property of the then minister. In 1805 a Countess of Huntingdon's minister was appointed, followed in

Former Presbyterian chapel, Swalwell.   (62)

1822 by a Congregationalist who gave the church an Independent polity; Presbyterianism was re-established after 1825. The meeting-house was considerably rearranged after 1862 and in 1898 it was superseded by a new chapel on the opposite side of the road. The former meeting-house, since used as a hall, was in 1974 awaiting demolition for road improvement.

The meeting-house of 1750 has rendered walls of brickwork on a stone plinth and a hipped slated roof formerly covered with pantiles. The SW front has two cross-framed windows flanking the original site of the pulpit, traces of two entrances, and other windows all with frames replaced in the 19th century; a stone tablet in this wall inscribed 'EBENEZER CHAPEL Built 1750' appears to be an insertion of the early 19th century. The SE and NW end walls each had two upper windows to light the galleries. In the NE wall is an original doorway, now blocked, and two windows, the upper probably inserted to replace one obscured by the erection of a manse, since demolished, against the NW wall. A vestry at the W corner is partly original. The interior (25½ft by 44ft) was drastically altered in the late 19th century when the pulpit was removed to the NW end and one gallery destroyed; no original features now remain apart from a moulded wooden ceiling cornice.

Plate: includes a pair of early 18th-century pewter plates inscribed 'Wood Side Meeting' and a later pair inscribed 'Swalwell Meeting'.

Forbes, J., *Presbyterian Church, Swalwell: A Story of its Birth and Pilgrimage, 1662-1933* (nd).

WITTON GILBERT

(63) WESLEYAN, Sacriston Lane (NZ 232457). Rendered gabled end with lancets. Opened 1832, perhaps later.

WOLSINGHAM

(64) BAPTIST, Market Place (NZ 076372). Built 1830-1, enlarged to front 1889. Rubble walls, gabled front of three bays with ashlar quoins. Original date tablet reset in side wall.

Clack and Pattinson (1978) 91-2. Douglas (1846) 259-60, 275-6.

(65) Former METHODIST, Whitfield Lane (NZ 075371). The former preaching-house built in 1776 stands in a lane off the S side of Front Street, adjacent to the garden of Whitfield House. It has rubble walls and the roof is covered with stone slates. The

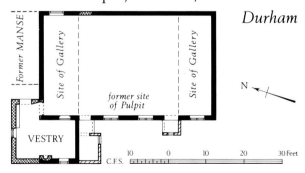

Ebenezer Chapel, Swalwell, WHICKHAM
Durham

Former MANSE

Site of Gallery

Site of Gallery

former site of Pulpit

VESTRY

N

10   0   10   20   30 Feet
C.F.S.

E side facing the lane is partly concealed by later buildings but has a blocked doorway near the S end. In the W wall are two tall windows with hung sashes and box shutters internally; S of them is a doorway with window over. Two windows in the N wall flank the site of the pulpit. The building was superseded by a new chapel on the opposite side of Front Street in 1836. It is now used as a carpenters' workshop.

Clack and Pattinson (1978) 34.

(66) WESLEYAN, Front Street (NZ 075372). The former chapel of 1836 stands adjacent to its successor of 1862. The former, now used for school purposes, is a plain building with pointed-arched windows and a sundial in the S gable. The later chapel, in the Gothic style, has a gabled S front divided into three bays by stepped buttresses rising to tall pinnacles.

Clack and Pattinson (1978) 34-7.

(67) Former PRIMITIVE METHODIST, 21-5 Silver Street (NZ 077374). Built 1825, converted to cottages after 1885.

Clack and Pattinson (1978) 70-2.

(68) Former PRIMITIVE METHODIST, Market Place (NZ 077372). 1885 by George Race, plain exterior with three tiers of windows and gabled centre bay. Closed 1978, now in commercial use.

Clack and Pattinson (1978) 70-3.

WOLVISTON   *Cleveland*

(69) WESLEYAN (NZ 454257). Brick walls, S front of three bays with round-arched windows, extended to E and front now partly covered by modern vestibule incorporating reset original tablet dated 1829.

WOODLAND

(70) WESLEYAN (NZ 066262). Built 1826, enlarged 1868 with addition of gabled single-storey rooms in front.

WHS, NEB LIV (1990) 16.

The County Palatine of Lancaster, extending historically from the Lancashire plain to the hills of lakeland, has a rich and varied background of religious dissent which remains evident in the numerous chapels and meeting-houses of early date and of different denominations. Many county families were noted for their recusancy in the 16th century while others adhered to the other extreme of Puritanism and eventual Presbyterianism. Some interaction between these two groups is to be seen in the earliest building to be noticed here, the Ancient Chapel of Toxteth (118) where, in 1618, the recusancy of local magnates combined with an aberrant ecclesiastical jurisdiction to permit the growth, nominally within the Established Church, of a puritan congregation. In spite of the eventual dismissal of the first minister, Richard Mather, this subsequently passed unhindered into the Presbyterian camp. From the vastness of some ecclesiastical parishes arose the need for a multitude of chapels-of-ease which were gradually provided during the 16th and 17th centuries at the expense of the inhabitants to whom also fell the choice and maintenance of 'godly preaching ministers'. The many chapels-of-ease in which nonconformist ministers continued to serve after the 1662 Act of Uniformity bear witness to the personal following which these Presbyterian ministers enjoyed.

Chowbent Chapel, Atherton (12) is a notable reminder of the tenacity with which dissenters held on to the older chapels – not until sixty years after the Restoration were they forced to provide a new meeting-house and then it was built in the style of a chapel-of-ease, as were many other local chapels of the period, with a bell-cote prominently placed on one gable. Walmsley Chapel (245) is another which originated in this manner as, for example, did the chapels at Ainsworth (188), Hindley (97), Platt (146) and Horwich (101). One of the earliest and most complete of these Presbyterian chapels is at Rivington (215), built in 1703 to accommodate a congregation displaced from the episcopal chapel. Other early chapels which still remain in recognizable form, though more radically altered, include Park Lane Chapel (4) of 1697, Gateacre Chapel (131) of 1700 and the small chapel in Park Street, Chorley (54), of 1725–7, all modernized by their Unitarian congregations in the 19th century. Lower Chapel, Darwen (70), of 1719, fared no better at the hands of its more orthodox inheritors while Tunley Chapel (281) of 1691 has been so changed that evidence for a former chancel comparable with Risley Chapel (66) of 1706–7, one of the most severe losses during

the course of this survey, is but speculation. The site of Thomas Jollie's chapel at Wymondhouses (178), built in 1688, is a reminder of the remote locations from which some of the more capable of the ejected ministers were still able to conduct a useful ministry, the fragmentary remains of the chapel at Hesketh Lane, Chipping (52), bearing further witness to the success of his work.

The only substantial urban meeting-house of early date to have survived until recent times was at Cross Street, Manchester (136), of 1694, but that was rebuilt after wartime damage. The much altered Cairo Street Chapel, Warrington (254), of 1745 serves rather to recall, through its later connection with the Warrington Academy, one of the influences by which so many nominally Presbyterian congregations came to accept a Unitarian ministry.

The exceptionally high number and quality of early Presbyterian chapels remaining in the southern part of the county is matched by a preponderance of Quaker meeting-houses in the northern regions which date from the early years of the movement. When, in 1652, George Fox found his way to Swarthmoor he laid the foundations of a society which flourished amongst the fells of lakeland and rapidly spread thence throughout the country. The earliest of these meeting-houses to remain is at Height (251), built in 1677, but the best surviving example, though not without alterations, is Colthouse (58) of 1688–9. Fox's own gift of a house to the Swarthmoor meeting (250) in the same year is of great denominational interest; other early meeting-houses in the region include Yealand Conyers (282) of 1692 and the much enlarged Lancaster meeting-house (108) of 1708. Further south the survival of the early meeting-house in St Helens (231) of c.1678, though internally gutted, is remarkable, while that at Crawshawbooth (207) of 1736 is unusually complete. Later examples of Quaker buildings which, though less numerous, are still worthy of note include Marsden (35) of 1763, Warrington (257) of 1829–30, and an essay in urban classicism at Mount Street, Manchester (141) of 1828–30.

The second half of the 18th century is marked by a greater diversity in denominational presence. Presbyterians and Independents continued to build, the former chapel at Elswick (80) of 1753 carrying with it a dimly remembered history linking it to a former episcopal chapel, while in Lancaster (107) the chapel newly built in High Street c.1776 marks the increasing divergence of belief within the ranks of the Old Dissent. Baptists, who had been particularly active in Rossendale, began to extend their influence and their meeting-house at Goodshaw Chapel (203), of 1760 and later, is, in the completeness of its fittings, a building of national importance. No early Methodist buildings now remain although former chapels in Warrington (258) of *c.*1778, Burnley (43) of 1788 and Salford (235) of 1790–1 were demolished during the period of this survey; the earliest now surviving is at Hoghton (100) of 1794, while that contrived in part of a barn at Southfield (155) in 1797 has a certain bucolic poignancy. A small group of chapels, mostly rebuilt, which remained attached to John Wesley's erstwhile associate Benjamin Ingham, is to be found in the vicinity of Colne, the earliest and largest being at Wheatley Lane (164) built in 1747–50. The Moravian church is represented principally by the late 18th-century settlement at Fairfield, Droylsden (77), which retains its character of orderliness and symmetry despite some rebuilding and the refitting of the chapel. The influence of the Countess of Huntingdon also appears briefly in Tyldesley Chapel (247) of 1789–90, a late example of the provision of what was effectively a chapel-of-ease in an otherwise void locality.

The 19th century, which witnessed a rapid growth in the population of the manufacturing regions of the county, saw a further proliferation both of chapels and denominations, with Congregationalists playing a prominent role especially in later years. In Liverpool, where orthodox members from the Ancient Chapel of Toxteth had set up a separate meeting, Great George Street Chapel (123) was built in 1840–1, an outstanding memorial in classical dress to a great preacher and an influential congregation. More often the now fashionable Gothic style was adopted, as by Edward Walters at Darwen (72) in 1847 and in a more archaeologically correct form at the now demolished Cavendish Street Chapel, Manchester (139) in 1848, as well as in an even grander manner for the socially aspiring at Broughton Park, Salford (234), in 1872–4 and Albion Chapel, Ashton-under-Lyme (7) in 1890–5.

Unitarians, at Upper Brook Street, Manchester (143) in 1839, set their seal on architectural orthodoxy by employing (Sir) Charles Barry and continued in even grander style with the full panoply of Gothic steeples and ornament at Hope Street, Liverpool, in 1849 (demolished 1963), Gorton (145) 1869–71, and Monton (78) 1873–5, culminating in the freer use of the style at Ullet Road, Liverpool (130), at the end of the century. Orthodox Presbyterians, strengthened by immigration from Scotland, now appear in numbers sufficient to support a building for the Church of Scotland in Rodney Street, Liverpool (129), in 1823–4; at Ramsbottom, St Andrew's (197) was built by a private benefactor in 1832–4 in the style of a Commissioners' church. Methodists also owed to mercantile patronage their grandest Gothic chapel at Summerseat (201)

of 1844–7 by James Simpson, unaccountably and regrettably demolished during the course of this survey; other chapels by Simpson are usually in a less expensive classical style, the best, also demolished, being Bold Street, Warrington (259) of 1850. Patronage on a smaller scale is also seen in the charming Wesleyan chapel at Scorton (158) of 1842, and many lesser Methodist chapels have points of interest such as the small Wesleyan chapel at Bilsborrow (21) which respects, if by chance, Wesley's preference for an octagonal plan.

Few of the other Methodist groups have left buildings of note: that at Baillie Street, Rochdale (224), of 1837, was of importance to the Wesleyan Methodist Association, while the Independent Methodists, of more local derivation, are seen at an early date in Oldham (163) and in the later, much repaired, chapel in Warrington (260). The last traces of the Methodist Unitarians in Rochdale (228) were obliterated by the demolition of their 1818 meeting-house but that at Padiham (176), of 1822, survives to confirm the limited resources available to them in their early years. The Strict Baptist followers of William Gadsby of Manchester were equally constrained in some of their work, notably at Hope Chapel, Rochdale (217), although in its present state the chapel attests more to the success of its second pastor; the chapel in Shaw Street, Liverpool (119), of 1847, with its simple pedimented front is also fully in accord with the architectural preferences of this branch of the denomination. Another society which found support in South Lancashire was that of the Church of the New Jerusalem, the 'Swedenborgians', whose former chapel of 1844 remains in Bolton (30) and several others were rebuilt later in the century. Derived from them were the 'Bible Christians' of Salford whose circular chapel in Every Street, Manchester (137), of 1823 was unique and a further tragic loss of recent years. The Catholic Apostolic Church lost one of its earliest and potentially finest buildings in the destruction by arson of the church in Liverpool (121), with its complete, if miniature, Gothic E end and contemporary stained glass. The continuation of architectural development and experiment into the opening years of the subsequent century is seen in the work of Edgar Wood at the First Church of Christ Scientist, in Victoria Park, Manchester (138), of 1903, and in the startlingly white but suitably seaside architecture of Fairhaven Congregational Chapel (133) of 1911–12.

Lancashire chapels and meeting-houses are as varied in their materials and their design as in their denominations. Old brickwork and stone slates appear in the flat lands of the south, red sandstone is found in the vicinity of Liverpool, millstone-grit in the Pennines and harder, less tractable, stones laid dry in the Furness fells. Tiles are little used in roofing but slates easily imported from North Wales are ubiquitous and soon supplanted any thatch which may have remained in use in the coastal regions of the Fylde. With such a rich choice of materials and an efficient system of distribution by canal and railway, chapel builders had every incentive to produce lasting monuments to their faith of a quality equal to any in the kingdom.

ACCRINGTON

(1) BAPTIST, Cannon Street (SD 759285). Gothic, with corner tower and spire; by George Baines, 1873–4, for a church which originated in the early 18th century.

B.Hbk (1886) 337. Whitley (1913) 102–3. Wylie, R. J. V., *The Baptist Churches of Accrington and District* (1923).

(2) NEW JERUSALEM, Abbey Street (SD 763284). A chapel built in 1807 was superseded by the present building in 1849. Gothic, with gabled front flanked by buttresses rising to open octagonal turrets. (Reported demolished *c*.1982)

Hindmarsh (1861) 185, 201.

AIGHTON, BAILEY AND CHAIGLEY

(3) WALKER FOLD CHAPEL, Chaigley (SD 671418). The chapel was built in 1792 primarily for use by a Charity school, but Congregational services were also held and a church was in existence by 1801. Scholastic use ceased *c*.1960 and services terminated *c*.1966; the building has since been converted to a house. It has rendered stone walls (24¼ft by 24¾ft externally) and a roof covered with stone slates. The original N front was of three bays with a central entrance between a pair of tall round-arched windows; the windows have now been altered, the heads rebuilt higher and a large porch added. The interior, formerly a single room without galleries, has been subdivided.

Inscription: on tablet in front wall, originally above entrance but now reset left of porch: 'Chaidgley Charity School – Established by mrs Ellin Haighton And Endowed by Miss Ann Haighton, the Only daughter of Mr Richd. Haighton, of London, the ground bought of Mr Richd. Haighton of Chaidgley, 1792'.

Miall (1868) 325. Nightingale II (1891) 217–23.

ASHTON-IN-MAKERFIELD   *Greater Manchester*

(4) PARK LANE CHAPEL (SD 569017). The chapel was built in 1697 for a Presbyterian congregation, latterly Unitarian, which may have originated some years before. The first minister, Thomas Blinston, appears to have come here from Frankland's Academy in 1695. The building was much altered during the 19th century, principally in 1826 and 1871–2. The walls are of brickwork with later rendering, and the roof is covered with stone slates. Very little of the original structure remains visible although the N, E and W walls are intrinsically of 1697 and the S wall was rebuilt on its original alignment in 1871–2. A model made in 1854 shows the exterior of the chapel in its former state with a bell-cote on the W gable and the S wall divided by two pilasters with a string-course below the eaves; there were four plain rectangular windows of two principal lights to the S with a doorway at the W end of the wall and a matching doorway, blocked in 1826, at the E end. The gabled E wall had a single window of two lights flanked by pilasters with an arch above. The N wall had two windows to the body of the chapel and a smaller one to the W below one end of a W gallery which was lit by two skylights in the roof. A cottage, probably of later date adjoining the chapel to the W, was subsequently enlarged for Sunday-school use and rebuilt in 1903–4 continuing the line of the chapel roof and with a new bell-cote at the W end. The outer walls are now divided by stepped buttresses and all the windows have been renewed.

The interior (42½ft by 18¼ft) was altered in 1826 when the roof was ceiled, a raised floor at the E end reduced to the common level and the pulpit, formerly centrally against the N wall, re-sited at the E end. In 1871–2 the roof was rebuilt, the original W gallery removed, the seating replaced and a new entrance made

Former Congregational chapel, Walker Fold. Before and after conversion to house.   (3)

centrally in the W wall.

Fittings – *Bell-cote*: on W gable, rebuilt 1903; bell in former bell-cote replaced 1801. *Book*: Bible with Apocrypha, bound with Book of Common Prayer, printed by Charles Bill and executrix of Thomas Newcomb, 1696. *Brasses*: on S wall (1) Rev. John Brownlow, nearly 60 years minister, 1788; on front of pulpit (2) 'This Chapel was Built in the Year 1697 Repaired in 1826 Renovated in 1871 George Fox, minister, Chapel Wardens William Barker Josiah Gaskell'; (3) 'In the Isle opposite the pulpit Lies Interred the Body of the Revd. Mr Sam'l Park...' 1775, tablet removed from the Presbyterian Chapel, Prescot, Lancs, 1896 (*see* (181)). *Collecting Shovel*: in vestry, one, with short wooden handle, 19th-century. *Font*: wood, given by William Taylor, 1873. *Fontlet*: pottery, Winchester Cathedral type, by Copeland, identical in detail with plaster model at Hawkshead, Lancs. (94), mid 19th-century. *Hat peg*: on front of pulpit, iron with heart-shaped terminal pierced with initials T. B. for Thomas Blinston, first minister, *c*.1700. *Inscriptions*: on doors of former pews, now dado, many initials, and date 1697; in vestibule, circular tablet dated 1867 from former school building N of chapel, superseded 1903. *Model*: in vestry, of chapel and annexe, cardboard, 1854. *Monuments*: in burial-ground (1) Thomas Pendlebury, 1724; (2) Henry Thomasson, 1724; (3) Elizabeth, widow of Henry Thomasson, 1726. *Paintings*: in vestibule, portrait in oils of the Rev. John Brownlow, minister 1727–88. *Pulpit*: reset in SE corner, polygonal with two tiers of fielded panels and moulded cornice, *c*.1697. *Seating*: doors and panelling from original pews reset as dado around walls.

Christian Freeman (June 1871) 88–90. Evans (1897) 198–9. Fox, G., *The History of Park Lane Chapel* (1897). Herford and Evans (1909) 112–13. Nightingale IV (1892) 44–52.

(5) CONGREGATIONAL, Gerard Street (SJ 578992), red-brick gabled front divided by buttresses, built 1867 for Richard Evans, colliery owner, by Alfred Waterhouse. Rebuilt 1977.

CYB (1868) 338. Nightingale IV (1892) 52–60.

ASHTON-UNDER-LYNE   *Greater Manchester*

(6) 'REFUGE CHAPEL', Albion Street (SJ 942992). Seceders from a recently formed congregation meeting in Providence Chapel, Dukinfield, Cheshire, reopened the former Methodist chapel in Harrop's Yard (*see* (8)) in 1815 for Congregational services. This was succeeded by 'Refuge Chapel', built in 1816–17, which was enlarged in 1827 by incorporating the original school-room and was in turn superseded by the first 'Albion Chapel' in 1835, which stood immediately in front of its predecessor. The earlier chapel, which alone remains, has brick walls and a slate roof. The gabled S front has two round-arched doorways with rusticated surrounds and a tablet inscribed 'REFUGE 1816' above a blocked central window.

Monuments: in burial-ground W of chapel, early 19th-century ledger stones.

Gordon (1896) 113–15. Nightingale V (1893) 296–306.

(7) 'ALBION CHAPEL', Stamford Street (SJ 943990). Built 1890–5 for the Congregational Church (now URC) formerly meeting in Albion Street (*see* (6)), much of the cost being met by Abel Buckley. Of stone in a late Gothic style by John Brooke, it

comprises a broad nave with narrow passage aisles, transepts, chancel, and a tall corner tower and spire at the front. The fittings, which are of exceptionally high quality, include glass by William Morris in the windows of the chancel and by Burne-Jones in the transepts.

CYB (1897) 168.

(8) METHODIST NEW CONNEXION, Stamford Street (SJ 940 989). Methodist preaching was introduced into Ashton in about 1741 and forty years later the first chapel was built in Harrop's Yard, an alley N of Cricket's Lane. This was a plain brick building with two tiers of round-arched windows and a central entrance in the broad front wall. In 1797 the Society transferred its allegiance to the New Connexion and in 1799 built the first chapel in Stamford Street. The present chapel on the same site was built in 1832; it has brick walls with two tiers of windows and a four-bay front with Doric porch and altered pediment.

The interior has a gallery around four sides supported by fluted iron columns and original box-pews throughout.

Fittings – Inscription: externally, in glass case, stone door lintel from Harrop's Yard Chapel, inscribed 'Can there any good [thing] come out of Nazareth? Come and see. John 1st 46th 1781'. *Monuments*: against W wall (1) Thomas Waterhouse, 51 years Methodist New Connexion minister, 1853, Mary his widow, 1866, and Joseph Saxton their grandson, 1851; (2) James Dean, tin-plate worker, 1819, *et al.*

Rose I (1967); II (1969).

(9) METHODIST NEW CONNEXION, Oldham Street, Waterloo (SD 932007). Built 1839 as a school-chapel, superseded 1968. Low-built brick front of five bays with pointed-arched windows.

Rose II (1969) 13–14, 58–9.

(10) WESLEYAN, Alt Hill Lane, Fairbottom (SD 940019). School-chapel built 1837: brick with broad three-bay front. Stepped seating right of entrance facing pulpit. *Inscriptions*: in chapel (1) 'Fairbottom Wesleyan Methodist Sabbath day school for children of all Denominations, erected 1837'; (2) texts from Exod. 20: 8, 12, dated 1837.

Rose II (1969) 32–3.

ASPULL   *Greater Manchester*

(11) WESLEYAN (SD 613080). Rendered brick with stone quoins, three-bay pedimented front with two tiers of round-arched windows, dated 1858. 'Wesleyan Schools 1859' behind.

ATHERTON   *Greater Manchester*

(12) CHOWBENT CHAPEL, Bolton Old Road (SD 679032). A chapel-of-ease to the parish church of Leigh was built at Chowbent in or about 1645, the nave at the expense of the local population and the chancel paid for by John Atherton, lord of the manor. At the Restoration the minister, James Woods, did not conform and, although the chapel was closed against him for a time, he regained possession and continued to hold services there until his death in 1695. The chapel remained in use by the Presbyterian congregation, with occasional services by the vicar of Leigh to maintain his claims, until 1721, when the dissenters were dispersed by Robert Atherton, lord of the manor, allegedly

Chowbent Chapel, ATHERTON

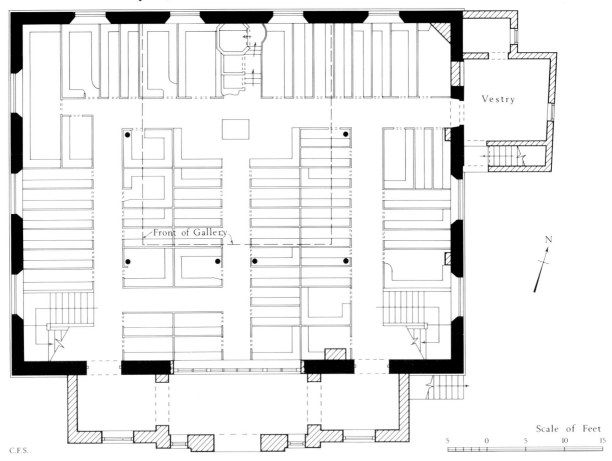

Vestry

N

Scale of Feet

C.F.S.

in retribution for the part played locally by the next minister, 'general' James Wood, and his supporters in suppressing the 1715 Jacobite rebellion. The chapel-of-ease was consecrated for Anglican use in 1723; it has since been rebuilt.

Chowbent Chapel was built in 1721–2 by the Presbyterian, latterly Unitarian, society on a site about 200 yards from the former chapel. The site was given by members of the Mort family whose seat at Wharton Hall had earlier served as an occasional meeting place for the congregation. The chapel has walls of brown brick with dressings of yellow sandstone; the roof is covered with slates. The N wall facing the road is of four bays with two tiers of round-arched windows separated by a platband and with rusticated quoins at the corners. The S front, now partly covered by a vestibule and organ chamber erected in 1901, previously had round-arched doorways in the end bays. The E and W walls are of three bays; in the former is a minor entrance with round-arched head and nail-studded door, now covered by a later vestry. The roof is gabled to E and W; on the W gable is a circular bell-cote with domed top supported by six slender columns.

The interior (42¾ft by 55¾ft) has galleries around three sides, reconstructed 1901, with bolection-moulded panelled fronts. The

galleries are supported by six timber columns with Doric capitals, four of which continue above to support the roof structure. Staircases in the SE and SW corners have turned balusters and moulded handrails. The pulpit is set centrally against the N wall. The plaster ceiling was renewed or embellished in 1901 (remade 1980). The roof is supported by three trusses with oak king-posts but many other members in softwood; the king-posts of the end trusses have assembly numbers in arabic numerals but Roman numerals elsewhere may indicate a reconstruction or some reuse of older material.

Sunday-school: E of chapel, 'Unitarian Sunday School Erected A.D. 1860 In Commemoration of the Centenary of the death of the Rev'd. James Wood who died Feb'y. 20th 1759'.

Fittings – *Bell*: one, in bell-cote on W gable. *Clock*: on front of S gallery, with brass dial, signed 'John Seddon, Frodsham', 18th-century. *Gates* and *Gate Piers*: at entrance from Bolton Old Road, rusticated stone piers surmounted by urns, early 18th-century; gates, pair, cast-iron by Picksley and Simms of Bedford, 1854. *Monuments*: in chapel (1) Thomas Bromiley William Sanderson, 1854, and Catherine his wife, 1839; (2) Thomas Sale, 1869, 'for sixty two years Clerk of this chapel in which his grandfather Thomas Sale had held the same office for fifty years'; (3) Rev.

Chowbent Chapel, Atherton.   (12)

Benjamin Rigby Davis, pastor, 1835; (4) Rev. James Wood, minister, 1759, large tablet above pulpit; (5) John Mort, 1788. In vestibule (6) John Taylor D.D., 1761, and Elizabeth his widow, 1761, signed 'William Bradshaw, Manchester'; (7) Adam Mort, and Martha his wife, both 1730, erected by John Mort, brass reset from burial-ground. In burial-ground, many 18th-century ledger stones. *Plate*: includes two cups of 1652 and 1653 with the initials of Robert Mort. *Pulpit*: three tiers, each desk with angled corners, fielded-panelled sides and moulded cornice; wide back-board divided by fluted pilasters. *Seating*: box-pews throughout, with fielded-panelled doors.

Baker, F., *The Life and Times of the Rev. James Woods...* (1859). Evans (1897) 7–8. Herford and Evans (1909) 77–83. Nightingale IV (1892) 95–108. Sharpe (1901) 54. Wright, J.J., *The Story of Chowbent Chapel* (1921).

AUDENSHAW   Greater Manchester

(13) METHODIST NEW CONNEXION, Audenshaw Road (SJ 917972). Built 1876 replacing 'Red Hall Chapel' of 1783 which stood opposite.

Rose I (1967) 23–4.

BACUP

(14) BAPTIST, Brandwood Road, Waterbarn (SD 846216). Pedimented ashlar front between terminal pilasters, two entrances, Venetian window centrally above. Dated 1847.

Whitley (1913) 197.

BARNACRE-WITH-BONDS

(15) FRIENDS, Calder Bridge, Bowgreave (SD 499438). Meeting-house of coursed water-shot masonry with slate roof built *c*.1828 largely at the expense of Richard Jackson, a cotton manufacturer, on a site behind his house. Plain windows in S front and rounded porch with double doorway inside to two rooms. Large meeting-room to W with original seating, smaller room to E with gallery over. Stable and shed detached to east.

Fittings – *Chandelier*: turned wood with iron core and sconces, early 19th-century. *Monuments*: in burial-ground, uniform headstones, early 19th-century and later.

Hewitson (1872) 518–20.

BARROW-IN-FURNESS   Cumbria

(16) CONGREGATIONAL, Abbey Road (SD 202700). 'Emmanuel', white rock-faced stone with red sandstone dressings; 1899. (URC, merger with Methodists proposed 1990).

(17) WESLEYAN, Abbey Road (SD 204702). Yellow sandstone with red sandstone dressings, corner tower and spire; opened 1899.

(18) Former PRESBYTERIAN, School Street (SD 202692). White stone with red sandstone dressings; gabled SW front with corner tower. 1874–5 by Paley and Austin. 'Presbyterian Lecture Hall, 1868' detached to left. (Derelict 1990)

BICKERSTAFFE

(19) FRIENDS' BURIAL-GROUND, Graveyard Lane (SD 421046), possibly associated with a former meeting-house at Stanley Gate (SD 4405), was in use from 1663. Square enclosure bounded in front by a low wall with gates, erected 1880; no monuments. *Inscription*: in front wall, with date 1665, late 19th-century. *Mounting Block*: inside gates, incorporating stone inscribed I C 1722.

BILLINGE-AND-WINSTANLEY   Greater Manchester

(20) WESLEYAN, Bispham (SD 527028). 'Erected 1845 by Wm. Holt, Bispham Hall'.

BILSBORROW

(21) WESLEYAN, Bilsborrow Lane (SD 517398). Low-built rendered walls and pyramidal slate roof, octagonal plan (14ft sides externally); plain windows with altered frames. Late 18th-century, said to have been built for pottery manufacture, purchased by Wesleyans 1810.

Wesleyan chapel, Bilsborrow.   (21)

BLACKBURN

(22) WESLEYAN, Heys (SD 669251). 'New Row' chapel, of rubble with ashlar dressings and modern rendering, was built in 1828. Broad three-bay front with two tiers of windows, crude swan-necked pediments to the lower openings, and central round-arched doorway. Shaped tablet in moulded surround above entrance inscribed 'G/W.T/1828/Wesleyan/Methodist/School Chapel'.

BOLTON   Greater Manchester

(23) BANK STREET CHAPEL (SD 718094). A Presbyterian society, now Unitarian, led by Richard Goodwin, ejected vicar of Bolton, met from 1672 in a house in Deansgate. The first meeting-house on the present site was built in 1696 on land behind the house of the then minister, Robert Seddon. The meeting-house was a rectangular building (about 30ft by 52ft) with the pulpit against the longer W wall and the E front concealed behind the house. The house was rebuilt *c*.1723 and in 1760 a wing was added to the front of the meeting-house covering the formerly intervening courtyard.

The present chapel of 1856 by George Woodhouse stands on the site of the earlier buildings. It has a gabled front with buttresses and lancet windows in a 13th-century style.

Baker, F., *The Rise and Progress of Nonconformity in Bolton*

(1854). Evans (1897) 24–5. Herford and Evans (1909) 57–9. Nightingale III (1892) 1–15. Street, C. J. et al., *Bank Street Chapel, Bolton* (1896).

(24) BAPTIST, St George's Road (SD 714095). 'Claremont' chapel, of brick and stone with a pedimented Italianate front, was built in 1868–9.

Whitley (1913) *passim*.

(25) CONGREGATIONAL, Blackburn Road, Astley Bridge (SD 716106). An 'iron chapel', opened 1877, was replaced by the present large and imposing perpendicular Gothic chapel by Jonathan Simpson in 1895–7. It was erected at the expense of W. H. Lever (Lord Leverhulme) and J. D. Lever and comprises a polygonal chancel, transepts, aisled nave and tall corner tower with spire supported by pinnacled flying buttresses. Fittings included an organ by Willis and stained glass by Henry Holiday in the chancel. (Derelict 1991)

CYB (1900) 144. Nightingale III (1892) 42–3.

(26) WESLEYAN, Knowsley Street (SD 715095). The 'Victoria Hall', on the W side of the street mostly concealed behind adjacent buildings but with a prominent tower at the entrance, is a large and elaborately designed mission hall, by Bradshaw and Gass. The principal room has a horseshoe-shaped gallery with much plaster enrichment on the front and supporting columns, and a vaulted plaster ceiling. The hall was built in 1898–1900 to serve the Wesleyan Mission which from 1892 had occupied the former Methodist chapel that stood to the S in Ridgway Gates.

Ridgway Gates Chapel, built in 1776, of brick with a broad front of five bays with two tiers of round-arched windows and a Venetian window between two doorways, was demolished in 1932 but a minister's house added at the N end of the chapel in 1791 still remains. John Wesley described the former chapel (*Journal* 22 July 1778) as 'the most beautiful in the country'.

Monuments: in courtyard S of Victoria Hall, ledger stones reset from front of chapel include (1) James, son of John and Frances Lomax, 1794, *et al.*; (2) Elizabeth Walker, 1799, *et al.*

Little, C. D., *The History and Romance of Our Mother Sunday School* (1935).

(27) Former WESLEYAN, Bridge Street (SD 718096). The chapel was built in 1803–4 by Peter Rothwell for the society formerly meeting in Ridgway Gates Chapel which was subsequently used for Sunday-school purposes. The walls are of brickwork. The pedimented S front is of five bays and has two tiers of round-arched windows; the entrances in the three centre bays have flanking columns with entablatures and a pediment to the central doorway. The side walls are each of five bays. Projecting at the N end is a singers' gallery with a wide Venetian window, now blocked, in the N wall. The interior (63ft by 50¾ft) was largely refitted in 1884.

Fittings – Monuments: in chapel (1) John Musgrave, 1864, with bust in low relief, signed 'Patteson, Manchester'; (2) Rev. George Marsland, 1849, signed 'Knowles, Manchester'; (3) William Cannon, 1867, signed 'Patteson, Manchester'; (4) Thomas Taylor, 1845, and Alle *(sic)* his wife, 1842, signed 'C. M. Seddon, Liverpool'. In extensive burial-ground numerous ledger stones including (5) children of George and Elizabeth Barns – Ann, 1795, Joseph, 1798, Thomas, 1809, Joseph, 1813, Mary,

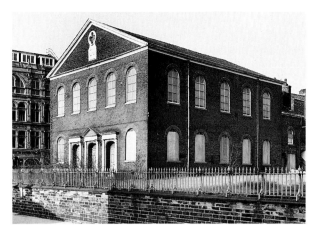

Wesleyan chapel, Bridge Street, Bolton.   (27)

1814, Peter, 1814, and James, 1814; (6) Rev. George Marsland, 1849, *et al.* *Plate*: includes cup and flagon dated 1803. *Seating Plans*: signed 'T. Ormrod, Architect, Bolton, March 1885'.

Little, C. D., *A Century of Service, 1850–1950* (1950).

(28) WESLEYAN, Darcy Lever (SD 735081). Low stone walls with lancet windows; front with stepped gable and two octagonal buttresses with battlemented turrets. Dated 1846, enlarged and internally realigned *c.*1870–80. (Derelict 1971)

(29) WESLEYAN, Delph Hill (SD 688106). Stone with lancet windows, built 1848, enlarged at both ends 1877, 1931.

(30) Former NEW JERUSALEM CHAPEL, Higher Bridge Street (SD 717097). A 'Swedenborgian' society formed in the late 18th

Former New Jerusalem Chapel,
Higher Bridge Street, Bolton.   (30)

century established a Sunday-school in 1797 and conducted services in a building in Bury Street where Samuel Crompton officiated as choirmaster; his chamber-organ is now in Hall i' th' Wood museum. The present chapel, built in 1844 and now used by Elim Pentecostal Church, is of brick with a pedimented front of three bays and tall round-arched windows.

Hindmarsh (1861) 200–1.

(31) Former PRESBYTERIAN, Bowkers Row (SD 718092). Built 1845–6; stone with lancet windows and prominent turret on a gable above the entrance.

BRIERCLIFFE

(32) BAPTIST, Haggate (SD 872354). Meetings which began about 1760 at Burwain's Farm soon attracted the support of William Smith, whose connections with the woollen industry in Scotland led the new church to adopt practices akin to those of the Scotch Baptists. This allegiance, with its plurality of preaching Elders, continued into the 20th century, the first stated minister being appointed in 1953.

The first meeting-house, built in 1767, stood 100 yards ESE of the present chapel. It was an almost square building with a S front of three bays, deep galleries around three sides and a tall round-arched window behind the pulpit. It was demolished after 1883.

The present chapel built 1865–6 is a large building with a pedimented front of four bays and two tiers of round-arched windows. In the burial-ground in front of the chapel are numerous tall monuments of the late 19th century.

Monuments: in burial-ground, close to site of first meeting-house (1) Abraham Nowell, minister, 1828, and Martha his widow, 1830; (2) John Robinson, 1829 *et al.*; (3) Robert Taylor, 1828, *et al.*; (4) Stephen Smith, 1802, and Mary his widow, 1848; (5) John Heap, 1813, and his sons John, 1812, and James, 1821; (6) John Smith, 1821, *et al.*; (7) William Smith, 1779, Betty his wife, 1771, their sons James, 1775, and John, 1813, and Grace, widow of the last, 1829.

Leaver, A., *Historical Fragments of Haggate Baptist Church 1767–1934* (1934). Shutt, W., *The Baptist Chapel, Haggate; Bicentenary Celebrations, 1760–1960*. Whitley (1913) 165–7, 335.

Baptist chapel, Haggate.   (32)

(33) BAPTIST, Lane Bottom (SD 877356). Ebenezer Chapel was first built in 1840 by seceders from the foregoing. A new chapel was built alongside in 1871–2, enlarged 1909, and the former chapel largely rebuilt 1886–7.

Shutt, *op. cit.* 12–13. Whitley (1913) 166, 329.

(34) FRIENDS' BURIAL-GROUND, Foulds House (SD 889360). Quaker meetings were held at Foulds House in the late 17th century with the support of John Ecroyd. Six burials are recorded in 'the orchard'. *Monument*: Elisabeth, wife of John Vipon, 1681, ledger stone.

RCHM, *Rural Houses of the Lancashire Pennines 1560–1760* (1985) 135.

BRIERFIELD

(35) FRIENDS, Walverden Road, Marsden (SD 857364). The meeting-house, built in 1763, replaces one of 1697 at Marsden Height (now a cottage). The walls are of water-shot masonry and the roof is slated. The W front has two tiers of mullioned windows of two lights, the lower range also being divided by transoms. The doorway, S of centre, has a triple keystone and flanking pilasters; to its left are three closely-spaced bays of windows and two more widely spaced bays to the right. The building was extended to the N in the late 19th century. The S wall is gabled and has four blocked windows and an original date tablet. The windows in the E wall have been altered or inserted.

FRIENDS' MEETING-HOUSE, MARSDEN   CFS 1979

The interior (56½ft by 32½ft) is divided into two rooms by a screen with vertically sliding fielded-panelled shutters. The larger N room has at the N end a 19th-century gallery supported by two cast-iron columns, and incorporating reused flat balusters in part of the front and staircase; this may be on the site of the original stand. The S room, refitted in the late 19th century, has a stand against the E wall formerly connected by a doorway in the screen to a matching but possibly later stand in the N room. An upper room at the S end, now closed and without regular access, originally served as a gallery. The roof is supported by four king-post trusses.

Monuments: in burial-ground, uniform headstones of 1839 and later.

(36) WESLEYAN, Colne Road (SD 847366). Four-bay pedimented front with paired entrances, segmental-arched upper windows and oval tablet dated 1861.

Moore (1899) 208–12.

(37) Former PRIMITIVE METHODIST, Burnley Road (SD 847364). Four-bay pedimented front with round-arched upper windows. Defaced tablet formerly dated 1864.

BROUGHTON WEST

(38) Site of BAPTIST, Scroggs (SD 2289). A Baptist meeting-house registered 1703, closed c.1823, survived in part as a farm building until c.1930. No traces found.

C & WT, NS XXXII (1932) 63–7. OS 25 in. map Lancs. VI.8 (1913) 'Sheepfold'.

(39) WESLEYAN, Broughton-in-Furness (SD 212875), with double bell-cote; dated 1875.

BURNLEY

(40) GENERAL BAPTIST, Colne Road (SD 843335). The church originated in 1776 when preachers from Birchcliffe, Hebden Bridge, began to hold services at Worsthorne. In 1779 a house in the market place in Burnley was registered for use and the first 'Ebenezer Chapel' built in 1787–8. This was enlarged in 1843 and converted for Sunday-school use when a new chapel was built alongside in 1860. A new Sunday-school was erected to the S of the chapel in 1872.

The former chapel ($30\frac{3}{4}$ft by $36\frac{1}{4}$ft), of stone with a hipped slate roof, has a broad W front with two doorways now converted to windows and other entrances inserted, and two tall

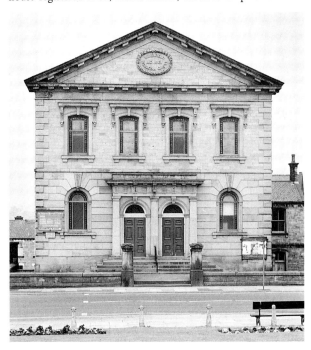

Wesleyan chapel, Colne Road, Brierfield. (36)

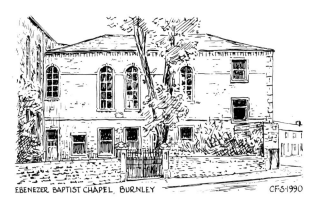

EBENEZER BAPTIST CHAPEL, BURNLEY   CF·S·1990

Former Primitive Methodist chapel, Burnley Road, Brierfield. (37)

round-arched pulpit windows. The walling appears to have been heightened in 1843; a house adjoins at the N end and the later chapel at the south. The latter has a pedimented W front of four bays.

Taylor (1818) II: 193–4, 278–80, 392–3. Whitley (1913) 158, 265, 272, 329. Wood (1847) 184.

(41) ÆNON CHAPEL, Red Lion Street (SD 842324), was built in 1851 for a Particular Baptist church. It was closed c.1989 and has since been converted to office use. Stone with Italianate front in three bays with rusticated lower stage, round-arched doorways with coved surrounds in side bays and with tripartite pedimented window centrally at gallery level. The rear wall, largely rebuilt, has a simple Venetian window above the site of the pulpit. The interior, now totally altered, formerly had a gallery, rounded towards the front, supported by Ionic columns. The roof is carried on four queen-post trusses.

Former Methodist chapel, Keighley Green, Burnley.
(*Photo: W. J. Smith/R. C. Cross Record of Pennine Buildings.*) (43)

'Ænon Chapel', Burnley.   (41)

(42) JIREH CHAPEL, Bootway (SD 842325). Small three-bay pedimented front in rusticated masonry, dated 1853. Built for a Particular Baptist church which originated in Crook Street.

(43) Former METHODIST, Keighley Green (SD 842328). Increased support following John Wesley's first visit to Burnley in 1784 led the society to acquire the site for a chapel which was completed in 1788. The chapel then had 271 sittings in 44 pews, most if not all in the gallery, with free seats or benches below. In the early 19th century the chapel was extended to the rear; pews were introduced to the ground floor between 1824 and 1828. A new chapel was built in Hargreaves Street in 1839–40, although the former building remained in use until 1842 when it was sold; it was subsequently converted to secular use.

The former chapel has stone walls and stone slates to the principal roof. The S front of five bays with rusticated quoins and two tiers of plain windows with altered frames had doorways in the end bays, one now removed, with pedimented stone heads. A house of three storeys at the E end was rebuilt in 1907 as 'Burnley Lads Club' incorporating one of the doorway surrounds from the chapel. The rear extension, which is separately roofed, has in the N wall a pair of round-arched pulpit windows, with cills

lowered, and plain windows at the ends of the former galleries.

The interior (40ft enlarged to 57½ft by 48¾ft) has been entirely altered but an 18th-century moulded plaster cornice remains in the S half of the building. (Demolished 1976)

Sundial: stone dial between upper windows of S front. (Removed before 1976)

Dolbey (1964) 91–2. Moore (1899) 53ff., 104ff.

(44) Former WESLEYAN, Todmorden Road, Fulledge (SD 848 324). Pedimented stone front with two Corinthian columns *in antis* between end bays. 1859–61 by James Robinson. Interior gutted after fire c.1980. (Roofless shell 1990)

Moore (1899) 144–8.

Former Wesleyan chapel, Fulledge.   (44)

(45) Former WESLEYAN METHODIST ASSOCIATION, Hammerton Street (SD 840323). Built c.1833 and sold to Baptists 1868 who still use it. Extended at front and side windows altered c.1868.

Whitley (1913) 213, 330.

BURY   *Greater Manchester*

(46) CONGREGATIONAL, Rochdale Road (SD 808109). Red brick with stone dressings, two four-light traceried windows above porch. 1885, by Maxwell and Tuke, on site of 1792 New Road chapel.

CYB (1866) 332; (1867) 355. Nightingale III (1892) 185–94.

Congregational chapel, Rochdale Road, Bury.   (46)

(47) WESLEYAN, Union Street (SD 805108). Brick with two tiers of round-arched windows; five-bay pedimented front with altered tympanum and late 19th-century porch across lower stage. Opened 1812, extended to rear and much altered in late

19th century and in recent years. Numerous ledger stones, early 19th-century and later, removed from burial-ground in 1974.

(48) WESLEYAN, Unsworth (SD 819078). Brick and stone, three-bay Ionic portico with flanking wings, four-bay sides with pedimented windows; built 1846. (Demolished since 1971)

(49) Former PRIMITIVE METHODIST, Walmersley Road (SD 809116). Three-bay pedimented front with pilasters and entablature blocks; dated 1865.

(50) Former NEW JERUSALEM CHAPEL, Walmersley Road (SD 809116). Close S of the last, gabled front with lancets, built *c.*1860 for 'Swedenborgian' society but transferred to Primitive Methodists *c.*1904.

CATON-WITH-LITTLEDALE

(51) WESLEYAN, Caton (SD 532646), round-arched windows with keystones, dated 1836.

CHIPPING

(52) Former INDEPENDENT, Hesketh Lane (SD 618413). The church formerly meeting here was one of several congregations in the district gathered by the Rev. Thomas Jollie. In 1689 the house of Christopher Parkinson at Hesketh Lane was registered for meetings. A new chapel was built in 1705 and continued in use until the late 19th century when part was demolished and the remainder converted to a cottage and an upper storey added.

Nightingale (II (1891)) illustrates the chapel before conversion when it was a long building with low walls having three plain windows at the front and two arched doorways between; the W end, which had a chimney stack on the gable, had become derelict, having earlier been separated from the chapel for use as a cottage or minister's house. The building has rubble walls and a slate roof. The S front, now about two-thirds of its original length, has a central doorway with a chamfered segmental-arched lintel dated MDCCV. A lintel of similar shape from the second doorway has been reset in the walling above the entrance; it is inscribed with the date 1705 and the text 'FOR HE LOVETH OVR NATION/AND HE HATH BVILT VS A SYNAGOGUE'. The two lower windows, formerly of two lights, have

Former chapel, Hesketh Lane, Chipping. Before and after conversion to house.   (52)

straight-chamfered jambs. In the E wall is a mullioned window of three lights. The N wall has near the centre of its original extent a window of two lights set close below the former eaves line, probably to light a central pulpit; near the E end of this wall at a lower level is a small window of two lights with hollow chamfered jambs.

The interior (now 19ft by 29ft) has no original features, but a stone fireplace with shaped stone jambs of the early 19th century may have been reset from the former W wall.

Miall (1868) 324–5. Nightingale II (1891) 210–17.

(53) CONGREGATIONAL, Chipping (SD 621432). 'Providence Chapel, erected by subscription, MDCCCXXXVIII', coursed stone with two plain doorways below round-arched windows. Chapel closed c.1882 but subsequently repaired and reopened.

Nightingale II (1891) 217–23.

PROVIDENCE CHAPEL, CHIPPING

CHORLEY

(54) PARK STREET CHAPEL (SD 583180). Although the minister of the parochial chapel, Henry Welch, was ejected for nonconformity in 1662, there is little evidence of any regular congregation in Chorley before 1719. In that year Chorley Hall, which, following the 1715 rebellion had been forfeited to the crown and purchased by Abraham Crompton of Derby, was registered as a 'Dissenters Meeting Place'. In his will dated 1724 Crompton left £150 in trust to build a chapel 'for a congregation of Protestant Dissenters, called Presbyterians' and an endowment for the maintenance of the ministry. The new chapel 'in a field called the Drenacres between Chorley Town and Chorley Hall' was registered in 1727. The congregation is now regarded as Unitarian.

The chapel stands on an obscure site on the S side of Park Street. It is a small building of stone with a broad ashlar front and roof covered with stone slates. The S front has two doorways with lintels and chamfered jambs and a pair of mullioned and transomed windows. The N wall has similar fenestration. The E wall is gabled and has a mullioned window but with an arched head and Y-tracery probably added in the 19th century.

The interior (27½ft by 42¼ft) was entirely refitted and re-oriented c.1902 when a red-brick organ-chancel was built at the W end. Prior to that date the pulpit was against the N wall with an organ and 'a little gallery for the singers' facing it between the doorways.

Fittings – *Monuments*: in burial-ground, dating from early 19th

Park Street Chapel, Chorley. (54)

Park Street Chapel
CHORLEY
Lancashire

N

Scale of Feet

5   0   5   10   15   20   25

original site of pulpit

C.F.S.

century. *Organ*: reputed to come from Liverpool pro-cathedral (St Peter's, Church Street), given 1902 by Sir William H. Tate, Bart., mid 19th-century. *Plate*: includes two two-handled cups of 1702 and 1747.

Evans (1897) 49–50. Herford and Evans (1909) 76. Nightingale II (1891) 1–10. *UHST* V (1931–4) 328–9.

(55) CONGREGATIONAL, Hollinshead Street (SD 585179). The chapel, built in 1792 for a congregation (now URC) formed about 1783, has been greatly altered and refitted. The walls (47½ft by 40¼ft externally) are of brickwork, heightened in 1877 and extended to the S in 1890. The N front of three bays with two tiers of round-arched windows has been rebuilt in recent years but omitting the keystones of the earlier design.

S of the chapel, in Byron Street, is the former 'Independent Sabbath School' dated 1836.

Nightingale II (1891) 10–19.

(56) Former CONGREGATIONAL, St George's Street (SD 584175). Built 1836 for seceders from the foregoing; occupied since *c*.1955 by a Baptist church. Stone walls with tall lancet windows. The interior has a gallery around three sides added *c*.1865; it was reseated *c*.1868–77. There is a school-room below the chapel.

Monument: E of chapel, to Lee Lee, 1837, 'one of the founders and senior deacon of the adjacent church'.

Nightingale II (1891) 20–5.

(57) WESLEYAN, Park Road (SD 584181). The chapel, built in 1842 to replace a smaller building in Chapel Street, has an ashlar front of five bays with a three-bay pediment and two tiers of round-arched windows. (Demolished 1977 and new chapel built on site)

CLAIFE   *Cumbria*

(58) FRIENDS, Colthouse (SD 359982). In 1658 a piece of ground was acquired for use as a burial-ground and as a meeting place.

Wesleyan chapel, Park Road, Chorley.   (57)

The present meeting-house stands within a walled enclosure of which the front boundary wall was heightened in 1769. It was built on a new site in 1688–9 in a traditional lakeland vernacular style with rendered rubble walls and a slate roof.

The E front has a gabled porch with segmental-arched outer doorway, altered or rebuilt in the early 18th century to incorporate a staircase; two tall windows to the principal room S of the porch were altered in 1790. In the S wall are two windows each with a mullion and transom and having a continuous moulded label above. One window at the N end of the W wall lights the smaller women's meeting-house, and is of three lights, also with a transom.

The interior (38¾ft by 24½ft) is divided by a screen with hinged shutters to the N and vertically sliding fielded-panelled shutters to the S of the early 18th century; at that period a floor was inserted above the N room cutting across the W window to

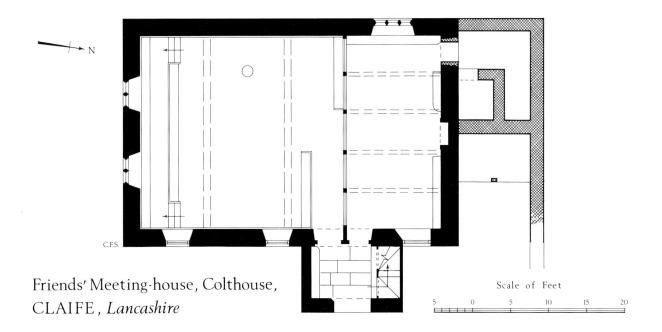

N

C.F.S.

Friends' Meeting-house, Colthouse,
CLAIFE, *Lancashire*

Scale of Feet

5   0   5   10   15   20

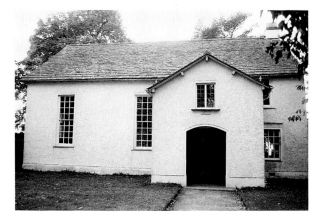

Friends' meeting-house, Colthouse.   (58)

provide a gallery which has an open balustraded front to the south.

Fittings – *Key*: to E door, 7¼ in. long, 18th-century. *Seating*: benches, many with backs and shaped ends added, 17th-century and later. *Stand*: in S room, pine panelled front, 19th-century. *Sundial*: the brass dial from a baluster sundial erected in forecourt 1824 is reported to be in the meeting-house.

Burial-ground: 200 yards S, a rectangular enclosure, much enlarged to S, is bounded at the N end by rubble walls incorporating stone seats.

Butler (1978) 126–31.

CLITHEROE

(59) Former CONGREGATIONAL, Shaw Bridge Street (SD 746418). Rubble with rendered front and slate roof; built 1815, galleries added 1818, superseded 1863 and subsequently occupied by Primitive Methodists and Salvation Army, now used for storage. Front with two tiers of round-arched windows with plain stone architraves, keystones and impost blocks; two doorways and four windows with five windows above. Rear wall formerly had two arched pulpit windows and five rectangular windows, all blocked.

Nightingale II (1891) 199–207.

(60) CONGREGATIONAL, Castle Gate (SD 743418). Gothic, by R. Moffat Smith, built 1862–3 to replace the foregoing. (URC)

CYB (1863) 307–8.

(61) WESLEYAN (SD 741417). Large pedimented front with rock-faced masonry, dated 1868.

Former chapel behind, surrounded on three sides by single-storey buildings, has rendered stone walls and a slate roof. The NW front is gabled and has two doorways, now internal, two segmental-arched windows above and a tablet between, now much decayed, inscribed 'The Ground on which this Chapel is erected was the voluntary gift of John Parker Esq. of Clitheroe in the year 1797. READER Remember the words of our Lord Jesus how he said [It is more blessed] to give than [to receive]. Acts [20:35].' The side walls have each four upper windows. Windows in the SE wall were altered in the late 19th century. The interior (50¾ft by 35½ft) has been converted for social use. Free-standing to NE, former 'Wesleyan School 1851'.

COLNE

(62) INDEPENDENT METHODIST (SD 878395). Late 19th-century; former chapel opposite, now builder's office, inscribed 'A.D. 1837 Bethel Chapel'.

(63) Former METHODIST, Colne Lane (SD 890399). The first chapel, built in 1777 for a society formed in 1758, was damaged by a severe storm during its erection, the W wall having to be rebuilt and a house built against it to strengthen the structure. It was opened by John Wesley before the fittings had been fully installed on which occasion further damage was caused by the collapse of one of the galleries. A new chapel was built in Albert Road in 1824 and the former building was then used by the Sunday-school until 1869; it was demolished *c*.1967.

The chapel had stone walls and a hipped roof covered with stone slates. The broad S front of six bays had a high ashlar plinth with rusticated masonry above, pilaster strips at the corners and a moulded cornice; the doorways in the end bays had open pediments and fanlights. The interior (approximately 30ft by 50ft) is thought to have had a gallery around three sides with the pulpit against one of the longer walls.

Dolbey (1964) 87–8. Moore (1899) 28–44, 168–72.

COLTON   *Cumbria*

(64) BAPTIST, Tottlebank (SD 314845). A mixed church of Independents and Baptists was formed in 1669 at the house of William Rawlinson of Tottlebank with Gabriel Camelford, the ejected curate of Staveley (George Fox's 'priest Camelford'), as Teaching Elder; the church was described as 'the Church of Christ in Broughton, Furness Fells and Cartmel'. Baptist tenets appear to have been adopted early in the 18th century, possibly during the pastorate of Thomas Richardson who came as an Independent in 1714 but was instrumental in the formation of an Association of Baptist Churches in 1719.

The chapel, which has low rendered rubble walls and a slate roof, was probably built in the early 18th century but has been greatly altered. In 1864 it was entirely refitted and about that date a wing was added at the back; a school-room was built at the SW end *c*.1894–5. The front wall may have had entrances in the end bays with three windows between but no structural evidence of this is now visible. The interior (20ft by 47½ft) has been reduced in length by the insertion of a vestry at the NE end.

Fittings – *Chairs*: two, ladder-back, late 17th-century. *Collecting Shovels*: two shallow square boxes with single handle.

Baptist Chapel at Tottlebank, COLTON
Lancashire

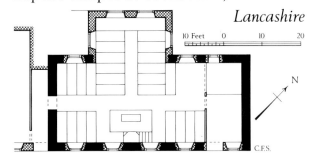

Communion Table: small, with stop-chamfered legs, early 18th-century. *Monuments*: in burial-ground NE of chapel (1) John Park, 1763, *et al.* with later brass to David Park, 1815; (2) John Atkinson, 1762; (3) George Drinkall, 1787, *et al.*; (4) Rev. John Sedgfield, 41 years pastor, 1765, and Elizabeth his wife, 1763, headstone with texts in Hebrew, Greek and English; (5) John Addison, 1793; (6) Benjamin Swainson, 1800, *et al.*; (7) Joseph, son of Thomas and Hannah Harbottle, 1864, pastor at Accrington and Oswaldtwistle.

Ivimey II (1814) 253, 260. Sunderland, F., *A Brief History of Tottlebank Baptist Church* (*c.*1948). Whitley (1913) *passim*.

(65) FRIENDS, Rookhow (SD 332895). The meeting-house was built in 1725 for the sole purpose of accommodating the business meetings of Swarthmore monthly meeting. It comprises a single

FRIENDS' MEETING-HOUSE, ROOK HOW   CFS 1971

meeting-house with a two-storeyed cottage at the N end and a large central porch. The walls are of rendered rubble and the roof is slated. The porch has a wide segmental-arched outer doorway and the principal room to the S has two large sash windows with small panes of crown glass at the front.

The meeting-house (31¾ft by 24ft, excluding the cottage) has a stand at the S end with central entrance and a small gallery opposite with an open balustraded front, now closed and incorporated into the cottage, with a staircase in the porch.

The cottage has a fireplace in the N wall with a circular stack on the gable. The roof is supported by three king-post trusses with braces. The forecourt is flanked on N and S by stables and a coach-house.

Fittings – *Ironwork*: on inner door to meeting-house, latch with hinged handle and plate with cut decoration and date 1725. *Seating*: six fixed benches remain on E side only with later backs. (Removed since 1971) *Spice Cupboard*: in cottage, with fielded-panelled door dated 1725.

Butler (1978) 137–40.

CROFT   *Cheshire*

(66) RISLEY CHAPEL (SJ 650930). The Presbyterian society which first met here was formed by Thomas Risley, a Fellow of Pembroke College, Oxford, who resigned his Fellowship on the passing of the 1662 Act of Uniformity. Although shortly after this event he accepted episcopal ordination, he was unwilling to proceed further and returned to his estate at Culcheth where he practised medicine and engaged in private preaching. In 1689 a barn at Culcheth was registered as a meeting-house and in 1706–7 the chapel was erected 'upon a piece of land called Fifty Croft in Cross Lane, in Culchett, near the dwelling-house of the said Thomas Risley'. Risley died in 1716 and was succeeded in the ministry by his son John. Under subsequent ministers the society came to accept heterodox doctrines until, in 1838, following a successful petition for the removal of the then Unitarian minister and trustees, the building passed into the care of what became the Presbyterian Church of England.

The chapel has walls of brickwork and the roof is covered with stone slates. It comprises a nave (38½ft by 20ft) and chancel (13¾ft by 15ft) in orthodox E–W alignment. The principal alterations have been the replacement of the N and S windows of the nave, probably after 1892 and perhaps as late as 1914, and the rebuilding

Risley Chapel, CROFT   *Lancashire*

C.F.S.

South Elevation c.1892 *showing original fenestration*

5 Feet   0   5   10   15   20   25   30

Risley Chapel, CROFT
Lancashire

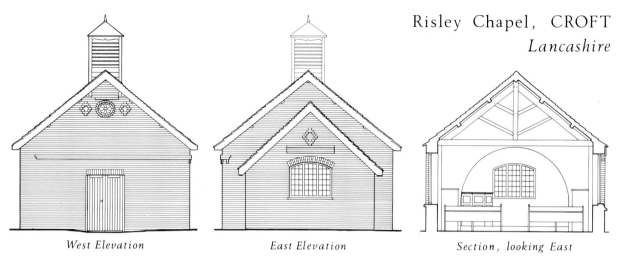

West Elevation   East Elevation   Section, looking East

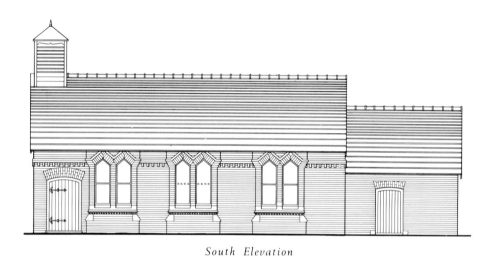

South Elevation

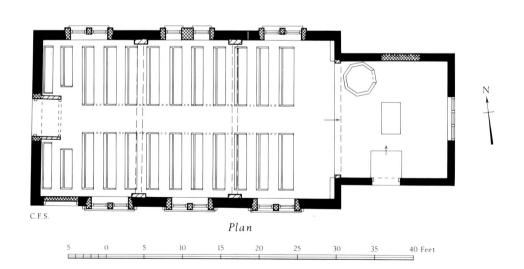

C.F.S.

Plan

5   0   5   10   15   20   25   30   35   40 Feet

Risley Chapel, Croft.   (66)

of the chancel arch and insertion of a W doorway in 1953. The *chancel* has an original E window with segmental-arched head and wooden frame of three lights; a similar window in the N wall has been blocked. Throughout the 19th century and later the chancel appears to have been divided from the nave by a partition of vertical boarding on the E side of the chancel arch and to have served as a vestry. Photographs of the arch before its rebuilding show a wide depressed arch with central keystone of early 18th-century character clearly intended to be open. The *nave* is of three bays and has externally to N and S a brick platband of two courses which formerly continued above segmental-arched windows. The roof structure, partly concealed until 1953 by an inserted plaster ceiling, comprises two king-post trusses and curved wind-braces above and below each purlin. The carpenters' assembly marks are in Arabic numerals. On the W gable is a square wooden bell-cote.

Fittings – *Bell*: one, in bell-cote, with date 1718, initials R. A. below and name 'Wiggan' opposite, for Ralph Ashton of Wigan. *Collecting Shovel*: one, with ogee-shaped opening to square box, short handle, 19th-century. *Monuments*: in burial-ground S of chapel (1) Rev. Thomas Risley M.A., 1716, table-tomb with late 19th-century inscription; (2) Rev. John Risley A.M., 1743, Hannah his wife, 1730, and Hannah their daughter, 1723, raised slab. *Pulpit*: octagonal, with two tiers of fielded panels, early 18th-century. *Seating*: box-pews with knob finials to ends next to centre aisle, partly remade but incorporating fielded-panelled doors carved with initials and dates I. W. 1706, R.L. 1706, 1759, P.D. 1706. I.P., [   ]06, C.H. I.C. [   ]706.

(Chapel closed September 1971 and immediately demolished; burial-ground remains)

AMST XXX (1986) 131–8. Nightingale IV (1892) 252–61.

(67) UNITARIAN, Lady Lane (SJ 639932). The small chapel built in 1839 by the congregation ejected from Risley Chapel (66) was demolished *c.*1960–5; the burial-ground remains.

Evans (1897) 63.

CRONTON   *Merseyside*

(68) WESLEYAN, Chapel Lane (SJ 495881). Walls of sandstone ashlar, pedimented front and round-arched side windows; dated 1845.

DALTON-IN-FURNESS   *Cumbria*

(69) Former CHRISTIAN BRETHREN, Ulverston Road (SD 233 742). Rendered walls, round-arched windows, gabled front to road; tablet dated 1868. Now Seventh-Day Adventist.

DARWEN

(70) LOWER CHAPEL (SD 694231). An Independent congregation, dispossessed in 1688 of the Upper Chapel which they had registered in the previous year, met in a barn at Bottoms until the erection of the present building in 1719. The accommodation was increased in 1754 by the erection of a gallery, and in the late 18th century the congregation (now URC) was reputed to be one of the largest in the county. In 1852–3 the chapel was seriously affected by mining subsidence and a new chapel was built in Duckworth Street. The old chapel, however, was retained in use; the front wall was entirely rebuilt

and the other walls heightened. A further drastic refitting in 1873–5 and subsequent alterations have left little of its original character.

The chapel (64¼ft by 40ft externally) has walls of gritstone rubble in shallow courses and a slate roof. The NE front wall, rebuilt in 1853, is gabled and incorporates a three-light mullioned window of 1719 above a porch added in 1873. The side walls have each five original windows of three lights with hollow-chamfered mullions below the remains of a continuous string-course; corresponding upper windows date from 1853. At the rear is a late 18th-century vestry with two ogee-arched windows in the SW wall.

The front and rear gables were formerly surmounted by ball finials and an elaborate bell-cote with one bell stood on the SE gable. All these features, which existed in the late 19th century, have since been removed.

Monuments: in extensive burial-ground around chapel, of 18th-century and later, including (1) Mary, wife of George Haydock, 1749, and Hannah her daughter, 1754; (2) Rev. Robert Smalley, 1791, also Ann, 1795, and Richard, 1800, children of Richard and Ann Smalley; (3) Thomas Ainsworth of Over Darwin, cotton manufacturer, 1785, and three children, 1785; (4) Fish Fish of Barons, Over Darwen, 1844, Ellen his widow, 1866, Intended Ann Fish, 1797, Thomas Fish, 1808, Robert Blake Fish, 1835; (5) John Shorrock, 1847, and Jenny his widow, 1858, stone slab raised on six cast-iron baluster legs; (6) Henry Polding, 1749, Ellin his wife, 1750, *et al.*; (7) Benjamin Mather, pastor, 1748/9, and Edward his son, 1746, with Latin inscription.

Nightingale II (1891) 239–61.

(71) BAPTIST, Bolton Road (SD 693217). Three-bay front with two fluted Roman Doric columns *in antis* to centre bay. Dated 1862.

Whitley (1913) 198, 333.

(72) Former CONGREGATIONAL, Belgrave Square (SD 692221). The 'Independent Meeting-house' was built in 1847 for a congregation formed in 1791 by seceders from Lower Chapel who first met in a chapel in Pole Lane. The meeting-house, designed by Edward Walters of Manchester in a 13th-century Gothic style, stands on a prominent site near the centre of the town. It comprises a nave and aisles aligned N–S, a single transept to the E and a lofty open porch at the N end above which over the N wall of the nave rises a triple gabled screen between octagonal turrets.

Monuments: in burial-ground (1) Rev. Joseph Hague, 'nearly 6 years Pastor of the English Reformed Church in Rotterdam and 4 years Pastor of Ebenezer Chapel in this village', 1835; (2) Betty Fish, 'the orphans' friend', 1854 *et al.*, obelisk.

CYB (1847) 172. Nightingale II (1871) 267–77.

(73) CONGREGATIONAL, Duckworth Street (SD 690225). Built 1852–3 for the majority of the church (now URC) formerly meeting in the Lower Chapel. Gabled front with tall pinnacles and traceried flying buttresses; four-bay loggia below large six-light window with curvilinear tracery. Probably designed by Raffles Brown of Liverpool. Bath stone dressings replaced by Longridge stone, 1868.

Nightingale II (1891) 261–4.

Former Congregational chapel, Belgrave Square, Darwen.   (72)

Congregational chapel (URC), Duckworth Street,
Darwen. (73)

(74) Former WESLEYAN, Railway Street (SD 693223), elaborate
three-bay front with giant Corinthian columns and pilasters
supporting a full entablature with pedimented centre; dated 1865.
(Converted to supermarket before 1971)

DENTON   *Greater Manchester*

(75) WESLEYAN, Two Trees Lane, Haughton Green (SJ 935942).
Three-bay brick front with rendered pediment dated 1810; two
bays deep, extended to rear, cottage attached.

Monuments: in burial-ground, many ledger stones of early 19th
century and later.

DOWNHAM

(76) Former WESLEYAN (SD 787441). Three-bay front with
round-arched doorway and two tiers of plain windows; built
1817. Now village hall.

DROYLSDEN   *Greater Manchester*

(77) MORAVIAN, Fairfield (SJ 901976). This extensive Settlement
was commenced in 1783 following concern over the uncertainty
of tenure of the site in Dukinfield, Cheshire (42); 54 acres of
farmland were acquired, the foundation stones of the chapel and
the Sisters' and Brethren's Houses were laid on 9 June 1784 and
by January 1785 the first house adjacent to the chapel was ready
for occupation.

The site is symmetrically planned with a central block of

building having the chapel on its S side bounded by roads to E, N
and W lined with two-storeyed cottages. Beyond these to the E,
in line with the chapel, is the former Sisters' House and balancing
it to the W, now rebuilt, was the Brethren's House. The road to
the N, 'Fairfield Square', has an entrance from the public road to
the N, adjacent to which was the former inn.

The chapel, or 'Congregation Hall', has walls of brickwork
with a hipped slate roof surmounted at the centre by a wooden
clock-tower with a domed roof; houses of two storeys adjoin to
east and west. The broad S front has a central pediment with
arched recess enclosing the main entrance and flanking wings,
each of two bays. The windows, formerly in two tiers with a
blind Venetian window above the entrance, were partly
conjoined and given new frames in 1908. The wings have
separate pedimented entrances which may not be original; that in
the W wing has been moved one bay to the west. The N wall has
four tall windows, unaltered in proportion, between pairs of
smaller windows in two tiers to the wings.

The interior (37ft by 86ft overall) was altered at various dates
in the 19th century and entirely changed in 1908 when it was
refitted and realigned. The wings were originally divided from
the chapel, that to the W having vestries on the lower floor and
that to the E containing a 'prayer hall'; the upper floors were
intended for possible conversion to galleries opening to the chapel
but this was never carried out. The pulpit was placed centrally
against the N wall, opposite the entrance, facing a small organ
gallery. E and W galleries were built within the original limits of
the chapel in 1865. In 1908 the pulpit, rebuilt *c*.1884, was re-sited
at the E end, the earlier galleries were removed and replaced by a
single gallery within the W wing, and the upper part of the E
wing, which with part of the roof space had earlier served as
dormitories for the girls' boarding-school, was converted to an
organ loft.

The former *Sisters' House*, E of the chapel, is of three storeys
with a S front of five bays which formerly had Venetian windows
at first-floor level in the end bays. It served from 1876 as the girls'
boarding-school and from 1906 to 1958 as a theological college.
The former *Brethren's House* was rebuilt in 1871 for the boys'
boarding-school, passing into use by the girls' school in 1906.

The *burial-ground* immediately in front of the chapel is laid out

Moravian chapel, Fairfield (77)

Monton Chapel.   (78)

in a regular pattern with separate plots on the W for male members and on the E for women and children. Monuments are uniformly numbered rectangular slabs with simple inscriptions and initials indicating the condition of the deceased; the earliest is 'No. 1 Henrietta Delamotte S.S. [single sister] Departed April 14th 1785'.

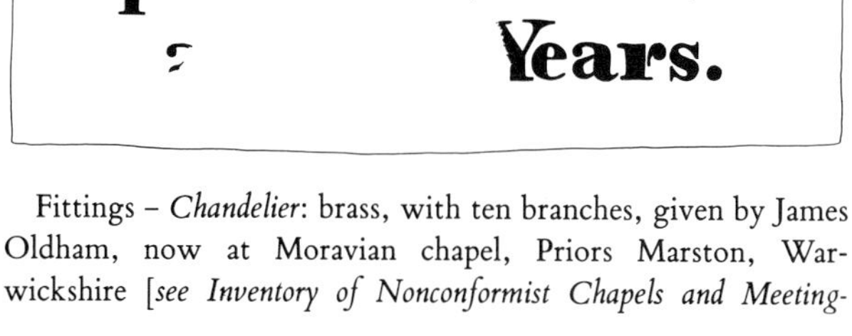

> ## No. 1.
> ## Henrietta Delamotte
> ## S.S.
> ## Depa r�557d April 14th,1785
> ## � Years.

Fittings – *Chandelier*: brass, with ten branches, given by James Oldham, now at Moravian chapel, Priors Marston, Warwickshire [*see Inventory of Nonconformist Chapels and Meeting-*houses in Central England (1986) I: 63], late 18th-century. *Organ*: in chapel, by Booth of Wakefield, 1860, remodelled 1869 and later, re-sited. *Sundial*: in burial-ground, baluster stem with horizontal dial, dated 1790.

England (1888) 22–6, Pls. 6–11. Mellowes, F. H., *A Short History of Fairfield Moravian Church* (1977).

ECCLES   *Greater Manchester*

(78) MONTON CHAPEL (SJ 765997). The Presbyterian (latterly Unitarian) congregation was formed in the late 17th century following the ejection of Edmund Jones, vicar of Eccles, who in 1672 took out a licence as a Presbyterian preacher. Meetings were also conducted by Robert Baldwin, ejected 1660 as vicar of Penrith and in 1662 as curate of Rainford; in 1689 Baldwin registered a barn at Eccles as a Presbyterian meeting place. The site for a permanent meeting-house was acquired at Monton Green and a building erected in 1697; this was sacked by a mob in 1715 and repaired with the assistance of a public grant. The first chapel was replaced in 1802 by a plain brick chapel with a bellcote above an end entrance.

The present building, of 1873–5 by Thomas Worthington, is a substantial Gothic structure of stone and slate comprising a polygonal chancel, transepts, a nave and aisles of five bays and a corner tower of three stages with a spire. The nave and crossing are covered by an open hammer-beam roof strengthened by iron tie-rods issuing from grotesque animal heads.

Fittings – *Bell*: one, in tower, from earlier chapel. *Font*: stone, octagonal, formerly at Hope Street Chapel, Liverpool, 1908. *Glass*: in chancel, *c*.1880; in transepts, four windows by H. Beiler of Heidelberg, mid 19th-century from former chapel; in clerestory windows of nave, figures of ancient and modern worthies intended to illustrate verses from the Te Deum and Benedicite, by Heaton, Butler and Bayne of London, 1893–9. *Monuments*: in vestibule, from former chapel (1) Frances, wife of John Coates, 1855; (2) Eliza Blackburne, 1864; (3) Rev. Robert Smethurst, 1846; (4) Catharine Leigh, daughter of John and Martha Booth, 1850. In burial-ground (5) Rev. John Chorley, 1764, Jane his widow, daughter of Sir Robert Duckinfield (*sic*), 1781, John, their son, 1826, and Ellen his wife, 1809; (6) Rev. Robert Smethurst, 1846, table-tomb; (7) Rev. Jeremiah Aldred, 1729, Mary his wife, 1729, and Jeremiah their son, 1727, inscribed floorslab or ledger stone reset above table-tomb.

Bleackley, J.R., *Short History of Monton Chapel...* (1969). Evans (1897) 175–6. Nightingale V (1893) 1–10. *UHST* II (1919–22) 32–46.

(79) Former METHODIST, Barton Road (SJ 765978). The original chapel built in 1796 (40ft by 30ft externally) was of two bays with an entrance at the SE end; it was enlarged to the NW and the walls heightened in the early 19th century. The walls are of brickwork with two tiers of round-arched windows, now in four bays to the side walls, the upper windows being partly in the wall heightening. A tablet in the NE wall is inscribed with the date of opening.

The interior has a continuous gallery of *c*.1840 with rounded ends, panelled front and thin supporting columns of cast-iron. The pulpit is at the NW end. The lower seating dates from the late 19th century.

At the rear is an extensive burial-gound with many headstones and ledger stones of the 19th century and later. (Chapel in use 1973 by the Church of the Nazarine)

Dolbey (1964) 81–2.

ELSWICK

(80) CONGREGATIONAL (SD 423383). A chapel-of-ease was built *c*.1650 'on the waste, or Leys' with an endowment of £50 per annum from the Committee for Plundered Ministers. At the Restoration it passed into use as a school but in 1672 'the meeting-house in Elswick Lees, in the parish of St Michael's' was registered for Congregationalists. From 1687 the congregation (now URC) was regarded as Presbyterian and appears in Evans's List under the ministry of Robert Moss. Towards the end of this ministry the old chapel, which stood about 600 yards S of the present buildings, was found to be no longer suitable and the first of the two existing chapels was erected in 1753 for 'Independents or Presbyterians'; this was heightened and enlarged in 1837. A second chapel was built on an adjoining site in 1873–4 and the former converted for use as a Sunday-school.

The former chapel of 1753 has stone walls with later rendering, ashlar quoins and a stone slate roof. The gabled N wall has a central porch surmounted by a stone bell-cote dated 1753, perhaps reset from the main wall, and a segmental-arched upper

Former chapel, Elswick. (80)

window behind, over which is a small tablet inscribed 'Renovated 1906'. The inner doorway has a pair of doors each with three fielded panels. The W wall has three original segmental-arched windows and a taller window in the extension to the south. Two original windows are exposed in the E wall which is partly covered by a later annexe. High in the S wall is a circular window of the late 19th century.

The interior (originally about 39ft by 24ft, extended to 54½ft) had in 1872 a gallery at each end with the pulpit centrally against the W wall with a window behind. Only the N gallery now remains with a mid 18th-century front having two ranges of fielded panels between moulded base and cornice.

The present chapel standing W of the former, designed by H.J. Paull, comprises a wide nave with transepts, organ chamber, E vestries and N porch with a tower on the N side rising to an octagonal turret with a short spire.

Fittings – *Book*: 'Geneva Bible', London 1594, reputed to have been chained in the Elswick Leys chapel, returned by private owner 1937. *Chair*: with fielded-panelled back and shaped rails, dated 1716, book-rest added for use as portable pulpit. *Monuments*: in burial-ground of former chapel, table-tombs and ledger stones of 18th century and later (Nightingale (I (1890)) records a monument to Rev. Robert Moss, 44 years minister, 1759).

CYB (1874) 423–4. Hewitson (1872) 410–18. *Lancs. CYB* (1924) 48–51. Nightingale I (1890) 78–92. VCH *Lancs.* VII (1912) 284.

Former Independent Chapel, ELSWICK
Lancashire

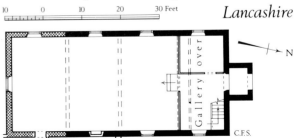

Dob Lane Chapel, Failsworth. First chapel *c.* 1698.   (81)

Dob Lane Chapel, Failsworth. Second chapel, 1878–9.   (81)

Dob Lane Chapel, Failsworth. Third chapel 1975.   (81)

FAILSWORTH   *Greater Manchester*

(81) DOB LANE CHAPEL (SD 886010). A nondescript brick chapel of 1975 replacing a minor Gothic chapel of 1878–9 by Adams and Son stands on the site of the first Dob Lane Chapel of *c.*1698. A school building erected 1846, enlarged 1860, remains at the rear. The Presbyterian congregation became Unitarian by the late 18th century.

Christian Freeman (September 1872) 136–7. Evans (1897) 85–6. Gordon, A., *Historical Account of Dob Lane Chapel, Failsworth...* (1904). Nightingale V (1893) 38–50.

(82) NEW JERUSALEM, Oldham Road (SD 902022). Gothic, 1889. Former 'Swedenborgian' chapel at rear facing Croft Street (derelict 1971); brick with corner pilasters, rusticated stone jambs to central round-arched doorway and tablet dated 1859. The former Sunday and Day School in Wicken Tree Lane is dated 1871.

(83) WESLEYAN, Oldham Road (SD 901021). Brick with open pediment to three-bay front; dated 1866.

FARNWORTH   *Greater Manchester*

(84) Site of INDEPENDENT, Church Street (SD 741058). The chapel, built in 1808 as the first place of public worship in Farnworth, was superseded by a new chapel in 1850, both on a site NE of Market Street. Only a few minor buildings, now in secular use, remain together with traces of the burial-ground. The first chapel had a bell-cote above the front gable and a Venetian window between the entrances.

Barnes, H. A., *The Story of Halshaw Moor Chapel* (1908). Dyson, S., *Rural Congregationalism...* (1881). Nightingale III (1892) 135–43.

(85) CONGREGATIONAL, Albert Road (SD 736054). Red brick, with three-bay pediment, pilasters and tall round-arched windows. Built 1862, galleries added 1871, school alongside 1872, enlarged 1891. (URC)

CYB (1863) 308–9 (erroneously described as 'Early English'); (1873) 428–9. Nightingale III (1892) 143–6.

FORTON

(86) CONGREGATIONAL (SD 488512). The formerly Presbyterian society (now URC) met until 1707 in Shireshead Chapel, a chapel-of-ease of Cockerham ($\frac{3}{4}$ mile east). The first chapel at Forton, built in 1707, was rebuilt *c.*1760 and its successor very considerably altered in 1870 and later.

The walls are of stone and the roof, rebuilt as a double roof *c.*1895, is covered with slates. A sketch published by Nightingale (1906) shows the chapel after the addition of a porch in 1870 with a N front of three bays with round-arched upper windows, single gables at the E and W ends and a small vestry to the west. The vestry remains with little alteration but the front now has two tall windows below gablets flanking the central porch. Two original round-arched windows in the S wall flanked the former site of the pulpit. Two tall windows at the E end probably replace two tiers of windows.

The interior (33$\frac{1}{4}$ft by 38$\frac{1}{4}$ft), re-pewed in 1870 with the pulpit re-sited at the W end opposite a small gallery, has been subdivided. The windows were reglazed in 1898.

A small outbuilding NW of the chapel, dated 1836, has an

CONGREGATIONAL CHAPEL, FORTON   CFS 1970

external flight of stone steps leading to an upper room formerly used for Sunday-school and weekday meetings.

Fittings – *Monuments*: in burial-ground (1) James, son of Eleazar Aray, 1721, ledger stone inscribed in raised capital letters; (2) Rev. James Grimshaw, 1838, and Jane his wife, 1836, table-tomb. *Mounting Steps*: in N boundary wall of burial-ground, double flight. *Panelling*: in chapel, fielded panels reused as wall-lining and pew backs. *Pulpit*: fielded-panelled front and sides, fluted pilasters and moulded dentil cornice, *c*.1760.

Hewitson (1872) 482–3. Nightingale I (1890) 181–91. Nightingale, B., *The Story of the Lancashire Congregational Union 1806-1906* (1906) facing 85.

FOULRIDGE

(87) Former FRIENDS (SD 89054235). The meeting-house described in VCH (op. cit. below) as 'Foulridge Dandy Shop' was converted to domestic use in 1979. It stands on the E side of the road N of Ivegate. All door and window openings date from the early 19th century or later although the fabric of the rubble walls may be earlier.

VCH *Lancs* VI (1911) 548.

(88) WESLEYAN, Mount Pleasant (SD 880433). Rubble walls and stone slate roof, chapel at upper level approached by external staircase with cottage below. Built or converted 1822; formerly a pair of two-storeyed cottages.

Moore (1899) 225.

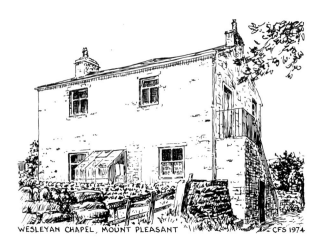

WESLEYAN CHAPEL, MOUNT PLEASANT — CFS 1974

GARSTANG

(89) CONGREGATIONAL, Croston Road (SD 491455). The chapel, built for a newly formed congregation (now URC), was opened 4 August 1779. It remained private property until 1867, when it was purchased by the church and drastically remodelled. The walls are of roughly squared and coursed rubble and the roof is slated. The S front is gabled and has a later porch. The E and W sides, originally of three bays, have tall round-arched windows probably replacing two tiers of smaller windows. The N end was extended by one bay in the late 19th century to provide a vestry and choir gallery.

The interior (36ft by 23¾ft) has N and S galleries with arcaded fronts of Romanesque design; prior to the 1867-8 refitting the galleries extended around three sides and there was a tall pulpit at the N end. The roof is supported by two king-post trusses.

The 'Congregational School', a detached building dated 1903, stands E of the chapel.

Fittings – *Books*: in vestry (1) Anon., *The Biographical and Martyrological Dictionary* . . . (Newcastle upon Tyne, 1790), inscribed 'For the use of the Minister of the Independent Chapel, Garstang, For the time being – Jany 25th 1787 [*sic*]'; (2) James Durham, *A Learned and Complete Commentary upon the Book of the Revelation* . . . (Glasgow, 1788), inscribed as above but undated; (3) Matthew Henry, *Exposition of the New Testament*, 2 vols. (Edinburgh, 1772), inscribed as last; (4) John Brown, *The Self-Interpreting Bible* . . . (Edinburgh, 1778), inscribed 'For the use of the Minister of Garstang for the time being – Bound by Mr. Robt. Gardner Lancaster £1-5s.-0d. Jan. 25th 1787 Geo. Richardson Minister' (title page missing); (5) William Jenkyn, *An Exposition of the Epistle of Jude* (Glasgow, 4th edn. 1783), inscribed as (2) above; (6) Benjamin Keach, *A Key to Open Scripture Metaphors* . . . (London 1779), inscribed as (4) above except price '£1-10s.-0d.'.

Fittings – *Monument*: in burial-ground, William Armstrong, 1809, Betty his wife, 1805, *et al. Seating*: in S gallery, two ranks of box-pews, centre pews altered, early 19th-century.

Hewitson (1872) 482–4. Nightingale I (1890) 191–203.

GOOSNARGH

(90) CONGREGATIONAL, Inglewhite (SD 547398). Stone with rendered sides 'erected A.D. 1826'. Gabled front with rusticated quoins, central entrance and platband below two small round-arched gallery windows.

Hewitson (1872) 583. Nightingale I (1890) 163–5.

(91) WESLEYAN, Whittingham Lane (SD 558364). Three-bay gabled front with round-arched openings, dated 1832.

Hewitson (1872) 77–8.

HAVERTHWAITE   *Cumbria*

(92) WESLEYAN, Backbarrow (SD 355852). Drystone walls of slate rubble with pointed-arched windows; defaced tablet dated 1850.

HAWKSHEAD   *Cumbria*

(93) BAPTIST, Hawkshead Hill (SD 338988). The first Baptist church meeting here originated with a church formed at Torver (*see* (239)) in 1678; about 1770 the centre of Baptist activity was transferred to Hawkshead where, in 1709, under the guidance of George Braithwaite, William Dennyson's house at Hawkshead Hill was registered as a meeting-house. The cause failed *c*.1833 but was re-formed a few years later as a mission station of the Coniston church. The chapel was reopened in 1977 after a long period of virtual disuse.

The chapel, which is set between adjoining buildings, may be the conversion of a 17th-century cottage. It has rendered rubble walls and a slate roof; in the front wall are two pointed-arched windows of the early 19th century with a tablet between bearing the false date of erection, 1678, and 'restored A.D. 1876'. The entrance, at the right-hand end of the front, is in a large lean-to porch.

BAPTIST CHAPEL, HAWKSHEAD HILL   CFS 1971

The interior (28½ft by 17ft) has a gallery adjacent to the entrance approached by a staircase in the porch with straight string, turned balusters and plain newels with ball finials; the staircase has been considerably repaired or renewed. There is a small vestry at the rear; most of the back wall is covered by the wing of an adjacent cottage.

The fittings were largely replaced in the late 19th century and subsequently but two 18th-century *coffin stools* remain in the gallery.

Ivimey II (1814) 253. VCH *Lancs.* VIII (1914) 380. Whitley (1913) 114, 190, 336.

(94) Former UNION CHAPEL, Hawkshead (SD 352981). A cottage at one corner of The Square was converted to a chapel in 1862 for an undenominational congregation; it was subsequently offered by a private owner to the Methodist Free Church, which declined it; it then passed to the Wesleyans and has since continued in Methodist use.

The chapel, largely concealed by adjacent buildings, has a small porch towards The Square and two round-arched windows at the back. The interior has a gallery with balustraded front next to the entrance.

Fontlet: plaster with inset china bowl, scale model of Winchester Cathedral font reputedly made for the Cambridge Camden Society, 1840.

HEYWOOD   *Greater Manchester*

(95) CONGREGATIONAL, Bamford (SD 860125). The chapel, built in 1801 for a recently formed congregation (now URC), was almost entirely rebuilt in 1842; subsequent alterations included the erection of an organ chancel in 1881. A Sunday-school was built alongside in 1861.

The front wall, of 1842, is of stone with a gable across three bays, gablets between pinnacles to narrow end bays, tall lancet windows, and a central porch which encloses a gallery staircase.

The interior has a gallery around three sides supported by cast-iron columns of quatrefoil section. The pews and gallery fronts date from the late 19th century.

Fittings – *Monuments*: in chapel (1) John Fenton, 1840, and Ann his wife, 1831; (2) Robert Kay, 1834. *Sundial*: in front of chapel, octagonal column with small horizontal dial, illegible from over-painting. Manchester maker, early 19th-century.

Anon., *Historical Notes on Bamford Chapel and Sunday School* (1801–1926). Nightingale III (1892) 254–62. Yates, J. T., *Bamford Chapel 1801–1976* (1976).

(96) NEW JERUSALEM, Church Street (SD 858107). A 'Swedenborgian' society which first met in Heywood in 1812 built a chapel in Oak Street in 1814. After some financial problems the chapel was let to Congregationalists in 1823, the former society meeting elsewhere. A new chapel was built on a leasehold site in 1828; it was enlarged in 1838, refronted and partly refitted in 1866 and extended to the rear along Temple Street in 1885.

The chapel is a square building of brickwork with a stone front and hipped roof with central valley or flat. In the side walls are four tall round-arched windows. The interior has a gallery around three sides supported by cast-iron columns. (Derelict 1971, since demolished)

Monuments: in chapel (1) John Wild, 'one of the earliest members of this society and for many years its leader', 1859; (2) James Ashworth, 1855, and Alice his widow, 1865, 'in whose house the doctrines of the New Church were first publicly preached in Heywood', signed 'A. Norbury, Hope St., L'pool'.

Hindmarsh (1861) 216. Nightingale III (1892) 263.

HINDLEY   *Greater Manchester*

(97) PRESBYTERIAN, Presbyterian Fold (SD 618047). The first place of worship in Hindley was a chapel-of-ease built in 1641 to serve the parish of Wigan. This property was administered by trustees, the majority of whom after 1685 were Presbyterians and who, although failing in an attempt to register the building as a dissenting meeting-house, appointed a minister of that persuasion to the chapel in 1690. In 1698 after protracted litigation the trustees and their nominee were dispossessed and the house of William Hilton was registered as a temporary meeting place.

The first Presbyterian chapel, or 'Hindley New Chapel', which stood on the present site was registered at Michaelmas 1699. It was built by Richard Crook of Abram and remained his personal property until 1717 when it was placed in trust. The building is reported to have fallen into 'a very dilapidated condition' during the pastorate of William Davenport (1765–78) when relations between the minister and congregation were exacerbated by a dispute over money collected in part for the erection of a new chapel in Wigan. Building accounts show that the Hindley chapel was rebuilt or largely reconstructed, possibly on the original foundation, in 1788. It was greatly altered in 1877, when the interior was refitted and a large Sunday-school was erected at the E end. The society has long been regarded as Unitarian.

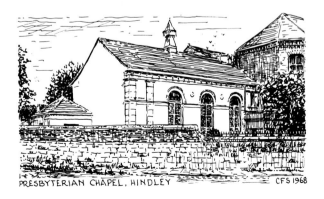

PRESBYTERIAN CHAPEL, HINDLEY   CFS 1968

The chapel has walls of brickwork rendered in stucco and a slate roof. The front wall faces S and has three tall round-arched windows of 1788 with altered frames and a doorway in a later porch to the right. Before 1877 this wall extended further to the E and had a pair of round-arched doorways at that end; the wall was embellished with rusticated pilasters and a Doric entablature in 1877. The N wall has two plain round-arched windows. The W wall is gabled and has no openings; a small vestry projects at this end. The E wall is obscured and partly encroached upon by the Sunday-school.

The interior (37ft by 24¼ft), entirely refitted in 1877, has a gallery at the E end and a square pulpit against the W wall.

Fittings – *Bell-cote*: above E gable, hexagonal base, super-structure now removed, had six columns supporting a dome containing one bell. *Inscriptions*: in vestry, three square wooden panels in 18th-century frames inscribed (1) 'Anno Dom 1700 Haec Capella fuit fundata per Richardum Crook De Abram'; (2) with scriptural texts in Greek and Hebrew; (3) with shield-of-arms of Crook. *Monuments*: in chapel (1) Rev. Joseph Bourn, 19 years minister, 1765; (2) Rev. Jonathan Hodgkinson, 33 years minister, 1812.

Evans (1897) 104–5. Herford and Evans (1909) 90–1. *HSL & CT* LXII (1910) 67–118. *L & CAST* LXVII (1957) 45–74. Nightingale IV (1892) 7–13. *UHST* VII (1939–42) 31–49, 66–7, 139–62.

(98) PARTICULAR BAPTIST, Market Street (SD 617044). Rendered pedimented front of three bays; dated 1854.

(99) INDEPENDENT, Bridge Croft (SD 621047). Built 1838 for seceders from St Paul's Congregational Chapel; brick and slate with tall pedimented wing on S side between two tiers of round-arched windows; extended to W for Sunday-school 1882. Refitted 1885. (Demolished since 1969)

Nightingale IV (1892) 21–3.

HOGHTON

(100) WESLEYAN, Chapel Lane (SD 622269). The chapel, built in 1794, was much altered and enlarged in the 19th century. The walls are built of sandstone ashlar and the roof is slated. The S front, now of five bays, was originally of three bays only with a central doorway, now blocked, and small square upper windows. In the early 19th century the chapel was extended 12½ft to the E, reusing the original quoins at the new corner and adding a second entrance which was further altered in 1887–8 by the addition of a round-arched surround and blind tympanum inscribed with the date of erection. A wing on the N side, on the axis of the enlarged chapel, was also added in the early 19th century to provide a vestry with singers' gallery above.

The interior (originally 24ft by 29½ft) has a gallery in the E extension with a panelled front supported by two turned wood columns. There appears to have been a second gallery at the W end until 1888 when the pulpit, possibly on the N side, was re-sited at this end. The N wing is separated from the body of the chapel by a solid wall to the lower floor, but the gallery above has a panelled front with a single stone Tuscan column on panelled die rising centrally to support the original eaves; the gallery is closed by later shutters.

WESLEYAN CHAPEL, HOGHTON   CFS1970

NE of the chapel is a mid 19th-century schoolhouse of two storeys with rendered stone walls, rusticated quoins, and a stone bell-cote on the S gable. The upper floor is approached by an external stair at the S end.

Fittings – *Candlesticks*: two, on backs of seats in N gallery, turned wood standards, 2ft high, early 19th-century. *Clock*: on front of N gallery, signed 'H. Crossley, London', early 19th-century. *Collecting Shovels*: two, circular boxes with turned handles, 17 in. overall, signed 'E. Titley, Blackburn', three, rectangular boxes, plain handles, 28½ in. overall. *Monuments*: in burial-ground, NE of chapel (1) John Crossley, 1812, Alice his fifth wife, 1823, *et al.*; (2) John, son of William and Priscilla Bennett, 1813, *et al.*; against E wall (3) James Horrocks, 1801; N of vestry (4) John Harrison, 1821, Mary his widow, 1840, and Anne their daughter, 1823, table-tomb on six legs.

Painting: in vestry, water-colour of chapel from SE before alteration to doorways, signed 'Albert Riley, 1888'. *Pulpit*: semi-octagonal with moulded base and cornice, reset on dwarf base, brought *c.*1960 from Clayton Street Wesleyan Chapel, Blackburn, late 18th-century. *Seating*: in N gallery, early 19th-century box-pews; in E gallery iron-framed benches; in body of chapel, late 19th-century pews with dwarf doors. *Sundial*: in burial-ground NE of chapel, stone column with brass dial and gnomon, signed 'J. Hardy, Preston, 1810'. *Tables of Decalogue*: on W wall, painted metal, late 19th-century.

HORWICH   *Greater Manchester*

(101) NEW CHAPEL (SD 656108). Horwich Chapel, a chapel-of-ease of the parish of Deane, was occupied in the late 17th century by a Presbyterian congregation which retained possession until 1716. In that year the dissenters were obliged to erect a new meeting-house for themselves, known as Horwich New Chapel. The church (now URC) became Congregational by the early 19th century.

The chapel has walls of squared stone and a slate roof. Although dating in part from 1716 the chapel was greatly altered or enlarged in 1805 (or possibly 1803), drastically refitted in 1888, and further altered in 1906 when a large chancel and vestry were added at the N end.

The S front is gabled and was formerly surmounted by a hexagonal wooden bell-cote, demolished in 1952; there are two doorways with a three-light mullioned window between and three similar windows above, all dating from 1805. Although the

New Chapel (URC), Horwich.   (101)

chapel is said to have been extended to the S in 1805, the lower half of this wall may date from the early 18th century, as evidenced by a change in the size of the quoins, and the enlargement or 'rebuilding' may have been a general heightening. The side walls have windows to the lower stage only, all of two lights except one on the E side which is of three lights.

The interior (34¾ft by 39ft) has a gallery around three sides with a late 19th-century cast-iron front. The ceiling has been raised, exposing the lower part of the roof trusses.

A detached Sunday-school is dated 1877.

Monuments: in burial-ground (1) James, 1802, and Hannah, 1804, children of the Rev. James and Hannah Kenworthy, also Joseph Dutton Kenworthy, 1838; (2) Elizabeth, daughter of the Rev. William and Ellen Wilsdon, 1846, buried in Abney Park Cemetery, John Richard Wilsdon, 1852, and William Wicklow Wilsdon, 1856; (3) Rev. James Kenworthy, 1828, 27 years minister, and Hannah his wife, 1824.

Antrobus, J. K., *A Revised History of New Chapel, 1716–1966* (1966). Nightingale III (1892) 90–110.

(102) ÆNON CHAPEL, Chapel Street (SD 644114). Small stone chapel, broad three-bay front with round-arched doorway and flanking windows, and plain upper windows. Built *c*.1830 for Wesleyans, used by Baptists from 1890 but now Pentecostalist.

Whitley (1913) 223, 337.

ÆNON CHAPEL, HORWICH   CFS 1974

INSKIP-WITH-SOWERBY

(103) BAPTIST, Inskip (SD 455380). This congregation is said to owe its origin, in part, to the defection of the Congregational minister at Elswick, the Rev. Timothy Senier, to the Baptists in 1795. Regular preaching was commenced at Roebuck in 1815 under the aegis of the Yorkshire and Lancashire Itinerant Society and a chapel was built at Inskip in 1817.

The chapel has stone walls, rendered at the sides. The front wall has a single round-arched window above a small later porch; traces of a mid 19th-century heightening are visible in the gable.

Hewitson (1872) 431-3. Long, A. J., *Hitherto: or the History of the Baptist Church at Roebuck from 1815-1817 and at Inskip from 1817-1917* (1917). Nightingale I (1890) 89–90. Whitley (1913) 173, 266, 337.

KIRKBY IRELETH   *Cumbria*

(104) CHRISTIAN BRETHREN, Kirkby-in-Furness (SD 235832). Rubble with pointed-arched windows and gabled front with tablet inscribed 'Christian Meeting House 1876'.

KIRKLAND

(105) STRICT BAPTIST, Nateby (SD 465447). Late 19th-century on site of 1838 chapel. *Monument*: in burial-ground, John Shaw, 1839, table-tomb.

Hewitson (1872), 515–18. Paul (1961) 168–84. Whitley (1913) 338.

LANCASTER

(106) ST NICHOLAS STREET CHAPEL (SD 478617). The Presbyterian, latterly Unitarian, congregation which originated in the late 17th century had a meeting-house in St Nicholas Street by the early 18th century. This stood behind other property on the S side of the street. It was rebuilt in 1786 to a design by a Mr Hurd; in 1874 it was altered and refitted and an apsidal chancel was built at the W end. It was demolished in 1965 and a new meeting-house erected in Scofforth Road. The chapel in St Nicholas Street had stone walls, the N side was of three bays with a broad pediment and tall round-arched windows. *Plate*: includes a two-handled cup of 1715.

Evans (1897) 127. Herford and Evans (1909) 97–9. Hewitson, W., 'Lancaster Unitarian Chapel', *Lancaster Observer* (September–December 1890). Nightingale I (1890) 209–22.

(107) CONGREGATIONAL, High Street (SD 476615). A congregation of orthodox dissenters (now URC) was formed about 1770, possibly as a result of the growth of heterodox preaching at the Presbyterian meeting. The meeting-house in High Street (formerly Mount Street) was built *c*.1776; it was greatly enlarged to the rear in 1833 and a school-room built below the extension. In 1851 various alterations were made, including reseating and enlargement of the gallery.

The walls are of coursed stone and the roof is covered with slates. The broad W front has rusticated quoins and five bays of windows, the upper tier round-arched with plain surrounds, keystones and impost blocks. The central doorway was superseded *c*.1851 by a pair of entrances in the adjacent bays and a stone with the false date of erection, 1772, inserted between; the former entrance was restored *c*.1900

Congregational chapel, Lancaster.   (107)

The interior (originally 37¾ft by 44½ft) was lengthened to 60ft in 1833. There is a gallery around three sides with a panelled front supported by wooden columns; the rear gallery has been enlarged.

Fittings – *Model*: architect's model for Centenary Congregational Chapel (1879, by Hetherington and Oliver). *Monuments*: in chapel (1) Peter Samuel Charrier, 19 years pastor here and 17 years at Bethesda, Liverpool, 1826; (2) Dorcas, wife of John Walmsley, 1781; (3) Robert Gardner, 1814, signed 'S. Franceys & Son L'pool'. *Pulpit*: mahogany rostrum, mid 19th-century perhaps incorporating earlier material. *Seating*: box-pews throughout of 1851.

Nightingale I (1890) 222–35.

(108) FRIENDS, Meeting-house Lane (SD 473617). Quaker activity in Lancaster dates from the early years of the society, one of its promoters being John Lawson, a merchant of Lancaster, who in 1652 protected George Fox from assault by the mob. The first meeting-house on the present site was built in 1677; it was mostly rebuilt in 1708 on a much larger scale by William Stout and Robert Lawson to accommodate the general meeting for the northern counties. This forms the nucleus of the existing building which was further extended to the E in 1779 and at the opposite end a few years later.

The walls are of coursed squared stone, rendered at the front, and the roof is covered with stone slates. The S front has a two-

Friends' meeting-house, Lancaster.   (108)

storeyed polygonal porch of the late 18th century; one bay to the left of this, the porch bay, and three to the right, delimit the extent of the 1708 building (externally 72¾ft by 37¾ft); the windows formerly had stone mullions and transoms, now replaced throughout by hung sashes. The later 18th-century work is represented by two additional bays at each end. The E wall is gabled and has a plain Venetian window lighting the back of the stand. The W wall has one window of the late 18th century. The N wall is covered by modern extensions.

The interior comprises two rooms separated by a passage with a stone wall to the W but a shuttered partition on the E opening to the principal room. The latter had a gallery along the N side, now removed, and a further gallery, now closed, above the passage. The E and S walls have a dado of 19th-century panelling; the stand at the E end has been removed. The W room has been entirely altered. The room above the porch was built for a record room and has a small fireplace with a late 18th-century surround. The roof is supported by late 18th-century trusses with king-post and braces, two collars and tie-beam, and has four purlins to each slope.

Fittings – *Inscription*: reset above inner doorway in porch, stone with raised numerals 1677 from first meeting-house. *Monument*: in porch, ledger stone removed 1951 from burial-ground at Moorside (SD 502630), to John Lawson of Lancaster, 1689. *Sundial*: S of meeting-house, fluted stone pedestal with square dial and gnomon, signed [?Wilson], 18th-century.

Muschamp, R., 'The Society of Friends in the Lancaster District in the seventeenth century', *L & CAST* XLII (1926) 21–41.

(109) Former WESLEYAN, Sulyard Street (SD 479617). Stone, with octagonal tower. 1873–4, possibly by Austin and Paley, on site of 1806 chapel. Now converted to residential use.

(110) INDEPENDENT METHODIST, Nelson Street (SD 480616). Three-bay front with large round-arched windows; dated 1829.

LATHOM

(111) WESLEYAN, Moss Lane (SD 456136). Broad three-bay front, rendered; opened 1813.

LEES   *Greater Manchester*

(112) ZION CHAPEL, High Street (SD 955046). Methodist New Connexion; first chapel built 1829, rebuilt 1852–3. Three-bay front with two tiers of windows, Venetian window above central doorway. (Demolition proposed 1979).

Monument: in burial-ground, John Bottomley, schoolmaster, 1830, with elaborately lettered inscription, signed 'Collier engraver', table-tomb.

Walker, W., *Builders of Zion* (nd; *c*.1920).

LITTLEBOROUGH   *Greater Manchester*

(113) INDEPENDENT, Summit (SD 946187). 'Ebenezer' Chapel dated 1834. Single entrance replaces two round-arched doorways in gabled end wall.

Kelsall, G. and Parry, K., *Looking back at Littleborough* (1981). Nightingale III (1892) 249–51.

(114) WESLEYAN, Temple Lane (SD 945184). 'Providence' Chapel, dated 1839; four-bay front to S with round-arched

Toxteth Chapel   LIVERPOOL
Lancashire

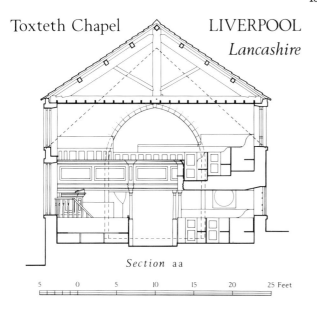

Section a a

5   0   5   10   15   20   25 Feet

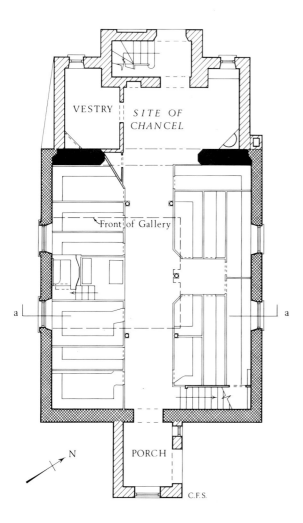

VESTRY   SITE OF CHANCEL

Front of Gallery

a   a

N

PORCH

C.F.S.

openings, originally with doorway between two windows facing small forecourt and further window to right. Derelict 1971.

(115) PRIMITIVE METHODIST, Summit (SD 946186). Rock-faced stone, ashlar dressings; round-arched windows grouped in front wall. Dated 1866.

LITTLE ECCLESTON-WITH-LARBRECK

(116) Former FRIENDS, Little Eccleston (SD 421404). The meeting-house, built in 1715 and closed in 1791, has brick walls; it was originally of a single storey but has now been heightened and converted to a cottage. The S front has been entirely refenestrated. A ceiling beam in the W room may indicate a former gallery at that end.

Abbatt (1931) 101, 112.

LITTLE HULTON   *Greater Manchester*

(117) Site of PRESBYTERIAN, Wharton Lane (SD 709039). Presbyterian services were held after 1662 at Wharton Hall, the seat of Robert Mort, where preachers included Matthew Henry and James Wood of Chowbent. The Hall was licensed for meetings in 1672 and continued as a preaching-place until the early 18th century. Wharton Chapel, first built in 1723, was a small building of three bays with a central entrance between a pair of round-arched windows on the S side, and a bell-cote above the W gable. The chapel was altered in 1866 by the addition of a Sunday-school on the N side and the bell-cote was renewed. The chapel was entirely rebuilt in 1900 and its successor demolished *c.*1970. The burial-ground remains.

Fittings – *Bell*: one, reported to have been inscribed '1723 Luke Ashton Fecit Wigan' (unlocated). *Monuments*: in burial-ground (1) John Farnworth, 1768; (2) John Farnworth junior, 1762, and Esther his daughter, 1758, table-tomb; (3) Betty, daughter of John Farnworth, 1758, and Richard Farnworth, 1758; (4) James Thornley, 1736; (5) Mary, daughter of James Hindley, 1734, and Mary her mother, 1735; (6) Rev. Mr Valentine, minister, 1754, Cicely his wife, 1751, *et al.*; (7) Thomas Carruthers 'of North Britain', 1728/9 and later inscription to Rev. James Stewart, 'minister of this chapel', 1864, *et al.*, table-tomb; (8) John Higson, 1767, Mary his wife, 1751, and Mary their daughter, 1758; (9) Jeremiah Hindley, 1763; (10) James Hindley, 1765, and Mary his wife, 1757. *Pulpit*: octagonal base on plain dwarf legs, six panelled sides with two tiers of fielded panels, reputedly from Wharton Hall but more probably early 18th-century, much repaired; given to Presbyterian Historical Society, 1913, location since 1978 unknown.

England (1888) 16, Pl. 4. Franks, E. H. E., *A Brief Sketch of the History of the Cause at Wharton 1662–1899* (1900). Nightingale IV (1892) 108–17. Nightingale, B., *The Story of the Lancashire Congregational Union 1806–1906* (1906) 29, Pl. facing 32. *PHSJ* I (1914–19) 7; X (1952–5) 154.

LIVERPOOL   *Merseyside*

(118) THE ANCIENT CHAPEL OF TOXTETH (SJ 364876). Toxteth Park, a former royal deer park several miles S of Liverpool, was converted to farmland at the beginning of the 17th century; in 1611 a school was commenced for the new community to which Richard Mather, then aged fifteen, was appointed master.

The Ancient Chapel of Toxteth. (118)

Toxteth was described at this period as 'a hamlet without a Chapell', forming a detached and extremely remote part of the parish of Lancaster. The provision of a place of worship was therefore a matter of urgency and a chapel was built by the inhabitants to which, after a brief period of further education at Oxford, Mather was invited in 1618 to become minister. Although duly ordained by the bishop of Chester, Mather was notorious in his support for the Puritan party, and was assisted in this both by the temper of his congregation and the anomalous ecclesiastical position of the chapelry. Additional preaching at Liverpool and Prescot eventually drew upon him episcopal demands for conformity in 1633–4, with which he was unwilling to comply, causing his enforced emigration in 1635 to New England where he continued to preach until his death in 1669.

Although nothing is known of Mather's immediate successor, or if one was appointed, Toxteth was sufficiently highly regarded by a Parliamentary commission in 1650 to be recommended, unsuccessfully, to be formed into a separate parish. At the Restoration the irregular or uncertain ecclesiastical status of the chapel assisted the minister, Thomas Crompton, and his co-pastor Michael Bristoe, in continuing in office without conforming, and permitted its licensing in 1672 as a Presbyterian meeting-house and its subsequent registration in 1689.

Exceptionally amongst Lancashire chapels-of-ease no attempt was made by the Establishment to reclaim the chapel which was reported in 1718 to be held on lease from Lord Molyneux. During the long ministry of William Harding (1737–76) maintenance of the building had been so far neglected that major repairs amounting to a substantial rebuilding had to be undertaken in 1774. Doctrinal questions also took on a greater prominence: with the appointment in 1776 of Hugh Anderson as minister, an evangelical minority seceded to form an Independent church in Liverpool (see (122)), leaving the chapel in the possession of a declining congregation and with, eventually, a Unitarian ministry. The chapel, formerly held by successive ministers as tenants at will, was placed in trust for Protestant Dissenters in 1827.

Toxteth Chapel, built in or about 1618, was greatly altered in 1774 when the outer walls were partly rebuilt and heightened. In 1841 a schoolhouse, which stood at the NW end, was superseded by the present porch and organ loft. The original building comprised a nave and chancel, of which the chancel arch is the principal remaining feature; at an early date the chancel was probably converted to a schoolhouse, which was itself rebuilt c.1795.

The chapel has walls of coursed sandstone and the roof, covered with stone slates, is surmounted at the SE end by a hexagonal wooden bell-cote. The SE wall is gabled and has a small porch of c.1918 covering the original entrance; above the porch is a round-arched window of 1774 and a circular recess in the gable. The SW wall facing Park Road was entirely rebuilt in 1774, but some of the stone quoins at each end, particularly to the NW, date from the original building. Two round-arched windows flank the pulpit with two similar windows immediately above; all have external wooden shutters. The NE wall, also largely of 1774, has two lower windows with stone lintels, one inscribed in recent times with the date 1650, and two round-

arched windows above. The NW annexe, entirely of 1841, has at the NW end two round-arched doorways, one false, and a range of three narrow windows below a gable.

The interior (25¾ft by 30¾ft) has in the NW wall a 12ft-wide two-centred arch of a single chamfered order which opened to the former chancel. In the roof space above the chapel and annexe the line of the original lower roofs remains visible on the wall above the chancel arch. The former chancel and its successor continued to be used for burials until 1835; some of the floorslabs are reset in the annexe which now forms the principal entrance and encloses a staircase to the gallery. The body of the chapel was realigned in the late 17th century with the pulpit centrally against the SW wall. The galleries were erected at various dates. The earliest gallery, at the SE end facing the chancel arch, dates from the mid 17th century or earlier and is supported by two acutely curved beams; before 1774 this gallery was approached by an external staircase against the SE wall. A corresponding NW gallery was added c.1700 and was formerly approached by a wooden staircase within the schoolhouse. A cross-gallery on the NE side was added c.1774 or later. All the galleries have fielded-panelled fronts above a bolection-moulded frieze and are supported by wooden columns. The roof is carried by two king-post trusses of 1774.

Fittings – *Bell*: formerly in bell-cote (loose in chapel 1978) dated 1751, unsigned but probably by Luke Ashton of Wigan.

EDWARD ASPINWALL OF TOCKSTETH PARKE ESQUIRE DEPARTED THIS LIFE IN MARCH THE TWENTIE NINTH A:D:1656

IT IS SOWNE A NATVRALL IT IS RAISED A SPIRITVALL BODY THERE IS A NATVRALL AND THERE IS A SPIRITVALL BODY FOR THIS CORRVPTIBLE MVST PVT ON INCORRVPTION AND THIS MORTALL MVST PVT ON IMMORTALITY SO WHEN THIS CORRVPTIBLE SHALL HAVE PVT ON INCORRVPTION AND THIS MORTALL SHALL HAVE PVT ON IMMORTALITY THEN SHALL BE BROVGHT TO PASSE THE SAYING THAT IS WRITTEN DEATH IS SWALLOWED VP IN VICTORY: I COR: CHAP: XV: VERSE: XLIV LIII:LIV:

The Ancient Chapel of Toxteth.   (118)

Brass: from floorslab, reset on SW wall, Edward Aspinwall, 1656. *Clock*: on front of NE gallery, late 18th-century. *Monuments* and *Floorslabs*. *Monuments*: on SW wall (1) Alice, widow of John Kennion, 1813, signed 'B. Baker'; (2) John Kennion, husband of the last, Collector of the Customs in Liverpool, 1785, with shield-of-arms; (3) Daniel Mather, 1782, *et al.*, brass tablet erected 1852; (4) Eliza, daughter of Dr Matthew Dobson, 1778, with Latin inscription. On NW wall (5) Jeremiah Horrox, 1641, 'the first to observe the Transit of Venus across the Sun's Disc', erected 1891. On NE wall (6) George Perry, merchant of Liverpool, 1771, Lydia [?Anne] his widow, 1801, and Peter Lacroy, her father, 1788, with shield-of-arms. On SE wall (7) Hugh Pringle, 1755, and Ursilla Ann Pringle, 1757, children of Hugh and Ursilla Pringle, Hugh Pringle, 1784, and Dorothy his widow, 1804. On SE gallery staircase (8) George Brown, 1839, Elizabeth his wife, 1832, and Thomas their son, 1860; (9) Rev. Robert Lewin, minister of Benns Garden Chapel, 1825, Mary his wife, 1816, three children, Mary Flanders, their servant, *et al.* In NE vestibule, (10) Joseph Brooks Yates F.S.A., 1855, and Margaret his wife, 1854. In burial-ground, monuments of 18th century and later include, SE of chapel (11) Edward Webster, 1738, and John Webster, 1764; (12) Hannah, wife of Edward Webster, 1830, *et al. Floorslabs*: in chapel (1) uninscribed, with indent of brass (see above) to Aspinwall, 1656; (2) Rev. John Brekell, 1769; (3) Richard Hampson, 1743; (4) Alice, widow of James Lawton, 1751 (or 1754); (5) John Haven, 1773; (6) Richard Hampson, merchant, 1743. At foot of NW staircase, reset upright from floor of schoolhouse (7) Thomas Whitfield, 1720, Alice his widow, 1735, their daughters Mary, wife of John Rigby, 1751, Margaret, widow of Nathaniel Litherland, 1769, *et al.*; (8) Peter Kennion, 1788, Elizabeth (Walker) his wife, 1782, their daughters Hannah, 1827, Elizabeth, 1835, *et al.*

Pulpit: with panelled front and back-board, late 18th-century. *Seating*: Box-pews throughout, mostly late 18th-century but incorporating some earlier material including pew door SE of pulpit inscribed DM 1650, perhaps for Daniel Mather, and pew door in NW gallery dated 1700. *Stair*: to pulpit, with flat shaped balusters, 18th-century.

Davis, V. D., *Some Account of the Ancient Chapel of Toxteth Park, Liverpool... 1618 to 1883...* (1884). Evans (1897) 139–41. Halley (1869) I: 244–51. *HSL & CT* LXXXVII (1936) 23–57. Nightingale VI (1893) 66–110: *UHST* III (1923–6) 412–14; V (1931–4) 351–83.

(119) STRICT BAPTIST, Shaw Street (SJ 358911). The church recently meeting in Shaw Street is the oldest Baptist congregation in Liverpool, where some evidence exists for meetings of this denomination from 1665. The present society, which until 1714 was attached to the older cause at Hill Cliff, APPLETON, Cheshire (8), dates its origin to 1700 in which year 'the house of Daniell ffabius alias Beanes practizer in Phisick Scituate in Everton in the County of Lancs' was registered for dissenters. Dr Fabius (or Fabeus) subsequently built a small meeting-house in Everton and in 1707 gave land there for a burial-ground. The chapel at Everton was registered 12 July 1714 and occupied until 1722, but the small burial-ground remained in use until 1825 when the adjacent public cemetery or 'Necropolis', now Grant Gardens (SJ 361914), was opened. In 1869 the old burial-ground, where Daniel Fabius was buried in 1718, was utilized as the site of 'Fabius Chapel' for a new Baptist cause, a proceeding strongly condemned by Picton ((1873) II: 400); this chapel has since been demolished.

In 1722 a new chapel was built at the S end of Byrom Street, on the E side close to the present junction with William Brown Street. A secession in 1747–8 led by the minister John Johnson resulted in the formation of a separate sect of 'Johnsonian' Baptists. The chapel was enlarged in 1773 shortly after the arrival as pastor of the notable hymn-writer Samuel Medley, whose successful ministry eventually occasioned the erection of a larger chapel 250 yards N in 1789. The older building, which then became 'St. Stephen's Church', was demolished in 1871.

Strict Baptist chapel, Shaw Street, Liverpool. (119)

On Medley's death in 1799 disputes arose over the appointment of a new pastor resulting in the establishment of separate societies in 'Lime Street Chapel' (subsequently Myrtle Street), and in Stanley Street where the former Johnsonian chapel was reoccupied. The major division in the church, however, came in 1839 when the pastor, C. M. Birrell, unsuccessfully attempted to introduce open communion and removed with a great number of supporters to Pembroke Chapel. In 1846 the surviving members were obliged to sell the Byrom Street chapel to the London and North-Western Railway Company who intended tunnelling below it, although as Byrom Hall it later reverted to use by another Baptist congregation.

The chapel in Shaw Street which was then built was opened 25 December 1847. Picton ((1873) II: 396) says that 'it is almost an exact reproduction of the Church of St. Matthias... Great Howard Street', built in 1834, and demolished in 1848. The walls are of red brick with stone dressings and the roof is slated. The front is of three bays with a pediment supported by pilasters; in the centre bay two tall unfluted Ionic columns *in antis* flank a recessed porch, and in each side bay is a single window with moulded architrave and cornice. The side walls are of five bays with tall windows divided at mid height, and lower windows to a basement school-room below the chapel.

The interior has a single rear gallery only, a complete set of original box-pews with central table pew and baptistery below, and a free-standing octagonal wooden pulpit on stem. (Proposed conversion to social use, 1992)

Fittings were reported to include an oil painting of Samuel Medley, his former pulpit now in the vestry, and a chair.

Paul (1961) 185–210. Picton (1873) II: *passim*. Sellers, Ian, *Salute to Pembroke* (1960). Sellers, Ian, *A History of Liverpool Baptists*, II: *The Minor Churches* (1962). *HSL & CT* IV (1852) 178–82; V (1853) 23–6. Whitley (1913) *passim*.

(120) TOXTETH TABERNACLE, Park Road (SJ 356886). Large polychrome brick Baptist chapel built 1870–1 for a new

congregation formed by the popular preacher W. P. Lockhart.
Whitley (1913) 242.

(121) CATHOLIC APOSTOLIC, Catherine Street (SJ 357895). 'The
Church of the Holy Apostles' is said by Picton to have been
'commenced in 1840, when the eastern portion was erected', but
the building was not completed until 1856 when the much
simplified plans of E. Trevor Owen, possibly associated with
G. B. Nicholls, were adopted. The original design, for which the
architect is not known, was for a cruciform church in the
Decorated style with E and W arms each of four bays, N and S
aisles, a polygonal apse and ambulatory to the E, short transepts
and a central tower and spire at the crossing. Of this ambitious
scheme only the work E of the crossing was completed. The
walls are of yellow sandstone and the roof is covered with slates.
The N and S bays of the aisles and clerestory have each one
pointed-arched window of three lights with cusped tracery; the
windows of the apse and ambulatory are of two lights. The bays
are divided by stepped buttresses with flying buttresses above the
aisles. The ambulatory is divided from the apse by an arcade of
two-centred arches above which and continuing along the N and
S sides is a miniature triforium. The chancel roof is supported by
hammer-beam trusses; the aisles and ambulatory are covered by
ribbed stone vaults.

The transepts, which appear to follow the general pattern of
the original design, have N and S windows of five lights with
tracery and a wide doorway to the south. The nave is of four bays
without aisles or clerestory, with a small tower adjacent to the S
transept which rose to an octagonal stone turret (removed
c.1971–4). The gabled W front is divided by stepped buttresses
with pinnacles and has a window of five lights above a central
doorway. Vestries and a small hall were built N of the chancel in
the late 19th century.

The fittings of the chancel represent the full development of
Catholic Apostolic worship and so must post-date the original

The Catholic Apostolic Church, Liverpool.
Window in ambulatory.   (121)

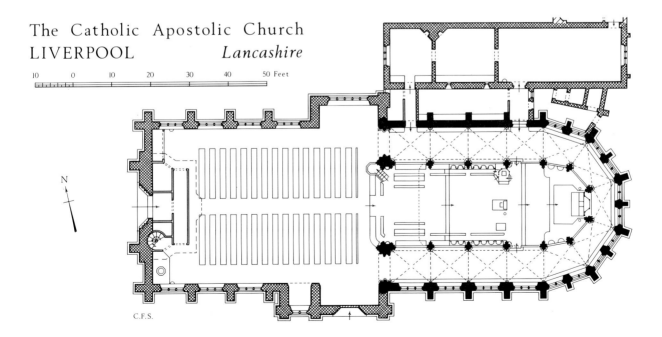

The Catholic Apostolic Church
LIVERPOOL   *Lancashire*

10   0   10   20   30   40   50 Feet

N

C.F.S.

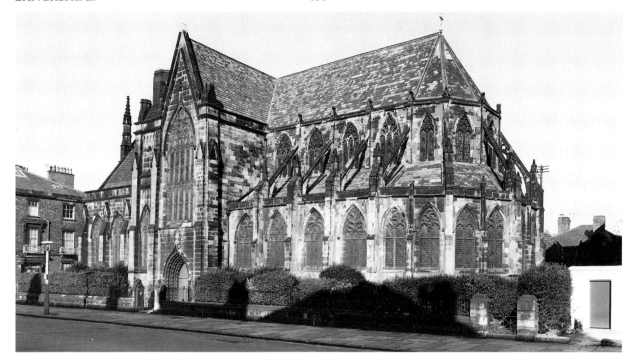

The Catholic Apostolic Church, Liverpool. (121)

building by several years. These include a stone altar with gilded Gothic tabernacle below an elaborately carved octagonal canopy flanked by standards for oil lamps, a hanging lamp in front of the altar and at the entrance to the sanctuary a hanging lamp of seven branches. N and S of the chancel are thirteen clergy stalls, the W pair with desks supported by kneeling angels. On the N side is the Angel's seat, a wooden canopied throne in front of which on the central axis is a prayer desk with adjacent lamp, and to the S the table of Prothesis. In the lower choir W of the sanctuary steps are the seats for deacons and choir, a lectern and stone pulpit. At the W end of the nave is a small organ gallery. The font, in the SW corner, is octagonal with traceried panels around the bowl.

Glass: the windows of the aisles, ambulatory and clerestory are filled with contemporary stained glass in kaleidoscopic patterns with linear borders and intermediate bosses of semi-floral or geometrical character. Incorporated in the windows of the ambulatory were five roundels of 15th-century Flemish glass, of which only three and part of a fourth survive. (Chapel severely damaged by arson 1986, fittings destroyed)

Picton (1873) II: 296.

(122) NEWINGTON CHAPEL, Renshaw Street (SJ 351902). The chapel was built in 1777 for the orthodox section of the congregation of Toxteth Chapel (118) following the appointment of Hugh Anderson as minister there in 1776. In 1811 the majority

of the congregation removed to a new chapel in Great George Street (*see* (123)) but Newington Chapel continued as a Congregational chapel until *c*.1871–2, when it was sold to German Lutherans. It passed into secular use in 1931 and was demolished *c*.1950. The chapel originally faced S towards Cropper Street, but in 1820 a new entrance was made towards Renshaw Street and a new N front built with traceried windows and a battlemented parapet; the earlier N gable behind the new front was dated 1777.

HSL & CT V (1853) 3–7; LXXXVI (1935) 63–8. Nightingale VI (1893) 139–56. Picton (1873) II: 271–2.

(123) Former CONGREGATIONAL, Great George Street (SJ 352 896). The first chapel on this site was built in 1811–12 for the congregation from Newington Chapel under the popular minister Thomas Spencer, who died from drowning before it was completed. Under his successor, Thomas Raffles, the congregation greatly increased and following the destruction by fire of the first chapel in 1840 the present much larger and more elaborate building was erected. This is a building of stone, designed by Joseph Franklin, the Corporation Surveyor, and comprises a large rectangular auditorium with a circular entrance lobby at the NE end. This last is surrounded externally by a ring of Corinthian columns and surmounted by a domed lantern. The side walls are divided by a giant order of Corinthian pilasters.

Former Congregational chapel, Great George Street.   (123)

Former Congregational chapel, Great George Street. (123)

Adjacent to the SE is a vestry wing added *c*.1870–80.

The interior (approximately 90ft by 60ft) has a coffered ceiling with blind central dome. There is a continuous gallery supported by cast-iron columns and upper galleries at each end with open balustraded fronts supported by cast-iron brackets. There are basement rooms below the chapel. (Chapel closed 1967 and converted to recreational use) .

Fittings – *Clock*: on front of NE gallery, signed 'T. Condliff, Liverpool'. *Model*: architect's plaster model with external detail only, 1840 (missing since 1967). *Monuments*: in NE lobby (1) Thomas Raffles D.D., Ll.D., 49 years minister, 1863; (2) James Kirkman Nuttall, 9 years pastor, 1900; (3) Rev. Thomas Spencer, 1811, signed 'W. Spence, L'pool'. *Organ*: in SW gallery, with classical case, *c*.1840. *Pulpit*: elaborately scrolled and enriched, *c*. 1840, enlarged. *Railings*: externally, cast-iron by Weber & Co., Liverpool. *Sculpture*: in lobby, white marble bust of Thomas Raffles. *Seating*: plain backs, scrolled ends, *c*.1900 refitting.

Nightingale VI (1893) 156–63. Picton (1873) II: 330–1. *HSL & CT* V (1853) 7–9.

(124) CONGREGATIONAL, Hunters Lane, Wavertree (SJ 391892). Built 1838–9 for a newly formed congregation, enlarged to front and galleries built 1868, repaired 1875. Sandstone with tall lancet windows to original part; bell-cote above front entrance, bell removed.

EM NS XVII (November 1839) 550. Nightingale VI (1893) 211–12.

(125) METHODIST CENTRAL HALL, Renshaw Street (SJ 352902). The first Methodist chapel in Liverpool, built in 1750 in Pitt Street, was rebuilt in 1803 and has long been demolished. A second chapel, on the N side of Mount Pleasant, NE of Central Hall, was built in 1790; in 1875, on the formation of the Liverpool Wesleyan Mission, it took the name 'Central Hall', continuing in this use until 1905 when the present Central Hall was opened; it was demolished *c*.1960–70. The Central Hall, a building of brick and terracotta, by Bradshaw and Gass, stands on the site of a Presbyterian chapel, latterly Unitarian, which had been built in 1811 and was sold following the removal of the congregation to Ullet Road in 1899 (*see* (130)).

Burial-ground of former chapel, NE of Hall, now public garden: columnar cenotaph erected 1905.

Picton (1873) II: 239. Rhind, J., *Unitarian Chapel, Renshaw Street, Liverpool* (1903). *HSL & CT* V (1853) 46–7. VCH *Lancs.* IV (1911) 49.

Former Wesleyan chapel, Great Homer Street, Liverpool. (126)

St Andrew's Church of Scotland, Liverpool.   (129)

(126) Former WESLEYAN, Great Homer Street (SJ 352917). Built 1839–40 to replace a chapel of *c*.1798 in Leeds Street, which was then demolished. The chapel (in use 1971 as 'Rydal Youth Centre') is of brick and stone; the broad ashlar front of seven bays has a five-bay pediment and recessed porch with two columns *in antis*. The interior, which had a gallery around three sides, was subdivided by an inserted floor, possibly in the late 19th century.

Picton (1873) II: 47, 420. *HSL & CT* V (1853) 47–8.

(127) Former WESLEYAN, Chapel Road, Garston (SJ 402848). Now part of Roman Catholic school. Built as 'Heald Chapel', 1837; long low building with rendered walls and broad five-bay front with four-centred arched windows and moulded labels.

(128) Former WELSH CALVINISTIC METHODIST, Burlington Street (SJ 344917). Built *c*.1840, sold to Congregationalists from Crescent Chapel 1859 for a mission hall (in use 1971 as a social club). Brick with ashlar front of five bays, three centre bays recessed with two Ionic columns to upper stage, rusticated lower stage obscured by a recent extension in common brick.

Nightingale VI (1893) 184–5.

(129) ST ANDREW'S, Presbyterian Church of Scotland, Rodney Street (SJ 354900). Scottish Presbyterians erected their first chapel in 1792–3 in Oldham Street; in 1823 the congregation divided over the choice of a minister, an appointment vested in the shareholders, and the majority of the seatholders left to form a separate society 'in strict connexion with the Church of Scotland'. The chapel which they then built in Rodney Street was designed by John Foster junior and opened in December 1824.

The body of the chapel has plain rendered walls with two tiers of round-arched windows. The front, of much greater elaboration, is of ashlar with two Ionic columns *in antis* between end bays which rise to domed classical pavilions above the two gallery staircases. The interior has a gallery around three sides supported by cast-iron columns with Doric capitals, continuing above as Corinthian columns to support the longitudinal valleys of the triple roof. The seating in the body of the chapel was renewed in the late 19th century; most of the gallery seating has been removed. (Chapel closed before 1974, severely damaged by fire November 1983)

St Andrew's Church of Scotland, Liverpool.
Interior of tower.   (129)

Monuments: in chapel (1) Harry Gordon, 1843; (2) George Campbell, merchant, 1836. In burial-ground (3) William Mackenzie, railway contractor, 1851, granite pyramid erected 1868.

HSL & CT II (1850) 69–84, 229–31.

(130) UNITARIAN, Ullet Road (SJ 377885). The Presbyterian, latterly Unitarian, society which had met successively in chapels in Castle Hey, Benn's Garden, and Renshaw Street (*see* (125)), acquired the present site in 1896. The chapel, opened 18 June 1899, and designed by Thomas and Percy Worthington, principally the latter, is of red brick with sandstone dressings in a free Gothic style. The front wall faces S and has a raised panel at the apex of the gable with a canopied niche. The central doorway is set between two windows with decorated tracery and has a rose window above. The building comprises an aisled nave of seven bays, faced internally with sandstone, a vestibule to the S and a choir and polygonal sanctuary at the N end. A hall to the E built in 1902 is linked to the chapel by a corridor or 'cloister', on the N side of which is a library with pointed barrel-vaulted ceiling.

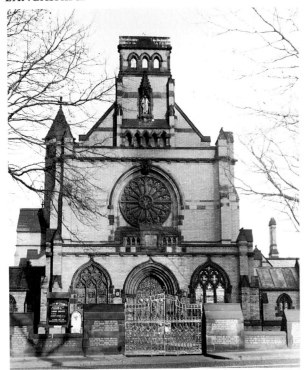

Unitarian chapel, Ullet Road, Liverpool.　　(130)

Fittings – *Books*: in library, include *bible*, printed by John Field, 1658, and Matthew Henry's *Exposition of the New Testament*, 2 vols. (1737). *Doors*: in S doorway and side entrances of vestibule, faced with beaten copper, by Richard Rathbone. *Font*: oak, hexagonal, elaborately carved with winged angels and on the cover a trinity of cherubim supporting a metal cross, 1906, by Ronald P. Jones. *Glass*: in sanctuary, by Morris & Co. *Lighting Fittings*: in nave, electroliers, *c*.1900.

Monuments: in 'cloister', removed from Renshaw Street Chapel (1) Robert Preston, 1833; (2) William Roscoe, 1831, erected 1856, with white marble bust; (3) Joseph Blanco White, 1841; (4) Charles Beard, minister, 1888; (5) John Hamilton Thorn, minister, 1894, and Hannah Mary his wife, 1872; (6) Edward Roscoe, 1834, and Margaret his widow, 1840, signed 'I. Gibson, Rome'; (7) William Caldwell Roscoe, 1859; (8) William Rathbone, 1868, signed 'J. H. Foley, R.A., London 1874'; (9) William Durning, 1830, and Jane his wife, 1830; (10) Henry Booth, 1869, 'whose vigorous capacity and varied ingenuity [is] fittingly commemorated by the railroad system of this kingdom'.

Paintings: in library and vestry, fresco ceiling paintings of the Pursuit of Truth and the Cardinal Virtues, by Gerald Moira, 1902. *Plate*: includes two cups of 1755.

Holt, A., *Walking Together: A Study in Liverpool Nonconformity (1688–1938)* (1938). Jones, R. P., *Memories of the Origin, and Building of Ullet Road Church, Liverpool* (1896–1899) (pamphlet, nd).

(131) GATEACRE CHAPEL (SJ 427877). A society of Protestant Dissenters was meeting at Gateacre by 1690, in which year both Thomas Collins, who received a grant of £8 from the

Presbyterian Fund, and Thomas Crompton, formerly of Toxteth Chapel, were holding services. The chapel, built in 1700, was registered without denominational name, and although a more rigid Presbyterian attachment was intended by a trust deed drawn up in 1787 specifically excluding 'Quakers, Anabaptists, Independents, Methodists and any other religious sect whatsoever', this was never ratified and the cause thereafter became effectively Unitarian.

The chapel has walls of red sandstone and a modern roof covered with green slate. It was much altered during the 19th century, particularly in 1885, when the roof and the bell-cote at the W end were renewed. The walls were raised by about 3ft, possibly in the early 18th century when the W gallery was inserted. The E and W walls are gabled; in the W wall is a round-arched doorway, set asymmetrically, with three altered or inserted windows above. In the N wall are two windows with heightened segmental-arched heads flanking the original site of the pulpit. In the S wall are three windows, formerly of three mullioned lights, but all now altered with arched heads, two raised higher. A vestry was added at the E end in 1872. The roof structure of 1885 was further altered or replaced during a subsequent renovation completed in 1954.

The interior (29¾ft by 42¼ft) was reseated in 1863 and later. The pulpit, moved to the E end in the mid 19th century, is now set in the NE corner. The gallery across the W end has a fielded-panelled front above a moulded entablature without original intermediate supports.

Fittings – *Bell*: one, in bell-cote, reported to be inscribed 'come away, make no delay. A. R. 1723', by Abraham Rudhall II. *Door*: in W doorway, two hinged leaves, 18th-century. *Monuments* and *Floorslabs*. *Monuments*: in chapel (1) William Shepherd Ll.D., 56 years minister, 1847, with marble bust; (2) Thomas Fletcher, 1850, Anna his wife, 1835, *et al.*, erected 1897; (3) Thomas Rodick, 1855, his wives Ann (Fell), 1816, and Judith (Preston), 1834, and nine children, with bust. *Floorslab*: in front of former site of pulpit (1) James Whittle, minister, 1702. *Plate*: includes a two-handled gadrooned cup of 1704, bought 1746, also a pair of two-handled cups of 1762 from the Kay Street meeting-house, Liverpool. *Pulpit*: octagonal, fielded-panelled sides with shaped tops, moulded base and cornice, early 18th-century.

Evans (1897) 92–3. Nightingale VI (1893) 192–207. Thornley, J. L., *Gateacre Chapel, Bicentenary Celebration . . .* (1900). *UHST* VI (1935–8) 380.

FRIENDS' MEETING HOUSE, CARTMEL　　　　CFS 1990

Congregational chapel (URC), Fairhaven. (133)

LOWER ALLITHWAITE   *Cumbria*

(132) FRIENDS, Cartmel (SD 383786). Built 1859 to supersede the meeting-house at Height (*see* (251)). Rendered stone walls with rusticated dressings. Gabled porch with dwarf buttresses and dated tablet above round-arched doorway. Interior with open rafter roof (ceiling inserted *c*.1970). Original fittings. Reputedly designed by Alfred Waterhouse.

Butler (1978) 135–6.

LYTHAM ST ANNE'S

(133) CONGREGATIONAL, Fairhaven (SD 347274). Built 1911–12 to designs by Briggs, Wolstenholme and Thornley for a church (now URC) which first met in 1903 at the house of Luke Walmsley. The walls are faced externally with white ceramic tiles. Square plan with shallow transepts, domed roof and ceiling, and tall domed campanile above the main entrance. The windows are filled with stained glass by Abbot & Co., designed by Charles Elliott, with representations of biblical scenes, figures of religious reformers and related subjects, to a scheme devised by Luke Walmsley.

CYB (1906) 185; (1912) 130–1. Mason, D. H., *Fair Domes of Fairhaven* . . . (1988). Walmsley, L. S., *Fighters and Martyrs for the Freedom of Faith* (1912).

(134) CONGREGATIONAL, Bannister Street, Lytham (SD 368273). Gothic with corner turret and spire, 1861–2 by Poulton and Woodman. (URC)

CYB (1862) 310–11; (1863) 291–3.

(135) WESLEYAN, Park Road, Lytham (SD 365273). Stone front dated 1868 with two giant Corinthian columns *in antis* between end bays. Enlarged 1901.

MANCHESTER

(136) CROSS STREET CHAPEL (SJ 839983). The chapel standing on the E side of Cross Street was built in 1959 to replace a chapel on the same site which suffered war damage in December 1940 and was subsequently demolished.

The Presbyterian society, which since the late 18th century has supported Unitarian doctrines, owes its origin to the work of Henry Newcome, preacher at the collegiate church from 1656 until 1660, who was licensed under the 1672 Indulgence as a preacher at his own house and in a barn at Coldhouse; several other ejected ministers are also named as having taken out

Cross Street Chapel, Manchester. In 1942.   (136)

licences in Manchester at this date. In 1687 Newcome was preaching in the house of Mr Barlow and later in Thomas Stockton's barn.

The present site, described as 'part of a parcel of land commonly called Plungen's Meadow', was acquired in 1693 and the new meeting-house opened 24 June 1694. It had a gallery at the N end erected by two members of the congregation who were reimbursed by the proceeds from pew rents. On 10 June 1715 the building was sacked by a Jacobite mob which destroyed all the internal fittings but left the outer walls standing. It was repaired and reinstated with the assistance of a government grant of £1,500 and reopened 8 May 1716.

The chapel, which had brick walls with stone dressings, was originally approximately square on plan with a frontage of 60ft. The W front of three bays had a central pedimented doorcase and a Venetian window above. The N wall was of five bays with two tiers of windows and a central doorway with rusticated surround. The pulpit was against the S wall and galleries were on the other three sides. In 1788 a further bay was added to the S which included a fourth gallery behind the pulpit. In 1798 an organ was placed in the S gallery. Considerable internal alterations were made in 1864 when the chapel was reseated, the pulpit lowered, the S gallery removed and a larger organ erected, and a doorway on the W side of the S extension replaced by a window.

Fittings – *Chandeliers*: five, brass, gift of Thomas Butterworth (destroyed 1940). *Monuments*: some ledger stones of 18th century and later remain in the burial-ground. *Plate*: includes a set of three cups, three footed plates and a flagon, all 1718, given by N. Gaskell, one cup and flagon of 1752, and one two-handled cup of 1789.

Baker, T., *Memorials of a Dissenting Chapel . . .* (1884). Evans (1897) 165–7. Johnson, H. H., *Cross Street Chapel, Manchester . . .* (1922). Macartney, M. (ed.), *Practical Exemplar of Architecture* (6 ser., 1928) Pls. 46, 47. Nightingale, V (1893) 81–107. Wade, R., *The Rise of Nonconformity in Manchester . . .* (1880).

(137) CHRIST CHURCH, Every Street (SJ 857980). The chapel was built in 1823 by James Scholefield, a disciple of the Rev. William Cowherd, minister of the (Swedenborgian) New Church in Peter Street, who had separated from that denomination in 1809 to form a distinct society of 'Bible Christians' which then met in King Street, Salford. Scholefield was a former preacher at King Street who also practised medicine and supported the Chartist movement. The chapel appears to have become disused following the death of Scholefield in 1855 and the closure of the burial-ground, from which a considerable revenue had derived. In 1902 the chapel and adjacent house were bought by Manchester University Settlement for use as a youth club, which continued until *c*.1975. (By 1981 the house had been demolished but the shell of the chapel remained in a badly damaged state)

The chapel is a circular building (58ft in diameter) of brick with a conical slate roof. Above the original entrance on the SW side, now replaced by a window, is a stone tablet inscribed 'Christ Church erected Anno Domini MDCCCXXIII'. A corresponding doorway probably existed on the NE side. To the SE is a further doorway in a later porch. A house of two storeys

Christ Church, Every Street, Manchester.   (137)

and basement, contemporary in date with the chapel, adjoins the NW; side entrances between the house and chapel may be additions of *c*.1926–8. The interior has a plaster ceiling with central ceiling rose of the early 19th century, but was otherwise drastically refitted in 1926–8, at which period and subsequently the burial-ground to NE and SW was largely cleared of monuments.

Monuments: in NE burial-ground, reset against boundary wall (1) Andrew McConnochie, 1853; (2) William Appleyard, 1846. (A 'large obelisk' to 'Orator Hunt', erected 1842, and another to some of the committee responsible for its erection, have both long disappeared.) In front of house (3) Rev. James Scholefield, 1855, 'Minister of the Society of Bible Christians 42 years and the founder of Christ Church Every Street', Charlotte his wife, 1835, and their children George Frederick, 1835, James Cowherd, 1835, Marcus Henry, 1835, Amelia Rebecca, 1854, and John Daniel, 1855, upright slab.

Hindmarsh (1861) 145–8, 190–200. Stocks, M. D., *Fifty Years in Every Street: The Story of the Manchester University Settlement* (1945).

(138) Former CHRISTIAN SCIENCE, Victoria Park (SJ 857957). The 'First Church of Christ Scientist' in Daisy Bank Road, now used for educational purposes, was built in 1903 to designs by Edgar Wood. The walls are of brick with stone dressings, the front wall of the main block is rendered and the roofs are tiled.

Former Christian Science Church, Victoria Park,
Manchester.   (138)

The building comprises a tall preaching nave with passage aisles and shallow transepts approached between low splayed wings containing cloakrooms and a meeting-room; the gallery staircase is in a low drum tower to the right of the round-arched entrance. Some of the original fittings, also designed by the architect, including chairs and lectern, are now in the Whitworth Art Gallery, Manchester.

Nicholson and Spooner (c.1911) 246.

(139) Former CONGREGATIONAL, Cavendish Street (SJ 842970). The church formerly meeting here claimed descent from the first Independent church in Manchester, which was formed in 1753–6 in a Baptist meeting-house in Coldhouse and opened its first chapel in Cannon Street, formerly Hunters Croft, in 1761. The society divided in 1788; the majority of those who then remained at Cannon Street eventually removed in 1807 to a new chapel in Grosvenor Street, and in 1912 to 'Roby' Chapel, Dickenson Road, rebuilt 1975; a minority, who in 1807 retained possession of Cannon Street, built a new chapel in Chorlton Road in 1861. The seceders of 1788 built a chapel in Mosley Street from which in 1848 they removed to Cavendish Street.

Congregational chapel, Cavendish Street, Manchester.   (139)

Cavendish Street Chapel, built to accommodate the increased congregation attracted by the preaching of Dr R. S. McAll and Dr Robert Halley, is a large building of stone in the 13th-century Gothic style by Edward Walters of Manchester. It comprises a nave and aisles, with transepts, polygonal organ apse, and a tall corner tower with broach spire. The interior, 125ft in length, designed to accommodate '1,500 adults in pews and 600 children', has galleries above the aisles and an open timber roof. Behind the chapel is the former day school for 700 pupils with a hall on the upper floor. (Chapel demolished 1973–4).

Fittings – Glass: in principal window of NW front, naturalistic patterns of flowers and foliage with formal panels and inscribed scrolls, c.1848. Monuments: in chapel (1) Rev. Robert Stephens McAll Ll.D., 12 years pastor, 1838, inscribed sarcophagus-shaped tablet surmounted by Greek Doric column. In vestibule (2) Robert Spear, 1819; (3) Mary Newall, 1821; (4)

John Star Jones, 1833, and Sarah his widow, 1839; (5) John Wittenbury, 1805, and Alice his widow, 1810.

CYB (1849) 211–12. Nightingale V (1893) 107–32, 137–47.

(140) Former CONGREGATIONAL, Stockport Road, Longsight (SJ 865960). A congregation was formed in 1834 and the first chapel built in 1841. This was superseded by 'Ivy Chapel', built in 1853 to designs by Travis and Mangnall. The walls are of stone; the SW front has two octagonal turrets rising to crocketed spirelets flanking a three-bay triple-gabled arcade which originally formed an open loggia based, at some remove, on the W front of Peterborough Cathedral. The plan comprises an aisled nave of five bays including one-bay transepts and a rectangular organ apse. A gallery at the front has been removed; provision was also made for galleries above the aisles. (Demolished 1972)

Monument: Jonathan Sutcliffe F.S.A., 33 years minister at Albion Street Chapel, Ashton-under-Lyne, and 4 years here, 1859.

CYB (1854) 279; (1860) 208. Nightingale V (1893) 158–65.

(141) FRIENDS, Mount Street (SJ 838980). The present meeting-house, built in 1828–30 by Richard Lane, is the successor to buildings of 1693, 1732 and 1795. It is a large building of brick with a five-bay ashlar front; the three-bay centre has giant Ionic columns and a pediment. The interior, now greatly altered, formerly comprised two interconnected meeting-houses on the axis of the entrance, the larger at the rear being 58ft square with side galleries supported on cast-iron columns. The former burial-ground surrounding the meeting-house, in use from 1796 to 1856, has been entirely cleared of monuments.

Inscription: on door lintel in boundary wall to N '1828, Friends Meeting House'.

Foulds, E. V. et al., Mount Street, 1830–1930 (1930). Lidbetter (1961) Fig. 30 (plan).

Friends' meeting-house, Mount Street, Manchester.   (141)

(142) Former WESLEYAN, Grosvenor Street (SJ 848974). Large rectangular brick chapel with battlemented parapets, stone pinnacles and four-centred arched windows, built in 1820. In 1824 it became the head of the Manchester south circuit, said at the time to have been the wealthiest circuit in British Methodism. The society was disbanded in 1927 and the chapel has since been in commercial use. It was severely damaged by fire in 1974. It originally had galleries around three sides.

Former Wesleyan chapel, Grosvenor Street, Manchester.   (142)

Huddleston, J. H., *History of Grosvenor Street Wesleyan Chapel, Manchester 1820–1920* (1920).

(143) Former UNITARIAN, Upper Brook Street (SJ 848969). Unitarian seceders from Cross Street Chapel in 1789 built a chapel in Mosley Street from which they moved to the present building in 1839. This chapel, now used by Jehovah's Witnesses and previously by Welsh Baptists, is a stone building in a 13th-century Gothic style designed by (Sir) Charles Barry. It comprises a single preaching nave of seven bays divided externally by gabled buttresses with small square turrets at the corners and a tall deeply-recessed arch at the SW front embracing the entrance with a two-light traceried window above it. Inside the ceiling has a pointed barrel vault with moulded ribs; there is a small gallery next to the entrance and passage galleries at each side which may be of later date. (Interior reported subdivided since 1971)

Fittings – *Glass*: in NE window, representation of Christ and the twelve apostles. *Inscription*: on stone tablet reset internally, from chapel in Granby Road, 'Welsh Baptist Meeting House Erected 1835'. *Monuments*: in burial-ground (1) Emily Adele, daughter of John James and Hannah Taylor, 1839, *et al.*; (2) Rev. Abraham Bennett, 1846, and Esther his widow, 1850; (3) Rev. William Turner, nearly 6 years minister of Hanover Square Chapel, Newcastle upon Tyne, 1859, and Anne his daughter, 1850. *Organ*: by Alex. Young and Sons, Manchester.

Davis, E. W., *Our Church's Origin, Upper Brook Street Free Church and Sunday School* (1915). Evans (1897) 172.

Former Unitarian chapel, Upper Brook Street, Manchester.   (143)

Former Unitarian chapel, Upper Brook Street, Manchester. (143)

(144) Site of BLACKLEY CHAPEL (SD 852030). The chapel, first built in 1697, repaired after damage in the Sacheverell riots of 20 June 1715, and rebuilt in 1884 by the then Unitarian congregation, has been demolished. Some late 18th-century ledger stones and other *monuments* remain in the burial-ground on the W side of Chapel Lane.

Booker, J., *History of Blackley Chapel* (1854). Evans (1897) 22–3. Nightingale V (1893) 27–37.

(145) GORTON CHAPEL (SJ 889959). Although the early history of the dissenting congregation (now Unitarian) is obscure, there is some evidence for their occasional use of the chapel-of-ease in the years after 1662. The first Protestant Dissenters' chapel at Gorton was built *c.*1703 and stood on a site SE of the present building, bounded on N and W by a brook and on the SE by Far Lane. This was a rectangular building of stone with a vestry or cottage wing at one side; above the entrance at one end was a plain Venetian window.

The former chapel was superseded in 1869–71 by a new building, 'Brookfield Church', which stands on higher ground adjoining Hyde Road. This is a large Gothic building of stone in the 14th-century style by Thomas Worthington and largely paid for by Richard Peacock M.P. of Gorton Foundry. It comprises a chancel, nave, N and S aisles with organ chamber N of the chancel and vestry to the S, and a tower of four stages with broach spire on the N side above the principal entrance. The nave arcades of six bays are supported by polished granite columns.

Fittings – *Bells*: in tower, eight. *Font*: dated 1891. *Monuments*: in present chapel (1) Martha, wife of John Wilson, 1850; (2) George Grimshaw, 1807, *et al.*; (3) John Grimshaw, 1861; (4) George Worthington, 1828, and Bridget his widow, 1846; (5) Rev. George Henry Wells, 44 years minister, 1888. Externally on N wall of organ chamber (6) Richard Peacock, C.E., M.P., 1889, erected by the employees of Gorton Foundry. W of chapel, (7) Joseph Peacock, 1875, Richard Peacock, 1889, and Ralph Peacock, 1928, gabled Gothic aedicule of limestone and polished granite surmounted by angels blowing trumpets. In burial-ground surrounding site of former chapel, many slabs and other monuments of 18th century and later, including (8) Rev. William Dodge Cooper, 13 years minister, 1801. *Mounting Steps*: NE of chapel, including reused stone with date 1703. *Plate*: includes a pair of two-handled gadrooned cups of 1720.

Christian Freeman (January 1872), 9–11. Cottier, F., *The Story of Gorton Chapel and Brookfield Church 1703–1871–1953* (1953). Evans (1897) 167–8. Nightingale V (1893) 50–62.

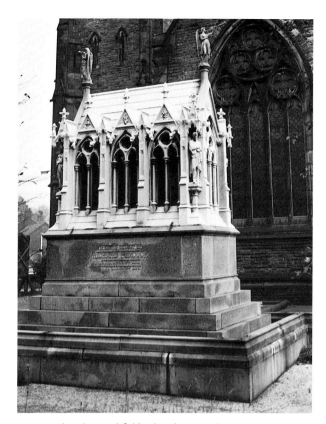

Gorton Chapel (Brookfield Church), Manchester.
Monument to Richard Peacock.   (145)

(146) PLATT CHAPEL (SJ 856945). A chapel-of-ease built at Birch in Rusholme in the late 16th century, and treated as a private chapel by the Birch family on whose estate it stood, served as a place of worship for Independents and Presbyterians and was licensed for their use in 1672 as 'A private oratory belonging to Thomas Birch Esqr. of Birch Hall'. It was registered as a meeting-house in 1689, but on the death of Thomas Birch in 1697 the dissenting congregation were dispossessed and met in temporary premises until the acquisition of the present site in 1699, described as 'part of a close known as Blake Flatt bounded on the south by the ancient Nico Ditch'. The first chapel, built 1699–1700, was replaced by the present building in 1790–91. It was altered by the then Unitarian congregation in 1874–6, when the N vestry was replaced by a small apse and a new vestry was built on the W side, the E entrance was blocked and a new doorway made at the S end; it was also partly refitted and re-roofed.

The chapel has walls of red brick and a slate roof. The E wall facing the road is of three bays with windows set in shallow arched recesses; the original doorway was in the S bay. On the W side the 'Worsley Chapel' of 1790–1 projects at the centre, and the later vestry adjoins to the south. The S wall was refenestrated in the late 19th century and is surmounted by a brick bell-cote of that period.

The interior (48ft by 30ft) has an original gallery at the S end with shaped front and lower dentil cornice. (Chapel closed

c.1972, since used by Manchester Amateur Photographic Society)

Fittings – Bell: in bell-cote, one, said to be dated 1718. Hatchment: in Worsley chapel, shield quartering the arms of Worsley of Platt. Monuments: in chapel on N wall (1) Godfrey Gottschalck, 1881, and Emma his wife, 1874, recording a bequest of £3,000, surmounted by a bust of Mrs Gottschalck; (2) William Robinson, 1832, Jane (Siddall) his widow, 1838, and Maria Robinson their niece, 1865; (3) Charles Schwind, 'drowned 1882 in the wreck of the Douro off Cape Finisterre'; (4) Eliza Leys, 1920, and Harold Schwind her son, 1873, brass; (5) Henry Finch, 1704 'one of the ejected ministers', modern tablet; (6) Joseph Willcox, 1897, brass. In burial-ground many ledger stones of early 18th century and later including (7) Obadiah Hulme, 1732/3; (8) Thomas Elcock, 1743/4. Plate: includes a shallow two-handled cup of 1641 and a florally ornamented two-handled cup of 1660. Pulpit: square with quarter-rounded fluted columns at front corners, late 18th-century.

Evans (1897) 169–71. Nightingale V (1893) 147–58. Swindells, E., *The History of Platt Chapel 1700–1950* (1950).

MIDDLETON

(147) CONGREGATIONAL, Market Place (SD 872061). 'Providence Chapel', of 1859–60 by James Simpson, has a pedimented front of four bays. The walls are of brickwork with stone dressings; the pediment has a polychrome frieze of blue, black and white brick. 'Providence School' of 1879, on adjacent site, replaces the former chapel of 1836 which had been converted in 1860 'to the uses of the Sunday schools, week-evening services, and lectures'. (URC)

CYB (1861) 268. Nightingale V (1893) 275–9.

(148) COUNTESS OF HUNTINGDON'S CONNEXION, High Street (SD 872065). The chapel, inscribed 'St. Stephen's 1824', is said to have originated with the work of the Rev. J.K. Foster. As Nightingale records that the Congregational church (*see* above) met from 1828 in a former chapel of the Countess's Connexion, continuous occupancy of this building may be in question. The plain brickwork of the side walls is of the early 19th century; the front was greatly altered c.1900.

CYB (1862), obituary of J.K. Foster.

(149) WESLEYAN, Long Street (SD 870061), on W side. The chapel, school and lecture-room, of 1899–1902 by Edgar Wood,

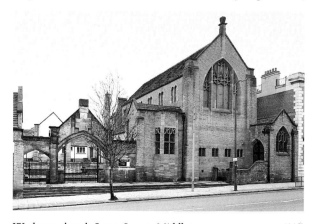

Wesleyan chapel, Long Street, Middleton.   (149)

Baptist chapel, Ogden.

(150)

stand around a courtyard which is approached through a segmental Gothic archway. The chapel, in header bond brickwork with minimal stone dressings, comprises an aisled nave and chancel separated by a chancel arch. The brickwork of the walls is exposed internally. Fittings which are contemporary with the building include – *Chairs*: pair, with tall inlaid backs. *Font*: circular bowl on polygonal support. *Lectern*: wood. *Pulpit*: stone with angel supporting desk.

Nicholson and Spooner (*c*.1911) 156–7.

MILNROW   *Greater Manchester*

(150) BAPTIST, Odgen (SD 952121). This congregation was commenced as an offshoot of the newly formed Baptist church in Rochdale and the first meeting-house was erected in 1783. A new chapel was built alongside the former in 1861–2, and the first building was replaced in 1897 by a larger Sunday-school which incorporated fragments of the 1783 meeting-house.

The first meeting house (30¾ft by 27¼ft) occupied the rear part of the present Sunday-school building; it had stone walls with round-arched windows having moulded imposts and keystones. The SW front was of four bays, probably with a central entrance represented by the existing basement doorway and two tiers of windows. The SE wall of four bays remains to its full height but has had an upper storey of matching windows added in 1897. The NW wall survives internally to a height of about 10ft and includes the remains of four windows similar to those described. In 1897 this building was heightened and extended to the NW. The former *bell-cote*, reset on the front gable, is of stone with eight short columns supporting an ogee top and ball finial.

The present chapel, adjacent to NE, has a gabled front of three bays with plain round-arched windows and a side wall of five bays. There is a continuous round-ended gallery and a rostrum pulpit opposite the entrance. (Demolished *c*.1972)

Monuments: in basement of Sunday-school (1) Abraham Hargreaves, 1846, *et al*. In burial-ground, monuments of late 18th century and after, including (2) Enoch Garside, 1863, *et al*. with footnote reference to adjacent stone.

Whitley (1913) 132–3, 273, 350.

(151) WESLEYAN, Rochdale Road (SD 924128). Ashlar front of five bays with round-arched upper windows. Opened 1860.

MOSSLEY

(152) METHODIST NEW CONNEXION, Market Place (SD 970 023). Chapel of 1834 rebuilt 1964. *Inscription*: tablet from Wyre Street Sunday-school reset externally, inscribed 'Methodist New Connexion Sabbath School for Children of all Denominations, built 1823 enlarged 1836'.

(153) UNITARIAN, Stamford Road (SD 973026). Low gabled front, two doorways with heavily rusticated arches and five-light window between. Tablet in gable 'Christian Church and Sunday School built 1852'.

NELSON

(154) WESLEYAN, Carr Road (SD 859378). The first chapel of 1826–7, which stood in Railway Street, was superseded by the present building in 1865 but continued in use as a Sunday-school until 1873. The chapel, dated 1864, has a pedimented front of four bays with altered entrances and two tiers of segmental-arched windows. The Sunday-school, free-standing to NW, of 1872–3 also has a pedimented front but with round-arched upper windows. The 'Wesleyan Peace Memorial Institute' in Cross Street is dated 1918.

Bentley, J., *This was Nelson* (1985).

(155) WESLEYAN, Southfield (SD 878368). The Methodist Society at Southfield may have originated in the work of William Darney, who resided here from 1768. William Sagar, of Southfield House, extended his hospitality to John Wesley on several occasions and in 1777 assisted in building the first Methodist Chapel in Colne (*see* (63)). The preaching-house at Southfield occupies part of a barn erected by Sagar in 1797 which is a traditional building of stone with a roof covered in stone slates. Centrally at the front is a tall segmental-arched opening with a small simple Venetian window above; to right and left are two tiers of windows, the upper ones also of a simple Venetian pattern. The keystone of the central arch is inscribed 'W & E SAGAR 1797'. The front half of the barn to the right of the entrance which forms the preaching-house is occupied on the lower floor by a Sunday-school room and by the meeting-room above, which extends with stepped seating above the barn entrance. Further accommodation comprising a vestry and scullery with storage space above was added to the E in the early 19th century, enclosing a stone staircase to the upper floor which may formerly have been external.

The interior (34¾ft by 13½ft at upper level) was much altered and refitted in the late 19th century; it appears to have had at an earlier date a small W gallery, part of the present upper floor being an insertion.

Moore (1899) 45–6, 213. *WHS, L & CJ* II (1970–4) 126–9. *Methodist Recorder* (1 May 1986).

(156) Former INDEPENDENT METHODIST, Scotland Road (SD 860379). 'Salem Chapel', 1892–3 by Thomas Bell of Burnley. Salem School adjacent dated 1800, reconstructed 1929.

(157) Former INDEPENDENT METHODIST, Barkerhouse Road (SD 864381). Dated 1885 in roundel of arched window above paired entrances.

NETHER WYERSDALE

(158) WESLEYAN, Scorton (SD 502487). In the early 19th century the Society received the support of George Fishwick who, with his brother, had established a mill in Scorton in 1809. The chapel, erected in 1842 by George Fishwick at his own expense, is an important example of a small patronage chapel. The walls are of ashlar with rusticated quoins and the roof is covered with blue slate. The E front of three bays is symmetrical with a rusticated porch between two round-arched windows each of three lights below a lunette. Three similar windows occupy the W wall and two, the lower lights now blocked, are in the S wall; the N wall is partly covered by a contemporary vestry. The N and S gables are surmounted by elaborate stone finials. A long panel over the entrance is inscribed 'WESLEYAN CHAPEL'.

The interior originally had a pulpit at the N end but the space has now been divided by a partition to form a small room at that

Wesleyan chapel, Scorton.   (158)

end. The seating rises on a stepped platform to the S which may be original.

Fittings – *Monument*: externally on E wall, left of porch, George Fishwick of Springfield, 1854, with long laudatory inscription. *Plate*: pair of cups, 1796, gift of George Fishwick, 1842.

Hewitson (1872) 524–5.

NEWTON-LE-WILLOWS

(159) CONGREGATIONAL, Crow Lane (SJ 586957). The first chapel on this site was converted for use as a Sunday-school following the erection of a new chapel in 1887–8 designed by W. & J. Hay of Liverpool. The latter was demolished *c*.1960–70 and the former has reverted to its original use.

The chapel, opened 12 May 1842, was designed by Sir James Picton. The walls are of red sandstone ashlar; the N front is gabled and has two entrances and a large rose window above. The side walls are each of five bays with tall lancets having cast-iron frames and iron panels at their base decorated with plain shields.

Monuments: in railed enclosure between front porches (1) Richard Evans of Haydock, 1864, *et al.*; in burial-ground (2) Richard Evans of Haydock, 1864, tall granite obelisk 'erected by his workmen as a memorial of their appreciation of him as a kind friend and Christian master'; (3) William Stevenson, 1844, *et al.*, table-tomb; (4) Rev. William Spencer Bell, 1861, dwarf obelisk.

Nightingale IV (1892) 144–50.

Congregational chapel, Crow Lane, Newton-le-Willows. (159)

OLDHAM   *Greater Manchester*

(160) CONGREGATIONAL, Greenacres (SD 949054). The church meeting here was gathered in the late 17th century by Robert Constantine, ejected curate of Oldham who, in 1672, took out a licence to preach 'in a thatched house at Greenacres'. In 1699 a house and barn were converted to a meeting-house which was partly destroyed in the Sacheverell riots of 21 June 1715, and subsequently repaired. This was replaced in 1784 by a new chapel

which had a bell-cote above the gabled front and two tiers of round-arched windows.

The present chapel, on the site of the former, was designed by R. Moffat Smith and built in 1854. It is cruciform on plan with lancet windows and a tower in one angle with corner pinnacles and flying buttresses supporting a central spirelet. An extensive burial-ground lies to the east.

Monuments: in burial-ground, principally of the 19th century, include (1) Rev. William James, 1788, and Rev. Robert Jinkinson, 1803, mid 19th-century replacement, a fragment of earlier stone is reset against S wall of chapel; (2) Anne, wife of Rev. John Detheridge Casewell, Baptist minister in Oldham, 1841; (3) Martha, wife of Rev. Thomas Brierley, pastor of Queen Street chapel, Oldham, 1844; (4) Rev. Joseph Galland, 38 years minister, 1843, Elizabeth his widow, 1856, and Robert their son, 1845; (5) James Wild, died '11th of October (O.S.) 1860', buried in burial-ground of the German Colony, Alexanderoffskey, St Petersburg, Alice his wife, 1843, and John Wild his nephew, 1891.

CYB (1855) 266–7. Nightingale V (1893) 230–45. Waddington, G.G., *A History of the Independent Church at Greenacres* (1854).

(161) CONGREGATIONAL, Union Street (SD 928049). The church, now URC, formed 1816, met from 1823 in a chapel in Queen Street. The present building of 1855 by R. Moffat Smith is of stone with a central tower having a wide arched entrance and six-light traceried window above. The tower is rectangular and was formerly surmounted by a small turret and crocketed spire, now removed. Galleried interior with cast-iron arcades; 'orchestra' gallery and organ with Gothic case behind site of pulpit.

Bridge, A. and Lee, G., *Centenary History of Queen Street Congregational Church* (1920). *CYB* (1856) 255. Nightingale V (1893) 245–51.

(162) Former WESLEYAN, Greenacres Road (SD 938052). Brick with stone dressings, pedimented front of four bays with two tiers of windows, the upper range with segmental pediments on brackets, paired entrances at centre. Built *c*.1860, by James Simpson. The original round-ended continuous gallery remains, supported by cast-iron columns. Former Wesleyan School of 1866 on adjacent site to E, by Edward Potts of Oldham. Both buildings are now in commercial use.

(163) INDEPENDENT METHODIST, George Street (SD 92390485). The society formed *c*.1805–6 built the present chapel in 1815–16. The building, of brick, comprises a galleried chapel with four tall windows in the front and rear walls and eight habitable basement rooms below with three original doorways to the rear. The chapel has side and rear galleries of the mid 19th century and box-pews of that period which probably replaced plain benches. (Closed August 1990)

Anon. *Centenary Souvenir of the Establishment of Independent Methodism in Oldham, 1816–1916* (1916).

OLD LAUND BOOTH

(164) INGHAMITE, Wheatley Lane (SD 839384). One of the societies formed by Benjamin Ingham after his separation from

Independent Methodist chapel, George Street, Oldham.　(163)

the Moravians was at Wheatley Lane, where the church claims to have been founded by Ingham on 1 May 1750. The chapel, said to have been built between 1747 and 1750, has stone walls and a roof covered in blue slates. A small cottage of two storeys was added at the NE end later in the 18th century and the whole building considerably enlarged to the NW in 1897.

The original structure has a long frontage to the SE with doorways in the end bays and four windows between, all with plain stone surrounds with round-arched heads, impost blocks and keystones. The gabled SW wall was rebuilt and extended to the NW in 1897.

The interior (originally $24\frac{1}{4}$ft by $60\frac{3}{4}$ft) was enlarged in 1897 by the addition of a two-bay aisle at the SW end of the NW side. The roof structure was also replaced at this date and the interior refitted.

Fittings – Collecting Shovels: two types, one with handle 20in. overall. *Cupboard*: in lower room of cottage, now vestry, NW of fireplace, with fluted angles and shaped door panel, mid 18th-century. *Monuments*: in chapel, William Hartley, 1822, *et al.*, signed 'Patteson, Manchester'; (2) Jonathan Hargreaves, 1805, and Jane his widow, 1828, with shield-of-arms, signed 'Webster's, Kendal'; (3) three children of Thomas and Nancy Hargreaves, 1812, 1814, 1818; (4) Lawrence Hargreaves, 1844, and Jane his wife, 1829, signed 'Patteson, Manchester'; (5) Robert Hargreaves, 1814, *et al.*, signed 'Webster's, Kendal'. In extensive burial-ground to S, monuments of 18th century and later, including (6) in paving next to SE wall, Ruth, wife of John Nutter, 1753. *Painting*: in vestry, on glass, exterior of chapel from SW, mid 19th-century. *Sundial*: on S corner, *c*.1800.

Thompson (1958) 94–7.

(165) WESLEYAN, Wheatley Lane (SD 831376), built 1824, rebuilt or enlarged 1863, 1867. School 1859.

Moore (1899) 159–62.

ORMSKIRK

(166) Former PRESBYTERIAN, Chapel Street (SD 416081). A society which dated its origin to the ejection of the vicar, Nathaniel Heywood, in 1662, built a meeting-house on this site

in 1696 which was superseded in 1783 by a chapel in Aughton Street, sold by Unitarian trustees *c.*1890 and since demolished. The earlier building, which stood on the W side of the street S of the Congregational chapel, is believed to have survived until *c.*1969.

Evans (1897) 195–6. Nightingale IV (1892) 180–96. VCH *Lancs.* III (1907) 264.

(167) CONGREGATIONAL, Chapel Street (SD 416082). Opened 1834. Brown brick with stone dressings and low pitched slate roof. Three-bay gabled front with stone finial and porch between two tall windows with moulded four-centred arched heads. Contemporary gates and railings next to street.

Nightingale IV (1892) 198–205.

CONGREGATIONAL CHAPEL, ORMSKIRK CFS 1971

(168) Former WESLEYAN, Chapel Street (SD 416081). Built 1810, brick with round-arched windows in side walls, front concealed. Superseded 1878 by 'Emmanuel', Derby Street (SD 417083).

ORRELL   *Greater Manchester*

(169) CONGREGATIONAL (SD 530043). 'Salem Chapel' built 1824, largely rebuilt 1905; original date tablet reset in back wall.

Inscription: on square tablet reset in front boundary wall 'I W M 1710'. *Monuments:* in burial-ground (1) Mary Maria Jones, 1840; (2) Ellen Bibby, 1852, *et al.*

Nightingale IV (1892) 37–44.

OSWALDTWISTLE

(170) BAPTIST, New Lane (SD 734269). 1878 by George Baines, free Renaissance with tall pilasters and open pediment. (Destroyed by fire 1987) *Monument:* in vestibule, Joseph Harbottle, pastor, 1864.

B.Hbk (1887) 331. Whitley (1913) 351.

(171) CONGREGATIONAL, Belthorn (SD 718246). 1818, rebuilt 1884–5 by John Yates of Blackburn. Some early 19th-century monuments in burial-ground.

CYB (1868) 299–300, obituary of J. H. Unwin. Nightingale II (1891) 120–7.

(172) WESLEYAN, Rhyddings (SD 741276). Mount Pleasant Chapel, built 1846 by James Hacking of Enfield 'architect and sole contractor' for a society formed in 1796. Tall three-bay ashlar front, with projecting pedimented centre, porch formerly open

Baptist chapel, Oswaldtwistle.   (170)

Wesleyan chapel, Rhyddings.   (172)

with two Roman Doric columns. Chapel enlarged and refitted in late 19th century.

Hargreaves (1883) 103–12.

(173) FREE METHODIST, Nab Lane, Stanhill (SD 726277). Tall round-arched windows; tablet 1864 on side wall.

OVER WYRESDALE

(174) Former FRIENDS (SD 548553). The first meeting-house here was built in 1709 and superseded in 1883 by a larger building added at right angles to it by Harrison and Hall. Both buildings have now been converted to domestic use. The original meeting-house has rubble walls and a roof covered with stone slates. On the S side is a low gabled porch with two windows, formerly of three lights, to the right, and one window to the left, all

variously altered. A doorway has been pierced in the E gable wall, possibly on the site of a three-light window, reusing the former lintel. The interior (36½ft by 18½ft) has been subdivided; in the W wall is an original fireplace which may have served a small room at that end.

PADIHAM

(175) WESLEYAN, Bank Street (SD 791340). The first Methodist Society in Padiham was formed in 1748 and a preaching-house erected in 1758; this was superseded in 1779 by a more substantial chapel with a four-bay front and two tall windows in round-arched recesses flanking a central pulpit. The third successive chapel built in 1847 faces Bank Street. This has an ashlar front of five bays with slightly projecting wings and a three-bay Ionic portico covering the two entrances. The interior, remodelled in 1867, has a continuous oval gallery supported by cast-iron columns. Behind the chapel is the *Wesleyan School*, dated 1840, which was enlarged in 1861 and partly rebuilt in 1871. There is a burial-ground at the rear. (Chapel and school derelict 1971, demolished before 1974)

Dolbey (1964) 89. Moore (1899) 46–50, 176–82.

(176) Former METHODIST UNITARIAN, West Street (SD 790 339). The 'Cookite' society was formed in 1806 when meetings were held in a room in Back Lane, now East Street. The chapel, built 1822–3 on the site of a cottage where the first Methodist meetings had been held in 1748, is a plain building of stone with a central doorway to the N and two upper windows. In the S wall are two round-arched windows which flanked the pulpit. The E and W walls are gabled; the latter has been refaced in brickwork. The interior, now used for storage, retains the remains of a gallery added in 1836.

Fittings – *Inscription*: above N doorway, on stone tablet, 'To us there is But One GOD even the FATHER/1 Corinth chap'r 8th verse 6th/1822'. *Monuments*: in burial-ground (1) Ellen, wife of Elijah Bridge, 1844; (2) Ann, wife of Christopher Lacock, 1840, John their son, 1839, and daughters Sabin, 1833, and Ann, 1843; (3) George Watson, 1851, and Fanny Agnes, infant daughter of Henry and Nancy Holland, 1851; (4) Thomas Rushworth, 1850, 'a teacher in this Sabbath School'; (5) John Astin, Sunday-school teacher 'desirous of benefiting others by the spread of knowledge

FORMER COOKITE CHAPEL, PADIHAM   CFS 1974

he bequeathed the whole of his books to the Chapel Library', 1846; (6) John Monk, 1838; (7) Hiram, 1839, and Nicholas, 1846, sons of Thomas and Mary Waddington (Jenkins (1906) op. cit. below refers to burial below pulpit of James Pollard, minister, 1848, with slab marked 'JP', also monuments in burial-ground to ministers John Robinson, 1848, and Henry Dean, 1855). *Sundial*: formerly on W wall, erected 1836, missing.

Jenkins, J. E., *History of Unitarianism in Padiham, 1806–1906* (1906). McLachlan (1919).

(177) UNITARIAN, West Street (SD 790338). Stone Gothic with corner tower and spire, by Virgil Anderton, built 1872–4 to replace the foregoing. *Glass*: in S window incorporating portraits of ministers John Robinson and James Pollard. *Monument*: Rev. James Pollard and Rev. John Robinson, 1848, formerly above pulpit in earlier chapel, removed here 1874.

Christian Freeman (October 1871) 152–3. Evans (1897) 197. Herford and Evans (1909) 109–11.

PENDLETON

(178) Site of CONGREGATIONAL, Wymondhouses (SD 764388). Thomas Jollie, ejected curate of Altham, bought a small farmhouse at Wymondhouses in 1667. An Independent church formed at Altham in 1649 was then continued here and in 1688 Jollie erected a 'new little chappell' which was completed in two months; it was registered as a meeting-house in 1689. This building formed a wing on the NW side of the present farmhouse. It remained in regular use until c.1869 but eventually fell into decay and was totally demolished c.1890. The work of Thomas Jollie is commemorated on a modern tablet above the SE doorway of the farmhouse.

Inscriptions: on stone in outbuilding 'T:I 69' for Thomas Jollie; on two loose fragments of stone various biblical references including 'EPHE[   ]5 CHAP[   ] Ve[   ]' within crude shield. A tablet formerly above the entrance to the chapel is now reset in the chapel at Barrow (see (273)).

Fishwick, H. (ed.), *The Note Book of the Rev. Thomas Jolly* (Chetham Soc. NS XXXIII, 1894). Johnston (1905) 89–123. Nightingale II (1891) 185–96.

PENKETH   *Cheshire*

(179) Former FRIENDS, Meeting Lane (SJ 565880). The meeting originated c.1667–9 following visits by George Fox and the present site was acquired in 1671 for use as a burial-ground. The first meeting-house of 1681 was replaced in 1736 by the existing building, now used since 1975 as a Community Centre. This has brick walls with later rendering to the S, with stone base and quoins and a more recent slated roof. Three segmental-arched windows in the S wall and two in the N may have been altered in the 19th century. The S porch, dated 1736, has two round-arched openings to S and E.

The interior (41¼ft by 26½ft) has a W gallery and an original corner fireplace in the space below. Some early 18th-century fielded panelling remains as a dado to the principal room rising at the E end where the stand has been removed.

Monuments: in burial-ground, many uniform round-topped headstones including (1) Alexander Chorley, 1801; (2) Samuel

South Elevation

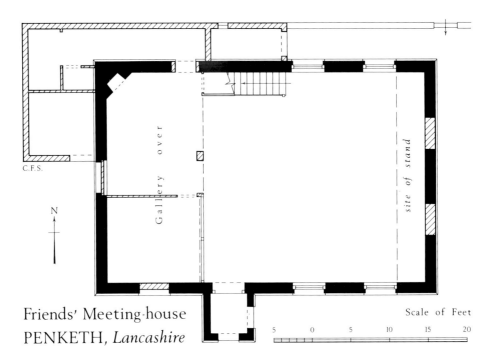

C.F.S.

N

Gallery over

site of stand

Friends' Meeting-house
PENKETH, *Lancashire*

Scale of Feet

5   0   5   10   15   20

Fothergill, 1772. *Sundial*: on S porch, painted stone dial with motto 'ut hora sic vita', 18th-century.

VCH *Lancs*. III (1907) 413.

POULTON-WITH-FEARNHEAD   *Cheshire*

(180) Former WESLEYAN, Padgate (SJ 625896). The chapel, now two cottages, 263 and 265 Padgate Lane, was built in 1831 for a society which had formerly met in hired rooms; it was superseded in 1875 by the present chapel on a new site (SJ 628899). The walls are of brickwork and the roof slated. The N front has a central round-arched doorway with keystone and impost blocks and a fanlight; a second cottage doorway was inserted *c*.1875. The windows have flat-arched brick heads.

Former Wesleyan chapel, Padgate.   (180)

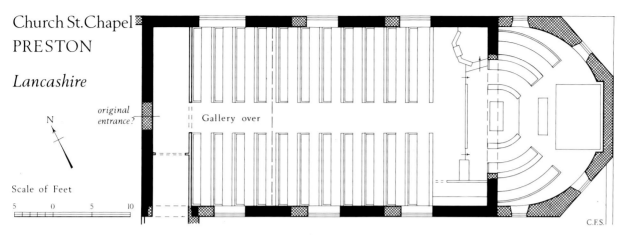

Church St. Chapel
PRESTON

Lancashire

N

original entrance?   Gallery over

Scale of Feet

5   0   5   10

C.F.S.

PRESCOT   *Merseyside*

(181) Former PRESBYTERIAN, Atherton Street (SJ 468929). The chapel, registered 7 October 1756 as a 'new building in a new street leading from Eccleston Street to the Moss', was built for the convenience of some members of the church in St Helens. It was closed in 1879 after many years in Unitarian hands, and sold in 1896 to Wesleyans who used it as a school. It was demolished before 1968.

The chapel was built of brick, and had a broad front of four bays with two tiers of round-arched windows and entrances in the end bays. A gallery was added above the entrances in the 19th century 'by the proprietors of a sailcloth manufactory in Prescot, to accommodate their work people and apprentices'. Nightingale records several *monuments* to former ministers, including a brass to Samuel Park, 1775, now in Park Lane Chapel, ASHTON-IN-MAKERFIELD (*see* (4)).

Evans (1897) 205–6. Nightingale IV (1892) 150–6.

PRESTON

(182) Former PRESBYTERIAN, Church Street (SD 544296). The chapel, reputed to have been erected *c*.1716–18 for a society of whose earlier existence little is known, may be the 'new building in Preston' registered for Samuel Crane as a dissenters' meeting place in 1723. The society, which eventually became Unitarian, had a second meeting-house at Walton-le-Dale, 2 miles SE, built by Sir Henry Houghton in 1719, which continued in use until *c*.1800 when it was converted to cottages. The Preston chapel has walls of brickwork, partly rendered, and the roof is covered with slates. It was much altered in the late 19th century, when a minister's vestry and Sunday-school room were built at the NW end and an organ chamber at the opposite end; it was also re-pewed. Further buildings were added to the NW in 1905 and alterations made to the organ chamber in 1912.

The original entrance was at the NW end, now covered by later buildings facing Percy Street. The side walls have each three windows, originally low openings with segmental-arched heads which remain visible on the NE side; lunettes were added above four of the windows, probably in the 19th century.

The interior (43½ft by 22½ft) has been much altered and refitted and a flat plaster ceiling was inserted in the 19th century. A gallery at the NW end was also rebuilt at that period and the upper part of the NW gable wall removed. The original roof structure survives with two king-post trusses and two purlins to each slope with short straight wind-braces above and below. The upper part of a blocked window is visible internally in the SE gable. (Chapel closed 1975)

Monuments: in chapel, removed 1954, are listed by Nightingale. In burial-ground (1) Mrs Mary Hoghton, 1793, ledger stone.

Evans (1897) 206–7. Herford and Evans (1909) 114–16. Nightingale I (1890) 9–21.

(183) Former CONGREGATIONAL, Guildhall Street (SD 540291). A chapel in Fishergate opened in 1790 was superseded by the present building in 1825–6. The chapel, which originally faced Cannon Street, was extended to the rear in 1851–2; in 1887 it was greatly altered by the erection of a new frontage to Guildhall Street, the interior was refitted and the pulpit moved to the opposite end. The walls are of brickwork with stone dressings, the 1887 front is of ashlar.

The original front is of five bays with a three-bay pedimented centre; two-storeyed wings of *c*.1852 or later project from the end bays. The side walls, of five bays extended to eight, have two tiers of windows and basement windows to the north side. The present frontage has a three-bay portico with giant Corinthian columns. (Chapel derelict 1972)

Inscription: in E pediment 'Independent Chapel Cannon St. 1825 Enlarged 1852'.

Nightingale I (1890) 21–47.

(184) WESLEYAN, Lune Street (SD 537294). Built 1817 to replace a chapel of 1787 in Back Lane. Brick, with later ashlar front of 1862 by Poulton and Woodman. The front comprises a cavernous arched loggia with paired Corinthian columns supporting the arch and raking cornices between flanking bays with two tiers of round-arched windows.

Richardson, W. F., *Preston Methodism's 200 Fascinating Years* (1975).

(185) WESLEYAN, Garstang Road (SD 536307). Brick with stone dressings, semicircular portico; built 1861–2, probably by Poulton and Woodman.

Wesleyan chapel, Lune Street, Preston.   (184)

PRESTWICH   *Greater Manchester*

(186) CONGREGATIONAL, Newtown Street (SD 823039). Red brick with chapel raised high above ground-floor school-room. Plate tracery to principal window in front gable. 1881 by Alfred Waterhouse for church founded 1862 previously meeting from 1865 in Rooden Lane.

Nightingale V (1893) 26–7.

QUERNMORE

(187) Former FRIENDS (SD 522593). Two plain windows in front and doorway to right, 1863; stand with central entrance against gable wall to left. (Converted to cottage since 1972)

RADCLIFFE   *Greater Manchester*

(188) PRESBYTERIAN, Ainsworth (SD 763102). Cockey Chapel, a 16th-century chapel-of-ease to Middleton on the site of the present parish church, $\frac{1}{4}$ mile W, remained in occasional use by dissenters until the early 18th century. The ejected minister, John Lever, continued to preach there, although in 1672 he licensed a new house close to Cockey Chapel 'soe near it that the Congregations may hear one another Sing Psalms'. In January 1715 dissenters registered 'new buildings in Ainsworth' as a meeting place and in March 1719 part of the present site '30 yards long and 20 in breadth in Ainsworth lying at the end of a close called Oakes Nooke' and 'the edifice newly erected' were placed in trust. The Presbyterian chapel was 'enlarged' in 1773 and further altered and partly refitted in 1845. The congregation have long supported a Unitarian ministry although retaining the original denominational designation for the building.

The chapel, of *c.*1718 but largely rebuilt in 1773, has walls of coursed squared stone and the roof is covered with slates. The S wall has a band of larger stones at mid-height which may indicate a substantial heightening or rebuilding of the early 18th-century structure. The windows are of three lights with mullions and moulded labels to the lower tier. At the W end of the wall is a blocked doorway. The N wall, of similar fenestration, which is laid water-shot, may date from the late 18th century. The present entrance, centrally in the E wall, dates from 1845; it may replace two earlier entrances in this wall of which only faint traces remain. The W wall is rendered.

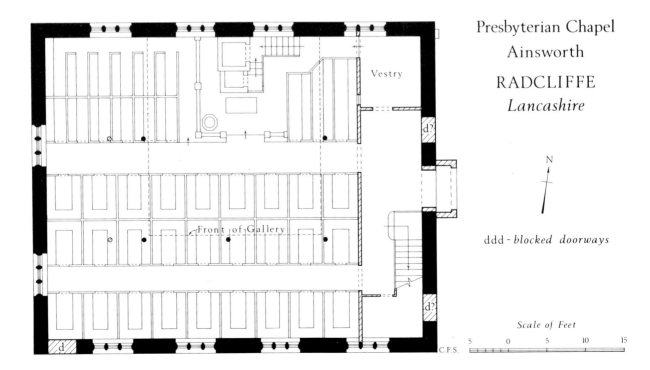

Presbyterian Chapel
Ainsworth
RADCLIFFE
Lancashire

N

ddd - *blocked doorways*

Scale of Feet

Vestry

C.F.S.

Presbyterian chapel, Ainsworth.   (188)

The interior (38ft by 49ft) has a gallery around three sides supported by five turned wood columns and approached by a late 18th-century staircase. The lower seating was replaced in 1845. There is a plaster ceiling divided by three cased tie-beams; the roof is supported by late 18th-century king and queen-post trusses.

Fittings – *Baptismal Basin*: pottery fontlet, type of St Mary Magdalene, Oxford, signed 'J. Flack', mid 19th-century. *Bell* and *Bell-cote*: on apex of W gable, square stone bell-cote with ball finial, containing one bell. *Book*: Bible, printed by T. Wright and W. Gill, Oxford, 1770. *Brass*: on pew 19, David Heaton, 1784, and Margaret his wife, 1770. *Candle Sconces*: on pulpit, two at corners of lower desk, moulded baluster stem with urn finial surmounted by eagle, adjustable candle bracket with detachable scroll ornaments, 18th-century. *Clock*: on front of S gallery, signed 'PR CLARE Fect. Manchester 1774'.

Monuments and *Floorslabs*. *Monuments*: in chapel on N wall (1) Rev. Joshua Dobson, 35 years pastor, 1767, and Elizabeth his widow, 1767; (2) Rev. Joseph Bealey, 27 years pastor, 1813, Rev. James Whitehead, over 41 years pastor, 1859, and Rev. James Thornely Whitehead, 11 years pastor, 1898, son and grandson of the first, erected 1904. Externally near E doorway (3) Thomas Baron, 1786, Mary his widow 1822, and Rev. Titus Baron, their son, 1799, table-tomb. In burial-ground to S and E, ledger stones and other monuments of early 18th century and later, including (4) Rev. Peter Seddon, 1731, Elizabeth his widow, 1749, and Rebekah their daughter, 1735, table-tomb; (5) Lawrence Greenhalgh, stonemason, 1797, *et al.*, flat slab with symbols of craftsman's tools, try-square, dividers, folding rule, chisels and mallet, signed 'LG'. *Floorslabs*: in S aisle (1) Thomas Davenport of Tottington, 1771, Margaret his wife, 1771, and Edmund their son, 1771; (2) Alice, wife of John Kirkman, 1731, Ann their daughter, 1729, Mary (?second) wife of John Kirkman, 1757, Thomas their son, nd, John Kirkman, 1766, and Peter, son of John and Mary Kirkman, 1786; (3) William Kirkman, 1725/6, and his children Thomas, 1717, George, 1718, and Rebecca, 1719; (4) Mr (Joseph) Whitworth, minister, 1721; in N aisle (5) John Aspinwall, 1728, and Ann Darbishire his sister, 1763; (6) Edmund Davenport, 1749, Elizabeth his widow, 1778, and their children Alice, 1726/7, John 1730, Ellen, 1736, and Betty, 1736; (7) William Kirkman senior, 1720/1; (8) Daniel Hamer, 1727, Esther his widow, 1732, and their children Esther, 1722, Samuel, 1722, Esther, 1727, and Rachel, 1733.

Plate: includes a pair of two-handled cups of 1776. *Pulpit*: against N wall, oak, in two tiers; lower desk square with fluted corner pilasters, shaped fielded panels and moulded cornice, late 18th-century; upper desk square with fluted quarter-round corner columns and plain fielded panels, 19th-century; back-board, three panels, late 19th-century replacing single panel. *Seating*: in gallery, box-pews, late 18th-century. *Miscellaneous*: on painted wooden board 'NOTICE. The Pew and seat holders are respectfully informed that the payments will become due next Sabbath day'.

A *cottage* NE of the chapel of three storeys with mullioned windows, with date stone 'NBA 1773', was demolished in 1973.

Evans (1897) 1–2. Gordon., A. (ed.), *Freedom After Ejection: A Review (1690–1692) of Presbyterian and Congregational*

Nonconformity in England and Wales (1917) 61, 383. Herford and Evans (1909) 44–7. Nightingale III (1892) 115–27.

(189) STAND CHAPEL (SD 795055). Although Thomas Pyke, rector of Radcliffe, was ejected in 1662, he removed to Blackley and there is little evidence of the existence of a regular Presbyterian society in 'Pilkington' (as the township was then known) before the late 17th century. The present chapel, erected in 1952, stands on the site of a chapel of 1819, destroyed by enemy action in 1940; this was a rebuilding of the first chapel of 1693. The society is now Unitarian.

Fittings – *Bell*: broken 1940, fragments remain, formerly inscribed 'Henry Penn made me, 1708'. *Inscription*: reset in wall near entrance, 'Conditum A.D. 1693/Renovatum A.D. 1818'. *Monuments*: in burial-ground S of chapel, several ledger stones of late 18th century. *Plate*: includes a two-handled gadrooned cup of 1706, given 1759. *Miscellaneous*: carved stone, loose, inscribed '1606 I.W. M.L/I.W'.

Evans (1897) 229–30. Gordon (1917) op. cit. 59, 62. Herford, R.T., *Memorials of Stand Chapel* (1893). Herford and Evans (1909) 128–30.

(190) CONGREGATIONAL, Four Lane Ends (SD 764123). Round-arched doorway between two windows, 1832; much altered and enlarged 1930.

(191) WESLEYAN, Bury Street (SD 795077). The chapel on N side of street was built in 1839 at the expense of Mrs Mary Bealey. The walls are of stone faced with ashlar to S and W and are surmounted by battlemented parapets. The S front is of three bays divided by octagonal buttresses rising to two-stage turrets;

Wesleyan chapel, Bury Street, Radcliffe.   (191)

Wesleyan chapel, Bury Street, Radcliffe. (191)

above the central doorway is a tall window with three cusped lights with an ogee label. The side walls to E and W have each three windows with traceried heads. There is a short chancel at the N end.

The interior has a S gallery with separate entrances and staircases in the front corners. The chancel is divided from the rest of the chapel by a four-centred arch with attached shafts and ornamented with Gothic paterae. The ceiling, in five bays, has a ribbed plaster vault springing from moulded semi-octagonal corbels. (Demolished c.1977–8)

Fittings – *Communion Rail*: cast-iron, Gothic, c.1839. *Glass*: in N window of chancel, with painted representation of crucifixion, 1839. *Monuments*: in chapel (1) Richard Bealey, 'who died at this College on the 22nd Novr. 1848' in 12th year of his age, tablet removed from Wesley College, Sheffield, 1907; (2) Mary, widow of Adam Bealey, 1858. *Organ*: in E transept, probably formerly in S gallery, Gothic case, c. 1839. *Pulpit*: wood, octagonal on cross base, probably re-sited from central position, 1839. *Sculpture*: marble statuette of John Wesley, presented to Mrs Mary Bealey, 1850.

(192) METHODIST NEW CONNEXION, Ainsworth (SD 761102). Rebuilt 1892, original date tablet 1847 reset in boundary wall.

(193) NEW JERUSALEM, Stand Lane (SD 791065). Yellow stone with two domed turrets at front, 1879 by Thomas Thorp of Whitefield, replacing chapels of 1803 and 1841. *School*, brick, built 1815, rebuilt 1850.

RAINFORD
Merseyside

(194) CONGREGATIONAL (SD 482011). Although Roger Baldwin, curate of the chapel-of-ease, was ejected in 1662, nonconformists under James Bradshaw, ejected curate of Hindley, occupied the parochial chapel from c.1672 to 1702. A separate meeting-house was then built for the Presbyterian, subsequently Congregational, society (now URC) which was replaced by the present chapel on the same site in 1867. The chapel has walls of yellow and red sandstone with a corner tower rising to an octagonal turret and spire.

Inscription: tablet from former School reset in wall of modern church hall, opposite chapel, 'DR 1847', for David Rosbotham. *Monuments*: in burial-ground, many reset ledger stones, including (1) Richard Mather, 1728, with shield-of-arms; (2) Nathan Tyrer, 1749, and Elizabeth his widow, 1784; (3) Rev. Tatlock Mather, 39 years minister, 1785, Margaret, widow of Rev. Benjamin Mather, 1783, *et al.*; (4) Rev. John Toothill, 50 years minister, 1839, and Sarah his widow, 1852; (5) John Naylor, 1727, Isabell his widow, 1734, *et al.*

Huyton, A., *A History of Rainford Congregational Church, 1577–1967* (1967). Nightingale IV (1892) 170–80. VCH *Lancs.* III (1907) 385–6.

(195) PRIMITIVE METHODIST, Crank (SJ 506997). Small stone chapel, now 'Alder Lane Mission', scrolled tablet inscribed 'Erected by William Pendlebury 1857'. Box-pews. *Monuments*: in burial-ground include (1) William Pendlebury, 1873, and William Pendlebury, junior, 1863. House adjacent dated 'WP 1848'.

RAMSBOTTOM

Greater Manchester
(except (199) Stubbins)

(196) DUNDEE CHAPEL, Holcombe (SD 786166). A Presbyterian congregation, gathered by Henry Pendlebury after his ejection in 1662 as minister of the chapel-of-ease of Holcombe, met in 1672 in the court house in Holcombe which was licensed for preaching. Subsequently a meeting-house was fitted up at Bass Lane, possibly Bast House (SD 804152). Dundee or Holcombe Chapel was built for this society in 1712 and opened on 5 August; it is referred to in the Dob Lane Chapel briefs (Gordon (1904) op. cit. below, 89) for 21 September 1712 when 14s. 8d. was collected 'for the new Chappell at Holcombe'. After 1731 the chapel at Bury became the principal Presbyterian meeting-house for the district and support for the largely Independent ministry at Dundee was greatly reduced. In 1798 a new minister removed with most of the remaining congregation to the newly built Park Chapel (SD 801161, rebuilt 1897) but a remnant remained at the former place. In the early 19th century the brothers William and Daniel Grant, calico printers from Strathspey, who had opened a mill in Ramsbottom, began to take a benevolent but autocratic interest in Dundee Chapel which they rebuilt, forcing the Independent minister to resign and replacing him by a succession of orthodox Presbyterians. In 1832–4 William Grant built 'St Andrews Church' (*see* (197)), to which the congregation removed until their ejection in 1869. The chapel reverted to its original use from 1869 to 1873 when a new Presbyterian Chapel, also St Andrews, was built, and again reverted in 1913 after the new and elaborate Gothic chapel became structurally unsafe. Dundee Chapel then continued in Presbyterian use until 1971 when the congregation united with Dundee Congregational Church, formed in 1885 by seceders from the former. It has since been sold.

The chapel has walls of coursed squared stone. The SE gable wall alone remains from the 1712 building; it was covered c.1790 by a cottage which rose higher than the chapel and served as a party wall. When the chapel was rebuilt c.1809 the new walls were made higher, all three periods being visible in this wall in 1978 after the demolition of the cottage. One original mullioned window remains in this wall of three arched lights, with flat sunk spandrels and a moulded label, since cut away. The early 19th-century work has two tiers of round-arched windows and a doorway at the NW end. The interior has a deep NW gallery. School-rooms were added against the NE wall in the late 19th century. (Demolished 1978)

Monuments: in burial-ground (1) John Cunliffe, 1824, 'designer and architect', Phoebe his wife, 1822, their sons James, 1812, and Charles, 1822, and grand-daughter Helen, 184[ ], ledger stone,

broken; (2) Edward Hamer, 1756; (3) Ann, wife of John Barnes, 1734; (4) Peter McFarlane, 1827, Nancy his widow, 1830, *et al.*, with masonic symbols; (5) Abraham Wood, 1777, Elizabeth his wife, 1746, *et al.*; (6) Andrew MacLean D.D., 40 years minister, 1869, and Jane Houston his widow, 1901, marble pillar, desecrated.

Elliott, W. H., *The Country and Church of the Cheeryble Brothers* (Selkirk, 1893). Gordon, A., *Historical Account of Dob Lane Chapel . . .* (1904). Mackelvie (1873) 484–5. Nightingale III (1892) 154–67. *Reform* (February 1974) 16–17.

(197) Former PRESBYTERIAN, Bolton Street (SD 789163). The parish church of St Andrew was built in 1832–4 at the expense of William Grant for the Presbyterian congregation formerly worshipping in Dundee Chapel; it remained the private property of the Grant brothers whose heir and nephew William Grant dispossessed the congregation in 1869, obliging them to return their former building, and in 1871 transferred it to the Church of England.

This is a substantial Gothic 'patronage chapel' of squared stone with lancet windows and buttresses in the Early English style. It comprises a large undivided nave of five bays and a W tower between staircase vestibules. A small polygonal sanctuary may replace a vestry of similar design. There is a deep W gallery which extends into the centre stage of the tower.

Fittings – *Bells*: in tower, one dated 1834, by Mears of London, four added 1871, by Mears and Stainbank. *Clock*: in tower, with provision for drives to four dials on faces of tower, (drive to E face not connected) and fifth drive to dial on gallery

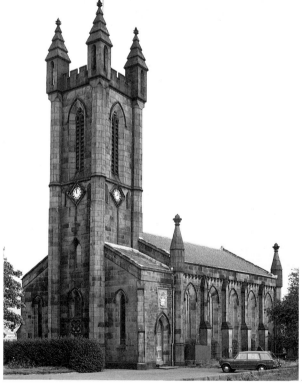

Former Presbyterian chapel, Ramsbottom.   (197)

front, signed 'Buchanan 1834'; a cast-iron beam in the clock chamber is inscribed 'This Clock is the gift of JOHN GRANT ESQ. of Nuttall Hall and was made at Ramsbottom Print Works under his Inspection'. *Glass*: loose in box, from former E window which had seven traceried lights; photographs record a central figure of Christ with two children, St Andrew to right, another figure to left, and shield-of-arms in tracery. *Monument*: on E wall, William Grant of Springside, 1842, 'the founder of this church', with bust and shield-of-arms, signed 'Knowles, Manchester'. *Plate*: includes a set of two cups, flagon, alms dish and baptismal basin, given 1834 by Miss Isabella Grant. *Seating*: in nave, original box-pews in three ranks, no centre aisle; in gallery, two large private pews with loose chairs for Grant family, doors inscribed 'Nuttall Hall', centre rank of pews for singers.

Anon., *The Case of the Forcible Seizure of St Andrews Presbyterian Church, Ramsbottom (The Church of the Cheeryble Brothers) and its Alienation to the Church of England* (Manchester, 1906). Elliott (1893) op. cit. above.

(198) Former BAPTIST, Bolton Street (SD 791168), three-bay pedimented front, segmental-arched cornice to centre bay, 1861.

(199) CONGREGATIONAL, Stubbins (SD 796185). Gothic with nave, transepts and corner tower and spire; 1866–7 by James Maxwell of Bury at the expense of James Porritt, mill owner.

Congregational chapel, Stubbins.   (199)

Monument: in burial-ground to James Porritt, 1896, *et al.* (Demolished since 1975)

CYB (1867) 365–6. Nightingale III (1892) 238.

(200) WESLEYAN, Market Place (SD 791170). Two recessed centre bays with round-arched doorways between pedimented wings. Dated 1874, by John Garnett.

(201) WESLEYAN, Summerseat (SD 795148). The chapel, built *c*.1844–7 at the expense of John Robinson Kay of Walmersley House, is an exceptionally complete work in the perpendicular Gothic style by James Simpson. The walls are of grey ashlar and the roofs are covered with slates. The plan comprises a wide unaisled nave with galleried transepts and a shallow eastern chancel flanked by vestries. An octagonal mausoleum was built against the S wall of the nave *c*.1872.

The exterior is richly decorated with buttresses rising to tall carved pinnacles, the W end of the nave being further elaborated by a pair of octagonal turrets with open-work tops. The principal E window of the chancel is of five lights with perpendicular tracery in a two-centred arched head; the transept windows are of three lights and those of the nave of two lights with cusped tracery. The chancel is divided from the nave by a four-centred arch with moulded responds, foliage capitals and moulded bases. All windows have internal hood-moulds and stops. The mausoleum, approached from the nave, has a wooden vaulted ceiling with central boss carved with a monogram of the initials of John Robinson Kay and his wife Mary. E and W of the chapel is an extensive burial-ground with numerous monuments. A later 'Methodist School' stands to the south. (Chapel demolished *c*.1977)

Fittings (all of *c*.1847 unless stated) – *Book*: on communion table, *Book of Common Prayer* (Oxford, 1846), inscribed 'Wesleyan Methodist Chapel, Summerseat, July 23rd 1847'. *Chairs*: in chancel, pair, with arched legs, arms, and tall, square, padded and buttoned backs with cresting. *Collecting Shovels*: four, with quatrefoil box and short handle. *Communion Table and Rails*: four shafted legs, plain upper rails; contemporary kneelers and quatrefoiled communion rails. *Font*: stone, octagonal bowl with quatrefoil panels on ring of circular shafts. *Gates, Gate Piers and Railings*: along N boundary contemporary iron railings and stone gate piers. *Glass*: in all windows, plain opaque glass with coloured borders and tracery lights. *Inscription*: on loose tablet from previous chapel, 'Summerseat and Brooksbottom Wesleyan Chapel', 1830' (see *Local Historian* XVII (1987–8) 496).

Monuments: in chancel (1) Rev. John Prusho Hetherington, Wesleyan missionary, 1861, signed 'J. Smith, Colquitt St., Liverpool'; in nave below W window (2) brass to 'John Robinson Kay, and Mary his wife, of Walmersley House, through whose influence and generosity this chapel and the schools adjoining were built, and by whose benefactions and devoted services the work of Wesleyan Methodism and the cause of education in this neighbourhood were promoted and sustained. Erected by voluntary contributions June 1894.' In mausoleum (3) John Robinson Kay, 1872, Mary (Hamer) his widow, 1883, large monument of polished granite, marble and inlaid stones surmounted by cross slab; also brasses to their children and grandchildren.

Pulpit: wood, octagonal on shafted stem. *Sculpture*: below W

Wesleyan chapel, Summerseat

(201)

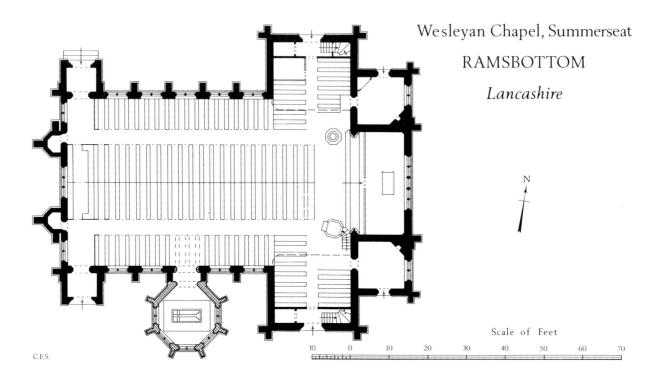

Wesleyan Chapel, Summerseat

RAMSBOTTOM

Lancashire

N

Scale of Feet

10   0   10   20   30   40   50   60   70

C.F.S.

Wesleyan chapel, Summerseat (201)

window of nave, alabaster panel with three angels, *c*.1894. *Seating*: in nave and transepts, pew ends with poppy-head terminals and doors; Kay family pew, W end of centre rank, upholstered with buttoned red baize and with full-height end doors.

Powell, K., *The Fall of Zion, Northern Chapel Architecture and its Future* (1980) 37–40.

RAWTENSTALL

(202) BAPTIST, Cloughfold (SD 824229). The church meeting in 'Sion Chapel' derives from the 'Church of Christ in Rossendale' formed in the late 17th century by William Mitchell and David Crossley. The first chapel of *c*.1700 was rebuilt in 1839. The chapel, dating principally from an 'enlargement' of 1852, has a three-bay front, formerly pedimented, with quoins and tall round-arched windows flanking a porch. Monuments in burial-ground of early 19th century and later. (Chapel demolished *c*.1980, church meets in 1901 Sunday-school)

Parry, A.J., *History of the Cloughfold Baptist Church from 1675 to 1875* (1876). Whitley (1913) 71–99, 266, 332.

(203) BAPTIST, Goodshaw Chapel (SD 815263). The hamlet of Goodshaw Chapel takes its name from one of the numerous chapels-of-ease in the parish of Whalley which was erected 'in a

certain place in the Forest of Rossendale called Morell Height' about 1545. The first evidence of nonconformist preaching here is in 1685–6 when William Mitchell was imprisoned for holding a conventicle in the chapelry, but his later work was centred on Bacup and elsewhere in the vicinity. In 1748 John Wesley preached at the parochial chapel, and a Methodist society was formed of which the principal supporters included members of the Butterworth family. A failure in the local organization led these to unite with the Baptists and it is possible that this may have influenced subsequent events. The church latterly meeting here originated at Lumb in an adjacent valley to the E, about 1742, encouraged by Joseph Piccop of Bacup, where a chapel was built at Bully Tree in 1750. In 1760 the church removed to Goodshaw Chapel, commencing the present chapel in that year and furnishing it in part with material taken from their former meeting-house. The chapel was enlarged to the front about 1800 and an adjoining cottage to the W was similarly extended in 1809 to provide classrooms. In 1864 a new chapel was built on Burnley Road and the former building subsequently was used only occasionally. By 1970 the chapel had become derelict but in 1975 it was taken into guardianship by the Department of the Environment and major works of repair were completed in 1984.

The chapel has coursed gritstone walls and a slate roof with

The Old Baptist Chapel, Goodshaw

RAWTENSTALL

Lancashire

Scale of Feet

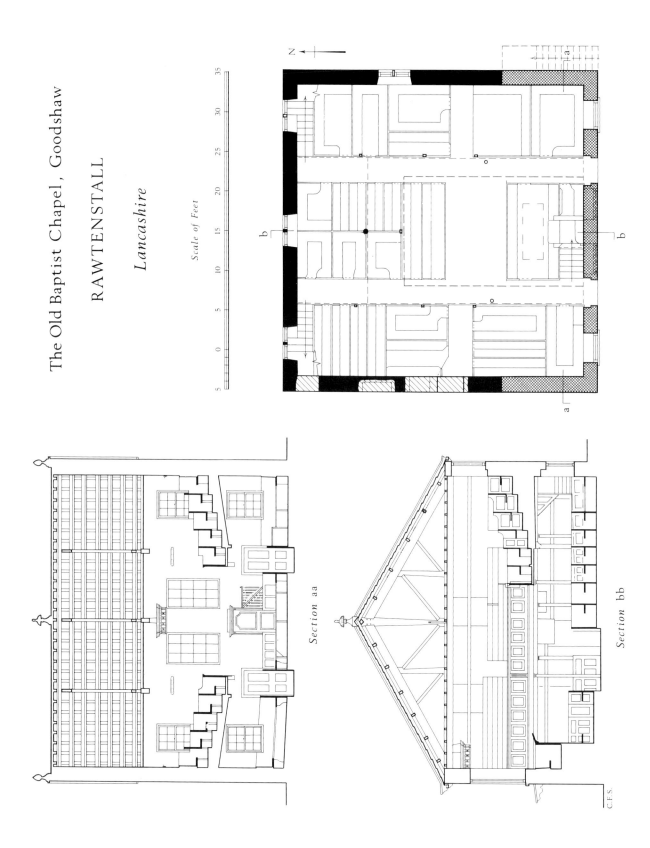

Section aa

Section bb

C.F.S.

The Old Baptist Chapel, Goodshaw Chapel. Before restoration.   (203)

renewed ball finials. Of the original building, the rear N wall and the gabled end walls to E and W survive, the latter being a party wall to the now-demolished former cottage. The enlargement of *c*.1800 comprises the present S front and the return walls of the extension against each of which was an external gallery staircase.

The S front, of water-shot walling, has two doorways with shaped stone corbels carrying flat hoods, two large pulpit windows between and smaller windows in the end bays, all with plain ashlar lintels and jambs and with renewed frames. The N wall was heightened *c*.1800. It has three original stone-mullioned windows of two lights to the lower level and had two similar upper windows in the end bays; these last were raised and two intermediate windows inserted in the early 19th century to light the cross gallery. The E wall is gabled and has shaped stone kneelers; it has a lower window of two lights centrally to the original work; fragments of the broken-off external stairs remain in the wall to the S and the blocking of the gallery doorway. The W wall incorporates the blocked remains of a cottage fireplace and doorways to the chapel as well as the former upper doorway to the gallery. The S wall of the annexe as extended in 1809 to align with the new frontage had a window in each of the three floors and an external doorway adjacent to the chapel.

The interior (originally 24½ft by 36¾ft, enlarged to 36¼ft by 36¾ft) has a flat plaster ceiling with three exposed ceiling beams. The pulpit stands between the front windows and has in front a large pew for the singers and communion table. A gallery around three sides has been enlarged on several occasions. The side galleries, approximately contemporary with the original structure, were later joined by a cross gallery to the N; all galleries were then extended inwards and subsequently the side galleries were lengthened to the S with the enlargement of the chapel. The gallery staircase in the NE corner has been altered and now covers a former internal doorway to the cottage. The floor of the chapel is paved with stone flags in the aisles and boards below the pews. The roof structure, of *c*.1800, comprises three king-post trusses; the original E gable has stone corbels internally to support the ends of two purlins to each slope of the former roof.

Fittings – *Chandelier*: two tiers, brass, 18th-century. *Clock*: on front of N gallery, signed 'JNO. WATSON, BLACKBURN'. *Communion Table*: with six turned legs and shaped brackets below end rails, drawers added, frame originally 9ft long, shortened, late 18th-century.

Monuments: in chapel, on E wall (1) William Nutter, 1824, stone tablet; on W wall (2) Rev. John Nuttall, 1792, 'he was the Honoured Instrument of gathering and establishing this Church, in which he laboured 45 years with Diligence and Success', wooden tablet. In burial-ground, S of chapel, (3) John Nuttall, 1766, inscribed 'John Nuttall/Lies here and thats/enough, the candels out also/the snuff: his souls with God/You need not fear, and what/remains, is interd here', headstone laid flat; (4) Richard Hudson, 1775, flat slab; (5) Henry Taylor, 1783, *et al.*, flat slab. Numerous other monuments in the extensive burial-ground date principally from the early 19th century and after.

Pulpit: on S wall, square with quarter-round fluted columns at corners; high canopy with Doric frieze. *Seating*: box-pews throughout including much late 18th-century fielded panelling;

the gallery pews are unpainted, pew doors are numbered.

Brandon, V. and Johnson, S., 'The Old Baptist Chapel, Goodshaw Chapel . . .' *Antiquaries Journal* LXVI (1986) 330–57. Jefferson, J., *A Brief History of the Church and Congregation Worshipping in the Baptist Chapel, Goodshaw* (1860). Whitley (1913) 129–30, 254.

(204) BAPTIST, Sunnyside (SD 809247). Rock-faced ashlar with steep pediment; built 1851 for seceders who left Goodshaw Chapel (203) in 1847.

(205) BAPTIST, Burnley Road (SD 811259). The church formerly meeting at Goodshaw Chapel removed in 1864 to a new chapel on this site which has now been demolished. The Sunday-school, built 1875 rebuilt 1886, remains at the rear of the site.

(206) STRICT BAPTIST, Goodshaw Fold (SD 808266). 'Rehoboth' chapel, built 1852 for a church originating in the work of John Kershaw of Rochdale, stands on a sloping site with rooms below and principal entrance at the upper level. Three-bay gabled end with two round-arched windows.

Strict Baptist chapel, Goodshaw Fold.   (206)

(207) FRIENDS, Crawshawbooth (SD 811254). A 'newly erected' building in the Forest of Rossendale was registered as a meeting-house for Quakers in 1716, but the present building appears to be entirely of 1736. The walls are of coursed stone and the roof is covered with stone flags. The S front, of four bays, has a gabled porch with a window to the left of three lights and a two-light window above; to the right two large windows have straight-chamfered mullions and diamond glazing, re-leaded in 1975. The N wall has a similar large window to the main room, a small blocked window near the E end and, at the W end, a three-light square-mullioned window with a longer, formerly mullioned, window above. The E wall is gabled and surmounted by a stone stack. The W wall is covered by a later taller cottage; there was formerly an upper doorway, possibly external, to the gallery at this end of the meeting-house.

The interior (32¾ft by 24½ft) is divided into two rooms by a substantial partition with double shutters below an open balustraded gallery front. Short stone return walls at the end of the partition are pierced to the S by a doorway to the lower W room, and to the N by a later upper doorway approached by a flight of stone steps. The roof is supported by two trusses, that to the E having a king-post.

Friends' Meeting-house, Crawshawbooth
RAWTENSTALL, *Lancashire*

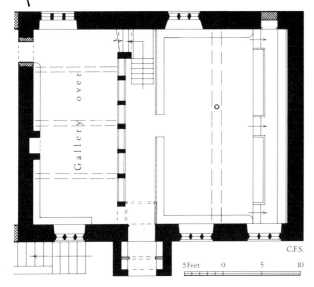

Friends' meeting-house, Crawshawbooth.   (207)

Fittings – *Chair*: plain panelled back and arm rests, 17th-century. *Door*: in porch, vertical boards pegged to three rails, early 18th-century. *Stand*: at E end, with open balustraded front to upper tier. *Table*: refectory table with turned legs, 17th-century.

R. H., *Crawshawbooth Friends' Meeting House* (nd). Newbigging (1893) 220.

(208) FRIENDS BURIAL-GROUND, Chapel Hill (SD 819236). Rectangular enclosure 43ft by 31ft bounded by high stone walls with traces of stone seating around inner face. Gateway to N with tablet above inscribed 'FRIENDS Burial Ground 1663 – The walls Rebuilt 1847'. No monuments visible.

(209) WESLEYAN, Bacup Road, Longholme (SD 812 228). Classical gritstone chapel of 1841–2 by James Simpson of Leeds, with three-bay portico and giant Ionic columns. Interior with horseshoe-shaped gallery, now with inserted floor, but

gallery seating remains. *Burial-ground* with monuments of 1840s and later.

Jessop (1880) 280–1.

(210) Former WESLEYAN, Rakefoot, Crawshawbooth (SD 812252). Large pedimented stone front with twin round-arched entrances and triplet of upper windows in centre bay, built 1866–7.

Jessop (1880) 343.

(211) WESLEYAN, Newchurch (SD 836225). The chapel, with foundation stone dated 1871, now much reduced and re-fronted stands on the site of a chapel of 1806. *Monuments*: in burial-ground include ledger stones to (1) Titus Baron, 1813; (2) Lawrence Nuttall, 1813, *et al.*; Mary Turner, 1809; (4) David Hoyle, 18[   ], and Mary his wife, 1822, *et al.*

Jessop (1880) facing 184, and *passim*.

(212) Former FREE METHODIST, Haslingdon Road, Rawtenstall (SD 808227). Built in 1855–7 in opposition to Longholme Chapel (209) and similar in design but in the Corinthian style.

(213) BANK STREET CHAPEL, Rawtenstall (SD 812229). Rebuilt 1971, on site of 1853 Gothic chapel, for a Unitarian congregation of Independent or mixed origin whose first meeting-house was built in 1757. *Gates* and *Gate Piers*: 1853.

Evans (1897) 208. Hague and Hague (1986) 110–12. Herford and Evans (1909) 117–19. McLachlan (1919) 54–9.

(214) BETHLEHEM CHAPEL, Newchurch (SD 835224). Built 1865 in Gothic style to supersede a chapel of 1808–9, enlarged 1822, for a Unitarian congregation of Cookite (Methodist Unitarian) origin. Sunday-school, 1874, on site of former chapel. *Monuments*: in burial-ground, of early 19th century and later. (Chapel demolished since 1981)

Evans (1897) 185. Hague and Hague (1986) 90. Herford and Evans (1909) 105–8. McLachlan (1919) *passim*.

RIVINGTON

(215) RIVINGTON CHAPEL (SD 627145). A chapel-of-ease to the parish of Bolton was built in Rivington in the early 16th century; from this building, now the parish church, the minister, Samuel Newton, was ejected for nonconformity in 1662. Nonconformists shortly afterwards regained possession of the building, Newton remaining until his death in 1682, and with the support of Hugh, Lord Willoughby of Parham, a local magistrate, continued to use it until the end of the century. By 1702 the episcopalians had recovered possession of the chapel-of-ease and in the following year the dissenters, loosely described as Presbyterians but more recently Unitarian, built the present chapel a short distance from the former.

The chapel has walls of coursed stone and a stone slate roof with wooden bell-cote at the W end. The broad S front has two doorways with lintels, one angularly cambered, and between them a pair of mullioned-and-transomed windows. Two such windows occur in each wall, those in the gabled ends having diamond-leaded panes, while the others are rectangularly leaded.

The interior (27½ft by 50ft) has a flat plaster ceiling with three exposed ceiling beams. The pulpit, which has been reduced in size, is centrally against the N wall facing a canopied pew of the Lords Willoughby on the opposite wall between the front

Rivington Chapel.

(215)

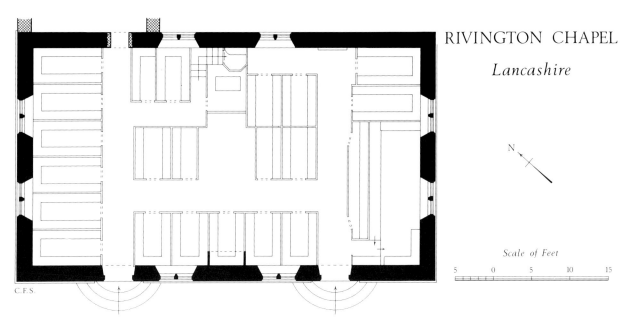

RIVINGTON CHAPEL

Lancashire

N

Scale of Feet

5   0   5   10   15

C.F.S.

Rivington Chapel.   (215)

Evans (1897) 210–11. Herford and Evans (1909) 120–5. Higson, P. J. W., 'Some leading promoters of Nonconformity . . . ' *L & CAST* LXXV-VI (1965–6) 135–8. Nightingale III (1892) 81–98.

ROCHDALE   *Greater Manchester*

(216) Former BAPTIST, West Street (SD 902138). The first Baptist church in Rochdale, gathered in 1773 by members of the Bacup church, met from 1775 in a meeting-house in Town Meadows. The present chapel, which replaced the former in 1833, has walls of red brick; the front is of three bays with a recessed porch having two Doric columns *in antis*. It has a galleried interior with an organ apse added *c*.1870–80. A new chapel was built in 1990 on the site of a Sunday-school of 1873; the former chapel is now in commercial use.

Ivimey IV (1830) 566–7. Robertson (1875) 133–5. Whitley (1913) 352, 353.

(217) HOPE CHAPEL, Hope Street (SD 897139). Supporters of William Gadsby, excluded from Town Meadows Chapel in 1808, were formed by Gadsby into a separate Strict and Particular Baptist Church in the following year under the pastorate of John Warburton. The church is best known for the lengthy ministry of his successor, John Kershaw, 1817–70.

Hope Chapel, built in 1810–11, was a cause of early financial embarrassment, the lower part remaining with only plain benches and a single coat of rough plaster on its walls until 1820, when conditions improved. Kershaw's popularity then attracted growing numbers and the chapel was increased to its present size by enlargement to the front in 1848. Some further renovation was carried out in 1869.

The chapel has walls of red brick and a slate roof. The S front of 1848 has a tall, wide, round-arched central window and two narrow side windows, each divided by a stone panel at gallery

windows. The seating is entirely of panelled box-pews of the 18th century. There are no galleries. A small two-storeyed annexe of the late 18th century adjoins to the north.

Fittings – *Bell* and *Bell-cote*: one bell, inaccessible, in restored hexagonal wooden bell-cote. *Brass*: on front of Willoughby pew, to Rt. Hon. Hugh Lord Willoughby of Parham F.R.S., 1765. *Inscription*: in frame, on broken and repaired stone recovered in mid 19th century from local walling 'Ye Revde Samuele Neutone ys driven from ye Church on Bartholomew Sonday 1662'. *Library*: formerly in upper room of annexe, commenced *c*.1821, books dispersed, copy of rules remains affixed to cupboard door. *Monuments*: in chapel (1) large obelisk-shaped monument on N wall, removed 1831 from Horwich chapel-of-ease, with lengthy inscription to the 11th to 15th Lords Willoughby of Parham (1691–1765) and others. In burial-ground many monuments of 18th century and later.

Hope Chapel, Rochdale. (217)

level. A central entrance replaces two round-arched doorways with fanlights. The N wall of 1810 has plain round-arched windows in the end bays, the central section has been rebuilt and, more recently, a chimney breast has been removed. The interior of the chapel (originally 33ft, enlarged to 54¾ft, by 38¾ft) was refitted in 1848. It has a continuous round-ended gallery supported by cast-iron columns and a vestry below the N gallery. Attached to the W is the former manse, originally one room in depth, of three storeys, the attic room being accessible only from the chapel gallery, while the cellar, which serves as a boiler house, has dual access.

The Sunday-school, free-standing to W, is a long, low building with round-arched windows and end doorways, built 1855, replacing one of 1828; it was enlarged to N and a W wing added in the late 19th century. (Sunday-school sold for secular use *c.*1987)

Fittings – *Inscription*: on N wall, externally, reset tablet 'Hope Chapel 1810'. *Monuments*: in chapel (1) John Kershaw, pastor, 1870; in Sunday-school (2) John Kershaw, 1870, 'erected by the committee, teachers and scholars'; in chapel yard (3) William Gadsby, 1844, 'interred at Rusholme Road Cemetery, Manchester', flat slab; (4) William Kershaw, 1834, Margaret, wife of John Kershaw of Hope Chapel, 1850, and five infant children of John and Ann Kershaw, 1845–54. Also numerous other ledger stones. *Painting*: in vestry, oil portrait of John Kershaw, *c.*1846.

Kershaw, J., *Memorials of the Mercies of a Covenant God* (1870). Paul (1961) 61–117.

(218) CONGREGATIONAL, Moore Street (SD 898131). Low five-bay front above basement, central doorway with tablet above inscribed 'Sunday School 1829'. Built as branch of Providence Chapel Sunday-school; now used as chapel.

Robertson (1875) 141.

(219) CONGREGATIONAL, Heywood Road, Castleton (SD 879 105). Built 1870 for congregation formed 1866. (URC)

Nightingale III (1892) 253–4.

(220) FRIENDS, George Street (SD 901137). The plain stone meeting-house of 1808 was demolished in the late 1960s. *Monuments*: in burial-ground include (1) John Bright, 1889; (2)

Elizabeth (Priestman) his first wife, 1841.

(221) Former WESLEYAN, Union Street (SD 896136), built for a Society whose first preaching-house was erected in Toad Lane *c.*1760, followed in 1793 by the first Union Street Chapel. The present chapel, now in industrial use, was built in 1825–6 with a seating capacity of 1,650. The walls are of brickwork with two tiers of round-arched windows. The front, of five bays, has a central segmental-arched recess of three bays; the lower stage is covered by a porch of 1910.

Morley, J. A., and Orrell, W. W., *Wesleyan Chapel, Union Street, Rochdale: A Record of the Society, 1746–1926* (1926). Robertson (1875) 151–7.

(222) WESLEYAN, Edenfield Road, Bagslate (SD 862145). Pedimented front with paired pilasters between flanking quadrant vestibules; 1870 replacing chapel of 1810.

(223) FREE METHODIST, Bagslate Moor (SD 868142), opened 1837, drastically altered 1973.

(224) Former WESLEYAN METHODIST ASSOCIATION, Baillie Street (SD 899135). Large brick chapel opened 1837 with five-bay pedimented front, central doorway with fluted Doric columns and pediment, side doorways added *c.*1912. Gallery added 1840. Seating capacity 1,800. (Closed *c.*1965–70, since demolished)

Dolbey (1964) 151–4.

(225) Former WESLEYAN, Healey Stones (SD 890155). Built 1877; NE tower. Reset in boundary wall, date tablet 1822 from Wesleyan Sunday-school.

(226) FREE METHODIST, Spotland (SD 884141). On W side of Rooley Moor Road, with elaborately detailed pedimented front of 1896.

(227) BLACKWATER STREET CHAPEL (SD 895135). By Henry Bowman 1856–7 for a Presbyterian later Unitarian congregation whose first meeting-house on this site was built in 1717. Gothic with small bell-cote, and S aisle; N aisle added 1890. (Demolished 1972; congregation moved to new building on site of Clover Street Chapel)

Fittings – *Glass*: in E window, by Burne-Jones (eight figures reset in new chapel in Clover Street). *Inscription*: below W window of S aisle, tablet erected 1909 reproducing a stone formerly in previous building with date 1717 and text from Mic. 6:8. *Monuments*: external (1) William Hastings, 1820, *et al.*; (2)

Former Unitarian chapel, Clover Street, Rochdale. (228)

Friends' Meeting-house

ST. HELENS

Lancashire

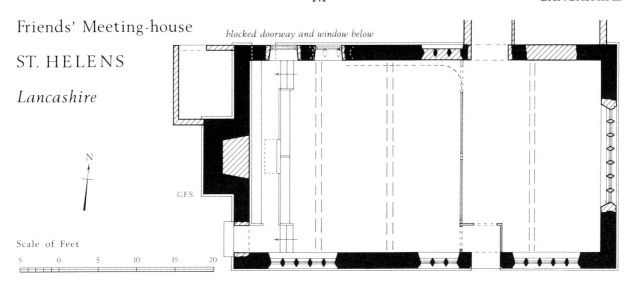

blocked doorway and window below

N

C.F.S.

Scale of Feet

5   0   5   10   15   20

John Lane, 1841, *et al.*

Christian Reformer (1868) 104–5. Evans (1897) 211–12. Herford and Evans (1909) 126–7. Nightingale III (1892) 240–4.

(228) CLOVER STREET CHAPEL (SD 894136). Brick with three-bay front and central entrance, tablet below upper window 'Unitarian Chapel 1818'. Built for a 'Cookite' or Methodist Unitarian congregation, formed by Joseph Cooke after his expulsion from the Methodist ministry, which previously occupied Providence Chapel, High Street. The congregation united with Blackwater Street in 1890 and the chapel was then used as a Sunday-school. (Rebuilt 1974)

Evans (1897) 213. McLachlan (1919). Nightingale III (1892) 240–4.

ROUGHLEE BOOTH

(229) Site of WESLEYAN, Rough Lee (SD 840401). The chapel, built 1823 but demolished since 1960, stood behind a row of cottages. *Monuments*: in small burial-ground include one to John Hargreaves, 1846, raised slab in railed enclosure.

Moore (1899) 213–14.

ROYTON   *Greater Manchester*

(230) FRIENDS' BURIAL-GROUND, Heyside (SD 932073). Corner of Shaw Road and Turf Lane, with 19th-century brick boundary wall. The site, in use since the late 17th century, was also occupied by meeting-houses of 1784 and 1884, both now demolished. *Monuments*: of mid 19th century and later. Unmarked burials include Sophia, mother of John Bright, 1806.

Ward, J., *A Retrospect of the Oldham Meeting of the Society of Friends* (1911).

ST HELENS   *Merseyside*

(231) FRIENDS, Church Street (SJ 515952). St Helens, or 'Hardshaw', was the seat of a monthly meeting in existence by 1678. A meeting-house near St Helen's Chapel was in use by 1680 and this was registered for Quakers as 'the house of George Shaw' in 1689. The present building, clearly of 17th-century

origin, was probably built in or before 1678; it was totally reconstructed internally in the mid 18th century and further modified in the late 19th century. It has walls of ashlar and the roof is covered with stone slates. The broad S front is entirely domestic in character with three stone-mullioned windows of five, three and five lights to the ground floor joined by a moulded string-course and two smaller upper windows of six and three lights at the ends. The doorway has a segmental-arched head and keystone.

The N wall has been much altered; two tall sash windows were inserted near the W end in the 19th century, below which a 17th-century window of three lights has been removed and a doorway near the W corner blocked; further E is a blocked window of three lights and moulded label balancing the similar window on the front. A modern wing projects to the rear. The E and W walls are gabled; that to the E has a larger mullioned-and-transomed window inserted in the late 19th century, the W wall is dominated by a massive stone chimney breast.

The interior (45½ft by 24¼ft) has been entirely altered and all floors or galleries removed. A mid 18th-century stand at the W end conceals the site of a large fireplace. The roof structure with four king-post trusses dates from the 19th century.

Friends' meeting-house, St Helens.   (231)

Fittings – *Stand*: front incorporates pierced flat balusters, 18th-century. *Sundial*: over S doorway square stone dial with iron gnomon, heavily painted, with date 1753.

(232) WELSH CHAPEL, Sutton Oak (SJ 530940). Low gabled brick front of three bays; side walls and cottage at rear all constructed of squared blocks of industrial slag. Mid 19th-century.

SALFORD   *Greater Manchester*

(233) CONGREGATIONAL, Chapel Street (SJ 832986). Five-bay brick front with two wide round-arched doorways with fanlights, dated 1819. Original stone balustrades and iron gates at front. Much rebuilt with loss of upper storey after wartime damage. (URC)

Nightingale V (1893) 213–17.

(234) CONGREGATIONAL, Broughton Park (SD 832022). Built in 1872–4 at the expense of several manufacturing families formerly attached to Richmond Chapel, Salford, to serve a new and fashionable residential district and hence of superior size and elaboration. Stone in the 14th-century Gothic style by S. W.

Welsh Chapel, Sutton Oak, St Helens.   (232)

Congregational chapel (URC), Broughton Park, Salford. (234)

Congregational chapel (URC), Broughton Park, Salford.   (234)

Dawkes, comprising an aisled nave with shallow transepts, a dominant tower and spire at the SE corner and triple gabled vestries with upper lecture hall at the N end with a polygonal staircase projection. The nave is of five bays, the arcades have pointed arches enriched with ball flower ornament above stone piers with clustered shafts and foliated capitals. (URC. Closed 1989, derelict 1991)

Anon., *Broughton Park Congregational Church...A Jubilee Souvenir* (1924). *Archaeological Journal* (1987) 26–9. CYB (1876) 441. Nightingale V (1893) 195.

(235) Former METHODIST, Gravel Lane (SJ 835988). Built 1790–1, superseded by a new chapel nearby in 1891 and subsequently in commercial use. Brick and slate with five-bay W front and two tiers of round-arched windows, gable rebuilt. N wall of six bays. S wall three bays only, the SE corner cut back in late 19th century for railway viaduct to Exchange Station. (Demolished since 1971)

FORMER METHODIST CHAPEL, GRAVEL LANE, SALFORD. CFS 1971

STRETFORD
Greater Manchester

(236) CONGREGATIONAL, Chorlton Road (SJ 829959). The chapel of 1860–1 by Poulton and Woodman has been demolished; part of the school premises were converted for church use c.1976. The church formerly met in Cannon Street (Hunter's Croft), Manchester, remaining as a remnant when the majority moved to Grosvenor Street Chapel. In the present building is a *monument* to the Rev. Caleb Warhurst, 1765, 'by whose labours under God this Place of Worship, together with the first Church assembling in it had the Rise'. (URC)

CYB (1862) 296. Nightingale V (1893) 107–32. *Reform* (December 1977) 5.

TOCKHOLES

(237) CONGREGATIONAL (SD 658230). Small chapel of rock-faced masonry with tall Y-traceried lancets, front porch and two-storeyed vestry annexe to rear with stone bell-cote; built 1880 to replace a meeting-house of 1710. An earlier Presbyterian meeting-house in 'Tockley' is named in a licence of 1672 for the Rev. John Harvie as 'erected for that purpose'.

Fittings – Bell: in bell-cote, inaccessible but possibly from earlier chapel. *Collecting Shovels*: three, with circular trays and handles, 19th-century. *Inscriptions*: in gallery, on reused panelling from former pews, ten sets of initials carved in relief with dates 1710 and 1711. *Monuments*: in burial-ground (1) Moses Cocker,

1825, Jane his widow, 1840, and Peggy their daughter, 1857, table-tomb; (2) Lawrence Haslam, 1769, Jane his widow, 1788, and Deborah their daughter, 1823, 'She Bequeathed to this Chapel the Sum of Twenty Pounds for a Sermon to be Preached on the 27th Day of March Annually', table-tomb; (3) James Mayo, 1791, Thomas, drowned (nd), Joseph, and Benjamin, sons of James and Jane Mayo, and Jane Jepson, 1825, table-tomb; (4) John Watson, 1762, James Wilkin, 1812, Mary his first wife, 1762, and Mary his second wife, 1822, table-tomb with earlier ledger stone below; (5) Rev. John Penkethman, 1848.

Nightingale, B., *History of the Old Independent Chapel, Tockholes...* (1886). Nightingale II (1891) 42–53.

(238) Site of BETHESDA CHAPEL (SD 657229). Built 1803 for seceders from the foregoing, closed c.1823, used as Sunday-school from 1851 and replaced by small mortuary chapel 1900. *Inscription*: reset in boundary wall, date tablet from chapel 'Bethesda Chapel 1803'. *Monuments*: in burial-ground (1) Rev. Robert Abram, 1852, and Mary his widow, 1869, table-tomb; (2) James Cocker, 1814, Betty his wife, 1805, Benjamin their son, 1806, *et al.*, box-tomb; (3) Ralph Richardson, 1819, Lydia his daughter, wife of James Riding, remainder obscured.

Nightingale (1886) *op. cit.*

TORVER
Cumbria

(239) Former BAPTIST, Sunny Bank (SD 290926). Largely rebuilt 1875 on the site of an earlier chapel. A Baptist church was first formed at Torver in 1678 by two of the elders of the Hexham church; it later had links with Hawkshead and was eventually re-formed as a preaching-station to Coniston.

Douglas (1846) 100–1. Whitley (1913) 113–19, 190.

TOTTINGTON
Greater Manchester

(240) CONGREGATIONAL, Greenmount (SD 778143). The first chapel, now a school, in Brandlesholme Road, was built in 1848; it is of six bays with round-arched windows in panelled recesses and has a former bell-cote at one end and a corresponding stack at the front. It was extended in 1880. The present chapel nearby in Holcombe Road, of 1886 by Woodhouse and Potts of Oldham, is of stone in the early Decorated style. It has a gabled front and corner tower with broach spire. To the right of the entrance is a polygonal staircase wing. (URC)

CYB (1867) 348. Nightingale III (1892) 211–15.

(241) ST JOHN'S FREE CHURCH OF ENGLAND, Kirklees Street (SD 776131). Gabled front with two entrances in pedimented portico; bell-cote on gable. Dated 1867. Former school alongside built 1869, enlarged 1905.

TRAWDEN

(242) FRIENDS' BURIAL-GROUND (SD 905390). Square walled enclosure in corner of Methodist cemetery; stone lintel inscribed 'I S: 1688' reset in front boundary wall. No monuments.

(243) INGHAMITE, Winewall (SD 911398). Three-bay stone front with round-arched doorways and windows, dated 1860. Former chapel nearby dated 1752 on lintel of former doorway, much altered and enlarged.

Thompson (1958) 65.

(244) WESLEYAN (SD 912388). The chapel of 1810, enlarged

1890, was demolished 1951. Some early 19th-century *monuments* remain in the burial-ground, including William Nelson Ash, infant son of William Ash, Methodist Minister, and Ann his wife, 1821.

Moore (1899) 173–4.

TURTON

(245) WALMSLEY CHAPEL (SD 704156). A chapel-of-ease within the parish of Bolton was in existence by 1552 to serve the district then known as Walmsley. Michael Briscoe, an Independent, appears to have served as curate at Walmsley from about 1648, though provoking much Presbyterian opposition, until the period of the Restoration. An Independent church continued in being and it is possible, though not proven, that dissenters retained some hold on the episcopal chapel until the early years of the following century.

The present chapel, 200 yards W of the main road, was built in 1713 during the pastorate of James Milne, also an Independent.

WALMSLEY CHAPEL, TURTON. CFS1968

The congregation now support a Unitarian ministry. The walls are of stone and the roof is covered with blue slates. The addition of galleries in the later 18th century may have been accompanied by a general heightening of the walls. Further major alterations took place in the late 19th century including re-roofing *c.*1860, much internal refitting *c.*1875 and the addition of a porch at the E end.

The site slopes steeply down to the W and the three lower windows in the side walls to N and S, each stone-mullioned of three lights, are stepped down to conform to the slope, perhaps formerly accompanied by a sloping or stepped floor internally with the pulpit at the W end. Three upper windows each side, generally similar to those below, are aligned horizontally. The W wall, of watershot construction, may have been rebuilt in the late 19th century and has a window of that period. The E wall, largely covered by the porch, has a stone bell-cote above the gable of *c.*1860 and a tablet dated 1713. S of the chapel is Walmsley School, dated 1851.

The interior (37¾ft by 32ft), much refitted in the late 19th century and given an open roof structure at that time, has galleries at the E end and along the N and S walls; these have fielded-panelled fronts supported by timber columns. The front of the E gallery, of the mid 18th century, is more elaborately moulded than the others and has fluted intermediate panels; its original supports have been replaced. The side galleries were added in 1783–8.

Fittings – Bell: in bell-cote, inaccessible. *Floorslabs*: in chapel, S of pulpit (1) Robert Milne, 1721, Rev. James Milne, twenty-four years minister, 1730, 'E. M.', 1735, 'J. M.', 1736; in vestibule (2) Ann daughter of William and Ellen Pilkington, 1787, *et al.*; (3) William Pilkington, 1770, and Ellen his widow, 1788. *Seating*: below side galleries, box-pews, late 18th-century.

Evans (1897) 246. Herford and Evans (1909) 136. Nightingale III (1892) 44–64.

(246) Former WESLEYAN, Bolton Road, Edgworth (SD 740 165). Square with three-bay gabled front and two tiers of round-arched windows. Built 1828, converted to Sunday-school after 1865. (Under conversion to five dwellings 1990)

TYLDESLEY   *Greater Manchester*

(247) TYLDESLEY CHAPEL (SD 691020). The chapel, later known as Top Chapel, was the first place of worship to be erected in

Walmsley Chapel, TURTON, *Lancashire*

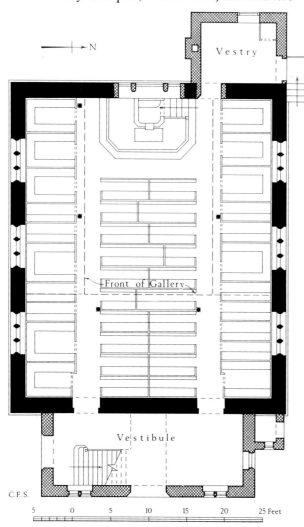

N

Vestry

Front of Gallery

Vestibule

C.F.S.

5   0   5   10   15   20   25 Feet

Tyldesley. It was built in 1789–90 on land donated by Thomas Johnson for the use of a minister in the Countess of Huntingdon's Connexion. In 1919 the congregation joined the Presbyterian Church of England and in 1978 the chapel was transferred to a Pentecostal church. The walls are of brown brick. The N front has two entrances with two tiers of plain Venetian windows between and a rebuilt bell-cote on the gable, now of brick but reported to have been earlier supported on four pillars. In the side walls are three wide round-arched windows, the upper glazing possibly altered, and in the S wall blind windows with brick tracery patterns.

Tyldesley Chapel.   (247)

The interior (approximately 60ft by 38ft) has been much changed and now has galleries of various dates around three sides and box-pews to the lower floor. The pulpit is said to have been originally on the W side with the communion table opposite. There are basement rooms below the chapel.

Bell: one, in bell-cote, inaccessible.

PHSJ II (1920) 17–23.

(248) UNITARIAN, Astley (SD 696004). Brick with round-arched windows; gabled front. Dated 1865. Sunday-school 1883.

ULVERSTON   *Cumbria*

(249) Former CONGREGATIONAL, Soutergate (SD 286787). The chapel, opened 8 July 1778 with a gallery added in 1839, is a plain building with rendered walls and low round-arched windows; it is now partly concealed behind a two-storeyed school building in the Tudor style built against the front wall in 1847.

Nightingale I (1890) 249–66.

(250) FRIENDS, Swarthmoor (SD 284769). Friends met from 1652 in a room at Swarthmoor Hall. In 1687 George Fox acquired the present site, comprising some buildings and three acres of land 'called Pettis' at Swarthmoor, which he then gave to

the society with instructions to convert one of the buildings for a meeting-house to be used only when Swarthmoor Hall was no longer available. The meeting-house was registered in 1689 and brought into regular use in 1690.

The walls are of rendered rubble and the roof is slated. Some traces of late 16th or early 17th-century work remain in the eastern part of the building but the remainder, while possibly incorporating some earlier structure, is largely of the late 17th century or after. The S front has a gabled porch with outer lintel inscribed 'EX DONO:G:F:/1688'. To the right are two windows of earlier date, of two lights with ogee-moulded stone mullions below a continuous moulded string-course, and two similar windows above. Left of the porch are three windows, perhaps originally with mullions and transoms but enlarged and replaced in 1829 by hung sashes and more recently by metal frames. The N wall is blank except for a small window, now below the gallery stair, with a substantial oak frame and two chamfered wood mullions, possibly of the late 16th century. The W wall is blank and partly hung with slates. The E wall is partly covered by a lower stable range; in the gable are two windows with wooden frames, each formerly with two wooden mullions.

The interior (54¼ft by 24ft) is divided by a passage flanked by screens with hinged shutters of *c.*1814 opening to the principal meeting-house on the W and the smaller women's meeting-house to the east. The latter has a fireplace with four-centred arched lintel. The staircase against the N wall dates from the 19th century and may replace a circular vice, of which slight traces

Friends' meeting-house, Swarthmoor.   (250)

Former Friends' meeting-house, Height. (*Photos: Bryan Horner, 1953.*)

(251)

remain in the NE corner. The gallery, or upper room, at the E end has shutters opening to the main room; it was given a sloping floor in the early 19th century.

The roof is supported by simple triangulated trusses with collars, carrying three purlins to each slope.

Fittings (some now at Swarthmoor Hall) – *Bed Frame*: in gallery, named in Fox's benefaction, 17th-century. *Book*: 'Treacle Bible', 1541, gift of George Fox (now in Friends' House, London). *Chairs*: two, with panelled backs and arms, one named in Fox's benefaction, 17th-century. *Chests*: two – (1) 'Fox's sea chest', rectangular wooden chest with flat lid, 17th-century; (2) wooden chest with arched lid, formerly covered with leather and ornamented with brass pins to form the inscription '1675/G. F.'. *Coffin Stool*: one, turned legs and moulded rails, late 17th-century. *Monuments*: in burial-ground, a few uniform round-topped headstones of 19th century and after. *Seating*: in large meeting-house, open-backed benches with shaped ends, 19th-century; in gallery, plain back-less benches, 19th-century. *Stand*: early 19th-century.

Butler (1978) 123–5. *C & WT*, NS VI (1906) 237–83. Richardson, J., *Furness Past and Present* I (1880) 188–91.

UPPER ALLITHWAITE   *Cumbria*

(251) Former FRIENDS, Height (SD 407848). The meeting-house was built in 1677 by Lawrence Newton at a cost of £106. 9s. 7d. Stables were built in 1691, in 1712 a cottage was added at the N end and about 1772 new window frames and some internal partitions were provided. The building was sold in 1922 but remained with little internal alteration until c.1964, when the front windows were altered and the seating, stand and a screen were removed.

The walls are of rendered rubble and the roof is slated. The E front has a two-storeyed gabled porch with semicircular arched entrance and small upper window; to the left are two altered and enlarged windows to the main meeting-house and to the right two tiers of windows to the women's meeting-house and gallery.

The interior (approximately 43ft by 23ft) is divided by a passage with a staircase opposite the entrance and an original panelled screen with shutters to the N; it formerly had to the S a screen inserted c.1772. Prior to 1964 the principal room had a stand at the S end with panelled back, open railed front with central entrance, and two ranks of open-backed benches.

Burial-ground: SE of meeting-house on opposite side of lane, walled enclosure with three flat stones and others upright with uniform rounded tops, 19th-century. *Inscription*: on porch 'LN/ANNO/DOMINI/1677'.

Butler (1978) 131–5. Wakefield, A. M., *Cartmel Priory and Sketches of North Lonsdale* (1909) 17–28.

WARDLE   *Greater Manchester*

(252) WESLEYAN (SD 912171). The first chapel, built 1808–9, stands close to its successor of 1874. Both are of stone with two tiers of round-arched windows but in their degree of elaboration they differ widely. The former has a plain three-bay front with central entrance, stone band below the upper windows and a smaller window in the gable; it was formerly surmounted by a square wooden bell-cote, now removed. The present chapel has

an open porch with paired Roman Doric columns, two doorways, conjoined upper windows and a lunette in the pediment; the interior has been subdivided.

Anon., *Centenary Souvenir of the Wardle Wesleyan Chapel, 1809–1909* (1909).

(253) Former WESLEYAN, Pot House Lane (SD 902163). Small three-bay building, now cottage, with round-arched windows and tablet over doorway inscribed: 'POTTERY WESLEYAN METHODIST SUNDAY-SCHOOL 1823 – Train up a child in the way he should go and when he is old he will not depart from it.'

WARRINGTON   *Cheshire*

(254) CAIRO STREET CHAPEL (SJ 60558810). Robert Yates, rector of Warrington, was ejected in 1662 and subsequently gathered a Presbyterian congregation which in 1672 licensed a room in the Court House for its meetings. In 1689 the society had the use of a barn formerly belonging to Lawrence Eccleston, and in 1703 occupation of the present site near the corner of Cairo Street and Sankey Street was confirmed in a lease from the Earl of Warrington to the minister, Charles Owen, of 'all that late erected building or meeting-house situate on a certain parcell of ground on the backside of a messuage or dwelling house in Sankey Street'. A house then occupied by a blacksmith whose smithy protruded into Sankey Street was bought about 1719 for use as the manse.

The present chapel, on the site of the former, was built in 1745 and originally was approached by a passage from Sankey Street; Cairo Street, to the W, was laid out in 1846 and then formed the principal access. The chapel was much altered and refitted c.1860 and later. The congregation have supported a Unitarian ministry since the late 18th century. The close connection between this congregation and the Warrington Dissenting Academy, commenced through the efforts of the minister, John Seddon, in 1757, is recalled by some of the memorial tablets on the walls of the chapel.

The chapel is a plain building of brown brick with a slate roof. The N and S walls are gabled. The N wall, partly covered by a building on the site of the manse, retains its original entrance over which is a blocked round-arched window, and in the gable a window to an attic room formerly annexed to the manse. The S wall has two doorways with wooden surrounds having pilasters, Doric entablatures and pediments, a large central round-arched window with keystone and renewed frame, and a circular window in the gable. The side walls, each of four bays divided by brick pilasters, have two tiers of round-arched windows with later wooden frames.

The interior (38¼ft by 57¼ft) was greatly altered, refitted and realigned c.1860 and later. The pulpit was originally set centrally against the W wall and a gallery extended the full length of the E wall. There are now no galleries and the seating faces north. There is a flat plaster ceiling with moulded cornice. The roof, of four bays with three king-post trusses having queen struts and diagonal braces, is accessible only via the adjacent property.

Fittings – *Clock*: on S wall, circular face, kidney-shaped case, 18th-century, repainted. *Inscription*: on wood, loose, probably from former pew, 'K W. 1689'. *Monuments*: in chapel, on N wall

Cairo Street Chapel, Warrington. (254)

Cairo Street Chapel, Warrington. Monument (5) to
Edward Garlick. (254)

(1) William Woodcock, 1777, Ann his widow, 1785, and
Johnson their son, 1784, erected 1790 by their daughter Amy
Fisher; on E wall (2) Holbrook Gaskell, 1842, signed 'W.
Spence, Liverpool'; (3) John Galway, of Portaferry, Ireland,
student in Warrington Academy, 1777; on S wall (4) Rev. John
Aikin, D.D., Professor in Warrington Academy, 1780, tablet
with apron and shaped cheeks, top missing, Latin inscription,
signed 'B. Bromfield'; on W wall (5) Edward Garlick, of
Virginia, student in Warrington Academy, 1758, erected by his
uncle, Edward Garlick, tall tablet with shaped cheeks and open
pediment surmounted by urn; (6) Rev. William Broadbent, over
30 years pastor, tutor in dissenting academies at Daventry and
Northampton, 1827, erected by his widow, also to Rev. Thomas
Biggin Broadbent A.M., his son, 1817; (7) John Andrews
Wilson, student in Warrington Academy, 1760, erected by his
father, Joseph Wilson of Rivington, square tablet with
elaborately decorated cheeks and apron, surmounted by obelisk
with portrait roundel in low relief and urn finial. In burial-
ground S of chapel are several table-tombs of late 18th century
and after. (For a full record of the internal monuments, but with
some minor errors in transcription, and a list of others, see
Bulmer (1980) *op. cit.* below.) *Plate*: includes two tall 18th-
century standing cups, one of 1735, with secondary donatory
inscriptions.

The Warrington Academy was conducted from 1757 to 1762 in a
large early 18th-century house at the S end of Bridge Street
(SJ 60728788). The house, of three storeys and attics with a front
of five bays, enlarged to the N by one bay in the mid 18th
century, was moved intact to a new site 20 yards N in 1981.
From 1762 until its closure in 1786 the academy occupied a new
building at one end of Academy Street; demolished late 19th
century.

Bulmer, J. R. (ed.), *The Unitarian Chapel, Cairo Street,
Warrington* (1980). Evans (1897) 250–1. Hague and Hague (1986)
42–3. McLachlan, H., *Warrington Academy, its History and
Influence* (Chetham Soc., NS CVII, 1943). Mounfield, A., *Early
Warrington Nonconformity* (1922). Nightingale IV (1892) 206–27.

(255) CONGREGATIONAL, Bewsey Street (SJ 604886). Brick with
tall corner tower, 1873 by George Woodhouse. (URC)

Hawthorne, J., *Centenary of Wycliffe Congregational Church*
(1951). Nightingale IV (1892) 227–42.

(256) Former COUNTESS OF HUNTINGDON'S, Winwick Street
(SJ 60628870). St John's Chapel was built in 1807 for seceders
from the church of St James, Latchford, who were served by
ministers in the Countess of Huntingdon's Connexion and
others until 1851, when a Congregational church was formed.
The latter removed in 1851 to Salem Chapel, Golborne Street.
The chapel was reopened in 1854 by the Presbyterian Church in
England; it is now in commercial use.

The walls are of brick with two tiers of round-arched
windows, those in the side wall having their original frames with
intersecting glazing bars. The front was rendered and otherwise
embellished *c.*1854.

Nightingale IV (1892) 246–8.

(257) FRIENDS, Buttermarket Street (SJ 608882). A meeting-
house in Buttermarket, built in 1725, was superseded by the
present building in 1829–30. This stands on an enclosed site on

Wycliffe Congregational Chapel (URC), Bewsey Street, Warrington.   (255)

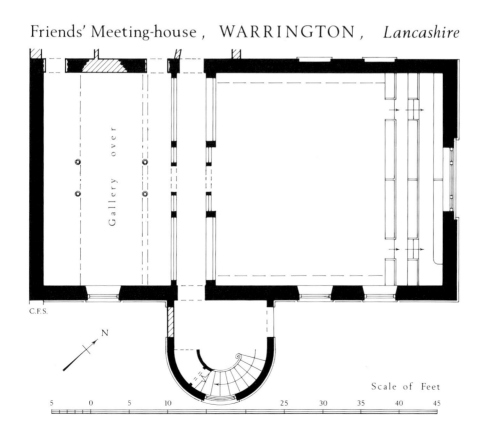

Friends' Meeting-house, WARRINGTON, *Lancashire*

C.F.S.

N

Scale of Feet

5   0   5   10   25   30   35   40   45

Friends' meeting-house, Warrington.   (257)

FORMER METHODIST CHAPEL, BANK STREET, WARRINGTON   CFS1971

the S side of the street. The walls are of red brick and the roof is slated. The SE front has a semicircular porch enclosing the gallery staircase flanked by tall hung-sash windows to the two principal rooms. The larger room, to the NE, has a wide segmental-arched window with tripartite frame in the end wall with the contemporary stand below. The walls are lined with a panelled dado and formerly had wall-benches. The rooms are separated by a passage with hung shutters. The ceiling of the women's meeting-house at the SW end terminates in a deep plaster cove above the possible site of a second stand. There is a gallery over the passage and SW room.

A detached *meeting-house* 30 yards E, sometime used for a

Quaker Adult School, with adjoining cottage, is thought to have served a Southcottian congregation in the early 19th century.

(258) Former METHODIST, Bank Street (SJ 60758817). Methodist meetings in Warrington commenced in the mid 18th century in rented premises. The first regular preaching-house, built in 1755 in Back Dallam Lane, survived as a cottage until the early 20th century. This was superseded in 1778 (possibly 1782) by the chapel in Bank Street, which remained in use until 1850. It subsequently served as a County Court, Ragged School, and latterly as Bethel Free Church.

The chapel has brick walls and a slate roof. The side walls to N and S have two tiers of round-arched windows with plain impost

Wesleyan chapel, Bold Street, Warrington.   (259)

Wesleyan chapel, Bold Street, Warrington.   (259)

blocks, moulded keystones, continuous stone cills, and wooden sashes with intersecting glazing bars. A rectangular projection at the E end has, at the lower level, a vestry or communion window with three-centred arched brick head enclosing a tripartite frame with hung sashes having pointed-arched heads to each light; above is a round-arched window. The W front is covered by an early 19th-century extension of three storeys with a rendered front wall of five bays, the N bay more widely spaced and separately roofed, with a wide round-arched central entrance, plain hung-sash windows and a moulded eaves cornice.

The interior (53¼ft by 43½ft) has been divided by the insertion of a floor at gallery level and the subdivision of the lower space. The plaster ceiling retains an original large central roundel ornamented with swags and fluting. The roof is supported by three trusses with king-posts, queen struts and diagonal braces. Below part of the chapel is a storage cellar with external access. (Demolished 1974)

WHSP VIII (1911–12) 57–61, 81–5.

(259) WESLEYAN, Bold Street (SJ 604881). Built 1850, by James Simpson of Leeds, to supersede Bank Street Chapel. Red brick with stone dressings, four-bay front with two tiers of round-arched windows, the upper range with pedimented surrounds, and five-bay sides. Large interior (80ft by 60ft) with continuous round-ended gallery and original seating including substantial box-pews. Coffered ceiling with enriched cornice. Vestries were added in 1854, ministers' houses 1856, Sunday-school and chapel-

keeper's house, 1884. The original two-decker pulpit was replaced by a large rostrum in 1900; the first organ, installed 1856, was replaced in 1907. (Demolished 1973)

Sellers (1976) No. 6.

(260) INDEPENDENT METHODIST, Cairo Street (SJ 605880). The first chapel at 'Friars Green' was built in 1802 for a society of Independent Methodists formed of Quakers and Wesleyan seceders originally designated 'Quaker Methodists'. The present chapel, which stands on the same site, was built in 1859–60 but it

Wesleyan chapel, Warton.   (261)

has been much altered. In 1879 a floor was inserted at gallery level and the lower storey converted to school-rooms; it was further altered in 1912. In 1938 the whole structure was strengthened by thickening some of the outer walls and adding many buttresses.

The chapel has brick walls with two tiers of round-arched windows with keystones and impost blocks. The end bays of the E front are gabled. Some traces of the former gallery structure remain.

Monuments: in chapel (1) James Whittle, 1816, and Ann his widow 1822, cast-iron tablet; (2) Peter Phillips, 1853, itinerant preacher.

Kendall (1905) I: 545. Durant, W., *The Story of Friars' Green Church* (1951).

WARTON

(261) WESLEYAN (SD 502726). Opened 1835; rubble and slate, two round-arched windows in each side wall, frames renewed since 1960.

WESTHOUGHTON   *Greater Manchester*

(262) CONGREGATIONAL, Park Road (SD 658058). Brown brick with lancet windows, 1853. *Monument*: in burial-ground to Joseph Sykes Carter, minister, 1860. (URC)

Nightingale IV (1892) 123–7.

(263) FRIENDS, Wigan Road (SD 649053). Built 1823, with rendered brick walls and a slate roof. Small porch with two inner doorways to the principal W room and a smaller E room with later loft or gallery over approached by an external staircase. The rooms are separated by wooden screens with hinged shutters. (Demolished 1972)

(264) INDEPENDENT METHODIST (SD 631076). Sunday-school dated 1861, with 'Independent Methodist or Free Gospel Chapel' of 1867 behind.

WHEELTON

(265) WESLEYAN, Blackburn Road (SD 608223). Stone and slate, three-bay front with pedimental gable, lunette tablet 'Wesley Chapel 1842', round-arched windows. Later porch.

WHITEFIELD   *Greater Manchester*

(266) CONGREGATIONAL, Besses o' th' Barn (SD 809052). Large chapel of 1865 at the junction of Bury New Road and Bury Old Road. Brown brick with black and yellow bands and stone dressings. Plate-traceried wheel-windows to W front and N and S transepts. (URC)

WHITWORTH

(267) HALL FOLD CHAPEL (SD 882177). The church meeting here originated as a Presbyterian society in the late 17th century, possibly in connection with Whitworth Chapel, a chapel-of-ease to Rochdale, where some evidence for a non-conforming ministry has been claimed. In 1833 the church joined the Lancashire Presbytery but in 1847 it became Congregational (now URC). The first chapel, which stood further W in the burial-ground on the opposite side of the road, was erected in 1718; it had two tiers of windows of three lights and a bell-cote on the front gable. It was demolished in 1849.

Congregational chapel (URC), Besses o' th' Barn.   (266)

The second chapel of stone in the Romanesque style, designed by David Russell of Rochdale, was opened in March 1850. The E front is gabled and has terminal pilaster buttresses rising to pinnacles, two doorways alternating with three round-arched windows, and a large circular window centrally above. The interior ($56\frac{3}{4}$ft by 45ft) has a continuous round-ended gallery and

Hall Fold Chapel, Whitworth.   (267)

Hall Fold Chapel, Whitworth. (267)

an arched recess at the W end for the organ. The pulpit was replaced in 1882 by a large rostrum but the original seating in box-pews remains throughout. (Demolished since 1970; adjacent Sunday-school converted)

Fittings – *Inscription*: on tablet in vestibule, 'Hallfold Chapel A.D. 1849'. *Monuments*: in chapel, Rev. Thomas Robinson, 23 years minister, 1819, Elizabeth his wife, their infant daughter, and Richard their son, 24 years minister at Witham, Essex, and subsequently here, 1858, all buried 'beneath the aisle of the former chapel'; in burial-ground W of chapel, late 18th-century ledger stones. *Organ*: 'Erected A.D. 1868'.

Nightingale III (1892) 269–79. Stott, R. C., *Hallfold Congregational Chapel, Whitworth, 1698–1948* (1948).

(268) Former PRIMITIVE METHODIST, Tong Lane (SD 885184). Small stone chapel with wide round-arched windows, 1850.

(269) Former UNITED METHODIST, Market Street (SD 884176). Stone with pedimented front, 1878; earlier Sunday-school behind.

WIGAN   *Greater Manchester*

(270) Former CHURCH OF CHRIST, Rodney Street (SD 584054). A society of Christian Brethren was formed in Wigan in 1841. The present building, inscribed 'A Christian Meeting House. 1858', is of brick with two tiers of round-arched windows. The front faces S and has at the E end an arched passage to the rear and at the W end a former house of three storeys with separate arched entrance. The principal accommodation comprises the chapel,

Church of Christ meeting-house, Rodney Street, Wigan. (270)

which is at first-floor level and has a segmental-arched plaster ceiling, and a large school-room on the ground floor. (Closed 1989, sold 1991)

Robinson, W. and Crook, R. K., *Centenary of the Church of Christ, Wigan, 1841–1941* (1941).

(271) Former CHURCH OF CHRIST, Albert Street, Newtown (SD 567050). Three-bay gabled front of brown brick with tall white

Former Church of Christ meeting-house, Albert Street, Wigan.   (271)

brick pilasters and arches with keystones. Built 1878. Now gymnasium.

(272) PRIMITIVE METHODIST, Whelley (SD 599069). Brick, centre bay rises in advance of pediment; 1868. (Derelict 1991)

WISWELL

(273) CONGREGATIONAL, Barrow (SD 739385). Small stone chapel built 1876 to supersede, and as a memorial to, Thomas Jollie's chapel at Wymondhouses (*see* (178)). Tablet from latter incorporated in front gable is inscribed 'T:I/LUKE:VII:V/1688'. *Seat*: in chapel, 'Jollie's chair', short pew incorporating panelled back of uncertain date.
   Nightingale II (1891) 196–9.

Congregational chapel, Barrow.   (273)

(274) Former CONGREGATIONAL, Wiswell (SD 746374). Built 1831, altered 1874, closed 1879, converted to cottages Nos. 4 and 6 Chapel Fold, 1882. Front formerly with two doorways, a window centrally between and four round-arched windows above.
   Nightingale II (1891) 196–9.

WITHNELL

(275) FREE METHODIST, Abbey Village (SD 641225). Square gritstone chapel with gabled three-bay front and lancet windows; deep gallery left of entrance facing original pulpit. Built 1848 to serve model industrial village.

WOODPLUMPTON

(276) WESLEYAN, Moor Side (SD 491358). Plain three-bay gabled front, simple Venetian window over entrance. Opened 1819.
   Hewitson (1872) 554–5.

WORSTHORNE WITH HURSTWOOD

(277) WESLEYAN, Worsthorne (SD 874324). Low gabled front dated 1837. Larger chapel built 1875–7, demolished 1984. *Monuments*: in front of earlier chapel include (1) John Hitchon, stonemason, 1852 and Ellen his widow, 1853, signed 'H. S'.

WRAY-WITH-BOTTON

(278) Former FRIENDS, Wray (SD 602677). Rectangular building of rubble with stone slate roof; built 1704, sold 1958 and since used as meeting-room for Methodist chapel. Side walls of four bays with mullioned-and-transomed windows, entrance on N side with former stable to north. Interior ($36\frac{3}{4}$ft by 20ft) has a plaster ceiling, fireplace at E end with corbelled lintel, and platform for altered stand opposite.

Former Friends' meeting-house, Wray.   (278)

Fittings – *Door*: in N doorway, 19th-century but with early 18th-century lock reused. *Monuments*: in burial-ground to S, four round-topped headstones of 1838 and later, also burial mounds. *Noticeboard*: on W wall facing road, with decayed painted inscription intimating that 'a Free Library illustrative of the History and Principles of the Society of Friends is Kept on the premises'.

(279) WESLEYAN, Wray (SD 601677). Coursed stone with entrance in rendered gable-end wall. Broad front to road with three three-light windows under labels; the centre window

Tunley Presbyterian Chapel (URC), Wrightington.   (281)

replaces original entrance and has a reset tablet below dated 1848. Contemporary rostrum pulpit.

(280) Former FREE METHODIST, Wray (SD 603675). Dated 1867, converted to cottage.

WRIGHTINGTON

(281) TUNLEY CHAPEL (SD 538124). Built in 1691 for a Presbyterian society which traced its origins to the ejection in 1662 of Jonathan Scholefield as curate of 'Douglas Chapel', a chapel-of-ease in the parish of Eccleston. The Wilson family of Tunley Hall were early supporters of the cause and the chapel appears to have been erected at the expense of Thomas and Elizabeth Wilson, the latter placing it in trust in 1703 after her husband's death, reserving for herself the right to approve a choice of minister. During the later 18th century heterodox doctrines prevailed but in 1797 the chapel was reported to have been 'given up by trustees to kirkmen, under the advice of the parson of the parish'; the congregation sided with the United Secession Church and more recently was associated with the Presbyterian Church of England. (Now URC)

The chapel, which has suffered greatly from refurbishment in the late 19th century and after, is a rectangular structure of coursed stone with a stone slated roof. The side walls have each three windows of four lights, some with decorative plaster cheeks, and simple stone labels. The entrance originally on the S side was re-sited at the W end in the 19th century. Prior to 1880 a small vestry of 1691 stood to the E which, by analogy with Risley Chapel (see (66)), may have been intended at first as a chancel.

The interior (37¾ft by 21¾ft) has been entirely refitted since 1880. Nightingale refers to a small original W gallery with a pew dated 1691 and to other contemporary pews including two large pews of the Wilson family at the opposite end. The roof is supported by two trusses with quadrant-moulded tie-beams and diagonal braces.

Fittings – Bell and Bell-cote: above W gable, both replaced 1881; the former bell inscribed 'SJ EC 1691' was later placed for

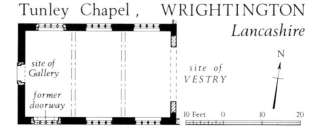

Tunley Chapel, WRIGHTINGTON
Lancashire

safe-keeping with the Presbyterian Historical Society, which suffered it to be recast in 1954 for use elsewhere. *Monuments*: in burial-ground, mid 18th-century and later.

Nightingale IV (1892) 23–7. *PHSJ* IV (1931) 240; X (1955) 184–93.

YEALAND CONYERS

(282) FRIENDS (SD 504745). The meeting-house was built in 1692 but refitted after a fire in 1737; the roof was renewed in 1842 and cloakrooms and kitchens added at the E end in 1967. The walls are of rendered rubble and the roof is covered with slates. The front faces S and has an original gabled porch with moulded kneelers and arched outer doorway inscribed with the date of erection. Two sash windows to the left of the porch have moulded surrounds and were probably filled with stone mullions and transoms. To the right are two storeys of windows, each formerly of two lights.

Two inner doorways in the porch open respectively to the large meeting-house to the W (26½ft by 22ft) and a much smaller room to the E with a fireplace against the end wall. The rooms are separated by a structural wall pierced by two shuttered openings and a modern doorway. Above the E end is a gallery with open fielded-panelled front, partly closed below by similar panelling and supported by fluted wood piers.

Fittings – *Doors*: inside porch, two, of nine and six fielded panels, heavily scratched with initials and dates from 1771. *Seating*: in gallery, open-backed benches, altered, 18th-century; lower benches late 19th-century. *Stand*: at W end, with fielded-panelled back, *c*.1737.

Southall (1974) 49–50.

Unlike the corresponding border county of Cumberland, Northumberland exhibits a close affinity with Scotland in its religious development and is unique in the number of old-established orthodox Presbyterian congregations which reflect in their varied historical allegiance the several parties that developed by secession from the established Church of Scotland. The great progress made by Methodism, particularly in the 19th century in the industrial and mining areas of the south-east of the county, is equally remarkable and, although the general picture remains of a predominantly Presbyterian dissent, the number of Methodist congregations listed in Kelly's *Directory of Northumberland* (1910) was 271 compared with only 79 Presbyterian. Congregations of other denominations at that date included Congregationalists 21, Salvation Army 19, Baptists 15, Brethren 13, and Friends 4.

Although many 18th-century meeting-houses survive in the county only that of the Friends at Coanwood (31), of 1760, has been spared a major refitting in the following century. The long and narrow proportions of Kielder (51), Bavington (14), Norham (66), Branton (50) and Birdhope-craig (69) are to be found elsewhere in the north of England; of these Bavington, in particular, retains clear evidence of its original arrangement. Larger meeting-houses of greater depth occur in the major towns, of which the

Low and Middle meeting-houses in Berwick (21, 22) and the two in Wooler (87, 88) are noteworthy, together with that at Etal (37) enlarged in 1806, which, although serving a country congregation, is of town proportions. Ten chapels were recorded, with dates from 1783 at Glanton (38) to 1836 at Berwick (23), in which the standard elevation occurs of two doorways with a pair of tall windows between and two smaller ones above the entrances; the Low Meeting-house at Berwick (21), although dated 1719, was probably refronted in this period.

Gothic elements were not widely adopted until the mid 19th century, although the Wesleyans used two-centred arched windows in Berwick (19) in 1797 and the former Presbyterian chapel in Clavering Place, Newcastle (64), of 1822, with its four-centred arched openings, is equally of note. Later conformity to the prevailing Gothic fashion is evident at Wallace Green, (24), of 1858–9, while Cubitt's Baptist chapel at Jesmond, (60), of 1889, now demolished, was a good example of the work of this architect.

With few exceptions stone is used for walling throughout the county; the only major examples of brickwork recorded were the extension of *c.*1800 to the chapel in Cottingwood Lane, Morpeth (58), and Brunswick Chapel, Newcastle (62), of 1820–1. Most of the buildings are now covered with blue slates.

ALLENDALE

(1) FRIENDS, Allendale Town (NY 834557). Rubble with rusticated quoins, doorway between three hung-sash windows at front; lobby and two rooms separated by shutters, triple-entry stand to larger room. Built 1868 on foundations of a meeting-house of 1735.

(2) WESLEYAN, Keenley (NY 804567). A Methodist society gathered by Christopher Hopper first met in a room in his farmhouse at Hindley Hill. John Wesley visited the society there in 1749. In 1754 a chapel was built at Keenley, claimed to be the second preaching-house to be erected in the northernmost counties of England. This appears to have had living accommodation below the principal room which was approached by an external staircase. The present chapel on the same remote site was built in 1874; it has a gabled front with three-centred arched doorway in a gabled porch and pointed-arched side windows.

Curnock (1938) III: 57, 429. Dolbey (1964) 72–3.

(3) WESLEYAN, Allendale Town (NY 836558). Gabled front of three bays with slightly projecting centre; round-arched windows, grouped above entrance. Built 1875–7.

(4) Former WESLEYAN, Catton (NY 828577). Broad five-bay front with central gabled porch and pointed-arched windows; built 1870.

(5) Former PRIMITIVE METHODIST, Allendale Town (NY 838 559). The chapel in Dawson Place, dated 1878, is now a library. It has pointed-arched windows with intersecting glazing bars and a row of seven memorial stones beneath. Attached to one end is the previous chapel of the early 19th century, of three bays with two tiers of sash windows; recess above doorway for former inscription tablet.

(6) PRIMITIVE METHODIST, Catton (NY 831575). Polygonal front with dodecagonal spirelet; dated 1882.

(7) Former PRIMITIVE METHODIST, Sinderhope (NY 844524). 'Jubilee Chapel, 1860'; three-bay front with rusticated quoins and round-arched windows. Small cottage below with access at rear

on sloping site. Stepped seating to left of entrance. (Under conversion to house, 1990)

ALNWICK

(8) SION MEETING-HOUSE, St Michael's Lane (NU 187132). The congregation formerly meeting here originated about 1729 in a secession from the Presbyterian meeting in Pottergate. A meeting-house built in Bondgate in 1736 was enlarged in 1768 and sold in 1816, following the erection of the present chapel. In the late 18th century the congregation was loosely attached to the Relief Church but by the beginning of the following century had adopted an Independent polity in which the church continued until its cessation c.1950–60. The building is now in commercial use.

Sion Meeting-house, Alnwick. (8)

The meeting-house has stone walls and a hipped slated roof. The broad front wall of four bays, facing E, has two tiers of windows with three-centred arched heads; at the centre of this elevation is an oval tablet inscribed 'SION MEETING HOUSE ERECTED 1815'. The entrances are in narrow wings at the N and S ends. The interior originally had a gallery on three sides and the pulpit against the longer W wall; in 1866 the galleries were replaced by a single deeper S gallery with pulpit opposite.

CHST V (1911–12) 149–50. Tate II (1869) 172–80.

(9) METHODIST, Chapel Lane (NU 186132). Methodist meetings in Alnwick commenced c.1744 and a small square preaching-house of brick, called the 'new room', was later built in Green Batt. This was succeeded in 1786–7 by the present building in Chapel Lane. A subsequent decline in the fortunes of the society led to the insertion of a floor at gallery level; in 1886 a 'restoration' was carried out, recorded on a tablet on the rear SE wall.

The chapel has walls of squared stone and the roof, gabled to NE and SW, is covered with slates. The front wall has two entrances with late 19th-century barge-boarded porches, and a tall three-centred arched window of two lights above each; over an inserted bay window between the entrances is a tablet inscribed 'WESLEYAN CHAPEL 1786'. The interior (40¾ft by 48½ft), entirely altered in the late 19th century, comprises a chapel at first-floor level with Sunday-school rooms below. *Pulpit*: loose on ground floor, five sides with two tiers of fielded panels, late 18th-century.

Tate II (1869) 193–200. *WHSP* VII (1909–10) 63–9, 88–96.

(10) PRESBYTERIAN, Pottergate (NU 184135). The congregation (now St James's URC) originated in the late 17th century. The former meeting-house was replaced in 1894–5 with a Gothic building of stone by Hicks and Charlewood with a substantial corner tower and prominent octagonal turret and spirelet.

Fittings – *Alms Dish*: pewter, badly worn, inscribed on rim 'HEB XIII 16 LUKE 12 33 REMEMBER THE POOR 1689', diam. 12¼in. *Plate*: includes a pair of plated two-handled cups, dated 1795, and a pair of pewter flagons 'made in Edinburgh'.

Tate II (1869) 159–71.

(11) Former PRESBYTERIAN, Lisburn Street (NU 185130). The chapel was built in 1840 for a congregation supported by the Relief Presbytery of Kelso which had met from 1837 in a building in Percy Street; after 1847 it became known as the Second United Presbyterian Church of Alnwick. In 1884 the chapel was reopened by a Baptist congregation which still uses it. The building has a plain domestic exterior of stone with ashlar facing to the principal elevations and two tiers of windows.

Catherall, G. A., *A Short History of the Baptist Church in Alnwick, 1883–1957* (1957). Mackelvie (1873) 99. Tate II (1869) 192.

(12) Former UNITED PRESBYTERIAN, Clayport (NU 185132). The congregation formerly meeting here was gathered in 1753 in connection with the Associate (Burgher) Presbytery of Edinburgh. Three meeting-houses on other sites, in Canongate, Clayport Street, and Green Batt, preceded the erection of the present chapel in 1846–7. In 1955 the congregation united with Pottergate and the building is now used as an auction room. The chapel has stone walls, the front is gabled between two octagonal crenellated towers, and the principal windows have pointed-arched heads with intersecting glazing bars; in the gable is a cusped octofoil opening and a tablet below with the date 1846.

Anon., *Clayport Presbyterian Church, Centenary 1847–1947* (1947). Mackelvie (1873) 98–9. Tate II (1869) 181–92.

Former United Presbyterian chapel, Clayport, Alnwick. (12)

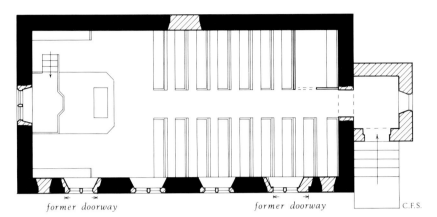

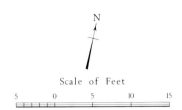

N

Scale of Feet

5   0   5   10   15

former doorway   *former doorway*   C.F.S.

ANCROFT

(13) Former PRESBYTERIAN, Ancroft North Moor (NT 963456). Rubble walls with dwarf pinnacles at the corners. Gabled front with two pointed-arched entrances, now concealed, central window with Y-tracery, tablet inscribed 'ANCROFT ENGLISH PRESBYTERIAN CHURCH ERECTED FOR THE REV. W. RYDER 1845'. Three pointed-arched windows in side walls. *Bell*: one, externally in front gable.

BAVINGTON

(14) PRESBYTERIAN, Great Bavington (NY 984803). The congregation (now URC) originated in the late 17th century and claims to have had amongst its early preachers Robert Blunt, ejected vicar of Kirk Harle. A meeting-house, in existence by 1693, was replaced by the present building in 1725. Drastic alterations in 1869 involving complete refenestration and refitting have left little original work beyond the masonry of the outer walls. The walls are of rubble and the roof is covered with slates. The original front wall facing S had two entrances with narrow windows adjacent and possibly two windows between; traces of the original openings remain between the four tall windows, each of two round-arched lights, inserted in 1869. The present entrance in a 19th-century porch against the E gable wall has a

reused lintel to the outer doorway inscribed 'DD EB 1725' and the later inscription 'A F [for Alex. Forsyth, minister] 1869'. The W gable wall originally had two tiers of windows, now replaced by a window similar to those in the S wall. The N wall, now blank, has a blocked window centrally below the eaves. The interior (18½ft by 39¾ft) has been entirely refitted. There were probably galleries at the E and W ends and the pulpit may have stood against the S wall.

Fittings – *Communion Tokens*: five types are known (Herdman (1901) Nos. 6–10) including the only saucer-shaped token. *Plate*: includes two cups with baluster stems of 1655 and 1658, a pair of mid 18th-century pewter flagons and a large pewter dish. *Sundial*: on S wall, early 19th-century.

Black (1906) 314–16. Page, A. H., '*Whose light must never die*', *A Brief Account of the Congregations of North Middleton and Great Bavington* (1962).

BELFORD

(15) PRESBYTERIAN, Nursery Lane (NU 110338). The congregation (now URC) originated in 1776 in a secession from the Church of Scotland; the chapel, possibly on the site of a meeting-house converted from a cottage, has a broad rendered front with two tall round-arched pulpit windows characteristic of the early 19th century.

Mackelvie (1873) 108.

BELLINGHAM

(16) PRESBYTERIAN (NY 838837). Stone with some brick banding, 1882–3 by W. L. Newcombe replacing a chapel of 1806. (URC)

Mackelvie (1873) 536.

BERWICK-UPON-TWEED

(17) Former BAPTIST, 1–3 Walkergate (NT 99725305). The chapel was built in 1810 for a church formed in 1803. In 1858 the church moved to the former Congregational chapel in Castlegate and their first chapel has since been converted to a shop. Ashlar front with rusticated quoins, eaves cornice, scrolled corbels to end gables and platband below three tall round-arched upper windows; lower openings replaced by shop front. Interior subdivided and ceiling lowered.

Scott (1888) 372.

Great Bavington Presbyterian Chapel (URC).   (14)

(18) Former CONGREGATIONAL, Castlegate (NT 99705315). The chapel was built 1848–9 for an existing congregation which shortly afterwards disbanded; in 1858 it was taken by the Baptists from Walkergate (*see* (17)). It has stone walls and a slated roof, a gabled front with grouped lancets and empty bell-cote, and pairs of lancets in the side walls. (Demolished since 1980)

CYB (1900) 200, obituary of Rev. W. D. Knowles. Scott (1888) 372.

(19) WESLEYAN, Walkergate (NT 999531). The chapel was built in 1797 for a society in existence by 1748 which formerly met in the Town Hall. In 1825 the interior was altered to increase the seating capacity, and in 1871–8 it was further altered and the manse which stood in front of the chapel was rebuilt to provide minor accommodation. In 1921 the Wesleyans sold the building to the Primitive Methodists formerly meeting in College Place (*see* (20)). The chapel, which has stone walls and a slate-covered roof, stands behind a forebuilding of similar materials with a S front of three bays in two storeys and a central arched entrance

Wesleyan chapel, Walkergate, Berwick-upon-Tweed.   (19)

with the dates 1797, 1878. The W wall of squared stone has five tall pointed-arched windows; the original entrance, now blocked, was below the altered centre window, the cill of which is inscribed with the date of erection. The interior (46ft by 25¼ft), entirely refitted in the late 19th century, has a S gallery. The roof has five original trusses with tie-beams and collar-beams and double purlins with tusk tenon joints to the principal rafters.

WHSP XXXIII (1961–2) 161–9.

(20) Former PRIMITIVE METHODIST, College Place (NT 998532). The chapel together with a school-room and manse were built in 1830 for a newly formed society. In 1921 services were transferred to the former Wesleyan chapel (*see* (19)). The building, now in commercial use, has stone walls and a slate roof. The ashlar front has two end entrances and two tall windows between, all with round-arched heads, circular windows above the entrances and a large central roundel, perhaps for an inscription. The interior, nearly square, has been gutted, but formerly had a gallery around three sides and the pulpit centrally against the front wall. (Demolished since 1980)

WHSP XXXIII (1961–2) 161–9.

(21) The LOW MEETING-HOUSE, Hide Hill (NU 000528). The oldest nonconformist congregation in the town originated in the late 17th century amongst the supporters of the Rev. Luke Ogle, ejected vicar of Berwick. Until 1719, when the meeting-house in Hide Hill was erected, services had been held in the Grammar

Former Presbyterian Low Meeting-house,
Berwick-upon-Tweed.   (21)

School. The congregation was seriously disturbed after 1845 by a legal action as a result of which the minister, who supported the cause of the Free Church of Scotland, was dispossessed and the meeting-house held to be in trust for dissenters in connection with the established Church of Scotland; the minister and the majority of the congregation then left to form a separate cause (*see* (23)). The remainder of the congregation were joined in 1879 by the *High Meeting* which had been formed in 1724 and whose meeting-house, long since demolished, stood behind the E side of High Street (NT 998530). The combined congregation removed in 1897 to St Andrew's, Greenside Avenue (*see* (26)) and the Low Meeting-house now serves as a garage for the Brown Bear Inn.

The meeting-house, which stands well back from the street on the SE side of Hide Hill, has walls of rubble with an ashlar front and a hipped slated roof. Although built in 1719 it was much altered in the 19th century. The W front, which has a high rusticated plinth, two doorways with small windows over, and two tall round-arched windows between, is dated 1719; it closely resembles Zion Chapel (23) of 1835–6 and may have been refronted at that period. The rear wall of four bays now has two tiers of windows, replacing four taller windows. The interior (42¼ft by 48½ft) has been entirely gutted and the roof rebuilt, but traces remain of galleries, perhaps inserted, around three sides and of the site of the pulpit against the front wall. The *Berwick Directory* of *c*.1806 describes it as 'a pretty meeting-house, well seated, with an excellent gallery and pews painted in stile'. (Demolished since 1980)

Black (1906) 298–300. Palmer III (1803) 55–8. *PHSJ* XII (1960–3) 170–8.

(22) The MIDDLE MEETING-HOUSE, Chapel Street (NT 999530). The Middle Meeting was commenced about 1756 by Thomas Monteith, sometime usher in the grammar school and later proprietor of a private school. After 1788 the Presbyterian congregation was connected with The Relief Church. A division in 1835 over the appointment of a new minister led to the erection of Zion Chapel (*see* (23)) and the meeting appears to have been discontinued shortly after 1900. The building has since been used as a bakery and latterly as a motor repair shop.

The meeting-house built in 1756 has walls of sandstone rubble, heavily pointed and with a cement rendering to the front; the roof, hipped with a centre valley, is covered with tiles. The N

Former Presbyterian Middle Meeting-house,
Berwick-upon-Tweed.   (22)

front had two doorways with two windows between and four
above, all with segmental-arched heads and keystones, and a
central circular tablet which may have carried an inscription.
Four taller but similarly detailed windows occupy the rear wall;
the E and W sides are of three bays with two tiers of windows.
The interior (45½ft by 55ft) has a flat plaster ceiling with
moulded cornice and a gallery along the E, N and W sides.

Mackelvie (1873) 100. Scott (1888) 371.

(23) ZION CHAPEL, Bank Hill (NT 997530). The chapel was
built in 1835–6 by seceders from the Middle Meeting who
formed a second Relief congregation but which disbanded by
1852. The building was then purchased in 1853 for the
Presbyterian Church in England (now URC) by the supporters
of the Rev. Alexander Murdoch, minister of the Low Meeting,
following his ejection for nonconformity to the established
Church of Scotland; the chapel has stone walls and a hipped slate
roof. The front wall has a tall rusticated plinth and moulded eaves
cornice, two entrances with round-arched windows above and a
pair of similar but taller windows between, the windows being
joined in pairs with arched and moulded labels. The interior is
nearly square with a gallery around three sides and the pulpit
against the slightly longer front wall.

PHSJ XII (1960–3) 23–4. Scott (1888) 372.

Zion Chapel (URC), Bank Hill, Berwick-upon-Tweed.   (23)

(24) PRESBYTERIAN, Wallace Green (NT 999532). The
congregation, which originated in 1769, was at first connected
with the Associate (Burgher) Presbytery of Edinburgh; it
subsequently adhered to the Presbyterian Church of England
(since 1972 St Andrew's, Church of Scotland). The first meeting-
house was built in Golden Square about 1771–2 and enlarged
c.1796–7. The present building, of stone in a 14th-century Gothic
style with low tower and tall spire to the designs of J. D. and I.
Hay of Liverpool, was opened June 1859.

Fittings – Collecting Shovel: in URC History Society
collection, box with oval opening and long handle, 4½ft overall.
Monuments: to ministers of this congregation, in adjacent parish
churchyard S of S porch (1) Rev. Alexander Dickson, 'Minister
of the Associate Congregation of Golden Square Berwick', 1780;
(2) Robert Balmer D. D., S. T. P., 'Minister of the First United
Secession Congregation in this town and Professor of Systematic
Theology to the United Secession Church', 1844.

Black (1906) 298. Mackelvie (1873) 100–1. Scott (1888) 371–2.

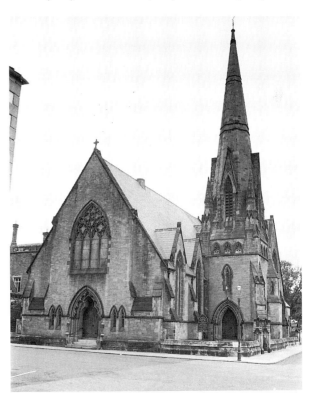

Presbyterian chapel, Wallace Green, Berwick-upon-Tweed. (24)

(25) Former PRESBYTERIAN, Church Street (NU 001530). The
Anti-Burgher meeting-house, subsequently St Aidan's
Presbyterian Church of England, was built in 1812 for a
congregation which had previously met monthly 'in Mr.
Dickinson's School near the Scotch Gate'. It has rubble walls and
a hipped slate roof. The SW front has two entrances now
concealed by later buildings, narrow windows above and two tall
round-arched windows between; a smaller window has been
added at the centre. The interior is approximately square with a
gallery around three sides and pulpit against the front wall;

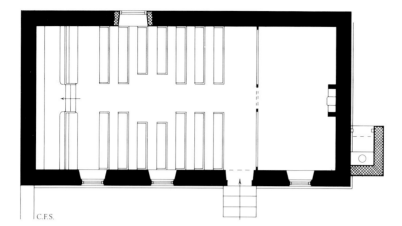

Friends' Meeting-house

COANWOOD

Northumberland

N

Scale of Feet

5   0   5   10   15

C.F.S.

seating replaced in late 19th century. Fittings include two pewter alms dishes, early 19th-century.

Berwick Directory (c.1806) 83. Mackelvie (1873) 101–2. Scott (1888) 372.

(26) PRESBYTERIAN, Greenside Avenue (NT 997531). St Andrew's, Church of Scotland, stone Gothic, by 'Mr Gray of Berwick'; cruciform with small turret on N gable, was built 1896–7 for the united congregation of the Low and High Meetings (*see* (21)). Wall tablet erected 1897 records benefactions by Joseph Watson (1716–52), seven times mayor, and Cecily, widow of George Lindsay, mariner, in 1745, to the constituent congregations. (Demolished 1990, congregation united with Wallace Green)

Black (1906) 300–2. Scott (1888) 370.

BLANCHLAND

(27) WESLEYAN, Baybridge (NY 957500). Rock-faced stone walls and slate roof; triangular-headed lancets and gabled porch inscribed 'Providence Wesleyan Chapel 1867', possibly by S. S. Teulon.

BLYTH

(28) WESLEYAN, Bridge Street (NZ 315816). Brick with stone dressings, three-bay pedimented front between recessed wings in two-tier elevation; attached Corinthian columns to upper stage. 1868 by F. R. N. Haswell. (Demolished c.1988)

Ancient Monuments Society *Newsletter* (Autumn 1988). Craster, H. H. E., *A History of Northumberland* IX (1909) 366.

(29) PRESBYTERIAN, Waterloo Road (NZ 311814). The original meeting (now URC) commenced about 1774. Ebenezer Chapel in Church Street, built 1814, was succeeded in 1874–6 by the present building of brick in the Gothic style with a corner tower and spire, by Thomas Oliver. A second Presbyterian congregation formerly existed, founded in 1820 in connection with the United Secession Church, which in 1828 built a chapel at Waterloo, followed in 1864 by one in Bridge Street.

Fittings – *Communion Tokens*: two types, one dated 1829 belonging to the Secession congregation, the other dated 1865 inscribed 'English Presbyterian Church' (Herdman (1901) Nos. 42–3). *Plate*: includes three late 18th-century pewter cups, one dated 1777, and a matching pewter flagon also of this date.

BROOMHAUGH AND RIDING

(30) Former BAPTIST, Broomhaugh (NZ 022615). The church formerly meeting here was of early origin and probably derived from the Hexham church. The chapel, now used by Methodists, has stone walls and a gabled front of three bays with two lancet windows and central doorway with plain stone surround, above which is a tablet inscribed 'BAPTIST/JUBILEE CHAPEL/ BUILT/AD 1842'.

Monuments: in burial-ground at rear of chapel (1) John Angus, late of Styford, 1752, and Deborah his wife, 1745, erected by their son Rev. John Angus, flat slab on four stone supports; (2) John Usher, 1708, raised stone slab; (3) John Angus, of Broomley, 1821, Mary his widow, 1859, two sons and two daughters; (4) George Angus, of Hindley, 1838, Grace his widow, 1841, *et al.*, tall monument with shaped finial; (5) Rev. William McLean, 6 years pastor, 1856.

COANWOOD

(31) FRIENDS (NY 709590). The meeting-house dated 1760 stands on a remote site 3 miles S of Haltwhistle. It has stone walls and a slated roof with a verge of stone slates. The S front has ashlar quoins to the corners and to the doorway, and plain stone surrounds to the windows. The date of erection is carved on the lintel above the entrance. The interior (39ft by 18¼ft) is divided into two rooms by a partition with hinged fielded-panelled shutters. The principal room to the W has a stand at the W end with central entrance between two tall open-backed seats with shaped ends, and plain open-backed benches. The smaller E room has a fireplace and iron hob grate. In the meeting-house is a small *library* formerly comprising 106 books with catalogue and loans record from 1824. *Burial-ground* to S contains monuments of 19th century and later.

CORBRIDGE

(32) Former PRIMITIVE METHODIST (NY 989644). Rubble with rusticated quoins and surrounds to pointed-arched windows; dated 1867. Now used by Brethren.

EMBLETON

(33) PRESBYTERIAN (NU 232226). Stone and slate, dated 1833. Broad W front with two tall pointed-arched windows and

Friends' meeting-house, Coanwood.   (31)

smaller openings to right and left; single entrance to left in later porch. Altered and lunette added in N wall 1924. *Collecting Shovel*: URC History Society collection, 3¾ft overall. (URC)

FALSTONE

(34) PRESBYTERIAN (NY 723876). This congregation (now URC) together with that at Kielder, formerly known collectively as 'North Tyne', may have originated in the late 17th century with the preaching of William Veitch, the Scottish covenanting minister. A church was formed in 1709, possibly with a meeting-house at Kielder (see (51)). In 1735 a new meeting-house was built at Falstone 'on a site given by the proprietor of Hawkhopehill', for which a collection had been taken up in the parish church at Melrose in December 1734. The present building dates from 1807 but drastic alterations of 1876 have left little evidence of its original appearance. The walls are of rubble and the roof is slated. At the E end is a tower with pyramidal roof and a S doorway with two-centred arched head and the dates 1709, 1807, 1876 above. The N and S walls have each four round-arched windows, the centre two being widest, and an original tablet with date 1807 on the S side. The interior was entirely refitted in 1876.

Fittings – *Communion Tokens*: two types, dated 1729 and 1801. *Inscriptions*: on small lead tablet in modern frame inscribed on both sides (a) 'This House in the Communion of the Church of Scotland Rebuilt 1807. for 420. Pounds The Revd. James Wood Minister Stipend 100 L. yearly. Price of a fat wether 30 Shs. of a stone (24 lb) of wool 31½ Shs. wheat 70 Shs. per quarter. Number of Communicants about 400 of Souls about 1000.' (b) 'First built 1709. Ministers since Revd. Messrs. Deane 1st, Wetherston 3d, Dryden 2d, and Murray 4th. Wm. Robson. Wm. Oliver, Wm. Crozer, Builders 1807'. *Plate*: includes four pewter cups and four flagons dated 1769.

Campbell, M. G., *An Historical Sketch of Falstone cum Kielder Presbyterian Church* (c.1900). Dodds, M. H. (ed.), *A History of Northumberland* XV (1940) 262–4.

FEATHERSTONE

(35) WESLEYAN, Park Village (NY 686616). Three-bay front, 1850, two bays added to left.

FORD

(36) PRESBYTERIAN, Crookham (NT 916382). The meeting-house, built in 1745 for a congregation (now URC) formed in 1732 by secession from Etal, was rebuilt in 1932–3; 'Crookham Presbyterian School', a separate building near the chapel, of stone with round-arched windows, is dated 1856. *Collecting Shovel*: in URC History Society collection, box with ogee opening and long handle, 3ft overall. *Communion Tokens*: five types known; the earliest is dated 1752.

(37) Former PRESBYTERIAN, Etal (NT 925393). The Presbyterian congregation at Etal was formed about 1694; a meeting-house erected c.1703 was largely rebuilt in 1806. The cause was abandoned about 1947 and the building subsequently used as a joiner's shop. It is a large structure of stone with gabled ends and slate roof. In the N front are two doorways, one altered, two windows between and three above. A tablet on this wall is inscribed '*REBUILT*/Anno Domini 1806/the Rev. D. Aitken/MIN.' but the masonry below the level of this tablet appears to be older and might date from c.1703. In the S wall are two tall round-arched windows and two tiers of smaller windows at each end. The interior (35½ft by 59ft) has a moulded plaster cornice. The pulpit stood against the S wall but this and all but a fragment of the galleries which continued around the other sides have been removed. (Conversion to visitor centre for castle, proposed 1991)

Presbyterian chapel (URC), Falstone.   (34)

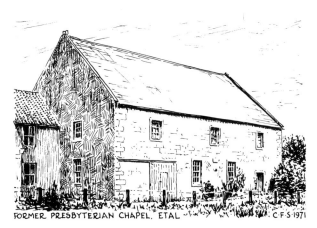

FORMER PRESBYTERIAN CHAPEL, ETAL   C·F·S·1971

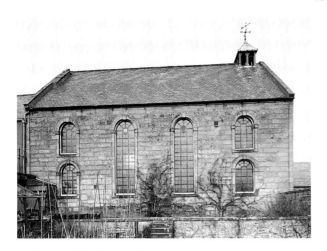

Presbyterian chapel (URC), Glanton. (38)

GLANTON

(38) PRESBYTERIAN (NU 069145). The congregation (now URC) originated in 1781 as a secession from Branton (*see* (50)), the seceders occupying a granary until 1783 when the present chapel was erected. The walls are of stone and the roof is slated. The N wall facing the road, into which an entrance had been pierced in 1867, was further altered in 1911 by the addition of a wide porch. The original entrance front, facing S, is less altered and has two doorways now converted to windows, with windows above and two tall windows between, all with round-arched heads with keystones. In each gabled end is a blocked circular window, that to the E now occupied by a clock dial. At the E end of the roof is a small bell-cote. The interior (28¼ft by 46½ft) originally had the pulpit against the S wall and galleries along the other three sides; in 1867 the pulpit was re-sited at the W end and N and W galleries were removed. The surviving E gallery is original and has a reeded panelled front with a fluted architrave and shaped dentils. The roof is supported by king-post trusses. *Plate*: in URC History Society collection, includes a plated flagon dated 1829.

Dodds, M. H. (ed.), *A History of Northumberland* XIV (1935) 501. Macdonald, W. K. H., *Glanton Meetin'*, *The Story of the Presbyterian Church at Glanton, Northumberland* (1932).

HALTWHISTLE

(39) Former PRESBYTERIAN (NY 709642). A T-shaped building of stone with a slate roof has an entrance in a gabled S wing and a tablet over the front upper window inscribed 'ENGLISH PRESBYTERIAN CHURCH 1862'; the chapel may incorporate work of an earlier date. The congregation (now URC), founded in 1744, removed to a new chapel (NY 705640) built in 1899–1900. *Plate*: in URC History Society collection includes a pair of pewter cups with baluster stems dated 1745.

HARBOTTLE

(40) PRESBYTERIAN (NT 933046). The Coquetwater congregation, in existence by 1713, met until 1756 in a converted cottage. The meeting-house then erected is described as having a thatched roof and all the windows and doors on the S side. The present

chapel, dated 1854, of rubble with ashlar dressings and a slate roof, has a gabled front with partly corbelled octagonal bell-cote and lancet windows. (Closed by 1992)

Fittings – in URC History Society collection. *Collecting Shovel*: wood, 4½ft overall. *Plate*: pair of pewter cups dated 1766.

Dodds, M. H. (ed.), *A History of Northumberland* XV (1940) 468.

HAYDON

(41) CONGREGATIONAL, Haydon Bridge (NY 842646). Stone with a three-bay pedimented front dated 1863; by John Potts of Haydon Bridge. Rusticated quoins and surrounds to side windows, pointed-arched openings, with moulded labels at front.

CYB (1865) 296.

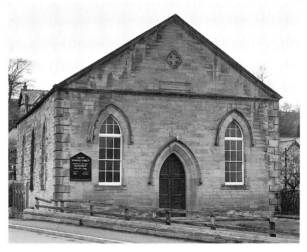

Congregational chapel, Haydon Bridge. (41)

(42) Former WESLEYAN, Haydon Bridge (NY 842643). Gabled front with paired lancets, dated 1873.

(43) PRIMITIVE METHODIST, Haydon Bridge (NY 842645). Broad five-bay front dated 1863, 'enlarged 1884'.

HEALEY

(44) Former FRIENDS', Winnowshill (NY 995529). The society formerly meeting here originated in 1751, when a new meeting was settled at the house of Ann Makepeace at Newbiggin in the parish of Shotley. The present building was erected in 1766. After 1823, when the meeting was discontinued, it was altered for domestic use; it now serves as a shelter for farm stock. The meeting-house (27½ft by 15¼ft) has rubble walls and a stone slate roof; it has been much altered but traces of the original entrance remain centrally in the NW wall.

Burial-ground to SE, rectangular enclosure with rubble boundary walls and blocked gateway to NW; modern tablet on SE wall records 55 burials between 1718 and 1877. No monuments.

Hodgson, J. C., *A History of Northumberland* VI (1902) 220.

Former Friends' meeting-house, Winnowshill.   (44)

HEDLEY

(45) Former WESLEYAN, Hedley on the Hill (NZ 080593). Broad three-bay front with gabled porch formerly dated 1837 and annexe to right. Converted to house.

HENSHAW

(46) WESLEYAN (NY 764646). Successive chapels of 1840 and 1897 stand adjacent.

HEXHAM

(47) Former PRIMITIVE METHODIST, Beaumont Street (NY 935640). Stone and slate with gallery staircases in rounded bastions flanking altered entrance; 1909 by Cackett and Dick. Now in commercial use.

(48) PRESBYTERIAN, Hencotes (NY 93356398). A Presbyterian congregation in connection with the Church of Scotland which had been formed in 1702 built a chapel in 1825 on the N side of Hencotes. In the late 19th century this society combined with a United Presbyterian church and the chapel passed to other use. It was demolished *c*.1960. The chapel had a pedimented front of three bays divided by pilasters; tablets inscribed 'SCOTCH CHURCH 1825' are reset in the boundary wall of a car park on the site, adjacent to a former Sunday-school of 1909 now used for worship. (URC)

HORSLEY

(49) CONGREGATIONAL (NZ 094660). The church (now URC) traces its origins to the ejection in 1662 of Thomas Trurant, vicar

Former Primitive Methodist chapel, Beaumont Street, Hexham.   (47)

of Ovingham. The meeting-house, which may have been built in the late 17th century and had a gallery dated 1729, was rebuilt in 1890.

Archaeologia Aeliana XIII (1887) 33–64.

INGRAM

(50) Former PRESBYTERIAN, Branton (NU 046164). The meeting-house built *c*.1756 for a congregation originating in 1691

Former Presbyterian chapel, Branton. (50)

replaced a building of *c*.1720 on a new site. It is a long T-shaped building of squared stone with a slated roof, the principal area (24ft by 64¼ft) having six tall round-arched windows in the front wall with entrances beneath the two end windows. The rear wing (26½ft by 24ft) is probably later. The interior, refitted 1872, has galleries in the wing and at the extremities of the front range. The roof is supported by king-post trusses with braced principals. (Chapel closed 1978)

Fittings – *Baptismal Basin*: base metal, inscribed 'THE PROPERTY *of the Presbyterian Congregation at Brampton NORTHUMBERLAND 1810*', diameter 10in. *Collecting Shovels*: wood, with long handles, 5ft overall, 19th-century. *Communion Tokens*: two types, dated 1756 and 1845. *Plate*: includes four two-handled cups and two flagons, base metal, dated 1810. *Sundial*: on front wall, 1781.

Dodds, M. H. (ed.), *A History of Northumberland* XIV (1935) 392–3. *PHSJ* XIII (1964–7) 18–25; XIV (1968–72) 196–200.

KIELDER

(51) Former PRESBYTERIAN (NY 624948). The former meeting-house at 'Lightpipe' or 'Waterhead' has rubble walls and a modern corrugated-iron roof. It is said to have been built about 1709 for a congregation formed in that year which may have derived from the activities of the covenanter William Veitch in the late 17th century (*see* (34)). A new chapel was built in 1874 and the earlier building has been converted to farm use. The whole of the S wall and part of the N wall have been rebuilt but the interior (18ft by 41¾ft) retains fragments of wall plaster.

Dodds, M.H. (ed.), *A History of Northumberland* XV (1940) 263.

(52) PRESBYTERIAN (NY 624941). The chapel built 1874 to replace the meeting-house at Waterhead is of stone in a late Romanesque style by F. R. Wilson of Alnwick. It has a bell-cote on the W gable. (URC)

LONGFRAMLINGTON

(53) PRESBYTERIAN (NU 128015). Stone and slate with lancet windows and bell-cote on front gable; built 1854 for congregation (now URC) formed in late 17th century.

LOWICK

(54) PRIMITIVE METHODIST (NU 018398). Jubilee Chapel dated 1860, three-bay front of random rubble with cottage attached. (Closed by 1992)

(55) PRESBYTERIAN, Cheviot View (NU 014395). The congregation, now in union with the Church of Scotland, originally met at Bowsden under an ejected minister and removed in the early 18th century to Barmoor, where they built a meeting-house; the latter was abandoned *c*.1746 when a new meeting-house was built at Lowick, to be replaced in 1821 by the present chapel. A secession about 1847 led to the formation of a separate congregation which joined the Presbyterian Church in England but is now defunct. The chapel has rendered stone walls with stone quoins and a hipped slate roof. A two-light Gothic window in the front wall probably dates from a renovation of 1878, any earlier openings being concealed by the rendering.

Collecting Shovels: in URC History Society collection, from the seceding congregation, two, with open boxes and long handles.

MATFEN

(56) PRIMITIVE METHODIST, Ingoe (NZ 040750). Small three-bay chapel of stone with slated roof, end gables with shaped kneelers, original side-entry porch dated 1848 between plain widely spaced windows.

(57) Former WESLEYAN, Matfen (NZ 030720). Squared stone with gabled front dated 1840, large Sunday-school extension adjacent. (Converted to house by 1992)

MORPETH

(58) Former PRESBYTERIAN, Cottingwood Lane (NZ 197863). The congregation (now URC) formed in 1693 now meets in Bridge Street where the Gothic chapel (NZ 201859), of stone with entrance tower and spire, by M. Thompson of Newcastle, was built in 1860. The former meeting-house in Cottingwood Lane, built about 1732 (originally about 25ft by 54ft externally) and enlarged *c*.1800 (to 37ft wide), has stone walls with some later brickwork, and a slated roof. The SE front wall of brickwork with stone dressings is entirely of *c*.1800 and has the standard arrangement of two tall windows between end entrances. The NW wall of *c*.1732 has been heightened and the two gabled end walls show clear signs of enlargement. The interior has been entirely altered. *Monuments*: in front of chapel (1) James Marshall, 1829, Jane his wife, 1828, and James his son, 1827, headstone; (2) Rev. George Atkin, 1828, square monument with re-entrant corners and urn.

FORMER PRESBYTERIAN CHAPEL, MORPETH   C·F·S·1971

NEWBURN   *Tyne and Wear*

(59) WESLEYAN, Bell's Close (NZ 192644). Stone and slate, with lancet windows; gabled front wall with central entrance and gabled hood on stone brackets inscribed '1839 WESLEYAN CENTENARY CHAPEL'.

NEWCASTLE UPON TYNE   *Tyne and Wear*

(60) BAPTIST, Osborne Road, Jesmond (NZ 253660). Romanesque, with stone walls and slated roofs, large central tower with hipped roof. Built 1889 by James Cubitt for a church founded in the mid 17th century. (Demolished since 1975)

B. Hbk (1885) 161–3; (1887) 118–19. Boyle (1890) 261, 267–8.

(61) CONGREGATIONAL, St James's, Northumberland Road (NZ 251649). The church (now URC) formed in 1833 first met in

Baptist chapel, Osborne Road, Jesmond.   (60)

St James's Chapel, Blackett Street, a building of 1826 by John Dobson which they had bought following the disintegration of the preceding Presbyterian society. The chapel was rebuilt on the same site in 1858–9 by Thomas Oliver and Robert Lamb, but was superseded by the present building in 1882–4. This is a large and imposing structure of stone in a 13th-century style by T. Lewis Banks. The plan is cruciform with a (rebuilt) lantern tower and spire above the crossing.

Binfield, C., 'The building of a town centre church: St James's Congregational Church, Newcastle upon Tyne' *Northern History* XVIII (1982) 155–81. Boag, L. and Boag, H. (eds.), *St James's Past and Present* (1927). *CYB* (1859) 248; (1883) 391–2.

(62) WESLEYAN, Brunswick Place (NZ 24856452). Methodist building in Newcastle commenced with the erection in 1743 of 'The Orphan House', a multi-purpose building comparable with the New Room in Bristol, which comprised a preaching-room on the ground floor, smaller meeting-rooms on the first floor, suite of preachers' rooms above and a small amount of accommodation in an attic which John Wesley reserved for his own use. The Orphan House, which stood in Northumberland Street just outside Pilgrim Street Gate, was rebuilt in 1857 and its successor has now been demolished.

Brunswick Chapel, about 100 yards W of the site of the

Brunswick Chapel, Newcastle upon Tyne.

(62)

Brunswick Chapel, Newcastle upon Tyne.
Water-colour by T. M. Richardson.   (62)

Orphan House, was built in 1820–1 to accommodate the increased numbers for which the former preaching-room was no longer adequate. The design is after the style of the Rev. William Jenkins whose chapel in Waltham Street, Hull 'was, with some slight alteration of the plan, adopted as a model'; the work was supervised by George Spoor who was responsible for the 'working plans' (Stamp (1863) 204). The walls are of brick and the roof is slated. The E front, of five bays, has a three-bay pediment and swept parapets to the wings. The central entrance has a wide porch with Tuscan columns; two further entrances flanking it replace original windows. The two tiers of windows have round-arched heads of two orders. In the gable is a tablet inscribed 'METHODIST CHAPEL 1820'. The side walls are of six bays, the two centre bays projecting slightly. There is an apse at the W end. The interior has a large oval gallery supported by iron columns. The organ installed 1821 but replaced 1893 is in the W apse at gallery level, and the space below originally designed as a communion area with a circular W window has been altered. A collection of items of Methodist interest is kept in the vestry. (Subdivided and floor inserted at gallery level since 1971)

Dolby (1964) 140–2. Stamp, W. W., *The Orphan House of Wesley . . .* (1863). Tulip, W., *Brunswick Methodist Chapel . . . 1821–1971* (1971). *WHS, NEB* LIX (March 1993) 11–26.

(63) Former WESLEYAN, Blenheim Street (NZ 242639). Brick with stone dressings, five-bay front with two tiers of round-arched windows and tall parapet; three-bay porch added. Built 1838 for a society formed in 1831 which formerly met in a chapel in Westgate Street.

Stamp (1863) op. cit. 197.

(64) Former PRESBYTERIAN, Clavering Place (NZ 249638). The congregation formerly meeting here commenced in 1801 as an Anti-Burgher meeting by secession from a church meeting in The Close, and removed in 1872 to a chapel in Westmorland Road. The chapel in Clavering Place, now in industrial use, was built in 1822 on the site of a house fitted up for worship in 1813. It is a square building of brick with two tiers of four-centred arched windows in three bays above a basement storey; the front windows and central entrance are set in recessed bays with arched heads joined by a moulded string-course. The design is attributed to John Green.

Black (1906) 318–20, 357. Mackelvie (1873) 526–7.

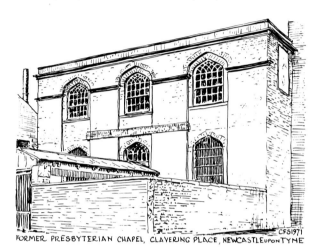

FORMER PRESBYTERIAN CHAPEL, CLAVERING PLACE, NEWCASTLE UPON TYNE

(65) PRESBYTERIAN, Burdon Terrace, Jesmond (NZ 251659). Gothic with stone walls and slated roofs, corner tower; built 1887–8 by W. L. Newcombe, for a Secession congregation which originated in 1744 and met successively in Sallyport Gate, Carliol Street, Barras Bridge, and Jesmond. (URC)

Black (1906) 321. Mackelvie (1873) 525–6.

NORHAM

(66) PRESBYTERIAN (NT 901472). The meeting-house was erected in 1753 for a society (now URC) in existence by 1737 which had been connected with the Associate congregation at Morebattle, Roxburghshire; it was drastically altered c.1860–70,

Presbyterian chapel (URC), Norham.   (66)

when a NE wing containing entrances, vestry and gallery was built against one of the longer side walls. The walls are of rubble and the roof, formerly thatched, is now covered with tiles. The original building (21ft by 52½ft) had five windows in the SW wall, now reduced to four and re-sited, and one at the SE end with another above it in the gable, traces of which are still visible. The interior has been refitted. *Monument*: Rev. James T. Anderson A.M., United Presbyterian minister, 1868. *Painting*: water-colour, view of meeting-house from SE, mid 19th-century.

Black (1906) 317–18. Mackelvie (1873) 97.

NORTH SUNDERLAND

(67) PRESBYTERIAN (NU 209315). Chapel built 1810 for an Associate (Burgher) congregation formed in 1808 by seceders from the Church of Scotland in Warenford. Rendered walls and hipped slate roof. Standard elevation of two entrances with tall round-arched windows between and smaller ones above. The entrances are covered by later porches; a vestry was added in 1843. (URC)

Black (1906) 356. Mackelvie (1873) 109–10.

OTTERBURN

(68) PRESBYTERIAN (NY 889930). The congregation was formed in 1831 by a disaffected member from Birdhopecraig as a branch of the United Secession Church. The chapel, built in 1833, was rebuilt in 1885 in stone with a gabled front and bell-cote with one bell. (Closed by 1992) *Plate*: in URC History Society collection, includes an early 19th-century cup of Sheffield plate.

Mackelvie (1873) 541.

ROCHESTER

(69) Former PRESBYTERIAN, Birdhopecraig (NY 821990). The former meeting-house adjacent to Redesdale Camp, 5 furlongs NW of the present chapel, is a long and narrow building (22½ft by 61ft externally) with rubble walls. The principal front faces S and includes a doorway with lintel dated 1682; it was much altered after 1826 on conversion to a coach-house and stables for Birdhopecraig Hall.

(70) PRESBYTERIAN (NY 828982). Built to supersede the foregoing for a (now URC) church claiming 1672 as its year of origin. Stone walls with ashlar front and hipped slate roof; three-bay, two-stage front with central entrance and tablet inscribed 'BIRDHOPE CRAIG SCOTCH CHURCH 1826'. Original pulpit and galleries.

STAMFORDHAM

(71) PRESBYTERIAN (NZ 079721). A society earlier meeting at Dalton, 2 miles E, which traced its origin to the preaching of John Owens, ejected vicar of Stamfordham, built a meeting-house c.1742–5 'at the east end of the village street'. In 1843 they joined the United Secession Church and in 1860 the present chapel was erected. This forms part of a continuous terrace; it has two tall round-arched windows in the S front. (URC)

Dodds, M.H. (ed.), *A History of Northumberland* XII (1926) 297–8. Mackelvie (1873) 544–5.

THROPTON

(72) PRESBYTERIAN (NU 028022). Stone, with short gabled spire

above entrance, 1863, by F.R. Wilson of Alnwick. Congregation founded 1799. (URC)

TWEEDMOUTH

(73) PRESBYTERIAN, West End (NT 992529). The meeting-house was built about 1783 for a newly established congregation of the Church of Scotland on a site given by Thomas Carr of Murton. It was extensively altered during the ministry of James Oliver (1870–9). The walls are of rubble and the roof is hipped and slated. The principal front to the S has the standard elevation of two entrances with tall windows between and smaller above, all with plain ashlar surrounds. The SW corner is splayed, perhaps due to site difficulties. The N wall facing the road has traces of three tiers of blocked windows, two tall round-arched windows inserted in the late 19th century, and an inserted doorway at the E end. The interior (36¼ft by 61½ft) has an original moulded plaster ceiling cornice but has otherwise been refitted c.1870 with pulpit at E end and a W gallery. *Monument*: between S windows, to John Mackay Wilson, 1835, author and editor of the *Tales of the Borders*, erected 1904. (Demolished since 1970)

Black (1906) 302–6.

(74) Former PRESBYTERIAN, West End (NT 993528). 'Scobie's Chapel', of stone with an ashlar front and hipped slate roof, was built c.1844 for an 'English Presbyterian' congregation founded in that year. The design with two semi-octagonal towers flanking the front wall resembles the United Presbyterian chapel in Alnwick (*see* (12)) and may be by the same architect. (Now 'Kingdom Hall' of Jehovah's witnesses)

(75) PRESBYTERIAN, Spittal (NU 003518). The congregation originated in 1745 when security precautions in Berwick restricted access to meeting-houses in the town; it has been variously attached to the Church of Scotland, the Relief Church, the United Secession Church and the Presbyterian Church of England (now URC). The meeting-house built in 1754 was rebuilt in 1878; the present building, 'St Paul's', is of stone with a corner tower and spire.

Black (1906) 306–7. Mackelvie (1873) 97–8.

TYNEMOUTH   *Tyne and Wear*

(76) BAPTIST, Howard Street, North Shields (NZ 356685). The church was formed in 1798 with the support of a church meeting at Tuthill Stairs, Newcastle; services were first held in a room in Walker Place and then at the Old Assembly Room in Stephenson Street until the erection of the present building in 1846. The chapel, which stands on the W side of the street, was designed by John Dobson; the gabled front of stone is divided by buttresses into three principal bays with round-arched windows and a central gabled entrance in the Romanesque manner.

Craster, H.H.E., *A History of Northumberland* VIII (1907) 377. Douglas (1846) 238–9, 242.

(77) Former CONGREGATIONAL, Front Street, Tynemouth (NZ 369693). Gothic, 1868, by Thomas Oliver, comprising nave, aisles, transepts and corner tower with spire. (Converted to shopping mall since 1971)

CYB (1866) 322.

(78) Former FREE METHODIST, Howard Street, North Shields

(NZ 357684). The chapel on the E side of the street, now public offices, is dated 1856. The front is of ashlar with a moulded cornice to the gable; two doorways and two tiers of windows are enclosed within three tall round-arched recesses.

Craster (1907) op. cit. 376.

(79) Former PRESBYTERIAN, Howard Street, North Shields (NZ 356684). The congregation formerly meeting here originated in 1759 as a secession from the Lower Meeting which subsequently expired. The seceders erected the High Meeting-house, which was replaced in 1811 by the present building sometimes known as the 'Scotch Church'; it is now used by the Salvation Army. The chapel, by John Dobson, has stone walls and a hipped slate roof. The E front has a three-bay ashlar façade with fluted Doric pilasters and entablature below an attic storey.

Craster (1907) op. cit. 373–4.

(80) PRESBYTERIAN, Northumberland Square, North Shields (NZ 356685). The congregation (now URC) formed in 1779 was admitted to the Associate Anti-Burgher Presbytery of Kelso in the following year; prior to the opening of the present chapel, 'St Columba's', in 1858 it occupied a varied succession of meeting places including the High and Lower Meeting-houses. The chapel, by John Dobson, stands on the S side of the square. It has an ashlar front of five bays with a rusticated lower storey; the upper storey has round-arched windows separated by Roman Doric columns which support an entablature and a balustraded parapet.

Black (1906) 321–3. Craster (1907) op. cit. 374. Mackelvie (1873) 532–3.

Presbyterian chapel (URC), Northumberland Square, North Shields. (80)

WARK

(81) PRESBYTERIAN (NY 861767). Stone and slate with lancet windows, gabled front with porch, and bell-cote with one bell; built 1875 for congregation founded 1788. (URC)

WARKWORTH

(82) PRESBYTERIAN (NU 248060). Chapel built 1828 for a congregation (now URC) then recently connected with the United Associate Presbytery of Newcastle. Stone walls with three-bay two-stage front of ashlar with pediment; central entrance with pilasters and cornice.

Black (1906) 356. Mackelvie (1873) 539.

WEST ALLEN

(83) WESLEYAN, High House (NY 790545). The chapel has rubble walls rendered to the SW and a slate roof; porch at NE side and gables to SE and NW both with chimney stacks. A stone lintel to a basement doorway in the NW wall is inscribed 'Ws C/AD/1829', the probable date of erection; a tablet in the SE wall records an enlargement in 1859.

Wesleyan chapel, High House. (83)

(84) WESLEYAN, Limestone Brae (NY 796498). Rubble walls, rendered front, and hipped slate roof. Round-arched windows, gabled porch dated 1825. Sunday-school added 1875.

(85) Former PRIMITIVE METHODIST, Whiteley Shield (NY 803 479). Small three-bay chapel of squared rubble with ashlar dressings and a slate roof. Broad front with rusticated quoins to corners, jambs of round-arched windows and to gabled porch. Tablet above entrance dated 1857. (Disused 1973)

Primitive Methodist chapel, Whiteley Shield. (85)

WHITTINGTON

(86) Former WESLEYAN, Great Whittington (NZ 005708). Stone walls with paired lancets; L-shaped plan with gabled front wing dated 1835. (Converted to house *c*.1988)

WOOLER

(87) PRESBYTERIAN, Cheviot Street (NT 992278). The congregation (now URC) which originated in the late 17th century erected the present meeting-house in 1778; the building was much altered *c*.1900 principally by the addition of a Gothic entrance, tower and spire and by alterations to the original fenestration. The walls are of stone and the roof is hipped and covered with slates; slight traces of former openings are visible in the outer walls. The Tower Hill meeting united with this congregation in 1903 and the Wester Meeting in 1952.

   Mackelvie (1873) 102–3. Vickers, K. H., *A History of Northumberland* XI (1922) 296.

(88) WESTER MEETING-HOUSE (NT 990281). The Presbyterian 'Wester Meeting' was formed *c*.1729 by some members from Cheviot Street and first occupied a meeting-house on the S side of High Street. The present building, erected in 1818, is now a Masonic Hall. The walls are of rubble with ashlar dressings and

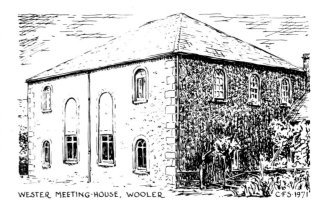

WESTER MEETING-HOUSE, WOOLER

the roof is hipped and covered with slates. The broad front wall has two original round-arched upper windows with others added and a wide late 19th-century porch. Two tall round-arched windows in the rear W wall, partly blocked, indicate the former site of the pulpit.

   Gregory, A., *Wester Meeting House, Wooler* (1894). *PHSJ* IX (1948–51) 199–202. Vickers, K. H., *A History of Northumberland* XI (1922) 297.

WESTMORLAND

Cumbria

Westmorland is a small, mountainous and essentially outward-looking county, the southern part having close ties with Lancashire, while the Eden valley provides easy access to Cumberland and Scotland and in the extreme south east affinities with the West Riding of Yorkshire are noticeable. Proximity to the early centres of Quakerism resulted in a spread of meetings in the later 17th century witnessed not only by a number of surviving meeting-houses but also by isolated burial-grounds, of which Newby (26) and Preston Richard (31) are referred to below. The earliest remaining meeting-house, at Great Strickland (9) of 1681, has been rendered totally unrecognizable on conversion to a bungalow, while that at Preston Patrick (30) of 1691, though still in use, was almost entirely rebuilt in 1869. The early 18th-century meeting-houses at Crook (8), Ravenstonedale (33), Shap (37), Tirril (38) and Mislet (45) have all been either demolished or converted to cottages, leaving only the much later meeting-house in Kendal (12) of 1816 as the building of greatest architectural interest of all denominations within the county.

At the time of Charles II's Declaration of Indulgence in 1672 the only licences taken out by dissenters were by Presbyterians and all were in the vicinity of Kendal. By the early 18th century the largest congregation was found in Ravenstonedale (32) where the patronage and protection of Philip, fourth Lord Wharton, Lord of the Manor and a notable benefactor of nonconformity, gave added strength and respectability to a church whose history epitomizes the struggles between Presbyterians and Independents which persisted throughout the 18th century. If the High Chapel at Ravenstonedale had not been 'restored' out of all recognition in 1867 it would more fully have complemented the history it enshrines. The much smaller, though equally ancient, congregation at Stainton (39) has also divested itself of most visible traces of antiquity in a chapel whose long and low proportions alone bear witness to its origin in the late 17th century. More easily recognizable for its early

date is Market Place Chapel, Kendal (10), one of the few surviving examples from the northernmost counties of an early 18th-century town meeting-house. The Presbyterian congregation, latterly Unitarian, has retained the exterior essentially intact but 19th-century and later refitting has deprived the interior of nearly all features of interest; the monuments in the burial-ground are, however, worthy of note.

The only buildings representative of the later 18th century are the former Inghamite chapels at Birks (41) and Kirkby Stephen (18) which, together with the slightly later one in Kendal (13) and the Sandemanian chapel at Kirkby Lonsdale (16), recall two little-known though related denominations. Most of the chapels of the early 19th century were built by Wesleyans; these are small but pleasant buildings, often of three bays, such as Cliburn (4) of 1832 and Ravenstonedale (35) of 1839, a type seen also in the rare Wesleyan Methodist Association chapel at Sandford (42) of 1848 and which continued in traditional style into the 1860s at Fell End, Ravenstonedale (36). All these have prominent date tablets; the inscription panels at Bolton (3), Kirkby Thore (20) and Long Marton (21) are also of interest for their iconographical content. Notable chapels of the later 19th century include Ranger's Italianate Wesleyan chapel of 1882–3 (14) and the Gothic Congregational chapel of 1896 (11), both in Kendal. The growing popularity of the Lake District resulted in a general extension of religious accommodation, represented here by two Congregational chapels in Windermere of 1857 (43) and 1880 (44), to serve the needs of visitors as well as residents.

The availability of good building stone throughout the county, used either as rubble or squared masonry, has meant that brickwork occurs only rarely even in the late 19th century. An exception is the Free Methodist chapel at Colby (6), of 1874, where yellow brick is used to face the principal elevation. Similarly, local slate or stone slates are used throughout for roofing.

APPLEBY

(1) Former WESLEYAN, Chapel Street (NY 682205). John Wesley visited Appleby in 1766 and described it as 'a county town worthy of Ireland, containing at least five and twenty

houses'. A Methodist society was formed in the late 18th century and the site in Chapel Street was acquired for the society by John Dent of Bolton in 1823. The former chapel, of rendered rubble with sandstone dressings and a slated roof, has a simple

Former Methodist chapel, Chapel Street, Appleby.   (1)

Free Methodist chapel, Colby.   (6)

pedimented front to the W of three bays; above the formerly round-arched entrance is a circular tablet dated 1823. (Roof and upper part of walls demolished since 1971)

(2) WESLEYAN, The Sands (NY 685205). Gothic with corner turrets, 1904.

BOLTON

(3) WESLEYAN (NY 636233). The chapel was built in 1818 by John Dent who had joined the Wesleyans in 1817 but later supported the Wesleyan Methodist Association to which the chapel eventually passed. The walls are of limestone with sandstone dressings. The low gabled front is of three bays with a porch inscribed 'Restored 1926', and an oval tablet in the main gable dated 1818 with symbolic ornament.

Burgess (1980) 41, 43.

CLIBURN

(4) WESLEYAN (NY 587249). Broad-fronted chapel of red sandstone in three bays. Pointed-arched windows with intersecting glazing bars, central porch and tablet above dated 1832.

CLIFTON

(5) WESLEYAN (NY 534266). Limestone with sandstone dressings. Gabled front with traceried window of three lights and sandstone finial at apex. Dated 1885.

COLBY

(6) FREE METHODIST (NY 665205). Yellow-brick front with sandstone dressings, pointed-arched doorway and windows. Dated 1874.

CROOK

(7) Former CONGREGATIONAL (SD 462952). Dated 1866, much altered on conversion to house.

Nightingale I (1890) 291–2.

(8) Site of FRIENDS (SD 437951). A meeting-house on this site was built in 1711, closed c.1830 and largely demolished by 1841. The surrounding burial-ground is bounded by a high rubble wall and has a covered entrance on the SW side.

Butler (1978) 117–19.

GREAT STRICKLAND

(9) Former FRIENDS (NY 557228). The former meeting-house SW of the Lowther Castle Inn has been drastically transformed in recent years and all appearance of antiquity totally destroyed on conversion to a bungalow. It was built in 1681 as a single room with the doorway in the N wall, and extended to the W by the addition of a smaller women's meeting-house with a further entrance in the front wall. Some time after the transfer of the meeting to Morland (see (22)) in 1806 the building was converted to cottages. The walls are of stone (21¾ft by 54¼ft externally) now entirely covered in cement rendering. When first inspected by the Commission in 1935 some original windows survived, including two mullioned windows each of three lights at the extreme ends of the N wall. *Burial-ground*: see Newby (26).

Butler (1978) 81–3. RCHM *Westmorland* (1936) 220, Great Strickland (4) 'Cottage'.

KENDAL

(10) MARKET PLACE CHAPEL (SD 516928). The Presbyterian, latterly Unitarian, society meeting here traces its origin to the preaching of the Rev. Richard Frankland, ejected in 1661 as perpetual curate of St Andrew's, Auckland (Bishop Auckland), County Durham. In 1670 he set up a dissenting academy at Rathmell in the West Riding of Yorkshire which, in 1674, he removed to Natland, two miles S of Kendal. In 1683 he was again obliged to move, eventually returning to Rathmell in 1689. The Kendal society, which was in existence by 1687, flourished under the long ministry of Dr Caleb Rotheram (1716–52), soon necessitating the erection of the present meeting-house. During the succeeding ministry of his son, also Caleb (c.1756–96), doctrinal changes led to an orthodox secession and the formation in 1763 of a separate Presbyterian society with support from the General Associate (Anti-Burgher) Presbytery of Edinburgh. In 1771, by a secondary secession, an Independent church was established. About 1810 a former minister of the last formed a Unitarian Baptist congregation which in 1820 was united with the meeting at Market Place.

The chapel stands behind buildings at the E end of Market Place and is approached through an archway beneath the former parsonage house of 1777. It was erected in 1720 and some

MARKET PLACE CHAPEL, KENDAL   CFS 1972

renovation was carried out *c*.1845 after threats to the title of chapels held by Unitarians had been lifted. The building was greatly altered in 1881–2 by the replacement of window frames, the erection of a porch and a total internal refitting. The walls are of rubble and are rendered in stucco with masonry lining which was first applied *c*.1845; the roof, which was also altered or repaired at that date, is covered with slates. The SW front and NE rear walls are each of five bays with two tiers of windows with renewed frames. The front wall has an original wooden moulded and bracketed cornice. In front of the three middle bays the porch of 1881–2 covers the two original entrances. The end walls are gabled; the SE wall has three windows to the lower stage and may have had a row of windows above; there are stone drip courses at both levels in the SE wall and above the lower windows of the rear wall. The NW end is partly covered by a low vestry beyond which is a school building of 1882.

The interior (35¾ft by 40ft) has been totally refitted. The pulpit was moved to a central position against the NE wall in the early 19th century; its former location is not known, nor does any structural evidence remain of the galleries for which the fenestration is clearly designed.

Fittings – Books: Baxter, R., *The Practical Works of . . . Mr Richard Baxter* (1707), 4 vols. folio, with leather label recording their gift in 1712 to Mr Audland, minister in Kendal, during his life and to his successors in the ministry after his death. *Collecting Shovels*: pair, octagonal with short handles, early 19th-century.

Monuments: all now external, many presumably re-sited from interior in 19th century (for complete transcriptions *see* Nicholson and Axon (1915) *passim*). In front courtyard, brass tablets from table-tombs (1) Deborah Blackstock, 1733; (2) Edward Blackstock, 1745; (3) Isabella Blackstock, 1731; (4) Daniel Scales of Skelsmergh, 1724, *et al*. In NW boundary wall at front (5) Mary, wife of C. Rotheram D.D., [1746], large monument with Ionic pilasters and shaped cheeks. Against SE wall of chapel (6) Samuel Gawthorp, 1788, and Ann his widow, 1803; (7) William Dawney, 1729; (8) Matthew Whitaker, 1773, *et al*. In burial-ground at rear, against boundary wall (9) Jane, wife of Rev. Edward Hawkes, 1847; (10) Andrew Henderson, 1799, and Ann his widow, 1800; (11) David Smith, late of Hereford, merchant, 1743, erected by his widow, Elizabeth, inscription panel flanked by fluted pilasters with Doric entablature and pediment. Against rear wall of chapel (12) Myles Harrison, [1730], John Harrison, [1737], and Benjamin [his son,

1731], elaborate architectural monument with pair of fluted Roman Doric columns carrying entablature blocks and segmental pediment, worn brass inscription tablet; (13) Rev. Caleb Rotheram D.D., 36 years minister, 1752, buried at Hexham; (14) Thomas Gibson, 1781, and Elizabeth Cookson his sister, 1781; (15) Sarah Garside, 1852, 'cut and erected by her surviving husband, W. C. Garside, engraver'; (16) John Patrick, 1763, *et al*. Against wall of Sunday-school (17) Anthony Strickland, 1765, and Agnes his widow, 1779, pedimented wall monument with fluted Ionic pilasters; (18) Rev. Caleb Rotheram, 40 years minister, 1796, *et al*.; (19) Dorothy, wife of Rev. Caleb Rotheram, 1770.

Plate: includes a pair of 18th-century pewter cups. *Rainwater-heads*: on front wall, two, inscribed 'AD/1720', 'AG'. *Seating*: in vestry, fragments of pew doors from former meeting-house, inscribed with initials and dates (1) 'S^{E}BR^{M}CE^{A}B' (2) 'EB * DB * 1709' (3) 'EI * EH 1691' (4) 'GA S^{W}A 1691 I^{A}R' (5) 'R^{W}D 1691'.

Evans (1897) 115–16. Nicholson and Axon (1915). Nightingale I (1890) 278–84.

(11) ZION CHAPEL, Highgate (SD 514924). The Congregational chapel, now URC, set back behind other buildings on the W side of the street was built for a congregation which originated in 1771 in a secession from the United Presbyterian church in Woolpack Yard. The chapel, of 1896 in the Gothic style by Stephen Shaw, has a gallery around three sides with timber arcades and an apsidal organ chamber.

The former chapel, now in commercial use, stands a short distance N, at the end of New Inn Yard; the walls are of stone with five round-arched windows to the E, now subdivided, and a porch dated 1844; it has been enlarged to the rear in a matching style.

Mackelvie (1873) 482–3. Nightingale I (1890) 290.

(12) FRIENDS, Stramongate (SD 518928). The first known meeting-house was bought in 1688, extended by the addition of a women's meeting-house in 1703 and further enlarged in 1707–8 and 1718. The present building, which stands in a retired position on the S side of the street, was built in 1816 to the designs of Francis Webster of Kendal. The walls are of limestone with the principal elevations of ashlar with moulded cornices; the roof is covered with slates and has a central valley. The NW front, partly concealed by adjacent buildings, is of three bays with round-arched windows to the lower stage and a doorway and porch at the left-hand end. The SE elevation is of five bays.

The interior comprises two meeting-houses and a wide passage at the NE end with entrances at front and rear and a double staircase to the galleries. The two rooms are divided by a partition of four arched bays with hung shutters and each room had a large tripartite window at the SW end behind the stand. The principal room to the SE is unaltered and a good example of its period. A tall gallery above the entrance passage continues along the SE side where it is supported by three reeded cast-iron columns; the gallery has an open balustraded front and contemporary seating. The stand at the SW end has three tiers of seating. The smaller room or 'women's meeting-house' was similarly arranged until 1934, when it was subdivided into two storeys of smaller rooms.

Butler (1978) 99–109.

Friends' meeting-house, Kendal. (12)

(13) Former INGHAMITE, High Beast Banks (SD 511924). The chapel dated 1844 and now used for secular purposes occupies the site of Pear Tree Barn which was converted to a meeting-house in 1756. The walls are of rubble with rusticated quoins and plinth. The W end has a pediment with moulded cornice and consoles. The windows, two at the W end and five on the longer N and S sides, are tall with round-arched heads and marginal glazing-bars.

Thompson (1958) 50–1, 55–8.

(14) WESLEYAN, Windermere Road (SD 514932). The Methodist society founded about 1787 first met in the old playhouse and from 1802 in The Fold, Stricklandgate. The first chapel on the present site was opened in 1808. It was a long building of five bays with doorways in the penultimate bays and two tiers of windows. The present chapel, of 1882–3 by W. Ranger of London, is of stone with a three-bay pedimented centre flanked by balustraded bays having cusped circular windows in the upper stage.

Jones, W. S., *Stricklandgate Methodist Church, Kendal* (1958).

KIRKBY LONSDALE

(15) WESLEYAN (SD 610788). Gritstone walls and lancet windows. Reset tablet over entrance dated 1834. Chapel rebuilt or greatly altered and refitted in late 19th century.

(16) Former SANDEMANIAN, Chapel Lane (SD 611787). An Inghamite society formed by a Mr Hunter first met in a private house in Mitchelgate. The former chapel in Chapel Lane, which dates from the early 19th century, was regarded as Sandemanian by the mid 19th century. It has walls of rubble and a slate roof. The chapel, at first-floor level with two cottages below, has three round-arched windows to front and rear, two with original glazing.

Thompson (1958) 52–3.

Former Sandemanian chapel, Kirkby Lonsdale. (16)

KIRKBY STEPHEN

(17) Former CONGREGATIONAL (NY 774086). Gothic, with corner turret and spire, built 1865 by Pritchett and Son of Darlington. Now used by Roman Catholics.

CYB (1865) 306. Nightingale I (1890) 305–9.

(18) Former INGHAMITE, Market Street (NY 775087). The late 18th-century meeting-house of rubble with a roof covered with stone slates stands concealed down a narrow alley off the E side of the street in 'Gregson's Yard' or 'New Inn Yard'. The society appears to have become Sandemanian before selling the building to Congregationalists who met there from 1810 to 1865. In the front wall is a round-arched doorway and at the rear are two tall windows which probably flanked the pulpit. It has been much altered by Congregationalists since 1865 for use as a Sunday-school and by others later.

Nightingale I (1890) 305–9. Thompson (1958) 36.

(19) WESLEYAN (NY 775084). 'Wesleyan Centenary Chapel A.D. 1839' with two tiers of round-arched windows and altered pediment. Sunday-school in similar style adjacent at rear dated 1879.

KIRKBY THORE

(20) WESLEYAN (NY 638256). Small chapel of red sandstone with broad three-bay front and large tablet dated 1828 above entrance. Refitted and porch added 1904. The land was given by the Crosby family who later joined the Wesleyan Methodist Association and attempted unsuccessfully to transfer the building to that allegiance. *Clock*: in recess opposite entrance, signed 'Geo. Wilson' and inscribed 'In Memory of The Revd. John Crosby of whose perseverance this Chapel is a standing Monument'.

Burgess (1980) 43. Sell (1986) 100–1.

LONG MARTON

(21) WESLEYAN (NY 667245). The chapel, of red sandstone with a hipped slated roof, occupies the upper floor of a two-storeyed building with a cottage below. It was built in 1818, the date on

Wesleyan chapel, Long Marton. (21)

two oval tablets in the side wall. The entrance is approached by a long flight of steps and surmounted by a tablet of extreme size with the name 'Methodist Chapel' and symbolic decoration. Two upper windows have been given round-arched heads and it is possible that the oval date tablets were originally sited above them. The interior was refitted in the late 19th century. *Clock*: in chapel, in recess in side wall, signed 'Geo. Wilson, Appleby'.

MORLAND

(22) Former FRIENDS (NY 601222). The meeting-house, SE of the village on the E side of Morland Beck, was built in 1805 for a meeting which commenced *c*.1766 and was joined in 1806 by the meeting from Great Strickland (*see* (9)). Meetings ceased in 1903; the building was sold in 1963 and converted to a cottage in 1971. The walls are of limestone rubble with red sandstone dressings. Three windows in the front wall with external shutters have all been reset lower in recent years. The interior, gutted in 1971, was formerly divided by a screen with hung shutters.

 Butler (1978) 83–5.

(23) WESLEYAN (NY 600223). Low walls of limestone with sandstone dressings. Three-bay gabled front with oval tablet dated 1819.

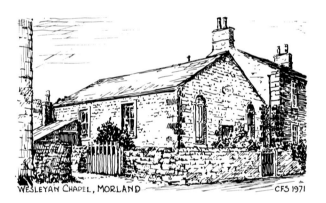

WESLEYAN CHAPEL, MORLAND CFS 1971

MURTON

(24) WESLEYAN (NY 730212). Small three-bay chapel with renewed date tablet of 1837 and late 19th-century Sunday-school attached.

NEWBIGGIN

(25) WESLEYAN (NY 629284). Rubble with contrasting red sandstone dressings. Three-bay gabled front with round-arched windows and porch canopy. Dated 1880.

NEWBY

(26) FRIENDS' BURIAL-GROUND (NY 585215). Small rectangular enclosure bounded by rubble walls, 2 miles ESE of the former meeting-house at Great Strickland (*see* (9)). *Monuments*: reset against boundary walls (1) Thomas Lawson of Great Strickland, 1691, 'Ludi Magister et Botanicus non imperitis', Francis [*sic*] his wife, 1693/4, and Jonah their son, 1683/4, former ledger stone with Latin inscription, partly recut; (2) Mary, wife of Thomas Wilson of Newby, and Thomas, son of Rowland Wilson of

Newby, undated, late 17th-century; (3) John Morland of Milne Flat, 1682, and Elizabeth his wife, 1672; (4) Sarah, wife of Thomas Laverick of Morland Low Field, 1792; (5) Robert Robinson of Newby Stones, nd, and John his son, 1772.

 Dictionary of National Biography, s.v. Lawson, Thomas. RCHM *Westmorland* (1936) 184.

(27) WESLEYAN (NY 589213). Rubble with dressed quoins, ashlar porch and stone-slated roof. Broad three-bay front with oval tablet dated 1853.

Wesleyan chapel, Newby. (27)

ORTON

(28) WESLEYAN (NY 624083). Three-bay gabled front with porch, dated 1833 but altered and enlarged in later 19th century.

PATTERDALE

(29) Former FRIENDS, Grisedale Bridge (NY 391163). Rubble and slate; built 1842 at the expense of George Head for joint use by Friends and Wesleyans, used exclusively by Friends from 1909 and closed 1964. Now in recreational use.

 Butler (1978) 93–4.

PRESTON PATRICK

(30) FRIENDS (SD 542840). The meeting-house built in 1691 was closed from 1833 to 1869 when it was entirely altered, refenestrated and a cottage added. The original outer walls of

Former Friends' meeting-house, Preston Patrick.
(Photograph pre-1869.) (30)

rubble remain but are now concealed by rendering, and the formerly stone-flagged roof has been re-covered in blue slates. A photograph taken before the alterations shows an entrance in the present position in the S front with one pair of windows to the right to light the principal room and two tiers of windows at each end. A gallery was approached by an external stone staircase at the E end. The interior (40¾ft by 19¼ft) is divided into two rooms: a large meeting-house to the E and a small kitchen to the W with separate access from a side-entry porch which incorporates a staircase to an upper room. The detached stables and coach-house date from the 19th century.

Fittings – *Door*: in porch, of nine fielded panels, *c*.1691. *Inscription*: wooden panel between inner doorways in porch, with original date 1691. *Stand*: late 19th-century, incorporating in the front 23 turned wood balusters of the late 17th century and some later plain panelling in the back.

Butler (1978) 109–12.

PRESTON RICHARD

(31) FRIENDS' BURIAL-GROUND, Birkrigg Park (SD 539865). At E end of Sepulchre Lane 1½ miles N of Preston Patrick meeting-house. First used 1651. Small walled enclosure with one ledger stone with damaged inscription to Anne, daughter of Isaac Cartmell, 170[?2].

RCHM *Westmorland* (1936) 197.

RAVENSTONEDALE

(32) THE HIGH CHAPEL (NY 722039). The church (now URC) originated in the late 17th century, drawn by the preaching of the Rev. Christopher Jackson, ejected rector of Crosby Garrett, and protected from molestation by the influence of Lord Wharton, Lord of the Manor. In 1692 it met, as a Presbyterian congregation, at the house of George Parkin where it appears that a meeting-house had been fitted up. In 1714 a short-lived, probably doctrinal, secession occurred, the seceders continuing to use the name Presbyterian. The remainder of the church adopted the style, although not the full polity, of Independency and in 1726 erected the present chapel. In 1734 the church was disturbed by the attempted expulsion of a minister and by a subsequent legal action, and the remainder of the 18th century is marked by a

continuing conflict between rival doctrinal influences. The adherents of Presbyterianism remained sufficiently powerful to secure the appointment in 1762 of a minister of the Church of Scotland, but from 1811 Independency again predominated. A major secession to the Wesleyans after 1835 led the remnant to reconstitute the church in 1838 on a firmer basis of Congregationalism.

The chapel of 1726 has rendered rubble walls and a slate-covered roof. It was drastically altered in 1867 and retains little of its early character; the minister responsible admitted afterwards that 'he shewed more zeal than knowledge in the affair'. The wide E front was originally of six bays with two tiers of windows, and doorways in the second and fifth bays; the former fenestration of the W wall is partly visible beneath the late 19th-century rendering. The former doorways and windows were blocked in 1867 and three tall round-arched windows with keystones and moulded imposts inserted in each of these walls. The N gable wall is blank and has shaped kneelers to a gable parapet. At the S end, in line with the chapel, is a two-storeyed addition of 1802 intended to accommodate a Sunday-school room on the ground floor, with habitable rooms above. This was also altered in 1867 to provide a new entrance lobby for the chapel and a school-room above approached by an external staircase. A stone bell-cote built *c*.1889 on the apex of the S gable replaces one of lighter construction first erected *c*.1813 above the original S wall of the chapel.

The interior (44½ft by 22¼ft originally) has been almost entirely refitted. A three-decker pulpit with sounding-board is said to have stood against the N wall. The addition of a gallery in 1731 is recorded on a contemporary brass tablet on the front of the present S gallery, inscribed 'This Gallery was Built/by the procurement of/The Reverend/Mr Ralph Milner/Anno Dom: 1731'. In the S wall of the present entrance lobby is a fireplace with plain stone surround of *c*.1802. Other fittings include *Bell*: in bell-cote, *c*.1813. *Chairs*: three, late 17th-century, given 1930. *Communion Table*: with turned legs, 18th-century. *Monuments*: externally against E wall (1) Henry Hewetson, 1783, Ann his widow, 1798, and their sons and daughters; (2) Richard Hewetson, 1813, Ann his wife, 1789, Henry their son, died at St Ann's Bay, Jamaica, 1799, Mary their daughter, 1824, *et al*. In burial-ground (3) William Shaw, 1799, Isabel his wife, 1773, and John their son, 1788, table-tomb; (4) Rev. John Hill, 19 years minister, 1809; (5) John Chamberlain, yeoman, of Greenside, 1827, *et al*.

CHST III (1907–8) 91–103, 217–19; IV (1909–10) 59. Nightingale I (1890) 309–18. Woodger, P. L. and Hunter, J. E., *The High Chapel, The Story of the Ravenstonedale Congregational Church* (1962; 2nd edn. 1987).

(33) Site of FRIENDS, Fell End (NY 734009). The meeting-house, built in 1705 on an isolated site 2 miles SSE of the village, closed in 1793 when the meeting was removed to Narthwaite. It was demolished in 1899. The few fragmentary remains on the site comprise part of the rubble walling of the SW end of the meeting-house and the foundations of an adjoining stable.

Butler (1978) 158–62.

(34) Former FRIENDS, Narthwaite (SD 702974). The meeting removed here from Fell End in 1793 was accommodated from

The High Chapel, Ravenstonedale (URC).　　　　(32)

1823 in an upper room of a newly erected barn. The room at the W end of the barn is approached from rising ground at the rear; it has a window in the S wall and plaster ceiling following the roof slope. No fittings remain.

Butler (1978) 161–2.

(35) WESLEYAN (NY 724039). Three-bay chapel of rubble and slate with round-arched windows. Built following a secession of members and the minister, Rev. William Hasell, from the High Chapel. Tablet above central entrance inscribed 'Wesleyan Centenary Chapel A.D. 1839'.

(36) WESLEYAN, Fell End (SD 723994). Three-bay front with round-arched windows, dated 1861.

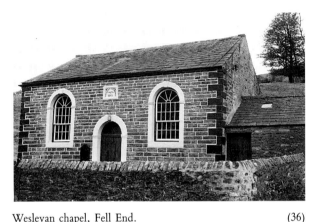

Wesleyan chapel, Fell End. (36)

SHAP

(37) Former FRIENDS (NY 563150). The meeting-house built in 1704 was closed in 1778 and sold in 1802. It has been much altered and partly rebuilt on conversion to a house of two storeys but some of the walling and a ceiling beam in the N room at the front may be original.

Butler (1978) 88–90.

SOCKBRIDGE AND TIRRIL

(38) Former FRIENDS, Tirril (NY 501267). The meeting-house built in 1731, to which a porch was probably added in 1733, was enlarged to the NE, the porch rebuilt and the interior entirely refitted in 1801. The meeting closed in 1861 and the building was converted to a cottage in 1932.

The walls are of rubble, partly rendered, and the roof is covered with slates. In the front wall are three windows with dressed surrounds, one altered, all of 1801; one window in the rear wall is also of this date. The lintel of the outer doorway of the porch is reset and is carved with the date 1733. The interior (40ft by 16¾ft) is divided unequally into two rooms separately approached through a pair of doorways inside the porch and separated by a partition of sliding shutters. The burial-ground lies immediately in front but contains no visible monuments.

Butler (1978) 90–3.

STAINTON

(39) STAINTON CHAPEL (SD 526859). Two licences were issued in 1672 for Presbyterian meetings in the parish of Heversham, one being for John Hinde's house, probably the same John Hind of Stainton whose house was registered 13 January 1698/9 under the Toleration Act. An earlier certificate, 8 October 1696, was granted for a house built by Myles Addyson. Although possibly of Presbyterian origin the church (now URC) had an Independent minister by the early 18th century.

The chapel was erected c.1698. It has rendered rubble walls and a slated roof. Four small regularly spaced windows in the E wall and two now flanking the pulpit at the N end are original but with renewed frames; three larger windows have been inserted on the W side. At the S end is a two-storeyed addition with a stable below and vestry or school-room above. The interior (18½ft by 35¾ft) was refitted about 1870 when, as Nightingale says, 'the earthen floor [was] replaced by a boarded one and the pulpit moved from the [E] side facing the road to its present position'. The roof is supported by three roughly shaped trusses of late 17th-century character.

Fittings – *Communion Table*: oak, with turned legs and guilloche ornament around upper rail, modern top, otherwise c.1698. *Door*: to stable, with wrought-iron hinges, early 18th-century. *Monuments* and *Floorslabs. Monuments*: on W wall (1) Thomas Greenhow of High House, 1838. In burial-ground N of chapel (2) Richard Greenhow, 1839, and Hannah Louisa, 1840, children of Rev. David and Mrs Margaretta Jones; (3) Alice Greenhow, 1873; (4) H. K., 1841. *Floorslabs*: in chapel (5) T. G., 1838; (6) R. G., M. G., T. G. *Plate*: includes a two-handled cup

Former Friends' meeting-house, Sockbridge and Tirril. (38)

Stainton Chapel (URC). (39)

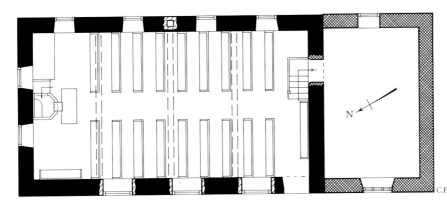

Independent Chapel
STAINTON
Westmorland

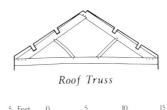

Roof Truss

C.F.S.

Stainton Chapel. Carved rail from pew door. (39)

of 1733. *Seating*: portion of pew door fixed to front of pulpit, with carved rail bearing initials and date 'I D E D 1698'. Other similarly inscribed fragments now missing are recorded by Nightingale as: 'T W M P 98; E B [1] 6 M F 99; H S E S 98; E I T 1698; 16 I P 98'. (Interior stripped, close-carpeted and floorslabs concealed, 1990)

Nicholson and Axon (1915) 438–45. Nightingale I (1890) 291–5.

TEBAY

(40) WESLEYAN, Gaisgill (NY 639053). Rendered rubble, built 1841 originally of three bays with round-arched windows; matching bay added to left and adjoining Sunday-school built 1901.

WARCOP

(41) Former INGHAMITE, Birks (NY 719151). The chapel, now converted to a barn, stands on an isolated site. It was built *c*.1757 by James Richardson and registered in 1760. The walls are of rubble and the roof is slated. In the broad NW front wall are two tall segmental-arched pulpit windows between end entrances with gallery windows above. In the gabled end walls are the

remains of gallery doorways formerly approached by external staircases. The interior (28ft by 43ft) had a flat plaster ceiling. The outline of the pulpit is visible on the wall between the front windows. A fireplace in the NE wall indicates the site of the vestry below an end gallery. The roof is supported by four king-post trusses. The burial-ground in front of the chapel, in use from 1758 to *c*.1848, contains no visible monuments.

Thompson (1958) 45–52.

Former Inghamite chapel, Birks. (41)

Wesleyan Methodist Association chapel, Warcop. (42)

(42) WESLEYAN METHODIST ASSOCIATION, Sandford (NY 729 162). Rendered rubble, three-bay front with tablet above central entrance inscribed 'Association Chapel Built A.D. 1848'.

Former Inghamite Chapel at Birks
WARCOP
Westmorland

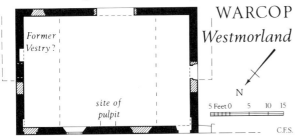

Former Vestry?

site of pulpit

C.F.S.

WINDERMERE

(43) Former CONGREGATIONAL, Troutbeck Bridge (NY 405 001). Rubble with ashlar dressings, gabled front with small wheel-window and bell-cote with one bell. Built 1857 and later. Chapel and detached Sunday-school now converted to nine dwellings.

Nightingale I (1890) 299.

(44) CONGREGATIONAL, Lake Road (SD 411979). 'Carver Memorial', 1880 by Robert Walker, in memory of William Carver of The Priory, Windermere. Gabled front, corner tower with plain pinnacles and short square spire. (URC)

CYB (1881) 468–9; (1884) 411–12. Nightingale I (1890) 300. *The Building News* (20 April 1888) 581.

(45) Former FRIENDS, Mislet (SD 432997). The meeting-house built in 1701, but perhaps incorporating an earlier dwelling at the W end, was closed in 1821 and has long been converted to a cottage. It has rendered stone walls (22ft by 34½ft externally) and a slate-covered roof. The S front has a gabled porch with original boarded inner door; two enlarged windows to the right lit the principal room and two windows to the left below a rough slate label have also been altered. On the W gable is a large chimney stack. The interior is divided unequally by a wooden partition W of the entrance which has removable panels and is contemporary with the building. Over the W room is a loft or former gallery.

Butler (1978) 115–17. RCHM *Westmorland* (1936) 246.

The county is described in accordance with its pre-1974 boundaries and is divided into the three Ridings which constituted separate county administrations. The City of York, though formerly most closely linked to the West Riding through a shared Lord Lieutenancy, while occasionally appended to the East or North Ridings for the convenience of authors, is here accorded that primary position to which it is entitled. Notable monuments include the late 17th-century St Saviourgate Chapel (1) with its unique and ambitious cruciform plan, the remains of an early Methodist preaching-house in Aldwark (6) and several

19th-century buildings by J. P. Pritchett, as well as two important and well-preserved examples of the work of James Simpson in Centenary Chapel (9) and Priory Street (10). The demolition of the Friends' Meeting-house (5) has deprived the city of one of the more outstanding urban buildings of that denomination.

EAST RIDING   *See page 191.*

NORTH RIDING   *See page 203.*

WEST RIDING   *See page 226.*

YORK   *N. Yorks.*

(1) PRESBYTERIAN MEETING-HOUSE, St Saviourgate (SE 606 520). Four preachers who had been appointed under the Commonwealth to serve at the Minster and All Saints, Pavement, were ejected in 1660. Of these Peter Williams continued to be active in York, where he enjoyed the protection of Lady Lister and later of Lady Watson, the widow of a former Lord Mayor. At Lady Watson's house in St Saviourgate, both Peter Williams and Ralph Ward, chaplain to Sir John Hewley, held weekly meetings, the house being licensed in 1672 for Independents as were the houses of Peter Williams and others for Presbyterians. Williams died in 1680 but Ward continued to preach in spite of persecution and imprisonment until 1692. The Presbyterian society which arose from these beginnings and which by the 19th century had accepted a Unitarian ministry was not at first notable for its strength of numbers, but with support from Lady Hewley, who possessed 'a spacious pew directly fronting the pulpit', and other benefactors, the present chapel was built in 1692–3. The building remained essentially unchanged until 1859–60 when it was entirely refitted under the direction of George Fowler Jones.

The chapel is cruciform on plan with brick walls and slate roofs. A low tower at the crossing has a pyramidal roof, formerly with a weathervane, and two windows to each face with flat-arched brick heads, most now blocked. The front SE arm and the transepts were re-roofed at a lower pitch in the mid 19th century or before and the SE gable replaced by a hip; the roof over the NW arm remains in its original state. The SE doorway has a brick surround and moulded brick cornice, above is a round-arched window with mid 19th-century frame and brick surround; the other windows are similar. In the end wall of the SW arm a pair of windows replaces one at the centre; the three remaining gabled walls have each a brick platband at the base of the gable and a blocked oval window above.

The interior ($72\frac{1}{2}$ft by $57\frac{3}{4}$ft) has a small SE gallery with open balustraded front. Prior to 1859–60 the pulpit stood against the W corner of the tower and the chapel was filled with box-pews except at the NW end where the communion table was enclosed within a table-pew. The vestry in the W angle replaces a smaller room on this site. Before alteration each arm had a segmental plaster barrel vault which survives above the flat plaster ceiling of the chancel. The tower is supported by four segmental-pointed arches; it was formerly ceiled at a higher level and had a substantial cornice above the heads of the upper windows.

Fittings – *Chair*: in vestry, upholstered seat and back, arms with turned supports, reputedly Lady Hewley's, 17th-century.

Presbyterian meeting-house, St Saviourgate.   (1)

Presbyterian Meeting-house, St Saviourgate, YORK

Yorkshire

Scale of Feet

5 0 5 10 15 20

N

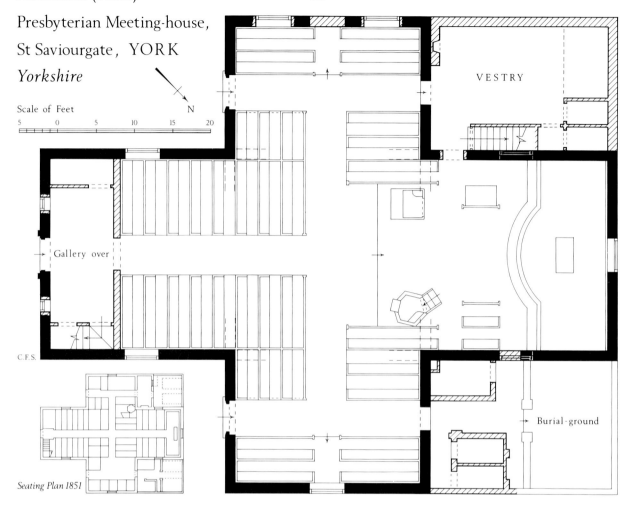

VESTRY

Gallery over

C.F.S.

Burial-ground

Seating Plan 1851

Monuments and *Floorslabs*. *Monuments*: in chapel (1) John Harland Fox, 1851; (2) Rachel (Wyndlow), widow of Rev. Edward Sandercock, 1790, erected by William Chaloner, seated female figure with symbols of hope and learning, signed 'Regnart, Cleaveland St., Fitzroy Square, London'; (3) Mary, widow of William Leach, 1805, Samuel Cowling, 1807, Nancy (Leach) his widow, 1819, their children, Charles, 1807, John, 1824, Rachel, 1841, and Catherine, 1847, and David, son of Thomas and Catherine Ward, 1850, signed 'Bradeey' [*sic*]; (4) William Cowling, merchant, 1847, Martha Amelia his widow, 1852, and Samuel their son, 1828, erected 1860, signed 'Bradley'; (5) Rev. John Kenrick, M.A., F.S.A., 1877, and Lætitia (Wellbeloved) his widow, 1879; (6) Rev. Edward Sandercock, 1770; (7) Varley Bealby, 1836, and Ann (Driffield) his widow, 1850, with shield-of-arms, signed 'Skelton'; (8) Robert Driffield, 1816, Mary (Whitaker) his wife, 1806, and Samuel their son, 1806, signed 'C. Fisher, York'; (9) Catherine (Harrison), widow of Rev. Newcome Cappe, 1821, signed 'Taylor, York'; (10) Rev. Newcome Cappe, 45 years minister, 1800; (11) Mary Duckworth, 1819; (12) Ann, wife of Rev. Charles Wellbeloved, 1823, and Anne Wellbeloved, 1846, signed Skelton, York; (13)

Rev. Charles Wellbeloved, 66 years pastor, 37 years Professor of Theology in Manchester New College, 1858, signed 'Skelton, York'. In vestibule (14) removed from Welburn, near Malton, 1877, John Mason 'the finest preacher of Unitarian Christianity in this village', 1828, signed 'R. Bradley'. In burial-ground N of chapel (15) Charles Wellbeloved, 1858, Ann his wife, 1823, and Anne their daughter, 1846; E of chapel (16) Harriet, daughter of [   ], 18[ ]6; (17) Margaret, wife of Daniel Fraser, gentleman of St Helens parish, York, 1827. *Floorslabs*: in vestibule (1) Robert, son of Robert and Mary Driffield, 1772, infant; in chapel at SE end (2) Joshua, son of Samuel Taylor of Moston near Manchester, 'who died in this city upon a journey', 1765.

Paintings: in vestry, portraits of Rev. Newcome Cappe and Rev. Charles Wellbeloved. *Plate*: includes a pair of two-handled gadrooned cups of 1694, a pair of plates, 1673, given by Andrew Taylor 1696, and flagon, 1790. *Pulpit*: hexagonal, with bolection-moulded panels, moulded capping and panelled base, *c*.1693.

Dale, B., *Historical Sketch of Early Nonconformity in the City of York* (1904). Evans (1897) 264–5. Kenrick, J., *Memorials of the Presbyterian Chapel, St Saviourgate, York* (1869). Miall (1868) 387–8. Rushton (1967) 245. RCHM *City of York* v (1981) 55–6.

(2) BAPTIST, Priory Street (SE 59835150). Reputed to be the first Gothic Revival nonconformist chapel in York, 1867–8 by William Peachey; roof rebuilt at lower pitch and upper stage of tower removed *c*.1939.

Darsley, R. R., *A Short History of Baptists in York, 1646–1987* (1987).

(3) Former INDEPENDENT, Grape Lane (SE 603520). Built 1781 for seceders, including the minister William Wren, from the Countess of Huntingdon's chapel in College Street; subsequently occupied from 1798 by the Methodist New Connexion, from 1806 by Particular Baptists and from 1820 to 1851 by Primitive Methodists. The chapel, of brick, stood on an irregular concealed site; it had brick walls and a gallery added in 1800. Derelict 1963; since demolished.

RCHM *City of York* v (1981) 54. VCH *York* (1961) 407.

(4) Former CONGREGATIONAL, Lendal (SE 601520). Built 1816 to designs by C. Watson and J. P. Pritchett of York for a congregation originating with a secession from Grape Lane Chapel which had met from 1796 in a newly built chapel in Jubbergate. In 1839 the majority of the then much-expanded congregation built Salem Chapel, facing the E end of St Saviourgate (demolished 1963), but a remnant remained as the nucleus of a new church which continued to use Lendal Chapel until 1929. The building has since been converted to shops and offices.

The walls are of brick and the roof is hipped and covered with slates. The front of five bays has a three-bay pediment, round-arched upper windows with a continuous cill but the lower part has been entirely altered. The SE side wall is of five bays with two tiers of windows. Centrally at the rear is a wide semicircular projection with domical roof, added to provide additional seats 'in a handsome circular gallery behind the pulpit'.

Miall (1868) 389. RCHM *City of York* v (1981) 54. Royle, E. (ed.), *A History of the Nonconformist Churches of York* (1933). VCH *York* (1961) 407.

(5) FRIENDS, Friargate (SE 604516). A visit to York by George Fox in 1651 was followed by a rapid growth in local support for Quaker beliefs and by the establishment of a meeting which, until 1674, met in hired premises. In that year a building on the present site was converted for use as a meeting-house and in 1678 this was further altered and an adjacent building fitted up as a second and larger meeting-house for the York Quarterly Meeting. The latter was replaced in 1718 by a new meeting-house of brick, its S wall standing on the remains of the precinct wall of the mediaeval Franciscan Friary and its W side adjoining the earlier meeting-house. In 1816–17 the premises were largely

Friends' meeting-house, Friargate.   (5)

rebuilt though incorporating much of the E wall of the former large meeting-house and retaining a small record closet added in 1797. Additional accommodation was erected to the W in 1884–5 following the construction of Clifford Street.

The meeting-house, completed in 1817 to the designs of C. Watson and J.P. Pritchett of York and fully described by Alexander ((1820) op. cit. below), has brick walls and a slate roof. The N front to Friargate is of five bays with a pediment and two tiers of blind windows above a former open portico subsequently concealed by a covered vestibule. The E wall of 1718, heightened and extended to the S in 1817, has five windows at gallery level and one below at the S end; the record closet, which projects at the former SE corner, is of brick with a stone slate roof and has a window in its S wall. The S wall has three upper windows and the W wall has four windows at gallery level above the roof line of the smaller meeting-house. The interior, of trapezoidal plan, has a gallery around three sides, rounded to N, with balustraded front supported by cast-iron columns. The stand, at the S end, with seats widened in the late 19th century, has above it a canopy with fielded-panelled soffit supported by cast-iron brackets. A smaller meeting-house to the W dates from 1886. (Both buildings demolished 1980)

Burial-ground: on NE side of Cromwell Road, Bishophill (SE 602514), purchased 1667, is surrounded by a high brick wall with stone coping having an arched entrance at the SE end. Monuments are uniform 19th-century headstones, formerly aligned but re-sited since c.1980 and the N part redeveloped for housing.

Alexander, W., *Observations on the Construction and Fitting Up of Meeting Houses etc. for Public Worship* . . . (1820). Allott, S., *Friends in York* (1978). Lidbetter (1961) *passim*. RCHM *City of York* III (1972) 48; V (1981) 52–4. VCH *York* (1961) 405–6.

(6) Former METHODIST, Aldwark (SE 607520). John Nelson of Birstal is credited with having introduced Methodism to York in 1744. The society met in various buildings before the erection of the first permanent preaching-house in 1759. This building, in use until c.1804, known also as 'Peasholme Green Chapel', is now in commercial use. Some responsibility for the work was taken by William Alwood, a trustee and one of the York preachers, to whom John Wesley wrote on 29 March 1759 'I believe each window may stand eight foot (the bottom of it) from the ground, and be four foot broad and six or seven high, arched at the top'.

The walls are of red brick and the roof is hipped and covered with pantiles. The broad front wall faces SE and, though much altered, has the remains of a wide round-arched window centrally below the eaves between two similar windows set lower down; other openings including an upper window to the extreme left may be later, perhaps c.1775 when additional galleries were constructed. The rear wall has been entirely refenestrated but one earlier arch remains at the lower level.

Lyth (1885) 91ff. RCHM *City of York* V (1981) 52. Telford, J. (ed.), *The Letters of the Rev. John Wesley* IV (1931) 55, 60; VCH *York* (1961) 408–9.

(7) Former WESLEYAN, Skeldergate (SE 602515). 'Albion Chapel', built in 1816 and superseded by a chapel in Priory Street in 1856–7, is a plain brick building with a five-bay front having a

pedimental gable, two tiers of round-arched windows, and entrances in the penultimate bays. It is said to have been designed by the Rev. John Nelson.

Lyth (1885) 228. RCHM *City of York* III (1972) 47. VCH *York* (1961) 409–10.

(8) Former WESLEYAN, Front Street, Acomb (SE 571512) (now Nos. 91, 93). Built 1821, superseded by Trinity Chapel 1879, converted to two shops and dwellings and re-fronted 1881.

RCHM, *City of York* III (1972), 48.

(9) WESLEYAN 'CENTENARY CHAPEL', St Saviourgate (SE 60555195). The chapel was built in 1839–40 at the suggestion of the trustees of New Street Chapel (the now-demolished successor to Peaseholme Green Chapel) to celebrate the centenary of Methodism. The architect was James Simpson of Leeds. The walls are of light-coloured brick with stone dressings at the front and brown brick at the sides. The SE front is of five bays with a central pedimented portico having four giant Ionic columns, and terminal pilasters to the flanking bays with a continuous entablature. The two tiers of windows have rectangular moulded frames.

The interior seating 1,500 has a continuous round-ended gallery and a full complement of box-pews. The rostrum pulpit and organ are of later date.

Chapels Society *Newsletter* 6 (June 1992). Lyth (1885) 255–7. RCHM *City of York* V (1981) 410.

(10) Former WESLEYAN, Priory Street (SE 59885151). The chapel, built in 1856 and intended to rival Centenary Chapel in its quality and accommodation, was also designed by James Simpson but in the more restrained Classical manner he had then adopted. The walls are of red brick with stone dressings with two tiers of round-arched windows under cornices with segmental pediments to the upper tier and an elaborately detailed cornice overall. The front is of five bays with triple entrances. The interior seating 1,500 has a continuous round-ended gallery with original seating, but the lower floor was refitted in the early 20th century and the pulpit replaced by a large mahogany rostrum. The chapel has been used since c.1982 by the Assembly of God.

Lyth (1885) 266–8. VCH *York* (1961) 410.

Former Wesleyan chapel, Priory Street. (10)

Wesleyan Centenary Chapel.

(9)

(11) Former PRIMITIVE METHODIST, Acomb Green (SE 572513). Small chapel with rendered walls, built *c*.1846 and converted to Friends' Meeting-house 1912.

RCHM *City of York* III (1972) 47. VCH *York* (1961) 406.

(12) Former PRIMITIVE METHODIST, Little Stonegate (SE 603 520). 'Ebenezer Chapel', opened in 1851 but converted for industrial use in 1901, was designed by J. P. Pritchett of York. The broad front to the street is of brick with stone facings above a rusticated ashlar basement. The end bays project slightly and have above the entrances wide round-arched windows to light the staircases; the four intermediate bays have two tiers of sash windows in moulded frames and others below to light a Sunday-school room below the chapel.

RCHM *City of York* V (1981) 52. VCH *York* (1961) 414.

(13) Former PRIMITIVE METHODIST, Victor Street (SE 601513). 1879–80 by William Peachey. Red brick with yellow-brick dressings, segmental bowed ends and two tiers of arched windows separated by pilasters.

VCH *York* (1961) 414.

(14) SALVATION ARMY, Gillygate (SE 602525). Brick 'citadel' with battlemented parapets, five-bay centre with segmental-

Salvation Army Citadel, Gillygate.   (14)

arched doorway and recessed wings, built 1882–3, architect Edmund J. Sherwood.

VCH *York* (1961) 417.

The eastern division of Yorkshire is not notable for any wealth of early meeting-houses; those congregations able to claim an origin in the 17th century have left few traces of their former buildings. One such is the Baptist church in Bridlington (18), where a fragmentary structure in Applegarth Lane requires more than a little of the eye of faith to discern the evidence for its first place of worship. A more substantial, though still somewhat enigmatic building in Dagger Lane, Hull (59), dated 1698, offered more convincing proof of the antiquity of dissent in a city whose places of worship of all periods and denominations have suffered grievously from demolition over many years and to which catalogue this too has been added during the period of this survey. A few former Quaker meeting-houses of the 18th century remain of which the earliest, at Welwick (100), dates from 1718 and another at East Cottingwith (28) from 1789. The former Baptist chapel at Driffield (30) remains substantially intact in spite of a century of other use, but the larger and slightly earlier chapel of 1770 at Bishop Burton (14) is included as another notable loss of the post-war years; the former chapel at Hedon (45), of 1801, a building with some architectural pretensions, stands in marked contrast to that of the Scotch Baptists in Beverley (8) which more closely resembles the meeting-houses of the Quakers. The chapels of the old-established Presbyterian or Independent churches at Cottingham (44) and Swanland (96), which in the early 19th century replaced their earlier meeting-houses, are both buildings of considerable size and notable architectural quality.

Methodism, restricted almost entirely to the Wesleyan and Primitive Methodist connexions, filled the gap left by the failure of the older dissent, providing small chapels in great numbers throughout the 19th century. The earliest surviving Methodist chapel, however, dates from the closing years of the life of John Wesley; dating from 1786, it stands in a typically concealed situation in Market Weighton (69) close to its successor of 1868. Several small Wesleyan chapels also remain or have been recorded from the last decade of the 18th century, such as East Heslerton (47), an unusual building of 1794, and Acklam (1) and Uncleby (66) of 1794 and 1796 which presage the many small three-bay chapels of the 19th century with entrances between a pair of windows, low eaves and the pulpit to right or left of the doorway facing a few rows of stepped seating. The most remarkable of these later chapels, though recently converted to a house, is at Burton Agnes (23), a three-bay chapel of 1837 in which Gothic elements with pointed windows and intersecting glazing bars are freely applied to the standard design. Such stylistic detailing, which was largely confined to the Wesleyans, was evident on the Market Weighton chapel and on such other chapels as Ellerton (34) of 1822 and Wold Newton (104) of 1839.

The larger Wesleyan chapel at Newport (73), of 1814, set back behind a range of building which contained the earlier preaching room, has recently had some of its glazing restored to an approximation of its former Gothic state; this and the chapel at Stamford Bridge (94) of 1828 illustrate the two-storeyed elevation arising from the provision of galleries. The flamboyant architecture of the later 19th century is here represented by the Wesleyan chapel of 1884 in St John's Street, Bridlington (19), and many other examples of this style may be found in the growing suburbs or watering-places of that period.

Brickwork is the most commonly used material for walling throughout the region with a few examples of stone where that was readily available. Slate is the most usual roofing material but pantiled roofs are of frequent occurrence; the absence of plain clay tiles is noticeable but patent concrete tiles have been used in several instances as a replacement for older materials.

ACKLAM
N. Yorks.

(1) Former WESLEYAN (SE 782616). Small chapel built 1794, repaired 1909 and closed 1966; now Anglican. Coursed stone walls and pantiled roof. Broad slightly irregular W front in three bays. Pointed-arched window with intersecting glazing bars in S wall. Two blocked windows in N wall formerly flanked the pulpit. Interior (26¾ft by 21¼ft) refitted. *Monument*: Nic.

Butterfield, 1796, probably removed from East Acklam church.
Neave and Neave (1990) 45.

(2) Former PRIMITIVE METHODIST (SE 786617). 'Zion Chapel 1821'. Squared stone with hipped pantiled roof. Entrance and two sash windows in N wall; two similar pulpit windows at E end. Seating formerly stepped up to W with room below having an external doorway (now blocked) in S wall.

Former Wesleyan chapel, Acklam.　　　(1)

ALDBROUGH　　　*Humberside*

(3) Former PRIMITIVE METHODIST (TA 240387). Hipped roof; three-bay front with round-arched openings. Dated 1850.

ATWICK　　　*Humberside*

(4) Former PRIMITIVE METHODIST (TA 191509). Three-bay front, dated 1856.

BARMBY MOOR　　　*Humberside*

(5) WESLEYAN (SE 779490). Three-bay front with arched and keystoned openings. 1869 by T. Grant, replacing chapel of 1807.

BARMSTON　　　*Humberside*

(6) WESLEYAN (TA 163590). Plain chapel of rendered brick with sash windows in gabled ends. Tablet in N gable 'WESLEYAN CHAPEL 1839 *Sir Henry Boynton Bart. gave the Ground for this Chapel to the Wesleyans*'.

BEEFORD　　　*Humberside*

(7) Former CONGREGATIONAL (TA 126540). Built 1810, enlarged 1857. Rendered gabled front with quoins and traces of arched windows with keystones. Much altered.

BEVERLEY　　　*Humberside*

(8) Former SCOTCH BAPTIST, Walkergate (TA 033397). The meeting-house, built in 1808, stands on the W side of the street opposite the end of Morton Lane. The walls (39¼ft by 24¾ft externally) are of brick with modern rendering, the roof is pantiled and gabled. The two longer walls have each three sash windows; there is an entrance on the E side and another flanked by two blocked windows at the N end. (Recently used by Jehovah's Witnesses, subsequently a restaurant)

(9) WESLEYAN, Toll Gavel (TA 034396). Italianate, 1891 by Morley and Woodhouse.

(10) Former FREE METHODIST, Trinity Lane (TA 038395). The chapel, now a Masonic Hall, was built in 1856. Rendered pedimented front of three bays with giant Corinthian pilasters.

BEWHOLME　　　*Humberside*

(11) PRIMITIVE METHODIST (TA 166500). Dated 1839; much rebuilt and heightened 1863.

BIELBY　　　*Humberside*

(12) Former WESLEYAN (SE 790437). Gault brick with hipped roof, three-bay front with small oval tablet dated 1837. *Sundial*: above entrance, painted stone dial with iron gnomon, inscribed with latitude and longitude, motto 'Soli Deo Omnis GLORIA[M]', signed 'J. SMITH, DELIN BIELBY, 1838'. (Converted to house since 1983)

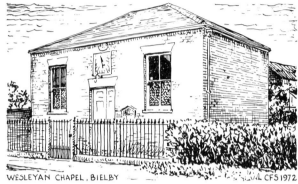

WESLEYAN CHAPEL, BIELBY　　　CFS 1972

BILTON　　　*Humberside*

(13) WESLEYAN, Wyton (TA 176332). Built 1841. Three-bay front with round-arched windows; central arch inscribed 'WESLEYAN CHAPEL'.

Wesleyan chapel, Wyton.　　　(13)

BISHOP BURTON　　　*Humberside*

(14) BAPTIST, Callas (SE 989396). The chapel built in 1770 for a church formed in 1764 was demolished *c*.1955. The walls were of brick and the hipped roof was covered with pantiles. The broad N front had two end doorways below flat-arched heads with keystones and small gallery windows above; centrally between, at mid-height, was a sash window with round-arched head and keystone.

　Shipley (1912) 68, 203, Plate facing 205.

(15) WESLEYAN, Pudding Gate (SE 989397). Rendered walls with round-arched windows and pedimented front; dated 1840.

BISHOP WILTON   *Humberside*

(16) Former WESLEYAN (SE 796551). Much altered *c*.1900; original tablet 'BETHEL 1810' in front wall.

BLACKTOFT   *Humberside*

(17) Former WESLEYAN (SE 845242). Small three-bay chapel dated 1839. (Conversion to house proposed 1989)

BRIDLINGTON   *Humberside*

(18) Former BAPTIST, Applegarth Lane (TA 176678). The Baptist Church formed in 1698, which since 1874 has occupied a chapel in Quay Road, claims to have met in its earliest years in a building in Applegarth Lane of which some reputed fragments and a small burial-ground remain. Meetings were transferred to a new location in Bayle Gate in the early 18th century.

The earliest structure (about 13½ft by 15ft externally) has low brick walls, much rebuilt, and a pantiled roof. The front wall, which may date in part from *c*.1700, faces the burial-ground; it has a central doorway and a small window to the left. The gabled end wall facing the lane has some early brickwork in its lowest courses but the rear wall and the other gabled end are entirely of the late 19th century.

The burial-ground is bounded by brick walls; fixed to the rear wall is a tablet recording the restoration of the site by Bridlington Corporation in 1938. *Monuments*: (1) Milcah, wife of John Furby junior, 1840; (2) William Chester, 1829. (Shipley illustrates a further stone to Robert Prudom (first pastor), 1708.)

BM XIII (1821) 196–8. *B. Hbk* (1875) 350. Douglas (1846) 115–17. Shipley (1912) 63–6, 201–3.

(19) WESLEYAN, St John's Street (TA 176676). Yellow brick with yellow-sandstone dressings, gabled front between turrets. 1884 by Joseph Earnshaw.

(20) Former PRIMITIVE METHODIST, St John's Street (TA 176 677). Gabled front between pyramidal turrets. 1877 by W. Freeman, replacing chapel of 1834.

Neave and Neave (1990) 47. Woodcock (1889) 49–50, 56.

Wesleyan chapel, St John's Street, Bridlington.   (19)

BUBWITH   *Humberside*

(21) WESLEYAN (SE 715362). The chapel, built 1796 and enlarged 1870, was demolished *c*.1973. The walls were of brick; the front had a pedimented gable and a pointed-arched doorway between two windows.

Neave and Neave (1990) 47.

(22) Former PRIMITIVE METHODIST (SE 713363). Gabled front, dated 1862. Now Parish Hall.

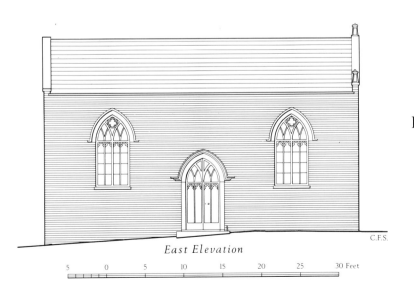

East Elevation

5   0   5   10   15   20   25   30 Feet

C.F.S.

Wesleyan Chapel,

BURTON AGNES,

Yorkshire E.R.

BURTON AGNES   *Humberside*

(23) Former WESLEYAN (TA 105631). The chapel standing 300 yards SE of Burton Agnes Hall has brick walls and a slate roof. The gable end facing the gates to the hall is ornamented with short stone finials and has a pair of windows flanking the pulpit with Perpendicular tracery under two-centred arched heads with moulded labels; in the gable is a tablet dated 1837 recording the gift of the ground by Sir Henry Boynton, Bart. The entrance front is of three bays with similarly arched openings but of less elaboration. Interior refitted. (Converted to house since 1985)

Former Wesleyan chapel, Burton Agnes.
After conversion to house   (23)

BURTON FLEMING   *Humberside*

(24) WESLEYAN (TA 083721). Red and yellow brick, 1883 (*pace* Methodist Statistical Returns) replacing 1806 chapel.
   Neave and Neave (1990) 48.

(25) Former PRIMITIVE METHODIST (TA 084721). Small three-bay chapel dated 1838; in lane SE of 1902 successor.

BURTON PIDSEA   *Humberside*

(26) Former WESLEYAN (TA 248314). Hipped pantiled roof, round-arched windows. Defaced tablet 'WESLEYAN CHAPEL/BUILT 1847/RESTORED [?1909]'.

CATWICK   *Humberside*

(27) Former WESLEYAN (TA 128454). Opened 1839. Rendered front with two original round-arched windows; entrance re-sited.

COTTINGWITH   *Humberside*

(28) Former FRIENDS, East Cottingwith (SE 703426). The meeting-house built in 1789 was leased in 1897 for use as a Board School and sold in 1921; it is now the village hall. The walls are of brick and the roof is covered with pantiles. The longer N and S walls have each two segmental-arched windows with original doorways centrally between in slightly projecting wall panels; the N entrance is now blocked and that to the S covered by a later porch. Two windows have been inserted in the W gable wall. The building (originally 33¼ft by 20¼ft externally) was enlarged at the E end after 1897. *Burial-ground*: to N, contains one monument, loose, to William Webster, 1854.

(29) Former WESLEYAN, East Cottingwith (SE 704424). Brick and pantile, originally of three bays with flat-arched heads to the windows; octagonal gable openings. Built 1796, extended to N and entrance re-sited 1868. (Closed 1973)

DRIFFIELD   *Humberside*

(30) Former BAPTIST, King Street (TA 026576). A meeting-house built in 1788 for a recently formed church was superseded in 1862 by a new chapel in Middle Street South. The former building, since used as a Masonic Hall and from 1987 as 'Cass Hall' by the Women's Royal Voluntary Services, has walls of brown brick and a pantiled roof.

The plan is rectangular (36¼ft by 23¾ft externally) but with a rounded NE corner. The E and W walls are gabled; at the E end is an original doorway and above it a circular gallery window set in the site of a wider round-arched opening. In the S wall are two further round-arched windows, another in the N wall is now blocked. The W wall, covered by a minor extension, had two windows flanking the site of the pulpit. A single gallery at the E end has been converted to an upper room.

Monuments: in burial-ground to S, 17 headstones, including (1) Michel [*sic*] Nicoles, 1794; (2) James Normanton, 32 years minister, 1848, Mary his mother, 1835, Fanny his sister, 1825, and Mary Conyers his niece, daughter of John Laybourne, 1854; (3) Thomas Jackson, schoolmaster, 1834, and Jane his wife, 1829.

(31) CONGREGATIONAL, Exchange Street (TA 025578). 1866-7 by H.J. Paull.
   Miall (1868) 256.

EASINGTON   *Humberside*

(32) WESLEYAN (TA 402192). Long front wall with round-arched windows and two entrances; triangular tablet on porch 'built 1850, restored 1901'.

(33) Former PRIMITIVE METHODIST, Back Street (TA 399191). Four-bay front with round-arched openings; tablet dated 1851.

ELLERTON   *Humberside*

(34) WESLEYAN (SE 706398). Opened 1822. N front of three bays with gabled porch and pointed-arched windows with intersecting glazing bars. Two altered windows in S wall; W wall rebuilt. The pulpit at E end faces stepped seating.

Wesleyan chapel, Ellerton.   (34)

ELVINGTON
N. Yorks.

(35) Former WESLEYAN (SE 701476). 1809–10, much altered.

FANGFOSS
Humberside

(36) WESLEYAN, Bolton (SE 771522). Yellow brick with stone dressings, broad three-bay front with gabled porch and round-arched openings with 'jewelled' keystones. 1869 by T. Grant.

(37) Former WESLEYAN, Fangfoss (SE 766532). Yellow brick with hipped slate roof and bracketed eaves. Round-arched windows with 'jewelled' keystones. Dated 1865.

Former Wesleyan chapel, Fangfoss.   (37)

FOLKTON
N. Yorks.

(38) Former WESLEYAN, Flixton (TA 043796). Altered three-bay front with round-arched openings; built 1841, closed 1929.

(39) Former PRIMITIVE METHODIST, Flixton (TA 042796). Three bays, windows with splayed lintels; dated 1841.

FRIDAYTHORPE
Humberside

(40) WESLEYAN (SE 875592). 'Centenary Chapel' dated 1840; central entrance re-sited.

(41) Former PRIMITIVE METHODIST (SE 875590). Built 1851. Converted to bungalow since 1932.

FULL SUTTON
Humberside

(42) Former WESLEYAN (SE 746554). Two sash windows with flat-arched heads; windows and two-centred arched doorway

Former Wesleyan chapel, Full Sutton.   (42)

with intersecting glazing bars in fanlight. Built 1828. (Converted to house since 1974)

GOODMANHAM
Humberside

(43) Former WESLEYAN (SE 890431). Three-bay front with two pointed-arched windows, semicircular-arched doorway and round window over. Built 1828, door and window arches remade 1964. Converted to cottage since 1961.

HALTEMPRICE
Humberside

(44) ZION CHAPEL, Cottingham (TA 044329). The Presbyterian, latterly Congregational, church (now URC) originated in the late 17th century and suffered from a short-lived orthodox secession during the ministry of the Rev. Edward Dewhirst (1775–84), whose Arian views were disapproved and who, according to Miall, was buried in the churchyard 'in a reversed position'. The present chapel, of 1819 by Appleton Bennison, has a gabled front of gault brick in three bays with two tiers of round-arched windows and entrances in flanking wings.

Miall (1868) 250. Neave and Neave (1990) 48.

Zion Chapel (URC), Cottingham.   (44)

HEDON
Humberside

(45) Former BAPTIST, Magdalen Gate (TA 190287). The origin of the church formerly meeting here is obscure, but it may have been allied to the Scotch Baptists. The chapel built 1801 was used

Former Baptist chapel, Magdalen Gate, Hedon.   (45)

by Wesleyans 1812–18 and Primitive Methodists 1819–73. From 1873 a Baptist congregation attached to George Street, Hull, appears to have met here. The building is now used by the Royal British Legion.

The walls are of brick and the roof is hipped and covered with pantiles. The front wall, facing N, is of three bays; the centre bay, which projects slightly and may formerly have been finished with a pediment, has a round-arched window with intersecting glazing bars and a large oval tablet above it carved with the date 1801, 'Built by subscription', and quotations from Eph. 1: 22 and Matt. 18: 20. Two doorways in the end bays have round-arched heads and blind fanlights.

HEMINGBROUGH   N. Yorks.

(46) WESLEYAN (SE 674307). Two-storeyed gabled porch between tall round-arched windows. Inscribed 'Erected 1836, rebuilt 1848'.

HESLERTON   N. Yorks.

(47) WESLEYAN, East Heslerton (SE 924767). Tall narrow-fronted chapel of brick with a hipped slate roof, built in 1794, extended to rear and heightened in 1840. Lofty interior; gallery of 1840 above entrance with steeply raked contemporary seating.

HOLME UPON SPALDING MOOR   Humberside

(48) WESLEYAN, Selby Road (SE 802384). Built 1826–7 to replace a chapel of 1787. Pointed-arched windows, doorway re-sited.

(49) Former PRIMITIVE METHODIST (SE 804383). 'Zion', 1880.

HORNSEA   Humberside

(50) Former FRIENDS, Back Westgate (TA 199476). A house was registered for meetings in 1711 and the present building (35¾ft by 15¾ft externally) acquired by the society in 1750; it has long been converted to a cottage. The walls are of brick on a rubble plinth and the roof is pantiled. The S front has been refenestrated and a former doorway blocked.

HOWDEN   Humberside

(51) CONGREGATIONAL, Bridge Gate (SE 748284). The chapel built in 1795, enlarged and altered in 1837, re-fronted 1878, was demolished in 1980.
    Miall (1868) 282–3.

(52) WESLEYAN, Hail Gate (SE 750284). The chapel built in 1832 replaces a preaching-house of 1786. The front is of three bays with a simple pediment and two tiers of windows with flat-arched heads. (Demolished 1974)

(53) Former PRIMITIVE METHODIST, St John's Street (SE 747283). Simple 1837 chapel alongside 1872 Gothic successor; both derelict 1984. (Demolished 1988)

HUMBLETON   Humberside

(54) Former WESLEYAN, Flinton (TA 220362). Three bays with flat-arched windows and re-sited entrance; dated 1855.

(55) PRIMITIVE METHODIST, Humbleton (TA 228345). Asymmetrical front with two round-arched windows. 'Primitive Methodist Jubilee Chapel, 1860'.

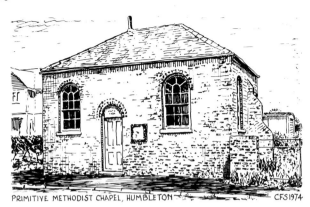

PRIMITIVE METHODIST CHAPEL, HUMBLETON   CFS 1974

KELFIELD   N. Yorks.

(56) WESLEYAN (SE 596383). Three-bay front with round-arched doorway and later clock dial above. 1815, altered.

(57) Former PRIMITIVE METHODIST (SE 595385). Built 1852, shed doors inserted in front; traces of stepped seating to rear.

KELK   Humberside

(58) Former PRIMITIVE METHODIST, Little Kelk (TA 097596). Rendered front, dated 1861.

KINGSTON UPON HULL   Humberside

(59) Former INDEPENDENT, Dagger Lane (TA 098286). The first Independent church in Hull was founded in 1643; throughout the Commonwealth it occupied the chancel of Holy Trinity church, which building it shared with the Presbyterians who worshipped in the nave. After some years in other premises the Independents built a chapel in Dagger Lane in 1698. The church suffered a major secession in 1768, the seceders founding a new congregation which met successively in Blanket Row (1769–82), Fish Street (1782–1898) and subsequently at Princes Avenue. After 1768 the original church came under strong Swedenborgian influence and remained in that allegiance until the early 19th century when, after legal action, the building passed to an orthodox Presbyterian church which continued to use it until the late 19th century; this congregation then removed to Spring Bank and is now represented by 'St Ninians', Chanterlands Avenue. During the Swedenborgian period the manse and vestry were sold to the Minerva Lodge of Freemasons; these were rebuilt in 1958, the Lodge subsequently acquiring the remainder of the property.

The chapel is a plain structure of brick with a slate roof. It is almost entirely surrounded by later building, only the upper part of the W gable wall facing Dagger Lane remaining visible; this is in English-bond brickwork and has three segmental-arched upper windows and traces of three openings below. Under the central window is a square stone tablet inscribed 'This Chapel was built A.D. 1698' together with Hebrew inscriptions above and below. (Rebuilt as Masonic Lodge 1978 incorporating new tablet repeating former inscription)
    Darwent (1899). Miall (1868) 288–90, 292–3. Neave (1991) 10.

(60) Former CONGREGATIONAL, Hope Street (TA 095288). Built 1797 for a former minister of New Dagger Lane Chapel; altered

Former Independent chapel, Dagger Lane, Hull.   (59)

mid 19th century, closed 1903, destroyed by enemy action 1941. The building was almost square with the pulpit between the front entrances.

Miall (1868) 293. Neave (1991) 18.

(61) Former CONGREGATIONAL, Witham (TA 106293). Built 1830 for the Rev. Ebenezer Morley; later used by Primitive Methodists and other denominations until 1954 when it was converted to commercial use. Rendered walls and hipped roof, three bays with lower annexe in front, side facing Holborn Street

Former Congregational chapel, Witham, Hull.   (61)

of four principal bays. Two floors inserted.

CYB (1863) obituary of the Rev. E. Morley. Miall (1868) 293. Neave (1991) 60.

(62) Former WESLEYAN, Scott Street (TA 099295). Rendered walls with two tiers of windows; pedimented front with quoins and platband. Built 1850 replacing a chapel of 1804. In commercial use since 1910.

Neave (1991) 55.

(63) Former METHODIST NEW CONNEXION, Charlotte Street (TA 101291). Bethel Chapel, built 1799, re-fronted 1875, destroyed by enemy action 1941.

Neave (1991) 26.

(64) Former METHODIST NEW CONNEXION, Beverley Road (TA 089302). Zion Chapel, built 1849, low rendered walls with three-bay pedimented front. Two storeyed cottage at rear facing Cave Street. Now Pentecostalist.

Neave (1991) 67.

Former Methodist New Connexion chapel, Beverley Road, Hull.   (64)

(65) Former PRIMITIVE METHODIST, Wincolmlee (TA 100301). Built 1842, later occupied *c.*1879–80 by Salvation Army, now in commercial use. Rendered front of three bays with pediment and two tiers of round-arched windows.

Neave (1991) 53.

Former Wesleyan chapel, Uncleby.   (66)

KIRBY UNDERDALE   *Humberside*

(66) Former WESLEYAN, Uncleby (SE 811592). Brick and pantile; altered doorway between pair of sash windows. Built 1796, closed 1974, now workshop.

  Neave and Neave (1990) 59.

LEAVENING   *N. Yorks.*

(67) WESLEYAN (SE 787630). Three-bay stone front with altered window frames. Built 1824.

LUTTONS   *N. Yorks.*

(68) WESLEYAN, West Lutton (SE 932693). Rendered walls, hipped roof; built 1817, altered 1880.

MARKET WEIGHTON   *Humberside*

(69) Former METHODIST (SE 876418). On 23 June 1788 John Wesley 'preached, with much enlargement of heart, in the new chapel at Market Weighton'. The chapel, built in 1786, stands in a concealed position behind other buildings; in 1868 a new Wesleyan chapel was built next to the road and the former converted for the Sunday-school; it is now in industrial use. The walls are of brick ($30\frac{1}{4}$ft by $40\frac{1}{2}$ft externally) rendered at the front and the roof is hipped and covered with pantiles. The front wall, of three bays, has a central entrance with two-centred arched head and similar flanking windows all with intersecting glazing bars and square windows above. The interior has been refitted and a floor inserted.

  Curnock (1938) VII: 406. Neave and Neave (1990) 10, 38.

Former Methodist chapel, Market Weighton.   (69)

MELBOURNE   *Humberside*

(70) WESLEYAN (SE 751440). Built 1811. Front with entrance between two wide pointed-arched windows with later frames; extended by one bay and a third window added.

(71) Former PRIMITIVE METHODIST (SE 750441). Gabled front, two round-arched windows and obscured tablet formerly dated 1821. Extended to front and tablet perhaps reset in mid 19th century. Now used by Scouts.

MUSTON   *N. Yorks.*

(72) PRIMITIVE METHODIST (TA 095794). Gabled front with two upper windows, doorway below one. Dated 1824.

NEWPORT   *Humberside*

(73) WESLEYAN, Wallingfen or New Village (SE 857304). The first preaching-house of 1789 occupied the upper floor of a long brick building adjacent to the road. The present chapel, standing well back behind other buildings, was erected in 1814 and has a burial-ground in front. It is a square building of brick with a hipped pantiled roof. The S front of three bays has two pointed-arched doorways and a similarly arched window between, and three upper windows with semicircular-arched heads; new frames with intersecting glazing bars have recently been inserted. The interior has a gallery around three sides with original seating. The pulpit and lower pews were renewed in the late 19th century but the earlier back-board of the pulpit remains; this has an oval panel between reeded architraves below a segmental cornice. *Monument*: to Charles Bains, 1838, and Mary his widow, 1840.

Wesleyan chapel, Wallingfen.   (73)

NORTH CAVE   *Humberside*

(74) Former WESLEYAN (SE 892325). Pedimented front with round-arched windows and altered entrance. Inscribed 'Wesleyan Methodist Centenary Chapel 1839'.

NORTH DALTON   *Humberside*

(75) WESLEYAN (SE 936523). 'Centenary Chapel' dated 1839. Steeply gabled centre bay.

NORTH DUFFIELD   *N. Yorks.*

(76) WESLEYAN (SE 685368). The successive chapels of 1833 and 1876 stand adjacent. The former has a simple three-bay front with segmental-arched windows. The latter, of greater

elaboration, has a gabled front with stone dressings, buttresses, finials and pointed-arched windows.

NORTH FRODINGHAM — *Humberside*

(77) CONGREGATIONAL (TA 099531). The congregation originated about 1804 in connection with the church in Fish Street, Kingston upon Hull. The chapel, built in 1821, had two doorways with a single round-arched window between in the front gabled wall. The present building, which may incorporate work of that date, has been much altered and extended to one side. It has a double-gabled N front. A tablet in the back wall is inscribed 'BETHESDA 1821'. (Demolished since 1972)

Darwent (1899) 136–8.

NORTON — *N. Yorks.*

(78) WESLEYAN, Commercial Street (SE 796715). Stone Gothic with Y-traceried windows; 1857, designed by William Lovel 'Builder and timber merchant'.

Neave and Neave (1990) 55, 64.

(79) PRIMITIVE METHODIST, Commercial Street (SE 796715). 'Bethel' chapel, close E of last. Broad three-bay front; 1864, by John Gibson, rear school-room added 1884 which 'communicates with the chapel by means of patent revolving shutters'.

T. Bulmer & Co., *History, Topography and Directory of East Yorkshire with Hull* (1892). Neave and Neave (1990) 55, 63.

PATRINGTON — *Humberside*

(80) WESLEYAN, Greenshaw Lane (TA 314226). Dated 1811; rendered pedimented front added in late 19th century.

POCKLINGTON — *Humberside*

(81) Former CONGREGATIONAL, Chapmangate (SE 802491). Built c.1808, re-fronted 1879; now Pentecostal.

(82) WESLEYAN, Chapmangate (SE 803492). Brick with stone dressings, wide pedimented front of five bays with two tiers of windows. Three doorways behind Roman Doric portico. By Edward Taylor of York 1864.

Neave and Neave (1990) 55, 67.

RICCAL — *N. Yorks.*

(83) Former WESLEYAN, Chapel Lane (SE 622381). A small chapel built in 1798, of brick and pantile with a gabled end wall and later house attached at the opposite end, was converted to a cottage after 1864. It was demolished in 1972. (*Ex inf.* R. Moody)

RILLINGTON — *N. Yorks.*

(84) Former CONGREGATIONAL, Low Moorgate (SE 853744). 'Bethesda Chapel' opened 23 July 1818 is now in commercial use. Stone walls and pantiled roof; pedimented front of three bays with two doorways, lunette between, and three round-arched windows above. 'Restored' and rear gallery given open cast-iron front, 1875.

Miall (1868) 338–9.

(85) WESLEYAN, Low Moorgate (SE 852745). Gabled front with round-arched windows. Built c.1805, enlarged to front in late 19th century.

Bethesda Chapel, Rillington   (84)

Wesleyan chapel, Low Moorgate, Rillington.   (85)

RISTON — *Humberside*

(86) Former PRIMITIVE METHODIST, Long Riston (TA 126425). Plain rendered walls; entrance below gable. Dated 1836.

ROOS — *Humberside*

(87) WESLEYAN (TA 291306). Dated 1808, altered mid 19th century. (Reported demolished 1977)

ROWLEY — *Humberside*

(88) WESLEYAN, Little Weighton (SE 987339). Rendered front with porch between two round-arched windows; hipped roof. Built 1827–30, refitted late 19th century. Stepped seating.

SANCTON   *Humberside*

(89) WESLEYAN (SE 899393). 1815, enlarged to front 1840; later porch.

Methodist Recorder (Winter Number, 1896) 92–6.

SCAGGLETHORPE   *N. Yorks.*

(90) Former WESLEYAN (SE 835724). Stone façade of three bays. Pedimented centre with pointed-arched doorway and roundel with remains of painted inscriptions and date 1816; blind pointed windows in flanking bays.

SCAMPSTON   *N. Yorks.*

(91) WESLEYAN, West Knapton (SE 877756). The chapel is a *c*.1882 conversion of a brick and pantiled farm building of the 18th century, the blocked ventilating slits of which remain in the N and S walls together with two small former doorways in each of these sides. The present entrance is at the E end. Sash windows have been inserted in the side walls.

SEATON   *Humberside*

(92) PRIMITIVE METHODIST, Catfoss Lane (TA 162469). Plain three-bay front of 1837; entrance resited.

SHERBURN   *N. Yorks.*

(93) WESLEYAN (SE 958768). Built 1813–14, much altered or rebuilt 1868. Three-bay front to road with two tiers of round-arched windows and re-sited entrance. Sunday-school of 1882 adjacent.

STAMFORD BRIDGE   *Humberside*

(94) WESLEYAN (SE 712555). Dated 1828. Hipped slate roof; wide front of four bays with two tiers of round-arched windows and later porch. Two tall pulpit windows at rear. (The previous chapel of 1796 is reported to survive as a house (Neave and Neave (1990) 57).)

Wesleyan chapel, Stamford Bridge.   (94)

STILLINGFLEET   *N. Yorks.*

(95) WESLEYAN (SE 593408). Hipped roof. Three-bay front, entrance re-sited and date tablet removed. Opened 1820.

SWANLAND   *Humberside*

(96) CONGREGATIONAL (SE 997280). The chapel built in 1804 stands on the site of a meeting-house erected in 1694 for this originally Presbyterian congregation. Arian influences in the second half of the 18th century resulted in an orthodox secession *c*.1770, the seceders building themselves a new chapel elsewhere in the village; on the re-union of the congregations *c*.1804 the latter was converted to cottages.

The chapel, which faces S, has brick walls and a hipped slated roof. The front wall has two tiers of windows in five bays, the centre pair of simple Venetian form, and two doorways in porches added in 1840. Gabled wings to E and W were built in 1854. The rear wall, which formerly had two tall windows flanking the pulpit, was altered in 1928 by the substitution of a small preaching apse. The interior has an original gallery around three sides with fielded-panelled front supported by turned wood columns; the gallery seating has been removed and the lower pews renewed.

Fittings – *Benefaction Boards*: on N wall, two, recording gifts by Jeremiah Turner 1814, and anon., 1852. *Monument*: on E wall, to Rev. David Williams, 1827, Mary his wife, 1818, and their six children, signed 'Myers Wilson, Hull'. *Plate*: Patton (1943, op. cit. below) records two cups, one given by Thomas Watson, 1723, the other given by Jeremiah Turner, 1789.

Miall (1868) 369. Patton, J. G., *A Country Independent Chapel* (1943).

(97) Former PRIMITIVE METHODIST (SE 998282). On confined site behind houses, with hipped roof and narrow three-bay front; tablet on side wall dated 1828 'Built on Ground the Gift of H. Sykes Esqr.'.

THIXENDALE   *N. Yorks.*

(98) Former WESLEYAN (SE 842611). Three-bay rendered front, 1837, altered or rebuilt 1906.

WARTER   *Humberside*

(99) Former WESLEYAN (SE 869503). Early 19th-century, enlarged to front 1878. Converted to house since 1974.

WELWICK   *Humberside*

(100) Former FRIENDS, Humber Lane (TA 344207). The meeting-house, now 'White Cottage', stands on the E side of the lane. It was built in 1718, closed 1818 and was used for a time in the mid 19th century as a school. It was converted to a cottage *c*.1910. The building is nearly square (26¾ft by 28ft externally) with walls of brick covered by later rendering. The W front has stone quoins at the corners. The windows have been altered and the interior is subdivided by a substantial N–S spine wall which may be an insertion.

WESTOW   *N. Yorks.*

(101) Former WESLEYAN (SE 755654). The chapel of 1793, standing in a back lane 100 yards NNE of its successor of 1906, has been converted for use as a workshop. The walls (30½ft by 25½ft externally) are of coursed squared rubble to the front and one end, the other end rebuilt in brick and the rear rendered. One

Congregational chapel, Swanland.

(96)

original doorway below a flat-arched brick head faces the road. Neave and Neave (1990) 59.

WILBERFOSS   *Humberside*

(102) WESLEYAN (SE 731508). Hipped roof; three-bay front with round-arched openings and later porch. Date tablet, 1841, with crude ornament of winged cherubs.

WILLERBY   *N. Yorks.*

(103) PRIMITIVE METHODIST, Staxton (TA 019792). Built 1847; three-bay front with round-arched openings, extended to left with one matching window and refitted in later 19th century.

WOLD NEWTON   *Humberside*

(104) Former WESLEYAN (TA 045732). Three-bay front, pointed-arched windows with moulded labels and intersecting glazing bars, tablet above later porch inscribed 'WESLEYAN CENTENARY, 1839.' Gabled end walls with stone copings. Pulpit to left of entrance, stepped seating to right with small room below. (Converted to hall since 1980)

YEDINGHAM   *N. Yorks.*

(105) Former WESLEYAN (SE 893793). Rendered three-bay front with round-arched openings, dated 1842. Original cast-iron rainwater gutter with lion's head ornament.

YORKSHIRE (NORTH RIDING)

The northern division of Yorkshire extends from the east coast to the Pennine watershed, some 160 miles of varied scenery and building materials. It is noticeably lacking in large towns other than those of relatively recent growth such as Scarborough, or the Teesside conurbation of which Stockton-on-Tees was historically a part of County Durham. Some traces of the meeting-houses of early nonconformist congregations remain in smaller towns, principally at Malton and Whitby, but it is among the more scattered communities of the Pennines and the Cleveland Hills that the only 17th-century fragments are now to be found. In the extreme north west in Swaledale is the site of Smarber Hall Chapel (88) close to the Westmorland estates of its benefactor, Philip, Lord Wharton. At the other extreme, at Hutton-le-Hole (68) on the southern slopes of the Cleveland Hills are the remains, though scarcely recognizable in their rebuilt form, of the Friends' meeting-house of 1689.

Of the meeting-houses of the older denominations, those of the Friends are particularly notable in this county and provide examples covering a wide period. The early 18th-century meeting-houses at Countersett (14), Osmotherley (106) and especially Laskill (75) are typical specimens of the small stone-walled buildings suited to the needs of country meetings. By contrast, the brick-built meeting-houses at Kirkbymoorside (73) and Thirsk (136) of 1789 and 1799 represent solutions to the use of restricted town sites, traditional in layout but concealed from view and contributing nothing to the townscape. At Pickering (109), also in the eastern part of the county, the meeting-house of 1793 is on a less crowded site and makes use of the local building stone. Further east at Scarborough (119) the former meeting-house of 1801 carries the same simple planning into the 19th century. One of the best examples of a Friends' meeting-house in the North Riding is at Malton (80), of 1823, but other buildings of that period, notably Whitby (152) and Stockton-on-Tees (132), are also of interest, the last concealed behind a later forebuilding comparable with that at DARLINGTON (Durham (10)). The Carperby meeting-house (27) of 1864, although not outwardly typical, conforms to the then fashionable plan of an end entry between retiring rooms.

Only three Presbyterian meetings were noted in the early 18th-century list of dissenting congregations compiled by Dr John Evans (in Dr Williams's Library), and of these the two which became Unitarian, at Malton (83) and Whitby

(151), virtually rebuilt their meeting-houses in the late 18th century or after. Independent congregations, a few with Presbyterian antecedents, are more fully represented but apart from Kirkbymoorside (72) of 1792, the much altered building in Pickering (108) of 1789, and the fragmentary remains at Keld (97) of the same date, none of their chapels is earlier than 1800. Keld is notable for its mediaeval site and for its Inghamite origins. The later chapels are not generally remarkable although South Cliff, Scarborough (118) is of interest for its connection with Titus Salt. That only one Baptist chapel is recorded (77) is an indication of the weakness of the denomination north of the industrial valleys of the West Riding. The single Inghamite meeting-house at Gayle (57), very like a small Quaker building, is a rare reminder of a little-known denomination while the 'Calvinist Chapel' at Thornton Rust (143) is similarly exceptional.

Two-thirds of the chapels listed are Methodist; most are Wesleyan with a few Primitive Methodist buildings of rather late date. Several 18th-century chapels remain of which the earliest, at Osmotherley (107) of 1754, is a simple long and low rectangle hidden in the traditional manner in an alley behind houses. The first preaching-house at Stokesley (125) of 1766, although much altered, was a square building, possibly low-built though with a few architectural pretensions. Most notable were the three octagonal chapels which Methodists built in 1761-2 at Whitby, 1763 at Yarm (156), and 1764-6 at Thirsk. The sole survivor, at Yarm, the oldest Methodist octagon in existence, remains clearly recognizable in spite of heightening, extensions and internal alterations. The former chapel at West Tanfield (148), of 1798, should also be noted for the contrast between its simple domestic front and the Gothic successor standing close against it. Chapels which reflect the grander styles of the 19th century occur at Malton (81), of 1811, in which the straightforward Georgian tradition continues, Stokesley (126) of 1812, a very much grander building than its predecessor, and at Brunswick Chapel, Stockton-on-Tees (133), of 1823, in a design then very popular with Methodist architects and building committees. The full development of Classical forms is to be found in Westborough, Scarborough (120), of 1861-2, but more typical of the region are the many small chapels which remain in great numbers in the country districts. Many of these are simple three-bay buildings with a central entrance between windows, varied in form but low-built and without galleries. An unusually elaborate village chapel is Great Edstone (50), of 1823, in which free use is made of Gothic windows and the virtuosity of the mason is displayed in the scrolled hip terminals which also occur in one or two other chapels in the district. The repetition of a single design, presumably by the same builder, in 1814–15, is noticeable at Brompton (21), Morton-on-Swale (95), Newby Wiske (101) and Sandhutton (117), while the influence of recently erected buildings on the instructions given by chapel authorities is exemplified in the records of the rebuilding of Gunnerside chapel (91) in 1866.

Good supplies of building stone occur in the western parts of the Riding where stone slated roofs are also common. In the Cleveland Hills suitable stone is also found, some being used as rubble in minor positions, but with pantiles as the usual roofing material. In the plain north of York and the adjacent low-lying and coastal areas brickwork is found from an early period, but its use did not extend into the stone districts to any significant degree. Slate has frequently been used to replace the traditional roofing materials but the absence of plain clay tiles, unsuitable at the low pitch of most North Riding roofs, is readily apparent.

AINDERBY QUERNHOW   *N. Yorks.*

(1) Former WESLEYAN (SE 350810). Tiny brick box, dated 1848.

AISKEW   *N. Yorks.*

(2) PRIMITIVE METHODIST (SE 271885). Former chapel with three-bay polychrome brick front, 1869, adjacent to 1911 successor.

AMPLEFORTH   *N. Yorks.*

(3) WESLEYAN, East End (SE 585787). Coursed rubble with hipped slate roof. Opened 1819.

(4) PRIMITIVE METHODIST, West End (SE 581787). Three-bay polychrome brick front with segmental-pointed windows and gabled porch. Dated 1854.

APPLETON-LE-MOORS   *N. Yorks.*

(5) WESLEYAN (SE 736878). Gabled front with two windows, corner doorway and tablet dated 1832.

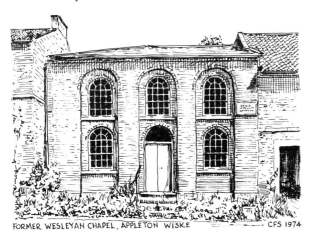

FORMER WESLEYAN CHAPEL, APPLETON WISKE   CFS 1974

APPLETON WISKE   *N. Yorks.*

(6) WESLEYAN (NZ 391046). Brick front with three round-arched recesses embracing two tiers of similarly arched windows and central doorway. Tablet dated 1821.

ARKENGARTHDALE   *N. Yorks.*

(7) Former CHRISTIAN BRETHREN, Eskeleth (NY 999038). Small mid 19th-century chapel with pointed-arched windows; now hostel.

Batty, M., *A View of Arkengarthdale* (1982) 41, 43–4.

(8) WESLEYAN, High Green (NZ 003025). Large chapel of 1883 by Leeming and Leeming of Halifax. The former Sunday-school to SE, now 'Lion House', dated 1923 may incorporate part of the structure of the earlier chapel of 1797.

Batty (1982) op. cit.

Wesleyan chapel, High Green, Arkengarthdale.   (8)

(9) Former PRIMITIVE METHODIST, Langthwaite (NZ 006024). Built 1839, closed *c.*1855 and much altered on conversion to two cottages. Traces of two round-arched windows flanking central entrances.

Batty (1982) op. cit.

(10) Former WESLEYAN, Whaw (NY 982046). Built 1840. Chapel at upper level with dated porch, cottage below.

Batty (1982) op. cit.

ASKRIGG   *N. Yorks.*

(11) PRIMITIVE METHODIST (SD 950913). Three-bay front with round-arched openings, dated 1869.

BAINBRIDGE   *N. Yorks.*

(12) Former CONGREGATIONAL (SD 934901). Gabled front with round-arched openings and clock face below small stone bell-cote with one bell; Sunday-school rooms below. Dated 1864.

(13) FRIENDS, Bainbridge (SD 934903). Rubble with stone-slate roof, S front with two sash windows to principal room and upper window to gallery above minor room and corridor. Built 1836 to supersede a meeting-house of 1700, fragments of which remain incorporated in the 1910 Temperance Hall (SD 932900).

(14) FRIENDS, Countersett (SD 919880). The meeting-house was converted from a barn in 1710 for a meeting formerly held at Countersett Hall. The walls are of rubble and the roof is covered with stone slates. The end walls are gabled and there is a low stone chimney stack at the SW end. The SE front, largely rebuilt in 1778, has three sash windows under rough stone labels and a doorway to the right. Earlier openings, now blocked, remain in the other walls; a later outbuilding adjoins to the south west.

The interior (30ft by 24½ft) has a flat plaster ceiling, a dado of 18th-century fielded panelling around the walls, and a stand at the SW end of unusual height raised by five steps above the floor and with two tiers of fielded panelling to front and back. Loose open-backed benches date from the 19th century.

Cooper, E., *The Quakers of Swaledale and Wensleydale* (1979). Hall, D.S., *Richard Robinson of Countersett, 1628–1693, and the Quakers of Wensleydale* (1989).

(15) WESLEYAN (SD 933902). Rubble with hipped stone-slate roof. Nearly square on plan with two tiers of round-arched windows in front. Dated 1836.

Wesleyan chapel, Bainbridge.   (15)

Friends' meeting-house, Countersett.   (14)

BARNINGHAM   *Durham*

(16) Former WESLEYAN (NZ 083102). Tall narrow-fronted gabled chapel of rubble. Two tall lancets in N front with doorway between and tablet dated 1815. Two Y-traceried windows inserted in each side wall with traces of earlier fenestration; W wall originally had entrance between plain windows with external stair to N leading to gallery doorway.

BARTON   *N. Yorks.*

(17) WESLEYAN, The Green (NZ 230087). Broad gabled front with round-arched openings; dated 1829.

BELLERBY   *N. Yorks.*

(18) WESLEYAN (SE 114929). Long low building with rendered walls and round-arched front windows. Dated 1839.

BILSDALE MIDCABLE   *N. Yorks.*

(19) WESLEYAN, Chop Gate (SE 559998). Concealed behind houses; gabled front with shaped kneelers and finial, round-arched windows with later stone Y-tracery. Dated 1858.

Wesleyan chapel, Chop Gate.   (19)

BRAWBY   *N. Yorks.*

(20) PRIMITIVE METHODIST (SE 739782). Squared stone with hipped slate roof. Three-bay front with sash windows. Tablet above entrance 'Ebenezer erected by Voluntary Subscription Anno Domini MDCCCXXXVIII'.

BROMPTON (Near Northallerton)   *N. Yorks.*

(21) Former WESLEYAN, The Green (SE 375963). Brick front, three bays with two tiers of round-arched windows, centre bay enclosed by tall shallow arch. Early 19th-century. Now converted to house.

BROMPTON (Near Scarborough)   *N. Yorks.*

(22) WESLEYAN, Sawdon (SE 943850). Small three-bay chapel dated 1823; windows altered.

BURRILL WITH COWLING   *N. Yorks.*

(23) WESLEYAN, Burrill (SE 240873). Brick and slate with wide eaves, gabled front with pointed-arched windows, later porch. Tablet dated 1837 inscribed 'We preach Christ crucified . . .'.

CARLTON   *N. Yorks.*

(24) WESLEYAN (NZ 509044). Squared stone with pantiled roof, gabled ends with stone copings and moulded kneelers. Opened 1818 but altered mid 19th century or later.

CARLTON HIGHDALE   *N. Yorks.*

(25) WESLEYAN, Horsehouse (SE 046811). Three-bay front with stone lintels above sash windows, doorway with simply moulded pilasters and tablet above dated 1828.

CARLTON MINIOTT   *N. Yorks.*

(26) WESLEYAN (SE 394810). Brick and slate; side wall originally of three bays with former central entrance, now blocked, and tablet above dated 1838.

CARPERBY-CUM-THORESBY   *N. Yorks.*

(27) Former FRIENDS, Carperby (SE 006898). The meeting-house, of rubble with ashlar dressings and a slate roof, has been suggested as possibly the work of John Hall Thorp of Leeds. The front wall, of three bays with two tiers of windows, has rusticated quoins and a heavily moulded pediment with large shield-shaped tablet dated 1864. Two storeys of rooms at front with central entrance passage leading to meeting-room with plain balustraded stand between corner fireplaces on rear wall. Converted to secular use since 1985.

Former Friends' meeting-house, Carperby.   (27)

(28) Former WESLEYAN (SE 005897). Set back E of the 1890 chapel is its predecessor of 1826. This has a central doorway between two formerly tall windows, now divided between two storeys. Both chapels now converted to houses.

CLAXTON   *N. Yorks.*

(29) PRIMITIVE METHODIST (SE 694601). Three-bay brick front with round-arched windows; dated 1850.

COTHERSTONE
Durham

(30) FRIENDS (NZ 015194). The meeting-house, standing remote from other buildings at the corner of a field, was built in 1796. It is rectangular (40¼ft by 23¾ft externally), with stone walls and a stone-slated roof gabled to E and W with stone copings and moulded kneelers and with a small chimney stack at the W end. The S wall has three round-arched windows and a porch added or altered in the early 19th century with similarly arched doorway and fanlight. Separate doorways inside the porch give access to the principal room to the E and the smaller to the W, separated by screens. At the E end is a contemporary stand with central entrance and panelled floor. *Monuments*: in burial-ground to S, 19th-century and later.

FRIENDS' MEETING-HOUSE, COTHERSTONE. CFS 1972

CRAKEHALL
N. Yorks.

(31) Former WESLEYAN, Great Crakehall (SE 243899). The chapel, built in 1839 to replace one of 1783, has squared stone walls and a hipped slate roof. Front wall with rusticated quoins, semicircular-arched doorway, now altered, between two tiers of windows; the upper windows have round-arched heads. A square inscription tablet above the entrance has been defaced. Superseded by new chapel opposite 1951.

Hird's Annals of Bedale III (1975) 423.

CROPTON
N. Yorks.

(32) PRIMITIVE METHODIST (SE 756890). Zion chapel, dated 1852; three bays, central entrance re-sited.

DANBY
N. Yorks.

(33) FRIENDS, Castleton (NZ 688081). A meeting-house adjacent to Didderhowe House (NZ 685076) was superseded in the late 18th century or earlier by one in Castleton which was closed in 1927 and demolished *c.*1940. The latter (about 52ft by 18ft) comprised two rooms divided by screens.

(34) WESLEYAN, Danby (NZ 707086). The chapel rebuilt in 1901 replaces one of 1811 of three bays with round-arched windows. It stands between the early 19th-century manse and the 'Wesleyan Jubilee School' of 1887. The school has one arched window matching those of the former chapel and has above the entrance a square *sundial* dated 1811, part of the lintel of the former chapel doorway.

EASBY
N. Yorks.

(35) WESLEYAN (NZ 577086). Small chapel opened 1842 attached

to end of earlier house. Gabled end wall with obelisk finials and pair of pointed-arched windows; plain front with similarly arched doorway.

Wesleyan chapel, Danby. Before 1901. (34)

Wesleyan chapel, Easby. (35)

EASINGWOLD
N. Yorks.

(36) WESLEYAN, Chapel Street (SE 529696). 1815 rebuilt 1974. *Monument*: John Scaife, 1839, fluted pillar.

(37) Former PRIMITIVE METHODIST, Spring Street (SE 529700). Large chapel with brick front of five bays with two tiers of round-arched windows enclosed in tall arched recesses. A single doorway supersedes the original entrances in the penultimate

Primitive Methodist chapel, Easingwold. (37)

bays. Dated 1840, interior refitted late 19th century. (Converted to flats since 1974)

EAST AYTON — N. Yorks.

(38) PRIMITIVE METHODIST (SE 989849). Rubble with hipped slate roof, three-bay front with wide corner pilasters of ashlar and eaves band, round-arched doorway, windows with intersecting glazing bars. Partly defaced tablet above entrance dated 1842.

Primitive Methodist chapel, East Ayton. (38)

ELLINGSTRING — N. Yorks.

(39) WESLEYAN (SE 175837). Rendered three-bay front dated 1848.

FEARBY — N. Yorks.

(40) WESLEYAN (SE 193810). Three-bay gabled front of stone with small square tablet dated 1849 'Worship God'.

FLAXTON — N. Yorks.

(41) PRIMITIVE METHODIST (SE 679622). Brick with hipped pantiled roof; three-bay front with later porch. Opened 1817.

FYLINGDALES — N. Yorks.

(42) CONGREGATIONAL, Robin Hood's Bay (NZ 952049). Ashlar with gabled three-bay front, two tiers of pointed-arched windows. Painted oval tablet dated 1840 above porch. (URC)

(43) Former METHODIST, Robin Hood's Bay (NZ 953050). John Wesley refers in his *Journal* (19 June 1784) to the society at Robin Hood's Bay as the first to be formed in the district but whose growth was disturbed by internal dissensions; he 'preached in the new preaching house' on 28 June 1779. The original building (26ft by 41ft externally) occupied the front (SW) part of the present site and may always have had the pulpit centrally on the longer front wall. Successive enlargements between *c*.1836 and 1857 greatly extended the building to the NE and culminated in the rebuilding of the remaining parts of the original structure. A joint in the masonry of the NW wall indicates the limit of the 1779 preaching-house. The chapel was superseded by another on a new site in 1936, but it still retains many of its 19th-century fittings.

The walls are of stone and the main roof, hipped to the NW, is covered with pantiles. The front wall, rebuilt *c*.1857, is of ashlar

with rusticated quoins and has two windows with flat-arched heads and a single doorway to the right. The date 1779 appears on a partly defaced mid 19th-century tablet below which a sundial has been removed. The first enlargement, increasing the depth of the chapel by about 10ft, is indicated by the surviving masonry of the gabled SE wall and by the present span of the front section of the roof. A second enlargement to the rear appears as a separately roofed structure with two tiers of windows in the back wall, comprising a ground-floor school-room and gallery extension above.

The interior (51ft deep) has a gallery around three sides with splayed corners and panelled front with applied mouldings above a wide cove; it is supported by turned wood columns with Roman Doric capitals. The early 19th-century gallery pews remain complete, stepped up on all sides and rising high at the rear.

Former Methodist chapel, Robin Hood's Bay. (43)

GLAISDALE — N. Yorks.

(44) METHODIST, Great Fryup (NZ 738050). The chapel built in 1789 was refitted and partly refenestrated in the late 19th century and a school-room wing added to one end. The walls are of squared stone and the roof is covered with local slates. The front wall has two round-arched windows with intersecting glazing

METHODIST CHAPEL, GREAT FRYUP   CFS·1972

bars and a gabled side-entry porch between. In the rear wall are two similar windows with the arches of former windows above. In the exposed gabled end is a blocked rectangular window. The extension is of two storeys above a small stable. The interior (32ft by 27ft) has been entirely refitted with stepped seating and shutters opening from the ground-floor school-room. The roof is supported by three trusses with king and queen-posts and three tusk-tenoned purlins to each slope.

(45) WESLEYAN, Glaisdale (NZ 758044). Squared stone and slate with gabled SW front, small porch, tablet dated 1821 and blocked upper window; one round-arched window with intersecting glazing bars in each side wall. Later Sunday-school buildings at rear. The burial-ground was given to the Trustees in 1850 by Thomas Breckon, a fact recorded on a stone next to the porch and the date on a gate pier; it was extended in 1905. *Monuments*: include Jane (Frank), wife of Thomas Breckon, 1850, 'The first corpse buried here', headstone with urn in low relief.

(46) Former PRIMITIVE METHODIST, Houlsyke (NZ 735080). 'Zoar' chapel dated 1852, squared stone and slate with two round-arched front windows and doorway to left. (Drastically altered on conversion to house 1980)

Primitive Methodist chapel, Houlsyke.   (46)

(47) WESLEYAN, Lealholm (NZ 761076). Wide NW front with three pointed-arched windows with intersecting glazing bars in bull-nosed stone surrounds with conjoined cills; similarly arched doorway with tablet above dated 1839. Gabled ends with stone coping and kneelers carved with head masks reputed to be the work of John Castello (Rushton (1967) 262).

GREAT AYTON   *N. Yorks.*

(48) Former CONGREGATIONAL (NZ 558107). A Presbyterian meeting-house which stood here from the early 18th century passed into Congregational use *c*.1813 after the death of the last, then Unitarian, minister. The chapel, rebuilt *c*.1852, has walls of squared stone and round-arched windows; in 1879 the front was obscured by a new forebuilding of dark brick with scrolled

inscriptions including 'Hinmers Memorial Schools' commemorating a former minister. Converted to two houses since 1972 and inscriptions defaced.

Miall (1868) 225–6.

(49) FRIENDS, High Green (NZ 563106). A meeting-house on the present site erected 1722 for a meeting commenced in the late 17th century has been used since 1841 in conjunction with the adjacent Friends' School. The building, which has stone walls and a wide three-centred arched entrance to the N, was greatly altered and extended to the E in 1967. *Monuments*: in burial-ground, date from 1825.

GREAT EDSTONE   *N. Yorks.*

(50) WESLEYAN (SE 708839). The chapel dated 1823 at the E end of the village is a nearly square building (24ft by 20¾ft) with squared stone walls, ashlar dressings and a slated pyramidal roof. Three-bay N front with pointed-arched doorway and Y-traceried windows; two windows in S wall of three lights with intersecting tracery and one similar window in E and W walls now blocked internally. The roof is surmounted by a stone finial and has stone copings to the hips with scrolled lower terminals. Interior refitted in late 19th century.

GREAT HABTON   *N. Yorks.*

(51) WESLEYAN (SE 758762). Long gabled building with walls of squared limestone and wide eaves. Entrance at centre of side wall; windows at ends only. Opened 1847.

GRISTHORPE   *N. Yorks.*

(52) Former WESLEYAN, Lebberston (TA 081823). Squared stone and hipped pantiled roof; three windows in front wall, doorway dated 1826 covered by later porch.

GUISBOROUGH   *Cleveland*

(53) Former FRIENDS (NZ 610157). Behind 183 Westgate. Built 1768, sold 1815 and converted to cottages. Largely rebuilt and front wall set back since 1981. Jamb of former doorway remains adjacent to passage from street.

HAWES   *N. Yorks.*

(54) CONGREGATIONAL (SD 875898). 'Bethel Chapel' built 1851. Rendered walls with narrow round-arched windows, gabled front with clasping two-stage corner buttresses and Romanesque entrance in ashlar surround.

Miall (1868) 270–1.

(55) Former CONGREGATIONAL, Widdale (SD 826878). A school and schoolhouse built in 1856 were sold to Congregationalists in 1863 as a place of worship but with provision for a continuing educational use. From *c*.1900 the conduct of the school passed to the School Board and the local authority. In 1912 the formal responsibility for maintaining Sunday services was transferred to the Wesleyans. The chapel is now solely in Methodist use.

The building has rubble walls and a stone slate roof. The chapel has two round-arched windows at the front and a similarly arched doorway to the left with date stone above. The cottage is of two storeys with a central doorway.

Whitehead (1930) 384–5.

Wesleyan chapel, Great Edstone.   (50)

WIDDALE CHAPEL   CFS.1974

(56) FRIENDS (SD 875899). A small meeting-house built in 1710 on the site of a house bought 1698 was enlarged to the W in 1746 and enlarged and refronted in 1816. It was closed in 1931 and demolished in 1955 for road improvement.

A detached burial-ground remains NW of the Congregational chapel. This is a rectangular enclosure with a modern tablet dated 1680–1943.

Hall (1989) 61–4.

(57) Former INGHAMITE, Gayle (SD 872893). Low rubble-walled and stone-slated meeting-house (38ft by 22½ft externally), rendered at front and one end, built in the mid 18th century by

James Allen, d.1804, one of Benjamin Ingham's preachers, who, with his congregation, defected to the Sandemanians in 1759; the building is now used as a Village Institute. Three plain windows in front and rear walls and one in gabled end, with doorways at extreme ends of front wall.

Monuments: in burial-ground include (1) Oswald Allen, 1831, Jane his wife, 1797, and John Allen, 1810; (2) Oswald Allen, 1780, Margaret his widow, 1782, and Matthew their son, 1814;

Former Inghamite chapel, Gayle.   (57)

(3) John Scarr, 1795; (4) Anthony Whaley of Hawes, 1782, Susanna (Allen) his first wife, 1765, their children Ann, 1765, and Richard, 1776, also Rachel (Jackson) his second wife, 1776, headstone with engraved brass inscription plate; (5) Isaac Metcalfe, 1791, *et al.*, table-tomb; (6) Mary, wife of Leonard Allen 17[?7]5 *et al.*; (7) John Routl[?edge], 1781, and Ann his widow, 1797; (8) Thomas Jackson, 1793, Elizabeth his widow, 1812, and Eleanor their daughter, 1831.

Thompson (1958) 61, 73ff.

(58) WESLEYAN, Gayle (SD 870893). Rubble and slate; built 1833, refronted 1879. Two round-arched windows in rear wall.

HAWNBY   *N. Yorks.*

(59) METHODIST (SE 542894). The chapel dated 1770 and the adjacent hamlet of Lower Hawnby are reputed to have been built by Methodists evicted from cottages in the village (¼ mile N). The walls are of coursed stone and the roof, heightened in the 19th century, is covered with pantiles. The original height of the walls is marked by the remains of a stone corbel at each corner, one only retaining its full mouldings. The N front had a doorway near the W end, re-sited and the dated lintel reused in the late 19th century. There were formerly two windows in the S wall, one now blocked and replaced at upper level. The interior (22ft by 18¾ft), entirely refitted in the late 19th century, has a gallery at the W end.

HAWSKER-CUM-STAINSACRE   *N. Yorks.*

(60) WESLEYAN, Hawsker (NZ 925077). Hipped roof with stone copings to hips and moulded kneelers at corners. Three-bay N front, gabled porch with tablet dated 1831. Extended to W in 1912.

HELMSLEY   *N. Yorks.*

(61) Former FRIENDS, Bridge Street (SE 614838). Quaker meetings formerly held in Ampleforth were removed to Helmsley in 1797. A permanent meeting-house built in 1812 stands behind houses on the E side of the street and is approached through an archway. It has walls of coursed rubble with ashlar dressings and a slate roof. The W end is gabled and has a large circular tablet dated 1812 above a central sash window. In the S wall are three similar windows and a later white-brick porch with double doors. Following the closure of the meeting in 1841 the building was leased to Primitive Methodists. The interior was refitted in the late 19th century. (Sold 1984 for Arts Centre)

HIGH ABBOTSIDE   *N. Yorks.*

(62) Former METHODIST, Cotterdale (SD 833941). Early 19th-century, formerly with stepped seating, converted to cottage 1972.

HINDERWELL   *N. Yorks.*

(63) PRIMITIVE METHODIST, Runswick Bay (NZ 810162). Rendered stone walls, irregular plan, built 1829.

(64) CONGREGATIONAL, Staithes (NZ 781188). 'Bethel' chapel built 1823 but possibly enlarged or rebuilt *c.*1835 has squared stone walls and a hipped slate roof. Three-bay front with two tiers of four-centred arched windows with plain hood-moulds

Congregational chapel, Staithes.   (64)

and central doorway with chapel name in bold block-serif lettering above.

Miall (1868) 368. Rushton (1967) 232.

HUBY   *N. Yorks.*

(65) Former FRIENDS (SE 567658). The meeting-house built in 1702 and placed in trust in 1712 was closed in 1851. It was used by Primitive Methodists in the early 20th century, subsequently as a workshop and more recently as a garage and annexe to a house. The walls are of brick; the S wall originally had a doorway between two windows. The interior (about 37ft by 18½ft) was divided into two rooms; now much altered.

HUTTON BUSCEL   *N. Yorks.*

(66) WESLEYAN (SE 970840). Three-bay chapel with date stone of 1822 reset in late 19th-century porch. Sunday-school added at W end in 1952.

(67) Former WESLEYAN, Wrench Green (SE 965895). Heightened and refenestrated, porch added 1903, date tablet 1845 reset and subsequently partly defaced on conversion to a house in 1961.

HUTTON-LE-HOLE   *N. Yorks.*

(68) Former FRIENDS (SE 705898). A meeting-house registered in 1689 was superseded by a building on the present site in 1698 which continued in use until *c.*1849. This was sold in 1859 and rebuilt in 1864 as a large two-storeyed house. The rear wing, which occupies the site of the meeting-house, incorporates some 17th-century material, notably the chamfered jambs of a partly

blocked doorway and a lintel roughly inscribed with the date 1698.

FHSJ XLIX (1959–61) 105–9.

HUTTON RUDBY   *N. Yorks.*

(69) Former METHODIST, North End (NZ 467064). The chapel, now converted to a house, is thought to date from 1759; it has two tiers of windows flanking a central entrance and traces of former doorways adjacent to front corners. Pointed-arched window in rendered rear wall between two tiers of sash windows.

KILBURN HIGH AND LOW   *N. Yorks.*

(70) WESLEYAN, Kilburn (SE 515793). Re-fronted in yellow brick, late 19th century. Original oval tablet, dated 1838, reset above rear entrance.

Anon., *Memorials of Early Methodism in the Easingwold Circuit* (1872) 45–8.

KIRBY WISKE   *N. Yorks.*

(71) WESLEYAN (SE 375850). Brick with hipped roof. Doorway with inscribed lintel dated 1825 between flat-arched windows. Paired stone corbels for former eaves gutter cut back. Stepped seating rises left of entrance.

KIRKBYMOORSIDE   *N. Yorks.*

(72) Former CONGREGATIONAL, Tinley Garth (SE 695865). 'Bethel Chapel', dated 1792 on a tablet in the front wall, remained in use until *c*.1950 but is now used for storage. The walls (32¼ft by 43¾ft externally) are of rubble with squared stone at the front and the roof is pantiled. The exterior is little altered with gabled ends E and W having moulded eaves corbels and stone coping. The wide S front has two windows with three-centred arched heads and plain imposts flanking the site of the pulpit and a similarly arched doorway near each end. The N wall is blank. The E and W walls have each a window matching those in the front wall superseding windows at two levels of which the arched heads of the former upper windows remain.

Miall (1868) 298.

(73) FRIENDS, West End (SE 695864). This site was acquired by

Former Congregational chapel, Kirkbymoorside.   (72)

Friends in 1690 for use as a burial-ground on part of which a meeting-house was then built. The building fell into disrepair in the late 18th century and was repaired and reconstructed in 1789–90. The meeting-house, standing behind houses on the S side of the street, has walls of coursed rubble and a hipped slate roof. The wide W front has a brick porch of *c*.1840 with round-arched entrance and lean-to roof. Immediately N and S are sash windows with wooden lintels and further S is the blocking of a former doorway. There are two sash windows in the E wall and a tripartite window of later date at the S end facing the former burial-ground.

Inside the porch is a staircase to the gallery with moulded newel and reeded balusters, and two doorways each with six fielded panels. The interior of the meeting-house (47½ft by 18ft) is divided into two rooms by a wooden partition with vertically sliding shutters and central doorway. The principal room to the S has a stand at the S end with fielded-panelled front and a N gallery with open balustraded front of *c*.1840. The N room had a stand at the N end, the site indicated by a rise in the panelled dado which lines both sections of the building.

Fittings – *Books*: include *A Journal of the Life of Thomas Story*

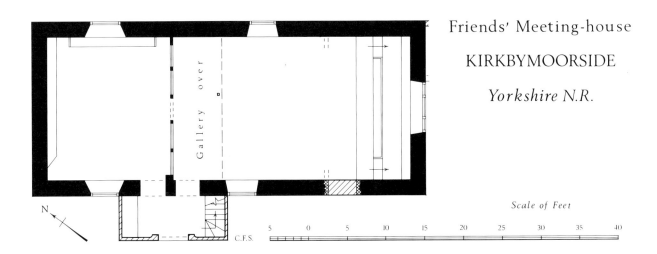

Friends' Meeting-house

KIRKBYMOORSIDE

Yorkshire N.R.

Gallery over

N

C.F.S.

Scale of Feet

5   0   5   10   15   20   25   30   35   40

(Newcastle upon Tyne, 1747). *Seating*: in gallery, three plain benches, early 19th-century. *Sundial*: on S wall of porch, square with Roman numerals and inscription 'J. RUSSELL *Dd.* MDCCCX'.

(74) Former PRIMITIVE METHODIST, West End (SE 696865). Tall brick building with external stairs to entrances. 1861 by George Styan of York.

LASKILL PASTURE   *N. Yorks.*

(75) Former FRIENDS, Laskill (SE 564908). The meeting-house built in 1733 retains few original fittings. It was little used in the later years of the 19th century and until 1954 was principally occupied for Methodist services. The building, which stands high above the road, has walls of squared stone, possibly heightened, and a pantiled roof. The end walls are gabled with stone copings and moulded kneelers and the SW front has a doorway between two windows, all with large rectangular stone lintels. A stable which stood at the SE end has been demolished.

Former Friends' meeting-house, Laskill Pasture.   (75)

The interior (27¾ft by 15¼ft) was divided by a possibly secondary partition into two rooms of equal size. A dado of vertical boarding rises at the NW end to indicate the former position of a stand; a plaster ceiling has been inserted. The SE room has a fireplace in the end wall and traces of a former stand against the NE wall; there is a small loft with boarded floor at this end.

Monuments: below right-hand window of front wall, two walling stones inscribed (1) 'Here Lieth the/Body of Eliz Clark/Departed this Life/1738'; (2) 'Joseph Clark/died in 1739'.

McDonnell, J. (ed.), *A History of Helmsley, Rievaulx and District* (1963) 225–8.

LASTINGHAM   *N. Yorks.*

(76) WESLEYAN (SE 730904). Broad W front with three windows and doorway covered by later porch. *Sundial*: dated 1804.

MALTON   *N. Yorks.*

(77) BAPTIST, Wells Lane (SE 787716). 'Salem Chapel', brick with hipped slate roof, has a three-bay front with two tiers of

round-arched windows. Built 1822–3, gallery added after 1840.

Rushton (1967) 244. Shipley (1912) 208.

(78) Former CONGREGATIONAL, Saville Street (SE 78647170). The church originated in 1813 in a major doctrinal secession from Wheelgate Chapel. 'Ebenezer Chapel', built in 1814–15 and much altered internally *c*.1860, was closed *c*.1970. The front wall of brick with stone dressings, now rendered, is of five bays with giant Ionic pilasters and a three-bay pediment. In the rusticated lower stage are three segmental-arched windows, with round-arched windows above.

Miall (1868) 313. Rushton (1967) 107–12, 150–60, 187–90, and *passim*.

(79) Former FRIENDS, Spital Street (SE 78537189). A meeting-house acquired in 1677 was superseded in 1823 and demolished in 1882, when a Friends' Adult School was built on the site. This was destroyed by fire in 1973. The W end wall of the former meeting-house, of rubble, remains in the boundary wall of the site.

(80) FRIENDS, Greengate (SE 78727189). The meeting-house built in 1823 stands on the N side of Greengate from which it is concealed by a high brick boundary wall. The walls are of brick in Flemish bond with a moulded timber eaves cornice and the roof is hipped and slated. The S front is of six bays with flat-arched sash windows, conjoined cills and a doorway with blind panel above. The interior is divided into two rooms by screens flanking a central passage; the larger room to the W has a low stand at the W end, with fielded-panelled front surmounted by a

Friends' meeting-house, Greengate, Malton.   (80)

Friends' meeting-house, Greengate, Malton.   (80)

Former Presbyterian chapel, Wheelgate, Malton (from Hargrove, *c.* 1903).   (83)

dwarf balustrade. The E room has wall benches around three sides. Midway above the central passage is a short gallery linking the two meeting-houses at an upper level but not apparently serving any other practical function. A low wing at the E end of the building accommodated a small library.

Fittings – *Inscription*: stone tablet at S end of passage, dated 1823. *Monuments*: in burial-ground, large flat slabs of slate, of uniform size, 19th-century. *Painting*: small water-colour drawing by George Nicholson, 1824, of the 1677 meeting house, showing a low stone building, with a thatched roof, chimneys at each end, and a central doorway between two three-light mullioned windows.

(81) WESLEYAN, Saville Street (SE 78667168). Brick, five-bay front with three-bay pediment; tablet inscribed with date 1811 and Latin motto. Two tiers of round-arched windows, three doorways in centre bays, two replacing windows, the central doorway flanked by tall thin Tuscan columns supporting an entablature. The interior is approximately square with a gallery supported by cast-iron columns. Much refitted and false ceiling inserted at gallery level.

(82) Former PRIMITIVE METHODIST, Spital Gate (SE 78577187). Stone and pantile, two tiers of sash windows, early 19th-century.

(83) Former PRESBYTERIAN, Wheelgate (SE 78697183). 'Wheelgate Chapel', standing behind other buildings SE of the junction of Wheelgate and Greengate, was first built in 1715 for a small society of dissenters which seems to have included both Independents and Presbyterians. After a long period of stagnation the cause was revived in 1771 by the Rev. Samuel Bottomley; increased support necessitated an enlargement of the chapel c.1783 which was then found to be structurally unsound and resulted in an almost complete rebuilding. A gradual change from the end of the 18th century in the doctrinal views of the minister and part of his congregation led to a major orthodox secession in 1813 resulting in the formation of a separate Congregational Church (*see* (78)). The remaining members came to be regarded as a Unitarian society which survived until 1952. The building is now used by the Elim Pentecostal Church.

The chapel (46¾ft by 28¼ft externally) has walls of brick to E and S but of coursed limestone rubble on the N and W which may represent part of the 1715 building. The roof is covered with pantiles. The E front is gabled and has moulded stone kneelers; a late 19th-century porch covers the entrance; above are two windows with flat-arched heads, keystones and renewed sashes with marginal glazing, and a small blind window in the gable. The S side is of three bays with two tiers of windows similar to those described. The N wall is blank except for a small blocked window near the E end. The W wall is narrower than the body of the chapel and may represent the original width of the building. The interior, refitted in 1877, has a rostrum pulpit and E gallery. (All window frames replaced since 1972)

Fittings – *Monuments*: in burial-ground E of chapel include (1) [   ] Wells, 1792, and [   ], wife of William Wells, [?1770]; (2) William Wells, 1822, *et al.*; (3) Mary King, 1821, and Joseph King, 18 [   ]. *Plate*: cup, of Sheffield plate, c.1800.

Evans (1897) 164–5. Hargrove (c.1903). Miall (1868) 313. Rushton (1967) 107–10, 222.

MARRICK   N. Yorks.

(84) WESLEYAN, Hurst (NZ 052027). The chapel in a remote situation near the hamlet of Washfold was built c.1815 to serve a former mining community; it is now used principally as a hostel. The walls are of rubble and the roof is covered with stone slates. The S front has a round-arched doorway between two tiers of sash windows. The pulpit was against the W wall with a gallery, now floored across, around the other three sides; the supporting posts remain.

Wesleyan chapel, Hurst.   (84)

MARTON   N. Yorks.

(85) PRIMITIVE METHODIST (SE 735832). 'Bethel' chapel, of brick with ashlar plinth and quoins, was built in 1821 and rebuilt 1870; the original date stone is reset in the back wall. A clock above the entrance is signed, internally, 'A. Morley, Crompton'.

MASHAM   N. Yorks.

(86) Former FRIENDS, Quaker Terrace (SE 223809). The meeting-house built in 1708 and closed in the early 19th century eventually passed in 1871 to the Primitive Methodists. The walls are of rubble. The S front has a central doorway between two later, altered, windows. In the N wall are two original windows, now blocked. Much changed and floor inserted on conversion to commercial use.

(87) Former PRIMITIVE METHODIST, Silver Street (SE 224809). Late 19th-century, with shaped gable. Now post office.

MELBECKS   N. Yorks.

(88) Site of SMARBER HALL CHAPEL, Low Row (SD 973976). About 1690 Philip, Lord Wharton, fitted up a shooting-lodge in Swaledale known as 'Smarber Hall' as a meeting-house for a Presbyterian, subsequently Independent, congregation; it was superseded by the present Congregational chapel (*see* (89)) in 1809. The meeting-house stood on the hillside N of the main road half a mile W of Low Row chapel. The site, which is marked by a modern stone tablet, comprises a rectangular enclosure (55½ft by 15ft) bounded N, S, and W by drystone walls and on the E by a stone barn of 17th-century date and domestic in origin, probably a cottage attached to the former meeting-house. Traces of wall plaster remain internally in the barn together with evidence of the earlier fenestration. The N wall of the enclosure

also retains traces of wall plaster and the splayed jamb of a window at the E end. A stone seat around the enclosure is of recent date. *Monument*: John Brown, 1868, headstone.

(89) CONGREGATIONAL, Low Row (SD 980978). The chapel built in 1809 to replace the foregoing was altered and refitted in 1874. It has walls of coursed stone and a stone-slate roof. The gabled E front is surmounted by a late 19th-century bell-cote with mace-head finial, and contains one *bell*; low gabled porch between two tall round-arched windows with circular light in gable and inscription tablet added 1874. Three similar windows in each side wall. Enlarged to rear in late 19th century with vestry and organ gallery behind pulpit.(URC)

Fittings – *Benefaction Tablet*: brass 'to commemorate the singular zeal, generosity and perseverance displayed in the erection and completion of this Chapel by Thomas Parke Esq. of Highfield House in the County of Lancaster, a native of Lawrow', 1809. *Monuments*: in chapel, painted wood with marbled surrounds (1) John Scott, 1841, Mary his widow, 1847, and John their son, 1811; (2) Rev. John Allanson '30 years minister of this chapel', 1836, Susannah his wife, 1830, and their children Ann, 1829, Sarah, 1828, Susanna, 1830, Ann, 1830, John, 1834. *Plate*: base metal, set of two plain cups, flagon and two plates given 1841.

Miall (1868) 311–13. Whitehead (1930) 148–59.

Congregational chapel, Low Row.   (89)

(90) Former FRIENDS, Low Row (SD 979978). A meeting-house built 1729 and closed by 1851 stood adjacent to the Congregational Manse 100 yards SW of the foregoing. Parts of two stone walls remain incorporated into the present garage, and other fragments built into the manse may also be from this source.

(91) WESLEYAN, Gunnerside (SD 950981). The Wesleyan society in Gunnerside originated *c*.1760 in a class-meeting in connection with a society then gathered at Blades; the first preaching-house was built 1788–9 and superseded by the present chapel in 1866. The former building of stone had an asymmetrical front with rusticated quoins, two lower windows with doorway to right and three small windows above. The present chapel, designed by George Dougill, a joiner, whose instructions were to base his design on the chapel at Reeth (*see* (115)), is a large building of

Wesleyan chapel, Gunnerside.   (91)

stone with three-bay pedimented front, surmounted by a mace-head finial, rusticated quoins and two tiers of round-arched windows, paired above the central entrance. The sides are of three bays.

Batty, M., *Gunnerside Chapel and Gunnerside Folk* (1967).

MELMERBY   *N. Yorks.*

(92) Former WESLEYAN (SE 337770). Brick and slate; gabled ends with stone coping and moulded kneelers. Three-bay front with sash windows and inscribed door lintel dated 1826.

MICKLEBY   *N. Yorks.*

(93) CONGREGATIONAL (NZ 801130). The chapel built in 1811 has coursed stone walls and a pantiled roof with gabled ends and ball finials. A slightly later cottage is attached to the east. The N front has two plain windows; to the left is an external staircase to the gallery. The chapel and cottage entrances are enclosed within an arched recess. The interior has an original gallery with panelled front and box-pews. The pulpit has been incorporated into a late 19th-century rostrum. *Collecting Shovels*: pair, with turned handles, 19th-century.

Miall (1868) 314–15. Rushton (1967) 231–2.

MIDDLEHAM   *N. Yorks.*

(94) PRIMITIVE METHODIST Market Place (SE 127878). The chapel, dated 1836 on a partly defaced tablet, is a plain two-storeyed building of rendered rubble. The ground floor is occupied by a cottage and the chapel is at first-floor level approached by a staircase in the SE corner immediately inside the entrance. Three ranks of original numbered pews stepped up in five tiers face a late 19th-century rostrum against the longer N wall. A large singers' pew occupies the NW corner.

MORTON-ON-SWALE   *N. Yorks.*

(95) Former WESLEYAN (SE 328921). Brown brick with hipped slate roof. Three-bay front in header bond brickwork with two tiers of round-arched windows and wide arched recess enclosing the central doorway and window over. Dated 1815 on keystone of doorway.

Primitive Methodist chapel, Market Place, Middleham.   (94)

MOULTON   *N. Yorks.*

(96) Former WESLEYAN (NZ 236038). Low three-bay chapel dated 1835. Gothic successor 1863, now farm store, 100 yards S opposite gates to Manor House.

MUKER   *N. Yorks.*

(97) KELD CHAPEL (NY 893011). The mediaeval Keld Chapel mentioned by Leyland in 1540 had fallen into disuse by the late 17th century and is reported to have been in ruins by *c.*1706. As a

Primitive Methodist chapel, Market Place, Middleham.   (94)

Keld Chapel.   (97)

result of preaching by Benjamin Ingham and Edward Stillman in the late 18th century, a new Independent church (now URC) was gathered which appears to have had some early links with the Moravian society at Fulneck, although not formally associated with that denomination. The old chapel was rebuilt *c*.1789 for the use of this congregation, enlarged in 1820, a school-room was built 1842 and a house attached to the chapel enlarged 1853–4.

The chapel, which has stone walls and is roofed with stone slates, was partly rebuilt and refitted in 1860. The S front, of this date, has two round-arched windows, and to the left a two-storeyed porch with bell-cote, round-arched doorway and upper window. At the E end a short pulpit-chancel extends beyond the line of the former end wall. The W end is covered by a two-storeyed house of the mid 19th century. The N wall of the chapel was heightened in 1860 but most of the random rubble walling is of the late 18th century or earlier. Two round-arched windows with ashlar surrounds, one at mid-height and one higher up to the W, are of the late 19th century but replace windows a little lower but in similar relative positions. A third window low down at the W end may occupy the site of an earlier opening. The interior ($32\frac{1}{4}$ft by $20\frac{3}{4}$ft), which may represent the size of the earlier chapel, has a W gallery approached by a staircase in the S porch.

Fittings – *Bell*: one, in bell-cote. *Monuments*: in chapel (1) Edmund Alderson Knowles of Low Row, 1835, recording a bequest to Keld Chapel of a field in Kisdon called Broken Intake as a permanent endowment for its successive ministers; (2) Rev. Edward Stillman, 48 years minister, 1837, and Grace his wife, 1830. In burial-ground (3) William Rukin of Angram, 1827, and others later. *Sundial*: above S doorway with painted dial dated 1840, initials [?A.] G. and location 'Lat. 54°. 2′. 28 N., Lon. 2.9.22. W.'.

England (1888) 6. Miall (1868) 297–8. Whitehead (1930) 304–14.

(98) Former CONGREGATIONAL, Thwaite (SD 891982). Rubble with ashlar dressings and slate roof; gabled front with bell-cote and mace-head finial, two doorways in arched ashlar surrounds with double-arched window between. 1863–4 by T. Ambler. (Converted to cottages since 1972)

Whitehead (1930) 315–20.

(99) WESLEYAN, Keld (NY 891010). Three-bay front of stone with ashlar quoins and rusticated pointed arches to windows. Dated 1841.

NEWBY   N. Yorks.

(100) WESLEYAN (NZ 506123). Plain three-bay brick front, 1826.

NEWBY WISKE   N. Yorks.

(101) WESLEYAN (SE 367878). Brick with hipped slate roof. Three-bay front with two tiers of round-arched windows and wide arched recess to centre bay enclosing entrance and upper window; later porch. Opened 1814.

NEWHOLM-CUM-DUNSLEY   N. Yorks.

(102) WESLEYAN, Newholm (NZ 867105). Squared stone with pantiled roof. Front altered; originally had a round-arched doorway with scrolled tablet above dated 1832 between two

WESLEYAN CHAPEL, NEWHOLM   CFS 1974

similarly arched windows with intersecting glazing bars. Doorway re-sited and other windows added in late 19th century. (*Pulpit*: said to have come from Methodist chapel, Church Street, Whitby (153) built 1788. Dolbey (1964) 90)

NORTHALLERTON   N. Yorks.

(103) CONGREGATIONAL, High Street (SE 369938). 'Zion' Chapel is approached through an archway behind buildings on the W side of the street. It was built 1818–19 and altered 1864. Three-bay brick front with two tiers of round-arched windows enclosed in tall arched recesses; porch added 1864. In S wall two close-set arched windows, one blocked, with date tablet between.

Miall (1868) 325.

Congregational chapel, Northallerton.   (103)

(104) WESLEYAN (SE 368942). Brick and stone, Gothic with gabled front, 1864–5 by Wilson and Crosland of Sheffield.

The previous chapel, possibly of late 18th-century date, was sold for Baptist use in 1866; it had brick walls and a hipped pantiled roof, and five-bay sides with large round-arched windows at the upper level.

B.HBk (1890) 137. Shipley (1912) 175–6, illus. facing 167.

NORTH COWTON   *N. Yorks.*

(105) WESLEYAN, The Green (NZ 284039). Brick with rendered gabled front. Opened 1827.

OSMOTHERLEY   *N. Yorks.*

(106) FRIENDS, West End (SE 454973). The meeting-house, which stands well back behind other buildings on the N side of the street, was built in 1723. Friends' use ceased between 1854 and 1890 when the building was used by Independents and Primitive Methodists. Since 1942 it has been occupied principally as a hostel.

Friends' meeting-house, Osmotherley.   (106)

The walls (36½ft by 20¾ft externally) are of stone and the roof is covered with pantiles. The front faces S and has two doorways and three windows with later frames. The end walls are gabled and have copings and shaped kneelers. A lean-to extension was added to the E in 1948.

The interior has a gallery at the E end with a low shuttered front and a former women's meeting-room below; the shutters between the two rooms have been removed. In front of the meeting-house is a rectangular burial-ground enclosed by stone walls and containing ten headstones of 20th-century date.

(107) Former METHODIST (SE 457973). The former preaching-house stands behind buildings E of the Cross and is approached along a cobbled passage between houses. A modern wooden tablet above the entrance is inscribed 'Built 1754 Restored 1935'. The walls (42ft by about 20ft externally) are of coursed stone and the roof is pantiled. The longer S front has three plain windows with lintels and renewed frames and doorway between the W pair with stone lintel bearing an original carved date 1754. The W end is gabled with stone coping and shaped kneelers; a small window off-centre in the gable has been blocked. A later cottage adjoins to the east.

PICKERING   *N. Yorks.*

(108) CONGREGATIONAL, Hungate (SE 79728395). A Presbyterian or Independent society existed in the 18th century with a meeting-house in Willowgate; this seems to have died out before the commencement of the present church whose origins have been traced to evangelical preaching in the neighbouring parish church of Middleton.

The chapel in Champley's Yard off the N side of Hungate, partly concealed by a two-storeyed yellow-brick Sunday-school of 1867 built at one end, was erected in 1789. A gallery was added in 1797 and a N gallery for use of Sunday-school children in 1814. About 1814 the building was extended to the S, a small vestry was built in 1826 and another gallery added in 1839. The chapel has walls of coursed limestone rubble with ashlar dressings and a slate roof. The E wall has three large pointed-arched windows of 1789 and a further similar window in the extension with doorway to the S and an upper window. The interior (originally 34ft by 27ft) has been largely refitted in the late 19th century but some earlier seats remain in the gallery which continues around the N, S, and W sides. The pulpit is at the S side end with vestry below the S gallery. *Clock*: with circular face and long pendulum case, late 18th-century.

Miall (1868) 331–2. Rushton (1967) 97–106 and *passim*.

(109) FRIENDS, Castlegate (SE 79828435). A meeting-house acquired in 1680 which stood on the site of No. 1 Undercliffe was superseded by the present building in 1793. This has walls of squared stone and a hipped slate roof. The wide S front has a gabled porch with three-centred arched outer opening, two inner doorways and a tablet with date of erection; there are two large sash windows left of the porch and a similar window to the right. The N wall has three further windows but the end walls are blank. The interior (50ft by 24ft) is divided by a passage between shuttered partitions; the larger W room has a gallery with balustraded front above the passage and formerly had a stand against the W wall; the smaller E room, which has a separate doorway from the porch, has a stand of late 19th-century date against the N wall.

Rushton (1967) 212–13.

Friends' meeting-house, Pickering.   (109)

(110) WESLEYAN, Hungate (SE 798839). In 1790 Methodists had the use of a preaching-house and cottage in Willowgate. The first chapel on the Hungate site was built in 1812 and replaced by the

present building in 1891. This has a gabled stone front between wings.

Rushton (1967) 257–9.

(111) PRIMITIVE METHODIST, Potter Hill (SE 795841). Four-bay pedimented front, built 1884–5.

Rushton (1967) 267–9.

PRESTON-UNDER-SCAR   N. Yorks.

(112) WESLEYAN (SE 070912). Three-bay front with altered round-arched windows; opened 1805. *Gates* and *Railings*: in front of chapel, wrought-iron with scrolled finials, early 19th-century.

RAVENSWORTH   N. Yorks.

(113) WESLEYAN (NZ 141078). Small building of squared rubble; two pointed-arched windows in the E and W walls. Opened 1822; refitted late 19th century.

REETH, FREMINGTON AND HEALAUGH N. Yorks.

(114) WESLEYAN, Healaugh (SE 017990). Set back on S side of road; three-bay front with gabled porch, dated 1843.

(115) WESLEYAN, Reeth (SE 039993). The chapel opened in 1796 was much altered or possibly rebuilt *c.*1866, in which year it was recommended as a model for the rebuilding of Gunnerside Chapel (*see* (91)). Stone walls with rendered sides and stone-slate roof. The front wall of three bays has two tiers of round-arched

Wesleyan chapel, Reeth.   (115)

windows, rusticated quoins and a narrow shaped gable between corner ball finials.

SALTON   N. Yorks.

(116) PRIMITIVE METHODIST (SE 717801). In terrace of houses facing the Green; red brick and pantile, three bays, dated 1858.

SANDHUTTON   N. Yorks.

(117) WESLEYAN (SE 383820). Brick walls and hipped tiled roof. Three-bay front with stone plinth and platband, two tiers of round-arched windows and wide arched recess enclosing doorway and upper window. The doorway has rusticated jambs and a wide fluted semicircular arch with fanlight; above is a repainted tablet dated 1815.

Wesleyan chapel, Sandhutton.   (117)

SCARBOROUGH   N. Yorks.

(118) CONGREGATIONAL, Ramshill Road, South Cliff (TA 041 877). Large Gothic structure of stone with nave, aisles, transept and tall corner tower and spire. Built 1864–8 to designs of Lockwood and Mawson under the patronage of Titus Salt. (URC)

CYB (1865) 298. Miall (1868) 344. Rushton (1967) 242.

(119) Former FRIENDS, St Sepulchre Street (TA 047889). A meeting-house built in 1676 in Low Conduit Street was superseded in 1801 by the present building; a new meeting-house was erected in York Place in 1894 and the 1801 building came to be used by an adjacent school. The walls are of brick and the roof is hipped and slated. The S front has a central entrance with double doors, two flat-arched sash windows to the left and one to the right. The rear wall is similarly fenestrated. The interior, now gutted, was divided by partitions into two rooms each with

a stand against an end wall. (Meeting-house in York Place demolished 1988)

Rushton (1967) 208–12.

(120) WESLEYAN, Westborough (TA 038882). Large classical chapel by W. Baldwin Stewart, opened 1862. Pedimented portico with giant Corinthian columns between blind corner bays surmounted by pedimented pavilions from which domed roofs have been removed.

Rushton (1967) 264.

SHERIFF HUTTON WITH
CORNBROUGH   *N. Yorks.*

(121) WESLEYAN, Sheriff Hutton (SE 648663). The chapel erected in 1794 was rebuilt in 1979.

Anon., *Memorials of Early Methodism in the Easingwold Circuit* (1872) 61–74. *Methodist Recorder* 19 July 1979.

SKIPTON-ON-SWALE   *N. Yorks.*

(122) WESLEYAN (SE 366798). Built 1810–11, extended and much refitted but with some original box-pews.

STILLINGTON   *N. Yorks.*

(123) Former WESLEYAN (SE 584679). Three-bay brick front with narrow pediment and two tiers of round-arched windows; central doorway with tablet above dated 1844. Sold 1972 for conversion to flats.

STOKESLEY   *N. Yorks.*

(124) GOSPEL MISSION, North Road (NZ 521086). Early 19th-century; brick with hipped roof, round-arched doorway with fanlight between two tiers of sash windows. Interior divided into two storeys.

(125) Former METHODIST, Levenside (NZ 523085). John

Wesley's first recorded visit to Stokesley was in 1752 and by 1761 a 'little society' had been formed. On 11 July 1766 Wesley wrote in his *Journal* 'about nine I preached in the new house at Stokesley; but it would by no means contain the congregation'. The first preaching-house has been provisionally identified as a building (26ft square externally) on the N side of Levenside near the W end. The front wall, bounded by rusticated quoins, has been rendered and entirely altered with the insertion of two garage doors and two plain upper windows. The upper part of the N wall has been rebuilt or heightened, the lower part is of ashlar with rusticated quoins, in the middle is a central projecting chimney breast to the left of which is a doorway and to the right, a blocked window. The original masonry is also visible in a covered passage along the E side where a wide opening has been blocked in brickwork.

WHS, NEB LVIII (September 1992) 13–16.

(126) Former WESLEYAN, Brewery Terrace (NZ 522086). The second Methodist chapel, superseding the preaching-house in Levenside, was built in 1812 and succeeded by the present chapel in High Street in 1887; it was then converted for use as a brewery. The former chapel has brick walls with stone dressings and a pantiled roof. The elegant S front is of three bays with rusticated quoins, plinth, double platband and moulded cornice; the centre bay projects slightly and has a pediment with large inscription tablet, now rendered over; pedimented door-case with pilasters and round-arched opening, and Venetian window above with intersecting glazing bars. The side bays had two tiers of sash windows with moulded architraves. The gabled end walls have each two round-arched windows to the lower stage and two plain sash windows above. On the N side is a central wing gabled to N, with a blocked upper window.

The interior (36ft by 43ft) was greatly altered for brewery purposes. Part of the plaster ceiling remains with a central roundel and evidence of a gallery staircase in the SE corner. The

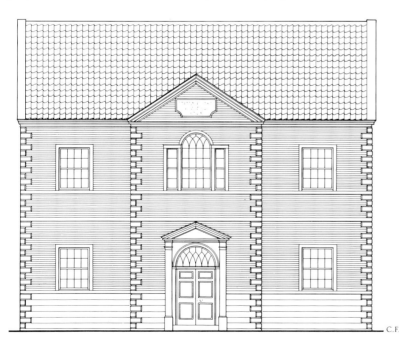

Former Methodist Chapel

STOKESLEY

Yorkshire N.R.

South Elevation (restored)

Scale of Feet

C.F.S.

N wing was occupied by a vestry with organ and singers' gallery above. The roof is supported by four trusses. (Demolition proposed 1978)

SUTTON-UNDER-WHITESTONECLIFFE   N. Yorks.

(127) WESLEYAN (SE 487825). Squared stone with hipped slate roof, three-bay front with round-arched windows, dated 1850.

TEESSIDE   Cleveland

(128) CONGREGATIONAL, Eston (NZ 554185). Rock-faced stone walls and slate roof. Gabled front with bell-cote (bell missing), pointed-arched doorway and Y-traceried window above. Built 1858 'from designs furnished gratuitously by Mr Joseph B. Blossom of Middlesbrough'.

    CYB (1859) 253.

(129) FRIENDS, Norton (NZ 446222). The meeting-house on the E side of the Green has brick walls and a pantiled roof. The front wall, rendered and entirely altered in 1902, has five round-arched windows and a modern tablet giving the date of erection as 1671. The earliest structure visible in the rear wall is of 18th-century brickwork in English garden wall bond. The meeting-house (36½ft by 20¼ft externally) has been extended to the north. In the E wall are two windows with flat-arched heads and renewed cills and an altered doorway near the former N corner. The stand at the S end is of the early 19th century; it has a central entrance flanked by moulded balusters and a panelled front with dwarf balustraded top.

(130) WESLEYAN, Meldyke Lane, Stainton (NZ 481142). Small three-bay chapel of rendered brick, dated 1840.

(131) CONGREGATIONAL, Norton Road, Stockton-on-Tees (NZ 445195). Rendered three-bay front with giant pilasters and pediment, dated 1845. Two tiers of windows, round-arched above, joined at intermediate level and below by recessed panels. (Demolished since 1972)

(132) Former FRIENDS, Dovecot Street, Stockton-on-Tees (NZ 443190). A meeting-house built in 1701 was superseded by the present building on a new site in 1814. A two-storeyed building of 1840–50 very similar in design to DARLINGTON (see Durham (9)) stands to the S adjacent to the street, of brick with stone dressings and a hipped slate roof; five bays with entrance in projecting centre bay. The meeting-house behind is a plain brick

Friends' meeting-house, Stockton-on-Tees.   (132)

building with gabled ends and a slate roof; it comprises one large meeting-room with two round-arched windows to the rear, replacing earlier fenestration, and a two storeyed section to the east. The principal room had a stand at the W end. (Now in use as offices)

(133) Former WESLEYAN, Dovecot Street, Stockton-on-Tees (NZ 44351898). 'Brunswick Chapel' of 1823, S of the Friends' meeting-house, is of brown brick with stone dressings and a slate roof. The design is in the style of the Rev. William Jenkins. The front is of five bays with two tiers of round-arched windows, the centre bay projects slightly and has a pediment above a panelled frieze and swept parapets above the end bays. The lower part of the front is covered by a later porch. The sides are of four bays with a projecting two-bay centre. Behind the chapel facing William Street is a two-storeyed Sunday-school dated 1824. (Closed by 1977)

Wesleyan chapel, Stockton-on-Tees.   (133)

THIRN   N. Yorks.

(134) WESLEYAN (SE 217859). Three-bay front with pointed-arched doorway in gabled porch. Dated 1835.

THIRSK   N. Yorks.

(135) Former CONGREGATIONAL (SE 431821). 'Salem Chapel', 1866 by W. A. Bourne, on site of defectively built chapel of 1845. Brown brick with red and white-brick dressings. (Now sports club)

    CYB (1868) 329–30. Miall (1868) 370–1.

(136) FRIENDS, Kirkgate (SE 428822). A meeting-house built in 1701 was superseded in 1799 by the present plain building on the E side of the street which includes a cottage at the W end. The walls are of brick and the roof is slated. The wide S front has four sash windows with flat-arched heads; the lower part of the wall is covered by a low porch of the late 19th century. In the E wall facing the burial-ground are two sash windows and a small window high in the gable. (Interior altered 1985)

(137) Former PRIMITIVE METHODIST (SE 429820). The first Methodist chapel in Thirsk was an octagon built in 1764–6 at St James's Green; both it and its Wesleyan successor of 1816 have been demolished. The Primitive Methodist chapel of 1851, now converted to a showroom, has a brick front with simple

pedimented gable and four round-arched upper windows. The gallery remains around three sides with pulpit and organ loft behind.

THORALBY   *N. Yorks.*

(138) Former WESLEYAN (SE 001868). Rubble and stone slate, of three bays, with round-arched windows, cottage adjacent to left. Built 1823, superseded by new chapel nearby (also now closed) in 1889. (Under conversion to cottage 1990)

(139) Former PRIMITIVE METHODIST (SE 002865). Small three-bay chapel of rubble with round-arched windows and tablet dated 1849 above doorway. Converted to tractor shed since 1963 and all front openings destroyed.

THORNTON-LE-CLAY   *N. Yorks.*

(140) Former FRIENDS (SE 685652). Built *c*.1743, closed 1861 and now used as garage for adjacent house 'Miles Croft'. Brick and pantile with doorway and one window remaining in S wall under flat-arched brick heads. Interior (39ft by 18ft) divided into two rooms by shuttered screen.

(141) WESLEYAN (SE 684652). Three-bay front with later porch and altered glazing. Opened 1822.

THORNTON-LE-MOOR   *N. Yorks.*

(142) PRIMITIVE METHODIST (SE 389881). Three-bay brick front with partly defaced tablet dated 1836.

THORNTON RUST   *N. Yorks.*

(143) Former CALVINISTIC INDEPENDENT (SD 974888). Rubble with stone-slate roof, comprising chapel with school-room below, now much altered and refenestrated on conversion to house. Tablet in front wall, below long label over site of former upper windows, inscribed 'THIS CALVINIST CHAPEL and SCHOOL ROOM were ENDOWED and ERECTED By JOHN TOMLINSON of this place AD 1827'. Semicircular heads of two former pulpit windows remain in rear wall.

Former Calvinist chapel, Thornton Rust.   (143)

TOPCLIFFE   *N. Yorks.*

(144) WESLEYAN, Church Street (SE 400760). Three-bay front with ball finials to pedimented gable; two tiers of round-arched windows. Dated 1840.

WARTHILL   *N. Yorks.*

(145) WESLEYAN (SE 675552). Three-bay front, doorway blocked and re-sited, 1841.

WESTERDALE   *N. Yorks.*

(146) WESLEYAN (NZ 666059). Three-bay front with side-entry porch. Dated 1849.

WEST SCRAFTON   *N. Yorks.*

(147) PRIMITIVE METHODIST (SE 073837). Three-bay front with plain stone doorway and tablet above dated 1866.

WEST TANFIELD   *N. Yorks.*

(148) WESLEYAN (SE 269790). The original chapel, now the Sunday-school, stands at right angles to its more grandiose successor. It has walls of squared rubble and a stone slated roof. The S front is of three bays with round-arched lower openings with keystones, that of the central doorway being dated 1798; three plain sash windows above. The rear wall has two tall round-arched windows with keystones and impost blocks. A house adjacent to the W has been heightened and is now of two storeys and attics. The interior (27¾ft by 32½ft) has an original gallery around three sides supported by five turned-wood columns. The gallery front is panelled and has a fluted pilaster in the centre of each face. The pulpit formerly stood against the N wall.

The present chapel, by W. J. Morley in the Gothic style with corner tower and spire, is dated 1901.

(149) WESLEYAN, Nosterfield (SE 277804). Rendered front with two round-arched windows and side-entry porch to right. Built 1813, much altered 1897.

WEST WITTON   *N. Yorks.*

(150) WESLEYAN (SE 061884). Rendered gabled front with two tall round-arched windows and later porch. Gable has stone kneelers with spiral ornament and lozenge-shaped tablet dated 1842. Sunday-school of 1884 adjacent.

WHITBY   *N. Yorks.*

(151) OLD CHAPEL, Flowergate (NZ 899110). The Presbyterian, latterly Unitarian, congregation originated in the late 17th century and built a chapel in Flowergate *c*.1715–18 which stands behind other buildings on the S side of the street. The chapel was largely rebuilt in brick in 1812 with a pantiled roof but a fragment of the earlier masonry walling remains at the S end. The S wall is gabled, the early 18th-century masonry being rendered externally but visible in the roof space where some internal wall plaster survives; a square depression at the apex of the original gable may represent the seating for a small bell-cote or finial. The S wall was extended to the E in 1812 and pierced with a round-arched window. The E wall has two semicircular-arched windows and a similarly arched doorway near the N end

Wesleyan chapels, West Tanfield.   (148)

with a small gallery window above. The W and N walls are mostly concealed by adjacent buildings.

The interior (36¾ft by 24¼ft) was 16 ft wide before enlargement. A gallery at the N end is supported by two columns and has an early 19th-century panelled front; later shutters have converted the gallery to an upper room and the space below has been altered to form a vestibule. The chapel was reseated in the late 19th century but a few fragments of earlier pews and panelling remain.

Fittings – *Chair*: with carved back and arms, dated 1690. *Plate*: includes a two-handled cup of 1718 and two plates of 1735. *Pulpit*: semi-octagonal with ogee-shaped panels of applied mouldings and moulded cornice, *c*.1812.

Evans (1897) 254–5. Miall (1868) 379. Rushton (1967) 219–20.

(152) FRIENDS, Church Street (NZ 901110). A meeting-house was built on this site in 1670. This was superseded by the present building in 1813–14. The walls are of squared stone and the roof is slated. The E end has a low pitched gable with wheel-window, two large round-arched windows below to the principal room, and two segmental-arched recesses beneath. The main entrance in the N wall has a pair of doors leading to a lobby between the two meeting-rooms; the W room has a sloping ceiling below a gallery.

FHSJ Supplement (1913) 'State Papers 1658–72', 303. Rushton (1967) 206–8, 218.

(153) METHODIST, Church Street (NZ 900112). An octagonal preaching-house built in 1761–2 in Henrietta Street which ultimately collapsed from subsidence was replaced in 1788 by a new chapel in Church Street. This was a large broad-fronted building of six bays with two tiers of pointed-arched windows and a small pediment across the centre bays. It was described by John Wesley (*Journal*, 12 June 1788) as 'the most curious house we have in England' from its situation at the head of a flight of forty steps; in 1790 he calls it 'one of the most beautiful chapels in Great Britain'. It was superseded in 1814 by Brunswick Chapel (rebuilt in 1891) but reopened after 1833 and remained in use until *c*.1918. After a lengthy period of neglect the chapel was demolished in 1959.

The steps leading to the chapel remain, in part, adjacent to the 1901 'Wesley Hall'.

Curnock (1938) VII: 400; VIII, 73–4. Dolbey (1964) 90–1. Rushton (1967) 253–7.

WRELTON   *N. Yorks.*

(154) WESLEYAN (SE 768860). Coursed stone with hipped slate roof, stone coping to hips with scrolled lower terminals. Three-bay front with round-arched windows and gabled porch. Tablet dated 1840, later clock above.

(155) PRIMITIVE METHODIST (SE 767861). Three-bay brick front

with segmental-arched windows, small porch and centre gablet with inscription 1869 around clock face.

YARM   *Cleveland*

(156) METHODIST, Chapel Yard (NZ 420129). The Methodist interest in Yarm dates from 1748 when John Wesley paid his first visit to the town. A preaching-house, believed to have been a converted hayloft behind the house of George Merryweather in High Street, was superseded by the present octagon chapel in 1763. The site was conveyed to Merryweather on 18 June 1763 and the building was probably completed by the end of that year; John Wesley preached in it on 24 April 1764 and in his *Journal*

Methodist chapel, Yarm.   (156)

described it as 'by far the most elegant one in England'. In 1815 the walls and roof were raised, a gallery was added and a new pulpit provided. A large forebuilding incorporating gallery staircases was built in 1873 (rebuilt *c*.1965) and an organ chamber and singers' gallery were added at the rear in 1896.

The chapel has brick walls and a pyramidal slate roof surmounted by a late 19th-century ventilator. The brickwork has a decayed yellow surface colouring, with red-brick dressings to the corners of the walls and jambs of the windows of the original part. The walls have in each exposed side a tall round-arched window with late 19th-century frame of two pointed lights; shorter but otherwise similar windows with continuous cills level with the original wall-head occur in the later upper walling. The front is covered by a modern brick and glass porch of two storeys replacing a wider triple-gabled front in white brick of 1873. A corresponding rear wing for the organ chamber has rendered walls and a gabled roof.

The interior (39½ft wide) is a regular octagon with horseshoe-shaped gallery covering seven sides, the eighth side being pierced by a wide semicircular-arched opening to the organ chamber. The fittings are all of 19th-century date: the rostrum pulpit supported by Gothic columns and the gallery fronts with trefoil-headed panels may be of *c*.1815 but the gallery columns, the seating and the wooden ceiling are of *c*.1896.

Love-feast Cups: two pairs, blue Chinese ornament on white background, each cup with one handle, one pair rounded, one angular, marked on base 'W & S/SONGEA'.

Dolbey (1964) 105–7. Wright, J., *Early Methodism in Yarm* (1949).

The West Riding is by far the most extensive and highly populated part of Yorkshire, a county which is comparable in size with the principality of Wales. The greatest concentration of population is in the southern half of the region, particularly around the industrial centres of Leeds, Bradford, Sheffield and Doncaster which witnessed a rapid expansion in manufacturing industry in the 19th century and a corresponding increase in the demand for fuel from the Yorkshire coalfield. In the 17th century these districts had shared in the prosperity of the woollen trade and nonconformist preachers, such as Oliver Heywood, found willing hearers amongst the sheep farmers and independent clothiers of the Pennines.

The earliest chapels recorded here, at Bramhope (77) and Great Houghton (148), date from the period of the Commonwealth. These were built as private chapels for Presbyterian worship and continued to be served by nonconformist ministers after the Restoration. Comparable with them is Bullhouse Chapel near Penistone (325), of 1692, an exceptionally fine example of a Pennine chapel in the vernacular style serving the needs of a large rural community in the manner of a chapel-of-ease. Small early 18th-century chapels built for Presbyterian congregations remain, though variously altered and without original fittings, at Winterburn (133), at Eastwood near Todmorden (428), and at Fulwood on the outskirts of Sheffield (379).

Nowhere in the Riding is the vernacular style of building more apparent than in the earliest Friends' meeting-house of 1675 at Brigflatts near Sedbergh (358) in the extreme NW corner of the county, where a traditional lakeland building and a notable Quaker interior unite in a monument of outstanding national importance. The much smaller meeting-house at Farfield (2), of 1689, also survives in a complete state. Other meeting-houses of the period, at Settle (367), Skipton (386), Rawdon (5), Airton (6), Askwith (10) and Salterforth (353), have suffered from varying degrees of alteration; although Warmsworth (446) of 1705 has remained largely intact it too is now threatened by domestic conversion. Friends' meeting-houses of the later 18th century, at Newton (311) and Calf Cop (28), continued in the earlier tradition, but more sophisticated details are to be found in the exterior of 'Sawley' meeting-house (151) of 1777. The two most notable meeting-houses of the 19th century, at Ackworth (1) and Woodhouse Lane, Leeds (268), illustrate the requirements of large congregations associated respectively with a Friends' school and a large urban meeting.

Presbyterian buildings of the mid 18th century include Stannington Chapel (52) of 1742–3, with a spectacularly ornate exterior, and Westgate Chapel, Wakefield (441) of 1751–2, in which a move away from traditional meeting-house architecture is apparent. This move is further seen in the original non-denominational Stainland Chapel (124) of 1754–5, and at Lydgate Chapel (199) of 1768, where an almost parochial appearance has resulted. Specifically Congregational churches which came into greater prominence in the later 18th century, either by secession from Presbyterian churches or as new societies, rebuilt many of their earlier chapels in the 19th century; the most important 18th-century survival is Square Chapel, Halifax (154) of 1772, remarkable for its size, materials, and the former elaboration of its internal decoration. Loxley Chapel (53), of 1787, is an interesting instance of a building intended for Anglican worship which early passed into nonconformist hands. Two former Baptist chapels also remain from the late 18th century, at Hebden Bridge (183) and Barnoldswick (17).

One denomination which, although not large in numbers, merits particular mention is the United Brethren or Moravian Church whose settlement at Fulneck (335) with its chapel of 1746–8 and ancillary buildings is the most complete example of its kind in England. Another smaller Moravian chapel remains at Wyke (456) but the 18th-century chapels at Gomersal (143) and Mirfield (298) have been rebuilt. Methodists, whose early history was closely interwoven with the Moravians, figure largely amongst the chapels of the late 18th century and after. The octagonal chapel at Heptonstall (193) of 1764, later enlarged, was one of the earliest to be built by Methodists on this plan, the first being at Rotherham in 1761. Other notable Methodist chapels of a more traditional design remain at Netherthong (200) and Eccleshill (121); the 18th-century chapels at Otley (322) of 1771 and Greetland (129) of c.1777–80 were demolished during the course of this survey. Chapels at Shelley (251) and Lindley (225) remain in a much altered state; a small chapel at Whiteley Wood near Sheffield (375) of 1789 is of additional interest in the history of Sheffield plate.

The proliferation of large nonconformist chapels which occurred in the wake of 19th-century industrial expansion in the West Riding has left numerous monuments to the wealth and aspirations of philanthropic industrialists and nameless benefactors as well as innumerable smaller buildings. Pre-eminent amongst Methodist chapels of the early 19th century is Carver Street, Sheffield (376), exceptional both for its quality and completeness; the former Wesleyan chapel in Queen Street, Huddersfield

(221) of 1819, an even larger building, represents a peak of Georgian achievement, while the former Ebenezer Chapel, Sheffield (377) of 1823, although partly shorn of its tower, is of importance for the early use of Gothic detail, a style which was continued at Leeds in 1844 by James Simpson in his chapel in Otley Road (276). More typical of Simpson's work are the chapels at Barnsley (22), Keighley (239), and Hanover Place, Leeds (273), all now either altered or demolished. The Wesleyan 'Model Deed' chapel at Sowerby Bridge (399) of 1832 was closed and the interior stripped during the course of this survey and Brunswick Chapel, Leeds (271), another notable town-centre chapel, has been demolished. Wesleyan chapels of a more homely pattern include the remote Harrop Fold chapel (152) of 1819, Mytholmroyd (188) of 1825, and many small three-bay chapels, such as Leathley (259) of 1826. The large bow-fronted chapels at Barnsley (21), as altered in 1811, and Gomersal (141) of 1827 are unusual, while the hexagonal chapel of 1845 at Monk Fryston (299) appears to be unique. Of the chapels of the other branches of Methodism the New Connexion Mount Sion chapel, near Halifax (170) of 1815, and the flamboyant turreted front of Boulderclough chapel (404) of 1897 are especially notable.

A few Particular Baptist chapels of the 19th century are noteworthy: Hall Green chapel (236) of 1824–5 and West Lane (235) of 1844, both in Haworth, may usefully be compared; Salendine Nook, near Huddersfield (216) of 1843 illustrates the growing requirements of a large and flourishing congregation; the former chapel in Harris Street, Bradford (60), of 1873 by Lockwood and Mawson, shows the continued Baptist preference for a monumental Classical style. The General Baptist New Connexion, which owed its origins to the work of Dan Taylor in the West Riding, is represented by the chapel at Queensbury (336) of 1820 and by the later 19th-century chapels at Shore (427), Heptonstall Slack (192) and Birchcliffe at Hebden Bridge (186); the last is an exceptionally magnificent building in spite of some internal alteration.

Congregational chapels of the early 19th century are many and varied, one of the earliest being Zion Chapel, Flockton (134) of 1802, with others at Grassington (145), Tosside (139) and Horton (214). Town chapels of note include Sion Chapel, Halifax (155) of 1819–20, Highfield Chapel, Huddersfield (219), and Zion Chapel, Wakefield (443), both of 1843–4. The Gothic style, first found with this denomination at Burley in Wharfedale (231) in 1839, continues at Warley (165) and Rawdon (4) in 1845 and 1846; the style was best exhibited in the new 'Square Church', Halifax (154) of 1855 by Joseph James, now largely demolished, and in Lockwood and Mawson's chapel at Lightcliffe (81), built in 1871 for Sir Titus Salt. The work of the same architects and patron is found earlier, but in the Classical idiom, in the palatial chapel at Saltaire (380), the epitome of industrial patronage; a comparable example of architectural patronage was responsible for the contemporary chapel at Luddendenfoot (397).

The continued use of older Presbyterian meeting-houses by congregations which had become Unitarian was followed by a period of rebuilding, particularly after the passing of the Dissenters' Chapels Act. One of the earliest instances was the rebuilding of Mill Hill Chapel, Leeds (260) in 1847–8 in the Gothic style by Bowman and Crowther. In the later rebuilding of the much-altered Northgate End Chapel, Halifax (153) in 1872, the same style was used, though without a comparable degree of success. By far the grandest of all the Gothic chapels in the West Riding is that built not for one of the older congregations but for the once poor 'Cookite' society of Methodist Unitarians in Todmorden (436) in 1865–9. This was the gift of the sons of John Fielden as a token of filial piety, and was built to the designs of John Gibson, its lofty tower and spire dominating the town and marking a peak of nonconformist architectural achievement unsurpassed by any other contemporary English chapel.

A wide variety of date and style is to be expected in an area as extensive as the West Riding. The most noticeable feature, especially in the earlier periods, is the prevalence of the Pennine tradition of building with the availability of good supplies of building stone, particularly millstone grit, throughout all the upland districts. This is accompanied by the use of stone slates for roofing which continued to be available in the southern Pennines at least until the mid 19th century. Brickwork is only found in general use in the eastern parts of the Riding, but its adoption as a fashionable material is to be seen at Wakefield (441) in 1751–2 and at Halifax (154) in 1772.

ACKWORTH   *W. Yorks.*

(1) FRIENDS (SE 442173). Ackworth School, the first Quaker public school to be established as a result of a decision by the 1777 Yearly Meeting, was opened in 1779 as a mixed boarding-school for children 'whose parents are not in affluence' (Barber (1879) op. cit. below, 82). The school buildings, acquired through the enthusiasm of Dr John Fothergill, had been erected in 1758 in connection with the Hospital for Foundling Children in London but this use ceased *c.*1773. A meeting-house was fitted up in the E wing in 1780. In 1846–7 an appeal was launched to improve the school premises 'by raising the boys' wing, so increasing the airiness of the Schoolrooms, adding to their number by taking the Meeting-house for that purpose, and erecting a new one in its place' (Barber (1879) op. cit. below, 155).

Friends' meeting-house, Ackworth.   (1)

The present meeting-house, built in 1847–8 for the use of the school and for local Friends, stands on the N side of the entrance courtyard. The architect is thought to have been Joseph Wood. The loggia of the courtyard with paired Tuscan columns continues across the S front of the building, which is of three bays with a pediment and has sash windows in moulded frames above triple entrances.

The interior (69¾ft by 45ft) has a gallery around three sides, rounded to the S, with a partly open balustraded front supported by cast-iron Ionic columns. The stand at the N end has a plain panelled front and two stepped entrances below a coved canopy.

The seating throughout comprises open-backed benches.

Barber, J. H. (ed.), *A Narrative of the Proceedings at the Celebration of the Centenary of Ackworth School* (1879). Foulds, E. F. and Milligan, E., *200 Years of Quaker Education at Ackworth* (1979). Lidbetter (1961) *passim*.

ADDINGHAM   *W. Yorks*

(2) FRIENDS, Farfield (SE 076518). The meeting-house, dated 1689 above the entrance, stands in one corner of a small walled burial-ground given for Friends' use some years before by Anthony Myers. Regular meetings ceased *c*.1840 and the building has since been put to only minor uses. It is a small building of rubble with a stone-slate roof gabled to NE and SW. On the SE side is a doorway with chamfered jambs between windows of three and four lights.

The interior is undivided (25ft by 19ft) with the stand at the NE end having a raised central bench with three turned balusters at the front. The roof is supported by a single king-post truss with braces to the ridge.

Monuments: in burial-ground, include a row of five table-tombs with sides of coursed stone and capstones with moulded or chamfered edges (1) Anthony Myers, 1697/8, and Elizabeth Myers, 1688; (2) George Myers, 1714; (3) Mary, wife of George Myers, 1737; (4) Sarah, daughter of George and Mary Myers, 1687, and George their son, 1739; (5) no legible inscription. Also three loose slabs (6) Sarah, daughter of George Myers, died 'the

Friends' meeting-house, Farfield.   (2)

Friends' meeting-house, Farfield. *Water-colour by H. Sterling Howard, 1888.*   (2)

2 day of the XI Month called January 1687' (perhaps superseded by (4) in 1739); (7) dated 1705; (8) dated 1709.

Arnold (1960) 105–6, 112. *Bradford Antiquary* VII (1933) 252–5.

(3) Former WESLEYAN, Chapel Street (SE 076500). The chapel was first built about 1778 on land 'on the E side of Lidget Lane' acquired in that year. It was greatly enlarged or rebuilt in 1808 and extended to the rear in 1834. Little recognizably 18th-century work survives, but two former doorways in the W front with round-arched heads and rusticated surrounds are of that period though possibly reset. The outline of a similarly arched opening formerly visible at the W end of the S wall, which could have been the earlier front, may mark the site of one of these doorways.

The gabled W front now has a late 19th-century central entrance and two tiers of plain windows above. The side walls are of three bays. The interior, which has a gallery around three sides supported by iron columns, was refitted and an organ chamber built to the E in the late 19th century. (Converted to flats since 1972)

Monument: in burial-ground, square stone mausoleum with inscriptions to George Oates Greenwood of Netherwood House, 1845, William Greenwood 1866, and Ann his wife 1850.

Lemmon, W., *Methodism in Addingham*, 2nd edn. (1973).

AIREBOROUGH   *W. Yorks.*

(4) CONGREGATIONAL, Rawdon (SE 206402). 'Benton Park Chapel' built 1846 partly at the expense of Henry Forbes; Gothic, by J. Clark of Leeds. Gabled front with central entrance between blind arches and band of arcading above. Contemporary manse to E demolished since 1970.

CYB (1847) 170–2. Miall (1868) 337.

(5) FRIENDS, Rawdon (SE 208401). The meeting-house was built in 1697. It was enlarged to the rear, possibly in the early 19th century, and in 1840 £235 was spent on re-roofing, altering the

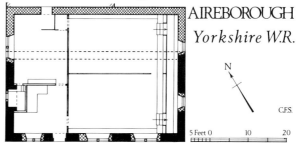

Friends' Meeting-house at Rawdon
AIREBOROUGH
Yorkshire W.R.

Friends' meeting-house, Rawdon. (5)

windows and removing a pillar which had supported the ceiling. The SW front has an original doorway with chamfered joints and dated lintel; the windows have all been raised and the stone frames renewed in 1840 and the wall heightened. The steeper pitch of the original roof is visible in the gabled end walls.

The interior (originally 43ft by 19ft) is divided into two rooms by sliding shutters. At the NW end are the remains of an original fireplace. The principal room, with plain pine seating, is bisected by a low panelled division on the main axis of the meeting-house for the separation of the sexes.

Monuments: in burial-ground, removed in 1932 from a burial-ground at Dibhouse (approximately SE 197412), (1) Joshua Overend, 1696; (2) Nathaniel Overend, 1696.

Barringer, J. A., *Rawdon Meeting* (1897; reprinted from *The Friend*). Lidbetter (1961) 83. Southall (1974) 59–60.

AIRTON
N. Yorks.

(6) FRIENDS (SD 903592). The meeting-house built at his own expense by William Ellis and opened in 1700 is an extension to the NE end of a 17th-century cottage. The walls are of rubble and

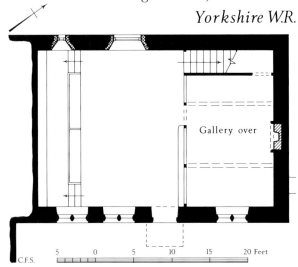

Friends' Meeting-house, AIRTON
Yorkshire W.R.

5 0 5 10 15 20 Feet

C.F.S.

Gallery over

the roof is covered with stone slates. The SE front, which is concealed from the road, has a doorway with chamfered jambs and arched lintel inscribed 'W^{E}A 1700'; three lower windows and one lighting the NE gallery are of two lights with straight-chamfered mullions. The NW wall is pierced by an early 19th-century window and by a small window at that end of the stand.

The interior (30¾ft by 19¾ft) is divided by a screen with hinged shutters. In the room below the gallery is a stone fireplace with plain chamfered shelf. The gallery has an open panelled front. The burial-ground to the NE has uniform headstones of the 19th century and later.

APPLETON ROEBUCK
N. Yorks.

(7) WESLEYAN (SE 552422). Brick with hipped pantile roof, broad three-bay front dated 1818. Gallery left of entrance. (Altered and refitted 1991)

APPLETREEWICK
N. Yorks.

(8) PRIMITIVE METHODIST, Howgill (SE 061594). Stone with shaped kneelers to end gables. Two doorways below round-arched windows in end wall, cottage below. Dated 1836.

ASKHAM RICHARD
N. Yorks.

(9) WESLEYAN (SE 536478). Brick and pantile, broad three-bay front with four-centred arches to doorway and windows. Opened 1842.

ASKWITH
N. Yorks.

(10) Former FRIENDS (SE 171479). Low stone-walled meeting-house built 1705 with mullioned windows of three and four lights in S front and doorway between with chamfered jambs and lintel. Three-light window, now blocked, in E wall above site of stand. Interior (36¼ft by 18¼ft) entirely altered during use as farm outbuilding or c.1965 on conversion to a house. This was also used in the late 19th century as a Primitive Methodist chapel.

Seals (1974) 17.

(11) WESLEYAN (SE 170484). The chapel stands on the site of the village school, rebuilt c.1832. The lower storey of the new building continued in public and scholastic use but the upper storey was built at Methodist expense as a chapel; it is approached by an external staircase with iron balustraded handrails.

Seals (1974) 17.

ASTON CUM AUGHTON
S. Yorks.

(12) Former WESLEYAN, Aughton (SK 454866). Broad three-bay front, partly defaced tablet 'erected July 1843'; later porch with pilasters and pediment.

(13) WESLEYAN, Rotherham Road, Swallownest (SK 451854). Low stone walls with lancet windows. Opened 1848.

AUCKLEY
S. Yorks.

(14) WESLEYAN (SE 650012). Rendered brick and pantile; broad three-bay front, dated 1832.

AZERLEY
N. Yorks.

(15) Former WESLEYAN, Mickley (SE 258770). Rubble and pantile, three-bay front with small round-arched windows in

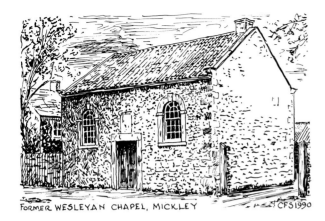

FORMER WESLEYAN CHAPEL, MICKLEY   CFS1990

ashlar surrounds with keystones. Date tablet defaced. Early 19th-century.

BADSWORTH   *W. Yorks.*

(16) WESLEYAN (SE 463148). Three-bay front, altered; oval tablet dated 1830.

BARNOLDSWICK   *Lancashire*

(17) Former BAPTIST, Walmgate (SD 876466). The Baptist church in Barnoldswick originated in the late 17th century as a branch of the Rossendale church, becoming autonomous in 1711. In 1693 a cottage which still stands at right angles to the former chapel, and a barn adjacent to it, were bought by David Crossley and apparently used as a meeting-house until the present building was erected in 1797. A new chapel, 'Bethesda', was built in Manchester Road in 1852 (SD 877466) and in 1879 another Baptist chapel was built in North Street (SD 876464) for a secession of 1868; the two societies reunited in 1911.

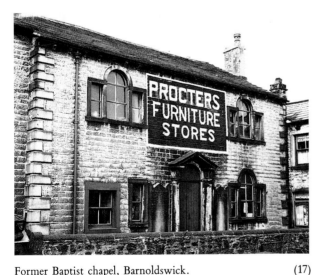

Former Baptist chapel, Barnoldswick.   (17)

The former chapel in Walmgate, now in commercial use, has stone walls and a stone-slate roof. The front wall has rusticated quoins, a central round-arched doorway with an open pediment supported by Roman Doric columns, and two tiers of plain

Venetian windows each side, one now altered. In the rear wall is a pair of pointed-arched windows flanking the site of the pulpit and windows above and below the returns of the former gallery; one lower window, now blocked, has been used as a doorway.

The interior ($27\frac{1}{4}$ft by 36ft) has no original fittings; a gallery around three sides has been removed. The roof is supported by two king-post trusses.

Monuments: externally on front wall (1) John Dean, 1839, and Christopher his son, 1843; (2) William Dean, 1838. A small walled burial-ground in front of the chapel contains several table-tombs of the late 18th and early 19th century including (3) Rev. Nathan Smith, 1831, *et al.*; (4) William Mitchell, 1795, Ann his widow, 1822, and two children; (5) Rev. John Parker, late minister at Wainsgate, 1793, and Alice his widow, 1804.

Shipley (1912) *passim*.

(18) INDEPENDENT METHODIST, Walmgate (SD 876465). Pedimented stone front, paired doorways with columnar surround. Dated 1892.

BARNSLEY   *S. Yorks.*

(19) 'SALEM CHAPEL', Blucher Street (SE 344062). The chapel, dated 1825, was built for Congregationalists who removed to a new chapel in Regent Street in 1856 and sold the former building to the present occupants, the Wesleyan Reform Church. Square stone building with three-bay pedimented front and two tiers of plain windows.

Monuments: in burial-ground (1) Marian Gunyon, 1834, and Jane her sister, erected by William Gunyon 'tea dealer, Barnsley', table-tomb; (2) Thomas Harrison, 1848, Anna his wife, 1839, and Samuel their son, 1845, table-tomb.

CYB (1857) 245–6. Miall (1868) 227.

(20) FRIENDS, Huddersfield Road (SE 342069). A meeting-house at Monk Bretton ($1\frac{1}{4}$ miles ENE) built in 1698 was superseded in 1815 by one on the present site which was rebuilt in 1969.

Monuments: in burial-ground, presumably from Monk Bretton, capstones from five table-tombs, some with moulded edges, including (1) with framed border, 1681; (2) William Fletcher, 1689, and Hannah his daughter, 1690; (3) Samuel Nickelson, late 17th-century.

Former Wesleyan chapel, Westgate, Barnsley.   (21)

(21) Former WESLEYAN, Westgate (SE 342064). The chapel, built 1792–4 to replace a meeting-room in Eastgate, was greatly enlarged and reorientated in 1811 to designs by John Whitworth of Barnsley. It was superseded in 1846 by a new chapel in Pitt Street and then sold to Primitive Methodists. It is now used by Barnsley Boys' Club.

The original building, of stone, faced Westgate and had a broad N front with two end doorways, small gallery windows above and two round-arched windows between which flanked the pulpit. In 1811 the walls were heightened and extended to the south. The new bowed S front, of three bays between staircase wings, has two tiers of round-arched windows and a former doorway at the centre approached from lower ground by a curved and divided flight of stone steps.

Kendall (1905) I: 488.

(22) WESLEYAN, Pitt Street (SE 342062). By James Simpson, 1845–6. Stone with rusticated quoins and moulded cornice. Five-bay front with two tiers of windows; open porch of three bays with Ionic columns. The interior has a rounded gallery, panelled ceiling and basement rooms below. (Subdivided 1979; closed 1982 following structural failure and since demolished. *Organ*, 1849, re-erected in Baptist Chapel, Sandy, Bedfordshire, 1987)

Wesleyan chapel, Pitt Street, Barnsley.   (22)

(23) Former WESLEYAN PROTESTANT METHODIST, Blucher Street (SE 344062). Opposite 'Salem'; 1829 by John Whitworth, enlarged and re-fronted 1901 by Herbert Crawshaw. In commercial use since 1958.

BATLEY   *W. Yorks.*

(24) WESLEYAN, Birstall (SE 226262). The first Methodist preaching-house on this site was built in 1750 for a society formed by John Nelson, a native of Birstall who became a notable itinerant preacher; it was rebuilt in 1782 and replaced by the present building in 1846. The chapel is a large building with stone walls and a slate roof. The SE front is of five bays with terminal pilasters, a three-bay pediment, two tiers of round-arched windows and entrances in the end bays; the sides are of six bays.

The interior originally had a continuous gallery with rounded ends; this has now been altered at the NW to form an organ loft and choir gallery. Some original seating remains including seats

Wesleyan chapel, Birstall.   (24)

for door-keepers near the front entrances. Below the SE end of the chapel is a small basement. At the rear is a separate Sunday-school of 1885.

In the burial-ground is a small brick building, 9ft square externally, with stone-slate roof, doorway to S and windows in E and W walls. In one corner is a fireplace with iron hob grate and a tablet with moulded cornice above inscribed 'JOHN NELSON's STUDY A.D. 1751'. There are wall benches around three sides.

Fittings – *Monuments*: in chapel (1) John Nelson, 1774, with portrait bust, signed 'Walsh and Lee, Leeds', erected 1846; (2) Eliza, daughter of Rev. H. Beech, 1835, and Mary Jane, daughter of Rev. James Hickson, 1830, signed 'Walsh and Dunbar, Leeds'; (3) Joseph Scholefield, 1849, machine maker, signed 'Bromley, sculptor, Leeds'. *Pulpit*: mahogany with octagonal top and corner columns, *c*.1846, reset. *Sundial*: in front of 'John Nelson's study', cylindrical stone pillar with moulded necking and square top, inscribed 'John Nelson, 1750'; gnomon renewed.

(25) UNITED METHODIST, Commercial Street (SE 243243). 'Zion Chapel', dated 1869, by Walter Hanstock and Michael Sheard of Batley. Elaborately detailed ashlar front of five bays with three-bay pedimented centre and triple-arched doorways.

BAWTRY   *S. Yorks.*

(26) Former WESLEYAN, Church Walk (SK 652930). Brick and slate, three-bay front with pedimental gable and two tiers of windows. Early 19th-century.

(27) Former PRIMITIVE METHODIST (SK 653932). Broad three-bay front and hipped roof, dated 1862.

BENTHAM   *N. Yorks.*

(28) FRIENDS, Calf Cop, Lower Bentham (SD 650702). Meetings begun *c*.1652–3 were held from 1686 to 1718 in a converted barn. In 1692 land was bought to enlarge the burial-ground and in 1717 it was proposed to build a new meeting-house 'at or as near the higher burying place as possible'. In May 1718 the purchase of land at Calf Cop was reported to Brighouse Monthly Meeting, and materials from the former meeting-house were reused in the

new building which was completed in that year.

The meeting-house was rebuilt on or near the site of its predecessor in 1768–70 but apparently replaced by the present building c.1797–8. This has rubble walls and a stone-slate roof with chimney stacks on the gabled ends. The E front has a low pedimented porch; the lintel of the inner doorway reused from the first building is dated 1718. Left of the porch are two sash windows with ashlar surrounds to the principal room and two tiers of smaller windows to the right. A window in the S wall, centrally behind the stand, has been blocked.

The interior (36¼ft by 20¾ft) comprises two principal rooms separated by a passage with a gallery staircase at the W end. The larger room to the S has a fielded-panelled dado and contemporary stand; the entrance from the passage is flanked by fluted pilasters over which is a moulded cornice and an open balustraded front to the gallery. The roof is supported by three trusses with tie and collar-beams and later king-posts. (Interior much altered 1975–6)

Burial-grounds: one adjacent to meeting-house with uniform headstones; the site of an earlier burial-ground about 250 yards S is marked by an inscribed stone.

(29) Former FRIENDS, High Bentham (SD 666693). Rendered pedimented front with porch between two tall windows, 1864. (Closed 1975, now Youth Club)

BEWERLEY   N. Yorks.

(30) CONGREGATIONAL, Bridgehouse Gate (SE 155654). When built in 1814 the chapel had a front to S of five bays with a central entrance and two tiers of windows all with four-centred arched heads; a cottage was later built to the left. In 1879 the chapel was entirely transformed with a Gothic W front, an inserted floor to accommodate school-rooms below the chapel, and enlargement of the S windows; the doorway and heads of the upper windows to the S alone appear to remain largely unaltered.

Monuments: in burial-ground S of chapel (1) Edward Gill, 1868, Ann his wife, 1847, and their children Matthew, 1820, and Elizabeth, 1825; (2) John Hardcastle, 1853, Ann his wife, 1817, and Elizabeth their daughter, 1847; (3) William Wood, 1825, Elizabeth his wife, 1822, *et al.*, table-tomb in railed enclosure; (4) William Ripley, 1829, Christiana Margaret his widow, 1864,

and their children John, 1816, William, 1819, Margaret, 1825, and Owen, 1825, table-tomb in railed enclosure.

Miall (1868) 328–9. Whitehead (1932) 125ff.

BILLINGLEY   S. Yorks.

(31) WESLEYAN, Chapel Lane (SE 436047). Three-bay gabled front with oval tablet dated 1818.

BILTON   N. Yorks.

(32) Former WESLEYAN, Bickerton (SE 451506). Small stone chapel, gabled front with shaped kneelers, dated 1826. Converted to cottage.

BINGLEY   W. Yorks.

(33) BAPTIST, Park Road (SE 109395). Square corner tower and pyramidal spire. Built 1876.

Shipley (1912) 186–7.

(34) CONGREGATIONAL, Ferrand Lane (SE 106393). Plain four-bay building with two tiers of windows. Built c.1818, extended to SW with two-storeyed cottage below. Sunday-school built 1862. Some early 19th-century ledger stones remain in burial-ground S of chapel.

Miall (1868) 230–1.

(35) WESLEYAN, Mornington Road (SE 111394). Gothic, with NW tower and spire; 1874, by J. P. Pritchett of Darlington.

(36) Former PRIMITIVE METHODIST, Hill Street (SE 11053905). 'Zion', 1853, pedimented front with Venetian window between two entrances: tripartite window above. (Derelict 1970)

(37) INDEPENDENT METHODIST, North Terrace (SE 11173893). Four-bay pedimented front with paired doorways, and two tiers of windows. Roundel in pediment inscribed 'EBENEZER 1868 CHRISTIAN BRETHREN'. (This designation was used locally by Independent Methodists until c.1900 (Vickers (1920) 164).)

(38) BAPTIST, Cullingworth (SE 067367). Built 1837, enlarged 1870 and 'entirely renovated' 1909. Original date tablet reset in later pediment.

Shipley (1912) 192–3.

(39) WESLEYAN, Cullingworth (SE 067368). Stone with hipped

Wesleyan chapel, Cullingworth.   (39)

roof, five-bay front with two tiers of round-arched windows. Dated 1824. *Sundial*: on front wall, 1832, with equations of time.

(40) Former WESLEYAN, Eldwick Crag (SE 128420). Small three-bay chapel with round-arched openings, c.1815.

(41) CONGREGATIONAL, Harden (SE 087383). Pedimented front with two tiers of round-arched windows above a basement; 1865.
Miall (1868) 270.

(42) Former WESLEYAN, Wilsden Old Road, Harden (SE 087 381). Three-bay gabled front, early 19th-century, heightened.

(43) WESLEYAN REFORM, Harden (SE 086382). Gabled front with two tiers of round-arched windows in three bays and two doorways between. Dated 1853.

(44) CONGREGATIONAL, Wilsden (SE 091365). The first chapel built in 1795 was converted to Sunday-school use in 1816 when a new chapel was built close by. The latter, with a broad front of three bays, was a roofless ruin in 1970 after damage by fire and has since been demolished. The earlier building (originally 46¾ft by 35ft externally) has been extended to the west. The S front of six bays with two tiers of plain windows, the upper ones heightened, formerly had doorways in the penultimate bays.
Miall (1868), 380.

BIRSTWITH   *N. Yorks.*

(45) Former METHODIST, Kettlesing Bottom (SE 228574). Built 1790, superseded by present Wesleyan chapel to N in 1931 and converted to cottages. Gabled front behind sunken railed forecourt; central entrance blocked, front refenestrated and rendered, pair of cottage doorways in side wall face lane at upper level. Former School of 1835 opposite later chapel.

BLACKSHAW   *W. Yorks.*

(46) WESLEYAN, Blackshaw Head (SD 959276). The chapel, built in 1815, was entirely refitted and reorientated in 1899; a Sunday-school added against the W end in 1838 was rebuilt in 1912. The original front facing S had three windows and two doorways alternately to the lower stage and four windows above. In 1899 a new entrance was made at the E end and the pulpit, formerly between two tall windows in the N wall, was set against the W wall. There is a continuous gallery.

BLAXTON   *S. Yorks.*

(47) WESLEYAN (SE 670004). Rendered brick and pantile, broad three-bay front dated 1834.

BLUBBERHOUSES   *N. Yorks.*

(48) WESLEYAN, Hardisty Hill (SE 170559). Gable entrance with two gallery windows over. Opened 1838, refitted late 19th century.

BOLTON BY BOWLAND   *Lancashire*

(49) CONGREGATIONAL, Holden (SD 771496). The chapel was built in 1766–8 and placed in trust for Presbyterians or Independents. A house for the minister was built at the N end in 1777 replacing accommodation under a former N gallery. In the late 19th century and after the chapel was greatly altered internally and in 1909 the manse was converted for use as school-rooms and the front wall rebuilt in alignment with the chapel.

The walls are of stone with later rendering and the roof is slated. The W front has three large upper windows and two small irregularly spaced windows below, all with round-arched heads. The interior formerly had the pulpit at the S end and a deep gallery to the N; this arrangement was reversed c.1882–4. The pulpit was superseded by a rostrum c.1916 but the former back-board remains. The S gallery has a fielded-panelled front of the late 18th century.

Fittings – *Chandelier*: Nightingale (II (1891)) records a 'huge brass chandelier' brought here from the former meeting-house in Bingley when the latter was superseded c.1818; now removed. *Monuments*: in burial-ground W of chapel (1) Rev. Henry Driver, 1860, *et al.*; (2) Edmund Lord, 1842, and Mary his widow, 1843; (3) Rev. Benjamin Sowden, 1813, and Esther his widow, 1833.
Miall (1868) 277. Nightingale II (1891) 232–8. Whitehead (1930) 174–88.

BOROUGHBRIDGE   *N. Yorks.*

(50) Former WESLEYAN, Aldborough (SE 406662). Three-bay gabled front, altered entrance; 1864.

BOSTON SPA   *W. Yorks.*

(51) WESLEYAN, Spa Lane (SE 433455). Gabled front with three graduated round-arched windows above entrance; school-rooms below. Opened 1847, roof austerely rebuilt c.1970 without the original deeply overhanging eaves.

BRADFIELD   *S. Yorks.*

(52) UNDERBANK CHAPEL, Stannington (SK 296887). Stannington Chapel, as this is more properly called, was built in 1742–3 in succession to an earlier building which stood nearby. The first chapel has been presumed to have been fitted up in 1652, following the will of Richard Spoone who in that year left some property in trust to provide for the maintenance of a preaching minister in Stannington, the appointment to be subject to the approval of the trustees and three neighbouring ministers. The distance from the parish church of Ecclesfield and its chapel-of-ease at Bradfield were evidently factors in determining this bequest, no doctrinal conditions were made although a puritanism consistent with the period may be inferred.

At the Restoration the minister, Isaac Darwent, was ejected for nonconformity, but not until 1663, and he remained a tenant of the chapel lands until 1666. Until 1689 and for some years thereafter, the ministers or curates of Stannington Chapel adopted a sufficient degree of conformity not to attract undue attention from the episcopal authorities whose claims to jurisdiction were ill-defined and eventually abandoned. In 1746, soon after the erection of the new chapel, a letter was sent seeking to terminate some parochial charges still levied on the former building; in this it was claimed that 'the chapel has been a Protestant Dissenting meeting place for religious worship and as such was licensed by several justices of the peace and was never consecrated by any Diocesan Bishop . . . It has been an old barn, and it was so called in the licence. I suppose it was converted into a place of religious worship by the neighbourhood and repaired and supported sometimes by one, sometimes by another, as long

Underbank Chapel, Stannington.   (52)

as it was possible of being supported upon such rotten ground as it stood upon. And now there is a new one erected, every stick of it new, and the old one laid aside.'

The dissenting interest in Stannington received support in the early 18th century from Thomas Marriot of Ughill, a burgess of Sheffield, who in 1714 added to the endowments of the chapel. His nephew, the writer of the above letter, bore most of the cost of the new building, referring to it as 'the place I have built for a meeting place, to be a place for them for the public worship of Almighty God ... after the dictates of their own consciences'. The trust deed of 14 February 1743 devotes the property to 'Protestant Dissenters of the Presbyterian or Congregational denominations', but of these the former prevailed and, in common with many similar congregations, it has been served by a Unitarian ministry since the late 18th century. The chapel figured largely in the 'Socinian controversy' of the early 19th century which culminated in the Dissenters' Chapels Act of 1844.

The new chapel, built by Thomas Marriot the younger and opened 2 June 1743, is externally one of the finest examples of its period. The walls are of squared local stone with ashlar dressings and the roof is hipped and covered with stone slates with a central lead flat. The walls have a low plinth, quoins and a moulded stone cornice. The S front of six bays has two tall round-arched windows flanking the site of the pulpit, doorways to right and left with deep lintels decorated with keystones and cornices

above, circular windows over each, and two tiers of rectangular windows in the end bays. The other three walls had each two tiers of two-light square-mullioned windows in three bays, but the fenestration at the W end has been altered by blocking the centre windows and substituting tall round-arched windows for those in the side bays.

The interior (32ft by 42ft) was entirely stripped in 1867; prior to that it had galleries around three sides, a pulpit against the S wall and a miscellany of box-pews to the lower floor. In the refitting a deep gallery was provided at the E end and the pulpit placed against the W wall. Further rearrangement of the W end occurred in 1921, with the introduction of a large organ, and in 1952, when its place was again taken by a central pulpit.

A cottage of two storeys adjoining the chapel at the SW corner is approximately contemporary. Further to the S is a School building of 1853.

Fittings – *Communion Cloth*: with embroidered inscription 'Stannington Chapel October 1st 1854'. *Doors*: in S wall, two, each with six fielded panels, mid 18th-century. *Glazing*: in two windows at N end of gallery, original rectangular leaded glazing. *Monuments*: in chapel (1) Charles Hinde, 1856; (2) Rev. Peter Wright, 40 years pastor, 1854; in burial-ground (3) Hannah, wife of John Hawksworth, 1784; (4) Rev. Samuel Smith, 1761; (5) Ruth, wife of Samuel Smith, 1757; (6) Edward, son of Rev. Edward and Jane Gibson, 1791; (7) Thomas, son of Elizabeth Birch, 1790. (Monuments in the front burial-ground were uprooted and flattened *c*.1979) *Plate*: includes a two-handled cup of 1751.

Christian Freeman (August 1871) 120–1. Evans (1897) 230–1. Miall (1868) 360–1. *UHST* III (1923–6) 160–5. Wood, F. T., *A History of Underbank Chapel, Stannington* (1944).

(53) LOXLEY CHAPEL (SK 303902). The chapel stands 2¾ miles E of the former chapel-of-ease, now the parish church, of Bradfield. It was built in 1787 as a proprietory chapel by the supporters of the Rev. Benjamin Greaves. Greaves, who is earlier reported to have served as *locum tenens* to John Fletcher at Madeley, Shropshire, was apparently dismissed from his assistant curacy at Bradfield for evangelical enthusiasm. Before the chapel was completed Greaves was appointed to the Derbyshire living of Stoney Middleton (10 miles SW) although for a time he continued his charge at Loxley. Work on the chapel was completed only with the help of a loan from Greaves's brother George, a London stockbroker, who as mortgagee appointed the next minister. About 1801 the building was leased by the congregation which appointed a Congregational minister, formed an Independent church (now URC) in 1804 and in 1820 purchased the freehold of the chapel. In 1821–2 the eastern bay was divided into two storeys and converted for use as a Sunday-school. A complete re-roofing and internal refitting was carried out in 1890–1.

The chapel is a large building with stone walls having a double platband and moulded cornice, and a hipped slated roof. The broad S front of five bays has a wide round-arched doorway at the centre, now altered to a window, with a Venetian window above. The W wall, also of five bays, has smaller round-arched doorways in the penultimate bays, a tripartite window between and a Venetian window above. The E wall has a large Venetian window at mid-height flanked by blind panels. The windows in the N wall are plain.

The interior of the chapel (originally 72¼ft by 48¼ft) has been reduced in length by 16½ft as a result of the separation of the E bay by a substantial cross-wall. The large E window, the original focus of the chapel, is flanked internally by shallow recesses. The remaining body of the chapel has an original gallery around three sides with fielded-panelled front and dentil cornice above; it is supported by late 19th-century cast-iron columns.

Fittings – *Chairs*: two with shaped and carved back rails, one with carved panelled back and arms, 17th-century. *Monuments*: in chapel (1) William Fearn Storrs 'one of the founders of the Independent Church at Loxley', 1870; in E room (2) George Augustus, son of George Augustus and Sarah Wood, 1846, *et al.*; (3) Aaron and Mary, 1836, children of Francis and Sarah Wood; (4) Elizabeth, daughter of Francis and Elizabeth Wood, 1805, *et al.* In burial-ground (5) Rev. Daniel Dunkerley, 1820, 18 years minister, and Alice his widow 1822; (6) Rev. John Hanson, 1851, 18 years minister. *Pulpit*: hexagonal with fluted frieze and dentil cornice, late 18th-century, reduced in height.

Lee, J., *Historical Sketch of Loxley Chapel* (*c*.1907). Miall (1868) 360.

(54) CONGREGATIONAL, Oughtibridge (SK 307933). Low gabled stone front of three bays. Renewed tablet 'Zion 1833'. (URC)

Miall (1868) 328.

(55) WESLEYAN, Brightholmlee (SK 298950). Gabled front with round-arched lower windows, two plain windows above, tablet dated 1807.

Loxley Chapel. (53)

(56) PRIMITIVE METHODIST, Dungworth (SK 280899). Broad three-bay front; 1850; altered.

(57) Former WESLEYAN, Low Bradfield (SK 262917). Three bays with traces of painted inscription on platband 'WESLEYAN CHAPEL Built AD 1817'. Two tall round-arched pulpit windows at back have been altered. Superseded in 1898 by Gothic chapel opposite.

BRADFORD   *W. Yorks.*

(*See* also CLAYTON, ECCLESHILL, IDLE, NORTH BIERLEY, THORNTON)

(58) CHAPEL LANE CHAPEL, Town Hall Square (SE 163329). A Presbyterian society formerly meeting at Little Horton or Wibsey (*see* (314)) built the first meeting-house on this site in 1718–19 using some materials from the demolished Howley Hall, Batley. This was a rectangular stone building with two entrances in the broad front wall and mullioned-and-transomed windows next to the corners to light the gallery staircases. It was superseded in 1869 by a Gothic chapel by Andrews, Son, and Pepper; in 1971 the now Unitarian society moved to a new building in Russell Street (SE 158324). The former chapel has been demolished. *Monument*: at Russell Street, Rev. John Dean, 1813, and Penelope his widow, 1832. *Plate*: includes a two-handled gadrooned cup of 1703.

Christian Freeman (1869) 56, 59. Evans (1897) 28–9. Hargrove (*c.*1903). Miall (1868) 235–6. Scruton (1889) 47–52. Smith, A. C., *Chapel Lane Chapel, Bradford, 1719–1919* (1919).

(59) Former BAPTIST, Westgate (SE 159333). A church was formed in 1753 and the first meeting-house erected in 1755. The present building was commenced in 1782, after which the earlier meeting-house remained in use as a school-room. The chapel, which originally seated 700, was enlarged in 1817 to 60ft by 50ft, again in 1839–40 and finally in *c.*1853, when the capacity was said to be 1,400 'besides excellent accommodation for the children of the school in the upper gallery'. The church removed *c.*1900 to a new chapel in Carlisle Road; the former building is now in commercial use.

The chapel has stone walls, rendered at the sides, and a slate roof. The E front, which represents the final phase of enlargement at this end, has rusticated quoins, two former doorways and two upper tiers of windows with a Venetian

window in the gable. The interior had a gallery around three sides with an upper gallery at the E end.

B. Hbk (1900) 368. Dowson, H., *The Centenary, A History of the First Baptist Church, Bradford, from its Commencement in 1753 . . .* (*c.*1854). Ivimey IV (1830) 563–6. Scruton (1889) 62–6. Shipley (1912) 117–19.

(60) Former BAPTIST, Harris Street (SE 170331). 'Sion Jubilee Chapel' was built in 1873 to supersede the first Sion Chapel of 1823 which stood in Bridge Street. The design by Lockwood and Mawson includes an elaborate classical frontage of five bays with a three-bay pedimented centre. The date tablet from the earlier chapel is reset in the side wall.

Dowson (*op. cit.*) 52–5. Scruton (1889) 66–8. Shipley (1912) 123–4.

(61) Former BAPTIST, Little Horton Lane (SE 159323). 'Trinity Chapel' was built in 1857 by some members of Westgate chapel to mark their centenary. Pedimented front with three deeply splayed round-arched entrances.

Shipley (1912) 128–9.

(62) BAPTIST, Highgate, Heaton (SE 140355). 1896, by John Jackson of Bradford. Gothic with short corner tower. Concentric seating. Burial-ground opposite.

B. Hbk (1896) 301–2. Shipley (1912) 129.

(63) Site of CONGREGATIONAL, Horton Lane (SE 161328). The chapel of 1863 by Lockwood and Mawson, superseding a late 18th-century meeting-house, has been demolished. The former Sunday-school of 1861, in the Jacobean style by the same architects, has been converted to offices.

CYB (1864) 289–90. Miall (1868) 236–7.

(64) Former CONGREGATIONAL, Manor Row (SE 162335). 'Salem Chapel' built 1835–6 has a pedimented front with broad terminal pilasters and stylized acroteria on the base of the pediment. Before alteration *c.*1888, when the congregation moved to a new chapel in Oak Lane and let the former to the Bradford School Board, there was a small central porch with a pair of Doric columns, lunette above, and a sarcophagus in a shallow recess in the main pediment. At the rear is a small segmental apse. (Mezzanine windows inserted to side walls 1990)

Anon., *Salem Congregational Church . . .* (1936). Miall (1868) 237.

Former Baptist chapel, Westgate, Bradford.   (59)

Salem Chapel, Bradford.   (64)

(65) Former CONGREGATIONAL, Upper Park Gate (SE 169333). 'College Chapel', built in 1839 and now much rebuilt for commercial use, has a bowed front of stone in three bays with a rusticated basement and blind attic storey with small pedimented feature at the centre.

CYB (1866) 324. Miall (1868) 237–8.

(66) Former CONGREGATIONAL, Great Horton Road (SE 149 323). Octagonal; 1890–1 by T. C. Hope of Bradford.

CYB (1891) 212–13.

(67) Former FRIENDS, Fountain Street (SE 160335). Earlier meeting-houses in Bridge Street and Wakefield Street were superseded in 1877 by the present building by Lockwood and Mawson. Front of five bays with moulded cornice; three-bay recessed porch. Interior gutted and one side wall removed; under conversion 1990.

(68) Former WESLEYAN, Leeds Road (SE 168330). Methodist meetings in Bradford began in 1756 and the first regular preaching-house, an octagon in Horton Lane (SE 160329), was built in 1766. In 1811 the society moved to a chapel in Kirkgate, soon supplemented in 1825 by Eastbrook Chapel, a Gothic building by Joseph Botham of Sheffield. The latter was replaced in 1903–4 on an enlarged site by Eastbrook Hall, a central hall for the Wesleyan Mission, designed by W. J. Morley and Son.

Stamp (1841) 89–92, 102–4.

Former Methodist chapel, Leeds Road, Bradford (from Stamp, 1841). (68)

(69) WESLEYAN, Great Horton Road (SE 143317). The chapel built in 1814 was greatly enlarged to the front in 1862. It has a pedimented centre of three bays with giant Corinthian columns and staircase wings with urns at the corners.

Monument: between front columns, ledger stone to Thomas Ramsden, 1854, Sarah his wife, 1835, and their children Joshua, 1807, John, 1810, David, 1817, and Ellen, 1817.

(70) Former WESLEYAN, Park View Road, Manningham (SE 146 351). 'St John's'; Gothic with corner tower and spire, by C. O. Ellison, 1879.

(71) Former METHODIST NEW CONNEXION, Great Horton Road (SE 158328). Elaborate Italianate front of five bays with three-bay pediment and colonnaded porch. 1877 by Hill and Swann of Leeds. Now 'Grove Library'.

(72) Former PRIMITIVE METHODIST, Rooley Lane, Bowling (SE 180311). The former chapel, behind its successor of 1886, has a five-bay front dated 1823. Burial-ground with early 19th-century table-tombs.

(73) Former WESLEYAN REFORM, Bakes Street, Great Horton (SE 143318). 'Built 1851, Enlarged 1852' for a society which seceded from the Wesleyans in 1849 but became Congregational by 1865. Five-bay front with hipped roof, two tiers of round-arched windows with Venetian windows at centre. Interior floored at gallery level c.1955–60 but baize-lined box-pews remain in gallery. (URC)

Miall (1868) 238–9.

Former Wesleyan Reform chapel (URC), Great Horton. (73)

(74) MORAVIAN, Little Horton Lane (SE 156318). Built 1838 to supersede a building opposite in use from 1742; 'improved and reseated 1872'. Stone with crow-stepped front gable, small bell-cote removed.

England (1887) 13–14, Pls. 1, 2.

Former Presbyterian chapel, Infirmary Street, Bradford. (75)

(75) Former UNITED PRESBYTERIAN, Infirmary Street (SE 159 335). Built 1848 for a congregation formed in 1847. Pedimented stone front with Tuscan columns and widely splayed round-arched windows. (Interior gutted, converted to restaurant before 1985)

Mackelvie (1873) 488–9.

BRAITHWELL   *S. Yorks.*

(76) WESLEYAN, Austwood Lane (SK 532946). The chapel opened in 1799 was enlarged and re-roofed in the early 19th century. The walls are of stone and the roof is hipped and slated. The N front (30¾ft wide originally) alone dates from the 18th century and has a doorway with rusticated jambs between blind recesses. Two round-arched windows have been inserted into the front wall and the building extended to the east.

WESLEYAN CHAPEL, BRAITHWELL   CFS 1972

BRAMHOPE   *W. Yorks.*

(77) BRAMHOPE CHAPEL (SE 249436). Although the precise status of this chapel may be questioned, it is included here as an important example of Puritan building during the years of the Commonwealth which, for a brief period following the Restoration, continued to be served by nonconforming ministers.

The chapel was erected in 1649 by Robert Dyneley of Bramhope Hall ostensibly as a chapel-of-ease for the parish of Otley but in fact as a private or proprietory chapel. The building

remained Dyneley's property but the appointment of a 'godly and able minister' lay in the hands of trustees. An annual stipend of £40 was provided by the enclosure of common land. The first minister, Jeremiah Crossley, continued in office without conforming at least until 1665 and possibly until his death about 1671. Oliver Heywood, a frequent visitor to the Hall, also preached here. Another nonconforming minister, Robert Pickering, later minister at Morley Chapel, is named as 'chaplain to Robert Dyneley'. No attempt was made to license the building under the 1672 Indulgence and the provision of a font in 1673 may indicate the date at which, in spite of Robert Dyneley's evident preferences, a conforming minister was appointed. The chapel continued in Anglican use until 1881, when it was superseded by St Giles's Church. After a period of neglect and severe storm damage in 1962 it was placed in the care of the local authority and thoroughly repaired. The principal structural alterations date from the early 19th century, when the walls and roof structure were raised by a few feet and a flat plaster ceiling, now removed, was inserted.

The chapel is a long low building of coursed stone with a stone-slate roof and rebuilt bell-cote on the W gable. The S front has two segmental-arched doorways and four mullioned windows with arched lights in rectangular recessed openings. There are similar windows in the other walls, that at the E end being of five lights, and a small single-light pulpit window in the N wall immediately below the line of the former eaves.

The interior (60ft by 17½ft) has rendered walls and an open roof with king-post trusses. The seating is divided by a central aisle which widens at the E end where an early 19th-century stone altar replaces the original communion table. The pulpit stands against the N wall slightly E of centre. Below the altar is an arched burial vault of the early 19th century.

Fittings – *Altar*: stone, with shield-of-arms on W face, Rhodes with inescutcheon of Smith, for Anne Rhodes née Smith, erected after her death in 1827. *Bell*: in bell-cote, modern, replacing a bell dated 1872. *Communion Rails*: plain iron rails and gate, *c.*1840. *Font*: short cylindrical pillar on square base with octagonal bowl and plinth, dated 1673. *Monuments*: on N wall (1) Esther, wife of Christopher Smith, 1814, and Ann their daughter, wife of William Rhodes, 1827, recumbent female figure signed 'J. Gott'; (2) Christopher Leyland, 1837; (3) John Silvester, 1781, and

5   0   5   10   15   20   25   30 Feet

BRAMHOPE CHAPEL, *Yorkshire W.R.*

N

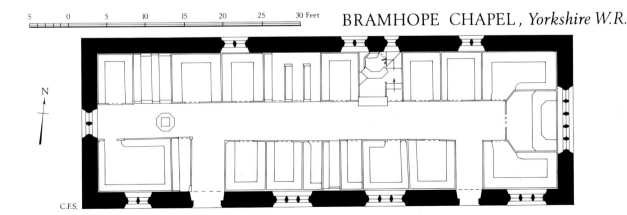

C.F.S.

Bramhope Chapel before restoration. (*Photos: G. B. Wood, 1944.*)

Elizabeth his widow, 1801; (4) Caroline Esther, daughter of William and Ann Rhodes, 1846; on E wall (5) Sarah, wife of Rev. Robert Dyneley, 1807; (6) Rev. Robert Dyneley, 1810; (7) Christopher Smith, 1846; on W wall (8) James Driver, 1818, and Ann his wife, 1814.

Pulpit: octagonal with two tiers of panelling, back-board with arched panel, moulded canopy with angle pendants, mid 17th-century. *Seating*: original work includes a few benches on N side with plain thick ends, and a pew S of pulpit with turned finials; other box-pews are principally of the 18th century, including clerk's desk in front of pulpit, but incorporate some earlier material; the partitions next to the outer doorways have mid 17th-century panels carved in low relief.

Miall (1868) 243–4. *The Bradford Antiquary* III (1900) 325–34. *Thoresby Society Publications* IX (1899) 228–45.

(78) WESLEYAN (SE 250433). Gothic with corner tower and spire, 1895–6 replacing a chapel of 1838, now demolished, 100 yards west.

Seals (1974) 17–18.

BRAMLEY
S. Yorks.

(79) Former WESLEYAN (SK 488924). Stone with hipped slate roof, three-bay front (24¾ft wide) with two round-arched windows with keystones, third window above entrance blocked and replaced by clock dial, door surround altered. Built by M. Waterhouse 1785, greatly altered and extended to rear in 19th century. (Converted to house *c*.1976)

BRAYTON
N. Yorks.

(80) WESLEYAN, Snaith Road (SE 606303). Three-bay brick front; dated 1844.

BRIGHOUSE
W. Yorks.

(81) Former CONGREGATIONAL, Leeds Road, Lightcliffe (SE 131 258). The congregation which first met from 1826 in the former Primitive Methodist chapel (82) moved to the present building on an adjacent site in 1871. The site was bought in 1869 by John Crossley and the new building erected with considerable financial support from Sir Titus Salt and his family, who occupied Crow Nest House. The chapel is a substantial stone building in the 14th-century Gothic style by Lockwood and Mawson. It comprises an aisled nave, N and S transepts, organ apse and E vestries, and a SW tower and spire. The nave is five bays in length, the W bay is closed to the S by the base of the tower, which forms the principal entrance, and to the N by a further porch. The N and S arcades of four bays have moulded two-centred arches supported by polished granite piers with elaborately carved capitals and a row of clerestory windows above; two taller arches open to the transepts and a wide 'chancel' arch spans the organ apse, which has a wheel-window in the E wall. (Converted to office use 1989; the church, now URC, meets in adjacent Sunday-school)

Fittings – *Bells*: in tower at base of spire, formerly six, now four re-hung for striking only. *Ringers' Board*: in tower, recording the first peal rung 29 March 1902. *Glass*: in E window, N and S windows of transepts and W window of nave with commemorative inscriptions to Andrew Scott

Former Congregational chapel, Lightcliffe. (81)

McLaurin, 1870, and Sir Titus Salt, Bart., 1876. *Inscriptions*: brass tablets on foundation stones in N and S lobbies, laid by Ada and Helen Salt, 22 August 1870. *Pulpit*: formerly central at E end, stone, octagonal with Gothic enrichment on central stem and four short columns. *Sculpture*: pottery bust of Sir Titus Salt, Bart., after model by John Adams-Acton, Copeland for J. Rhodes, 1877.

Miall (1868) 310–11. Nortcliffe (1978) 12–13.

(82) Former PRIMITIVE METHODIST, Leeds Road, Lightcliffe (SE 132258). 'Mount Zion' chapel dated 1823 was used as a chapel by Congregationalists from 1826 until 1871, then as school-rooms; latterly in industrial use. Stone with broad S front and two round arched windows flanking the site of the pulpit. (Demolished *c*.1979)

Monument: in burial-ground, John Jackman, 1856, Grand Master, Independent Order of Oddfellows.

Miall (1868) 310–11. Nortcliffe (1978) 13.

Former Primitive Methodist chapel, Lightcliffe. (82)

(83) PARK CHAPEL, Bethel Street (SE 146228). A Wesleyan chapel on this site built 1795 was temporarily occupied from 1799 by the Methodist New Connexion; they were ejected in 1811 and the original society returned. In *c*.1848 the society defected to the Wesleyan Reformers, joining the Free Methodists in 1857. The chapel was rebuilt in 1876–8 to designs by R. F. Rogerson. The front, of five bays between staircase towers, has round-arched upper windows. The interior has a continuous round-ended gallery.

Closed *c*.1984 and lower floor converted to general market. Gallery and upper fittings remain.

Howe, G., *A History of Park from 1791* (1978). Nortcliffe (1978) 37–9.

(84) Former METHODIST NEW CONNEXION (SE 145228). Built 1811, enlarged and re-fronted 1855. Front to Bethel Street, three bays with stone cornice and inscribed blocking course, two tiers of windows under moulded cornices. Rusticated quoins and surround to central arched entrance. Original tablet at rear inscribed 'Bethel Chapel 1811'. Superseded 1904, since in commercial use.

Howe (1978) op. cit. 9. Nortcliffe (1978) 38–9.

(85) WESLEYAN, Chapel Lane, Southowram (SE 116236). Built 1806, enlarged to N by two bays 1890. E front originally of five bays with two tiers of plain windows, doorways in penultimate bays. Date 1806 on central window cill.

Monuments: in burial-ground, several table-tombs and many ledger stones of early 19th century (1) Mary, wife of Aaron Akroyd, 1809, *et al.*; (2) Phebe, wife of John Fawcitt, 1810; (3) John, son of William Freeman, 1807, *et al.*; (4) Alice (Freeman), wife of Jonathan Richardson, 1808, *et al.*; (5) Job, son of Luke and Sarah Aspinall, 1819, *et al.*; (6) Joseph, son of Joseph and Susannah Denton, 1819, *et al.*; (7) Hannah, daughter of John and Mary Hemingway, 1823, *et al.*

(86) PRIMITIVE METHODIST, Waterloo Road (SE 141233). Pedimented front with later porch, 1864; converted to Sunday-school 1888 when larger chapel with octagonal steeple built alongside.

Nortcliffe (1978) 28.

BURNSALL   N. Yorks.

(87) Former WESLEYAN (SE 003613). Built 1840, superseded by new chapel to N in 1901 and greatly altered after 1965 on conversion to a house. Three-bay front with central entrance formerly flanked by two tall round-arched windows; date tablet reset in garden wall.

CATTALL   N. Yorks.

(88) Former WESLEYAN (SE 451541). Late 19th-century successor to an upper room in nearby Horbatt House.

CHAPEL HADDLESEY   N. Yorks.

(89) Former WESLEYAN (SE 582262). 'Centenary Chapel', three-bay brick front with pointed-arched openings, *c*.1839.

CLAPHAM CUM NEWBY   N. Yorks.

(90) Former INGHAMITE, Thin Oaks (SD 708685). A meeting formed here by William, son of Giles Batty, was in 1760 the venue of a general meeting attended by the Countess of Huntingdon, Benjamin Ingham and others to ordain elders and to transact other business relating to their societies. The farm, now 'Oaklands', was the former home of William's mother Mary (*née* Robinson).

The former chapel, scene of the 1760 meeting which attracted 'a large assemblage of people' (Seymour (1839) op. cit. below, I: 273), has been converted to a barn. It has walls of roughly coursed rubble (34¼ft by 49½ft externally) with gables to E and W ends. The S wall, reported to have had three windows, has been entirely rebuilt. A wide doorway has been pierced at the centre of the N wall, perhaps replacing pulpit windows. In each of the end walls is a small central doorway with blocked window above which lit the end galleries. The roof structure has been entirely renewed.

The former manse, now farmhouse, stands to the E; a burial-ground is believed to have existed S of the house.

Monuments: (1) 'Mary Daughter of C^r: & A^e: Batty of Thinoaks Who dy'd N^o: 23^d: Aged 2: 1762 Also Mary wife of Gyles Batty: A: 81:', ledger stone reset in wall N of house; (2) Paul Jackson of Lancaster, 1765, and Paul his son, 1765, loose fragments, found in barn 1927.

Lancaster Guardian (7 October 1977). Seymour (1839) I: 273–4. Thompson (1958) 59–60.

(91) Former SANDEMANIAN, Wenning Bank (SD 734678). Meeting-house with living accommodation, now private house. Built *c*.1760 for a meeting founded by James Allen, a former Inghamite supporter. Symmetrical stone front with central arched upper window.

Thompson (1958) 36.

CLAYTON   W. Yorks.

(92) Former WESLEYAN, Clayton Heights (SE 117306). Old Dolphin Chapel 'built by Subscription 1806' in part with loan from landlord of 'Old Dolphin' Inn. S front with two tiers of plain windows and later porch. Many early 19th-century monuments including table-tombs in burial-ground. (Closed 1980; Sunday-school, 1892, converted to chapel)

CLAYTON WEST   W. Yorks.

(93) STRICT BAPTIST, High Street (SE 259109). Broad front with three round-arched windows alternating with two doorways,

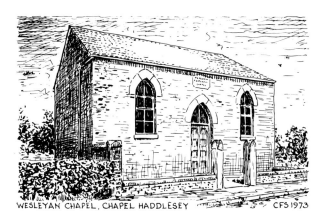

WESLEYAN CHAPEL, CHAPEL HADDLESEY   CFS 1973

dated 1840, to chapel and school. *Monument* in front to Joseph Higson, 1852, and Ann Higson Armitage, 1855.

CLECKHEATON   *W. Yorks.*

(94) CONGREGATIONAL, Providence Place (SE 191257). Although a group of dissenters was meeting in 1669 in the mediaeval Cleckheaton Chapel or 'Old White Chapel in the North' they did not succeed in an application to license the chapel in 1672. From that year, or before, Joseph Dawson, ejected curate of Thornton, gathered a society at 'Ye Closes', Egypt Farm, now 99 Drub Lane, Gomersal (SE 196269), whence in 1710 they removed to Cleckheaton. 'The Red Chapel' of brick which they then built in Scott Yard, Bradford Road, was rebuilt in 1780 and enlarged in 1815.

Congregational chapel (URC), Providence Place, Cleckheaton.   (94)

'Providence Place Chapel', built for this congregation in 1859, was designed by Lockwood and Mawson; it is an elaborate Italianate building with a pedimented front and open arcaded loggia of five bays with a giant order of Corinthian columns. Below the chapel are Sunday-school rooms and much other accommodation. (URC) (Closed 1992)

CYB (1860) 241–2. Miall (1868) 249. Peel (1891) *passim.* Tincker, D. C., *Providence Place Congregational Church* (1922). Turner II (1911) 661.

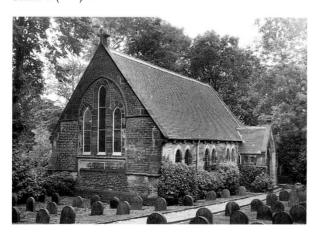

Friends' meeting-house, Scholes.   (95)

(95) FRIENDS, Scholes (SE 168250). Stone with paired lancets and gable finials; S porch. Built 1883 in simple Gothic style to designs by William Henry Thorp of Leeds for a recently formed meeting supported by the Crossland family.

Blamires, D., *A History of Quakerism in Liversedge and Scholes* (*c.*1971).

COLNE VALLEY   *W. Yorks.*

(96) BAPTIST, Pole Moor (SE 067159). A Baptist church, unable in 1788 to obtain land in Slaithwaite, acquired the present site, then waste-land two miles distant, from the freeholders of Scammonden. The first building of 1790 remains behind its successor of 1858–9; it comprised a chapel (30¼ft by 39¾ft) of four bays with a three-storeyed cottage attached to the west. The S front had two end doorways and two tiers of windows, the pulpit probably being central on this side. The second floor of the cottage is approached only from the former gallery.

The present chapel attached to the E has a front of three bays with a pediment. The interior has a horseshoe-shaped gallery, supported by marbled columns, and an organ gallery to the W; original box-pews remain throughout.

Monuments: in burial-ground to S, many table-tombs, ledger stones and other monuments of early 19th century and later including (1) Rev. Charles Bamford, first pastor, 1804, and Mary (Wrigley) his widow, 1815.

Shipley (1912) 232–4.

(97) BAPTIST, Scapegoat Hill (SE 088166). A school building erected 1849 by a section of the Pole Moor church was enlarged in 1863; in 1871 it was converted to a chapel and the present school built 1872–4, enlarged 1892. The chapel was rebuilt 1899–1900; a tablet from the first building with dates 1849, 1863, is loose in the chapel yard.

Haigh, N., *A Short History of the Baptist Church, Scapegoat Hill* (1921).

(98) STRICT BAPTIST, Slaithwaite (SE 081138). 'Providence Chapel' built 1816 was enlarged and re-fronted in 1886. Broad five-bay front with hipped roof and two tiers of windows; original walling at rear.

(99) Former WESLEYAN, Chapel Street, Slaithwaite (SE 082139). 'Centenary Chapel, 1839'. Three-bay front with platband and round-arched upper windows; hipped roof. Three-bay sides extended to rear. 'Wesleyan Schools' to NE with gabled front dated [?1871]. *Monuments*: in front of chapel, include Charles, son of Charles and Mary Wilkinson, 1846, *et al.*

Mallinson (1898) 76–8.

(100) FREE METHODIST, Slaithwaite (SE 081142). 'Ebenezer'; tall gabled front, *c.*1870.

CUMBERWORTH   *W. Yorks.*

(101) WESLEYAN, Cumberworth Lane, Denby Dale (SE 228087). Built 1799–1801 by a society formed when the Shelley Bank chapel (*see* (251)) passed to the New Connexion. Enlarged to rear 1839, refurbished and organ apse built 1877. The original chapel, of stone with a stone-slated roof (36¾ft by 49ft externally), has a broad pedimented front of five bays with two tiers of round-arched windows and a large inscribed tablet inserted in the

pediment in 1839. In that year the external length of the chapel was increased to 55 feet. A porch was added at the front in 1877.

Mallinson (1898) 71–3, 176.

DACRE
N. Yorks.

(102) CONGREGATIONAL (SE 192609). 'Providence Chapel' built 1827, of stone and slate, has a pedimental gable surmounted by a battlemented stone chimney stack. Upper windows in the front and side walls are blind. Interior refitted *c*.1897. (URC)

Monuments: in burial-ground (1) Thomas Atkinson, 1832; (2) Benjamin Grange, 1834; (3) Eliza, daughter of George and Sarah Whitley, 1831, *et al.*; (4) Samuel, son of Samuel and Grace Trees, 1839; (5) Elizabeth, widow of Thomas Grange, 1850, and William their son, 1830; (6) John, son of John and Margaret Swain, 1840, and Margaret their daughter, 1851. *Sundial*: in burial-ground, stone baluster-shaped pillar on circular base, horizontal dial inscribed 'GG 1828 Lat.51'.

Whitehead (1932) 166–88.

Providence Chapel, Dacre. (102)

(103) FRIENDS' BURIAL-GROUND (SE 186607). Rectangular enclosure S of Sand House Farm; dry-stone boundary walls and gateway on W side with lintel dated 1682. A meeting-house built 1696 and given to Friends 1697 stood against the N boundary. It was superseded in 1802 by a meeting-house at Darley (*see* (294)) and was demolished *c*.1860. The rectangular outline of the meeting-house is visible on the ground and structural masonry from its S wall has been reused. No *monuments* visible; earlier writers record (1) Wm. Clayton, 1706; (2) Ma. Bradley, 1730. *Sundial*: now at Adel, Leeds (*see* (269)).

Whitehead (1932) 163–6.

(104) WESLEYAN, Woodmanwray (SE 166612). Small isolated chapel near Dike Lane Head. Entrance at S end flanked by mean outbuildings; gabled end with renewed tablet dated 1839, small stone chimney stack at apex.

DARTON
S. Yorks.

(105) Former METHODIST NEW CONNEXION, Spark Lane, Mapplewell (SE 330100). Three-bay front, two tiers of round-arched windows, *c*.1850.

(106) Former FREE METHODIST, Spark Lane, Mapplewell (SE 329099). Low gabled front with two doorways and elaborately railed enclosure. Dated 1829.

DENBY
W. Yorks.

(107) FRIENDS, High Flats (SE 212075). From the mid 17th century Friends met at Lane Head, Kirkburton, where in 1695 the house of Joseph Firth, Hallroyd (now Lane Head House, SE 194090), was registered for meetings. The present site is believed to have been acquired in 1697 and a barn was converted for use as a meeting-house. The existing building of stone incorporates parts of a 17th-century structure, altered and extended to the W in the mid 18th century and heightened, re-fronted and partly refitted in the mid 19th century.

The S front is of ashlar with four plain sash windows and a porch, all of *c*.1850. The N wall has large quoins marking the end of the original building and three small blocked windows to the lowest stage. The former, lower, gables are visible at the E and W ends; in the latter is a blocked mullioned window of four lights. The interior comprises a single room (44½ft by 18½ft), the size of the original building, and a smaller room to the W above which an upper room extends into the meeting-room to form a gallery with fielded-panelled front and sliding shutters.

Fittings – *Chandelier*: twelve branches, of wrought iron with brass sconces, early 19th-century. *Monument*: fragment loose against N wall; to '[   ] wife of [   ] Dickinson', early 18th-century.

(108) WESLEYAN REFORM (SE 233081). 1908 with simple pedimented predecessor 'Zion Chapel, 1860' alongside.

DENHOLME
W. Yorks.

(109) BAPTIST, Southgate (SE 069339). Pedimented front; two porches with shaped gables. Dated 1866.

Shipley (1912) 127–8.

(110) INDEPENDENT (SE 070345). Built 1844, extended to rear 1896. Front with pedimental gable, paired entrances, centre window altered. (URC)

Miall (1868) 251.

(111) PRIMITIVE METHODIST, Denholme Gate (SE 070325). Two tiers of round-arched windows in three bays with doorways between. Dated 1834.

Primitive Methodist chapel, Denholme Gate. (111)

Congregational chapel (URC), Dent.   (112)

Congregational chapel (URC), Hallgate, Doncaster.   (117)

DENT   *Cumbria*

(112) CONGREGATIONAL (SD 704869). 'Zion Chapel' built 1835; rubble and slate. Round-arched entrance with two windows above in gabled end wall. Interior refitted 1895. (URC)

Miall (1868) 252. Whitehead (1930) 252–67.

(113) Former FRIENDS, Lea Yeat (SD 761869). Small meeting-house (36½ft by 33½ft externally) built 1701–3, altered *c*.1750 to provide a women's meeting-house at one side. Closed 1911, much altered *c*.1974 on conversion to a cottage. The S front originally had three windows; the entrance was in the W wall opening to a lobby.

Boulton, D., *Early Friends in Dent* (1986). Butler (1978) 152–4.

(114) WESLEYAN (SD 703871). Built 1834 on site of a Friends' meeting-house of 1700. Broad three-bay front; entrance re-sited, interior refitted.

Whitehead (1930) 255.

DEWSBURY   *W. Yorks.*

(115) WESLEYAN, Daisy Hill (SE 244217). 'Centenary Chapel' opened 1839; five-bay front with rusticated lower stage, plain ashlar above with terminal pilasters. Two tiers of round-arched windows, wide doorways in penultimate bays. Interior refitted and gallery closed by suspended ceiling.

(116) WESLEYAN, Briestfield (SE 229171). Three-bay front with round-arched openings; school-room below. Dated 1825.

DONCASTER   *S. Yorks.*

(117) CONGREGATIONAL, Hallgate (SE 578032). Built 1804, rebuilt or greatly altered 1874 and later. Three round-arched upper windows, Doric entablature and balustraded parapet. (URC)

Miall (1868) 255–6.

(118) FRIENDS, West Laithe Gate (SE 572031). Friends' meetings which began in a private house in French Gate in the late 18th century were strengthened by a decision of the Warmsworth meeting (*see* (446)) to move to Doncaster. In 1798 a barn was

acquired and converted for use as a meeting-house. Major alterations took place in 1897 when a building for the Friends' Adult School was added at the back.

The original building is of coursed rubble covered with later rendering. The front faces SE but an earlier entrance was in the NW wall and faced the burial-ground. The interior (60ft by 21ft) was formerly subdivided with the principal meeting-house at the NE end and a gallery opposite with women's meeting-house below. The roof is supported by six late 18th-century trusses with collars and pegged principals, but without tie-beams or ridge-piece. (Demolished *c*.1973)

Clark, H. M., *Notes on the Early History of Warmsworth and Doncaster Friends Meetings Houses* (1954).

Friends' Meeting-house, DONCASTER
Yorkshire W.R.

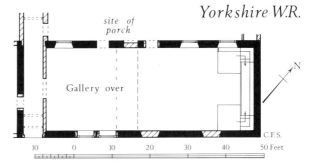

(119) WESLEYAN, Priory Place (SE 574032). The chapel built in 1832 superseded a preaching-house of 1770 which stood in St Sepulchre Gate. The front wall is of ashlar in five bays with a rusticated lower stage and round-arched upper windows. The interior has a shallow communion apse behind the later pulpit and a continuous round-ended gallery. (Much altered and floor inserted 1979)

Dolbey (1964) 127, 148–9.

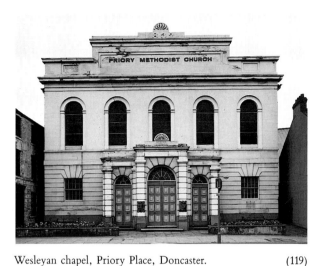

Wesleyan chapel, Priory Place, Doncaster.   (119)

(120) FREE CHRISTIAN, Hallgate (SE 577032). A plain brick chapel of 1912 concealed behind buildings on the S side of the street stands on the site of a small Presbyterian meeting-house of 1744. The latter had rendered walls and a pantiled roof; in the N and S walls were two round-arched windows with keystones and impost blocks.

Anon., *Notes on the Establishment of the Society of Protestant Dissenters...at Doncaster* (1892). Evans (1897) 73–4. Hargrove (*c*.1903). *UHST* VI (1935–8) 152–4.

Free Christian chapel, Hallgate, Doncaster. Before rebuilding. (From Hargrove (*c*. 1903).)   (120)

ECCLESHILL   *W. Yorks.*

(121) Former METHODIST, Lands Lane (SE 182364). The chapel, which was built largely through the efforts of Zachariah and Thomas Yewdall, Quaker converts of John Wesley, was opened in November 1775. On 26 April 1776 Wesley notes in his *Journal*: 'preached in the new chapel at Ecclesall [*sic*] to a people just sprung out of the dust, exceeding artless and exceeding earnest, many of whom seemed to be already saved from sin'. The power of the trustees to appoint and dismiss ministers was unsuccessfully resisted by Wesley (*Journal*, 2 May 1788). About

1823 land in Norman Lane was acquired for a burial-ground and in 1832 a vestry or cottage was erected alongside the chapel. In spite of a secession in 1838, the chapel remained in use until 1854–6 when it was superseded by a new building in Stony Lane. The chapel has since been used as a joiner's workshop.

The walls are of coursed stone in narrow courses with larger stone dressings and the roof is covered with stone slates. The S front has two plain doorways with gallery windows above and a pair of large round-arched windows with keystones and impost blocks which flank the site of the pulpit. The end walls to E and W are gabled with stone copings and shaped kneelers. The N wall has two square windows to the lower floor, one blocked, and two similar gallery windows above. All the windows have hung sashes.

The interior ($30\frac{1}{2}$ft by $36\frac{1}{4}$ft) has a flat plaster ceiling with moulded cornice and central roundel. A floor has been inserted at gallery level, but the original supporting beams remain for a gallery around three sides with square-section posts and moulded capitals below. The original roof structure includes three trusses with king and queen-posts and diagonal struts; two purlins each side have tusk-tenon joints to the principal rafters.

(Mrs Hammond, Norman Lane, kindly lent her notes on this building.)

(122) Former WESLEYAN, Stony Lane (SE 182361). Dated 1854, by James Simpson. Now Ukranian Orthodox.

(123) Former PRIMITIVE METHODIST, New Line, Greengates (SE 192372). 'Albion Chapel', built 1836 and much altered on conversion to a Liberal Club, had a broad front with four bays of windows in two tiers, the upper ones with round-arched heads and continuous cills. A further bay has been added to the right. The chapel may have been at the upper level with cottages below.

ELLAND   *W. Yorks.*

(124) STAINLAND CHAPEL (SE 082196). Now the parish church of St Andrew, Stainland Chapel was built in 1754–5, as a non-denominational proprietory chapel. It was supplied by Methodist and Independent ministers who were required by the trust deed to use the *Book of Common Prayer*, though the provision came to be neglected by the latter. John Wesley preached here on 21 April 1759, and records in his *Journal* 'It is a handsome building near the top of a mountain, and surrounded by mountains on all sides. It was filled from end to end. Mr Grimshaw read prayers and I preached on part of the Second Lesson.' Stricter enforcement of the provisions of the trust deed caused the Independents to form a separate society in 1813 (*see* (128)), and in 1838 the Wesleyans also erected a new chapel after which the trustees appear to have transferred the building to the Church of England; the new parish was constituted in 1843. The building was entirely refitted and a chancel built in 1888.

The chapel has stone walls and a slate roof. The original structure is of four bays with tall round-arched windows in the N and S walls, the cills now raised by about three feet. The former E wall, now removed, had a similar window asymmetrically placed to align with an aisle centrally between the S wall and the front of the N gallery. A tower at the W end, heightened in the mid or late 19th century and with ancillary accommodation added to N and S, may date in its lower stage from the previous

Former Methodist chapel, Eccleshill.   (121)

century. The interior (originally 38ft by 54ft) formerly had a tall canopied pulpit centrally against the S wall, a gallery round the other three sides, and the communion table in an enclosure below the E window. There is now a small gallery only at the W end.

Fittings – *Font*: dated 1842. *Monuments*: in NW vestry (1) John Bottomley, 1826, Betty his wife, 1815, and Hannah their daughter, 1807; (2) James Gledhill, 1792, recording a bequest of £100, part of the interest to be paid 'to the minister of Stainland Chapel for preaching a Sermon on Good-Friday. The remainder to be laid out in Linen Cloth and given to the Poor of Stainland'; (3) William Rothwell, 1817, and Mary his widow, 1821. In burial-ground, S of chapel, many monuments of late 18th century and after; N of chapel (4) headstone with winged cherub's head, to two infants, dated 1811. *Royal Arms*: on front of W gallery, Victoria. *Sundial*: on S wall 'Lat 53°40′ N Declination 15°0′ East. TIME IRRECOVERABLY FLIES 1826' with equations of time.

Hartley (1914). Miall (1868) 367. Watson (1775) 452.

(125) BAPTIST, Blackley (SE 102199). The first chapel was built in 1789 by James Cartledge, a member of the Salendine Nook church, as a thank-offering for the success of his coal-mining activities. In 1793 a gallery was added to the chapel and a church constituted which, after various troubles, was re-formed in 1798. A new chapel SE of the former was built in 1878–9.

The former chapel, now converted to cottages, has stone walls (42¾ft by 35ft externally) and a stone-slate roof. The end walls are gabled with stone copings and shaped kneelers. Above the

altered NE entrance is a blocked round-arched window and at the opposite end are two round-arched windows with keystones and imposts, also blocked, which appear to have flanked the pulpit. The longer SE and NW walls have two tiers of windows in five bays; the middle upper window in each wall was arched. The present chapel, dated 1878, has a pedimented front of four bays with two tiers of round-arched windows, and school-rooms below.

Monuments: in burial-ground, at SW end of former chapel in railed enclosure, nine table-tombs (1–9) and other monuments (1) Thomas Hadfield Woodhead, 1816, and John Woodhead his father, 1818; (2) John Cartledge, 1809, Betty (Woodhead) his wife, 1804, and Mary their daughter, 1798; (3) Hannah, widow of Jonathan Taylor, 'last surviving daughter of John Cartledge', 1860; (4) Mary (Woodhead), wife of John Cartledge, 1803, and Joseph Cartledge M.D., 1815; (5) James Cartledge, 1793; (6) Joseph Waterhouse, 1793, Ann his wife, 1807, Hannah their daughter, 1830, and Caleb Dickinson, 1870; (7) Dorothy Waterhouse, 1796, Charles Broadbent, 1832, *et al.*; (8) John Thomson M.D., 1818, with Latin inscription; (9) James Cartledge, 1828; (10) James Cartledge, 1827; (11) Dorothy Waterhouse, 1849. SE of former chapel (12) Mary (Lockwood), wife of Joseph Morton, 1793, Sarah (Mitchel), wife of Manuel Morton, 1795, *et al.*; (13) James Turner, 1797.

Anon., *Blackley Baptist Church, Elland – 175 Years of Witness* (1964). Shipley (1912) 234–5.

(126) CONGREGATIONAL, Elland (SE 110210). 'Providence

Chapel' built 1822–3, refitted or altered 1856 and later, has a gabled front of three bays with an arched recess enclosing the middle bay.

Miall (1868) 259.

(127) CONGREGATIONAL, Holywell Green (SE 088200). A school building in Tudor style by Joseph James was erected in 1853 principally at the expense of Joseph Crossley. It was also used for Sunday services and a church was formed here in 1867. A new chapel on an adjacent site in the Gothic style with corner tower and spire, by J. P. Pritchett of Darlington, built in 1872–4, was demolished c.1975.

CYB (1854) 281; (1872) 406. McKenzie, J. G., *History of Holywell Green Congregational Church, 1867–1917* (1917).

(128) Former CONGREGATIONAL, Stainland (SE 073193). 'Providence Chapel' was built 1813–14 by Independents formerly worshipping at Stainland Chapel (*see* (124)). The chapel, originally three bays in length, was enlarged to the rear by a similar amount in 1835–40 and a further bay added in 1863–73. In 1895 round arches were added to the upper windows of the side walls, a central entrance was made at the front and the interior was refitted.

The front wall has two original entrances which were set between three tall arched recesses, remade flush 1948, in the tops of which are lunette windows at gallery level. Two lower windows and a central doorway may be additions of the late 19th century. The wall appears to have been heightened and the gable rebuilt or added at the date of the first enlargement. (Chapel under conversion to tenements, 1989; many monuments in burial-ground broken or destroyed)

Monuments: in burial-ground, many ledger stones and other monuments of early 19th century and later, including in chapel (1) John Holroyd, 1819, Mary his widow, 1819, and Benjamin his brother, 1828. (2) Joseph Hepworth, 1854, Rebecca his widow, 1889, and their children, verse below with allusions to blacksmith's trade; (3) Joseph Shaw, 1825, Patience his widow, 1829, *et al.*; (4) Jeremiah Newton, 1819.

Allinson, M., *A Story of the United Reformed Church, Stainland*

Providence Chapel, Stainland.   (128)

(1984). Firth, N. M., *A Short History of Providence Congregational Chapel, Stainland, from 1914 to 1964 . . .* (1964). Haley, J., *Memorials of the Congregational Church at Stainland* (1864). Hartley (1914). Miall (1868) 367.

(129) METHODIST, Greetland (SE 088213). The chapel built 1777–80 was enlarged in the mid 19th century by the erection of an organ chamber on the N side and considerably refitted in 1897 when two new entrances were constructed. The walls are of coursed stone and the roof is covered with stone slates. The broad S front, of five bays with two tiers of windows separated by a platband, originally had entrances in the penultimate bays. The upper windows have three-centred arched heads, each formed of two stones. The E and W walls are gabled. A row of two-storeyed cottages adjoins the chapel on the E side.

The interior (36ft by 48¼ft) has a plaster ceiling divided into panels by moulded beams with central ceiling rose and ventilator. A gallery around three sides with splayed corners is a rebuilding of the late 19th century; it has a plain panelled front and is supported by cast-iron columns. The choir gallery behind the pulpit has a mid 19th-century fielded-panelled front divided by fluted pilasters. The roof is supported by four trusses with king and queen-posts and crossed braces; the purlins, four to each side, have tusk-tenon joints to the principal rafters. (Chapel demolished c.1975)

Fittings – *Clock*: in E gable with external dial and second dial below on gallery front, mechanism signed 'TITUS BANCROFT MAKER. 1822'. *Monuments*: in burial-ground S of chapel, 19th-century. *Pulpit*: mahogany, octagonal, on arcaded base with eight columns and leaf capitals, late 18th-century. *Sundial*: on S wall, square stone dial dated 1827 'Lat. 53° 41′ N Lon. 1° 55′W' with equation of time and motto 'Mind Heavenly things; for death hangs over every hour'. *Table*: in vestry, small mahogany side-table with rounded front corners, perhaps former communion table.

Chapman (1952) 19–20. Dolbey (1964) 86–7.

EMBSAY WITH EASTBY   *N. Yorks.*

(130) WESLEYAN, Embsay (SE 011539). 'Centenary Chapel, 1839'; much altered.

Providence Chapel, Stainland.   (128)

Methodist chapel, Greetland.   (129)

Methodist Chapel, Greetland   ELLAND, *Yorkshire W.R.*

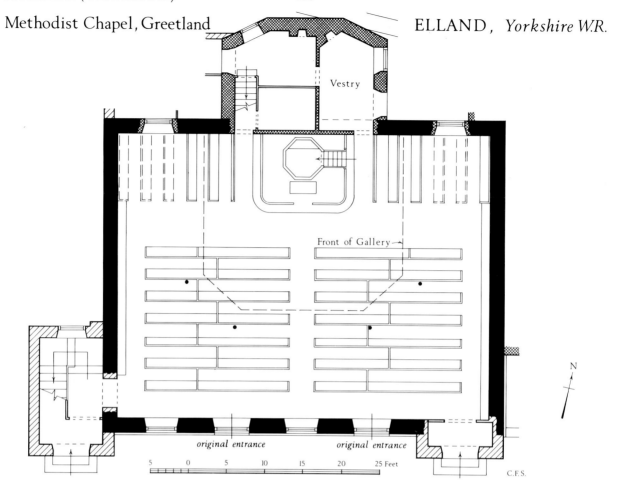

Vestry

Front of Gallery →

N

original entrance   *original entrance*

5   0   5   10   15   20   25 Feet

C.F.S.

(131) Former PRIMITIVE METHODIST, Eastby (SE 020544). Three-bay ashlar front with round-arched upper windows; early 19th-century. Converted to house.

FISHLAKE   *S. Yorks.*

(132) METHODIST NEW CONNEXION (SE 655134). 'Zion' dated 1834, brick with hipped roof and pointed-arched windows.

FLASBY WITH WINTERBURN   *N. Yorks.*

(133) WINTERBURN CHAPEL (SD 935587). The Presbyterian society formerly meeting here owed its origin to the interest of Mrs Barbara Lambert, daughter-in-law of Cromwell's Major General, John Lambert, whose house, Calton Hall ($1\frac{3}{4}$ miles W) served as a safe refuge for nonconformist preachers in the late 17th century. Oliver Heywood and Thomas Jolly both record visits to the Hall and the latter claimed to have dissuaded Mrs Lambert from joining the Quakers. Her particular concern for the society at Horton (*see* (214)) may, however, have delayed the formation of a regular congregation in Winterburn. In 1691 the Presbyterian Fund made a grant towards the provision of able ministers at Winterburn and elsewhere and in 1694 the house of Thomas Whalley was registered as a meeting-house.

The chapel was built by Thomas Whalley in 1703–4 and placed

in trust for Presbyterians. It stands on the site of one of two cottages known as Brigghouses which had been bought by Whalley for this purpose. Mrs Lambert gave an endowment for the chapel in 1708. The two 'Craven societies' maintained close links throughout the 18th century but by 1816, when a new chapel was built at Horton, Winterburn had fallen into decline; Congregational services were maintained with difficulty until 1880 when the chapel was closed. It was reopened in 1882 as an Anglican mission chapel for the parish of Gargrave although it remained Congregational property until 1917.

The chapel has rendered rubble walls with ashlar dressings and a stone-slated roof. The S front of five bays has a central doorway with chamfered jambs and a four-centred arched lintel in a square frame. The windows in two tiers are of two lights with straight chamfered mullions, the lower windows have hinge-pins for external shutters. The N wall has three similar windows at the upper level only. The gabled E wall is blank; at the SE corner is the chamfered jamb of a doorway probably related to the survivor of the two cottages on the site prior to 1703. The W end is covered by a late 19th-century vestry; traces of the sites of two windows one at each level are visible in the wall plaster.

The interior (20ft by 36ft) was 'thoroughly renovated' by Congregationalists *c.*1862 and no original fittings remain. The

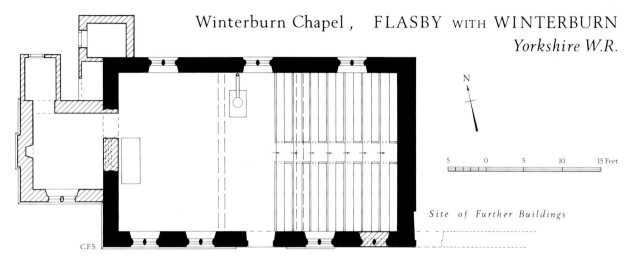

Winterburn Chapel , FLASBY WITH WINTERBURN
Yorkshire W.R.

N

5   0   5   10   15 Feet

Site of Further Buildings

C.F.S.

Winterburn Chapel.   (133)

pulpit was probably against the N wall and there may have been end galleries; the present layout of stepped seating at the E end dates from the 19th century. *Graffiti*: on plaster of E wall, large drawings in red line of cocks and other birds, and inscriptions '1784 John Gregson, Winterburn', '[ ] Gregson 1778'.

Miall (1868) 381. Nicholson and Axon (1915) 165. Whitehead (1930) 134–47.

Zion Chapel, Flockton.   (134)

FLOCKTON   *W. Yorks.*

(134) CONGREGATIONAL (SE 232149). A Presbyterian society existed in Flockton in the late 17th century with a privately built chapel with 'ceiled pews' and an endowed ministry. The present congregation (now URC) originated *c*.1800 and the chapel was built in 1802.

'Zion Chapel' has rendered stone walls; the S front of five bays with two tiers of arched windows has a simple pediment with a circular window. Two tall round-arched windows in the N wall flank the original site of the pulpit.

The interior has a gallery around three sides with splayed corners and contemporary box-pews; box-pews to the lower floor date from the mid 19th century. A lower organ gallery at the N end was built in the late 19th century.

Pulpit: incorporated into the centre of the organ gallery, of two tiers with upper desk supported at the front by two tall columns and clerk's desk below with panelled back flanked by pilasters.

Bielby (1978) 82–3. Miall (1868) 260–2.

(135) WESLEYAN, Barnsley Road (SE 244150). Three-bay front with round-arched windows, 1841. Extended and entrance re-sited in late 19th century.

FOUNTAINS EARTH   *N. Yorks.*

(136) Former PRIMITIVE METHODIST, Lofthouse (SE 101735). About 20 yards S of late 19th-century Wesleyan chapel, with two tall windows and doorway to left in front wall, of the mid 19th-century.

GARSDALE   *Cumbria*

(137) WESLEYAN (SD 741895). Gable end to road, dated 1830.

(138) PRIMITIVE METHODIST (SD 749896). Three-bay front dated 1841, between later buildings.

GISBURN FOREST   *Lancashire*

(139) CONGREGATIONAL, Tosside (SD 766559). 'Mount Sion Chapel' was built in 1812–13 for a congregation gathered by the Rev. Benjamin Sowden of Horton. The manse, adjacent to the chapel, also dates from the early 19th century. The walls are of

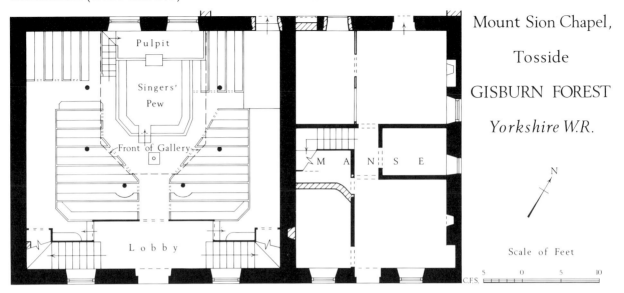

Mount Sion Chapel,

Tosside

GISBURN FOREST

Yorkshire W.R.

rubble, rendered at the front and the roof is covered with stone slates. The S front of the chapel is of three bays with two tiers of windows formerly with external shutters. The N wall has two windows flanking the pulpit and two at the ends of the gallery. There is a school-room behind the manse built *c*.1830–40.

The interior has a gallery around three sides with splayed corners and a panelled front supported by turned wood columns. In front of the late 19th-century rostrum pulpit is a singers' pew supported above floor level by dwarf columns. The gallery staircases were enclosed and square balusters removed in the late 19th century.

Inscription: on oval tablet above outer doorway 'Mount Sion, Chapel AD 1812'.

Miall (1868) 371–2. Whitehead (1930) 238–51.

Cooke, 1845, first minister; (2) Rev. David Wilson, 1864, 'pastor of the Independent Church, Birstal'.

Miall (1868) 262–3. Peel (1891) 206–12.

(141) WESLEYAN, Latham Lane (SE 205265). Broad bow-fronted chapel dated 1827 with side wings containing entrances and gallery staircases. Two tiers of windows formerly with hung sashes and marginal glazing replaced since 1970 by plain flush grilles. The interior has a gallery around three sides and a later organ chamber behind the pulpit. It was largely refitted *c*.1870–80 apparently by George Mallinson. *Monuments*: in burial-ground at rear, several table-tombs of early 19th century and later.

Bielby (1978) 77–8. Peel (1891) 200–1.

CONGREGATIONAL CHAPEL, TOSSIDE   CFS 1970

GOMERSAL   *W. Yorks.*

(140) CONGREGATIONAL (SE 208264). 'Grove Chapel' was built in 1825–6 on land given by James Burnley who also paid for the adjacent Sunday-school. The chapel was much altered and enlarged in the late 19th century. The NW front has three bays of round-arched windows in two tiers below a pediment. The Sunday-school is of four bays with a hipped roof.

Monuments: in burial-ground SE of chapel (1) Rev. John Hall

Wesleyan chapel, Latham Lane, Gomersal.   (141)

(142) UNITED METHODIST, Bradford Road, Birkenshaw (SE 202 287). Chapel *c*.1871, Sunday-school 1908 with reset tablet, 1822.

(143) MORAVIAN (SE 208253). The society which until 1755 formed part of the Fulneck congregation built the first chapel on

this site in 1751. A Single Sisters' house of that date was rebuilt on a new site in 1785 and again in 1798. Houses were built at each end of the chapel in 1793. The chapel was rebuilt on the same site in 1868–70 incorporating parts of the original end walls. It is a tall building of brick with a slate roof surmounted by a square louvre. The houses of 1793 remain at each end, of red brick with stone dressings. The former chapel had doorways at each end and three round-arched windows between.

Monuments: in burial-ground, 200 yards E, acquired 1790, small plain rectangular slabs in numbered series, male burials N, female burials S, of central path (1) No. 1, John Peel, 1790; (2) No. 2, Thomas Hanson, 1791; (3) No. 3, Peter Scaif, 1791; (4)

WESLEYAN CHAPEL, GRANTLEY   CFS1974

No. 4, Mary Gray, 1791; later stones are of greater elaboration, e.g. (5) No. 143, Mary West, 1810.

England (1887) 11–12, Plate 3. Heywood *et al.* (1955) 6–11.

GRANTLEY   *N. Yorks.*

(144) WESLEYAN (SE 232699). Small chapel of stone, three-bay front formerly with doorway to left, later central porch; early 19th-century.

GRASSINGTON   *N. Yorks.*

(145) CONGREGATIONAL (SE 004641). The chapel built in 1811 has rendered rubble walls and a stone-slate roof. The SW front has two round-arched doorways with fanlights and three small upper windows. The end walls have each three windows at gallery level and below. The interior has a gallery around three sides with splayed corners. The internal appearance has been adversely affected by alterations *c*.1980 including the introduction of a false ceiling and the renewal of the pulpit.

Monuments: in chapel on N wall (1) Rev. Richard Harper, 1829; in burial-ground (2) James Hudson, 1834, Abigail his widow, 1862, and five children, 1816–28, table-tomb on six baluster legs in walled enclosure next to entrance gate (dismantled *c*.1980); (3) William Tomson, 1816, headstone. *Seating*: in gallery, full set of pews with panelled and balustraded backs, 1811.

Whitehead (1930) 289–303.

Congregational chapel, Grassington.   (145)

Congregational chapel, Grassington. Interior before 1980. (145)

(146) WESLEYAN, Chapel Street (SE 003643). Although a chapel was opened in 1811 the present building was not completed until 1825. Front of three bays with two tiers of round-arched windows below pedimental gable. Gallery around three sides, re-fronted but retaining early 19th-century seating of steeply ranked box-pews.

(147) Former PRIMITIVE METHODIST, Chapel Fold (SE 003642). The chapel, dated 1837, stands above a cottage which rises to two storeys below the stepped seating which formerly filled the lower end of the chapel. Superseded 1907.

GREAT HOUGHTON   S. Yorks.

(148) GREAT HOUGHTON CHAPEL (SE 430065) is reputed to have been built in 1650 by Sir Edward Rodes, whose father Sir Godfrey Rodes was the first to occupy Great Houghton Hall. The hall built c.1580 for his fourth son by Francis Rodes of Barlborough, the prominent Elizabethan lawyer, stood to the E of the chapel; it was demolished c.1960. The first known minister was Thomas Johnson who received Presbyterian ordination in 1655; he was ejected in 1662 when vicar of Sherburn-in-Elmet. Richard Taylor, described as 'chaplain to Sir E. Rhodes', appears to have been here in 1662. Support for dissenting ministers was continued by Lady Rodes after her husband's death in 1666, notably Jeremiah Milner who officiated in 1672 and continued as chaplain to the family probably until his death and that of his

patroness in 1681. Nathan Denton, the last survivor of the ejected ministers, was a frequent preacher here in the late 17th century and was still an occasional visitor in 1713. How well a regular congregation was maintained in the later 18th century is not recorded although Miall (op. cit. below) suggests that a close connection existed with the Presbyterian society in Doncaster. At the opening of the 19th century R. S. Milnes, who had married the heiress to the property, through whom it descended to Baron Houghton and ultimately to the Marquis of Crewe, was said by Palmer (op. cit. below) to have engaged a minister 'to perform divine service once a month'.

About 1845 the chapel passed out of nonconformist use, becoming a chapel-of-ease to the parish church of Darfield.

The chapel is a long, narrow, rectangular building aligned approximately E–W with walls of soft sandstone partly repaired by rendering; the roof is now covered with artificial stone slates. The walls have a chamfered plinth, moulded string-course above the heads of the windows on all except the W side, and a corbelled battlemented parapet with rounded merlons which are grouped as central features on the N and S sides and rise in crow-stepped formation up the E and W gables. The W gable is surmounted by a stone bell-cote with a single bell.

In the E wall slightly S of centre is a window of three lights with straight-chamfered mullions divided by a transom and pointed-arched heads to the upper lights. Centrally in the gable is

GREAT HOUGHTON CHAPEL

Yorkshire W.R.

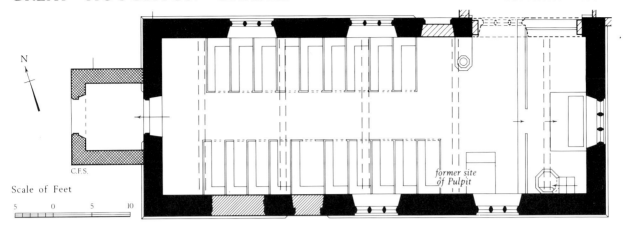

N

Scale of Feet

C.F.S.

5   0   5   10

former site of Pulpit

Great Houghton Chapel. Before addition of vestry.   (148)

a shield-of-arms with helm and mantling, now very decayed, bearing quarterly the arms of Rodes and Milnes. The N wall has three regularly spaced windows of like pattern, but that at the E end has been reset since 1960 in a modern vestry wing; a pointed-arched doorway between the eastern pair of windows has been blocked internally. The S wall repeats the features of the opposite wall but with the doorway nearer the W end; this has been blocked and an adjacent end window possibly removed. The W wall has a pointed-arched doorway inside a W porch of slightly later date but of the same general design.

The interior (55ft by 19¾ft) has been scraped and a plaster ceiling removed exposing five plain king-post roof trusses. A wide opening has been pierced at the E end of the N wall.

Fittings – *Pulpit*: octagonal with panelled sides in three tiers the middle range having arched panels and the upper tier being carved with formal enrichment; panelled back-board and octagonal tester; *c*.1650. *Seating*: box-pews with acorn finials, enriched upper panels to door and ends, original hinges; *c*.1650.

Ambler (1913) 61, Fig. 98. Matthews (1934) *passim*. Miall (1868) 264. Palmer III (1803) 446n.

GREAT OUSEBURN   *N. Yorks.*

(149) CONGREGATIONAL (SE 446619). Brick with gabled front and two circular windows to gallery. Built 1858 to replace a chapel of 1816.

Miall (1868) 264. Whitehead (1932) 237–51.

GREEN HAMMERTON   *N. Yorks.*

(150) Former CONGREGATIONAL (SE 459571). The chapel (approximately 32ft by 23ft externally) was built in 1797, a gallery was added in 1801 and in 1902 a porch, originally with a lean-to roof, was built at the S end and a Sunday-school room added at the rear. The building passed into Roman Catholic use *c*.1960–70.

The walls are of brick and the roof is covered with pantiles. The S wall is gabled and has a rebuilt porch between two round-arched windows. The E wall has three similar windows set in wide arched recesses.

Inscription: on E wall over centre window, stone tablet inscribed 'OPENED Oct. 8, 1797 with a TEXT from Prov. IX.1.'. *Monuments*: externally against E wall (1) Mark Ingham, 1805; (2) Ann, wife of William Hobson, 1851. *Sundial*: over original S doorway, small stone dial dated 1808.

Miall (1868) 264. Whitehead (1932) 232–50.

FORMER CONGREGATIONAL CHAPEL, GREEN HAMMERTON   CFS 1970

GRINDLETON   *Lancashire*

(151) FRIENDS, Sawley (SD 773467). A meeting-house at Newby, 3 miles E, was superseded in 1742 by the first building on the present site. The existing meeting-house, built in 1777, has stone walls with ashlar quoins and a stone-slated roof. It includes a small two-storeyed cottage at the SW end which was enlarged *c*.1870. The SE front of the meeting-house is symmetrical with a round-arched doorway between two windows of three lights with widely spaced square mullions. In the gabled NE wall is a secondary entrance with two gallery windows above.

The interior of the meeting-house comprises a single room (27½ft by 21¼ft) with a deep NE gallery which is closed above by hinged shutters; between the windows in the gallery is a contemporary fireplace with hob grate. The stand has a central entrance, and fielded-panelled front and back.

Friends' meeting-house, Sawley.   (151)

Books: include Besse's *Sufferings of the Quakers*, 2 vols. (1753), William Sewel, *History of the Quakers* (1722), and the *Works of William Penn*, 2 vols. (1726); in each volume of the last is inscribed the name of the original purchaser William Greenwood, the cost of the two volumes, one guinea plus eight pence carriage from London, and a record of their gift to his son, John Greenwood, 7th of 8th Month 1727.

(152) WESLEYAN, Harrop Fold (SD 749496). The chapel opened in 1819 stands on an isolated site. The walls are of rubble, coursed at the front, and the roof is covered with stone slates. The front wall has a doorway between two tiers of windows with renewed frames, and to the right a two-storeyed annexe for use as a vestry and Sunday-school room. The chapel is approximately square with a gallery above the entrance approached by a stone staircase, a fireplace in the end wall, and pulpit between two windows opposite the entrance.

WESLEYAN CHAPEL, HARROP FOLD   CFS 1974

HALIFAX   *W. Yorks.*

(153) NORTHGATE END CHAPEL (SE 094254). Several Presbyterian meetings were commenced soon after the Restoration in and around Halifax supported by Oliver Heywood and other ejected ministers including Eli Bentley, former vicar of Halifax. A society in Halifax which was in existence by 1693 may have been the successor to Bentley's congregation. This society acquired a close at the end of North Gate called 'Bell Croft' as a gift from the minister Nathanial

Northgate End Chapel, Halifax. (153)

Priestley. On this was built the first meeting-house opened 11 November 1696 by Oliver Heywood. The builder is named as Timothy Stock, the total cost being £200. The building was altered in 1762 when the walls were raised by some five feet, presumably to permit the addition of galleries. In 1817 the S wall was rebuilt, the roof renewed and the interior refitted. In 1847 the W end was rebuilt. By 1870 the congregation, which since the late 18th century had been regarded as Unitarian, were no longer satisfied with the condition or appearance of the chapel and decided on its replacement.

The earlier chapel was aligned east and west. The W front of 1847 had paired Ionic pilasters supporting a pediment, and a lunette window above the central entrance. The pulpit was against the longer S wall and galleries extended around the other three sides. At the E end was a lunette window at gallery level and a window below in front of which the communion table appears to have stood.

The present chapel by J. A. Davies of Leeds, opened in 1872, stands on the site of the former. It is of stone in the Gothic style with a gabled W front divided by buttresses and pinnacles. It comprises a nave, N and S transepts with galleries, and a short chancel. Below the chapel is a large school-room and alongside to the S is a hall, the 'Judge Stansfield Memorial Rooms', built in 1884. (Chapel and fittings sold by auction 13 November 1979; since demolished)

Fittings – *Brasses*: (1) Ann, widow of Samuel Heywood descendant of Oliver Heywood 'one of the founders of the Presbyterian churches in this neighbourhood', 1825; (2) Edward Ferguson, 1736, John his son, 1775, Ann (Threlkeld), wife of the last, 1773, and their children Martha, 1837, Edward, 1843, and Ann, 1846; (3) William Kershaw, 1837, and Hannah his widow, 1846; (4) James Lord, chapel warden, erected 1885; (5) John Richardson, 1825, his sisters Elizabeth Walton, 1840, and Mary Richardson, 1856, and Elizabeth (Walton), widow of Charles Ronayne, 1881; (6) Thomas Holmes, 1848, and Hannah (Ibbetson) his wife, 1841; (7) George Brown, 1839, and Elizabeth his wife, 1832; (8) Oliver Heywood, erected late 19th century.

Glass: in W window, figures of faith, hope, charity and fortitude, signed 'S. Evans, artist, West Smethwick, Birmingham', with memorial inscription below to Thomas Holmes

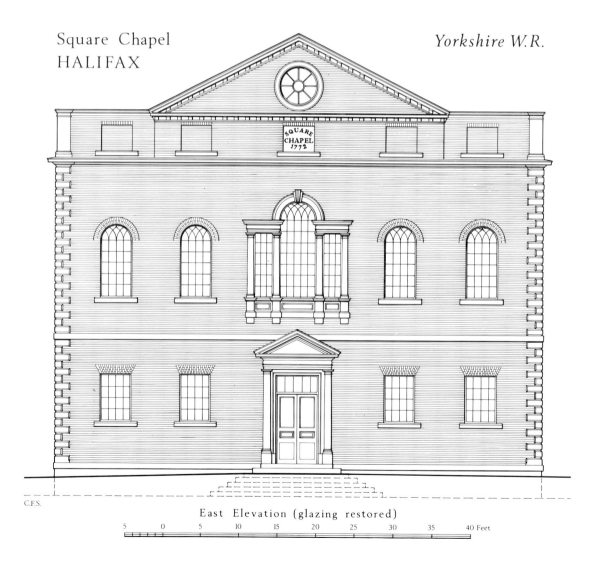

Square Chapel
HALIFAX

Yorkshire W.R.

SQUARE CHAPEL 1772

C.F.S.

East Elevation (glazing restored)

5   0   5   10   15   20   25   30   35   40 Feet

Edleston, 1857; in N windows with biblical scenes and memorial inscriptions below to Rev. William Turner, Richard Kershaw Lamb, 1870, James Stansfield.

Inscription: in basement school-room, reset in S wall, date stone of first meeting-house '1696' with later inscription 'rebuilt 1872'. *Monuments* (*see also* Brasses): in chapel on W wall (1) John Thomson M.D., 1818, white marble tablet with draped pedestal in low relief bearing a portrait roundel above a representation of Asclepius's staff, signed 'Chantry, sculptor, 1820'; (2) John Rhodes, 1818, white marble tablet with seated female weeper, draped urn in low relief with shield-of-arms, portrait bust on pedestal, signed 'Chantry sc. 1823'; on N wall (3) Rawdon Briggs, 1835, and Anne his wife, signed 'Ternouth sc. Pimlico, London'; (4) Rev. Joseph Ralph, 27 years minister, 1795, and Dorothy (Rhodes) his widow 1824; on S wall (5) Rev. William Turner Jnr. M.A., 25 years minister, former tutor at Manchester College, York, 1853; (6) Thomas Holmes Edleston, chapel warden, 1857, signed 'Morton Bros. Hx.'.

Panelling: fronts of N and S galleries, bolection-moulded panels separated by panelled pilasters, reused from galleries of former chapel. *Plate*: includes two cups of 1792. *Sculpture*: on bracket in basement school-room, bust of Rev. William Turner, 1853, by J. B. Leyland.

Christian Freeman (November 1872) 168–70. Evans (1897) 99–100. *Halifax Courier* (5 October 1872). Miall (1868) 265–6. Millson, F. E., *Two Hundred Years of The Northgate-End Chapel, Halifax, A.D. 1696, 1896* (1896).

(154) SQUARE CHAPEL (SE 096251). The Congregational church originated in the work of Titus Knight, a former collier and Methodist convert, who adopted Independency under the influence of the Countess of Huntingdon; with the support of William Grimshaw he built the first meeting-house in 1762. This stood behind a barn on the S side of Gaol Lane, 45ft by 24ft in size with a small forecourt on the W facing Chapel Fold. It was converted to three cottages in 1772 and has since been demolished. The much larger Square Chapel, opened May 1772, was built on a new site in Talbot Croft, S of a new 'square'; the name is thought to derive from the latter rather than its plan. It was built with assistance from several benefactors, of whom the principal subscriber and overseer of the works was James

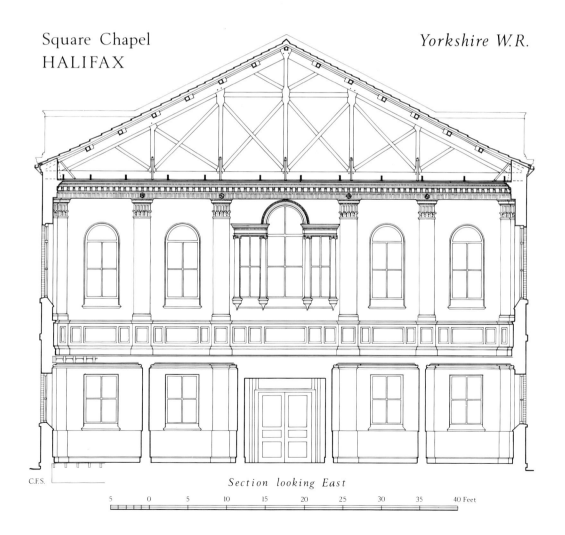

Square Chapel
HALIFAX

Yorkshire W.R.

C.F.S.

Section looking East

5   0   5   10   15   20   25   30   35   40 Feet

Square Chapel, Halifax.

(154)

Square Chapel, HALIFAX   *Yorkshire W.R.*

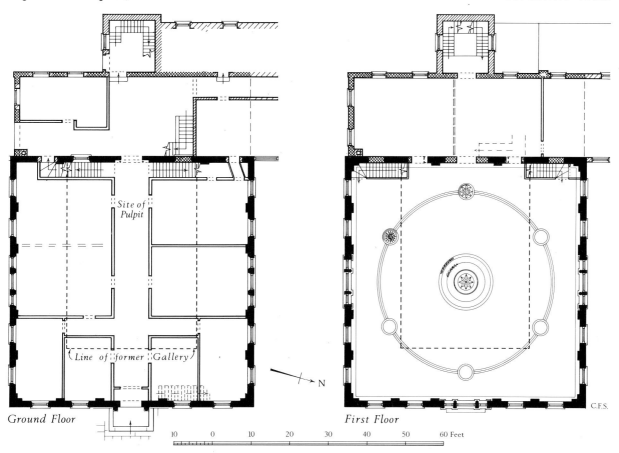

Ground Floor   First Floor

10   0   10   20   30   40   50   60 Feet

Kershaw, formerly a member of Northgate End. John Wesley visited the chapel shortly after it was opened, remarking in his *Journal* that it was larger than the Octagon Chapel in Norwich, 'full as superb . . . and finished with the utmost elegance'. The chapel was superseded in 1855 by a new Gothic chapel on an adjacent site and the former building was converted for Sunday-school use. The later chapel was closed in 1970 and severely damaged in a series of fires in 1970–2.

The former chapel of 1772 has walls of red brick with stone dressings and a slate roof. The E front, of five bays, has a stone plinth, platband and cornice, and stone quoins. A pediment over three bays incorporating a circular window rises above a tall parapet with blind rectangular recesses. The central doorway has a pedimented entablature supported by attached Roman Doric columns. Above it is a Venetian window with moulded details; other windows are plain with flat-arched heads to the lower tier and round-arched above. The W wall, similar to the foregoing but less elaborate and with a tripartite lunette in the pediment, is covered by a three-storeyed Sunday-school extension of the early 19th century and later. The N and S walls, also of five bays with plain Venetian windows centrally to the upper stage, now have no parapets though these are indicated on an early engraving.

The interior (60ft square) was greatly altered *c.*1855 when the

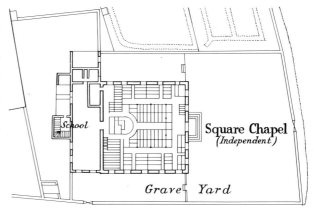

whole of the seating and gallery structure was removed and a floor inserted, minor rooms created on the lower floor and a single large meeting room above. The layout of the former seating is indicated on the 1:500 Ordnance Survey plan of 1850 (above) with a gallery on three sides and pulpit near the W end but standing well forward from the wall. Stone staircases remain in the NW and SW corners, the former bearing indications of reuse but the latter apparently original.

Much of the late 18th-century plaster decoration remains in the upper room. This has a flat plaster ceiling with elaborately moulded and enriched cornice, large circular band interrupted by six small circular ventilators, and a central roundel with Greek key ornament and inner circuit of oak leaves about the pendant base of a ventilator for the principal chandelier or a later gaselier. The walls are divided into bays by broad pilasters with fluted capitals having single bands of acanthus leaves; the bases and panelled dado below are mid 19th-century alterations. The three remaining Venetian windows (the W window is blocked) carry a full enrichment including intermediate columns and end pilasters with four-sided Ionic capitals. The roof is supported by five trusses of oak with pine tie-beams, having king and queen-posts and crossed braces.

The chapel of 1855 is an ambitious building in stone in the Gothic style of the 14th century by Joseph James. It comprises a wide aisle-less nave with end gallery, galleried transepts and an organ chancel behind the central pulpit. The tower in the angle between nave and S transept rises to a tall crocketed spire with corner pinnacles.

(Since 1972 the outbuildings of the 1772 chapel and the whole of the 1855 building except the steeple have been demolished. The 1772 chapel has been repaired and reopened in 1991 as a public concert hall)

Fittings – *Inscriptions*: painted on timbers of 1772 roof trusses, include 'Painter WM 1830 do. 1841', 'J Farrar 1844', 'Wm Foster 1810', 'AA Priestley 1876'. 'J Smith Painter April 18[7]6', 'J Thompson Plumber 1867', 'R H Parker 18[?94]'.

Monuments: in burial-ground E and S of 1772 chapel numerous ledger stones of late 18th century and after, including, near SE corner (1) [   ] Tayl[or], 8 Nov. 177[ ] 'The First Corps inter'd at this Place'; near NE corner (2) Rev. T. Knight, first pastor, 1793, Elizabeth his widow, 1806, and their children Martha, 1792, and John, surgeon, 1800. *Pulpit*: loose in upper hall, wood, square with fluted corners, pilasters with floral enrichment and panels with fluted borders, the front panel carrying a winged head and sunburst in high relief, 1772. *Sculpture*: loose behind chapel, stone representation of head and shoulders of a minister wearing gown and bands, possibly 18th-century.

Curnock (1938) V: 475. *CYB* (1858) 264–6. *Halifax Courier* (5 October 1872). Hanson, T. W., 'The Old Independent Chapel in Chapel Fold', *HAST* (1936) 29–52. Miall (1868) 267–8. Seymour (1839) I: 283–5.

(155) SION CHAPEL, Wade Street (SE 095254). The first chapel on this site was built at the beginning of the 19th century for a former Wesleyan preacher, David Barraclough. He conducted undenominational services there until 1813 when he became minister at Stainland chapel. After a brief occupation by a Southcottian congregation the chapel passed into Congregational use, at first from 1815 to 1816 as a temporary home for Square Church while their chapel was under repair and then for a distinct congregation. The chapel was rebuilt in 1819–20 and variously altered internally after 1829 and particularly in 1853. A Day School was built alongside in 1846 and a Jubilee Memorial Sunday-school erected in 1866. The chapel was closed *c*.1960 and has since passed into commercial use.

Sion Chapel, Wade Street, Halifax.   (155)

The chapel has ashlar walls and a hipped slate roof. The S front of three principal bays has a recessed centre with a colonnade of four attached Greek Doric columns and central entrance. The side bays have each a lunette window in an attic storey which is continued across the frontage and includes a rectangular window above the main entrance. The side walls have two tiers of windows above a basement storey. The former 'Sion Schools' of 1846, W of the chapel, have a broad front of seven bays with an arched central entrance rising to an Italianate turret.

Dale, B., *Jubilee Memorial of Sion Chapel and Schools* (1867). Miall (1868) 268–9.

(156) CONGREGATIONAL, Harrison Road (SE 091249). Built 1837 for seceders from Square Chapel. Two doorways with Venetian window between and round-arched windows above. (URC)
Miall (1868) 269.

(157) CONGREGATIONAL, Hopwood Lane (SE 084251). 'Park', built 1867–9 in the Gothic style by R. Ives and Sons, has a corner tower rising to an octagonal turret and spire. (URC)
CYB (1870) 372. Miall (1868) 269.

(158) Former FRIENDS, Highroad Well (SE 068252). The meeting-house built or converted in 1696 and superseded in 1743 stands on the S side of Gibbet Street just beyond the W extremity of the original township of Halifax. It was converted to two cottages in 1743, the S front was rebuilt and an outshot erected against the N wall. An original upper window, of six round-

FORMER FRIENDS MEETING-HOUSE, HALIFAX   CFS 1977

arched lights, now blocked and the mullions removed, remains at the W end. The interior (31ft by 19¼ft) has been entirely altered.

(159) FRIENDS, Clare Road (SE 093248). The meeting-house built 1743 to replace the foregoing has stone walls with rusticated quoins at the E end and shaped kneelers to the E gable. It was greatly altered in the 19th century, extended to the W, refenestrated and entirely refitted. The S front has traces of two former entrances and in the E wall at a low level are two blocked mullioned windows of four and two lights. The interior (45ft by 26¾ft), which was formerly divided into two meeting-houses, now comprises a single room with stand at the E end.

Monuments: removed from Highroad Well and from a private burial-ground at Shaw Hill, now fixed on S wall or reset internally (1) 'Mary wife of Jonathan Hallidy of Northourom', 1694; (2) Hannah, daughter of John Elam, 1694; (3) Elizabeth Laycock, 1703; (4) Jonathan Laycocke, 1696, recut; (5) Mathew Wright of Bradford, 1672, 'who give this parcel of ground for a burying place to the children of light called Quakers'. (Meeting-house sold for office use 1990)

Halifax Weekly Courier and Guardian (16 August 1952).

(160) Site of METHODIST, Church Lane, now South Parade (SE 096248). The first preaching-house built in 1752 in succession to a room at Cow Green opened in 1749 was rebuilt in 1777 and registered in July of that year as the 'New Preaching House, Church Lane'. It was enlarged in 1812 and superseded in 1880 by a new chapel in Prescott Street. The former building was demolished in the late 19th century for railway improvements.

Pulpit: from 1777 chapel, was removed 1885 to St Paul's Wesleyan chapel, Brighouse and thence in 1949 to Hill Street Unitarian chapel, Poole, Dorset (*see Nonconformist Chapels and Meeting-houses in South-west England*).

Chapman (1952) *passim*.

(161) HANOVER CHAPEL, Kings Cross Street (SE 089250). Former Methodist New Connexion chapel, now the Playhouse, built 1834, closed 1943. Front of three bays with broad terminal pilasters and narrow pediment. Porch with two Greek Doric columns.

(162) CONGREGATIONAL, Mixenden (SE 055280). The formerly Presbyterian Society meeting in Moor End chapel originated in the late 17th century with the preaching of Mathew Smith from Kipping Chapel who became its first pastor. The first meeting-house, which still survived in 1868 after conversion to cottages, stood half a mile from the present site. The first chapel at Moor End was built in 1717, rebuilt in 1810 and again in 1836. During the 18th century ministers of varying orthodoxy occupied the pulpit; a Congregational church (now URC) was formed *c*.1816.

The chapel, of stone with a hipped stone-slated roof, has a S front of three bays with a platband between two tiers of windows. Prior to 1890, when the upper windows were lengthened, a central entrance constructed and the interior entirely refitted, there were two outer doorways with moulded cornices and a three-light mullioned window between. Adjacent to the E is a fragment of earlier building, possibly of 1810 but incorporating a small oval window with stone surround inscribed with the initials and date 'MᔆS 1717' for Mathew Smith and Susan his wife. The interior of the chapel has a gallery around three

Congregational chapel, Mixenden.   (162)

sides supported by iron columns. An organ recess was built to the N *c*.1890. NW of the chapel is a Sunday-school with elaborately lettered tablets recording its erection in 1821 and enlargement in 1848. (Demolition of chapel proposed 1983)

Fittings – *Chairs*: two, late 17th-century. *Monuments*: in chapel on E wall (1) Rev. Thomas Smith, late minister of Selby, grandson of Rev. Mathew Smith, 'founder of this chapel', 1854; externally against W wall (2) Jonas Foster, 1778, Lydia his wife, 1785, Jonas their son, 1799, *et al.*; against S wall (3) John Garforth, 1770, *et al.*; (4) Thomas Evans, minister, 1779, with Latin inscription; (5) James Richie, minister, 1763, with Latin inscription; against E wall (6) Rev. John Smith, 1768; (7) Susanna Clay, 1781; in burial-ground (8) John Preston, 18 years minister, 1853, *et al.*, table-tomb; (9) William Smith 'who officiated as Clerk of this chapel for upwards of twenty years', 1821, *et al.* (A monument to Rev. Mathew Smith, 1736, is no longer visible). *Sundial*: on front of earlier building to E, dated 1771.

Armitage, H., 'Mixenden Chapel', *HAST* (1964) 1–15. Miall (1968) 316–20.

(163) CONGREGATIONAL, Northowram (SE 111267). The church (now URC) formed in 1672 now meeting in 'Heywood Chapel' owes its origin to the work of Oliver Heywood, minister of Coley Chapel whence he was ejected in 1662. He subsequently engaged in an extensive ministry, settling in Northowram in 1672 in a house which he had formerly occupied and which was licensed for Presbyterian preaching. An unsuccessful attempt was made to license Coley Chapel for dissenters in 1672. Heywood's cottage, 100 yards N, was used for meetings from 1672 to 1688. It was much altered in the late 18th century or after; in the front wall is a former door lintel inscribed 'OᴴA/EBENEZER/1677' for Oliver and Abigail Heywood.

The first chapel was erected largely at Heywood's expense between April and July 1688 on a site 45ft by 36ft, E of the present building, in the SE corner of a close called 'Well-Butts'. It is described as 'being 3 large bays with Bolings [large beams], 2 bays lofted'. In 1710 further land was acquired to enlarge the meeting-house to the W and in 1783 a third gallery was added. A sketch of questionable authenticity shows the chapel with six bays of windows in the front wall; in the inner bays is a pair of round-arched windows, presumably flanking the pulpit, with date tablet above while the outer bays have two tiers of windows and doorways adjacent to each corner.

The present chapel, built 1836–7, was enlarged to the W in 1853 by the addition of an organ chamber, the window frames were altered in 1887 and various changes made to the interior in 1863 and 1894. It is a plain building of stone with two tiers of windows. The E front is gabled and has a shallow arched recess enclosing the doorway and upper window of the central bay. The interior has a gallery around three sides and school-rooms below the chapel.

Fittings – *Book*: Bible with Apocrypha, folio, 'printed by Charles Bill and the Executrix of Thomas Newcombe deceased', 1701. *Inscription*: reset externally in S wall, tablet from former chapel with monogram OH for Oliver Heywood and date 1688. *Monuments*: in burial-ground E of chapel, against wall of cottage (1) Martha, wife of James Pollard, 1753, *et al.*, ledger stone; (2) Rev. Thomas Dickinson, 1743, Hannah his widow, 1765, their sons Thomas, 1754, and John, 1764, *et al.*, wall monument attached to surviving fragment of wall of former chapel; in burial-ground (3) Rev. Robert Hesketh, 1774, headstone with Latin inscription; (4) Dorothy Clark, 1819, table-tomb.

Pulpit: in chapel, incorporating steps, open-desk top and cupboards below, reputedly in use 1672–88 at Heywood's cottage, 17th-century. *Sundial*: reset in NW wall of burial-ground, square stone, upright dial dated 1780 with eagles and signs of zodiac.

Brayshaw, L., *Oliver Heywood, his Church and Chapel* (1972). Miall (1868) 325–7. Pearson, M., *Northowram, its History and Antiquities* (1898). Turner III (1883) 234; IV (1885) 128, 131, and *passim*.

(164) CONGREGATIONAL, Ovenden (SE 077274). 'Providence Chapel', built 1836–7, has been variously altered internally, notably in 1877–8 when the gallery was lowered. This is a plain stone building closely resembling the chapel at Northowram (*see* (163)) and probably by the same builder; the design was supplied gratuitously by Mathew Naylor. (URC)

Miall (1868) 270. Trigg, W. B., *History of Providence Congregational Church, Ovenden* (1937).

(165) Former CONGREGATIONAL, Warley (SE 057248). Presbyterian meetings commenced in the late 17th century and a permanent meeting-house was erected in 1705. The present chapel, dated 1845 but possibly incorporating earlier material, has a stone front of three bays divided by octagonal buttresses which rise to battlemented turrets. The windows have four-centred arched heads. In the rear wall above a large blocked window are two stones from the former chapel inscribed '1705', 'Repair'd 1805'. Small front gallery only. (Closed *c*.1973; under conversion to house 1986)

Miall (1868) 377–8.

(166) WESLEYAN, Keighley Road, Illingworth (SE 070289). The chapel of 1877, by James Farrar, replaces a chapel of *c*.1799 erected by Wesleyans who left Mount Sion, Upper Brockholes. (*see* (170)) when that passed to the New Connexion.

Moore, H., 'The story of Illingworth Moor Methodist Church', *HAST* (1969) 29–54.

(167) Former WESLEYAN, Luddenden (SE 042261). Polygonal front, two tiers of windows above basement, dated 1837. Now Working Men's Club.

(168) Site of WESLEYAN, Luddenden Dean (SE 030287). Plain three-bay chapel with gabled front and two tiers of windows, built 1828, demolished after fire 1954. Date tablet reset in burial-ground. Wesleyan School, 1878, 100 yards SE.

Monument: in burial-ground, Thomas Midgley, over 60 years a Wesleyan local preacher, 1897, Mary his wife, 1887, and their sons Matthew, 1837, and Foster, 1877.

Turner, W., *A Spring-time Saunter* (1913) 12–14.

(169) WESLEYAN, Mount Tabor (SE 053273). Gabled three-bay front with round-arched upper windows and later porch; opened 1820. Sunday-school 1835, rebuilt 1871. Large burial-ground.

(170) MOUNT SION CHAPEL, Upper Brockholes (SE 068297). Methodist meetings commenced about 1755 at the house of James Riley at Bradshaw, $\frac{3}{4}$ mile NE. In 1772 the need was seen for a permanent preaching-house and the present site, then waste ground at 'Tod-moor Green', was acquired. The first chapel, opened in 1773, was visited by John Wesley on 22 April 1774 who described it in his *Journal* as 'standing alone in a dreary waste'. In the disruption of 1796–7 the trustees and the majority of the society supported the Kilhamite reformers and successively held the property for the Methodist New Connexion. The chapel was rebuilt in 1815 although a cottage which formed part of the earlier structure remains at the W end.

Mount Sion Chapel, Upper Brockholes. (170)

The chapel has a broad S front of four bays with two doorways and two tiers of round-arched windows with late 19th-century frames. The end walls are gabled and have shaped kneelers. At the rear is a semicircular projection, added *c*.1840 to provide a vestry with singers' gallery above. The adjacent cottage is of two storeys with five-light mullioned windows to the south.

The interior (38ft by 43$\frac{1}{2}$ft) was refitted *c*.1881 by Leeming and Leeming of Halifax. There is a gallery around three sides with angled corners. The singers' gallery has a plaster semi-dome with moulded dentil cornice and swag decoration now largely concealed by the organ. In the W wall of the vestry is a blocked outer doorway.

Fittings – *Inscriptions*: On S wall, tablet recording the rebuilding in 1815; above vestry fireplace, tablet from earlier chapel with date 1773 and text from Psalm 100 (Common Prayer version). *Monument*: in front of chapel, Joseph and Susanna, children of John Child, 1779, Jonathan Child, 1781, and later inscription to Daniel Child, 1843; there is an extensive burial-ground. *Seating-plans*: in vestry, with pegs for allocation, 1881. *Sundial*: on S wall, dated 1773, 'Mount Sion'.

Bradley, J., *Mount Zion, Ogden 1773–1973* (1973). Moore, H., 'The story of Illingworth Moor Methodist Church', *HAST* (1969) 29–32.

(171) WESLEYAN REFORM, Wainstalls (SE 047283). 'Mount Pleasant', built 1857, has a low gabled front with central doorway between two plain Venetian windows. Sunday-school 1893. Walled burial-ground adjacent.

Wesleyan Reform chapel, Wainstalls.   (171)

HAREWOOD   *W. Yorks.*

(172) WESLEYAN (SE 323449). The society was formed *c.*1760 by John Pawson, then a builder employed on Harewood House. The chapel was built as a pair of two-storeyed cottages about 1755 as part of an intended industrial development for ribbon manu-facture; they were leased to Methodists in 1814. The front is of three bays with a central doorway.

WHSP XXVII (1949–50) 129–34.

HARROGATE   *N. Yorks.*

(173) BAPTIST, Victoria Avenue (SE 306551). 1882–3 by William Peachey. Corner tower with octagonal upper stage and spire.

(174) CONGREGATIONAL, Victoria Avenue (SE 302551). The church began with cottage meetings in the early 19th century. In 1821 a chapel was built known as 'Cross Chapel' from its cruciform plan; it was sold in 1831. The former chapel-of-ease on the Stray, built 1744, was then acquired and the materials used to build 'Providence Chapel', opened 1838. The present chapel, built on a new site in 1861–2, is a stone building by Lockwood and Mawson in the Gothic style with a corner tower rising to an octagonal turret and spire. The W front formerly had two doorways, now converted to windows; a doorway has been inserted into the W wall of the tower and a pinnacle on the W gable removed. The S wall has six individually gabled windows with head stops representing early nonconformist worthies and others.

Bell: Whitehead (op. cit. below) records that the bell in the tower came from St John's chapel-of-ease.

CYB (1863) 299, 302. Miall (1868) 270. Whitehead (1932) 253–82.

(175) WESLEYAN, Oxford Street (SE 302555). 1862, by Lockwood and Mawson. Five-bay pedimented front with giant Corinthian pilasters and attached columns.

(176) WESLEYAN, Park Road (SE 303545). Large Gothic chapel, built 1879, corner tower and broach spire added 1889.

(177) PRESBYTERIAN, Victoria Avenue (SE 303551). Built 1885. Nave with wooden clerestory, transepts and corner tower. (URC)

HARTWITH CUM WINSLEY   *N. Yorks.*

(178) FRIENDS BURIAL-GROUND, Hardcastle Garth (SE 227605). Rectangular enclosure bounded by stone walls; in use *c.*1658–1859.

Whitehead (1932) 46–7.

(179) Former WESLEYAN, Summer Bridge (SE 200625). Built *c.*1830. Converted to Board School 1894 when new chapel built and former date tablet re-lettered. Pedimental front gable, round-arched windows.

HATFIELD   *S. Yorks.*

(180) WESLEYAN, High Street (SE 664095). Brick with hipped roof; opened 1844.

(181) PRIMITIVE METHODIST, Goodcop (SE 731084). Small brick chapel with hipped pantile roof. Three-bay front, dated 1839; porch later.

PRIMITIVE METHODIST CHAPEL, GOODCOP   CFS 1974

(182) METHODIST NEW CONNEXION, Hatfield Chase (SE 718 106). 'Salem chapel', brick with hipped roof, three-bay front with pointed-arched windows and doorway, rebuilt 1851. Porch added 1893.

HEBDEN ROYD   *W. Yorks.*

(183) Former BAPTIST, Market Street, Hebden Bridge (SD 991 272). 'Ebenezer Chapel' was built in 1777 for the Rev. John Fawcett and some of his congregation from Wainsgate (*see* (438)) to serve the needs of the growing town. A new chapel was built in 1858 (*see* (184)) and the former building was subsequently used as a Sunday-school until 1873 and for social purposes; it was sold in 1919, used as a printing works and latterly for the sale of bric-à-brac.

Former Baptist chapel, Hebden Bridge.   (183)

The chapel has a broad stone front to the S with rusticated quoins and a platband between two tiers of windows. Between two pedimented doorways with eared architraves is a pair of round-arched pulpit windows with keystones and moulded imposts. The E wall is gabled and has a Venetian window centrally at each level. The W end is covered by the former manse, a contemporary though architecturally distinct building of three storeys, now much altered. The N wall is built into the hillside and has windows at gallery level only.

The interior ($35\frac{3}{4}$ft by $41\frac{1}{4}$ft) has been floored over at gallery level; it formerly had a gallery around three sides with angled corners. Original staircases remain in the NE and NW corners with moulded stone treads; the former had (in 1967) a handrail with a single turned baluster to each step. The roof structure, common to chapel and house, has four queen-post trusses with king-struts and collars.

Fittings – *Monuments*: in small burial-ground in front of chapel (1) William Greaves, 1801, Sarah his widow, 1807, *et al.*; (2) John Foster, 1814, Ann his widow, 1816, and John their son, 'author of the Essays "Decision of Character" on the Evils of Popular Ignorance', 1843; (3) Grace Townsend, 1785; (4) Sarah, daughter of John Fawcett of Brearley Hall, 1785, table-tomb; (5) Henry Riley, murdered 1818, flat slab supported by four turned stone legs. *Panelling*: some wall panelling remains at gallery level. *Sundial*: on front wall, square stone dial dated 1835, 'Lat. 53° 48' Decl. 3° 40' ', motto 'Quod petis umbra est' and equations of time.

Ivimey IV (1830) 568–75. Shipley (1912) 219–20. Williams, C. *et al.*, *A Brief History of the Baptist Church, Hebden Bridge, Yorkshire* (1878).

(184) BAPTIST, Hebden Bridge (SD 993272). Hope Chapel, built 1857–8 for the congregation at the foregoing, has a pedimented stone front of three bays with pilasters. The interior, partly refitted in the late 19th century, has a gallery around three sides.

Monuments: in gallery, removed from Ebenezer Chapel (1) Rev. John Fawcett D.D., 1817, signed 'S. Manning'; (2) John Fawcett, son of the last, 1837.

Shipley (1912) 219–20.

(185) Former BAPTIST, Brearley (SE 025259). Bethel Chapel, built 1845 for a newly formed Particular Baptist church, has a front of three bays with pedimental gable. It was converted to cottages following the erection of a new chapel further west. The latter, built 1875, closed 1976 and now in commercial use, has a basement room at the N side, formerly with stepped seating, for use as a day school.

Bingham, A., *Jubilee Commemorative Souvenir, 1875–1925* (1925). Jackson, A., *Brearley Baptist Church, Centenary 1875–1975* (1975). Livingstone, W. A., *These Sixty Years 1845–1905* (1905). Shipley (1912) 223–4.

Former Baptist chapel, Brearley.   (185)

General Baptist chapel, Birchcliffe, Hebden Bridge.   (186)

(186) Former GENERAL BAPTIST, Birchcliffe (SD 995274). A society gathered by Dan Taylor, a former Methodist, met from 1762 in a house in Wadsworth Lane (SE 005273). In the following year Taylor was baptized by General Baptists at Gamston, Nottinghamshire, and returned to reorganize his society as the first General Baptist church in Yorkshire.

In 1764 a chapel was built at Birchcliffe which was enlarged in 1793 by the addition of a larger gallery. The chapel was rebuilt in 1825. A new chapel, converted to a conference centre since 1974, was built on a new site 100 yards W in 1897-9; the earlier chapel has been demolished.

A sketch of the 1764 chapel shows a rectangular building with a mullioned-and-transomed window of five round-arched graduated lights in the gabled S wall and three windows each of three similarly arched lights in the W wall with a doorway between the right-hand pair; attached to the N end is a house of three storeys.

The chapel of 1825 had a broad W front of six bays with two tiers of round-arched windows, doorways in the penultimate bays and a pair of taller pulpit windows between. The former house, against the N wall, still stands and is dated 1855.

The chapel opened in 1899 is a large Italianate structure by Sutcliffe and Sutcliffe. The SW end is of three bays with a pediment between lower pedimented pavilions and an arcaded porch of five bays across the front. The interior is subdivided by arcades of four bays with polished granite columns and clerestory windows above. Galleries extend along each side and at the SW end. The central pulpit is in a NE chancel with baptistery behind. There are minor rooms below the chapel. Since 1974 lower seating has been removed and a floor inserted at gallery level.

Fittings – Inscriptions: on S wall of former manse, tablet reset from front of 1825 chapel 'BIRCHCLIFF CHAPEL Built Anno Domini 1764 Enlarged Anno Domini 1825 JEHOVAH-JIREH'; on fragment of walling of former Sunday-school S of above, two tablets (1) 'SUNDAY SCHOOL BUILT BY Subscription for the Instruction of poor Children A.D. 1827. The Ground (220 sq yds) was kindly given . . . by Richd Sutcliffe Esqr. of Lumb Bank, and Betty his Wife, youngest Daughter of the late Henry Cockroft Esq of Great Burlees . . . ' signed 'J. Brown, Lap'; (2) 'BIRCHCLIFF SCHOOL BUILT A.D. 1827. REBUILT AND ENLARGED A.D. 1871.'

Monuments: in 1899 chapel (1) Rev. Henry Hollinrake, 49 years pastor, 1855, erected 1857, signed 'Fisher, York'; in burial-ground W of former chapel (2) Thomas Tobson, 43 years Master of the Heckmondwike Subscription Schools, 1858, and Elizabeth his wife, 1834; (3) Charles Lord, 1863, Grace his widow, 1872, and Betty Smith their daughter, 1863; (4) Rev. Henry Hollinrake, 1855, Sally his widow 1860, Mary Elizabeth, daughter of Joseph and Grace Wheelhouse, 1852, and Emlie Wheelhouse, 1861, table-tomb; (5) John Lord, 1878, and Charlotte his widow, 1899. (Monuments in old burial-ground broken up 1980)

Anon., A Short History of Birchcliffe Baptist Church, Hebden Bridge (1899). B.Hbk (1898) 322-4. Shipley (1912) 216-18. Taylor (1818) II: 70-9, 178-82, 270, 385-7. Wood (1847) 182.

(187) STRICT BAPTIST, Osborne Street (SD 994272). 'Zion Chapel' built 1881-2 for a church formed 1839 by seceders from

Wainsgate (see (438)) stands on a steeply sloping site with two-storeyed cottages below the SW end.

Anon., Song of Zion (1982). Grace (June 1982) 5-7.

(188) WESLEYAN, Mytholmroyd (SE 012257). A Sunday-school commenced in 1799 by Baptists from Hebden Bridge was re-formed with the assistance of Wesleyans who subsequently assumed the sole charge. The present site 'in one corner of a large meadow called the Great Ing' was acquired in 1806 and a school or chapel erected. In 1814 this was found to be structurally unsafe and a new one was constructed in 1815. The present chapel was built on the SE side of the school-rooms in 1825 and the latter were rebuilt on an extended site in 1872.

The chapel has a broad NE front with two tiers of round-arched windows in four bays and two doorways between. The gabled SE wall has four bays of plain windows and similar windows occur on the SW side where a later organ chamber projects at the centre. The interior (44ft by 49ft) has a gallery around three sides with angled corners, supported by cast-iron columns. In 1895 the ceiling was rebuilt and the pulpit replaced by a wide rostrum. The roof is supported by four queen-post trusses, the purlins have tusk-tenon joints to the principal rafters. (Chapel demolished 1985 following structural failure)

Fittings – Love-feast Cups: seven, including two with two handles. Monuments: in front of chapel, table-tombs of early 19th century and later, large burial-ground at rear. Seating: to lower floor, complete set of early 19th-century box-pews, the central rank, lined with red baize, have mahogany desk fronts and cast-iron umbrella stands of various dates.

[Smith, A.J.], Mytholmroyd Wesleyan Methodist Church . . . (1906).

(189) Former WESLEYAN, Cragg Vale (SE 003234). Three-bay gabled front with two tiers of round-arched windows. Octagonal chimneys at apex of front and rear gables. School-room below chapel. Tablet in front gable dated 1835. (Converted to house after 1973)

Monuments: headstones against front wall (1) Henry Greenwood, 1881, Mary his wife, 1877, and Sarah their daughter, 1903; (2) Grace, wife of Henry Whitaker, 1873, and Mary Grace, daughter of John and Elizabeth Whitaker, 1875; (3) Sally, wife of Henry Fawthrop, 1845, and their sons, David, 1847, and William Henry, 1865; (4) John Barker, 1870, Mary his wife, 1842, and William their son, 1859. (Monuments now removed)

(190) Former PRIMITIVE METHODIST, Mytholmroyd (SE 015 262). A chapel built in 1837 and forming the upper storey of a pair of cottages with external staircase remained until after 1970 behind the 'Huntsman' Inn, in Midgley Road; it has since been demolished. It was superseded by 'Mount Zion' chapel (SE 014261) in 1887 which was demolished in 1970.

## HECKMONDWIKE	W. Yorks.

(191) CONGREGATIONAL (SE 222237). The 'Upper Independent Chapel' was built for a church formed in 1674 by Josiah Holdsworth, ejected rector of Sutton upon Derwent, Yorkshire. A meeting-house was provided c.1686 by conversion of a barn in Chapel Fold and a new one erected in 1701. This was superseded in 1761 by a meeting-house in the NW corner of the present

Wesleyan chapel, Mytholmroyd.   (188)

Upper Independent Chapel, Heckmondwike. (191)

burial-ground and in 1845 by another chapel on the present site.

In 1859 a separate building was opened for the use of day schools and a Sunday-school, and the chapel was rebuilt in 1888–90. A secession had occurred in 1786, when some members built a separate chapel in Westgate, known as 'Lower Chapel'; that was rebuilt 1866.

Upper Chapel, designed by a local architect Arthur A. Scott, is a large prominently sited building of stone with a pedimented portico with four giant Corinthian columns and flanking bays, one rising to an octagonal turret, each surmounted by a tall polygonal dome. The interior, seating 1,300, has a horseshoe-shaped gallery with elaborately panelled front supported by fluted iron columns, a large rostrum pulpit with semicircular railed communion space in front and an organ recess behind. The original lower seating comprises box-pews set in radiating pattern facing the pulpit. The school building alongside has a front of five bays with a three-bay pediment. (Chapel closed before 1977, conversion to secular use proposed)

Monuments: in large burial-ground at rear, table-tombs and other monuments of the 18th century and later; in front of chapel, more elaborate monuments of the later 19th century; reset in boundary wall between chapel and school, fragment of grave slab dated 1675.

Bielby (1978) Pls. 85, 86. Burnley, E. G. and Walker, J. W., *Upper Independent Church, Heckmondwike 1674–1924* (1924). *CYB* (1889) 222; (1891) Fig. 212. Miall (1868) 271–6.

HEPTONSTALL
W. Yorks.

(192) Former GENERAL BAPTIST, Heptonstall Slack (SD 977287). Seceders from the New Connexion in Hebden Bridge opened a disused Particular Baptist meeting-house adjacent to Robertshaw Farm in 1807 and built the first chapel on the present site in 1808. A manse for the first minister, James, son of the Rev. Dan Taylor, was built soon afterwards alongside the chapel and in 1819 the latter was enlarged by 6 yards to the rear, heightened, and partly refitted. The manse was extended to the S after 1827 and in 1834 a larger gallery was constructed in the chapel. The chapel was rebuilt in 1878–9. A separate Sunday-school of 1863 behind the chapel superseded the use of the earlier meeting-house which had served this purpose from 1810.

The original 'Zion Chapel' of 1808 had a broad E front of five bays with two tiers of plain windows and doorways in the penultimate bays; its size is stated to be 13 yards by 10 yards. The present chapel on the same site, by T. Horsfield of Manchester, has a gabled front of five bays with round-arched windows. The interior (approximately 65ft by $39\frac{1}{4}$ft) has a continuous gallery with an organ in the polygonal W end above two vestries. The ceiling is divided into large panels by deep moulded beams. (Chapel closed 1974; since altered internally)

The Sunday-school W of the chapel, dated 1863, has a low pedimented front of three bays with a porch.

Fittings – *Baptistery*: below platform in front of pulpit, metal tank with steps on N side and a further flight to W through

Upper Independent Chapel, Heckmondwike.   (191)

General Baptist chapel, Heptonstall Slack.   (192)

doors below pulpit with direct access to vestries. *Chair*: in pulpit, with carved back panel, shaped frame and arm rests, 17th-century. *Inscription*: tablet from former chapel reset in back wall 'Mount Zion built 1808 enlarged 1819'. *Monuments*: in burial-ground in front of chapel, many table-tombs, ledger stones and headstones of early 19th century and later. *Pulpit*: narrow rostrum with two staircases and doors below to allow passage from baptistery.

Brown, P. and Greenwood, J. W., *Heptonstall Slack Baptist Church, 1807–1957, Ter-Jubilee Celebrations* (1957). Shipley (1912) 222–3. Taylor (1818) II: 387–9. Thomas, E. G., *Centenary Souvenir of Heptonstall Slack Baptist Church 1807–1907* (1907). Wood (1847) 206.

(193) METHODIST, Northgate (SD 988282). William Darney, a shoemaker and evangelist from Scotland, began an itinerant ministry in the West Riding and East Lancashire in 1742, forming his converts into a number of societies one of which was at Heptonstall. In 1747 Darney placed his societies under the authority of John Wesley, whose first visit to the district was made in that year. The Heptonstall society met in a house at Northgate End and elsewhere until the erection of the present chapel in 1764. The chapel, built as a regular octagon in conformity with Wesley's ideals, was enlarged in 1802 by lengthening it to the rear. In the late 19th century vestries were constructed below the N gallery and early in the 20th century a large rostrum replaced the former pulpit and displaced the communion area which previously lay behind.

The chapel has stone walls and a slate-covered roof. Each bay has rusticated quoins at the corners and two tiers of plain windows separated by a platband at gallery level. The original round-arched entrance was blocked c.1802 and replaced by doorways in the adjacent bays.

The interior (36ft across, lengthened to 51ft) was refitted in 1802 and later. A loan of £160 in 1772 to build 'a loft or gallery in Heptonstall chapel' may indicate that the chapel did not at first

have galleries. These are said to have been supported by stone columns, but the present gallery has a fielded-panelled front supported by timber columns with moulded capitals. The roof structure probably dates entirely from 1802. It comprises two queen-post trusses with king-posts and four purlins to each slope with tusk-tenon joints to the principal rafters and half trusses to the angles. The novelty of the original structure is reported to have been such that the roof could not be constructed locally but had to be made by carpenters in Rotherham, where an octagon chapel had recently been built, and carried thence by road to Heptonstall.

Fittings – *Seating*: in gallery and central space below, box-pews of early 19th century, side pews below gallery installed 1903 in place of loose forms. *Tables of Creed and Commandments*: below pulpit, painted on plaster face of inserted brick wall, Lord's Prayer, Apostles Creed, and Decalogue, late 19th century.

Dolbey (1964) 101, 107–9. Gee, C. H., *Methodism in Heptonstall* (1939).

(194) WESLEYAN, Edge Hey Green (SD 964288). Dated 1891, tablet from earlier chapel (?1841) said to remain in back wall.

HIGH AND LOW BISHOPSIDE   *N. Yorks.*

(195) Former METHODIST, Park Road, Pateley Bridge (approximately SE 158656). The chapel, which was later converted to two cottages, was built in the late 18th century; it had four-centred arched windows. The building was demolished c.1960–70. (A stone dated 1776 and the original pulpit are reported to be in the present chapel)

Curnock (1938) V: 177. *Methodist Recorder* (Winter Number, 1906) 87.

HOLMFIRTH   *W. Yorks.*

(196) CONGREGATIONAL 'Lane Chapel', Holmfirth (SE 139081). Built 1889–90 to replace a chapel of 1778 erected for Independent members from Netherthong (*see* (200)). In burial-ground opposite, monuments including table-tombs of early 19th century.

CYB (1891) 217–18. Miall (1868) 277–8.

(197) CONGREGATIONAL, Honley (SE 136117). Rebuilt 1911. Monument in burial-ground opposite, Rev. James Potter, 35 years minister of Moorbottom chapel, 1872, and Mary his wife, 1844.

Miall (1868) 278–9.

(198) FRIENDS, Wooldale (SE 153091). The meeting-house, dating from the late 17th century, was largely rebuilt in 1783. The walls are of coursed stone and the roof is covered with stone slates. The S front has four large windows of 19th-century character and a small doorway of earlier date near the W end with chamfered jambs and altered lintel. The N wall has been heightened and partly covered by later buildings but is largely of the late 17th century.

The interior (36¾ft by 26¾ft) has a low stand at the E end. A gallery of 1783 at the W end has a fielded-panelled front supported by two Roman Doric columns; it is closed above and below by hinged shutters. (Much alteration and repairs, including entire renewal of roof structure, reported completed 1984)

Methodist chapel, Northgate, Heptonstall.   (193)

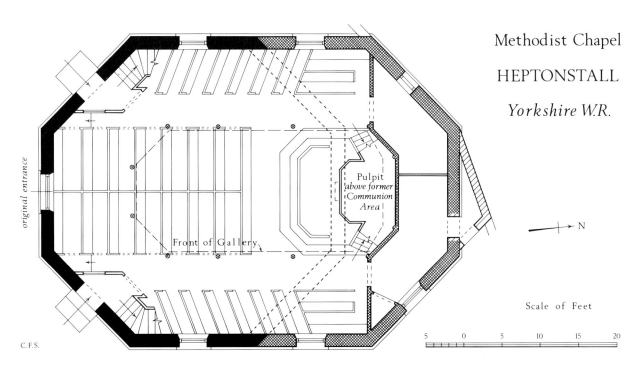

original entrance

Front of Gallery

Pulpit
*above former
Communion
Area*

Methodist Chapel

HEPTONSTALL

Yorkshire W.R.

N

Scale of Feet

5   0   5   10   15   20

C.F.S.

Friends' meeting-house, Wooldale. (198)

Monuments: in burial-ground, mid 19th-century and later, also many unmarked mounds (some earlier stones are reported to have been found built into the walling of the meeting-house). *Sundial*: free-standing S of meeting-house, stone pillar surmounted by 12-inch cube with dials on five faces, gnomons missing, dated 1802.

Bower, D. and Knight, J., *Plain Country Friends: The Quakers of Wooldale, High Flatts and Midhope* (1987).

(199) LYDGATE CHAPEL, New Mill (SE 159091). A small Presbyterian society which about 1690 was holding monthly meetings in the house of a blacksmith, John Armitage, encouraged by visits from Oliver Heywood, built a meeting-house at Lydgate in 1695. The society, which by the 19th century had a Unitarian ministry, is said to have rebuilt the meeting-house in 1768. The chapel, of stone with a slate roof, is three bays in length with gabled ends to which an E porch rising to the full height and surmounted by a bell-cote was added in 1848.

The W wall has two plain Venetian windows flanking the pulpit, the minor lights blocked in the 19th century. The N and S walls have each three round-arched windows with keystones and impost blocks. The original E end has shaped kneelers to the gable; the E doorway has a semicircular arched head with narrow flanking windows and a round-arched window above. The bell-cote, of stone, has six polygonal piers supporting a domed top with ball finial.

The interior (36¾ft by 24ft) is entered at the E end through a later lobby flanked by two narrow gallery staircases. The E gallery, erected in 1786, has a fielded-panelled front divided by fluted pilasters and supported by a pair of turned wood columns. The original pews are divided by a central aisle, wider at the W end next to the pulpit where some alterations, including the addition of iron communion rails, were made in the mid 19th century.

Fittings – *Books*: chained to communion table, *The Works of the Most Reverend Dr John Tillotson, Late Lord Archbishop of Canterbury*, 3 vols. (1712–20). *Chair*: with carved panelled back, dated 1689. *Glass*: in all windows, opaque white glass divided vertically by bands of yellow glass with intermediate squares of

Lydgate Chapel. (199)

Former Methodist chapel, Netherthong.   (200)

blue and red, *c.*1848. *Inscriptions*: on late 17th-century panels incorporated into pews in SW corner (1) 'BA'; (2) 'MM/1695'; (3) 'IOHN ARMITAGE 1695'; on S wall (4) 'EA'; on N wall, brass plates from pew doors (5) 'Jonas Hobson THURSTELAND 1800'; (6) 'Jno Hobson MITHAM BRIDGE 1800'.

Monuments: in chapel on S wall (1) John Morehouse, 1811, *et al.*; on N wall (2) Rev. Joseph Marshall, 49 years minister, 1814. Externally, against S wall (3) Rev. John Byram, 1709, and [Mary (Booth)] his wife, 1706, headstone recut or renewed; near W wall (4) Sarah, wife of Rev. Joseph Marshall, 1786, Joseph their son, 1786, *et al.*, table-tomb. *Pulpit*: square with chamfered and fluted corners, panelled back-board and square canopy with moulded cornice, re-entrant front corners, and knob pendant on soffit, late 18th-century. *Seating*: box-pews with fielded-panelled doors, late 18th-century.

Evans (1897) 158–61. Hargrove (*c.*1903). Miall (1868) 310. *UHST* x (1951–4) 181–4.

(200) Former METHODIST, Netherthong (SE 139099). A society including both Independents and Methodists, formed as a result of the evangelical preaching of the Rev. Henry Venn in Huddersfield, built a 'New Preaching House' here about 1769 which was registered in the following year. A division within the society soon left the building entirely in Methodist hands; John Wesley records (*Journal*, 6 July 1772) his preaching at 'the New house at Nether Thong'. The society was much weakened about 1848 by secessions to the Wesleyan Reformers. A subsequent revival led to drastic internal changes to the building in 1860–1. The adjacent chapel house was rebuilt in 1875 and further

Former Methodist Chapel, Netherthong
HOLMFIRTH, *Yorkshire W.R.*

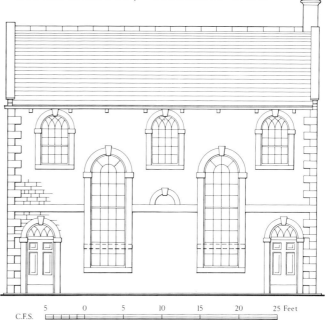

alterations to the interior were made in 1888. The chapel was closed in 1957.

The chapel stands on a steeply sloping site on the N side of a narrow valley. The walls and roof are of stone. The S front has two doorways, two tall windows flanking the site of the pulpit and three upper windows all with round-arched heads having square imposts and keystones. The windows have original glazing bars with intersecting bars to the upper tier. The principal windows have been lengthened and have between them a blind lunette, perhaps intended to enclose an inscribed tablet. The E wall was largely rebuilt in 1866 with two plain windows at each level. The N wall, facing a lane behind the chapel at gallery level, is of a single storey with two plain doorways, one blocked, and two windows.

The interior (34ft by 36ft) was entirely altered in 1861 when a floor was inserted at gallery level leaving the lower storey for Sunday-school use only. The original pulpit was destroyed in a fire in 1843 and the later subdivision and subsequent alterations have left no original fittings in position. The lower part of the chapel (23¾ft deep) does not extend below the N gallery which stands above unexcavated ground. The gallery appears to have continued along the E and W walls. The original roof structure remains with three trusses having king and queen-posts with raking struts and purlins with tusk-tenon joints to the principal rafters.

Fittings – *Gates* and *Railings*: in front of chapel, late 18th-century. *Monuments*: S and E of chapel, table-tombs and ledger stones from late 18th century; in NE corner of upper burial-ground (1) Abel Hobson, 1889, Betty his wife, 1839, and Ann

their daughter, [*sic*] 1856, aged 12, 'Her death was caused by a barbarous beating on the head, by her School Mistress, at Nether Thong School'.

Anon., *Echoes of the Past* (1897).

(201) WESLEYAN, Hade Edge (SE 146054). Broad four-bay front of single storey with pedimental gable, dated 1841. Burial-ground in front with tall obelisks and table-tombs.

(202) PRIMITIVE METHODIST, Gate Head (SE 175059). Small chapel with basement rooms, built 1836–7, extended at ends. *Sundial*: on S wall dated 1837.

(203) Former WESLEYAN, Hinchliffe Mill (SE 123070). Three-bay front with shaped gable and two tiers of windows above basement. Dated 1839. School of 1877 adjacent. (Drastically altered on conversion to housing since 1971)

(204) WESLEYAN, Holmfirth (SE 143083). Front of three bays with segmental pediment above recessed centre and paired entrances. Built 1871 with tablet from former chapel of 1810 reset in back wall. (Demolished 1971)

Monuments: in chapel (1) Rev. Aaron Floyd, 1836, signed 'H. Mares, Pimlico, London'; (2) Benjamin Butterworth, 1846, and Sarah his widow, 1859, signed 'Dennis Lee & Welsh, Leeds'; (3) George Gartside, 1844, and Mary his widow, 1874, signed 'Fisher, Huddersfield'. In burial-ground (4) Rev. Aaron Floyd, 1836, table-tomb; (5) Rev. Thomas Hill, 1857.

(205) WESLEYAN, High Street, Honley (SE 138119). 'Ebenezer

Wesleyan chapel, Thurstonland.

(210)

Chapel' dated 1826, four-bay front with two tiers of windows and pedimental gable. 'Wesleyan Schools' opposite dated 1878. (Reported demolished since 1971)

(206) PRIMITIVE METHODIST, Southgate, Honley (SE 140119). Dated 1842, much altered 1889. (Reported demolished since 1971)

(207) Former METHODIST NEW CONNEXION, Hall Ing Lane, Honley (SE 149123). 'Bethel Chapel', Woodroyd, dated 1840, has a three-bay front with pediment and round-arched windows. (Conversion to house proposed 1984)

Monuments: in front of chapel two table-tombs (1) Joseph Haigh, 1851, et al.; (2) Sarah Ann, daughter of Joseph and Ellen Haigh, 1852, et al.

(208) WESLEYAN, Jackson Bridge (SE 165073). Plain three-bay gabled front with two tiers of windows. Tablet in gable inscribed 'Methodist Chapel built by Subscription 1808'. Sundial: on S wall dated 1829. (Derelict 1971)

(209) Former FREE METHODIST, Netherthong (SE 139098). Zion Chapel, dated 1872.

(210) WESLEYAN, Thurstonland (SE 164104). Three-bay front with two tiers of plain windows, parapet with shaped ends and simple pediment; dated 1836. Rear wall with two round-arched windows flanking pulpit. Basement school-room below chapel.

Monuments: in front of chapel, table-tombs (1) Hannah, wife of John Chambers, 1844, et al.; (2) John Mitchell, 1846, and Ann his wife, 1837; (3) Robert Jenkinson, 1837, et al.; (4) Mary, wife of Charles Mitchell, 1842, et al.; (5) George Dearnley, 1843, et al.

HORSFORTH   *W. Yorks.*

(211) BAPTIST, Cragg Hill (SE 241375). Built 1803, heightened, and extended to rear, c.1830; early 19th-century house of three storeys adjacent. Sunday-school opposite dated 1864.

(212) WESLEYAN, Town Street (SE 237379). Dated 1867. Sunday-school behind may be former chapel of late 18th century, four-bay front with two tiers of windows; much altered on conversion, derelict 1970.

(213) WESLEYAN, Woodside (SE 251376). Gothic chapel of 1895. Former chapel alongside, single-storey with hipped roof and round-arched windows. Tablet on NE wall inscribed 'This Wesleyan Methodist Chapel was erected by Voluntary Subscription in 1839'. At right angles, and now linked to the former chapel, is an early 19th-century school building with blocked central entrance between pairs of round-arched windows.

HORTON   *Lancashire*

(214) CONGREGATIONAL (SD 856502). Presbyterian meetings of the 'Craven Society' were held at the house of John Hey, Pasture House (SD 873509), from c.1670 and actively supported by Mrs Barbara Lambert of Calton Hall (see (133)). In 1682 a meeting-house was built adjacent to Pasture House which continued in use until c.1717; it subsequently became a barn and was rebuilt in the late 19th century. A house in Horton was registered for meetings in 1710 but in 1717 a new meeting-house appears to have been erected on its site. This remained in use until 1816 when the present chapel was built, the cost being met from an endowment

Congregational chapel, Horton.   (214)

intended for the joint benefit of Winterburn and Horton chapels.

The meeting-house of 1717 remains, at least in part, as a two-storeyed cottage adjacent to the S of the chapel. The two upper window openings to the left of the entrance appear to have been longer and to have served the main body of the building. The interior ($30\frac{1}{4}$ft by $20\frac{3}{4}$ft) has at the S end the remains of the former gallery; a corresponding gallery at the N end may have been demolished when the present chapel was built.

The chapel of 1816 has a broad W front of four bays with two round-arched doorways and two tiers of windows. Two pointed-arched windows in the E wall flank the pulpit. The interior has a gallery around three sides with angled corners, and a panelled front supported by six thin cast-iron columns. The pulpit was replaced by a rostrum in the late 19th century; in front is a large singers' pew occupying much of the central space.

Fittings: – Inscriptions: on arched panel from pew door, fixed to E wall, 'RH 1718'; on tablet in arched recess behind pulpit 'This chapel opened Anno Domini 1816. Let no base Hireling here intrude, To feed Thy Flock with poisonous food, Kind Shepherd for Thy Flock prepare, Pure Living streams and Pastures fair – Come in ye Thirsty don't delay, Drink Wine and Milk from day to day, Sweet Jesus calls you come away, Flee now to Him this very Day.' Monuments: in front of chapel (1) Mary, wife of Robert Taylor, 1837, et al.; (2) Robert Wilson, 1794; (3) Mary, wife of Christopher Holgate, 1794; (4) William Ayrton Metcalf, 1814; (5) Thomas Metcalf, 1815. Seating: to lower floor, open-backed benches with arm rests, box-pews between entrances; in gallery complete set of box-pews incorporating reused fielded panels.

Miall (1868) 283–4: Whitehead (1930) 106–32.

HOYLAND NETHER   *S. Yorks.*

(215) WESLEYAN REFORM, Elsecar (SE 384002). 'Mount Zion', dated 1859. Three-bay pedimented front with upper doorway to first-floor chapel above cottages.

HUDDERSFIELD   *W. Yorks.*

(216) PARTICULAR BAPTIST, Salendine Nook (SE 106179). The congregation, in existence by the late 17th century, formed a section of the church meeting at Rodhill End and Stone Slack near Todmorden until its reorganization as a distinct church in

Baptist chapel, Salendine Nook.   (216)

1743. The first meeting-house on this site, built in 1739, was replaced in 1803 by a larger chapel and again in 1843 by the present building. Considerable alterations were carried out in the late 19th century, particularly in 1893–4.

The chapel is a large building of stone with a slate roof, formerly hipped. The front wall of three bays, partly covered by a wide porch of 1893–4, has a plain Venetian window between two round-arched windows at gallery level. A late 19th-century pediment replaces a cornice and parapet. The interior, largely refitted in the late 19th century, has a gallery around four sides, rounded at one end, supported by cast-iron columns which continue above the gallery fronts to support a segmental plaster barrel vault over the central space.

Fittings – *Monuments*: in burial-ground SW of chapel, many early 19th-century table-tombs and a few earlier monuments, including Rev. Joshua Wood, 1794, second minister. *Pulpit*: square with richly carved corner consoles, supported at front by two columns, 1843.

Stock, J., *History of the Baptist Independent and Congregational Church, Meeting in Salendine Nook Chapel, Huddersfield* (*c*.1874). Stock, P., *Foundations* (1933).

(217) BAPTIST, Lockwood Road, Huddersfield (SE 137153). A chapel was built in 1792 by Benjamin Ingham, a cloth merchant of Huddersfield, and a church formed in 1795 by transfer of members from Salendine Nook. The present chapel, built on the site of the former in 1851–2, has a front of three bays with a pediment between terminal pilasters, a central doorway with columns and entablature, and arched windows above. The interior has a round-ended gallery, and a complete set of contemporary box-pews. (Chapel subdivided at gallery level and lower seating destroyed 1986–8)

Monuments: in chapel (1) Rev. James Aston, 25 years pastor, 1830, and Mary his widow, 1836, signed 'Sanders, New Road, Fitzroy Square, London'; (2) Geoffrey Berry, 1850, and Sarah his widow, 1853, signed 'Fisher, Huddersfield'; (3) Benjamin Ingham, 1811, signed 'Fisher's, York'.

Former Congregational chapel, New North Road, Huddersfield.   (219)

Baptist Times (19 January 1989). Shipley (1912) 235–6. Stock (1933) op. cit. 396–8.

(218) Former BAPTIST, Milnsbridge (SE 117159). 'Ænon Chapel' was built in 1843–4 for a new congregation formed by members from Salendine Nook. The interior was much altered and vestries and organ chamber added *c*.1894. The chapel passed to industrial use in 1965 when services were transferred to a detached Sunday-school of 1883.

Three-bay front with bracketed lower haunches to pediment, two tiers of windows, and paired entrances replacing a single doorway. Gallery around three sides altered *c*.1894. (Demolished *c*.1981)

Fittings – *Baptistery*: with exit below site of pulpit, late 19th-century. *Monuments*: in burial-ground W of chapel, of mid 19th century and later.

Shipley (1912) 239–40.

(219) Former CONGREGATIONAL, New North Road (SE 139 172). The church formerly meeting in 'Highfield Chapel' originated in 1771 following the departure of the vicar, Henry Venn. Venn came to Huddersfield in 1759 and gathered around him a large body of enthusiastic evangelical supporters. On his acceptance of the living of Yelling, Hunts., these formed an Independent church and built the first chapel on this site which was opened in January 1772. This had a plain gabled front of three bays with two tiers of windows and sides seven bays in length. The present chapel, by Perkin and Backhouse, was built in 1843–4.

The chapel, of ashlar with a slate roof, has a broad S front of three bays between end pavilions with a giant order of Ionic columns *in antis* flanking the entrances. A 'singers' gallery', now the organ loft, was added at the back in 1846. The interior has a gallery around three sides. The seating was entirely renewed in 1907 on a horseshoe-shaped plan facing a rostrum pulpit of that date. (Converted to residential use *c*.1990)

Monuments: in burial-ground, around and at rear of chapel, include several memorials of late 18th-century date.

Bruce, R., *Centenary Memorial of Highfield Chapel, Huddersfield* (1872). *CYB* (1875) 120–4; (1909) 149–50. Miall (1868) 285–6.

(220) FRIENDS, Church Street, Paddock (SE 130163). A meeting-house was built here in 1770 and rebuilt 1898. A second meeting-house, adjacent to the former, erected in 1812, has stone walls and a hipped stone-slated roof. The front is of three bays with a central entrance and two tiers of blind windows.

Monuments; reset against front wall, two stones removed from a burial-ground in Brighouse in 1902 (1) Tabitha, daughter of Thomas Taylor, 1672; (2) Thomas Taylor, 1684, 'buryed on his own backside Apr. 30. 1684, a quaker, but a rich man' (Turner II (1881) 148); in burial-ground, small flat marker stones of early 19th century, and later headstones; (3) Mary Firth, 1806; (4) Robert Firth senior, 1819; (5) Robert Firth, 1828; (6) John Horsfall, 1827; (7) Thomas Firth, 1825; (8) Jane, wife of Thomas Firth, 1814. *Mounting-block*: inside front entrance gates, five steps, early 19th-century.

(221) Former WESLEYAN, Queen Street (SE 146165). The first Methodist chapel in Huddersfield was built in 1775 in Buxton Road. 'Bank Chapel' passed into the hands of the supporters of

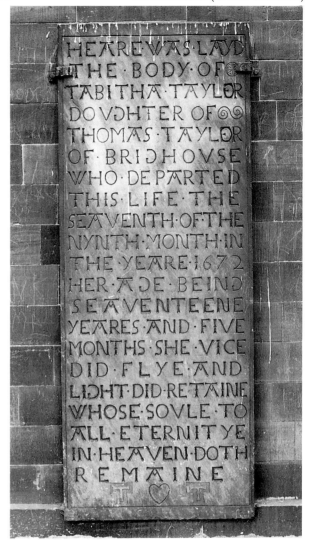

Friends' meeting-house, Huddersfield.   (220)

the New Connexion in 1797 and was only recovered by Wesleyans in 1814; it was rebuilt in 1837 and has been demolished since 1960. About 1798 a new chapel was built for the old society with assistance from the Wesleyan Conference; this was superseded in 1819 by the present building in Queen Street, claimed at the time to be the largest Methodist chapel in the kingdom, seating 2,400. It is now used for social purposes.

The chapel stands on the E side of the street set back in a courtyard flanked to N and S by houses of three storeys; a low wall with gate piers and urn finials next to the street has had its iron gates and railings removed. The W front is of seven bays with a five-bay pediment and two tiers of windows with a band of blind panels between the stages. In front of the central entrance is a porch with four fluted columns and above it a large round-arched window of three principal lights. In the frieze below the pediment is a tablet inscribed 'THE *Wesleyan Chapel* MDCCCXIX'. At each end of the frontage is a narrow two-storeyed bay with minor entrance. The rear wall of the chapel is

Former Wesleyan chapel, Queen Street, Huddersfield.   (221)

curved and has at the centre of each principal stage a plain Venetian window between four windows on each side. The lower windows retain their original hung sashes and glazing bars. There is a basement storey below the chapel.

The interior, refitted in the late 19th century, has a gallery of that period around three sides; a possible E gallery has been obscured by recent alterations.

Monuments: in chapel, on S wall (1) Mary (Bentley), wife of John Carr, 1832, with cartouche-of-arms; (2) Timothy Bentley, 1830, with shield-of-arms, signed 'Williams'; (3) William Bunting, 1866, and Harriet (Bentley) his widow, 1891; (4) Betsey, widow of Timothy Bentley, 1863; on N wall (5) David Shaw, 1841, signed 'Brine, London'; (6) Joseph Thornton, 1831, signed 'Williams'; (7) George Wilson, 1837, surmounted by sarcophagus and dove between palm trees, signed 'Walsh & Dunbar, Leeds'; (8) Rev. Mark Day, 1823, and Jane his wife, 1823, signed 'W. Williams'. On W end of S range of houses facing street (9) tablet erected 1938 to Rev. G. B. MacDonald, Superintendent Minister 1847–50, Hannah his wife, and their children Henry James, Alice, mother of Rudyard Kipling, Georgiana, wife of Sir Edward Burne-Jones Bart., Frederick William, President of Methodist Conference, Agnes, wife of Sir Edward Poynter Bart., Louisa, mother of Stanley Baldwin, and Edith, 'authoress'.

Mallinson (1898) 52, 123–4, 138–42.

(222) WESLEYAN, Almondbury (SE 168150). The chapel, built 1814–16 for a society originating in 1766, was rebuilt 1968. It had a front of four bays with two tiers of windows and a gabled parapet with shaped ends. A Sunday-school was built in 1824 and enlarged in 1842; an inscribed tablet of 1842 remains in a rebuilt annexe of 1900.

Hulbert (1882) 119–23. Mallinson (1898) 17–21, 54–7.

(223) WESLEYAN, Cowcliffe (SE 138188). Small, with gabled end; tablet dated 1836, signed 'J. Dawson'.

(224) METHODIST NEW CONNEXION, Deighton Lane (SE 165 195). Dated 1876; earlier burial-ground in front with table-tombs of 1822 and later.

(225) WESLEYAN, East Street, Lindley (SE 118185). The house of Joshua Dyson, now 14–18 West Street, 300 yards W of the chapel, was registered for preaching in 1773; it was superseded in 1795. The present chapel of 1867–8 by George Woodhouse of Bolton stands adjacent to its immediate predecessor which was converted for use as a Sunday-school.

The former chapel of 1795 has stone walls and a slate roof. It has been much altered by subdivision and by extension at each side. The front and back walls were originally of four bays with two tiers of windows separated by a platband. The cills of the upper windows have been lowered. The S front, which had doorways in the end bays, was altered c.1859 by the erection of a semicircular two-storeyed projection across the two middle bays which previously may have been filled by a pair of pulpit windows; the new work probably provided a vestry with an organ or singers' gallery above, the two round-arched pulpit windows being then reset at each side of the new wing. The first lateral extension to the W, also of the mid 19th century, replaced two cottages and a meeting-room above.

The interior (30¾ft by 42ft) had a gallery around three sides; the two remaining gallery columns are octagonal wood posts with moulded caps and bases above a tall plinth to pew height. Across the opening to the organ gallery is a semicircular arch with keystone.

Monuments: in burial-ground in front of former chapel, include table-tombs of 1801 and later.

Mallinson (1898) 35–7, 129–30.

(226) WESLEYAN, Lamb Hall Road, Longwood (SE 102173). The first chapel built in 1837 stood opposite the present building; it had a front of three bays with two tiers of round-arched windows and a pedimented parapet with shaped ends. The central doorway with stone pilasters and entablature remains *in situ* as a feature in the burial-ground, together with the parapet scrolls set upside-down at the sides and with the inscribed gable tablet above.

The present chapel, of 1903–4 by J. Berry, is in the Gothic style and comprises a preaching nave with transepts and an organ and vestry wing at the NW end behind the central pulpit. (Demolition proposed 1977)

Fittings – Glass: memorial windows with inscriptions to the Broadbent family; other windows with informal patterns of tinted glass at the head. *Seating*: in ends of pews, draw seats for occasional use.

Riley, A. E., *Longwood Methodist Church, Centenary Souvenir* (1937).

(227) Site of WESLEYAN, Outlane (SE 081177). The chapel of 1877 replacing one of 1822 has been demolished. Stone tablet from 1822 chapel now loose outside 1915 Sunday-school opposite. Monuments in burial-ground date from early 19th century.

(228) WESLEYAN, Wiggan Lane, Sheepridge (SE 156194). Much altered or rebuilt; original tablet dated 1822 reset above entrance to 1908 Sunday-school.

IDLE   *W. Yorks.*

(229) UPPER CHAPEL (SE 175379). A Congregational chapel, rebuilt 1850 on the site of Presbyterian meeting-houses of 1717 and 1791, was again rebuilt in 1956–7. A few ledger stones of *c.*1800 remain in the burial-ground. (URC)

Miall (1868) 294–5. Turner, J. H., *Nonconformity in Idle, with the History of Airedale College* (1876) 51–2.

(230) FRIENDS' BURIAL-GROUND (SE 172379). Trapezoidal enclosure with stone boundary walls and original doorway with lintel dated 1690. Stone seat around inner face of walls. *Monument*: Jeremiah son of Zachary Yewdall, [1690], ledger stone.

Lidbetter (1961) 6, Pl. 2. Turner (1876) op. cit. 27.

ILKLEY   *W. Yorks.*

(231) CONGREGATIONAL, Burley in Wharfedale (SE 166464).

Congregational chapel (URC), Burley in Wharfedale.   (231)

'Salem Chapel' built in 1839 owes its existence to the patronage of J. P. Clapham who lived at the Grange, the site apparently forming part of his estate. The walls are of stone with gabled ends, paired lancet windows in the side walls and gabled buttresses. Above the rear gable is a tall chimney finial; the front finial has been partly removed. (URC)

Monument: in burial-ground, now part of public park, William son of John and Isabella Allison, 1840, *et al.*

Miall (1868) 247.

(232) WESLEYAN, Burley in Wharfedale (SE 169463). The first chapel of 1816 stands near its more elaborate successor of 1867. The former, of three bays with two tiers of round-arched windows below a pedimental gable, was extended to the rear in 1832.

Seals (1974) 18.

(233) WESLEYAN, Ben Rhydding (SE 134476). Free Gothic with short tower, 1909 by Garside and Pennington.

KEARBY WITH NETHERBY   *N. Yorks.*

(234) WESLEYAN, Kearby (SE 338474). Small chapel with two cottages below, on sloping site. Gabled ends with shaped kneelers, oval tablet dated 1809 above entrance.

KEIGHLEY   *W. Yorks.*

(235) BAPTIST, West Lane, Haworth (SE 028374). The church

FRIEND'S BURIAL-GROUND, IDLE   CFS1989

was formed in 1752 as a result of the preaching of James Hartley. The chapel built in that year was enlarged in 1775 and replaced by the present building in 1844. This has a pedimented front with two tiers of round-arched windows and two doorways with pilasters and entablatures.

Monuments: in front of chapel (1) James Hartley, 27 years minister, 1780, and Ann his widow, 1788; (2) Rev. Isaac Slee, 1784, and Ann his widow, late wife of Rev. Benjamin Thomas, 1785; (3) Rev. Miles Oddy, 1841, and Martha his wife, 1832. In burial-ground (4) Sarah, wife of Miles Oddy, minister, [*c.* 1800], and John their son, 1805, table-tomb; (5) Michael Heaton, 1765, Mary his widow, 1771, John Heaton, 1801, and Dinah his widow, 1814.

Ivimey IV (1830) 579–82. Shipley (1912) 185–6.

(236) STRICT BAPTIST, Hall Green, Haworth (SE 032369). The chapel was built in 1824–5 and an organ gallery and vestries added 1840. Broad N front of five bays with pedimental gable and two tiers of round-arched windows. Entrances in penultimate bays have plain stone surrounds with keystones and impost blocks.

Monuments: in burial-ground, of early 19th century and later. *Sundial*: on S wall, 19th-century, repainted.

Day, Marjorie, *The Hall Green Story* (1974). Shipley (1912) 185.

(237) BAPTIST, Oakworth (SE 030396). Baptist meetings begun in 1819 in a room at Bogthorn were transferred to a new chapel at Mackingstone Lane in 1821. This is a plain building of stone with a gabled front of five bays incorporating a tablet inscribed 'ZION'S CHAPEL 1819', perhaps reset from the first meeting place. The chapel was converted to Sunday-school use when a new chapel, which has now been closed, was built nearby in Slack Lane (SE 028394) in 1879–80. The latter has a pedimented front of four bays with two tiers of round-arched windows.

Shipley (1912) 188–9.

(238) CONGREGATIONAL, East Morton (SE 098419). 'Bethel' chapel, 1845, single-stage elevation of five bays with three-bay pediment.

Miall (1868) 231.

(239) Former WESLEYAN, Temple Street, Keighley (SE 059412). The Methodist society in Keighley was formed in 1742 following

Former Wesleyan chapel, Temple Street, Keighley.   (239)

preaching by John Nelson of Birstall. The site of the present chapel was acquired in 1753 and the first preaching-house erected; in 1810 a new chapel appears to have been built against the S side of the former, facing W towards Chapel Lane. The 1753 building was superseded in 1846 by the existing chapel and in 1905 a new Sunday-school replaced the former chapel of 1810.

The chapel of 1846 is a large building with stone walls and slate roof in the classical manner by James Simpson of Leeds. The front of four bays with two tiers of round-arched windows has porches in the end bays with Tuscan columns *in antis* and paired pilasters flanking the windows above. The side walls are of six bays. The interior, which had a round-ended gallery, has been entirely altered. (Chapel sold in 1980 for conversion to a mosque)

Inscription: an oval tablet reset in W wall of former Sunday-school 'EDEN CHAPEL 1810'.

Dolbey (1964) 29.

(240) PRIMITIVE METHODIST, Green End Road, East Morton (SE 101422). Low building with round-arched windows, blocked doorway next to road with tablet above dated 1827; enlarged 1881.

(241) WESLEYAN, Exley Head (SE 048402). Porch inscribed 'Wesleyan School A.D. MDCCCLIIII'.

(242) WESLEYAN, West Lane, Haworth (SE 027374). The first preaching-house was built in 1758–9 by the Rev. William Grimshaw, perpetual curate from 1742, with the assistance of a legacy left for that purpose by Mrs Mercy Thornton of Leeds; it was not brought into regular use until Grimshaw's death in 1763. Increasing congregations in the early 19th century necessitated the erection of a gallery in 1805, apparently by the removal of an upper floor, and an enlargement in 1822. A new chapel built on the site in 1846 was enlarged in 1853 and demolished in 1951. Only the single-storeyed Sunday-school buildings of the mid 19th century now remain, part converted to a chapel.

The first chapel is reported to have been 12 yards long and 9 yards wide. Part of the side wall remains adjacent to a cottage, 56 West Lane, including the return of the front wall with plain quoins and a platband at mid-height. The second chapel was set further back on the site and had a front of four bays with two tiers of windows and end entrances.

Fittings – *Chair*: in present chapel, with tall carved back, formerly the property of William Grimshaw, 17th-century. *Inscriptions*: reset in outer wall of porch; on blind tympanum of plain Venetian window from first chapel 'To Us To Live is CHRIST To Die is Gain A.D. 1758'; above doorway 'This Chapel was Erected by the Revd William Grimshaw A.B. Minister of Haworth Church A.D. 1758', first word altered *c.*1846 to read 'The 1st'.

Baker, F., *William Grimshaw, 1708–1763* (1963) 252–3. Dews, D. C., *A History of Methodism in Haworth from 1744* (1981). Dolbey (1964) 25, 82.

(243) WESLEYAN, Marsh Lane, Oxenhope (SE 026357). Small Sunday-school built 1836, enlarged or rebuilt 1874.

(244) WESLEYAN, Scar Top (SD 995373). 'Sunday School', three-bay pedimented front, opened 1869.

KETTLEWELL WITH STARBOTTON *N. Yorks.*

(245) WESLEYAN, Kettlewell (SD 974724). Opened 1835, round-arched windows. *Monument*: in burial-ground, Jonathan Wear, 1847, and Jane his wife, 1839.

KIRKBURTON *W. Yorks.*

(246) Former CONGREGATIONAL, Dogley Lane (SE 188141). The chapel was built in 1816 for seceders from Shelley (*see* (248)), it was heightened in 1832 and a Sunday-school added at the S end. In 1882 the latter was rebuilt on a larger scale incorporating a new entrance to the chapel. The original building, which remains as part of the enlarged structure, was of a single storey; the W front has at the centre two semicircular arched windows with doorways to right and left now blocked and plain windows at each end. The interior was entirely refitted in the late 19th century. (Chapel closed before 1980)

Monuments: in chapel (1) Rev. William Lees, 1831; (2) Paul, son of Joah and Rachel Sugden, 1821, *et al.*; (3) Rev. Francis Egglestone Henson, 1881; (4) Rev. John Hughes, 1849. In front of chapel (5) John Ibberson, 1836, Susannah his widow, 1862, Clark their son, 1820, and Ann their daughter, 1841; (6) Martha, wife of James Statham, 1832, and Martha [?Ibberson], 1838.

Miall (1868) 254. Thomas, H., *The History of Dogley Lane Congregational Church 1816–1919* (1919).

(247) CONGREGATIONAL, Kirkheaton (SE 180182). The chapel built in 1818 is similar in design to the original Dogley Lane chapel with two round-arched windows at the front, two entrances each side now covered by a porch, and plain end windows. The interior has been refitted and the pulpit formerly between the front windows has been re-sited at one end; the walls are lined with a dado of panelling from the former pews.

The Sunday-school, opposite the chapel, was built in 1833 and enlarged 1885. (URC)

(248) Former CONGREGATIONAL, Shelley (SE 203112). The church formerly meeting here originated about 1793 when Calvinists, dissatisfied with a new incumbent at the parish church, commenced to hold separate meetings in a house at Lane Head. The chapel at Shelley was built in 1796, a cottage was added at one end in the mid 19th century and a detached Sunday-school was built in 1899. The chapel was refitted and the window frames renewed in the early 20th century. It was closed *c.*1974 and sold in 1977 for conversion to a house.

The chapel, of stone with a stone-slated roof, has a front of

FORMER CONGREGATIONAL CHAPEL, SHELLEY   CFS 1974

four bays (36¼ft wide externally) with two tiers of windows separated by a narrow platband, two end doorways and a pair of round-arched pulpit windows between. The rear wall has two tiers of three two-light windows with square mullions. The roof is supported by three queen-post trusses with an upper king-post above each collar.

Monuments: in front of chapel (1) Eliza, wife of George Benjamin Scott, pastor, 1847, and their children Benjamin Robert, 1841, and William Henry, 1843; (2) Joshua Williamson, 1832, Bathsheba his widow, 1836, and Martha their daughter, 1844.

Miall (1868) 361–2. Thomas (1919) op. cit. 1–10.

(249) Former FRIENDS, Lane Head (SE 194090). Lane Head House served as a meeting place for Quakers in the late 17th century prior to the erection of a meeting-house at High Flats (*see* (107)).

(250) WESLEYAN, North Road, Kirkburton (SE 197129). Built 1845 superseding 'Pontey' chapel of 1816. The pedimented front of three bays with Venetian window above a central doorway has been reduced in height leaving only the lower openings. Original tablet of 1845 reset in new gable.

Mallinson (1898) 108–10.

(251) METHODIST, Shelley (SE 202109). Methodist preaching in Shelley commenced in 1770 and the present site was acquired in 1783. The chapel built in 1785 was placed in a trust which foresaw a possible division in Methodism and gave to the trustees an unusual freedom of alignment with either party; this option was exercised following the Kilhamite agitation and the chapel passed to the Methodist New Connexion. The chapel was enlarged in the mid 19th century by the addition of an organ gallery and vestry against the front wall and later by a two-storeyed annexe at one end.

The broad S front appears to have been of four bays with end entrances and plain windows above and a pair of round-arched pulpit windows between, now reset in the side walls of the organ chamber. The back wall has three bays of windows formerly of two lights with square mullions.

The interior (30ft by 42¼ft) has a gallery around three sides with fielded-panelled front. The organ gallery has a lower balustraded front and an arched opening to the chapel. The gallery pews, some of which have balustraded backs and trellis balustrading inside the back windows, date from the early 19th century.

Mallinson (1898) 30–1. Packer (1897) 69.

KIRKBY OVERBLOW *N. Yorks.*

(252) Former WESLEYAN (SE 327492). Now house, with rusticated doorway in gable end and tablet dated 1843. Chapel probably at upper level with cottages below.

KIRK DEIGHTON *N. Yorks.*

(253) WESLEYAN, Lime Kiln Lane (SE 398502). Stone with three-bay front; opened 1819, much altered or rebuilt.

KNARESBOROUGH *N. Yorks.*

(254) CONGREGATIONAL, Briggate (SE 351568). A Presbyterian society formed in the late 17th century registered a barn in

Windsor Lane in 1697 for use as a meeting-house. The support of Lady Hewley, who had an estate nearby at Hay-a-Park, has been claimed for this society. Meetings ceased *c*.1730 and were only intermittently resumed *c*.1764. In 1779 the meeting-house was rebuilt on or near its former site and in 1782 a Congregational church was formed. The chapel was enlarged in 1817 and superseded by the present building on an adjacent site in 1864–5. The former chapel, later Sunday-school, has been rebuilt. The chapel opened in 1865 is in the Gothic style by Pritchett and Son of Darlington. (URC)

CYB (1865) 300. Miall (1868) 298–300. Whitehead (1932) 201–25.

(255) Former WESLEYAN, Bond End (SE 346572). The first Methodist chapel here, built in 1794, is a large square building of stone with pantiled roof. The gabled front originally had two tiers of flat-arched windows, doorways in the end bays, two windows between and three above. The side walls were two bays deep. In the rear wall were two pulpit windows. Superseded 1815; drastically refenestrated in recent years on conversion to cottages.

(256) Former WESLEYAN, Chapel Street (SE 351569). Plain gabled front of five bays, central doorway and four round-arched windows with plain windows above, dated 1815. The present chapel, on an adjacent site in Gracious Street, was built in 1868.

KNOTTINGLEY
W. Yorks.

(257) CONGREGATIONAL, The Croft (SE 503241). Salem Chapel; brick with rendered dressings, three arched windows in front above later porch. Built 1849 replacing chapel of 1807.

Monument: in burial-ground, Rev. John Denniston, 1859, 15 years minister, Mary Ann his widow, 1875, and five children.

CYB (1861) 210. Miall (1868) 300.

(258) WESLEYAN, Ropewalk (SE 502239). Rendered walls with four-bay front, round-arched upper windows and pedimental gable above cornice with small wooden bell-cote at apex. (Chapel reported demolished by 1981)

Monuments: in burial-ground (1) Thomas Cliffe, shipbuilder, 1851, Hannah his widow, 1861, Mary Elizabeth their daughter, 1856, and Mary, wife of their son John, 1855; (2) William Horracks, mariner, 1853, Mary his wife, 1852, *et al.*; (3) Richard Swan, master mariner, 1879; (4) Benjamin Womack, mariner, 1853; (5) John Wray, mariner, 1865; (6) John Walker, mariner, 1856, and Ann his widow, 1859; (7) John Senior, 1850.

LEATHLEY
N. Yorks.

(259) WESLEYAN (SE 234472). Small three-bay chapel of stone with hipped roof; front facing away from road has two large windows with doorway asymmetrically between and tablet dated 1826 with text from Matt. 24: 14. Original fittings, with pulpit left of entrance and stepped pews to right.

Seals (1974) 22.

LEEDS
W. Yorks.

(260) MILL HILL CHAPEL (SE 299335). The first meeting-house used by the Presbyterian, latterly Unitarian, society is said by Thoresby (quoted in Wicksteed (1847) op. cit. below, 35–6) to have been built soon after the 1672 Indulgence 'near the Park-

Former Wesleyan chapel, Bond End, Knaresborough. Of 1794. (255)

Former Wesleyan chapel, Chapel Street, Knaresborough. Of 1815. (256)

Present Wesleyan chapel, Gracious Street, Knaresborough. Of 1868. (256)

WESLEYAN CHAPEL, LEATHLEY   CFS 1974

Mill Hill Chapel, Leeds.   (260)

stile . . . adjoining to the Alms-house Garth'. Although reputedly opened on 25 March 1674 it was not in regular use until after 1687. A drawing on Cossins' map of c.1725 shows it with a broad front of seven bays with a porch at the centre of full height rising to a small tower, three doorways and two tiers of windows. The interior was reported to be divided in ecclesiastical fashion by pillars and arches. The chapel was much altered later in the 18th century when it was re-roofed and given a central pediment; the latter seems to have been partly obscured by the subsequent erection of an organ loft behind the pulpit which stood against the centre of the front wall.

The present chapel on the site of the former was built in 1847–8 in the Perpendicular Gothic style to designs by Bowman and Crowther. It is a long building of stone and slate with a gabled transept and principal entrance set centrally between the six bays of windows. The entrance bay is flanked by octagonal and stepped buttresses formerly rising to crocketed pinnacles which, together with much other superior ornamentation, have been removed.

The interior has a long nave with a short N chancel separated

Mill Hill Chapel, Leeds.   (260)

by a two-centred arch. The nave S of the central transept was separated from the body of the chapel c.1965-70 and converted to other uses.

Monuments: in burial-ground S and W of chapel (1) Rev. Joseph Cappe, 1747, his children, Sarah, 1738, William, 1740, Martha, 1741, *et al.*; (2) Joseph Rayner, 1757, *et al.*, table-tomb; (3) Eli Musgrave, 1778, Catherine his wife (nd), *et al.*, table-tomb; (4) Benjamin, son of George and Sarah Oates, 1746, *et al.*, with indent for brass; (5) Mary Ann, wife of James Watson, 1823, and Francis H. Balls, tutor in Rev. Joseph Hutton's family, 1826. *Plate*: includes a two-handled cup of 1718, one of a pair, the other now in private hands.

Evans (1897) 127-8. Miall (1868) 301-2. Schroeder, W. L., *Mill Hill Chapel, Leeds, 1674-1924* (1924). UHST III (1923-6) 276-9; VIII (1943-6) 181-3. Wicksteed, C., *Lectures on the Memory of the Just . . .* (1847).

(261) BAPTIST, Hough Lane, Bramley (SE 244350). Zion chapel, built 1846, replaced a chapel of 1808. Stone with paired Tuscan columns at entrance. (Partly demolished 1978)

Shipley (1912) 142-4, Fig. 157.

(262) BAPTIST, Low Road, Hunslet (SE 312318). The Tabernacle, built 1837, has a rendered front of four bays with two tiers of round-arched windows, and a hipped roof.

Shipley (1912) 147-8, Fig. 144.

(263) Former BAPTIST, Woodhouse Lane (SE 298345). 'Blenheim Chapel', Gothic with corner tower and square spire; 1863-4 by Cuthbert Brodrick.

Shipley (1912) 149-50.

(264) SALEM CHAPEL, Hunslet Lane (SE 303330). The first Independent chapel in Leeds, built in 1691 in Call Lane, was demolished c.1880 after a period of use by General Baptists. A second congregation was formed c.1755 under John Edwards, a former Wesleyan preacher, with support from orthodox seceders from Call Lane, who built the 'White Chapel' or 'Whitehall Chapel' in Hunslet Lane. In 1791 the major part of this society moved to the new Salem chapel which they vacated in 1841 on the erection of a Greek revival chapel in East Parade, moving thence in 1902 to Trinity, Woodhouse Lane (*see* (266)). Salem was subsequently occupied by another Congregational church and from 1891, under the joint pastorate of B. Smith and F. Wrigley, became a flourishing centre of inner-city mission. The chapel was much altered in 1907 on conversion to a 'Central Hall' with increased accommodation. In c.1975-80 the chapel was converted to workshops and a new meeting-room fitted up elsewhere in the building.

The chapel of 1791 (60ft square externally) has walls of squared stone. The original S wall facing Salem Place has rusticated quoins, a plinth and platband between two tiers of windows in three bays, the lower ones with round-arched heads. The W front, rebuilt on a semicircular plan in 1907, was previously of six bays with a four-bay pedimented centre. The N wall has been altered or rebuilt and later buildings adjoin to the east. The interior was refitted in 1907 with a gallery around three sides and hinged seating.

Guntrip, H. J. S., *Smith and Wrigley of Leeds* (1944). Miall (1868) 306-7. *Reform* (February 1980) 7.

(265) BELGRAVE CHAPEL, Cross Belgrave Street (SE 30303395). Built 1835-6 for Congregationalists formerly meeting in Albion Chapel. Closed c.1940-50 and converted to shops and offices. Brick with stone platband and moulded cornice; five-bay front entirely refenestrated but with faint traces of arched heads of original windows.

Miall (1868) 308-9.

(266) CONGREGATIONAL, Woodhouse Lane (SE 296346). 'Trinity', 1902 by Danby and Simpson in a free Perpendicular Gothic style; built to replace East Parade Chapel (1841 by William Hurst and W. L. Moffatt, demolished 1900). Nave, chancel and transepts with a prominent tower and spire at one side. (URC)

Binfield, C., *So Down to Prayers* (1977) 98-9. CYB (1847) facing 158; (1903) 155-6.

(267) Former CONGREGATIONAL, Upper Wortley Road (SE 271 328). Italianate, 1881 on site of Bethel Chapel opened 1815. Derelict 1972.

Monuments: in burial-ground (1) Eliza, daughter of James and Mary Hargreave, 1833, and her cousin William Hargreave Hardcastle, surgeon, 1844; (2) Rev. Robert Leslie Armstrong, 25 years pastor, 1856, *et al.*, table-tomb.

Miall (1868) 309.

(268) Former FRIENDS, Woodhouse Lane (SE 298344). Friends' meetings which began in the mid 17th century were being held by c.1690 in a building in Boar Lane. A new meeting-house was built in Water Lane in 1699 and enlarged in 1723 and 1775. In 1788 it was rebuilt, principally to accommodate the Quarterly Meeting. After the transfer of meetings to Woodhouse Lane the former building passed into commercial use.

The meeting-house in Woodhouse Lane, built in 1866-8 to designs by Edward Birchall, has a pedimented stone front of five bays with a low entrance vestibule between retiring rooms. The accommodation comprises two principal rooms with minor buildings around a courtyard at the rear. The major part of the building was sold in 1921 and is now used by the British Broadcasting Corporation.

Allott, W., 'Leeds Quaker Meeting', *Thoresby Soc. Miscellany* XIV Part 1 (1966). Mortimer, J. and Mortimer, R. (eds.), *Leeds Friends' Minute Book 1692 to 1712*, Yorks. Arch. Soc., Record Series, CXXXIX (1980).

(269) FRIENDS, Adel (SE 264393). Burial-ground acquired and meeting-house built 1868. *Sundial*: square stone pillar with chamfered and stopped corners, removed 1886 from burial-ground at Dacre (*see* (103)), late 17th-century with later base and cap; horizontal dial by J. W. Appleyard, 1887, gnomon missing, inscribed 'Watch for ye know not the hour'.

Allott (1966) op. cit. 61.

(270) ALBION CHAPEL, Albion Street (SE 300338). The first Methodist preaching-house in Leeds, the 'Old Boggard House', was built in 1751 and superseded in 1834 by St Peter's Chapel on an adjacent site near St Peter's Square (now demolished). A second Wesleyan chapel was built in Albion Street in 1802 from which the society moved in 1824 to Brunswick Chapel (*see* below). Albion was then occupied by Congregationalists but

since their removal to Belgrave Chapel (*see* (265)) in 1836 it has been in commercial use. The chapel has been much altered but the rear gable of brickwork remains visible above Nos. 25 and 26 Butts Court. (Demolished 1989)

Beckworth (1910) 8. Mayhall I (1860) 205.

(271) BRUNSWICK CHAPEL, Brunswick Street (SE 303341), was built in 1824–5 for the society formerly meeting in Albion Chapel (*see* (270)). The erection of an organ in the chapel in 1827 caused a major secession from the society and the formation of a distinct body of 'Protestant Methodists' which in 1836 united with the Wesleyan Methodist Association.

The chapel, of ashlar with a hipped slate roof, was designed by Joseph Botham. The walls have two tiers of round-arched windows separated by a platband. The N front of three principal bays has a slightly recessed centre with a doorway of late 19th-century appearance below the principal Venetian window; the flanking bays have original round-arched doorways to the lower stage and narrow round-arched windows above between paired Ionic pilasters. The S end of the chapel is elliptical.

The interior has a continuous round-ended gallery occupied at the S end by the organ in front of which is a wide rostrum pulpit of the late 19th century. (Demolished *c.*1980)

Fittings – *Monuments*: in chapel (1) Rev. Miles Martindale, 1824; (2) John Lawson, 1837, and Jane his widow, 1862; (3) Sarah (Smith), wife of George Morley, surgeon, 1836, and Ann her sister, 1847, signed 'W. Spence & Son, Liverpool'; (4) William Smith, 1868, and George his son, 1884; (5) Benjamin Pollard, 1860, tablet removed from St Peter's [Wesleyan] Chapel, 1910; (6) William Dawson, 1841; (7) William Gilyard Scarth, 1853, with portrait bust below; (8) Thomas Simpson, 1848; (9) William Watson, 1855, Sarah his widow, 1856, and Sarah their daughter, 1855; (10) Charles Smith, 1848. In burial-ground, many 19th-century ledger stones.

Organ: built 1827 by Joseph Booth of Wakefield, enlarged 1846 by Francis Booth, hydraulic blowing engines installed 1859. *Seating*: to lower floor, substantial box-pews, some with narrow separate tables, early 19th-century.

Mayhall I (1860) 309–10.

Brunswick Chapel, Leeds.   (271)

Brunswick Chapel, Leeds.   (271)

(272) WESLEYAN, Oxford Place (SE 297338). The chapel of 1835 by James Simpson was re-fronted and altered internally in 1896–1903 by George F. Danby and William H. Thorpe; the interior was entirely reconstructed in 1979. The original chapel had an E front of brick of five bays with two tiers of round-arched windows and pedimented doorways in the end bays. The W wall, of which four original bays remain, has a central doorway. The interior, prior to 1979, had a continuous round-ended gallery and a rostrum pulpit in front of a curved screen wall at the W end.

Monuments: in chapel (1) Edward Joy, 1862, and Ruth his wife, 1852, signed 'Alfred Bromley, Leeds'; (2) John Howard, 1848; (3) James Musgrave, 1844.

Methodist Recorder (17 May 1979).

(273) Former WESLEYAN, Hanover Place (SE 29053395), by James Simpson. Built 1847, of brick with stone dressings, four-bay front and sides with two tiers of round-arched windows with cornices to lower stage and open pediments above. Porch with paired Tuscan columns enclosing two doorways. (Upper part demolished *c.*1980)

(274) WESLEYAN, Farnley Hill (SE 251325). The original chapel built in 1797 has been much altered and extended. In 1819 a Sunday-school, since demolished, was erected against the SW side, and in 1828 a second school-room and caretaker's cottage were built against the NE side, the chapel was extended to the rear and the SE front wall rebuilt. The walls are of stone and the roof is hipped and slated. The front is of five bays with two tiers

of plain sash windows and two later porches against the end bays. The three middle bays project slightly; until 1968 these were finished with a pediment containing a clock dial over which, prior to 1915, was an open bell-cote. The NE annexe, partly extended to the front in 1921, formerly had a central doorway at first-floor level between a pair of plain Venetian windows; the corresponding annexe was of similar design.

The interior ($21\frac{1}{4}$ft, extended to $39\frac{1}{4}$ft, by $36\frac{1}{4}$ft) has a gallery around three sides with a polygonal front supported by cast-iron columns.

Former Wesleyan chapel, Hanover Place, Leeds.   (273)

Wesleyan chapel, Farnley Hill. Before 1915.   (274)

Fittings – *Inscription*: above doorway to Sunday-school, dated 1828. *Monuments*: in chapel (1) William Pawson, 1863, and Eliza Ann his wife, 1852; (2) Thomas Pawson, 1831, 'a principal instrument in the hand of God in the erection of this chapel and the adjoining school', and Elizabeth his widow, 1837; in Sunday-school (3) Richard Ellwand, 1850. *Pulpit*: with semicircular desk front and clerk's seat below, early 19th-century. *Seating*: in gallery, box-pews of 1828.

(275) WESLEYAN, Chapel Street, Halton (SE 351336). Opened 1840.

(276) WESLEYAN, Otley Road, Headingley (SE 278362). Built 1844, by James Simpson. Stone and slate in lancet Gothic style with nave, and aisles, transepts and short chancel. Gabled E front of three bays with buttresses rising to tall finials and pinnacles at corners and apex of gable. Open timber roof and iron arcade columns supporting side galleries which continue across the transepts and have a cross gallery at the E end. Fittings at W end much altered.

Seating: original box-pews, some with small narrow tables having Gothic decoration.

(277) Former METHODIST, Waterloo Road, Hunslet (SE 312 317). A chapel at the corner of Jack Lane was built in 1780 and enlarged 1819. After the erection of a new Wesleyan chapel in 1839 it passed to Independents and in 1846 was occupied by

Primitive Methodists. It is a plain brick building with original SE gable end but otherwise greatly altered for domestic use. (Demolished *c*.1977)

Beckworth (1910) 93–4.

Wesleyan chapel, Otley Road, Headingley.   (276)

(278) Former WESLEYAN, Dixon Lane Road, Wortley (SE 270 323). Chapel built 1846–7, stone with three-bay pedimented front and two tiers of round-arched windows with basement windows in side wall. Buildings behind include a Sunday-school of 1898 with earlier building alongside facing Green Road, and a former Free Methodist chapel dated 1855.

(279) Former METHODIST NEW CONNEXION, Woodhouse Lane (SE 300340). Brick with stone dressings, five-bay front with two doorways, altered windows and elaborately decorated pediment; by William Hill, 1858.

    Packer (1897) 7.

(280) Former METHODIST NEW CONNEXION, Whitehorse Street, Hunslet (SE 309321). Four-bay front of brick with stone dressings, two doorways with pilasters and entablatures; *c.*1846 probably by James Simpson.

(281) Former PRIMITIVE METHODIST, Brudenell Road (SE 288352). Timber-framed and weather-boarded with small three-stage tower and spire at corner. Erected *c.*1880 at their own cost by the brothers Benjamin and William Walmsley, builders, who had laid out the surrounding estate. Now Christadelphian.

    Beckworth (1910) 201.

(282) Former WESLEYAN METHODIST ASSOCIATION, Lady Lane (SE 305338). 1840, by James Simpson. Four-bay brick front between narrow end bays, two entrances and two tiers of round-arched windows. Much altered, in commercial use.

(283) Former WESLEYAN METHODIST ASSOCIATION, Town Street, Armley (SE 269334). Stone with three-bay pedimented front, round-arched windows. Built 1839–40, converted to commercial use.

(284) Former WESLEYAN PROTESTANT METHODIST, St Marks Street, Woodhouse (SE 294350). Brick with rendered front of three bays, polygonal organ chamber at back. Early 19th-century, much altered and possibly enlarged.

(285) Former FREE METHODIST, Victoria Road, Hyde Park (SE 287355). 1886 by W. S. Braithwaite. Now Pentecostalist.

LITTLE RIBSTON   *N. Yorks.*

(286) WESLEYAN (SE 386533). Stone with shaped gable kneelers, dated 1818.

LITTLE SMEATON   *N. Yorks.*

(287) Former WESLEYAN (SE 521168). Three-bay rendered front with porch, early 19th-century. Now youth club.

LIVERSEDGE   *W. Yorks.*

(288) Former FRIENDS, Quaker Lane, Hightown (SE 190241). Quaker meetings, which commenced in the mid 17th century following the visit of George Fox to Hightown in 1652, were principally supported by the Green family. In January 1700 a 'new erected house in Liversidge' was registered as a place of worship and in February 1701 the building then described as 'on the west side of Townend Lane' was transferred to the Society by Thomas Green for use as a meeting-house. Meetings ceased by the end of the 18th century and the building was shortly afterwards converted to cottages; it was sold in 1904.

    The former meeting-house, latterly a pair of cottages but now

FORMER FRIENDS' MEETING HOUSE, HIGHTOWN   W. /CFS 1972

combined into a single dwelling, is the conversion of an existing single-aisled hall of three bays dating from the early 17th century or before. The outer walls are of rubble, partly covered by later rendering, and the roof is finished with stone slates. All external features date from the 19th century.

    The interior (32ft square) includes an aisle or outshot, 14ft wide, on the N, the walling between that and the main body of the building incorporates two timber posts with straight braces to two original roof trusses over the S range. The beams supporting the upper floor were inserted in the 19th century.

Burial-ground: to S, small walled enclosure with modern tablet inscribed 'Friends Burial Ground 1700'; no monuments, last interment 1784.

    Blamires, D., *A History of Quakerism in Liversedge and Scholes* (1971). Peel (1891) 28–34.

(289) FRIENDS' BURIAL-GROUND, Sepulchre Hill (SE 182235). Irregular enclosure bounded at front by low wall incorporating on inner face a modern tablet with date 1665. *Monuments*: three ledger stones and one former capstone from table-tomb, all reset on low rubble plinths (1) Mary, wife of Thomas Greene, 1684, capstone; (2) Solomon, son of John Greene the younger, 1665, small ledger stone; (3) Bridget, wife of John Greene, 1665; (4) John Greene, 1669/70.

(290) WESLEYAN, Halifax Road, Hightown (SE 186240). Four-bay stone front with two tiers of round-arched windows and two porches; opened 1828. (Demolition proposed 1982)

LOFTHOUSE   *W. Yorks.*

(291) WESLEYAN, Leeds Road (SE 333258). Built 1840, enlarged or re-fronted 1870.

LONG PRESTON   *N. Yorks.*

(292) BAPTIST (SD 833584). Built 1833 for a church formed *c.*1782. Rubble walls with front of squared stone and hipped stone-slated roof. Front wall facing SW has plain stone quoins and a platband, two doorways and two upper windows; the side walls have each three large upper windows.

    The interior (35½ft square) has a very deep NE gallery with staircases from the front entrances between which is a tall late 19th-century rostrum with baptistery below. A vestry and minister's or caretaker's cottage occupy most of the lower area below the gallery. The principal seating, which is in the gallery,

Baptist chapel, Long Preston. (292)

comprises box-pews with plain panelled sides. (Demolished *c*.1970–5)

Shipley (1912) 109, 190.

LOTHERSDALE   *N. Yorks.*

(293) Former FRIENDS (SD 958460). The meeting-house of 1799, replacing one of *c*.1723, was closed in 1897 and sold in 1958 for conversion to a house. The walls are of rubble, partly rendered, and the roof is covered with stone slates. The building comprises a single meeting-room (30¼ft by 24¼ft) to the W with three tall sash windows in the S wall, and an original two-storeyed cottage to the E; between these parts is an entrance passage with double doors to the principal room. A gallery at the E end of the meeting-room has an open front of square balusters supported by two turned wood columns, the upper part formerly closed with shutters.

Bradford Antiquary V (1912) 233–46.

MENWITH WITH DARLEY   *N. Yorks.*

(294) Former FRIENDS, Darley (SE 208593). The meeting-house was built in 1802 superseding that at Dacre (*see* (103)); the building was sold in 1950 and is now in divided use for storage and social purposes. The walls are of squared stone and the roof re-covered in corrugated material. The S front has a gabled porch and three plain sash windows; similar fenestration to N; end walls gabled.

Interior divided by partition of shutters with principal room at E end. Roof trusses with king-posts and raking struts. To the E is a small contemporary stable.

Fittings – *Monuments*: in burial-ground to S, late 19th-century stones to families of Walker and Briggs, reset. *Mounting Steps*: against E wall of stable. *Sundial*: stone pillar at SE corner of meeting-house, dial missing, *c*.1802.

(295) WESLEYAN, Darley (SE 196596). Gabled end with central entrance, two upper windows and circular stone chimney at apex. Dated 1829. Sunday-school wing dated 1929.

(296) PRIMITIVE METHODIST, Darley (SE 203593). Dated 1841 above blocked doorway; octagonal stone chimney on gable; gable copings with scrolled ends.

MIRFIELD   *W. Yorks.*

(297) CONGREGATIONAL, Lower Hopton (SE 201192). A Presbyterian congregation founded in the late 17th century by the Rev. Richard Thorpe was re-formed in 1733 and the chapel, then at Hopton, was rebuilt. The present chapel of 1829 has a pedimented front of five bays and a three-bay porch with a pair of Roman Doric columns. (URC)

Miall (1868) 279–81.

(298) MORAVIAN, Wellhouse (SE 206211). In 1752 Moravians who had begun meetings in Mirfield in 1742 moved to Wellhouse and converted a building there for use as a chapel. This stood N of the present chapel on the site of Nos. 1–6 Wellhouse Stand. The first chapel on the present site, built 1800–1, was rebuilt in 1970. Wellhouse farmhouse, dated 1576, was used as a Single Brethren's house from 1768 to 1824 and other buildings appropriate to a Settlement were added or converted at subsequent periods.

The chapel of 1800–1 had a broad brick front of five bays with a three-bay pediment surmounted by a bell-cote. The principal windows had round-arched heads; a range of smaller upper windows served a dormitory above the chapel for a boys' boarding-school attached at the W end. A manse, built against the E wall of the chapel in 1837, still remains.

The former chapel was partly refitted internally in 1837 and entirely realigned in 1884.

Fittings – *Bell*: one, undated *c*.1800. *Monuments*: uniformly

Former Friends' meeting-house, Darley. (294)

Former Wesleyan chapel, Monk Fryston. (299)

numbered rectangular slabs in burial-ground, include (1) No. 1 Hannah Wheatley, 1794, S. S. (single sister); (2) No. 2 Samuel Mossley, 1794, M. B. (married brother).

England (1887) 10–11, Pl. 3. Heywood *et al.* (1955) 12–19.

MONK FRYSTON   *N. Yorks.*

(299) Former WESLEYAN (SE 506297). The chapel, of stone with a slate roof, was built in 1845 as a regular hexagon (35½ft wide) with a tall round-arched window at a high level on each face. In 1875 the building was extended to the S and refitted internally with seating stepped up to the N and a school-room at the S end. (Closed 1989)

Moody (1978) 8.

MORLEY   *W. Yorks.*

(300) MORLEY OLD CHAPEL (SE 264280). The present building of 1875 stands on the site of the church of St Mary in Morley Wood. The church, which is referred to in Domesday Book, had

Morley Old Chapel. Former chapel.   (300)

Morley Old Chapel. Royal Arms, 1664.   (300)

been reduced by the 13th century to the status of a chapel-of-ease to the parish church of Batley and its dedication changed to St Nicholas. The chapel, rebuilt after a fire in 1322, and much altered or rebuilt in the 16th century, became the property of the lords of the manor. In 1650 the Earl of Sussex granted a lease of the building to trustees with an endowment for a 'preaching minister'. After the removal of the minister, Christopher Etherington, in 1662, the chapel does not seem to have been in regular use and in 1672 an unsuccessful attempt was made to license it for dissenters on the grounds that it had 'stood vacant divers years'; however, some use by the established church is indicated by the Royal Arms of 1664 and by a prayer book *temp.* James II inscribed 'Morley Town's Book Common Prayer' mentioned by Wonnacott (op. cit. below). In 1689 the registration of 'a public place built by the Inhabitants of Morley' as a Presbyterian meeting-house could refer to the chapel which was certainly in nonconformist hands by the end of that century. A secession of Independents in the 18th century led to the erection of another chapel in 1764, superseded in 1834 by 'Rehoboth', Brunswick Street (SE 261281), which was destroyed by fire in 1977.

The former chapel was a low building with aisled nave and chancel, a small W gallery, bell-cote and mullioned windows with arched lights of 16th or early 17th-century date. Various

Morley Old Chapel. St Mary's in the Wood (from Smith, 1876).   (300)

alterations were made about 1865 but the structure became unsafe in 1872 and was demolished in 1874. The present building, named 'St Mary's in the Wood', is of stone in the Gothic style by Lockwood and Mawson. It comprises a nave of three bays with transepts, a short chancel, and a tower and spire at the SW corner.

Fittings – *Baptismal Basin*: two-handled bowl of biscuit-coloured pottery with floral ornament, on separate saucer, possibly late 18th-century. *Bells*: in tower two – (1) from former chapel, inscribed 'SOLI DEO GLORIA 1694'; (2) '1879 W BLEWS AND SONS'. *Clock*: loose in vestry, with swan-neck pediment to case, signed 'Stonehouse, Leeds', early 19th-century.

Monuments: in chapel (1) Benjamin Edward Knowles, 1841. In mausoleum S of chapel, monuments to Scatchard family including (2) Matthew, 1688, Elizabeth his widow, 1715; (3) Thomas, 1700, Jane his wife, 1691; (4) Samuel, 1760, Mary his widow, 1771; (5) Samuel, 1779, and Theodocia (Norrisson) his wife, 1767; (6) Thomas, 1771; (7) Watson, 1817, and Frances his wife, 1812; (8) Norrisson Cavendish, 1853, *et al.*; (9) Watson, 1855, *et al.*; (10) Watson Samuel, 1833. In burial-ground, many monuments of late 17th century and after, include: SE of chapel (11) Robert Pickeringe M.A., 'preacher of the Gospel att Morley', 1680, table-tomb; (12) John Halliday, 1677, and John, son of Jonathan Fothergill, 1742; (13) Samuel Baily, 'Minister of the Gospel at Morley and Topcliffe', 1675; (14) Alice, wife of Samuel Baily, 1674; (15) Elizabeth, wife of John Scur, 1679; (16) John Scur, 1684; (17) Ruth, wife of William Brook, 1724, and Ann their daughter, 1746, table-tomb; (18) William Robinson, 1695; (19) Stephen Thompson, 1675; (20) William Thompson, 1667; (21) Henry Greatheed, 1718, and Martha his widow, 1722; (22) Mary (Metcalfe), wife of Joseph Beaumont, 1689; (23) Mrs Elizabeth Craister, 1691; (24) Thomas Craister, 1681. S of chapel (25) Rev. Timothy Aldred, 54 years pastor, 1773; (26) Samuel Dawson, 1696; (27) Abraham Dawson, 1671, and Rev. Joseph Dawson his son, 1709; (28) John Dawson, 1741, with shield-of-arms; (29) Esther, wife of Joshua Crowther, 1693. N of chapel (30) Mercy Sargen, 1676; (31) John Lister, minister, 1707, and Bathshua his widow, 'niece to the late Lord Eure', 1732.

Painting: in vestry, water-colour sketch of Old Chapel *c*.1830. *Plate*: includes two two-handled cups of 1765 and 1808 and a

Wesleyan chapel, Wesley Street, Morley.

(303)

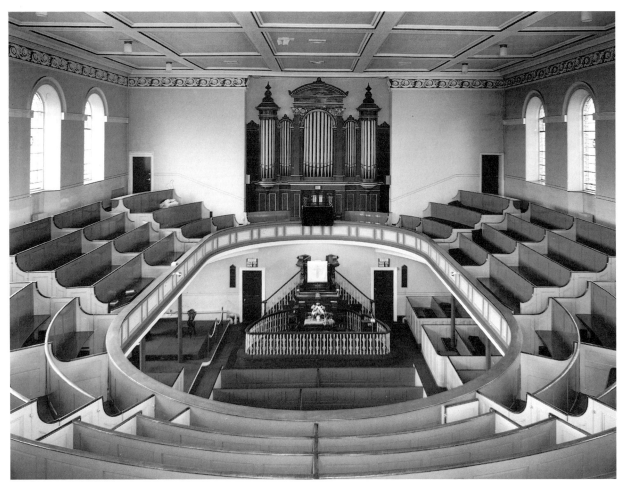

Wesleyan chapel, Wesley Street, Morley. (303)

plate of 1772. *Royal Arms*: painted on wood, Charles II dated 1664, from former chapel.

Miall (1868) 320–3. Smith, W., *The History and Antiquities of Morley* (1876) 124–73. Smith, W., *The Registers of Topcliffe and Morley* (1888). Wonnacott, J., *The History of Morley Old Chapel* (1859).

(301) BAPTIST, Church Street, Gildersome (SE 241294). The congregation, which originally formed part of the extensive church of Rossendale, built its first meeting-house in 1707. This was enlarged in 1787 and replaced by the present chapel, by Simpson and Son of Leeds, in 1866. The chapel has an elaborately pedimented front with five round-arched upper windows. Galleried interior with box-pews throughout. Alongside is a Memorial Hall, of 1887, by J. Reginald Naylor.

Bilbrough, W. R., *et al.*, *History of the Baptist Church at Gildersome in the County of York* ... (1888). Shipley (1912) 155.

(302) FRIENDS, Gildersome (SE 244291). Meetings began *c.*1660 and the first meeting-house was built 1709–10. The present building on a new site in Street Lane was erected in 1756–8 but greatly altered in the 19th century. It stands concealed behind a range of stables next to the road and is approached through a segmental-arched gateway with library room above. The walls and roof are of stone. The S front has two tiers of windows and two doorways. The interior (39½ft by 25¼ft) is divided into two rooms by a partition with fielded-panelled shutters. The principal room to the E has a stand incorporating 18th-century panelling. The roof is supported by four softwood trusses with queen-posts and tusk-tenon joints to the purlins.

Monuments: reset internally, two ledger stones removed from former burial-ground at The Nooks, ¼ mile E (1) Thomas Jefferson 'which departed this life the 27 of the 12 month called Adar 1662'; (2) Anthony Casson, 1667. In boundary wall (3) William [   ], 167[ ].

Morley Advertiser (16 January 1976).

(303) WESLEYAN, Wesley Street (SE 264276). The chapel of 1860–1 by James Simpson replaced a chapel of 1770 which had been variously enlarged. It has stone walls with a four-bay pedimented front with paired entrances and sides of six bays. The interior retains most of its original fittings including a continuous oval gallery, box-pews at both levels, mahogany pulpit, and organ with Classical case by Booth of Wakefield, 1863.

Smith (1876) 182–7.

(304) WESLEYAN, Churwell (SE 273295). The chapel of 1821 in Back Green has been beheaded.

(305) WESLEYAN, Westerton Road, Upper Green (SE 278253). Plain building with three-bay sides and hipped roof, opened 1838. Sunday-school in front c.1900.

(306) Former PRIMITIVE METHODIST, Fountain Street (SE 264 275). Classical stone front of five bays with three-bay pediment supported by giant Corinthian pilasters; 1885–6. Detached Sunday-school to right dated 1878. Both now in commercial use.

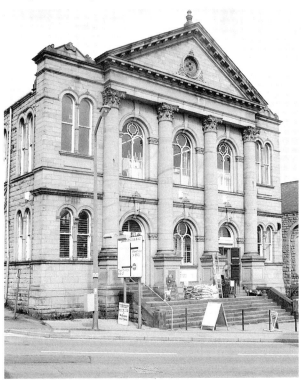

Former Primitive Methodist chapel, Fountain Street, Morley. (306)

(307) PRIMITIVE METHODIST, Haigh Moor (SE 283242). Broad three-bay front with round-arched windows; inscription 'Ebenezer . . . 1856'.

(308) Former UNITED METHODIST, Commercial Street (SE 266 277). 1896, by Thomas A. Buttery, superseding a Wesleyan Reform chapel of 1858.

(309) Former UNITED METHODIST, Churwell (SE 271294). Three bays with two tiers of round-arched windows; 'Mount Zion, 1861'; school-room dated 1871. Now in industrial use.

NEWTON   *Lancashire*

(310) CONGREGATIONAL (SD 697504). The chapel built in 1696 by Richard Lee of Birkett and enlarged or reconstructed c.1832 was almost entirely rebuilt in 1887. The early 19th-century rear wall survives with three round-arched windows with keystones and impost blocks. Prior to 1887 the front wall had two similar windows flanking the entrance. The original red-sandstone door lintel, reset inside the porch, is inscribed '1696 RL'. (URC)

Miall (1868) 324–5. Nightingale II (1891) 224–32. Whitehead (1930) 160–73.

(311) Former FRIENDS (SD 695505). The meeting-house and adjacent cottage, of rubble with a stone-slate roof, replaced at the front by slate, were built in 1767 with a legacy from John Brabbin who also built and endowed the Friends' School. They superseded a meeting-house of 1698. The S front of the meeting-house has a plain doorway between three two-light windows with squared mullions and one upper window at the E end. The cottage to the W is of a single bay with two storeys of windows; a tablet above the doorway is inscribed I^{B}M 1767.

The interior of the meeting-house (21ft by 27½ft) has a gallery at the E end with an open front of flat balusters; the space below the gallery is closed by shutters to form a separate room. The stand is continuous across the N wall. Some 18th-century seating remains; on the back of one bench is cut the inscription 'J B . . . . t 1826' for John Bright who was a pupil at the school. (Incorporated into adjacent cottage 1988)

Former *Friends' School*, 100 yards SE, with initials and date J^{B}M 1757, became the Congregational Manse in 1910 and was enlarged in 1928.

Burial-ground, 100 yards NW, walled enclosure with stone gateway, monuments late 19th-century and after.

Whitehead (1930) 165–6.

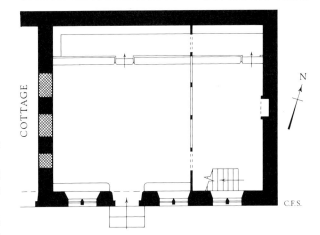

Friends' Meeting-house, NEWTON *Yorkshire W.R.*

NORMANTON   *W. Yorks.*

(312) BAPTIST, High Street (SE 385228). Red-brick with blue-brick and stone dressings; pediment with large inscribed tablet 'erected 1877'.

Shipley (1912) 172–3.

(313) PRIMITIVE METHODIST, Wakefield Road (SE 382224), opened 1850, re-fronted 1903. (Reported demolished 1981)

NORTH BIERLEY   *W. Yorks.*

(314) Former MEETING-HOUSE, Chapel Fold, Wibsey (SE 147 303). Early 17th-century house, now three cottages, with large ten-light mullioned window with transom to hall range. Said by

Former Meeting-house, Chapel Fold, Wibsey. (314)

England ((1887) op. cit. below) to have been used by Presbyterians from 1688 to 1719, i.e. the society which then moved to Chapel Lane, Bradford (*see* (58)), but perhaps by a congregation distinct from that at Little Horton (¾ mile NE) from which the Bradford society claims to derive. Occupied also by Moravians between 1760 and 1837 prior to the erection of a new chapel at Little Horton. The pulpit is reported to have stood against the hall window, one light of which remains blocked for this purpose, with a gallery around the other three sides.

England (1887) 13, Pl. 11. RCHM, *Rural Houses of West Yorkshire 1400–1830* (1986), 70, 72 and Plate 76.

(315) Former CONGREGATIONAL, Chapel Street, Wibsey (SE 152302). Opened 1841, refitted 1868. Four-bay sides with two tiers of plain sash windows, gabled front with doorways in end bays. Interior with late 19th-century horseshoe-shaped gallery

supported by cast-iron columns; large school-room below chapel. Roof supported by five trusses with king and queen-posts.

'John Paul Memorial School 1862' adjacent, with sculptured pediment; larger Sunday-school, 1887. Burial-ground in front of chapel with numerous table-tombs and other monuments; vandalized. (Demolition of chapel proposed 1985)

CYB (1861) 227. Miall (1868) 239.

(316) WESLEYAN REFORM, Holyroyd Hill, Wibsey (SE 153301), hipped stone-slate roof, four-bay front and two tiers of round-arched windows, mid 19th-century. (Demolition proposed 1986)

(317) WESLEYAN REFORM, Shetcliffe Lane (SE 178295). 'Bethel A.D. 1855', three-bay front with round-arched windows; Sunday-school later.

NORTON   S. Yorks.

(318) PRIMITIVE METHODIST (SE 548153). 'Zion chapel' dated 1845, rendered three-bay front, round-arched openings. Derelict 1972.

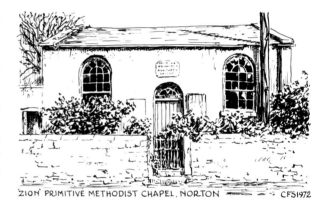

'ZION' PRIMITIVE METHODIST CHAPEL, NORTON   CFS1972

NORWOOD   N. Yorks.

(319) Former WESLEYAN, Brown Bank (SE 216538). The upper storey of a remotely situated cottage dating in part from the early 18th century was converted for use as a preaching-room in 1847. The porch is approached by an external flight of stone steps. The fittings, largely of the late 19th century, include stepped seating to the left of the entrance, a singers' pew, and a leaders' pew with balustraded front adjacent to the pulpit. (Reported closed and fittings removed for preservation, 1985)

OSSETT   W. Yorks.

(320) Former PRIMITIVE METHODIST, Queen Street (SE 278201). 'Mount Zion' 1863; three-bay front with pediment and two tiers of round-arched windows. Now in industrial use.

OTLEY   W. Yorks.

(321) CONGREGATIONAL, Bridge Street (SE 202458). Gothic with octagonal corner turret and spire, 1897–9, by T. H. and F. Healey of Bradford. Tablet from former chapel inscribed 'SALEM CHAPEL MDCCCXXV' reset inside boundary wall. (URC)

Briggs (1946) Pls. 7, 8. CYB (1900) 149. Miall (1868) 328.

Congregational chapel, Wibsey. (315)

Wesleyan chapel. Brown Bank.   (319)

(322) Former METHODIST, Nelson Street (SE 20354550). The preaching-house erected in 1771 for a society in existence by 1755 was visited by John Wesley 30 June 1772 who described it in his *Journal* as 'as neat as that at Hull'. It was superseded by a new chapel in Boroughgate (*see* (323)) in 1826 but remained in use by the Sunday-school until 1875. It subsequently became a Drill Hall.

The walls are of coursed stone and the roof is covered with slates. The S front is of three bays with a pediment and two tiers of windows separated by a platband. The central doorway has been widened; above it is a Venetian window with triple keystone and a small circular ventilator in the pediment; the other windows have plain stone architraves. In the N wall is a

Former Methodist chapel, Nelson Street, Otley.   (322)

large plain Venetian window, now blocked and covered by an external chimney breast. The side walls, which may have been partly rebuilt, are irregularly fenestrated.

The interior (47½ft by 38½ft) was much altered in the mid 19th century when a floor was inserted. (Reported demolished 1973)
    Seals (1974) 24–6.

(323) Former WESLEYAN, Boroughgate (SE 20374560). The chapel built in 1825–6 to supersede the foregoing was converted for a Sunday-school in 1876 and passed to commercial use in 1905. The front is of ashlar in four bays with round-arched upper windows. At the rear is an apsidal vestry with singers' gallery above having a blocked Venetian window centrally at the upper level. The interior (50½ft by 41ft) is divided by an inserted floor. The ceiling has enriched plasterwork with a ribbed vault above the apse. (Demolition proposed 1976)
    Seals (1974) 24–6.

PAYTHORNE   *Lancashire*

(324) WESLEYAN (SD 830518). Small three-bay chapel of 1830 with railed forecourt.

PENISTONE   *S. Yorks.*

(325) BULLHOUSE CHAPEL (SE 211027). The chapel, dated 1692, stands close to Bullhouse Hall, 2 miles W of Penistone. The hall was built in 1655 by Sylvanus Rich, a Puritan well acquainted with Oliver Heywood, who gave asylum or support to several nonconformist ministers after the Restoration. These included the Rev. Henry Swift, vicar of Penistone, who, although he suffered several periods of imprisonment between 1663 and 1666 and failed to comply with the full requirements of the 1662 Act of Uniformity, retained the living until his death in 1689 largely due to the support of the Riches and other local Puritan families. In 1672 the hall was licensed for use as a Presbyterian meeting place with Nathan Denton, ejected vicar of Bolton upon Dearne and later minister at Great Houghton, as the recognized preacher. Elkanah Rich inherited his father's estate in 1683 and a few years after the Toleration Act, when several local houses had been named as preaching-places, he built the chapel at Bullhouse: this was certified in April 1692 as 'a new house at Bullhouse in Penistone'. The first minister of the chapel, also described as 'chaplain to Mr Rich', was Daniel son of Nathan Denton who remained here until 1721. A later minister was Thomas Halliday, described in 1772 as 'chaplain to Hans Busk esq.' who had inherited the property by marriage and through whom it descended to the family of Lord Houghton. By the early 19th century the Presbyterian interest at the chapel had expired and the building seems to have been occupied by Wesleyan preachers for much of that century; the establishment of a Sunday-school in 1825 may be attributed to that denomination. The present Independent congregation has no external affiliation.

The chapel has walls of squared millstone grit and the roof is covered with stone slates. It has a chamfered plinth and eaves cornice and gables to the N and S ends with moulded kneelers and stone ball finials. A porch centrally on the E side has similar details; the outer doorway has a segmental-arched lintel but the inner has a voussoired arch of similar form. Each side of the porch are two windows of two lights divided by a transom, the heads

Bullhouse Chapel, Penistone.

(325)

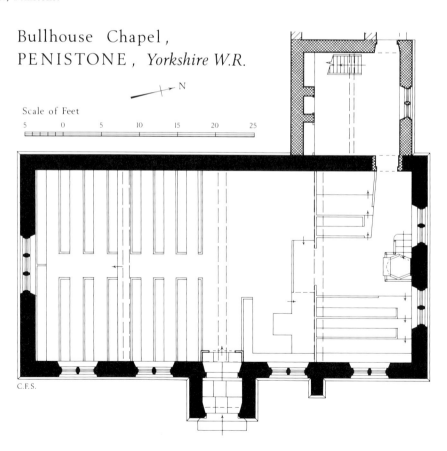

Bullhouse Chapel,
PENISTONE, *Yorkshire W.R.*

N

Scale of Feet

5   0   5   10   15   20   25

C.F.S.

of all lights being elliptically arched. A stepped buttress between the two northern windows may be an addition. Two similar windows in the N wall are joined at the head by a moulded label; in the S wall is a window of like pattern with a label but with three lights above and below the transom. The W wall is blank but attached at the N end is a small cottage of two storeys with a single room to each floor. This is of similar construction to the chapel, although a few years later in date, and has in the N wall one window with two arched lights to each room and an outer doorway on the W side with a plain lintel, now covered by additions.

The interior of the chapel (49ft by 24¼ft) has a squared stone face to the walls with traces of former whitewash but without evidence of original plastering; three cased tie-beams below the flat plaster ceiling are supported at their ends by short upturned brackets and wall-posts resting on moulded stone corbels. The pulpit stands between the N windows, the transoms of which are carved with the crest of a wyvern, for Rich, and a cross *botonny*. The seating was renewed *c*.1900.

Fittings – *Doors*: in inner doorway of E porch, pair, each with two applied panels with moulded edges outlined in nail studding, 1692; in outer W doorway of cottage, boarded with four applied panels and nail studding, original decorative iron hinges, *c*.1700; in inner doorway between chapel and cottage, with four fielded panels, *c*.1700. *Hat Pegs*: around walls of chapel, oak rails and pegs. *Inscriptions and Scratchings*: externally over inner doorway in porch, in square cartouche, 'APRIL 18 ANOD 1692' with numeral or letters II below; on N jamb of outer doorway, scratched initials IM with fylfot below. *Masons' Marks*: externally on chapel + A E I V; on cottage + △ H I ↓ V. *Music Stands*: various, three of iron with lyre-shaped tops and tripod legs and one of wood signed 'Weeldon's patent', mid 19th-century. *Picture*: photograph of teachers and scholars in front of chapel, taken on Jubilee of Sunday-school, 1875. *Pulpit*: wood, seven-sided with two tiers of bolection-moulded panelling above modern square base; panelled back-board and heptagonal canopy with scrolled brackets, moulded cornice with acorn pendants and crown of flat wood scrolls around central pillar with acorn finial, late 17th-century.

Ambler (1913) 84, Pl. CII. Matthews (1934) *passim*. Miall (1868) 329–30.

(326) NETHERFIELD CHAPEL (SE 242039). Although the vicar, Henry Swift, continued to occupy the living after 1662 without fully conforming, no regular nonconformist congregation was found in the village until the late 18th century. Netherfield Chapel was built by Congregationalists in 1786 but extensions to the N in the early 19th century, to the S in 1890, and to the E at a similar period have left little of the original building visible. The walls are of stone (32ft by 46ft externally), with two original windows with moulded stone surrounds remaining in the surviving fragment of the 18th-century S front; a pedimented stone doorcase and window above, reset in the 1890 extension may also come from this wall.

Monuments: in burial-ground (1) John Batley, dyer, 1798, Ann his wife, 1793, their sons Smith, 1792, John, 1794, and daughter Mary, 1811, table-tomb; (2) Rev. John Williams, pastor, 1900, Hannah (Wiggins) his wife, 1864, and Hannah their daughter,

1864, table-tomb; (3) Joseph Hadfield, 1807, and Mary his wife, 1799; (4) David Firth, 1800, Mary his wife, 1798, and Joshua their son, 1797.

Miall (1868) 330–1.

(327) METHODIST NEW CONNEXION, Hoyland Swaine (SE 262 048). The original chapel of 1807, a low stone building of three bays, was extended to the E and an upper storey added in 1850. The lower storey was converted to a cottage with the chapel above approached by external staircases on the N and S sides, the former now removed. A tablet above the original entrance is inscribed 'Beathel Chapel Erected 1807'. Sunday-school, 100 yards E, built 1814, much enlarged 1893.

Methodist New Connexion chapel, Hoyland Swaine.   (327)

POLLINGTON   *Humberside*

(328) WESLEYAN (SE 613197). Three-bay brick front, 1835.

PONTEFRACT   *W. Yorks.*

(329) FRIENDS, Southgate (SE 459220). The meeting-house built in 1698, demolished 1947, stood on the SE side of the road at the junction with Harrop Well Lane. The broad SW front facing the burial-ground had two windows to the right of the doorway under a continuous string-course and a third window to the left. *Monuments*: in burial-ground, rectangular marker stones with dates from early 19th century.

(330) WESLEYAN, Horsefair (SE 458221). John Wesley opened a new preaching-house here in 1772. The chapel on the SE side of the street, which may have been subsequent in date although possibly of the late 18th century, was of brick with a pedimented front, tripartite lower window between Ionic-columned front entrances and a Venetian window above. (Demolished 1962)

PUDSEY   *W. Yorks.*

(331) Former BAPTIST, Bagley Lane, Farsley (SE 222357). Built 1777 but much enlarged in 1784, 1836 and 1844 leaving no original work visible. Converted to Sunday-school 1869 and since 1906 in industrial use. Five-bay front dated 1836.

Ivimey IV (1830) 567. Shipley (1912) 156–8.

(332) BAPTIST, Richardshaw Lane, Stanningley (SE 220342). 'Salem Chapel' dated 1827 has a gabled front of five bays with

Moravian Settlement, Fulneck. From the air.   (335)

two tiers of plain windows. Enlarged 1838. (Proposed conversion to offices 1985)

BM (1838) 394. Rayner (1887) 110–11. Shipley (1912) 162.

(333) Former CONGREGATIONAL, Bradford Road, Stanningley (SE 217344). Small Gothic chapel of 1855 by Lockwood and Mawson.

CYB (1856) 265. Miall (1868) 368.

(334) WESLEYAN REFORMERS, Bradford Road, Stanningley (SE 218344). 'Olivet' chapel, opened 1856, has a low pedimented front of three bays.

(335) MORAVIAN SETTLEMENT, Fulneck (SE 222320). In the years preceding 1741 numerous religious societies had been formed in Yorkshire by Benjamin Ingham and Charles Delamotte. In that year a formal agreement was reached under which the supervision of these groups passed to the Moravian church and a centre for the continuance of the work was established at Smith House, Lightcliffe. A conflict of interest between Moravian and Methodist supporters soon led to the need for removal to more suitable premises and the present site, one mile S of Pudsey, was acquired by Ingham in January 1744. The Settlement, first named 'Lamb's Hill' and from 1749 'Gracehill', received its present designation in 1763 by a variation of the earlier name of the site, Fall Neck, to equate with that of the original home of the church in Silesia.

Use was first made of two houses existing on the site together with property to the W at Bankhouse, where a textile manufactory was established. The first chapel, N of its successor and now converted to housing, was in use from 1744 to 1748. The present chapel or Congregation Hall was begun in 1746 and the other principal buildings necessary for a fully developed settlement were built subsequently to form, eventually, a

Moravian Settlement, Fulneck. South front of chapel.   (335)

Moravian Settlement, Fulneck. Interior of chapel.   (335)

continuous terrace 300 yards in length with the chapel at the centre. The first of these were two detached 'choir houses' for the Single Brethren and Sisters W and E of the chapel, of 1749–52, both enlarged in 1758. Two other detached houses intermediately between these and the chapel were then built, that to the W probably in 1784–5 for the boys' boarding-school, and the intervening spaces filled by further houses, mostly of three storeys, in the later 18th or early 19th century. Boys' and girls' boarding-schools, commenced in London in 1741, settled at Fulneck in 1753 and 1755 respectively, initially occupying rooms below the chapel but since the late 19th century accommodated in the former choir houses to which further buildings have since been added. A mixed range of housing, including the first chapel, lies N of the principal terrace and a further range of houses, together with the village shop and the site of an inn, lies to the west.

The first chapel has stone walls and roof. The S front of five bays is bounded by quoins and has a platband between two tiers of windows. The entrance is central with a round-arched window above. The roof was formerly surmounted by a wooden bell-cote.

The Congregation House, including the chapel, reputed to have been designed by Edward Graves and his brother from Newark, is also of stone with the entrance centrally on the N side but with the principal elevation to the south. The S front is of four bays with two further bays at each end bounded by uniform quoins above a low basement storey and with dormer windows in the roof. Four tall round-arched windows light the chapel on this side. At the centre is a doorway to the basement and above it a blank stone tablet with broken pediment supported by pilasters. The N wall is partly covered by a two-storeyed porch of three bays added in 1770 which has a pedimented front surmounted by a stone bell-cote. The end bays, which comprise domestic accommodation, project as wings to each side of the porch.

The chapel, opened in 1748, has a plaster ceiling with decorative bosses and a moulded and enriched cornice. The pulpit is centrally against the S wall opposite the entrance: this and the E and W galleries were not completed until 1750; the matching N gallery, which may be contemporary with the porch, was extended forwards in the early 19th century. The gallery has a fielded-panelled front and dentil cornice which breaks forward on each side and is supported by Roman Doric columns. The E and W wings are of two storeys above a basement. The rooms below the chapel, which in the late 18th century served as classrooms, have been converted to dwellings; they include a large central room with an apse N of the entrance. A staircase connected the basement with the attic floor above the chapel where dormitory accommodation was provided by raising the roof structure to the level of the tops of the parapet walls; mortices for the former roof trusses are visible in the tie-beams.

The choir houses of 1749–52 are of identical design with walls of red brick and slated roofs. They are of three storeys and attics with seven-bay fronts to the S; the three central bays project slightly and are finished with pediments in each of which is a simple Venetian window. The same feature is repeated in the E and W gables.

Fittings – *Baptismal Basin*: plated base metal, two handles, 19th-century. *Bell*: one, in bell-cote. *Clock*: in N porch with external dials, *c*.1779. *Love-feast Cups*: handle-less cups with matching saucers in blue and white ornamental patterned china, all inscribed beneath 'Fulneck Jubilee April 19th 1855'. *Monuments*: in burial-ground E of the Terrace, uniformly numbered rectangular marker stones, all re-sited along edges of paths. *Organ*: in N gallery, removed from E gallery in 1803, by Snetzler, 1750, enlarged 1855, rebuilt 1929, original case. *Pulpit*: on octagonal stem, with balustraded stair to W, *c*.1750. *Seating*: pews erected 1888 replacing open-backed benches.

England (1887) 7–11, Pls. 4–6, 10, 13. Linstrum (1978) 243–4. Rayner, S., *The History and Antiquities of Pudsey* (1887) 233–77.

QUEENSBURY AND SHELF   *W. Yorks.*

(336) GENERAL BAPTIST, Chapel Street, Queensbury (SE 102 304). Services at Queensbury (formerly Queen's Head) commenced about 1772 by Dan Taylor were continued by his brother, John Taylor of Halifax, and a meeting-house was built in 1773. Galleries were added in 1792 and later. The present chapel, rebuilt on the same site in 1820, is of stone with a hipped roof. The broad front of five bays has two tiers of windows separated by a platband, entrances in the penultimate bays and a simple Venetian window between with a tripartite window above; below this last is a tablet with the dates of erection and rebuilding.

The interior has a gallery around three sides with angled corners. An organ chamber was built behind the pulpit *c*.1873.

Fittings – *Baptistery*: external, in front of chapel. *Chair*: with scrolled and panelled back and arm rests, associated with Dan Taylor, formerly at North Parade Chapel, Halifax, 17th-century. *Monuments*: in chapel (1) Rev. John Taylor 'the founder of the General Baptist Cause in this Neighbourhood', 45 years pastor, 1818, signed 'J. Rushton'; (2) Samuel Ibbotson, 1815, Mary his wife, 1811, and Mary their daughter, 1863; (3) John Ibbotson, 1818, and Mary Ann Ibbotson, 1835. The front of chapel, many table-tombs, including (4) Rev. Thomas Hall Hudson, pastor and missionary, 1876, Hannah his wife, 1832, and five children. *Sampler*: depicting present chapel, signed 'Hannah Stocks', mid 19th-century. *Seating*: to lower floor mid 19th-century box-pews; in gallery original box-pews formerly without cross access between the two sides.

Shipley (1912) 106, 120–1. Taylor (1818) II: 180, 182–8, 272–5, 390. Wood (1847) 182.

(337) UNION CROFT CHAPEL, Halifax Road, Ambler Thorn (SE 094295). Plain gabled chapel of 1842 built by seceders from the Methodist New Connexion who formed themselves into a Congregational church in 1846.

CYB (1846) 180–1.

(338) Former PRIMITIVE METHODIST, Wade House Road, Shelf (SE 123287). Broad six-bay front with two round-arched windows between doorways and plain end windows; opened 1821. School adjacent dated 1901.

Monuments: against front wall (1) Jonathan Jaggar, 1835, and Hannah his widow, 1843; (2) Joseph Bottomley, 1866, and Martha his wife, 1849. In front burial-ground, nine table-tombs and various ledger stones (3) George, son of John and Rebecca Flather, 1823, *et al.*; (4) John Shaw of Mill House 'one of the founders of this chapel', 1837, and Elizabeth his widow, 1859; (5) John Bartle 'one of the founders of this chapel', 1846, and Mary his widow. (Converted to secular use, and front monuments removed, before 1984)

PRIMITIVE METHODIST CHAPEL, WADE HOUSE   CFS 1974

(339) FREE METHODIST, Wade House Road, Shelf (SE 128289). 'Bethel Chapel' dated 1853. Four-bay front with two tiers of round-arched windows with original glazing bars; hipped slate roof. Large burial-ground in front.

(340) UNITARIAN, Pepper Hill (SE 112288). School-chapel built 1862, broad five-bay front with round-arched windows.

Hargrove (*c*.1903).

RATHMELL   *N. Yorks.*

(341) WESLEYAN (SD 805598). Three-bay front with entrance re-sited, dated 1846.

CONGREGATIONAL CHAPEL, NEWBY HILL   CFS 1972

RIMINGTON   *Lancashire*

(342) CONGREGATIONAL, Newby Hill (SD 821458). Broad six-bay front with round-arched windows, centre pair higher flanking pulpit, four plain windows high in back wall, later cottage at end. Built 1817.

Fittings – *Paving*: in front of gates from road, cobbles laid with inscription 'SC/1817' for 'Salem Chapel'. *Sundial*: between front windows, stone with arched top, motto 'Time flies swift away'.
   Miall (1868) 315. Nightingale II (1891) 207–10.

RIPON   *N. Yorks.*

(343) Former WESLEYAN, Coltsgate Hill (SE 311716). Brick with stone dressings, pedimented front of four bays with paired entrances, round-arched upper windows and carved enrichment in pediment. Built 1861, probably by James Simpson.

RIPPONDEN   *W. Yorks.*

(344) BAPTIST, Rishworth (SE 034182). The chapel built in 1803 for a newly formed congregation has stone walls and a stone-slate roof. The S front of three bays has a window of three lights between the entrances and three plain windows above. A wing incorporating an organ chamber was added centrally at the rear in the mid 19th century. A detached Sunday-school of 1898 stands to the north.

The interior (30ft by 40ft) has a gallery around three sides supported by cast-iron columns. The pulpit rostrum and lower seating, including a large family pew for the Whiteley family at the E side, date from the late 19th century but the original seating remains in the gallery.

BAPTIST CHAPEL, RISHWORTH   CFS 1977

Monuments: in chapel (1) Rev. Thomas Mellor, 36 years pastor, 1852, signed 'Fisher, Huddersfield'. In burial-ground, many ledger stones formerly in front have been removed to the side or rear, other monuments in front include (2) Joseph, son of Joseph and Rachel Shaw, 1826, *et al.*, table-tomb; (3) Mary, daughter of Eli and Lettice Pogson, 1846, table-tomb; (4) Rev. Thomas Mellor, 1852, Mary his widow, 1857, *et al.*; (5) John Taylor, 1824, Mary his wife, 1824, and Sally their daughter, 1817; (6) Thomas Henry, son of John and Elizabeth Whiteley, 1828, *et al.*, table-tomb.
   Shipley (1912) 221–2.

(345) CONGREGATIONAL, Ripponden (SE 035194). Gothic with octagonal turret and short spire above entrance, 1869 by Paull and Robinson.
   CYB (1870) 381.

(346) CONGREGATIONAL, Parrock Nook (SE 016182). Built 1832 for a congregation formed by members from Sowerby and in existence by 1824. Stone walls and roof with three-bay front, tall round-arched windows and three short windows above. Possibly heightened 1858 when galleries were added.

Inscription: above central entrance 'INDEPENDENT UNION CHAPEL 1832' with initials PW.
   Miall (1868) 340.

ROTHERHAM   *S. Yorks.*

(347) OLD MEETING-HOUSE, Downs Row (SK 429926). The former Presbyterian society, latterly Unitarian, originated in the late 17th century. The first regular meeting-house, built in 1706 largely at the cost of Thomas Hollis junior on land 'near the Beast Market', was much altered in 1841 to designs by James Hill; it was superseded in 1880 by a new Gothic chapel in Moorgate Street, 100 yards NE, by Flockton and Gibbs (now in other religious use).

Old Meeting-house, Rotherham.
(From Blazenby (1906).)   (347)

The Old Meeting-house, which later served as a day school but is now let for commercial use, stands on a concealed site at the end of a minor lane. The walls are of stone, rendered at the sides, and the roof is slated. Before 1841 the principal front faced W and was of six bays with tall cross-framed windows and with doorways with segmental pediments below the windows in the penultimate bays; two windows centrally on the E side flanked the pulpit. The roof was hipped and had a central flat or valley. In the 1841 alterations the roof was rebuilt with N and S gables, the E and W walls were refenestrated each with four round-arched windows, a vestry was added at the S end and a porch of sandstone with gallery above was built to the north.

The interior has been subdivided by a floor at gallery level. There is a flat plaster ceiling with moulded cornice and frieze with floral paterae of 1841.

Inscription: large tablet reset externally on E side of N porch, removed from Hollis School in Oil Mill Yard, recording the endowment in 1702 by Thomas Hollis senior of London of a school for poor children in Rotherham, the erection of the building in 1789 and its further endowment by 'several of the Trustees and other Protestant Dissenters'. *Monuments*: internally on E wall, reset here after sale of later chapel, eight monuments and brasses including (1) Sarah Ann McDermot, 1825; (2) Rev. Jacob Brettell, 43 years minister, 1862; (3) Elizabeth Favell, 1862. In burial-ground, several ledger stones of early 19th century and later.

Blazenby, W., *Rotherham: The Old Meeting-house and its Ministers* (1906). Evans (1897) 214. Miall (1868) 340–1.

(348) MASBROUGH CHAPEL, College Road (SK 423929). The Congregational church (now URC) formerly meeting here originated in 1760 as a secession by sixteen members from the Methodist society. The first chapel on this site, built largely at the expense of Samuel Walker, an ironmaster, was opened in 1764. The present building of 1777–80 was extended to the front in 1829–30 and further altered in the late 19th century. Since 1960 the chapel has passed to commercial use.

Rotherham Academy, later Rotherham College, founded 1795 as the successor of Northowram Academy, was early associated with this chapel. The first building, in College Road, paid for by John Walker, was superseded in 1876; the College amalgamated with Bradford College in 1888.

The chapel (originally 63¼ft by 46¼ft externally) has brick walls with stone quoins and a hipped slate roof. The architect is thought to have been John Platt. The lower stage of the original E front has, to the lower floor, two doorways with a tripartite window between; the upper part was brought forward in 1829–30 as an extension of the rear gallery. The new upper walling, which has three windows with stone architraves, is carried by an open loggia with five cast-iron columns and is closed by a wall at the S end. The loggia was enclosed by a glazed screen in the late 19th century and the gallery staircases brought forward into it. The side walls of the chapel have two tiers of windows matching those in the E front.

The interior has a continuous gallery rounded at each end with a 19th-century front supported by cast-iron columns. The seating has been removed.

Fittings – *Clock*: on front of E gallery, mechanism inscribed 'The Gift of Joseph Walker to the Meetinghouse in Masbrough A.D. 1778', dial later. *Monuments*: in chapel (1) Joseph Walker, 1801; (2) Mary (Walker), wife of Jonathan Walker, 1803, with shield-of-arms; (3) Jonathan Walker J.P., 1807, with male weeper resting against broken column, shield-of-arms below; (4) Joshua Walker, 1815, and Susanna his widow, 1831, with shield-of-arms; (5) Elizabeth Abney, 1850; (6) Edward Williams D.D., 18 years pastor and theological tutor, 1813; (7) Thomas Walker, 1828, and Mary his widow, 1844; (8) Rev. John Thorp, 13 years pastor, 1776, oval tablet; (9) George Glossop, 1809 and Sarah his widow, 1831; (10) Alfred Walker, 1824; (11) Rev. William Hendry Stowell D.D., pastor, president of college and theological tutor, 1858; (12) Rev. James Bennett D.D., 15 years pastor and theological tutor, 1862; (13) Samuel Walker 'The principal projector of those extensive Ironworks first founded at Masbrough in the year 1746 which now afford so singular an Example both of the public and private Benefit which may arise from the smallest beginnings when favoured by divine Providence, and prosecuted with Integrity, Foresight,

Masbrough Chapel, Rotherham. (*Photo*: *A. Smith, 1948*.) (348)

Regularity, and an active comprehensive Genius . . .', 1782, 'buried in the Cæmetery which he built for his body', and Mary his widow, 1798. In E loggia (14) Mary Winter, 1794, and members of Walker family, table-tomb. In burial-ground, in SE corner (15) mausoleum with pyramid roof and eared corners, uninscribed [Walker family], early 19th-century; N of last (16) Aaron Walker, 1777, Rhoda his widow, 1790, Rhoda their daughter, 1767, John their son, 1804, who died at Teflis, Georgia, and Samuel Walker, son of Jonathan and Mary Walker, 1782; (17) Nicholas Bramah, 1802, and Hannah his wife, 1780.

Chislett, C. J. (ed.), *Masbro' Independent Chapel, Bicentenary 1760–1960* (1960). Miall (1868) 341–3.

(349) WESLEYAN, Ship Hill (SK 429927). The first octagonal Methodist chapel was built in Rotherham in 1761. It was replaced in 1807 by a new chapel on the present site (formerly Talbot Lane) which was destroyed by fire in 1901. The chapel of 1903, by Morley and Son of Bradford, has a gabled E front with paired entrances and five-light traceried window above; there is a tower and spire at the SE corner.

RUFFORTH   *N. Yorks.*

(350) WESLEYAN (SE 529514). Three bays, 1843, re-fronted 1884, original tablet on porch.

Former Friends' meeting-house, Rylstone.   (351)

RYLSTONE
N. Yorks.

(351) Former FRIENDS (SD 964590). The meeting-house was built in 1711 for a meeting settled about 1653 which ceased in 1792. The building was sold in 1813 and subsequently was in farm use until *c*.1989 when it was converted to a house. It stands within a rectangular walled burial-ground with a gateway on the W side.

The meeting-house, of rubble with a stone-slate roof (37½ft by 23½ft externally) faces W; it has a central doorway, one two-light mullioned window to the right with a similar window above, and a pair of taller windows also of two lights to the left.

SADDLEWORTH
Greater Manchester

(352) CONGREGATIONAL, Delph (SD 986080). The first chapel on this site was built in 1746 for the convenience of some members of the church at Greenacres (OLDHAM, Lancashire), 3 miles SW, and originally described as Presbyterian. A gallery was added *c*.1765 and the building 'enlarged', in 1791. The present chapel, of 1865–6 by W. G. Habershon and Pite, has paired lancet windows at the sides and a stone bell-cote above the W gable.

The former chapel had two tiers of round-arched windows at the sides, a Venetian window at the W end and wooden bell-cote.

Fittings – *Bell*: one in bell-cote, possibly 18th-century. *Monuments*: in chapel (1) Rev. Noah Blackburn, 30 years minister, 1821; (2) Rev. Thomas Gurnill, 1769, brass, signed 'Tutty'; (3) John Cartside, 1852 with half-length portrait bust. In burial-ground many monuments of late 18th century and after, W of chapel (4) John Platt, 1773, Lydia his widow, 1779, Alice their daughter, wife of Richard Cropper, 1770, Sarah their daughter, 1770, and John Platt junior, 1808, table-tomb; against S wall (5) Edmund Scholefield of Castleshaw, 1749, 'Some years before he came to end his Race. He gave the greatest Sum to build this Place: A Preached Gospel lay his Heart so near, That he did much t'advance its Intrest here', table-tomb with panelled and balustered sides.

CYB (1866) 315. Miall (1868) 251.

SALTERFORTH
Lancashire

(353) Former FRIENDS (SD 890455). Long low building of stone erected 1715 in place of an earlier meeting-house. In the early 20th century it was leased to Wesleyans; it has now been converted to a house. The S front formerly had three plain windows with external shutters to the meeting-house, a minor doorway to the left and principal entrance between the right-hand pair; a contemporary cottage with former doorway and lower window at the front is attached at the E end. The N wall formerly had small square windows below the eaves. The interior (33½ft by 24¼ft), now divided, has two exposed ceiling beams; some wall-benches remain at the W end.

(354) INGHAMITE (SD 890455). Immediately E of the foregoing, rebuilt in 1932. The former chapel on this site was constructed in 1754 and had two entrances at the ends of the front wall with a pair of large windows between which flanked the pulpit. *Books*: the church is reported to possess Rev. Benjamin Ingham's family Bible.

[Baxter, T.], *Inghamite Chapel, Salterforth, Bicentenary 1754–1954, A Short History* (1954).

SAWLEY
Lancashire

(355) Former WESLEYAN (SD 775463). Barn converted 1867, part of long range of 18th-century building.

SCOTTON
N. Yorks.

(356) FRIENDS BURIAL-GROUND (SE 326596). A rectangular enclosure, 200 yards E of the Old Hall, is bounded by stone walls; the leasehold of the site was acquired by Friends in 1670. In the SE corner are the remains of a small square building.

Monuments: three stone table-tombs with moulded edges to capstones, dates illegible, late 17th-century (1) Ann, wife of George Watkinson, and Rachel, [   ]; (2) George, son of William Watkinson; (3) illegible; also three small headstones; (4) John, son of Joseph and Elizabeth Dodson of Knaresborough, 1736, segmental top; (5) Margaret, wife of Bossoll Middleton of Knaresborough, 1676, circular top; (6) Ann, wife of Matthew Hogg, 1672 or 1679, circular top.

FRIENDS' BURIAL GROUND, SCOTTON   CFS 1972

SEDBERGH
Cumbria

(357) CONGREGATIONAL (SD 658922). Rebuilt 1871, by Stephen Shaw of Kendal; some foundations of the earlier chapel of 1828 remain in the rear side wall. (URC)

Miall (1868) 344–5.

(358) FRIENDS, Brigflatts (SD 641912). A meeting near Sedbergh gathered by George Fox in 1652 centred on a community of flax weavers at Brigflatts. In 1660 a piece of land was acquired for use as a burial-ground and in 1674 the site of the present meeting-house was purchased.

The meeting-house, which was built in 1675, is a traditional building of stone rubble with a stone-slate roof. In external appearance it resembles the house of a yeoman farmer with stone-mullioned windows and a two-storeyed porch to the S with round-arched outer doorway and a small window above to an upper room. The windows in the end bays of the S wall are in two tiers, each of three lights, the intermediate bays to the right of the porch have two similar windows set at mid-height above the level of the stand and one small upper window.

The interior (21ft by 41ft) was originally undivided with a gallery in the W bay only, although the fenestration allows for a similar feature at the opposite end also. In 1714 the gallery was

Friends' meeting-house, Brigflatts.   (358)

extended across the N wall and at the E end, and a new staircase provided opposite the entrance. The W gallery was converted to a women's meeting-house in 1749 by the erection of a shuttered partition and the whole of that end was divided from the meeting-house in 1900 to provide a caretaker's cottage. Considerable repairs were carried out in the early 20th century, including the complete replacement of the roof timbers.

Fittings – *Galleries*: with open balustraded fronts, supported by turned wood posts. *Inscription*: on stone tablet on porch, 'ANNO DO. 1675', tablet renewed, previous tablet loose inside. *Monuments*: in burial-ground 100 yards NW, uniform headstones of 19th century and later. *Seating*: plain benches with open backs added, late 17th-century and later. *Stand*: against S wall, open railed front with simple finials to newels, centre access, late 17th-century.

Arnold (1960) 104–5, 111. Butler (1978) 146–52. Lidbetter (1961) *passim*.

(359) WESLEYAN, Cautley (SD 690942). Three-bay stone front with ashlar quoins and round-arched opening; dated 1845.

(360) WESLEYAN, Frostrow (SD 684914). Dated 1886, bell-cote on front gable.

SELBY   *N. Yorks.*

(361) CONGREGATIONAL, New Lane (SE 614323). 1865–6 by Pritchett and Son on site of former chapel of 1808. Red brick with gault brick dressings; tripartite front with wheel window. (URC)

  CYB (1867) 366. Miall (1868) 345–6.

Congregational chapel (URC), New Lane, Selby.   (361)

(362) Former FRIENDS, Gowthorpe (SE 613323). The meeting-house, partly concealed behind a modern shop front on the S side of the main street, was built in 1785 replacing a meeting-house acquired in 1692; it was enlarged *c*.1825. The building was sold

in 1951 following a period of use by the Brethren and has since been converted to a shop.

The walls are of brick, partly rendered (20ft by 50½ft externally); the roof is hipped and covered with corrugated asbestos. Five small sash windows and an inserted doorway face a public passage on the E side. The rear N wall has a wide round-arched window, now blocked.

Monuments: in burial-ground at rear, now public garden, several loose or reset ledger stones (1) Thomas Goodaire of Selby, late 17th-century; (2) inscribed within decorative border, 'Hic Jacet Johannes Hodgson Medicinæ Doctor qui Mortuus est 12th die February Anno Domini 1681'; (3) inscribed 'Hic Iacet Corpus Johannis Hodgson de Selby (. . . Medicinæ Practicus) qui moriebatis die 27ᵐᵒ Marii [?March] Anno Domini 1680', broken stone; (4) Jane, wife of Thomas Goodaire, 1688/89, and Jane their daughter, 1688/89.

(363) Former WESLEYAN, 56 Millgate (SE 614327). The preaching-house built in 1786 and visited by John Wesley in 1788 was superseded by a new chapel in James Street in 1817 (rebuilt 1882 and since demolished). The former building, which then passed to commercial use, was demolished in 1974. This was a large plain building of brick with a pantiled roof. The wall facing the road was of four bays with two tiers of windows; the entrance appears to have been in the gabled end wall to the right, later covered by further buildings.

(Information from Richard Moody.)

(364) Former PRIMITIVE METHODIST, Gowthorpe (SE 611322). Brick, tripartite gabled front with paired doorways and Venetian-traceried window over. Built 1862.

(365) ST MICHAEL'S CHAPEL, Millgate (SE 613327). Presbyterian, later Unitarian, chapel, built 1699, rebuilt 1903; now Gospel Hall. *Plate*: included two-handled gadrooned cup, 1707.

  Evans (1897) 219. Miall (1868) 345.

SETTLE   *N. Yorks.*

(366) CONGREGATIONAL (SD 822635). Zion Chapel, built in 1816 for a congregation formed in 1811, has rendered rubble walls with ashlar quoins and a hipped roof. The front wall is of three bays with a central doorway and two tiers of round-arched windows. The interior, reseated in the late 19th century, has a gallery around three sides.

  Miall (1868) 346–7.

(367) FRIENDS, Kirkgate (SD 818636). The present site comprising a 'burial-ground and meeting-house thereon' was conveyed to trustees in 1661. The meeting-house, rebuilt in 1678, has rubble walls and a stone-slate roof. It was refitted in the mid 18th century and further altered in the 19th century when the walls were raised by about three feet and the mullions and transoms of the windows were removed.

The E wall has a moulded string-course with three windows below and a doorway at the N end, now covered by a later porch, with a shaped lintel dated 1678; above the string-course are three smaller windows, one blocked. The S wall is gabled and has two windows of 19th-century date with an earlier blocked window between. In the N wall are two gallery windows of the 19th century.

Friends' meeting-house, Settle.   (367)

The interior (30¼ft by 19¾ft) has a deep gallery at the N end with a double thickness of shutters opening to the principal room. The stand against the S wall, altered in the 19th century, has 18th-century fielded panelling at the back.

Door: in E doorway, irregularly panelled with original hinges, late 17th-century.

Southall (1974) 32–3.

(368) Former PRIMITIVE METHODIST, Commercial Street (SD 822633). Small three-bay chapel on sloping site with two cottages below; early 19th-century.

SHEFFIELD   *S. Yorks.*

(369) UPPER CHAPEL, Norfolk Street (SK 355874). The formerly Independent, now Unitarian, congregation traces its origin to the ejection in 1660 of James Fisher, vicar of Sheffield. In 1672 several houses, including that of his son, appear to have been licensed for meetings. In 1678 a house known as 'New Hall' in Snig Hill was fitted up as a meeting-house, continuing in use until the erection of the present chapel in 1700–1; the house was subsequently converted to an almshouse, Hollis's Hospital. In 1714 about two hundred members withdrew, in objection to the appointment of a new minister by the trustees alone, and formed a Congregational church at Nether Chapel (*see* (370)), to which further seceders came from Upper Chapel in the later 18th century as the doctrinal orthodoxy at the latter diminished.

'New Chapel', as Upper Chapel was originally called, was built on land 'betwixt the Pepper Alley and the Alsop Fields'; it was registered in 1701 and the first trustees were appointed in 1704. The chapel was almost entirely rebuilt in 1847–8 to designs by John Frith. The surviving N wall of the original building is of brickwork, 60ft in length, in four bays with two tiers of windows. On the wall is a contemporary tablet inscribed 'BUILT IN 1700' and a later inscription 'enlarged 1847'. The 19th-century E front of ashlar has a pedimented centre between wings and a three-bay porch with Ionic columns. The interior has a gallery around three sides with a tall pulpit on columns at the W end and an organ in an apsidal recess at the back.

Monuments: in chapel (1) John Bagshaw, 1721, with Latin inscription, border of swags and cherubs' heads with death's head below; (2) John Rutherford, 1789; (3) Richard Greaves,

1835; (4) William Greaves, 1830, *et al.* Externally, on N wall (5) Rev. John Wadsworth, 1748, his only son Rev. Field Sylvester Wadsworth, 1759, Elizabeth, widow of the last, 1774, and William their son, 1759; (6) Field Sylvester, 1717, Rebekah his widow, 1723 (or 1725), William their son, 1723, and Rebekah their daughter, wife of [Rev.] John Wadsworth, 1735; against W wall (7) [Thomas Jollie], 1714, with shield-of-arms and Latin inscription, much decayed.

Plate: includes two two-handled cups of 1706 and 1784.

Evans (1897) 219–21. Manning, J.E., *A History of Upper Chapel, Sheffield* (1900). Miall (1868) 350–3.

(370) NETHER CHAPEL, Norfolk Street (SK 356874). The original building erected in 1715 for Congregational seceders from Upper Chapel was rebuilt in 1827 to designs by Watson, Pritchett and Watson of York; this was superseded in 1971 by a multi-purpose building incorporating a chapel for the united congregations from Nether Chapel and Queen Street (now URC).

Collecting Shovels: four, numbered '1, 2, 8, 11' part of larger set, inscribed 'NEW NETHER CHAPEL, opened August 19th 1828'.

Hawksworth, G.F.B., *The Central Congregational Church in Sheffield* (1971). [Johnson, T.F.], *Nether Church (Congregational) Sheffield, 1714–1964* (1964). Miall (1868) 353–5.

(371) CONGREGATIONAL, Queen Street (SK 354876). The chapel, built in 1784 by seceders from Nether Chapel, was demolished *c.*1965–70. The front was of brickwork in five bays with two tiers of windows and a large pediment with scrolled tablet dated 1784. *Plate*: (now at Norfolk Street) includes a pair of two-handled cups, in Sheffield plate, dated 1787.

Miall (1868) 356–7.

(372) Former CONGREGATIONAL, Westfield Terrace (SK 349 872). 'Mount Zion' chapel was built in 1834 for a newly formed congregation which in 1838 exchanged buildings with another Independent church then meeting in Leecroft Chapel. The chapel

Mount Zion Chapel, Sheffield.   (372)

Upper Chapel, Sheffield.   (369)

has been incorporated into the adjoining Royal Hospital. The E front, of ashlar in three bays, has a pedimented centre and recessed entrance flanked by a pair of Ionic columns *in antis*. (Demolition, excluding front wall, proposed 1983)

Miall (1868) 357–8.

(373) Former CONGREGATIONAL, Springvale Road, Crookes (SK 330878). Octagonal, in free Gothic style by W.J. Hale of Sheffield, 1906. (Converted to open-plan architects' office 1990)

CYB (1906) 192–3.

(374) 'ZION' CHAPEL, Tannery Street, Woodhouse (SK 420848). Plain rendered chapel with broad three-bay front partly covered by recent extensions; dated 1836.

(375) Former METHODIST, Whiteley Wood Road (SK 310846). The chapel was built in 1789 by Mrs Hutton, daughter of

Thomas Boulsover, the originator of Sheffield plate, for the work-people at Boulsover's mills. The walls are of coursed rubble and the pyramidal roof is covered with stone slates. The W front has a round-arched entrance between two windows with flat-arched heads, all blocked in stone. Centrally in N and S walls are square windows with renewed frames, and in the E wall is a round-arched window which has been converted to a doorway. The interior (24¼ft square) has no original fittings; it was already in use as a farm building by 1912.

Bradbury (1912) 3, 10.

(376) WESLEYAN, Carver Street (SK 350873). Methodist preaching in Sheffield began *c*.1741 and the first substantial chapel was built in Norfolk Street in 1780, rebuilt in 1908 as the 'Victoria Hall'. The second or 'New Chapel' in Carver Street was built in 1804–5 to designs by the Rev. William Jenkins. The

Wesleyan chapel, Carver Street, Sheffield.   (376)

Wesleyan chapel, Carver Street, Sheffield.   (376)

walls are of brick and the roof slated. The E front of five bays has a three-bay centre with a pediment within a larger gable, the roof possibly being intended to have hipped ends. The windows in two tiers are set in arched recesses, with a Venetian window above the central entrance.

The interior is spacious, with a continuous round-ended gallery supported by wooden columns. The organ is set in a recess at the W end. The seating was entirely renewed in the late 19th century and the pulpit and communion table were replaced or altered c.1919. (Chapel sold 1933)

Monuments: in chapel (1) Henry Longden, local preacher, 1812; (2) Joshua Gillatt, 1840, *et al.*; (3) Rev. John Walmsley, 1842, and Ann his widow, 1847; (4) Elizabeth Atkin, 1835; (5) Thomas Smith, trustee, 1831, and Martha his wife, 1823; (6) Rev. William Edward Miller, 1839, and Mary (Dunhill) his wife, 1833; (7) Charlotte Maria, wife of Thomas Beard Holy, 1837; (8) Thomas Holy, 1830, with portrait bust and shield-of-arms, signed 'E. Law sculpt. 1832'. In burial-ground numerous ledger stones, including on S side (9) Samuel Harris, 1833, 'a converted Polish Jew'.

Dolbey (1964) 135–7.

(377) Former WESLEYAN, Acorn Street (SK 351881). 'Ebenezer Chapel', built in 1823 to designs by Joseph Botham and now in commercial use, is a large building of stone with a hipped slate

Former Wesleyan chapel, Acorn Street, Sheffield.
Photo *c.* 1910.   (377)

roof. The front of five bays and the sides of six bays have two tiers of pointed-arched windows of three lights with stone-traceried heads. At each corner is an octagonal buttress formerly rising to a short turret and castellated parapets between. The porch, which projects centrally at the front, formerly rose to a tower with a window of four lights in the upper stage.

(378) Former METHODIST NEW CONNEXION, Scotland Street (SK 351878). Brick with five-bay front, central doorway replacing two earlier entrances and two tiers of round-arched windows. Narrow gable above parapet with large tablet dated 1828 and dates of earlier chapels 1764 and 1797.

(379) FULWOOD OLD CHAPEL, Whiteley Lane (SK 303852). A congregation of orthodox dissenters formed in the early 18th century may have met at the house of John Fox, Fulwood Hall, which was registered for meetings in 1714. In 1724 William Ronksley left a bequest of £400, of which the interest after four or five years was to be spent on the erection of 'a large and handsome Chapel...finished with a Pulpit and convenient seats near unto Birks Green' and the remaining capital to serve as an endowment. The chapel was served by ministers of varying persuasions until 1873 when the cause failed. The building was used briefly by Wesleyans, 1878-80, and by Congregationalists from 1899 to 1934, after which it was opened by the trustees for Unitarian worship.

The chapel is a modest building of coursed rubble with ashlar dressings. The broad front wall facing S has two doorways between four mullioned windows of two lights rebated for external shutters. Between the middle windows is a square tablet inscribed 'Built 1729 In Persuanc[e] of ye last Will of Mr W. Roncksley'. The E and W walls are gabled with shaped stone kneelers to the gable parapets, later buildings adjoin at each end. In the N wall are two windows of a single light flanking the original site of the pulpit.

The interior (24ft by 36¾ft) was entirely refitted in the late 19th century and in recent years.

The parsonage, adjacent to the E, is dated 1754.

Floorslab: a stone 'in east aisle' was reported (*UHST* VI (1935-8) op. cit. below) to be inscribed to the Rev. J. Gill, 1758, 30 years minister. *Stocks*: in front of chapel, stone posts and wooden crossbars with 18th-century locking strap, formerly on Birks Green, re-sited 1929.

Fulwood Old Chapel. (379)

Anon. *A Short History of Fulwood Old Chapel* (*c*.1964). Evans (1897) 90-1. Miall (1868) 359. *UHST* VI (1935-8) 194-204, 330-53.

SHIPLEY   *W. Yorks.*

(380) CONGREGATIONAL, Saltaire (SE 139381). The chapel opened in 1859 was built at the expense of (Sir) Titus Salt as the principal place of worship and centrepiece of his model village. The church (now URC) was formed in 1857. The chapel stands in a park-like setting close to the Leeds and Liverpool Canal and is aligned on the axis of the offices of the factory. The design is in the Classical idiom by Lockwood and Mawson with stone walls and slate roof. At the E end a semicircular Corinthian colonnade surrounds the circular entrance vestibule, above which rises a domed tower with eight columns to the principal stage and iron grilles filling the belfry windows. The N and S walls are divided into six bays by pilasters; a mausoleum was added against the S side *c*.1870. The W end is pedimented and has a small apsidal projection below with a blocked window at the centre.

The interior (90ft by 44½ft) (*see* Frontispiece) has an elaborately decorated high segmental-vaulted ceiling with cross vaults above the side windows. The E and W ends are each of three bays divided by pilasters. The centre bay to the W rises to a segmental arch; the apsidal recess beyond, now entirely filled by an organ, has doorways to N and S, the former serving a staircase from a basement vestry. The apse is flanked by a pair of attached columns and originally accommodated the pulpit as well as a smaller organ. The centre bay at the E end is similarly arched and has a small gallery above the vestibule intended to serve as a private pew. The N and S walls have attached columns between the windows. There are basement rooms below the chapel on the N side and a vestry below the W apse.

Fittings – *Bells* and *Ringers' Boards*: in tower, formerly six bells, removed *c*.1940; ringers' boards recording two peals of 5,040 changes, 1888 and 1889. *Clock*: in tower, with external dials to N, S and E. *Communion Table*: with marble top and claw feet. *Font*: white marble, shallow square bowl with acanthus enrichment around edge on fluted stem with moulded base and square sub-base. *Light Fittings*: suspended from ceiling, two larger gaseliers, ormolu with glass panels.

Monuments: in mausoleum (1) Sir Titus Salt, Bt., 1876, Caroline his widow, 1893, Titus Salt, 1887, and Caroline his widow, 1930, white marble monument with entablature and pilasters flanking standing figure of angel, signed 'John Adams-Acton, 1875'; (2) Whitlam, 1851, Mary, 1851, and Fanny Caroline, 1861, children of Sir Titus Salt; (3) Mary Jane Susan, wife of Edward Salt, 1870. *Sculpture*: in E vestibule, white marble bust of (Sir) Titus Salt with shield-of-arms, and in the base a representation of his factory, and alpaca ram and ewe flanking a cornucopia, 'presented to TITUS SALT Esquire by the Work-people in his employment...', 1856, signed 'T. Milnes, sculptor, London'. *Seating*: two ranks of pews with elaborately scrolled ends and claw feet.

Balgarnie, R., *Sir Titus Salt, Baronet* (1877) 139-42. Miall (1868) 239.

(381) SALVATION ARMY, Rhodes Place (SE 148377). Citadel with castellated stone front, dated 1892.

Congregational chapel (URC), Saltaire.   (380)

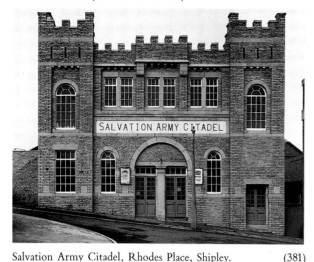

Salvation Army Citadel, Rhodes Place, Shipley.   (381)

United Methodist chapel, Midgley.   (382)

SITLINGTON   *W. Yorks.*

(382) UNITED METHODIST, Midgley (SE 272147). Red brick, yellow terracotta dressings, shaped gable. Dated 1910.

SKELMANTHORPE   *W. Yorks.*

(383) WESLEYAN, Commercial Road (SE 233105). Gothic 1896 with Sunday-school 1904, on site of earlier chapel. *Monuments*: in front of chapel, several low table-tombs of early 19th century.

(384) PRIMITIVE METHODIST, Pilling Lane (SE 235108). Low stone front with open pediment and two doorways. 'Erected 1836, enlarged 1864'.

SKIPTON   *N. Yorks.*

(385) CONGREGATIONAL, Newmarket Street (SD 992517). The present chapel of 1914–16 in a free Gothic style by James Totty of Rotherham stands on the site of chapels of 1777–9 and 1839. A few early 19th-century headstones have been reset against the side of the adjacent 1890 Sunday-school. (URC)

   CYB (1916) 151. Dawson, W. H., *Independency in Skipton* (1891). Miall (1868) 362–3.

(386) FRIENDS, The Ginnel (SD 991515). Friends' meetings commenced *c.*1652, the present site was acquired in 1692 and the meeting-house completed in the following year. The walls are of stone, now rendered, and the roof is covered with stone slates. The S front is of three bays with a central doorway with chamfered jambs and lintel, the latter carved with the date 1693 within a shield. The two windows have chamfered jambs and modern frames probably replacing mullions and transoms. The end walls are gabled and have stone copings with moulded kneelers; there is a stone chimney stack on the W gable.

Friends' Meeting-house, SKIPTON *Yorkshire W.R.*

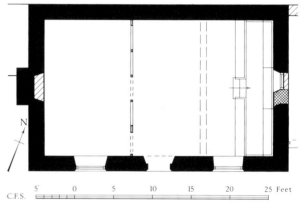

The interior (29½ft by 17¼ft) was subdivided in 1761 when a partition with hinged shutters was introduced and a ceiling constructed over the E part at the same period. The original stone flags remain below the present floor. The stand at the E end has been altered; it was formerly entered at the ends and had a raised centre. The roof is supported by two king-post trusses with cambered tie-beams incorporating re-used material dating from a partial reconstruction in the 19th century.

Seating: nine benches with shaped ends and open backs, probably a set provided in 1761.

Burial-ground: the ground in front of the meeting-house was formerly used for burials; another burial-ground which existed at Bradley, about 2 miles SE, was sold in 1876 to pay for the erection of a caretaker's cottage at Skipton.

   Anon., *An Account of the Charitable Trusts ... in Brighouse Monthly Meeting ...* (1920).

(387) Former WESLEYAN, Chapel Hill (SD 990520). Built 1791 and greatly enlarged and re-fronted 1811. Pedimented stone front

of three bays with two doorways and three round-arched upper windows with intersecting glazing bars.

(388) Former WESLEYAN, Gargrave Road (SD 989519). Five-bay front with three-bay pediment and giant Ionic columns; dated 1864.

(389) Former PRIMITIVE METHODIST, Gargrave Road (SD 987 518). 1879 superseding one of 1835 in Coach Street. Tablet from former chapel now in Skipton Museum. (Demolished since 1975)

SLAIDBURN *Lancashire*

(390) WESLEYAN (SD 713523). 'Built 1821, restored 1889'.

SNAITH AND COWICK *Humberside*

(391) WESLEYAN, Snaith (SE 645221). Large chapel in park-like setting. Walls of red brick and stone dressings; pedimented S front of five bays with giant Roman Ionic columns and pilasters, three round-arched entrances and two tiers of windows. Interior with continuous gallery and complete contemporary fittings.

SOUTH MILFORD *N. Yorks.*

(392) WESLEYAN, High Street (SE 496317). The chapel of 1840 was superseded by the present building in 1876; the back wall of the former remains as part of the Sunday-school. *Fontlet*: Winchester Cathedral pattern with domed lid, maker '[?A] Shaw & Son, Congleton, England'.

SOWERBY BRIDGE *W. Yorks.*

(393) BAPTIST, Butts Green (SE 045250). The chapel built in 1805 for a congregation of 'Johnsonian' Baptists formed about 1780 has been demolished since 1958. A few early 19th-century monuments remain in the burial-ground.

(394) Former BAPTIST, Norland (SE 067233). 'Bethel Chapel' dated 1865 was built for a congregation largely comprised of disaffected Methodists. Three-bay pedimented front with rooms below chapel.

Shipley (1912) 225–6.

(395) PARTICULAR BAPTIST, Steep Lane (SE 029237). The congregation originated in the mid 18th century by division from the Independent or Presbyterian society in Sowerby and did not adopt Baptist practices until 1779. The first meeting-house of 1751 was superseded in 1820 and replaced by the present building in 1874–5. The 1820 chapel had an E front of seven bays probably incorporating a house for the minister. The present chapel faces S and has a pedimented front with giant corner pilasters; the interior has a continuous gallery supported by cast-iron columns and a full complement of contemporary box-pews. Sunday-school adjacent at rear opened 1874. (Chapel reduced in height *c.*1988 following structural failure)

Fittings – *Inscriptions*: reset above outer doorway to Sunday-school, stone with date 1751 from first meeting-house and tablet from second chapel inscribed 'HEPHZIBAH 1820 . . .' *Monuments*: in burial-ground E of chapel (1) James Broadbent, 1761, Mary (Hellewell) his widow, 1763, Jonathon (*sic*) Hellewell her father, 1775, and later inscription to William, son of the first named, 1826, and Sarah his wife, 1790, table-tomb with panelled sides; (2) Rev. John Dracup, 28 years minister, 1795, and Rachel his widow, 1795, 'erected by subscription', table-tomb with

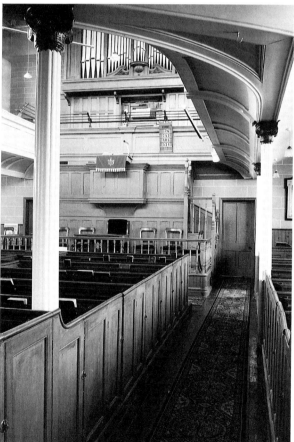

Particular Baptist chapel, Steep Lane. (395)

panelled sides; (3) Elisha Saltonstall, 1868, Hannah his widow, 1879, their children Joshua, 1821, Joshua, 1828, Joseph, 1832, Elisha, 1858, *et al.*, table-tomb on two wide stone piers; (4) Hannah, wife of John Firth and widow of Isaac Bottomley, 1836; (5) Tempest Oddy, 1835, Sarah his widow, 1844, Thomas Mitchell, 1862, and Hannah his wife, 1854.

Garside, A., *Fifty Years at Steep Lane, 1874–1924* (1924). Haigh, W., *An Historic Sketch of the Baptist Church, Steep Lane, Sowerby* (1890). Miall (1868) 366. Shipley (1912) 220–1.

(396) CONGREGATIONAL, Booth (SE 042275). A chapel was built in 1761 and shortly afterwards a church was formed by James Crosley, a convert of the Rev. William Grimshaw. The chapel was rebuilt in 1828 and a larger one constructed alongside it in 1869. A Sunday-school was built in 1850.

'Ebenezer' chapel dated 1828, of stone with a slate roof, has a gabled front of three bays to the SW with two tiers of windows including a Venetian window centrally at gallery level. At the NE end is a narrow wing containing vestries and organ chamber. The side walls are of four bays including windows to rooms below the chapel. The interior has been altered by the insertion of a floor at gallery level.

The 'Independent Sabbath School' dated 1850 adjoins the former chapel on the NW side and is approached by an external doorway at the upper level; below it is a caretaker's cottage.

The later chapel at the SE end of the group has a gabled front with a large wheel window between a pair of short staircase towers with pyramidal roofs. (Chapels demolished 1979)

Fittings – *Banner*: small Sunday-school banner late 19th-century. *Monuments*: in former chapel (1) William Crosley of

Congregational chapel, Booth, 1869.   (396)

Leeds, merchant, 1818, Nancy his widow, 1834, and their children, Harriet, Jane, Ann (infants), Mary 1803, Samuel, 1816, and William, 1831; (2) Samuel Crosley of Leeds, merchant, 1812; (3) Rev. James Crosley, 20 years pastor, 1782, oval tablet. In burial-ground to NE many monuments and table-tombs, some with cast-iron baluster supports of early 19th century and later.
Miall (1868) 232–3.

(397) CONGREGATIONAL, Luddendenfoot (SE 040245). The chapel built in 1859 at the expense of John Whitworth and his brother, local manufacturers, is of an unusual design. The broad N front facing the road has a central porch rising to a tower of three stages; the body of the chapel is of five bays with two round-arched windows each side of the entrance, and pedimented wings at each end in which are the vestries and a house for the minister.

The interior has an exceptionally elaborate segmental-vaulted ceiling with plaster enrichment. The organ and railed choir rostrum are at the E end and the seating comprises a complete set of original box-pews. There is no gallery. Below the chapel is a large school-room. (Now URC. Interior of chapel entirely altered by subdivision and removal of fittings, *c*.1982)

Monument: in chapel on W wall, to John Whitworth of Kirby Leas, Halifax, 1861, and Mary Ward his widow, 1887, signed 'Patteson, Manchester'.
Miall (1868) 311.

(398) CONGREGATIONAL, Sowerby (SE 038233). An Independent church was formed in 1645 by Henry Root, newly appointed curate of Sowerby Chapel from which he was belatedly ejected in 1663. A few years after Root's death in 1669 the church united with the Presbyterian congregation at Northow-

Former Congregational chapel, Booth, 1828.   (396)

Congregational chapel (URC), Luddendenfoot, Sowerby Bridge. (397)

Congregational chapel, Sowerby, Sowerby Bridge. (398)

ram under the pastorate of Oliver Heywood and a 'new built meeting-house' at Quarrell Hill erected by Joshua Horton was licensed in 1672. The Sowerby congregation dispersed before the end of the 17th century but was revived in 1719 when the present site was acquired and the first meeting-house erected on it in the following year. After various enlargements the building was superseded by a Gothic chapel by John Hogg, opened 1861. This is a stone building with paired doorways in the gabled front and an asymmetrical staircase turret which rises to a short spire. (Demolished c.1980)

Monuments: in chapel (1) Rev. James Hatton, 1840, signed 'Bromley, sculptor, Leeds and Halifax'; (2) William T. Brown, 1859; (3) Rev. Joseph Bottomley, 25 years pastor, 1866, brass. In burial-ground (4) William Broadbent, 1774, *et al.*; (5) Rev. Mr Wm. Dodge 'the first minister in this place', 1743, headstone laid flat; (6) Hephzibah, wife of Daniel Philipps, V.D.M., 1767, and their children Daniel and Theophilus; (7) Phebe Clee, 1769; (8) monument repeating inscription to Hephzibah Philipps, but with date 1765, also Phebe Clee, her aunt, and Hephzibah, her daughter, 1782; (9) John Siddal, 1793, Hannah his wife, 1787, *et al.*; (10) Susey, daughter of John Haigh, 1772, *et al.*

Miall (1868) 363–6. Smith, A., *History of Sowerby Congregational Church, 1645–1945* (1945).

(399) Former WESLEYAN, Bolton Brow (SE 065237). The chapel built on a new site in 1832 to supersede one of 1806 is a large building of stone with ashlar front and a hipped slate roof. The deeds of the property were drawn up in exceptional detail and were accepted by the Wesleyan Conference to serve as a Model Deed for their chapels. The site slopes steeply to the S where it is bounded by the canal of the Calder and Hebble Navigation. The original building of 1832 was extended to the S about 1868 and further altered internally in 1897.

The N front of five bays with recessed centre has a Venetian window between a pair of doorways and round-arched upper windows. The S wall rises through six storeys, with a two-storeyed canal warehouse and two 'basement' storeys below the chapel; the latter has three widely spaced windows at each stage including a simple Venetian window at the back of the former communion recess.

The interior has a gallery around three sides, supported by cast-iron columns, and a complete set of box-pews to the gallery and lower floor. The gallery formerly continued to the S end but the final bay was altered in 1897 when a partition wall with an arch enclosing the organ was erected and the communion area behind the pulpit converted for the accommodation of the hydraulic machinery of the organ. The panelled ceiling with three ceiling roses dates from c.1868. (Chapel closed and fittings removed 1979)

Fittings – *Fontlet*: white pottery with cover, 'St Mary Magdalene, Oxford', mid 19th-century. *Glass*: all principal

Wesleyan 'Model Deed' Chapel, Bolton Brow
SOWERBY BRIDGE   *Yorkshire W.R.*

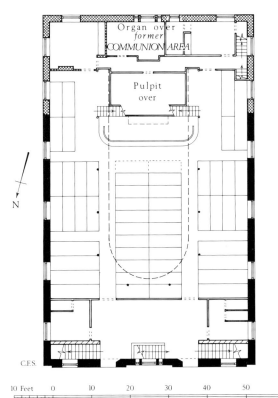

windows have inner hinged casements with borders of blue glass and floral paterae, *c.*1868. *Love-feast Cups*: pair, with two handles and moulded base, blue line decoration on white ground, inscribed 'Love Feast', 19th-century. *Monuments*: in chapel (1) John Sutcliffe, late of Willow Hall, Halifax, 1833 'This memorial ... adorns the edifice in which he stately worshipped,

Former Wesleyan chapel, Bolton Brow, Sowerby Bridge. Exterior from north.   (399)

and to the expenses of whose erection and support he was a most munificent contributor', marble monument with portrait head, kneeling female weeper and shield-of-arms. In burial-ground to E, many table-tombs and raised slabs; (2) Rev. Thomas Staton, 1863, Jane his widow, 1873, and Elizabeth their daughter, 1845; (3) Daniel Garnett, 1849, Judith his widow, 1857, David their son, 1836, *et al.*; (4) Mary, daughter of James and Ann Greenwood, 1817, *et al.*; (5) Samuel Morley, 1838, Hannah his widow, 1859, and Edwin Lumb their son, 1826. *Organ*: by James Binns of Bramley, opus 202, installed 1897, has last hydraulic blower in working order. (Removed to Christ Church, Sowerby Bridge, 1979) *Pulpit*: large varnished pine rostrum, 1897. *Seating*: box-pews, probably a complete refitting *c.*1868. *Seating Plans*: with pins for lettings, signed 'Lloyd and Son, architects, Sowerby Bridge'.

A Summary of the Proceedings of the Committee Appointed by the Conference to Enquire into the Eligibility of a Plan for the Settlement of Methodist Chapels etc ... (1832). Chapman (1952) 14.

(400) Former WESLEYAN, Burnley Road, Friendly (SE 053242). Single-storey with cottages below, *c.*1837; superseded 1890.
    Chapman (1952) 15. Chapman (1982) 4.

(401) Former WESLEYAN, Mill Bank (SE 036214). Built *c.*1865 for cotton workers at Cottonstones and Kebroyd; under conversion to secular use 1984.
    Chapman (1982) 4.

Former Wesleyan chapel, Bolton Brow, Sowerby Bridge. Exterior from south.   (399)

(402) Former WESLEYAN, Norland Town (SE 070230). Built 1819, transferred to Methodist Free Church 1850, subsequently enlarged and latterly greatly altered on conversion to house. Two round-arched windows in end wall. *Inscription*: on tablet reset in boundary wall 'MOUNT PLEASANT ERECTED BY SUB-SCRIPTION A.D. 1819'.

Chapman (1952) 16.

(403) WESLEYAN, Rooley Lane, Sowerby (SE 039232). A preaching-house built in 1787 was rebuilt in 1900; both this and a Sunday-school of 1876 have been demolished since 1952. Many early 19th-century *monuments* remain in the burial-ground including (1) John Crossley of Sowerby, 1814, 'one of the first members of a Methodist society in this town'.

Chapman (1952) 24, 33.

(404) Former METHODIST NEW CONNEXION, Boulderclough (SE 035239). The first chapel on this site was built in 1822 for a Primitive Methodist society; in 1834 it was leased by the New Connexion which eventually bought it and in 1897 replaced it by the present chapel. The first chapel was a plain stone building of three bays with a central doorway and two tiers of windows. The present building, designed by Sutcliffe and Sutcliffe, has two circular staircase towers with conical roofs flanking an open loggia of four arched bays. The chapel is at first-floor level with a school-room below. (Closed 1979, under conversion to two houses 1984)

Fittings – *Banner*: 'Sunday School and Band of Hope'. *Inscription*: tablet from former chapel, reset in wall behind platform of school-room 'BETHEL, 1822 . . . In this place will I give peace, saith the Lord of hosts', denominational names altered. *Monuments*: in burial-ground in front of chapel (1) William Thorp, 1824, Grace his widow, 1838, *et al.*; (2) William Hollos, 1834, James his brother, 1836, *et al.*; (3) Jonathan Hooson, 1854, Hannah his wife, 1840, and their daughters Ellen,

1846, Elizabeth, 1849, and Hannah, 1851. *Seating Plan*: with pins for lettings, dated August 1898.

(405) METHODIST NEW CONNEXION, Midgley (SE 028265). 'Providence Chapel', 1833 by Thomas Horsfield, on site of 'Union Chapel' built 1818. Oval date tablet from first chapel reset in organ recess.

Harwood, H. W., *History of Methodism in Midgley* (1933).

(406) Former PRIMITIVE METHODIST, New Longley (SE 053 220). 'Mount Zion' 1863, enlarged 1874, 1881, 1908. Three-bay pedimented front. Now house.

(407) FREE METHODIST, Tuel Lane, Sowerby Bridge (SE 059 237). Opened 1874, drastically altered 1979, destroyed by fire 1988; since rebuilt.

(408) FREE METHODIST, Luddendenfoot (SE 039250). Mid 19th-century, enlarged 1861, Sunday-school built behind 1879, demolished *c*.1972.

SPOFFORTH WITH STOCKELD   *N. Yorks.*

(409) WESLEYAN (SE 362510). 'Providence Chapel' dated 1810, enlarged to front and original date tablet reset.

STAINBOROUGH   *S. Yorks.*

(410) PRIMITIVE METHODIST, Crane Moor (SE 307016). 'Mount Gerezim'; broad three-bay front dated 1874.

STAINBURN   *N. Yorks.*

(411) WESLEYAN, Braythorn (SE 245490). Broad three-bay front dated 1836 with small walled forecourt; stepped box-pews. (Tablet defaced since 1974)

Seals (1974) 28.

Wesleyan chapel, Braythorn.   (411)

STANLEY   *W. Yorks.*

(412) CONGREGATIONAL (SE 353246). 'Zion', 1876; by J. T. Fleck for J. F. Fleck.

CYB (1876) 447.

(413) PRIMITIVE METHODIST, Kirkhamgate (SE 297229). Three-bay chapel, enlarged; original tablet, 1862, reset.

SWINEFLEET   *Humberside*

(414) WESLEYAN, Low Street (SE 768221). Brick and slate, built 1836 but front altered with addition of porch and flanking gabled

Former Methodist New Connexion chapel, Boulderclough.   (404)

wings in late 19th century. Semicircular rear wall with tall round-arched windows later subdivided. Original date tablet reset in rear boundary wall.

TADCASTER WEST   *N. Yorks.*

(415) WESLEYAN, High Street, Tadcaster (SE 485433). SE front of limestone ashlar between three-storeyed domestic wings, central round-arched doorway with platband above and continuous cill to upper windows. Tablet formerly inscribed 'WESLEYAN CHAPEL 1828'. Sunday-school behind dated 1886. (Demolition of school-room proposed 1980)

TEMPLE HIRST   *N. Yorks.*

(416) WESLEYAN (SE 605250). Gault brick with lancet windows, dated 1842; three bays, extended to east.

THORNE   *S. Yorks.*

(417) Former FRIENDS, Church Street (SE 689133). The meeting-house, built in 1749 on a concealed site to replace one of 1702, was closed in 1942 and has since been demolished. The walls were of brick and the roof slated. The front, of three bays, had two large sash windows in shallow recesses and a tall early 19th-century central porch incorporating a gallery staircase. Truncated end gables had stone copings with moulded kneelers. The interior (approximately 21ft by 27ft) had a stand opposite the entrance and a gallery around three sides. Some brickwork of the rear wall alone remains at the NE end of the site which is now largely covered by a prefabricated Pentecostal chapel.

(418) WESLEYAN, King Street (SE 687134). Brick with pedimented front. Built 1826; extended to rear mid 19th century and later, re-fronted 1898.

(419) Former UNITED METHODIST, King Street (SE 686134). Polychrome brickwork with pilasters and pediment; dated 1893, inscriptions defaced.

(420) Former PRIMITIVE METHODIST, South Parade (SE 688131). Simple brick chapel of 1859 with successor of 1907 to N in free Gothic style.

(421) Former UNITARIAN, Orchard Street (SE 687132). A congregation gathered by Richard Wright from 1805 erected a small chapel together with a burial-ground which was opened 28 June 1816. The society was dissolved about 1903 and the chapel was sold to a Congregational church which claimed to have been formed in 1800.

In 1903 the original chapel of brick (32ft by 28¾ft) was extended by 6 feet to the NW, re-fronted, and a lean-to vestry built at the rear. A separate Sunday-school was also erected at this date. (Chapel demolished 1972)

Monuments: below vestry floor, several early 19th-century ledger stones, including Thomas Husband, 1830, and Margaret his wife, 1829.

[Hadfield, G.], *The Manchester Socinian Controversy* (1825) 175. Miall (1868) 371. *Monthly Repository* XI (1816) 156–7, 247–9, 302, 420–1; XII (1817) 256–8, 652–4.

THORNTON   *W. Yorks.*

(422) CONGREGATIONAL, Market Street, Kipping (SE 103327). 'Kipping Chapel' built in 1843 stands on the site of a chapel of

1769; the congregation, which claims to have been in existence by 1672, previously met in a barn. The chapel has walls of stone in shallow courses and a hipped slate roof. The N front is of three bays with a large dated tablet above the entrance. Reset on the E wall is the tablet from the previous building 'KIPPING-CHAPEL Built in the Year 1769, Enlarged in the Years 1807 & 1823'. The interior has a continuous round-ended gallery supported by cast-iron columns. The pulpit is original but the seating was replaced in the late 19th century.

Monuments: in chapel (1) Rev. Samuel Hulme, 46 years minister, 1756, Mary his widow, 1775, and Susannah their

Kipping Chapel. Monument (2).   (422)

daughter, wife of Rev. Thomas Lillie, 1780; (2) James Anderton, 1822, Deborah his wife, 1817, and their sons John, 1815, and George, 1817, white marble tablet surmounted by bas-reliefs of weepers and an angel rising from a tomb, shield-of-arms below; (3) Rev. John Calvert, 20 years minister, 1816, painted wood with oval inscription panel, cornice and draped urn; (4) Elizabeth, widow of Rev. John Calvert, 1825, wooden tablet; (5) Hannah (Anderton), wife of John Cockroft M.D., 1836. In burial-ground, remains of 18th-century table-tombs and other monuments; (6) Joshua Rhodes, 1778, *et al.*; (7) James Patterson, 1785, *et al.*; (8) Jonas Craven, 1785, *et al.*; (9) Hannah Smith, 1788, *et al.*; (10) Jeremiah Holdsworth, 1798, *et al.*

[Dakin, D.S.], *Kipping Chapel, Thornton, A Brief History* ... (1922). Miall (1868) 23–43.

THORPE AUDLIN   *W. Yorks.*

(423) WESLEYAN (SE 480160). Long low frontage with porch dated 1838, cottage at end.

THURCROFT   *S. Yorks.*

(424) WESLEYAN, Laughton-en-le-Morthen (SK 522880). Yellow sandstone with hipped slate roof, central entrance flanked by small later vestries, *c.*1817.

WESLEYAN CHAPEL, LAUGHTON-EN-LE-MORTHEN   CFS 1974

TICKHILL   *S. Yorks.*

(425) WESLEYAN, Northgate (SK 591934). Three-bay ashlar front, drastically reduced in height and refitted, 1837.

TODMORDEN   *W. Yorks.*

(426) Former BAPTIST, Millwood (SD 946245). 'Rehoboth

FORMER BAPTIST CHAPEL, MILLWOOD, TODMORDEN   CFS 1984

Chapel', on N side of Halifax Road, was built in 1808 for a congregation recently formed by secession from an Inghamite church and which earlier had met in a chapel at Rodwell End which had been erected by a much earlier Baptist foundation. The Millwood congregation removed in 1877 to a new chapel (SD 942243), now rebuilt, and the former building has since been in commercial use. Broad front with two doorways, one altered, and a pair of pulpit windows between.

Briggs, H. *History of the Roomfield Baptist Church, Todmorden* (1908). Shipley (1912) 213–14.

(427) Former GENERAL BAPTIST, Shore (SD 914266). The congregation was gathered about 1770 by the Rev. Dan Taylor and the first meeting-house was built in 1777; this was much rebuilt in 1835 and greatly extended and refitted in 1871. The chapel stands within a large burial-ground high on the hillside above the Vale of Cliviger. The E front of 1871 is of three bays with a pediment; the two foremost bays are also of this date but the three bays to the rear date from 1835, although heightened and altered, and incorporate masonry in the lower courses of the side wall which may represent part of the original meeting-house. A large three-storeyed Sunday-school of the mid 19th century is attached to the S side. (Closed following structural failure *c.*1985)

Shipley (1912) 106–7. Taylor (1818) II: 179, 272, 389. Wood (1847) 192.

(428) Former PRESBYTERIAN, Eastwood (SD 959259). A society was formed here about 1693 by the Rev. Matthew Smith of Mixenden. In 1699 services began to be held in a room at Great House whence in 1704 some members of the congregation seceded to form a separate Baptist church at Rodhill End. In 1717 land was acquired at Bent Head, above Eastwood, and a meeting-house erected in 1719. The society was greatly reduced in numbers by the beginning of the 19th century but it was then revived under a Congregational minister and a new chapel built at Myrtle Grove, lower down the hillside, in 1807. That was demolished about 1838 for the erection of a railway station at Eastwood and superseded in 1840 by a further chapel on a new site (*see* (429)).

The former meeting-house at Bent Head, which after 1807 was converted into several cottages, is a building of stone in the local vernacular style. It included a cottage at the W end, originally of one bay but later enlarged, for the use of the minister. The S front of the meeting-house had two doorways with arched lintels and a pair of pulpit windows between with mullions and transoms, the lower parts now blocked, and a cottage doorway and windows inserted below. The E and W walls are gabled with stone parapets and moulded kneelers. In the E gable is a blocked window at gallery level of four lights below and two lights above the transom. The N wall has three original lower windows, each of three lights, and three upper windows each of four lights added or altered in the 19th century.

The interior (approximately 24ft by 39ft) was entirely altered in the early 19th century when intermediate walls with fireplaces and an upper floor were inserted.

Miall (1868) 257–8. Wood, H., *Congregationalism at Eastwood* (1940).

Former General Baptist chapel, Shore.

Former Presbyterian Meeting-house, Eastwood, TODMORDEN
Yorkshire W.R.

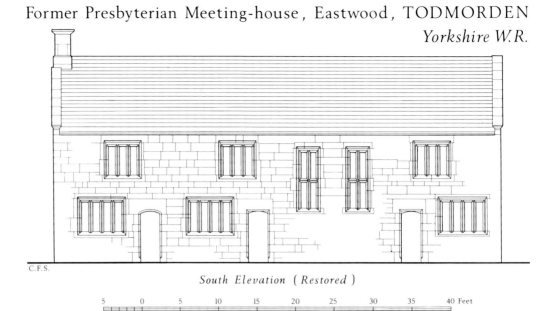

C.F.S.

South Elevation (Restored)

5   0   5   10   15   20   25   30   35   40 Feet

(429) CONGREGATIONAL, Eastwood (SD 965255). The chapel built in 1840 to replace the foregoing has a W front of three bays with giant pilasters and pediment. The side walls are of five bays with two tiers of round-arched windows and lower windows to school-rooms below the chapel. A bowed projection at the E end was altered in 1877 to form an organ chamber.

The interior has a gallery around three sides altered and refitted in 1885–6. (Chapel demolished 1970–1)

Monuments: in chapel (1) Rev. Amos Blackburn, 42 years pastor, 1864, and Hannah his wife, 1837, signed 'Fisher and Dyson, Halifax'. Externally on S wall (2) Margaret, widow of Rev. James Somerville of Branton, 1812; (3) Rev. Thomas Roberts, 1779, removed from the first meeting-house.

Miall (1868) 257–8. Wood (1940) op. cit.

(430) Former INDEPENDENT, Clough Foot (SD 910239). Chapel built 1854 for a church which developed from a Sunday-school commenced 1819; partly refitted 1869, closed 1988 and sold for secular use. Stone with hipped roof, round-arched windows and deep gallery around three sides; original box-pews throughout. Extensive burial-ground with many late 19th-century monuments.

(431) FRIENDS' BURIAL-GROUND, Shoebroad (SD 937235). The earliest known local meetings of Friends were at Mankinholes where land for a burial-ground was leased in 1667. In 1694 a meeting-house was provided at Shoebroad (alias Shewbroad) which continued in use until c.1808 when a new building was erected in Todmorden (*see* (432)). The burial-ground, 8 chains SE of Shoebroad Farm, is enclosed by stone walls.

Monuments: (1) John Scott of Rochdale, mercer, 1753, Sarah his widow, 1770, and Joseph their son, 1741, ledger stone; also five uniform headstones of 1865 and later to Oddie.

Holden, J., *A Short History of Todmorden* (1912) 126–8.

(432) Former FRIENDS, Honey Hole (SD 93622390). Built c.1808

to supersede the meeting-house at Shoebroad Farm; hipped roof and two-storeyed wing at the rear with a wide doorway, now blocked. Variously altered on conversion to two cottages.

(433) WESLEYAN, Mankinholes (SD 959237). The chapel built in 1814 was enlarged to the rear in 1870 and almost entirely rebuilt in 1911. The Sunday-school alongside is dated 1833. (Chapel demolished c.1980, school converted to house and many monuments destroyed)

Monuments: in burial-ground in front of chapel, many table-tombs with moulded stone supports include (1) Ann, wife of William Bentley, 1831; (2) Alexander Wild, 1820, and Betty his widow, 1828; (3) Joseph Wild, 1848, and Mary his wife; (4) Thomas, son of James and Ann Crawshaw, 1853; (5) Hannah, wife of Edmund Lord, 1845, and their children Edmund, 1835, and Betty, 1835; (6) Abraham Whitehead, 1835; (7) William Hooson, 1840; all with further inscriptions, also many ledger stones of early 19th century and later.

(434) FREE METHODIST, Lumbutts (SD 958234). The Wesleyan Methodist Association chapel, built in 1837, was largely rebuilt c.1870. *Monuments*: in burial-ground include (1) Sarah (Salmon), wife of John Wright, Wesleyan Methodist Association minister, 1843.

Wilkinson, R., *Unto the Hills: The Story of Methodism in Lumbutts, 1837–1987* (1987).

(435) Former METHODIST UNITARIAN (SD 93652395). A congregation loosely connected with the Cookite societies of Lancashire was formally constituted in 1823 and a 'new Unitarian Meeting-house' was built and opened in 1824. In 1828, when the society suffered severe financial problems, its chief supporter, the manufacturer and social reformer John Fielden, bought the building and maintained the services at his own expense. After the erection of a new chapel (*see* (436)) the meeting-house was converted for use as a Sunday-school. It is now in secular use.

The meeting-house has stone walls and a hipped roof, rusticated quoins at the corners and two tiers of plain windows. The NE front is covered by an extension built in 1899.

Monuments: in burial-ground (1) John Fielden, 1849, inscribed stone kerb; (2) Rev. James Taylor, 14 years pastor, 1856.

(436) UNITARIAN (SD 93552388). An urgent need for additional school accommodation within the original meeting-house (*see* (435)) was met in 1865–9 by erection of a new chapel by the sons of John Fielden, who had continued their father's support of the Unitarian society. The new building, standing on a prominent site 100 yards SW of its predecessor, was designed in the Gothic style by John Gibson of Westminster. The walls are of stone and the roofs are covered with slate. It comprises a S chancel with former vestry and organ chamber to the W and mortuary chapel, now vestry, to the E, an aisled nave of seven bays, N porch, and a tower and spire against the W wall.

The chancel has a pointed stone barrel vault and the adjoining chambers are also vaulted in stone; there is a small corner fireplace in the former vestry. Below the intended mortuary chapel is a cellar with external access, possibly intended for burial purposes. The chancel arch of three orders enriched with ballflower ornament is supported by attached marble shafts with foliage capitals. The nave and aisles are separately roofed and separated by arcades of pointed arches rising from circular piers of polished marble; in each bay of the nave is a pair of small cusped clerestory windows. The N front has three gables and a large traceried

Unitarian chapel, Todmorden.   (436)

circular window to the nave. The tower has open arches to the lowest stage and an entrance to the S bay of the nave. The base of the stone spire is pierced by tall arched openings and has traceried buttresses and pinnacles at the corners.

Fittings – *Bells*: in tower, eight, by Robert Stainbank, 1868, in wooden bell-frame, with carillon mechanism for striking hymn tunes in conjunction with tower clock. *Collecting Shovels*: six, wood, trefoil pattern with single handle. *Font*: carved white marble bowl supported by six coloured marble shafts on moulded bases. *Glass*: in chancel windows, by J. B. Capronnier, Brussels, 1868. *Inscription*: in paving below tower, on circular tablet 'Erected by Samuel, John & Joshua Fielden AD MDCCCLXVIII'. *Monuments*: in E aisle on W wall (1–3) three similar marble tablets to 'the three brothers who built and endowed this church', John Fielden of Dobroyd Castle, 1893, Joshua Fielden of Stansfield Hall, 1887, and Samuel Fielden of Centre Vale, 1889. Externally, W of chancel (4) Samuel Fielden, 1889, and Sarah Jane his widow, 1910; (5) Joshua Fielden, 1887, *Pulpit*: wood, octagonal on marble base with coloured marble shafts. *Ringers' Board*: in tower, recording first peal of Todmorden Change Ringers Society, 30 April 1870, and another 6 May 1871. *Seating*: in chancel, stalls with variously carved poppy heads.

Evans (1897) 242–3. Fox, A. W., *Annals of the Todmorden Unitarian Congregation* (1924). Herford and Evans (1909) 131–5. McLachlan (1919) 64–5.

WADSWORTH   *W. Yorks.*

(437) GENERAL BAPTIST, Blakedean (SD 958314). Concern for the needs of scattered moorland settlements NW of Heptonstall led the church at Heptonstall Slack (*see* (192)) to acquire this site in 1816 and to erect the chapel which was opened in December 1820. In spite of a serious decline in the local population after the mid 19th century occasional services continued to be held until 1959.

The chapel, which stands in a remote valley on the road to Widdop, has a symmetrical SE front of five bays with two tiers of round-arched windows and intersecting glazing bars. The side walls are gabled, that to SW is blank, the NE wall has two round-arched windows with external shutters which flank the pulpit. The NW wall against higher ground at the back of the chapel has a single doorway, dated 1820 on the lintel, giving direct access to the gallery.

The interior has a gallery at the SW end with a panelled front supported by a pair of moulded timber columns. The roof is

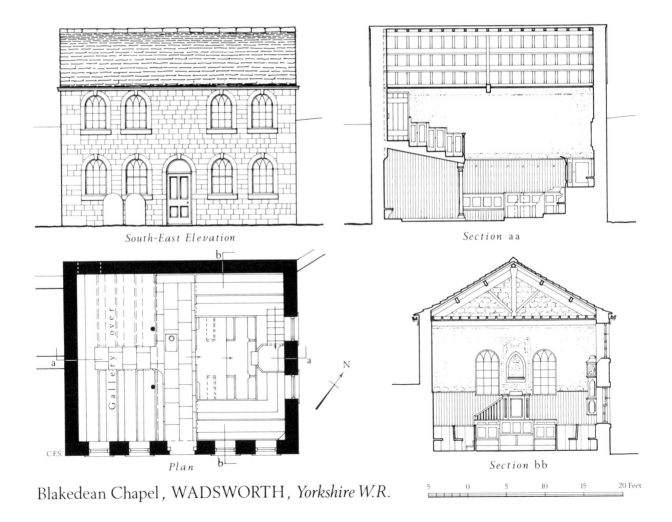

South-East Elevation

Section a a

Plan

Section b b

Blakedean Chapel, WADSWORTH, *Yorkshire W.R.*

5   0   5   10   15   20 Feet

Blakedean Chapel.   (437)

supported by a single king-post roof truss with braces. (Chapel demolished *c*.1972)

Fittings – *Clock*: long-case clock, probably acquired 1825, signed 'Gilyard, Burnley'. *Monument*: SE of chapel, James Mitchell of Alcomdam, 1825, *et al.*, table-tomb. *Pulpit*: square with splayed corners, fielded-panelled front and reeded angles, *c*.1820. *Seating*: in gallery, complete set of original box-pews; lower seating partly altered but including square singing pew in front of pulpit. *Sunday-school Banner*: wooden board, 1ft 3in by 8½in, on long pole, inscribed 'BLAKEDAIN SUNDAY SCHOOL'.

Thomas (1907) 143–51. Turner, W., *A Spring-time Saunter* (1913) 146–8.

(438) BAPTIST, Wainsgate (SD 998288). A small congregation tracing its origin to the influence of William Grimshaw's preaching was formed into a church in 1750. A meeting-house was built in 1751 at Wainsgate Farm in which the roof was supported by a stone arch after the manner of some local barns. The successful ministry of John Fawcett led to the transfer in 1777 of a large body of members to a new chapel in Hebden Bridge (*see* (183)). A further small secession in the 1830s led to the formation of a Strict Baptist church in Hebden Bridge (*see* (187)). The chapel at Wainsgate was rebuilt in 1815 and again replaced by the present building in 1859–60.

The chapel, of stone, has a pedimented front of three bays with two tiers of round-arched windows. The Sunday-school, attached to the rear, was built in 1834 but incorporates in its back wall a window of three round-arched lights under a single lintel which may remain from the first chapel.

Monuments: in burial-ground (1) 'M:W 1767' with later inscription to John, son of Henry and Grace Wadsworth, 1833; (2) John Whitaker, 1803 and Thomas his son 1799; (3) 'Mally' daughter of Simon and Grace Whitaker, 1797, *et al.*; (4) Stephen son of John Fawcett, 1771, table-tomb; (5) Richard Smith, first minister, 1763, and Judith his widow, 1783, table-tomb; (6) 'A.S. 1797', and William Sutcliffe, 1823; (7) Richard Sutcliffe, 1796, and Mary his widow, 1829; (8) Mary Crossley, 1797, *et al.*; (9) Grace, wife of John Pickles, 1789, and Martha his widow, 1816; (10) William Pickles, master of Rishworth Grammar School, 1823, and Mary his widow, 1848; (11) John Fawcett

YORKSHIRE (WEST RIDING)

327

D.D., 1817, Susannah his wife, 1810, John their son, 1837, and Ann his widow, 1850, and their grandchildren John Hargreaves Fawcett, 1816, Esther, 1811, and Eliza Ann, 1819.

Ivimey IV (1830) 576–8. Shipley (1912) 98, 214, 279.

(439) WESLEYAN, Crimsworth Dean (SD 996316). Small isolated chapel built 1865.

Greenwood, W.S., *Crimsworth Dean Methodist Chapel and Sunday School: Centenary Year* (1965).

(440) Former WESLEYAN, Pecket Well (SD 998297). Three-bay front with pedimental gable and two tiers of round-arched windows. Central doorway with eared pediment, dated 1834. (Under conversion to secular use 1991)

Monuments: in burial-ground include (1) John Greenwood of Parock, 1836.

WAKEFIELD   *W. Yorks.*

(441) WESTGATE CHAPEL (SE 329207). The Presbyterian, latterly Unitarian, society appears to have been formed by Joshua Kirby, ejected in 1662 as parish lecturer in Wakefield where he subsequently suffered for nonconformist preaching. In 1672 Kirby was licensed as a Presbyterian preacher at his own house. Also in 1672 Peter Nayler, ejected curate of West Houghton, Lancashire, was preaching at Alvethorpe, 1½ miles NW, which became the main centre of activity until 1697. In that year a new meeting-house was opened at Westgate End in Wakefield 'close to the beck at the junction of Alvethorpe Road and Westgate Common'. By 1751 the meeting-house, which had been built on an unsuitable site subject to flooding, had become ruinous and the present site was acquired.

The chapel, on the N side of Westgate, was built in 1751–2 at a cost of £1,161 which was met by subscriptions and the sale of burial rights. It was subject to considerable internal alteration and refitting in 1882. The walls are of brickwork and the roof is covered with slates. The S front of red brick has a broad pediment above three bays of windows surmounted by a domed circular bell-cote. The two doorways have pedimented surrounds with pilasters and a Doric frieze; between them is a Venetian window

Westgate Chapel, Wakefield.   (441)

Westgate Chapel
WAKEFIELD

Yorkshire W.R.

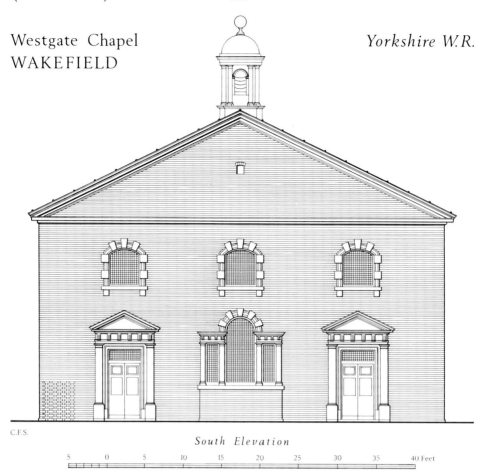

C.F.S.

South Elevation

5   0   5   10   15   20   25   30   35   40 Feet

with rusticated arch and above are three segmental-arched windows with rusticated surrounds, all with renewed glazing. The side walls have each three tall round-arched windows in arched recesses. The N wall has a tripartite lunette window in the pediment to light the roof space and four tall round-arched windows below.

The interior (54½ft by 48½ft) has a deep gallery at the S end with staircases in the SE and SW corners; the gallery may have been enlarged in 1882. The pulpit is centrally against the N wall behind which is a late 19th-century vestry. The boarded and panelled ceiling also dates from *c*.1882 but the original roof structure remains above; this is supported by six trusses with king and queen-posts with diagonal bracing, and a further truss at the S end to support the bell-cote. Below the chapel are burial vaults approached from a later burial-ground to the N by a ramp and tunnel below the intervening road. The vaults lie E and W of a central partly vaulted passage, the S end being possibly an extension of *c*.1810. The 90 vaults are arranged in three tiers; the earliest burials date from 1755, not all the spaces are occupied. The burial-ground N of chapel, given 1850, was sold for commercial use 1990.

Fittings – *Bell*: in bell-cote, one, not accessible. *Clock*: on gallery front, 18th-century. *Gallery*: panelled front of mid 18th century incorporated in later work; staircases have 18th-century

balusters. *Monuments*: in chapel on W wall (1) Benjamin Gaskell M.P., 1856; (2) William Stansfield, 1835. Externally S and W of chapel, several early 19th-century stones. In later burial-ground N of chapel (3) Joseph Horner, corn miller, 1850, broken fluted column on pedestal with testimonial inscription from the 'Working Men's Movement'; also several loose slabs removed *c*.1970 from former burial-ground at Westgate End; (4) John Scott, 1738, and Frances his wife, 1709; (5) Rev. John Aldred, 1760, and Mary his widow, 1761; (6) Mercy, widow of Thomas Elston late minister at Topcliff, 1719, Martha, widow of Japhet Heald, 1731, and Elizabeth, daughter of Hananiah Elston A.M., 1759. *Pulpit*: square with fluted corner columns and bolection-moulded panels, back with fluted pilasters and arched panel, square canopy with indented corners and moulded cornice arched on principal faces, mid 18th-century, body of pulpit lowered 25in. *c*.1882. *Seating*: all renewed *c*.1882, the earlier pews included a semicircular singers' or communion pew in front of the pulpit.

Evans (1897) 245–6. *Inquirer* (30 June 1990). Miall (1868) 375.

(442) Former BAPTIST, George Street (SE 331206). Built 1844 for a church formed 1836 which removed after 1937 to Belle Isle Avenue. The chapel, latterly occupied by the Assembly of God as 'Glad Tidings Hall', is of brick, the upper part divided by stone pilasters and having three small windows above the entablature.

Former Baptist chapel, George Street, Wakefield.   (442)

Monuments: in front of chapel, include (1) James Spawforth, 1847.

Shipley (1912) 164–5.

(443) CONGREGATIONAL, George Street (SE 334206). The church (now URC) was formed and the first chapel built on this site in 1782–3. The present 'Zion' chapel of 1843–4 designed by William Shaw has walls of ashlar, raised above a basement storey, with moulded cornice and parapet. A single tier of tall round-arched windows separated by pilasters forms a continuous arcade around the front and side walls. The front of five bays has a central entrance and the name 'ZION' on a raised panel of the parapet.

Inscription: above side entrance, oval tablet from former chapel dated 1782.

EM (August 1833) 337ff. Miall (1868) 375–6. Taylor, K., *Wakefield District Heritage* (1976) 94–5.

Zion Chapel, Wakefield.   (443)

(444) Former METHODIST, Thornhill Street (SE 33452051). The 'new house at Wakefield' opened by John Wesley 28 April 1774 was superseded by a new chapel in West Parade, built 1801. The

former preaching-house was sold to the Society of Friends in 1805. It was rebuilt *c*.1962.

Methodist Recorder (28 March 1907).

(445) WESLEYAN, Lawefield Lane, Westgate End (SE 324205). Brick, built 1827, with five-bay front bowed forward at the centre and two giant Ionic pilasters and entablature forming a prominent feature above the entrance. Original entrances in end bays converted to windows. Chapel extended to rear and refitted 1885.

WARMSWORTH   *S. Yorks.*

(446) Former FRIENDS, Quaker Lane (SE 546006). The meeting-house was built in 1705 by William Aldam and continued in use until about 1798 when the meeting was transferred to Doncaster. The building was re-sold in 1882 to the family of the original donor; it was again opened for meetings from 1912 to 1940 and has since been used for social purposes.

Former Friends' meeting-house, Quaker Lane,
Warmsworth.   (446)

The walls are of rubble and the roof is covered with slates. The S front has a central doorway between a pair of windows with renewed frames. The end walls are gabled with parapets and moulded kneelers. A lower stable at the W end with pantiled roof has been converted to a kitchen.

The interior (31ft by 18¼ft) is divided by an original partition with shutters. The front doorway opens directly into the larger W room which has a stand at the W end with two entrances and early 18th-century balustraded front, a dado of horizontal boarding around the walls and wall-benches to each side. The E room has a modern fireplace. (Conversion to private house proposed 1990)

Monuments: in burial-ground (1) Francis Smith, 1727; (2) Ann, wife of Thomas Smith, 1717, also 'the above mentioned T. Smith died the [   ] of the [   ] buried here in a Lead Coffin'; (3) large ledger stone against S boundary wall with worn inscription '[   ] M [   ] DOAM' for ?William Aldoam, early 18th-century.

Clark, H. M., *Warmsworth & Doncaster Meeting Houses* (1954).

WATH UPON DEARNE   *S. Yorks.*

(447) CONGREGATIONAL, West Melton (SE 424010). Built 1802; rendered walls and hipped roof, two doorways in front with Doric surrounds and small gallery windows above lacking former architraves. (URC)

Monuments: in burial-ground include (1) Jane Prior wife of

Rev. Benjamin Beddow, 1845; (2) Sarah (Hunt), wife of Rev. W. Tiler, 1836; (3) William Moorhouse, 30 years minister, 1840, Frances his wife, 1831), and Frances Dickens, 1826.

Chislett, C.J., *Masbro' Independent Chapel, Bicentenary 1760–1960* (1960) 27. Miall (1868) 378–9.

(448) Former WESLEYAN, Chapel Street (SE 434008). Stone with three-bay pedimented front, broad corner pilasters and two tiers of windows. Built 1810, present Gothic chapel alongside opened 1894.

WEETON　　　　　　　　　　　　　　　*N. Yorks.*

(449) Former WESLEYAN (SE 286469). Tall stone chapel (33½ft by 27½ft externally), built 1796, front wall rebuilt and rear refenestrated 1881; closed 1938, now in domestic use. *Inscription*: tablet in front wall, now removed, was inscribed 'The poor have the Gospel preached to them, 1796 – Benj Winterburn'.

Seals (1974) 29.

WENTWORTH　　　　　　　　　　　　*S. Yorks.*

(450) WESLEYAN, Wentworth Woodhouse (SK 387983). Three-bay front with pedimented porch dated 1834; hipped slate roof.

WETHERBY　　　　　　　　　　　　　*W. Yorks.*

(451) WESLEYAN, Bank Street (SE 403483). Rubble with ashlar front and hipped slate roof. Front wall, closely similar to Tadcaster (*see* (415)), in three bays with platband and continuous cill to upper windows. Large tablet inscribed 'WESLEYAN CHAPEL 1829'.

WHIXLEY　　　　　　　　　　　　　　*N. Yorks.*

(452) WESLEYAN (SE 446577). Rendered brick walls, gabled front with round-arched doorway and tablet above dated 1808. Round-arched windows in NW side wall indicate central pulpit between end galleries but interior altered and refitted in late 19th century. Original gallery at entrance.

(453) Former PRIMITIVE METHODIST (SE 446575). Brick and pantile, altered three-bay front dated 1866.

WIGHILL　　　　　　　　　　　　　　*N. Yorks.*

(454) WESLEYAN (SE 475469). Brown brick and slate, broad three-bay front dated 1828.

WYKE　　　　　　　　　　　　　　　　*W. Yorks.*

(455) CONGREGATIONAL (SE 158266). 'Westfield Chapel' dated 1824 has walls of stone in shallow courses and a slate roof. Three-bay front with altered gable, two tiers of plain windows and two doorways. *Monument*: in burial-ground, Rev. Benjamin Firth, first pastor, 1853. (URC)

Miall (1868) 383–4.

(456) MORAVIAN, Lower Wyke (SE 150259). The first chapel on this site built in 1753 was rebuilt in 1775 and a house for the minister added at the W end in 1795. The chapel has stone walls with later rendering and the roof is covered with stone slates. The broad S front has two tall round-arched windows flanking the pulpit and doorways at each end with gallery windows above. An organ chamber was added against the N wall *c*.1895. On the former W gable of the chapel, next to the later manse, is a square stone bell-cote with ball finial.

The interior (30¼ft by 41½ft) has separate E and W galleries each with a fielded-panelled front supported by a single wooden column. The roof is carried by three queen-post trusses with tusk-tenon joints to the purlins.

A house for Single Sisters, built N of the chapel in 1782, became a girls' boarding-school after 1805 and has now been converted to housing. Other buildings NE of the chapel include a former boys' school.

Fittings – *Baptismal Basin*: plated base metal, oval with two handles, 19th-century. *Monuments*: in burial-ground S of chapel, flat numbered marker stones, re-sited. *Plate*: includes a two-handled cup of 1803 from the Moravian chapel in Bath. *Pulpit*: centrally against S wall, late 18th-century. *Seating*: in galleries, box-pews erected 1824; lower pews now mostly late 19th-century but a few open-backed benches remain.

England (1887) 12. Heywood *et al.* (1955) 21–5.

Moravian Settlement, Wyke.　　　　　　　　　　　　　　　　(456)

ABBREVIATIONS

NBR	National Buildings Record
RCHM	Royal Commission on the Historical Monuments of England
URC	United Reformed Church

BIBLIOGRAPHICAL SOURCES
other than those fully titled in the text

Abbatt, D. 1931	*Quaker Annals of Preston and the Fylde, 1653–1900.*
Ambler, J. 1913	*The Old Halls and Manor Houses of Yorkshire.*
AMST	*Transactions of the Ancient Monuments Society* (New Series, from 1952).
Arnold, H. G. 1960	'Early meeting houses', *Transactions of the Ancient Monuments Society*, NS VIII (1960), 89–139.
B.Hbk	*The Baptist Handbook* (Baptist Union of GB and Ireland, from 1861).
Beckworth, W. 1910	*A Book of Remembrance Being Records of Leeds Primitive Methodism Compiled During the Centenary Year, 1910.*
Bielby, A. R. 1978	*Churches and Chapels of Kirklees.*
Black, K. M. 1906	*The Scots Churches in England.*
BM	*The Baptist Magazine* (from 1809).
Boyle, J. R. 1890	*Vestiges of Old Newcastle and Gateshead.*
Bradbury, F. 1912	*History of Old Sheffield Plate.*
Briggs, M. S. 1946	*Puritan Architecture and its Future.*
Burgess, J. 1980	*A History of Cumbrian Methodism.*
Butler, D. 1978	*Quaker Meeting Houses of the Lake Counties.*
C & WT	*Transactions of the Cumberland and Westmorland Antiquarian and Archaeological Society* (from 1874).
Chapman, E. V. 1952	*John Wesley & Co. (Halifax).*
Chapman, E. 1982	*Methodism in the Ryburn and Mid-Calder Valleys, 1786 to 1949.*
CHST	*Transactions of the Congregational Historical Society* (21 vols.; 1901–72).
Clack, P. A. G. and Pattinson, K. E. 1978	*Weardale Chapels.*
Cong. Mag.	*The London Christian Instructor, or Congregational Magazine* (from 1818).
Curnock, N. (ed.) 1938	*The Journal of the Rev. John Wesley, A. M. . . .* (8 vols.; 1909–16, reprinted 1938).
CYB	*The Congregational Year Book* (Congregational Union of England and Wales, 1846–1972).
Darwent, C. E. 1899	*The Story of Fish Street Church, Hull.*
DNB	*Dictionary of National Biography.*
Dolbey, G. W. 1964	*The Architectural Expression of Methodism: The First Hundred Years.*
Douglas, D. 1846	*History of the Baptist Churches in the North of England from 1648 to 1845.*
EM	*The Evangelical Magazine* (1793–1904).
England, J. 1887	*Yorkshire Moravian Chapels and Preaching Houses.*
1888	*Moravian Chapels and Preaching-Houses . . . Lancashire, Cheshire, The Midlands and Scotland.*
Evans, G. E. 1897	*Vestiges of Protestant Dissent.*
FHSJ	*Journal of the Friends Historical Society* (from 1903).
Gordon, A. 1896	*Historical Account of Dukinfield Chapel and its School.*
Hague, G. and Hague, J. 1986	*The Unitarian Heritage.*

Hall, D. S. 1989   *Richard Robinson of Countersett 1628–1693 and the Quakers of Wensleydale.*

Hall, J. 1883   *A History of the Town and Parish of Nantwich, or Wich-Malbank in the County Palatine of Chester.*

Halley, R. 1869   *Lancashire: Its Puritan and Nonconformity (2 vols.).*

Hargreaves, T. 1883   *The Rise and Progress of Wesleyan Methodists in Accrington and the Neighbourhood.*

Hargrove, C. c.1903   *The Unitarian Chapels of Yorkshire.*

Hartley, J. 1914   *A Brief Account of the Origin and History of Providence Congregational Church, Stainland . . . 1814–1914.*

HAST   *Transactions of the Halifax Antiquarian Society (from 1901).*

Hawkins, F. H. 1973   *The Presbytery of Durham.*

Herdman, E. F. 1901   *Sacramental Tokens of the Presbyterian Churches in England.*

Herford, R. T. and Evans, E. D. P. (eds.) 1909   *Historical Sketch of the North and East Lancashire Unitarian Mission and its Affiliated Churches 1859–1909.*

Hewitson, A. 1872   *Our Country Churches and Chapels.*

Heywood, T., Tysoe, F. H. and Lloyd, G. R. 1955   *Two Hundred Years of Christian Witness at Gomersal, Mirfield and at Wyke: 1755 to 1955.*

Hindmarsh, R. 1861   *Rise and Progress of the New Jerusalem Church.*

HSL & CT   *Transactions of the Historical Society of Lancashire and Cheshire (from 1849).*

Hulbert, C. A. 1882   *Annals of the Church and Parish of Almondsbury, Yorkshire.*

Inquirer   *The Inquirer (from 1942).*

Ivimey, J. 1811–30   *A History of the English Baptists (4 vols.).*

Jessop, W. 1880   *An Account of Methodism in Rossendale and the Neighbourhood.*

Johnston, J. 1905   *Pioneers of Lancashire Nonconformity.*

Kendall, H. B. 1905   *The Origin and History of the Primitive Methodist Church (2 vols.).*

Lancs. CYB   *Lancashire Congregational Year Book.*

L & CAST   *Transactions of the Lancashire and Cheshire Antiquarian Society (from 1884).*

Lidbetter, H. 1961   *The Friends' Meeting House.*

Linstrum, D. 1978   *West Yorkshire Architects and Architecture.*

Lyth, J. 1885   *Glimpses of Early Methodism in York and the Surrounding District.*

Mackelvie, W. 1873   *Annals and Statistics of the United Presbyterian Church.*

McLachlan, H. 1919   *The Methodist Unitarian Movement.*

Mallinson, J. 1898   *History of Methodism in Huddersfield, Holmfirth, and Denby Dale.*

Matthews, A. G. 1934   *Calamy Revised.*

Mayhall, J. 1860–c.75   *The Annals of Yorkshire from the Earliest Period to the Present Time (3 vols.).*

Miall, J. G. 1868   *Congregationalism in Yorkshire.*

Moody, C. R. 1978   *Chapels in the Selby Circuit.*

Moore, B. 1899   *History of Wesleyan Methodism in Burnley and East Lancashire.*

Neave, D. 1991   *Lost Churches and Chapels of Hull.*

Neave, D. and Neave, S. 1990   *East Riding Chapels and Meeting Houses.*

Newbigging, T. 1893   *History of the Forest of Rossendale (2nd edn.).*

Nicholson, C. and Spooner, C. c.1911   *Recent English Ecclesiastical Architecture.*

Nicholson, F. and Axon, E. 1915   *The Older Nonconformity in Kendal.*

Nightingale, B. 1890–3   *Lancashire Nonconformity . . . (6 vols.).*

Nortcliffe, D. 1978   *Buildings of Brighouse.*

Packer, G. (ed.) 1897   *The Centenary of the Methodist New Connexion 1797–1897.*

Palmer, S. 1802–3   *The Nonconformist's Memorial . . . (3 vols.).*

Paul, S. F. 1961   *Further History of the Gospel Standard Baptists, Vol. IV: Some Northern Churches.*

Payne, G. A. (1934)   *An Ancient Chapel: Brook Street Chapel, Knutsford, with Allostock Chapel, Nr. Knutsford.*

Peel, F. 1891   *Nonconformity in the Spen Valley.*

PHSJ   *Journal of the Presbyterian Historical Society of England (14 vols., 1914–72).*

Picton, J. A. 1873   *Memorials of Liverpool (2 vols.).*

Powicke, F. J. 1907   *A History of the Cheshire County Union of Congregational Churches.*

Rayner, S. 1887 — *The History and Antiquities of Pudsey.*

Richards, R. 1947 — *Old Cheshire Churches.*

Roberts, H. D. 1901 — *Matthew Henry and his Chapel, 1662–1900.*

Robertson, W. 1875 — *A History of Rochdale, Past and Present* (3rd edn.).

Rose, E. A. 1967–9 — *Methodism in Ashton-under-Lyne*, Vol. I: *1740–1797*; Vol. II: *1799–1914*.

Rushton, J. H. 1967 — *They Kept Faith: The History of Some Yorkshire Christian Congregations Including the Pickering and Malton Congregational Churches.*

Scott, J. 1888 — *Berwick-upon-Tweed, the History of the Town and Guild.*

Scruton, W. 1889 — *Pen and Pencil Pictures of Old Bradford.*

Seals, W. F. 1974 — *Methodism in the Otley Circuit, 1744–1974.*

Sell, A. P. F. 1986 — *Church Planting: A Study of Westmorland Nonconformity.*

Sellers, I. 1976 — *The Methodist Chapels and Preaching Places of the Warrington Circuit, 1750–1976.*

Seymour, A. C. H. 1839 — *The Life and Times of Selina, Countess of Huntingdon* (2 vols.).

Sharpe, E. (ed.) 1901 — *Pictures of Unitarian Churches.*

Shipley, C. E. (ed.) 1912 — *The Baptists of Yorkshire.*

Smith, W. 1876 — *The History and Antiquities of Morley.*

Southall, K. H. 1974 — *Our Quaker Heritage: Early Meeting Houses Built Prior to 1720 and In Use Today.*

Stamp, W. W. 1841 — *Historical Notices of Wesleyan Methodism in Bradford and Its Vicinity.*

Tate, G. 1866–9 — *The History of the Borough, Castle, and Barony of Alnwick* (2 vols.).

Taylor, A. 1818 — *The History of the English General Baptists* (2 vols.).

Thomas, E. G. 1907 — *Centenary Souvenir of Heptonstall Slack Baptist Church, 1807–1907.*

Thompson, R. W. 1958 — *Benjamin Ingham (The Yorkshire Evangelist) and the Inghamites.*

Turner, G. L. 1911–14 — *Original Records of Early Nonconformity under Persecution and Indulgence* (3 vols.).

Turner, J. H. (ed.) 1881–5 — *The Rev. Oliver Heywood, B. A., 1630–1702: His Autobiography, Diaries, Anecdote and Event Books* (4 vols.).

UHST — *Transactions of the Unitarian Historical Society* (from 1917).

Urwick, W. (ed.) 1864 — *Historical Sketches of Nonconformity in the County Palatine of Chester.*

VCH — Victoria History of the Counties of England. *Lancashire* (8 vols.; 1906–14).

Vickers, J. 1920 — *History of Independent Methodism.*

Watson, J. 1775 — *The History and Antiquities of the Parish of Halifax, in Yorkshire.*

Whitehead, T. 1930 — *History of the Dales Congregational Churches.*

1932 — *Illustrated Guide to Nidderdale and a History of its Congregational Churches.*

Whitley, W. T. 1913 — *Baptists of North-West England.*

WHS, L & CJ — *Wesley Historical Society; Lancashire and Cheshire Branch Journal* (from 1965).

WHS, NEB — *Wesley Historical Society; North-East Branch Bulletin* (from 1962).

WHSP — *Proceedings of the Wesley Historical Society* (from 1897).

Wood, J. H., 1847 — *A Condensed History of the General Baptists of the New Connexion.*

Woodcock, H. 1889 — *Piety Among the Peasantry: Being Sketches of Primitive Methodism on the Yorkshire Wolds.*

INDEX

Nathanial, 256b–258a; Rich, Elkanah,
297b; Rich, Sylvanus, 297b;
Ridgeway, Henry, 24a; Rodes family,
254a; Ronksley, William, 312a; Salt,
Sir Titus, 220b, 241a, 241b, 312b;
Scholefield, Edmund, 305a; Spoone,
Richard, 234b; Sutcliffe, John, 319a–b;
Sutcliffe, Richard, 268a; Sykes, H.,
200b; Tate, Sir William H., 85a;
Taylor, Andrew, 186b; Taylor,
William, 75a; Thornton, Mercy, 282b;
Tomkinson, John, 29a–b, 30a;
Tomlinson, John, 223a; Turner,
Jeremiah, 200b; Walker, John, 304a;
Walker, Joseph, 304a; Walker,
Samuel, 304a–b; Walley, Thomas, 33b;
Walmsley, Benjamin and William,
290a; Watson, Joseph, 162a; Watson,
Thomas, 200b; Whalley, Thomas,
250a–b; Whitridge, Joseph, 41b;
Whitworth family, 316b; Wilson,
Thomas and Elizabeth, 155a; Wright,
Mathew, 263a
Bentham, N. Yorks., 232b–233a; Calf Cop,
226a, 232b–233a
Berkeley Towers, Cheshire, 24a
Berwick-upon-Tweed, Northumb., 157b,
159b–162a, 172b; Wallace Green,
157b, 161b
Besses o' th' Barn, Greater Manchester, 152a,
152b
Beverley, Humberside, 191a, 192a
Bewaldeth and Snittlegarth, Cumbria, 41a–b
Bewcastle, Cumbria, 41b
Bewerley, N. Yorks., 233a–b
Bewholme, Humberside, 192a
Bickerstaffe, Lancashire, 78a–b
Bielby, Humberside, 192b
Billinge-and-Winstanley, Greater Manchester,
78b
Billingley, S. Yorks., 233b
Bilsborrow, Lancashire, 73b, 78b
Bilsdale Midcable, N. Yorks. see Chop Gate
Bilton, Humberside see Wyton
Bilton, N. Yorks., 233b
Bingley, W. Yorks., 233b–234a, 234b
Birmingham, W. Midlands, 258b
Birstall, W. Yorks., 232a–b, 252b, 282b
Birstwith, N. Yorks., 234a
Bishop Auckland, Durham, 61a, 176b
Bishop Burton, Humberside, 191a, 192b
Bishop Wilton, Humberside, 193a
Bispham, Greater Manchester, 78b
Blackburn, Lancashire, 78b, 98b, 122a, 136a
Blackley, Greater Manchester, 128b
Blackshaw, W. Yorks., 234a
Blacktoft, Humberside, 193a
Blanchland, Northumb., 162a
Blaxton, S. Yorks., 234a
Blennerhasset and Torpenhow, Cumbria, 41b
Blubberhouses, N. Yorks., 234a
Blyth, Northumb., 162a
Bolesworth Castle, Cheshire, 42b

Bollington, Cheshire, 5a, 22b
Bolton, Cumbria, 175b, 176a
Bolton, Greater Manchester, 73b, 78b–80a,
137b, 144a, 280b
Bolton by Bowland, Lancashire, 234a–b
Bolton upon Dearne, S. Yorks., 297b
Boltons, Cumbria, 41b
books and libraries, 6a, 18a, 42a, 66a, 75a,
94b, 96b, 110a, 128a, 131b, 139a,
147a, 154b, 162b, 177a, 212b, 256b,
264a, 274b, 305a
Booth, W. Yorks., 316a–b
Bootle, Cumbria, 38a, 41b–42a
Boroughbridge, N. Yorks., 234b
Boston Spa, W. Yorks., 234b
Bothel and Threapland, Cumbria, 42a
Boulderclough, W. Yorks., 227a, 320a–b
Bowden Downs, Greater Manchester, xvii, 2a,
3a, 4
Bowdon, Greater Manchester, 5a
Bowsden, Northumb., 168a
Bradfield, S. Yorks., 234b–237a; see also
Loxley; Stannington
Bradford, W. Yorks., 227a, 237a–239a;
architects, surveyors and builders,
237b, 238a, 297a, 304b; see also
Clayton; Eccleshill; Idle; North
Bierley; Thornton
Braithwell, S. Yorks., 239a
Bramhope, W. Yorks., xviii, xxi, 226a,
239a–241a
Bramley, S. Yorks., 241a, 319b
Brampton, Cumbria, 38a, 38b, 42a–b
Branton, Northumb., 157a, 165a, 166b–168a
Brassey Green, Cheshire, 1b, 33b
Brawby, N. Yorks., 206a
Braythorn, N. Yorks., 320b
Brayton, N. Yorks., 241a
Bredbury and Romiley, Greater Manchester see
Hatherlow
Brereton, Cheshire, 5b
Bridlington, Humberside, 191a, 191b, 193a–b
Briercliffe, Lancashire, 80a–b; see also Haggate
Brierfield, Lancashire, 80b–81b; see also
Marsden
Brigflatts, Cumbria, xviii, 226a, 305b–307a
Brighouse, W. Yorks., 241a–242a, 279a; see
also Lightcliffe
Brockley Moor, Cumbria, 51a
Brompton (near Northallerton), N. Yorks.,
204a, 206a
Brompton (near Scarborough), N. Yorks., 206a
Broomhaugh and Riding, Northumb., 162b
Broughton, Cumbria see Great Broughton;
Little Broughton
Broughton West, Lancashire, 81a–b
Broxton, Cheshire, 5b
Brussels, glass from, 10a, 326a
Bubwith, Humberside, 193b
builders see architects, surveyors and builders
Bulkeley, Cheshire, 5b
Burgh-by-Sands, Cumbria see Moorhouse
burial-grounds, detached: Baptist, 24b; Friends,

Society of, 35b, 53a–b, 78a–b, 80b,
137a, 141a, 143b, 180a–b, 181a, 244a,
265b, 281a, 290b, 305b, 324a
Burland, Cheshire, 5b
Burley in Wharfedale, W. Yorks., 227b,
281a–b
Burnley, Lancashire, 73a, 81b–82b, 119b, 327a
Burnsall, N. Yorks., 242a
Burrill with Cowling, N. Yorks., 206a
Burton Agnes, Humberside, xviii, 191b, 193,
194a
Burton Fleming, Humberside, 194a
Burton Pidsea, Humberside, 194a
Burwardsley, Cheshire, 5b
Bury, Greater Manchester, 83a–b, 130a, 131a

Caldbeck, Cumbria, 44a; see also Gillfoot;
Hesket Newmarket; Whelpo
Calton, N. Yorks., 250a, 277a
candle sconces, 18th-cent., 66a, 128a
candlesticks, 19th-cent., 98b
Capenhurst, Cheshire, 6a
Carlisle, Cumbria, xvii, 38b, 44b–45b
Carlton, N. Yorks., 206b
Carlton Highdale, N. Yorks., 206b
Carlton Miniott, N. Yorks., 206b
Carperby-cum-Thoresby, N. Yorks., 203a,
206b
Cartmel, Cumbria, 110b, 112a
Castle Sowerby, Cumbria, 45b
Caton-with-Littledale, Lancashire, 83b
Cattall, N. Yorks., 242a
Catwick, Humberside, 194a
ceramics see cups
Chadkirk, Greater Manchester, 1a, 5a
Chaigley, Lancashire see Walker Fold
chairs: 17th-cent., 20a, 86b, 137a, 147a, 181b,
185b, 224a, 236b, 263b, 272a, 274b,
282b, 302a; 18th-cent., 6b, 14b, 94b;
19th-cent., 119a, 131b; 20th-cent.,
119a; see also communion chairs
chandeliers: 18th-cent., 24a, 93a–b, 136a;
19th-cent., 78a, 244b; undated, 113a,
234b
Chapel Haddlesey, N. Yorks., 242a, 242b
**chapels and meeting-houses, dating from
before 1800**
BAPTIST
converted premises: barns, 10b–14a;
cottages, 96b–97a, 231a
18th-cent.: *1700–50*, 33b, 86b–87a;
1750–1800, 22a–b, 23, 64a–66a,
81b–82a, 118, 119a, 133a–136b, 194b,
231a–b, 237a–b, 243b, 247a–b,
265b–266a
CONGREGATIONAL OR
INDEPENDENT
converted premises, 7b–9a
17th-cent., 19a–20a, 53a
18th-cent.: *1700–50*, 45b–46b, 53b–54a,
83a–84a, 90a–b, 144a–b, 181a–b,
277a–b, 305a, 308a–b, 309;
1750–1800, 7a, 20a, 39a–b, 40, 59a–b,